MOON

U.S. CIVIL RIGHTS TRAIL

A TRAVELER'S GUIDE TO THE PEOPLE, PLACES, AND EVENTS THAT MADE THE MOVEMENT

Deborah D. Douglas

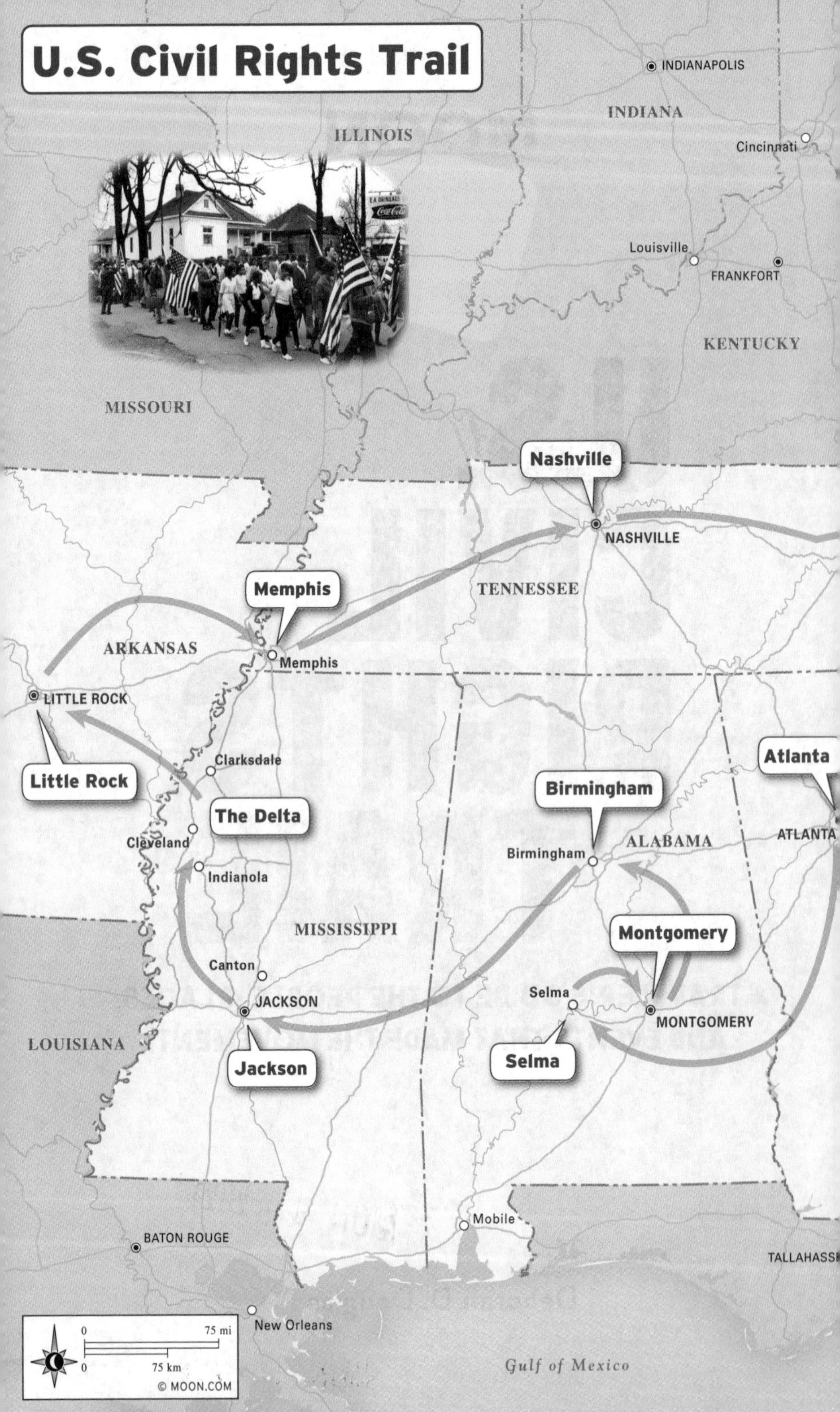

U.S. Civil Rights Trail
INDIANAPOLIS
INDIANA
ILLINOIS
Cincinnati
Louisville
FRANKFORT
KENTUCKY
MISSOURI
Nashville
NASHVILLE
TENNESSEE
Memphis
Memphis
ARKANSAS
LITTLE ROCK
Little Rock
Clarksdale
The Delta
Cleveland
Indianola
Birmingham
Birmingham
ALABAMA
Atlanta
ATLANTA
MISSISSIPPI
Montgomery
Canton
JACKSON
Selma
MONTGOMERY
LOUISIANA
Jackson
Selma
Mobile
BATON ROUGE
TALLAHASSEE
New Orleans
0
75 mi
0
75 km
© MOON.COM
Gulf of Mexico

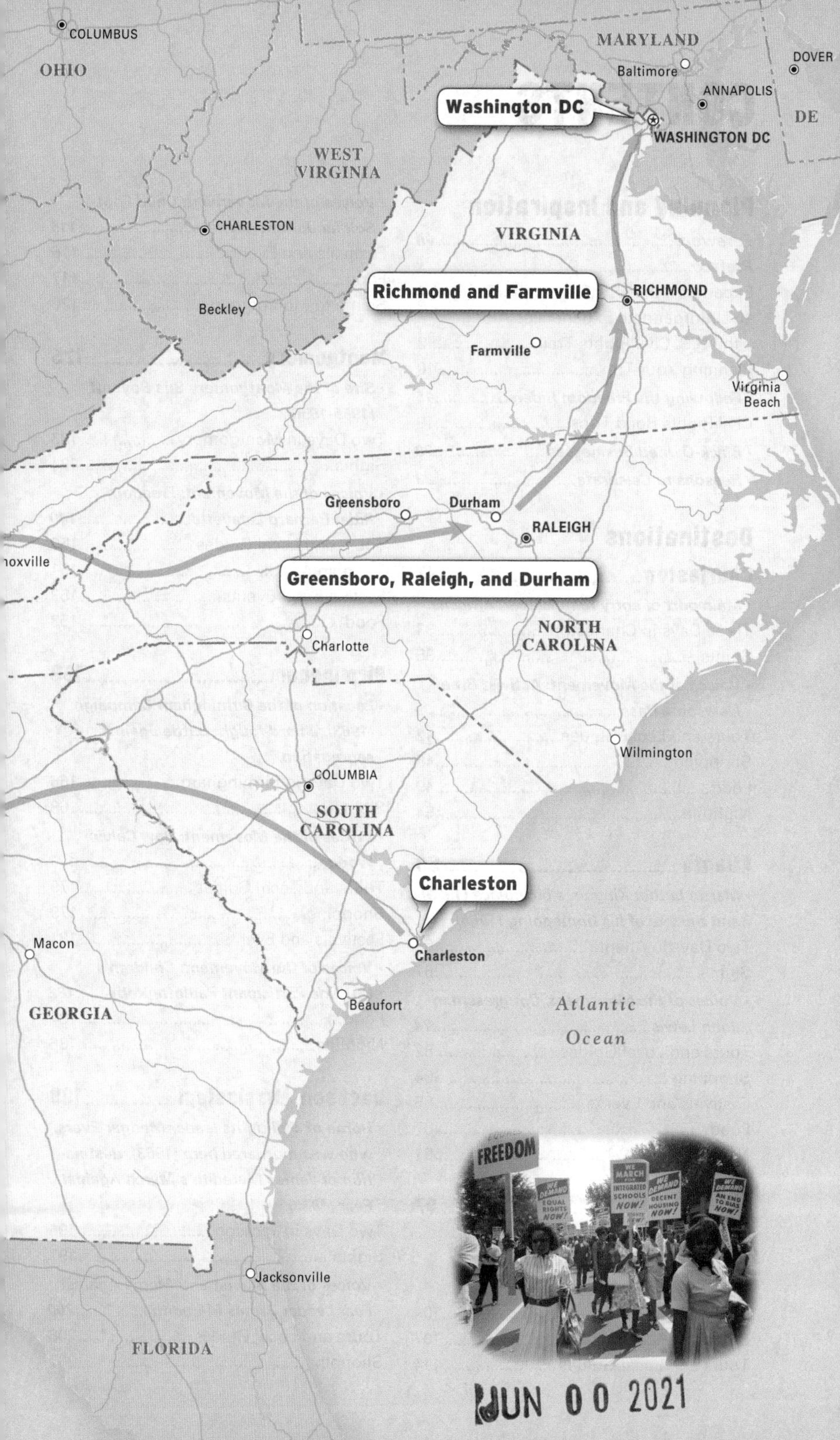
COLUMBUS
OHIO
MARYLAND
Baltimore
DOVER
ANNAPOLIS
DE
Washington DC
WASHINGTON DC
WEST VIRGINIA
CHARLESTON
VIRGINIA
Richmond and Farmville
RICHMOND
Beckley
Farmville
Virginia Beach
Greensboro
Durham
RALEIGH
noxville
Greensboro, Raleigh, and Durham
NORTH CAROLINA
Charlotte
Wilmington
COLUMBIA
SOUTH CAROLINA
Charleston
Charleston
Macon
Beaufort
GEORGIA
Atlantic Ocean
FREEDOM
WE DEMAND EQUAL RIGHTS NOW!
WE MARCH FOR INTEGRATED SCHOOLS NOW!
WE DEMAND DECENT HOUSING NOW!
WE DEMAND AN END TO BIAS NOW!
Jacksonville
FLORIDA

CONTENTS

Planning and Inspiration

Destinations

Photos (top to bottom): inside the Birmingham Civil Rights Institute; National Civil Rights Museum at the Lorraine Motel in Memphis; the Virginia Civil Rights Memorial by sculptor Stanley Bleifeld

Background and Resources

Although every effort was made to make sure the information in this book was accurate when going to press, research was impacted by the COVID-19 pandemic and things may have changed since the time of writing. Be sure to confirm specific details, like opening hours, closures, and travel guidelines and restrictions, when making your travel plans.

FOREWORD

What fascinates me most about history is how it helps us make sense of the present. History impacts us whether we are conscious of it or not. Becoming aware of it can then empower us to be more than passive, unwitting participants in events as they unfold around us.

Stepping foot on one of the historical sites listed in this guide, the Old Slave Mart Museum in Charleston, was pivotal to the awakening of my own sociopolitical consciousness—part of a series of events that culminated with me scaling the flagpole at the South Carolina State House in 2015 to lower the Confederate battle flag in an act of protest and civil disobedience. While I'd heard stories of my relatives who were enslaved in South Carolina, something about standing in a physical space where African people were bought and sold gave new clarity to the experiences of my ancestors. I imagined what it would mean to exit that space and be separated from my family forever, taken to a place where I might never see them again. The experience stirred my soul and made me feel connected to my ancestors on another level.

My visit to the Old Slave Mart Museum took place during the summer of 2013. Within a month, I would be arrested while participating in a sit-in at the North Carolina State House as part of the Moral Monday movement led by Rev. William Barber II and the North Carolina NAACP.

My visit also coincided with other key events that occurred during that fateful summer. The U.S. Supreme Court gutted the Voting Rights Act of 1965, and my home state of North Carolina wasted no time in seeking to pass new laws clearly designed to disenfranchise Black voters. This was also the summer that George Zimmerman was acquitted in the murder of Trayvon Martin, a Black teenager whom Zimmerman stalked, accosted, and shot while Trayvon was walking home from a convenience store. Like the many young people of the 1950s and '60s who saw themselves reflected in Emmett Till and felt compelled to rise up in protest, I saw myself in Trayvon. As Emmett Till's lynching helped inspire the civil rights movement, Trayvon's murder would prove to be a major catalyst for the modern movement popularly known as Black Lives Matter.

I jumped feetfirst into this modern movement, marching countless miles with countless others across the nation demanding an end to a racist system that had persisted for centuries. During this time, I continued to learn about every stride that had been made in this effort prior to now. The more knowledge I gained, the less distant the civil rights movement of the 1960s and the Black Power movement of the 1970s seemed. I considered my own life and my own place in time and asked myself: How much did I owe my freedoms to the actions and choices of those who came before me, those who recognized what was at stake in the times and places they lived? And what would be the consequences of my own actions or inactions?

For all the obvious parallels between past and present, in 2013 I still felt that what we faced was not on the same level as the violence and intimidation that confronted those who came before us. When I was arrested for participating in the voting rights sit-in at the North Carolina State House and found myself handcuffed in the back of a police van, I had no concerns that I would be physically harmed or killed. This only emboldened me to take further action. If those who'd come before me had risked life and limb for me to have rights that were now imperiled, who was I to balk at risking arrest in order to preserve those rights?

My sense that modern demonstrations were less dangerous than those from the past quickly evaporated, however. In 2014, I watched as people protesting the killing of an unarmed Black teenager named Michael Brown by a White police officer in Ferguson, Missouri, were met by a militarized police force armed with tanks, sniper rifles, and tear gas. It also seemed that each passing event unearthed another chilling similarity to the past. This was especially true in June 2015, when a White supremacist shot and killed nine Black people during a prayer meeting in Charleston's Emanuel African Methodist Episcopal Church. The violence of that event was something we'd not yet seen in the modern iteration of the movement—a terrorist attack akin to the 16th Street Baptist Church bombing that killed four little girls in Birmingham in 1963.

By 2015, two things were clear: that we weren't any more removed from violence or the threat of death than Black activists had been in previous generations, and that acts of racial terrorism can happen anywhere. It seemed that the more we demanded a reckoning on racial justice, the more we exposed the racist underbelly of our nation. One day before the terrorist attack in Charleston, the man who would become the 45th president of the United States descended a golden escalator to announce his candidacy, running on a platform of hate, anti-immigrant sentiments, and racist conspiracy theories about the nation's first Black president.

It was under these circumstances that I coordinated with a team of activists to lower the Confederate flag on June 17, 2015. There was never any doubt as to what that flag meant, and what it signaled to Black people in that region. It had been flying on the state house grounds since the 1960s, when it was raised as a statement of opposition to sit-in protests and an increasing pressure to end legal segregation in the state. I was a teenager in 2000 when, after a belabored act of compromise on the part of the South Carolina legislature, the flag was moved from its original location over the dome of the state house to a flagpole on the lawn. At the same time, the South Carolina Heritage Act was passed to further protect the flag's placement on state house grounds. Part of that law required a two-thirds approval in the state house to lower the flag for any reason—an impossibly high bar usually reserved for constitutional amendments. And so it remained in the aftermath of the Charleston massacre, flying high at the top of its 30-foot pole, even as the United States and South Carolina state flags were lowered to half-mast in recognition of the lives lost at Emanuel A.M.E.

My decision to lower the Confederate flag was both an act of civil disobedience and a way of demonstrating that we would not allow ourselves to be ruled by the acts of racial terrorism that have persisted for centuries. That act of protest became one of the most iconic moments of the modern movement, compelling the state of South Carolina to permanently remove the flag 13 days later and inspiring similar actions around the country. I couldn't have done any of it had I not been armed with an awareness of history and knowledge of the long-standing tradition of nonviolent civil disobedience that I consciously became a part of in that moment. As I scaled the flagpole in South Carolina, a Black woman descendant of people who'd been enslaved there, my climb symbolized the struggle of an entire people. As I brought the flag down, it was a reminder of all that we have overcome and will continue to overcome.

My hope for readers of this guide that has been so thoughtfully assembled by Ms. Douglas is that they find themselves similarly inspired and empowered by making physical connections with the places and history outlined herein. It's one thing to read about history in a book and quite another to find yourself physically present in a space where a certain event occurred, where the walls around you and the land beneath your feet bear witness to what happened and hold palpable energy that propels you forward toward a greater understanding of your own place in time.

—Bree Newsome Bass

PREFACE

I'm a product of the Great Migration, having grown up as a Black girl in the remnant aura of the civil rights movement. My childhood experiences included hearing my mother's memories of picking cotton, inhaling books belonging to family and friends who studied at historically Black colleges and universities (HBCUs), and heeding my grandmother's instruction to never fall asleep with a broom next to the bed, for fear a witch would ride my back in the night.

I also grew up hearing about the movement. These stories enthralled me, because I innately felt a part of them. It was up to kids like me, I felt, to wrest an education from White teachers who in the 1970s and '80s seemed perpetually perplexed at having to teach Black children. And when I saw Rev. Jesse L. Jackson on TV with his fly 'fro and fist raised, exhorting us to say and internalize the declaration "I am somebody!" it was more than a feel-good moment: The call to action was a challenge to an entrenched White power structure that held otherwise, despite the wins the movement produced.

So when the opportunity to travel the civil rights trail presented itself, I took it. I also prepared myself—for summer downpours, navigating remote roads, and the emotional weight of the journey. Standing in front of Bryant's Grocery & Meat Market in the Mississippi Delta, would I feel the lingering spectral energy of Carolyn Bryant, the White woman who told a lie on this site that got a child, Emmett Till, killed in 1955? I was also low-key worried about real people I might meet on a country road, given the nation's racially caustic environment. (I'm equally hyperaware standing in line for coffee up North, so it's not a Southern thing—it's a Black-in-America thing.)

Somewhere along the way, the question was raised: Why travel the civil rights trail when you can read books, watch films, listen to podcasts, and learn about the history in any number of other ways?

There's more than one good reason. In the spirit of the sage essayist, novelist, and playwright James Baldwin, who once said, "In the church in which I was raised, you were supposed to bear witness to the truth," some might travel the trail as witnesses, paying respects to voting rights martyrs Jimmie Lee Jackson, Rev. James Reeb, and Viola Liuzzo; to slain leaders like Martin Luther King Jr. and Medgar Evers; and to murdered children including Emmett Till, Addie Mae Collins, Denise McNair, Carole Robertson, Cynthia Wesley, Virgil Ware, and Johnny Robinson. Bearing witness is important: It's a critical step in addressing the structural underpinnings of racism.

Some might travel the trail to learn a story not told in our schools and history books. America has long labeled itself as a beacon for immigrants, but that doesn't quite fit the description of how African Americans came to be here, even though a full 13 percent of the population shares the burden of our history of enslavement. To travel the trail is to really know such facts—and it might help us begin to address our social programming. This journey is an exercise in curiosity, about what this country is really about and what we can do to make it better. It's part of a conversation that challenges the one-dimensional narratives we live with daily.

Finally, you might travel the trail to feel pride in the role Black Americans have played in shaping this country. Because, ultimately, the underlying question the trail addresses is: Just whose country is this?

When situated in historic spaces on the trail, connecting with other people, the realization that U.S. history is *our* history creates a palpable sensation. No longer are stories of lost family wealth or midnight road trips North disconnected happenstance. For those of us who grew up in Great Migration cities—New York, Chicago, Kansas City, and Detroit, to name a few—the trail satisfies our curiosity as to why so many of our friends and neighbors also had family Down South and why the rich soil beckoned us each summer.

There is power in connecting to the places where successful resistance began. Exploring the civil rights trail is a way of linking our lived experience to a time when Black Americans became united, committed, and stronger. Assimilation was never the goal: Being safe (physically and psychically), included, and valued as citizens who helped build this nation from the ground up is the whole point.

This book bears witness to the atrocities that occurred when everyday people took risks to pursue justice and equity. It also celebrates triumph over adversity, as well as the contributions African Americans have made to American culture. Finally, in looking forward to modern social justice movements, it might even help some of you decide for yourself what side of history you want to be on.

In each chapter you'll find:

- **Sights,** from churches where activists planned protests, to museums and monuments dedicated to the movement. Setting foot on some sites can be emotionally taxing, but sometimes it takes the presence of a narrative to fully understand the context of our existence as citizens of the U.S. and the world. The White House is also included, not only because Barack and Michelle Obama made history when they moved in, but because so many enslaved and free Black people actually *built* it. It is *our* house, and the civil rights movement proves why over and over again.
- **Tours by local guides** that focus on Black and civil rights history. The most compelling guides were themselves foot soldiers of the movement, including Selma's JoAnne Bland, who—at age 11—joined voting rights activists as they attempted to cross the Edmund Pettus Bridge on what came to be known as Bloody Sunday.
- **Restaurants, bars, and shops** that celebrate Black culture in America, from historic sites that fed movement leaders to modern Black-owned establishments. Every effort has been made to include Black entrepreneurs in these pages. In fact, unless stated otherwise, you can assume that all restaurants, bars, and shops in this book are proudly Black-owned.
- **Quotes and stories from activists, past and present** that bring the spirit of the movement to life. In the Voices of the Movement spotlights throughout the book, you'll hear from sit-in organizers, ministers, and Freedom Riders, including those who did time at Mississippi's notorious state penitentiary, aka Parchman Farm. Dwania Kyles, one of the first Black kindergarten students to desegregate an all-White school in Memphis, shares her experience, as does James Meredith, who risked his life to march from Memphis to

Jackson in a peaceful demand for voting rights in 1966. Bree Newsome Bass gives a modern perspective, explaining what compelled her to pull down the Confederate flag at the South Carolina State House in 2015.

- Last but not least: Need music for the road? We got y'all. My Get into the Rhythm **playlists** incudes songs, many of which sprang from our most sacred traditions, that either gave the movement momentum or speak to the issues it addressed.

The idea that our culture and history should linger as background music and imagery to a larger American story is a no-go. Our story is just too amazing for that. This journey is about cultivating a greater sense of belonging and of welcoming others into the America we helped to create; of feeling and knowing this is our home, too.

—Deborah D. Douglas

Experience the U.S. Civil Rights Trail

The U.S. Civil Rights Trail follows the twists and turns of a momentous era in U.S. history: the civil rights movement.

Our journey starts in Charleston—the main port of entry for many enslaved Africans—then winds through Southern cities and towns where demonstrators waged marches, boycotts, and Freedom Rides. At risk of being locked up (they were), bitten by trained dogs (that happened), or shot and killed (that happened, too), these courageous activists and workaday people of all ages caused our nation to fundamentally shift course and begin to truly embrace its stated ideals.

For travelers, the trail offers a wealth of opportunities to learn, contemplate, and grow. Stand in the footsteps of heroes at churches, courthouses, and sit-in sites. Expand your knowledge at museums and pay respect to slain martyrs at moving memorials. As you encounter unsung heroes like Pauli Murray, a queer Black woman who was an early challenger of "separate but equal," you'll see: There is so much more to this story than what is taught in school.

Any journey on the U.S. Civil Rights Trail will surely unleash a range of emotions, from anger to awe over the ability of human will to triumph over adversity. There's never been a more auspicious time to visit. The movement has served as inspiration and as a blueprint for action for many modern movements: #BlackLivesMatter, the fight for LGBTQ rights, and the March for Our Lives to end gun violence, to name a few.

Our journey ends in Washington DC, where some of the demands raised by movement leaders eventually found a hearing. But of course, it doesn't really end there. African Americans have always resisted oppression: The movement of the 1950s and '60s is just a part of a long through line that continues to this day. Traveling the U.S. Civil Rights Trail will challenge you to ask yourself: What parts of "America" as presented in our founding documents can be made real? Hopefully you'll agree that the answer is all of it.

In 1965, voting rights activists marched along Highway 80 from Selma to Montgomery.

10 Unforgettable Experiences

Along the U.S. Civil Rights Trail

1 Learning about the ways in which African Americans have shaped our country at the **National Museum of African American History and Culture** in Washington DC (page 416).

2 Walking in Martin Luther King Jr.'s footsteps at the **National Civil Rights Museum at the Lorraine Motel** in Memphis. Room 306, where he stayed before being assassinated on the balcony of this motel, has been frozen in time (page 286).

3 Contemplating where Memphis has been—as well as where it's headed now—at **I Am A Man Plaza,** where sanitation workers went on strike for better pay and working conditions in 1968. A sculpture by Cliff Garten commemorates the event (page 290).

4 Learning the truth—the whole truth—about the civil rights movement and much more at **The Legacy Museum: From Enslavement to Mass Incarceration** in Montgomery, Alabama (page 135).

5 Trying to summon the courage of the Little Rock Nine as you step foot onto the formerly segregated campus of **Little Rock Central High School** (page 255).

6 Grasping the terror of life for Black people in the Jim Crow South through dynamic exhibits at Jackson's **Mississippi Civil Rights Museum** (page 198).

7 Visiting Montgomery's **Dexter Avenue King Memorial Baptist Church,** where a young, charismatic man by the name of Martin Luther King Jr. stepped into the role of minister in 1954 (page 143).

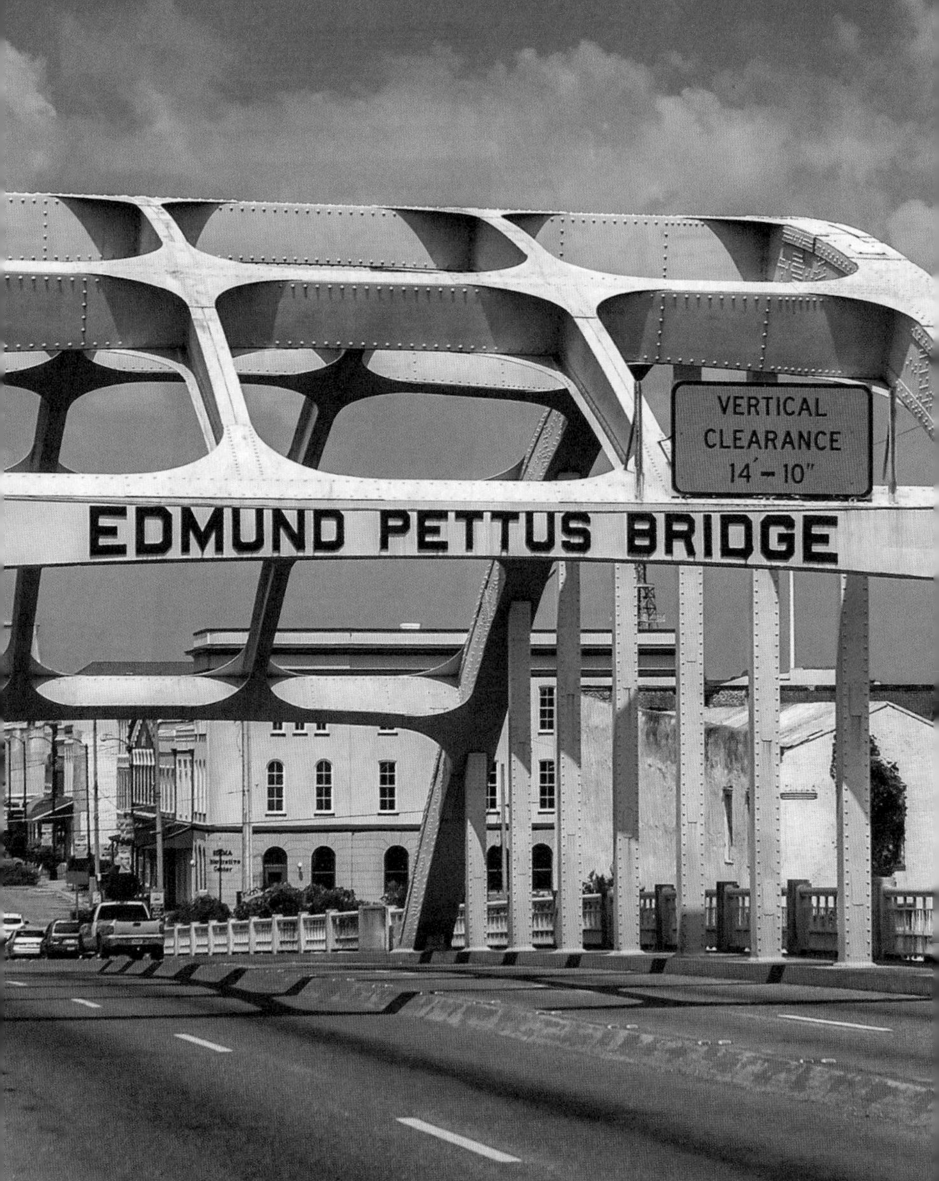

8 Walking across the **Edmund Pettus Bridge** in Selma, where peaceful voting-rights demonstrators faced violence at the hands of law enforcement in 1965 (page 109).

9 Honoring civil rights activists, as well as four young girls who died in a KKK bombing, at Birmingham's **16th Street Baptist Church** (page 168).

10 Observing a moment of silence outside the ruins of **Bryant's Grocery & Meat Market,** where a lie about Black teen Emmett Till turned murderous in 1955. The subsequent outrage is regarded as the catalyst to the modern civil rights movement (page 227).

PLANNING YOUR TRIP

Where to Go

CHARLESTON

Charleston's harbor—the main point of entry for many enslaved Africans—can be considered the starting place for the civil rights struggle. The sights here, including the **Old Slave Mart Museum** (a former market where the enslaved were bought and sold), and **Emanuel African Methodist Episcopal Church** (aka Mother Emanuel), where nine parishioners were murdered by a White supremacist in 2015, can be a lot to endure. Excellent **food** and tours led by **Gullah/Geechee guides** offer balance.

ATLANTA

Atlanta is where Martin Luther King Jr. was born, and where his homegoing was held after his assassination. It's also home to the Southern Christian Leadership Conference (SCLC), an important civil rights organization. Visitors to the city can walk in King's footsteps, visiting the **Martin Luther King Jr. Birth Home** as well as **Ebenezer Baptist Church,** where King was ordained at the age of 19, and where he was laid to rest in 1963. Still open for business is **Busy Bee Café,** where King liked to eat. Modern Atlanta is a diverse and thriving place that's open and accepting.

SELMA

Small-town Selma, Alabama, was a hotbed of voting rights activity during (and even before) the movement, culminating in a triumphant march toward the state capitol of Montgomery in 1965. Visitors can make an appointment to see **Brown Chapel A.M.E. Church,** where important marches departed, and walk across the **Edmund Pettus Bridge,** where marchers were met with violence on Bloody Sunday. It's also possible (and worthwhile) to drive along the march route to Montgomery, making a stop at the **Lowndes Interpretive Center** along the way.

MONTGOMERY

Alabama's state capitol was the site of a yearlong bus boycott, instigated when Rosa Parks famously refused to relinquish her bus seat to a White passenger in 1955. It's also where King rose to prominence as the pastor of **Dexter Avenue Baptist Church,** and where a crowd 25,000 gathered after the Selma to Montgomery march to demand voting rights at the state capitol building. Today, the city's museums include the **Rosa Parks Museum,** the **Freedom Rides Museum,** and **The Legacy Museum,** which draws an irrefutable through-line from enslavement to mass incarceration. It's a transformative place, as is the **National Memorial for Peace and Justice** that accompanies it—it's the first-ever memorial to victims of lynching.

BIRMINGHAM

Birmingham, Alabama, saw so much violence before and during the civil rights movement that the city earned itself a nickname: Bombingham. The city was the site of an intense, multifaceted campaign against segregation in 1963, known as the Birmingham Campaign. This is also where four young girls perished in a KKK bombing of 16th Street Baptist Church. Today, visitors can contemplate commemorative public art in **Kelly Ingram Park,** a site of mass meetings and rallies during the Birmingham Campaign, and learn more about local action at the **Birmingham Civil Rights Institute.** Meanwhile, **16th Street Baptist Church** still stands, and heretell, parishioners are still welcoming.

JACKSON, MISSISSIPPI

Mississippi's state capitol was home to Medgar Evers, an early martyr in the civil rights movement. Travelers can visit the **Medgar Evers Home Museum,** where Evers once lived and where he was assassinated in 1963. The **Mississippi Civil Rights Museum,** which opened in 2017, is another of Jackson's must-sees, with interactive displays that bring the movement to life.

Jackson was also the destination of James Meredith's March Against Fear in 1966. Marchers stopped in **Canton,** about 30 miles north of Jackson, and you can too: Here, The Congress of Racial Equality (CORE) Freedom House, which served as a refuge for marchers, has been transformed into the **Canton Freedom House Civil Rights Museum,** a tiny trove of civil rights artifacts, photographs, and memorabilia.

THE DELTA

As the site of 14-year-old Emmett Till's brutal murder, which, when publicized, incited outrage, it could be argued that the Mississippi Delta is where the civil rights movement took flight. Travelers today can pay respects to Till at **Bryant's Grocery & Meat Market,** where a false accusation against the child led to his murder. A pair of museums dedicated to Till provides context. The Delta is also the birthplace of the blues, which visitors can experience through museums, including the **Delta Blues Museum** and the **B. B. King Museum & Delta Interpretive Center,** and **blues clubs.**

LITTLE ROCK

Little Rock is famous as the site where nine Black high school students faced down hateful segregationists to integrate the local all-White high school. Still a functioning

inside the Birmingham Civil Rights Institute

school, **Little Rock Central High School** is also a national historic site that can be visited on a tour. Elsewhere in Little Rock, **Mosaic Templars Cultural Center** tells the story of the city's West 9th Street Historic District, a former hub of Black-owned businesses.

MEMPHIS

In 1968, King traveled to Memphis to support striking sanitation workers, who united under the powerful slogan, "I Am A Man." Pay tribute to these workers at **Clayborn Temple,** where they organized daily marches, and the adjacent **I Am A Man Plaza.** It was during this trip to Memphis that King's assassination took place at the Lorraine Motel, which has been transformed into the **National Civil Rights Museum at the Lorraine Motel,** a can't-miss sight.

Today, Memphis is a majority-Black city, and there is fun to be had here, whether on **Beale Street** or at the **Stax Museum of American Soul Music,** which celebrates Black musical forms.

NASHVILLE

Nashville is notable for the Nashville Student Movement, which coordinated a series of sit-ins in 1960 that led to Nashville being the first city in America to desegregate all public facilities. Learn about the student movement at the **Civil Rights Room at the Nashville Public Library** and pay tribute to local leaders like Diane Nash at the **Witness Walls** at the Davidson County Courthouse. Travelers can also enjoy a meal at the historic **Woolworth on Fifth** (a former sit-in site)—a delightfully transgressive experience.

GREENSBORO, RALEIGH, AND DURHAM

In 1960, a sit-in at Greensboro's segregated Woolworth's lunch counter set off a movement: Scores of nonviolent demonstrations across the South followed. The Woolworth's building, including a section of the original lunch counter, has been reimagined as the **International Civil Rights Center & Museum.** Other notable sights in this area include a collection of **murals** in Durham (including a set dedicated to local activist Pauli Murray), and the **Dr. Martin Luther King Jr. Memorial Gardens** in Raleigh, birthplace of the Student Nonviolent Coordinating Committee (SNCC).

RICHMOND AND FARMVILLE

Way back in 1951, 16-year-old Black student Barbara Johns orchestrated a walkout at her crowded, run-down high school to protest for a better campus. Johns's concerns reached the NAACP, and a subsequent lawsuit became part of the landmark Supreme Court case *Brown v. Board of Education.* Today, it's possible to visit the high school, now the **Robert Russa Moton Museum,** including the auditorium in which Johns implored her fellow classmates to walk out.

An hour away in Richmond, walk through the historic Black neighborhood of **Jackson Ward,** where the **Maggie L. Walker Historic Site**—former home of the first Black woman in the country to own a bank—is located.

WASHINGTON DC

Many pivotal events in civil rights history took place in our nation's capital, including the 1963 March on Washington for Jobs and Freedom, during which King delivered his famous "I Have a Dream" speech from the steps of the **Lincoln Memorial.** Nearby, the **Martin Luther King Jr. Memorial** pays tribute to the civil rights martyr. Meanwhile, the landmark **National Museum of African American**

WHERE TO LEARN ABOUT...

- **Women in the movement:** Visit Montgomery's **Rosa Parks Museum,** the **L. C. and Daisy Bates Museum** in Little Rock; the **Mary McLeod Bethune Council House,** first home of the National Council of Negro women, in Washington DC; and Nashville, where **Diane Nash** was a student leader in the sit-in movement. In these pages, you can also read about **Fannie Lou Hamer, Ella Baker, Pauli Murray,** and anti-lynching activist **Ida B. Wells.**

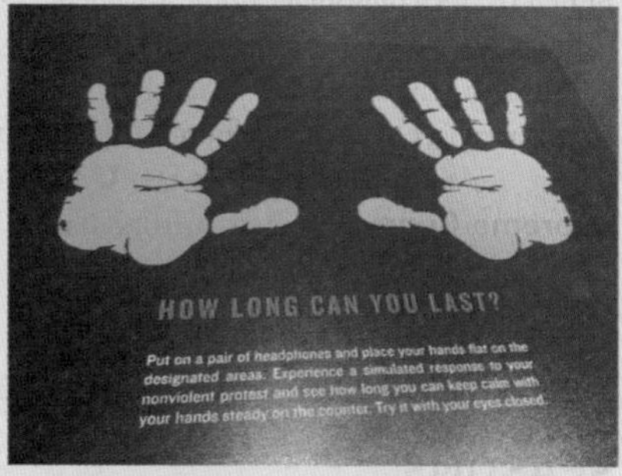

Atlanta's National Center for Civil and Human Rights invites visitors to participate in a simulated lunch-counter sit-in.

- **Student movements:** College students in **Nashville, Atlanta,** and **Greensboro,** where students were organized and impactful in their activism, are all good cities to visit.
- **Sit-ins:** Atlanta's **National Center for Civil and Human Rights** and Greensboro's **International Civil Rights Center & Museum,** located inside a former Woolworth's sit-in site, have exhibits on these nonviolent demonstrations.
- **Children in the movement:** Visit the **Robert Russa Moton Museum** in Farmville, Virginia, where 16-year-old student Barbara Johns led a walk-out in 1951. Learn about the Birmingham's Children's Crusade at the **Birmingham Civil Rights Institute**—or participate in the annual reenactment of the event, the **Anniversary Children's March,** in May. Take a tour with **Journeys for the Soul** in Selma. Tour guide JoAnne Bland participated in Bloody Sunday at the young age of 11.
- **School integration:** Visit the **Little Rock Central High School National Historic Site.** In this book, read first-person interviews with Memphis 13 student **Dwania Kyles** and Little Rock Central High students **Elizabeth Eckford** and **Sybil Jordan Hampton.**
- **Voting rights:** Visit Selma, specifically, the **Selma Interpretive Center,** the **National Voting Rights Museum and Institute,** and the **Sullivan and Richie Jean Sherrod Jackson Foundation and Museum.** Also relevant is the **Lowndes Interpretive Center** on the road to Montgomery, and the **Montgomery Interpretive Center at Alabama State University.**
- **Martin Luther King Jr.:** Visit **Atlanta,** where King was born; **Birmingham** and **Montgomery,** where he lived; and **Memphis,** where he was assassinated.
- **Your own roots:** Charleston's **International African American Museum,** scheduled to open in 2022, will facilitate genealogy research for African Americans. Washington DC's **National Museum of African American History and Culture** provides a similar service.

History and Culture opened to great fanfare in 2016. More than a museum, according to inaugural director Lonnie G. Bunch III, it's a pilgrimage home, to where it all began.

Some of the demands posed by civil rights activists eventually found a hearing in our nation's capital, at the **U.S. Supreme Court.** Engaged visitors may want to view a court session themselves, or even make an appointment to visit their representatives at the **U.S. Capitol.**

The district is not all museums, memorials, and politics: "Chocolate City" celebrates Black culture with a calendar of **festivals,** while go-go music, the heartbeat of DC, thrums in the Shaw neighborhood year-round.

When to Go

SEASONS

In **summer,** the entire region is marked by sticky and swampy weather with high heat and humidity. Rent a car with air-conditioning: You'll need it. Memphis rates among the hottest cities in summer, with highs reaching 91°F.

Washington DC is the coldest destination covered in this guide, with average low temperatures in **winter** dipping into the low 20s. It gets warmer as you go south. The transition from winter into **spring** that occurs in March is often marked by stormy weather, while Washington DC and Virginia may still experience wintery weather patterns. Atlanta, Memphis, Nashville, and Washington DC are the rainiest destinations in this guide, with more than 100 days of rain each year.

Bookmark **weather.gov** to search for local forecasts by town or ZIP code. They are pretty reliable seven days out.

When the six-month hurricane season starts in June, weaker tropical storms affect this region. Check **hurricanes.gov** for the latest information on tropical storms. There are also several radar apps, such as AccuWeather that are handy for when you are driving and wondering if it's best to pull over at a rest stop and wait for a storm to pass.

SPECIAL EVENTS

Several events along the trail draw crowds and/or are worth planning a trip around.

Spring

At 6:01pm on April 4 of every year, the **Dr. Martin Luther King Jr. Commemorative Ceremony** takes place at the National Civil Rights Museum at the Lorraine Motel in Memphis. Onlookers stand in the museum's courtyard as a new wreath is hung outside Room 306.

The **Selma Bridge Crossing Jubilee** in early May draws thousands of people every year. Also in May, the Birmingham Civil Rights Institute hosts an **Anniversary Children's March.** This reenactment of the 1963 Children's Crusade allows children and adults to walk in path of civil rights foot soldiers. It's an incredible experience.

Summer

In the Mississippi Delta, Clarksdale's **Sunflower River Blues and Gospel Festival** draws tens of thousands every August.

Fall and Winter

In Washington DC, the **Annual Legislative Conference (Congressional Black Caucus Weekend)** in the fall annually addresses many of the same issues from the civil rights movement. Also in DC, folks take the day of service aspect of **King Day** seriously, rolling up their sleeves for a variety of opportunities to volunteer. It's a good day to visit the district if you're in the mood to volunteer yourself.

FOLLOWING THE FREEDOM RIDERS

After the Supreme Court case *Boynton v. Virginia* officially desegregated interstate transportation facilities, a group of activists known as Freedom Riders set out on interstate bus rides to test the new ruling. On May 4, 1961, the original 13 Riders departed Washington DC for New Orleans, trading out for other Riders as they sustained injuries and stopping at a number of destinations covered in this guide along the way.

WASHINGTON DC TO ATLANTA

Upon leaving Washington DC, the Freedom Riders traveled through Virginia and North Carolina, stopping at cities including **Richmond** and **Greensboro,** and encountering some violence along the way. In **Atlanta** (page 91), Martin Luther King Jr. cautioned about violence ahead, but the Riders continued anyway.

ALABAMA

The Freedom Riders' arrival in Alabama was met with extreme violence, including a bombing in Anniston and beatings by the KKK in **Birmingham** (page 174). At this point, the Congress for Racial Equality (CORE) ceased the rides, but activists from **Nashville** (page 325) picked up where the CORE riders left off.

A group in **Montgomery,** which included John Lewis and Bernard Lafayette, was met by an angry mob who bashed Lewis over the head with a Coca Cola crate and put fellow Rider Jim Zwerg in the hospital. Lafayette suffered cracked ribs—read his account on page 140, or learn more in person at Montgomery's **Freedom Rides Museum** (page 139).

MISSISSIPPI

From Montgomery, the Riders headed to **Jackson** (page 215), where many were arrested and some were sentenced to time at **Mississippi State Penitentiary, aka Parchman Farm.** (Read first-person accounts of time in Parchman on page 244.)

AFTER THE RIDES

Although not all Riders made it to their intended destinations, their actions did not go unnoticed: The Interstate Commerce Commission, under the direction of Attorney General Robert Kennedy, mandated the end to segregation on interstate facilities, a ruling that took effect in November 1961.

Freedom Riders targeted segregated bus terminals like this one in Albany, Georgia, for nonviolent protests.

THE U.S. CIVIL RIGHTS TRAIL

The official U.S. Civil Rights Trail (www.civilrightstrail.com) launched in 2018 to commemorate sites where history was made during the civil rights movement. For travelers, the Civil Rights Trail website is a great planning tool. The "Plan Your Trip" feature (found by clicking on the Interactive Map tab) is especially helpful: Enter your start and end points to generate a list of all the sights along your route. Pick which sights you want to see, and a Google map shows driving directions between each stop. Other features include a timeline showing the narrative arc of this dramatic period in American history.

Not every site on the website is covered in our book, and vice versa: Whereas this book sticks mainly to the South—ground zero of the movement—the website covers turf from Kansas in the West to Delaware in the North and Florida in the South. Conversely, while the website sticks to sights associated with the movement in the 1950s through the passage of the Fair Housing Act of 1968, we've taken a wider view, stretching back to enslavement and all the way forward to the present day while also featuring shops, restaurants, and nightlife. Destinations in this guide that are also stops on the official Civil Rights Trail are designated as such in each chapter, and are listed below by city:

CHARLESTON

- Emanuel African Methodist Episcopal Church

ATLANTA

- APEX (African American Panoramic Experience) Museum
- National Center for Civil and Human Rights
- Ebenezer Baptist Church
- Martin Luther King Jr. National Historical Park and Martin Luther King Jr. Birth Home
- Jimmy Carter Presidential Library and Museum
- Martin Luther King Jr. Center for Nonviolent Social Change (The King Center)

SELMA

- Brown Chapel A.M.E. Church
- Edmund Pettus Bridge
- National Voting Rights Museum and Institute
- Selma Interpretive Center
- Selma to Montgomery National Historic Trail
- Lowndes Interpretive Center
- City of St. Jude Interpretive Center *

MONTGOMERY

- Alabama State Capitol
- Civil Rights Memorial Center
- Dexter Avenue King Memorial Baptist Church
- Dexter Parsonage Museum
- First Baptist Church on Ripley Street
- Frank M. Johnson Jr. Federal Building and United States Courthouse
- Freedom Rides Museum
- Holt Street Baptist Church
- Rosa Parks Museum
- The Legacy Museum: From Enslavement to Mass Incarceration
- National Memorial for Peace and Justice

BIRMINGHAM

- 16th Street Baptist Church
- Bethel Baptist Church
- Birmingham Civil Rights Institute
- Kelly Ingram Park

JACKSON

- Medgar Evers Home Museum
- Mississippi Civil Rights Museum
- Mississippi Freedom Trail
- Tougaloo College

* Covered under Montgomery on www.civilrightstrail.com

MISSISSIPPI DELTA

Bryant's Grocery & Meat Market
Emmett Till Interpretive Center
Emmett Till Intrepid Center
Tallahatchie County Courthouse

LITTLE ROCK

Little Rock Central High School National Historic Site
Little Rock Nine Memorial at the Arkansas State Capitol
Mosaic Templars Cultural Center
William J. Clinton Presidential Library & Museum
L. C. and Daisy Bates Museum

MEMPHIS

Beale Street Historic District
Clayborn Temple
Mason Temple Church of God in Christ
National Civil Rights Museum at the Lorraine Motel

NASHVILLE

Civil Rights Room at the Nashville Public Library
Clark Memorial United Methodist Church
Witness Walls
Fisk University
Griggs Hall at American Baptist College
Woolworth on 5th

GREENSBORO, NORTH CAROLINA

International Civil Rights Center & Museum
February One Monument

FARMVILLE, VIRGINIA

Robert Russa Moton Museum

WASHINGTON DC

Lincoln Memorial
Martin Luther King, Jr. Memorial
National Museum of African American History and Culture
Supreme Court of the United States
Howard University

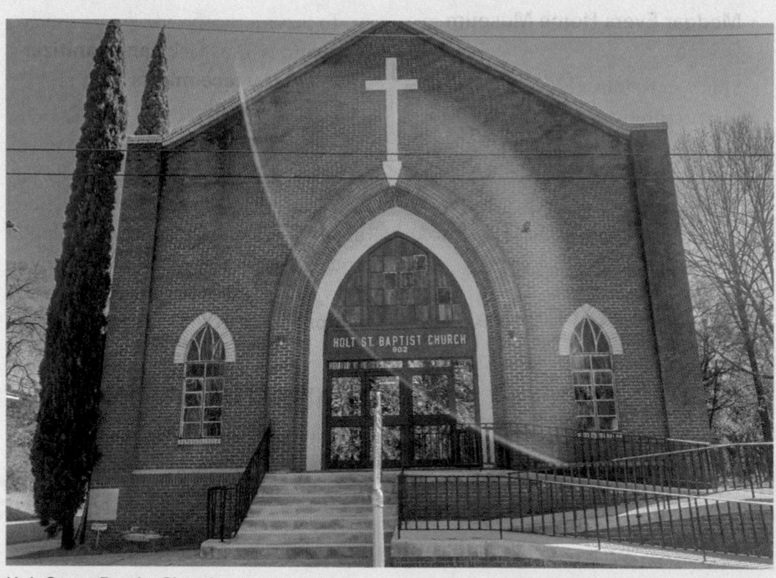

Holt Street Baptist Church

Before You Go

ADVANCE RESERVATIONS

Museums and Other Sights

It's possible to walk into many of the museums in this guide without an advance reservation, but for some places, reservations are either required or recommended.

- **National Museum of African American History and Culture** in Washington DC; reserving tickets two months in advance is a good rule of thumb.
- **The Legacy Museum** in Montgomery; during busy times—especially March, when the Bridge Crossing Jubilee draws crowds in neighboring Selma—you'll want to make reservations a couple weeks in advance.
- **Dexter Parsonage Museum** in Montgomery
- **Little Rock Central High School National Historic Site** in Little Rock
- **Medgar Evers Home Museum** in Jackson

Some museums (especially smaller ones), interpretive centers, and historic homes and churches are open by appointment only, as noted in the contact info throughout this guide. In general, try to reach out a week in advance to secure an appointment to visit.

Tours and Local Guides

Many tours and local guides require advance booking; you can't just show up at the departure site and join the tour, necessarily. Reach out to secure your tour spot about a week (or, at the very least, 48 hours) in advance. Getting a day-of tour isn't impossible, necessarily, but it can be challenge.

WHAT TO PACK

Be sure to pack:

- **Breathable clothing** (including underwear!) made of natural fabrics like cotton. This includes long-sleeved shirts and pants or skirts to protect from sun exposure and mosquitos.
- A **light jacket** for springtime
- **Walkable shoes** that won't pinch your feet.
- **Sunglasses**
- **Umbrella**
- **Bug repellent** containing DEET
- **Sunscreen** (to be applied before you layer on the repellent)
- If you're into **hats,** make yours crushable and wide-brimmed for sun protection
- **Charging cables** for your devices
- To prevent the spread of viruses such as coronavirus, pack **hand sanitizer** and several **face masks** made of breathable cloth

One final note: African American travelers will be familiar with traditionally tiny shampoo and conditioner bottles in hotel rooms: We know a quarter-size dollop of product won't do the job for our curly to kinky hair. Make sure you pack your fave **hair products** to ensure full coverage.

TRANSPORTATION

It's easy to get around Washington DC on public transit. Everywhere else, you'll pretty much need a car.

CIVIL RIGHTS ROAD TRIPS

Each chapter of this book includes a two- or three-day itinerary to help you make the best of your time in that city or region, but for a fuller experience of civil rights history, you'll want to visit more than one place. The trail is a car-centric affair, so plan on driving on all of the following routes.

THE GRAND TOUR: CHARLESTON TO WASHINGTON DC

Total length of trip: At least a month

More than likely, you'll explore the trail as a series of excursions or long weekends, but if you had a month to spare, you could have a transformational time exploring it in one go. This route starts in Charleston, heads through the South, and ends in Washington DC. Along the way, you'll learn about sit-ins, marches, and school integration; visit museums, monuments, and memorials; and still have time for dining and shopping at an inspiring collection of Black-owned businesses.

Below is the recommended route and suggested length of stay in each destination. This adds up to a total of 30 days, but note that you'll need longer to complete the trip, given the drive times between each destination. (At 7 hours, the stretch between Nashville and the Raleigh region of North Carolina is by far the longest):

- **Charleston:** 3 days
- **Atlanta:** 2 days; 5 hours from Atlanta
- **Selma and Montgomery:** 2 days in each city; 2.5 hours from Atlanta
- **Birmingham:** 2 days; 1.5 hours from Montgomery
- **Jackson, Mississippi:** 2 days; 3.5 hours from Birmingham
- **Mississippi Delta:** 2 days; 2 hours from Jackson
- **Little Rock, Arkansas:** 2 days; 2.5-3.5 hours from the Delta
- **Memphis:** 3 days; 2 hours from Little Rock
- **Nashville:** 2 days; 3.5 hours from Memphis
- **Greensboro, Durham, and Raleigh, North Carolina:** 3 days; 7 hours from Nashville
- **Richmond and Farmville, Virginia:** 2 days; 3 hours from Raleigh
- **Washington DC:** 3 days; 2 hours from Richmond

CELEBRATING KING: ATLANTA TO MEMPHIS

Total length of trip: 10 days

On this trip, you'll follow the arc of Martin Luther King Jr.'s life, starting in Atlanta's Auburn community where he was born and ending in Memphis, where he delivered his final speech the night before his assassination. The itinerary below suggests 10 days, but you'll likely want to work in a day or two to rest from all the driving.

Days 1-2

ATLANTA: KING IS BORN (1929)

Arrive: Hartsfield-Jackson Atlanta International Airport (ATL)

King was born into a multigenerational household full of love and purpose in Atlanta's Auburn neighborhood. Visit his childhood home, the **Martin Luther King Jr. Birth Home,** along with **Ebenezer Baptist Church,** which gave King a spiritual foundation and where he was ordained at age 19. Eat where he ate (the **Busy Bee Café**) while strategizing for a way to win.

BLACK-OWNED BUSINESSES

LaToya Tucciarone, founder and CEO of SustainAble Home Goods in Atlanta

Black creativity undergirds so much of what makes America excellent. Why not celebrate us by enjoying amazing apparel, food, and other products and services? Making a point to patronize Black-owned businesses is also a simple act to level the uneven playing field that exists nationwide. Favorites include:

RESTAURANTS

- **Slutty Vegan** in Atlanta, where lines of multicultural patrons extend out the door (page 90).
- **The Senator's Place** in Cleveland, Mississippi, serving up buffet-style soul food cooking (page 238).
- **Dame's Chicken and Waffles** in Greensboro and Durham, North Carolina, helmed by a couple of college buddies who put all kinds of spin on the classic dish (pages 360 and 372).
- **The Chicken Hut,** a neighborhood institution in Durham serving homecooked meals, including fried chicken (page 373).
- **Lannie's BBQ Spot** in Selma, where pulled pork sandwich topped with cracklings are the specialty. Family-owned Lannie's has been in business since the 1940s (page 117).
- **Chef Tam's Underground Café** in Memphis, where Chef Tamra Patterson's "soul-infused" menu items range from familiar (fried green tomatoes) to wildly creative (peach cobbler nachos) (page 306).
- **Ooh Wee Bar-B-Q,** a no-frills drive-thru barbecue stand that's a local favorite in Nashville (page 342).
- **Sweet Magnolia Gelato Co.,** whose products are available across the South. Find a branch in Memphis near the Civil Rights Museum (page 307).

BARS AND NIGHTCLUBS

- **Perfect Note** nightclub, located outside Birmingham in suburban Hoover, is a special spot that draws a diverse crowd (page 186).
- **Havana Mix Cigar Emporium** in Memphis, a father-and-son operation (page 311).
- **Downtown Cigar Company,** a cigar bar in Jackson (page 213).
- **Ground Zero Blues Club** in Clarksdale, Mississippi, co-owned by none other than Morgan Freeman (page 240).

SHOPS AND GIFTS

- **Nubian Hueman** in Washington DC's Anacostia neighborhood, a hip clothing boutique with a young clientele (page 443).
- **Mahogany Books,** which makes a point of promoting cultural awareness. It's located in the same building as Nubian Hueman in Anacostia, Washington DC (page 444).
- **Woodcuts Gallery & Framing** on Nashville's historic Jefferson Street, specializing in African American art (page 334).
- **Cocoa Belle Chocolates,** a gourmet brand available at **Bella Vita Jewelry** in downtown Little Rock (page 270).
- **SustainAble Home Goods** in Atlanta sells everything from kitchen supplies to textiles, with a section of the store dedicated to Black makers (page 84).

WELLNESS SERVICES

- **Lucid Living** in Richmond, Virginia, where owner Natasha Freeman provides healing sessions ranging from reiki to Thai bodywork (page 401).

You can also partake in tours led by African American guides in a variety of destinations in this book, including **I Am More Than... Tours** in Montgomery (page 150) and **Whistle Stop Tours** in Durham (page 371). Not ready to hit the road just yet? A number of Black-owned businesses will ship their products to you direct. Find a list on page 467.

Ground Zero Blues Club

Days 3-4

MONTGOMERY: FIRST PASTORSHIP (1954)

165 miles (2.5 hours) from Atlanta

It was in Montgomery where King helmed his first church, **Dexter Avenue King Memorial Baptist Church,** in 1954, at the age of now 25, and where he and wife, Coretta, started their family.

King proved to be an eloquent and succinct communicator who understood how to leverage the media spotlight. In the wake of Rosa Parks's arrest (1955), he was selected to lead the Montgomery Improvement Association (MIA), which directed the 381-day Montgomery bus boycott. Learn about the boycott in Montgomery at the **Rosa Parks Museum.**

Ten years after the bus boycott, Montgomery was the endpoint of the Selma to Montgomery march (which you'll learn about in Selma, your next stop). While you're here in Montgomery, swing by the **Alabama State Capitol** to see the site where King addressed a crowd of 25,000 at the march's conclusion.

Day 5

SELMA: SUPPORTING THE VOTING RIGHTS MOVEMENT (1965)

52 miles (1 hour) from Montgomery

Driving into Selma from Montgomery, you'll cross the **Edmund Pettus Bridge,** where peaceful voting rights demonstrators met violence at the hands of law enforcement on what came to be known as Bloody Sunday. Two days after this event, King led a symbolic march halfway across the bridge. A third march, also led by King, made it all the way to Montgomery five days later, where King addressed the massive crowd.

The 1965 Selma to Montgomery march for voting rights was the culmination of years of efforts. The **Lowndes Interpretive Center,** located before the bridge between Selma and Montgomery, is your first opportunity to learn about the local voting rights movement. In Selma, the **Selma Interpretive Center** provides further information. King stayed with the Jackson family on visits to Selma: their daughter, Jawana, has fond memories of "Uncle Martin." The Jackson's home has been preserved as the **Sullivan and Richie Jean Sherrod Jackson Foundation and Museum** and is open by appointment.

Days 6-7

BIRMINGHAM: ORGANIZING THE BIRMINGHAM CAMPAIGN (1963)

90 miles (2 hours) from Selma

From Selma, backtrack in time a couple of years to Birmingham, where King was invited by Rev. Fred Shuttlesworth to lend his weight to the local fight for civil rights. The resulting 1963 Birmingham Campaign would produce some of the most astounding imagery of the civil rights movement, the kind that could change hearts and minds. National media exposed horrific images of Black demonstrators, including children, being hosed by water cannons, attacked by canines, and battered by batons wielded by White police officers. While jailed in Birmingham, King wrote a now-famous letter in the margins of newspapers, responding to the demands of local White clergymen.

Learn about the Birmingham Campaign at the **Birmingham Civil Rights Institute,** and visit **Kelly Ingram Park,** a site where some of the most critical events took place. Today, a series of park installations pays tribute to civil rights participants.

REASONS TO CELEBRATE

Moving though they may be, visiting civil rights sites can create a feeling that rests heavy in your psyche. At some point, you will feel some kind of way. Balance the heaviness of the journey to the past with experiences infused with the joy of the present.

MUSEUMS

- **Stax Museum of American Soul Music:** This temple to soul music and other Black musical forms is located in the aptly named Soulsville neighborhood of Memphis, on the site where Stax Records once lived. Nearby climbing gym **Memphis Rox** makes a point to employ neighborhood youth, so you can feel like your workout is making a difference (page 295).
- **Madame C. J. Walker Beauty Shoppe and Museum:** This former beauty shop in Atlanta holds relics of Black beauty culture from eras-gone-by. Owner Ricci de Forest also hosts jazz-listening sets on-site (page 73).
- **ESSE Purse Museum:** Learn the story of women through the handbags they carried at this Little Rock museum. While the museum itself is not Black-owned, it takes care to include Black women in its storytelling, which is gratifying to see (page 267).

FESTIVALS AND CELEBRATIONS

- **Juneteenth:** While Juneteenth celebrations are now taking place nationwide, the Birmingham Civil Rights Institute's celebration has something for everyone: Live gospel and R&B and hip-hop music, walking tours, face-painting and bouncy houses, and educational programs that highlight Black history from enslavement to the civil rights movement. The institute historically hasn't charged admission on that day (page 183).
- **Howard Homecoming:** With live music, step shows, and the game itself, Howard Homecoming (held in Washington DC in October) is all about joy (page 450).
- **Black Love Experience:** Held in Washington DC every February, this celebration of Black culture is organized by a local Black business owner (page 447).

climbers at Memphis Rox

OTHER FUN STUFF

- There's no category to sum up **Metro PCS** in Washington DC, but it's certainly worth a stop: It's from this Shaw neighborhood store that owner Donald Campbell proudly blasts Go-Go music for all the neighborhood to hear. When new residents protested the noise, a movement, #DontMuteDC, emerged (page 443).

Days 8-9

MEMPHIS: KING'S ASSASSINATION (1968)

250 miles (3.5 hours) from Birmingham

In 1968, King traveled to Memphis to amplify the cause of striking sanitation workers. The workers exemplified those he wanted to help with the Poor People's Campaign, which would focus on economic and human rights for all people. In a stirring yet foreboding sermon at **Mason Temple Church of God in Christ** the night of April 3, 1968, King appeared to take stock of his mortality. The next day he was gone: assassinated by a sniper lying in wait across from the Lorraine Motel. Today, that hotel functions as the **National Civil Rights Museum at the Lorraine Motel,** where you can learn more about the movement and get a close-up view of King's room and the sniper's view from across the way as you consider where you stand.

Day 10

BACK TO ATLANTA

400 miles (6 hours) from Memphis

In addition to being King's birthplace, Atlanta was also his last home: In 1960, he returned from Birmingham to co-pastor with his dad at Ebenezer and focus his energy on the Southern Christian Leadership Conference (SCLC), and he lived here until his assassination in 1968.

With More Time

With more time, take a detour to **Nashville** on your way back to Atlanta to learn about the sit-in movement there. The detour will add about 60 miles (1 hour) to your drive time. Alternatively, **Selma,** which is 52 miles (1 hour) west of Montgomery, is a worthy add-on between Montgomery and Memphis. Plan for an extra day or two if you want to stop here.

TRACING THE MARCH AGAINST FEAR: MEMPHIS TO JACKSON

Total length of trip: 6 days

In 1966, James Meredith, donning a pith helmet and wooden walking stick, kicked off his March Against Fear—or a Walk Against Fear, as he called it—from Memphis. His purpose was to encourage Black people to attempt to register to vote. He planned to walk 220 miles to Jackson, Mississippi, down Highway 51; however, he was ambushed and shot the second day, and had to be hospitalized. Civil rights leaders picked up where Meredith left off.

This march was accomplished over three weeks and culminated with an eight-mile march from Tougaloo to the state capitol in downtown Jackson where 15,000 people, including local residents, converged. During this march, Stokely Carmichael's use of the phrase "Black Power" emerged as a point of contention. Regardless of the schisms, the march succeeded in registering thousands of Black voters. Now that's some Black power, yeah?

Day 1

MEMPHIS: MEREDITH DEPARTS

Arrive: Memphis International Airport (MEM)

There isn't much of Meredith to see in Memphis, though the **National Civil Rights Museum at the Lorraine Motel** features an extensive telling of his quest to get into the University of Mississippi. Its Black Power exhibit also features a video loop of the speech Stokely Carmichael delivered in Greenwood, Mississippi, during the march. For a Meredith-related sight, stop by the **Withers Collection Museum & Gallery.** Photojournalist Ernest Withers captured some of the movement's largest figures in his photographs, including Meredith.

Days 2-3

MISSISSIPPI DELTA: THE MARCH CONTINUES

100 miles (2 hours) from Memphis to Clarksdale

The straightest shot from Memphis to Clarksdale, your destination for the night, is to take US-61 South for about 76 miles (1.5 hours). Another option is to start out on Highway 51, as Meredith did, turning onto US-278 West in Batesville to reach Clarksdale. If you choose this slightly longer option, there's plenty to consider as you make your way south.

First, 26 miles after leaving Memphis, you'll pass through **Hernando, Mississippi,** where Meredith was shot on Day 2 of his march. From this bloodstained spot, civil rights leaders, including ministers King, Ralph Abernathy, Kelly Miller Smith, Andrew White, Ralph Jackson, and Bernard Lee, picked up where the wounded Meredith had to leave off.

The marchers decided on a new route toward Philadelphia, Mississippi. When they reached **Batesville** (39 miles south of Hernando), marchers celebrated with singing at the Panola County Courthouse. Retired Black farmer El Fondren, age 106, gave them something to sing about that day when he registered to vote for the first time in his life. As reporters thrust questions at the elderly man, one asked how he felt, to which Fondren said: "Me? I feel good." Some members of crowd hoisted Fondren in the air as marchers and locals shouted, "Hip, hip, hooray!"

From Batesville, the march proceeded in a zig-zag fashion, according to John Dittmer in *Local People: The Struggle for Civil Rights in Mississippi* (1994). Locals would join as the marchers moved through rural areas and towns. Mississippi Delta stops included the towns of Greenwood, Belzoni, Midnight, and Louise. In Philadelphia, King spoke at a memorial for Congress of Racial Equality (CORE) staffers James Chaney, Andrew Goodman, and Michael Schwerner, three Freedom Summer workers murdered by the Ku Klux Klan in 1964.

A good route for travelers is to head west from Batesville to **Clarksdale, Mississippi** (40 miles, 45 minutes) to find a room for the night. This is a good base from which to spend a couple of days exploring the Delta, including **Greenwood,** 60 miles (1 hour) to the south, which was a one of the stops on the March Against Fear—and the site where Student Nonviolent Coordinating Committee (SNCC) chairman Stokely Carmichael started speaking about Black Power on the night of June 16, 1966.

THREE- TO FOUR-DAY ROAD TRIPS

Overwhelmed by the vast geography of the trail? Below are good options for shorter trips:

- **Greensboro, Raleigh, and Durham** to **Richmond and Farmville** to **Washington DC**
- **Atlanta** to **Birmingham,** then **Montgomery** and **Selma**
- **Memphis** to **the Delta** and **Jackson**
- **Memphis** to **Little Rock**
- **Nashville** to **Memphis** to **the Delta**
- **Greensboro, Raleigh, and Durham** to **Charleston**

Day 4 (Morning)

CANTON, MISSISSIPPI: MEREDITH REJOINS THE MARCH

75 miles (1.5 hours) from Greenwood to Canton

Everyone, including Meredith, came back together in Canton, Mississippi, where a CORE Freedom House served as a safe space for marchers, including King. In Canton, 200 marchers met with 1,000 residents for a rally at the courthouse. Violating a promise to remain peaceful, state troopers peppered marchers (who were trying to set up camp at a local elementary school) with tear gas and beat the ones who refused to move.

Stop in Canton yourself to visit the **Canton Freedom House Civil Rights Museum,** located in the former Freedom House marchers once used as a refuge. When you're done exploring, continue on to Jackson. On your way there, you can stop at Tougaloo College, as marchers did, and visit **Woodworth Chapel,** where a good deal of civil rights organizing occurred.

Day 4 (Afternoon) and Day 5

JACKSON, MISSISSIPPI: MARCH FINALE

27 miles (30 minutes) from Canton to Jackson

The March Against Fear ended with a rally at the Jackson State Capitol. Attended by 15,000 people, it was the largest civil rights demonstration in Mississippi's history.

Spend an extra day in Jackson, exploring the **Mississippi Civil Rights Museum** and visiting the **Medgar Evers Home Museum,** a moving tribute to an early martyr of the movement who dedicated himself to making Mississippi a safer place for Black people to live.

Day 6

BACK TO MEMPHIS

220 miles (3 hours)

From Jackson, it's a straight shot back to Memphis on I-55 North.

With More Time

With an extra day or two, you might consider starting or ending your trip in **Little Rock,** 140 miles (2 hours) west of Memphis. It's not related to the Meredith story, but as the home of the famous Little Rock Nine, it's a good place to learn about school integration.

Charleston

As the main point of entry for forcibly displaced Africans who hailed from areas like Senegambia, Angola, and Congo, the lush coastal city of Charleston is in many ways the beginning of the story of the civil rights struggle. Almost half of enslaved Black people shipped to America entered through Charleston, where they were sold like animals and separated from families—first in public, then behind closed doors in rooms, yards, and marts. Enslaved Africans then toiled in rice fields and were prone to malaria, suffering exceedingly short life spans due to grueling work in muddy fields in the scorching sun.

CHARLESTON'S TOP 3

1. Meditating on "liberation theology"—the concept that God loved enslaved Black people and wanted them to be free—at **Emanuel African Methodist Episcopal Church,** the oldest Black church south of Baltimore (page 40).

2. Learning about Gullah culture and Black history in Charleston on one of Alphonso Brown's **Gullah Tours** (page 44).

3. Feasting on Southern classics at **Bertha's Kitchen,** a Black-owned business (page 52).

Photos (top to bottom): Emanuel African Methodist Episcopal Church, Alphonso Brown's Gullah Tours, Bertha's Kitchen. Previous: Emanuel African Methodist Episcopal Church

Charleston is foundational to the understanding of the African presence in the United States and a subsequent spirit of resistance that refused to be extinguished. This mindset stretched from the colonial period to the Civil War to the civil rights movement. This is where Robert Smalls, then enslaved, commandeered the Confederate steamship *Planter* the night of May 13, 1862, and sailed past Fort Sumpter to deliver the vessel and its cargo of enslaved men, women, and children to the U.S. Navy. He also delivered Confederate navy code books and became the first Black captain of the U.S. Navy, appointed by Abraham Lincoln. He later served in the South Carolina legislature and the U.S. Congress.

Charleston is the home of Emanuel African Methodist Episcopal Church, affectionately called Mother Emanuel, the oldest independent Black Christian congregation south of Baltimore, founded in 1816 by Morris Brown out of an African worship movement co-founded by Denmark Vesey. Vesey and 34 enslaved men were tried for planning a revolt to free Black people by killing White slave owners. The church itself was rebuilt in 1891 after the Civil War and sadly became the site of a modern-day massacre: In 2015, eight members and Emanuel's pastor were attending Bible study when they were shot to death in a racially motivated act of domestic terror by a young White man welcomed into the sanctuary. The post-racial world so many people imagined the 20th century civil rights movement or the 21st century election of a Black president to represent fell away to reveal the most-racial realities of the African American experience and the country's violent landscape of White supremacy.

Today, laid-back Charleston shares narrative space with those who marvel at its European architectural influences, relationship to the Founding Fathers, and general "Old World" feel, and those who instead focus on the city's role in powering the economic engine of America with free Black labor. Because nearly half of enslaved Africans brought to the New World came through here, the city is a natural draw for those researching their roots. The International African American Museum (which, at the time of writing, was set to open at Gadsden Wharf in early 2022) is a great reason to put Charleston on your list of travel must-sees: The museum's Center for Family History will provide resources to help African Americans trace our lineage, a particular challenge in our community.

Sunday service at Emanuel African Methodist Episcopal Church

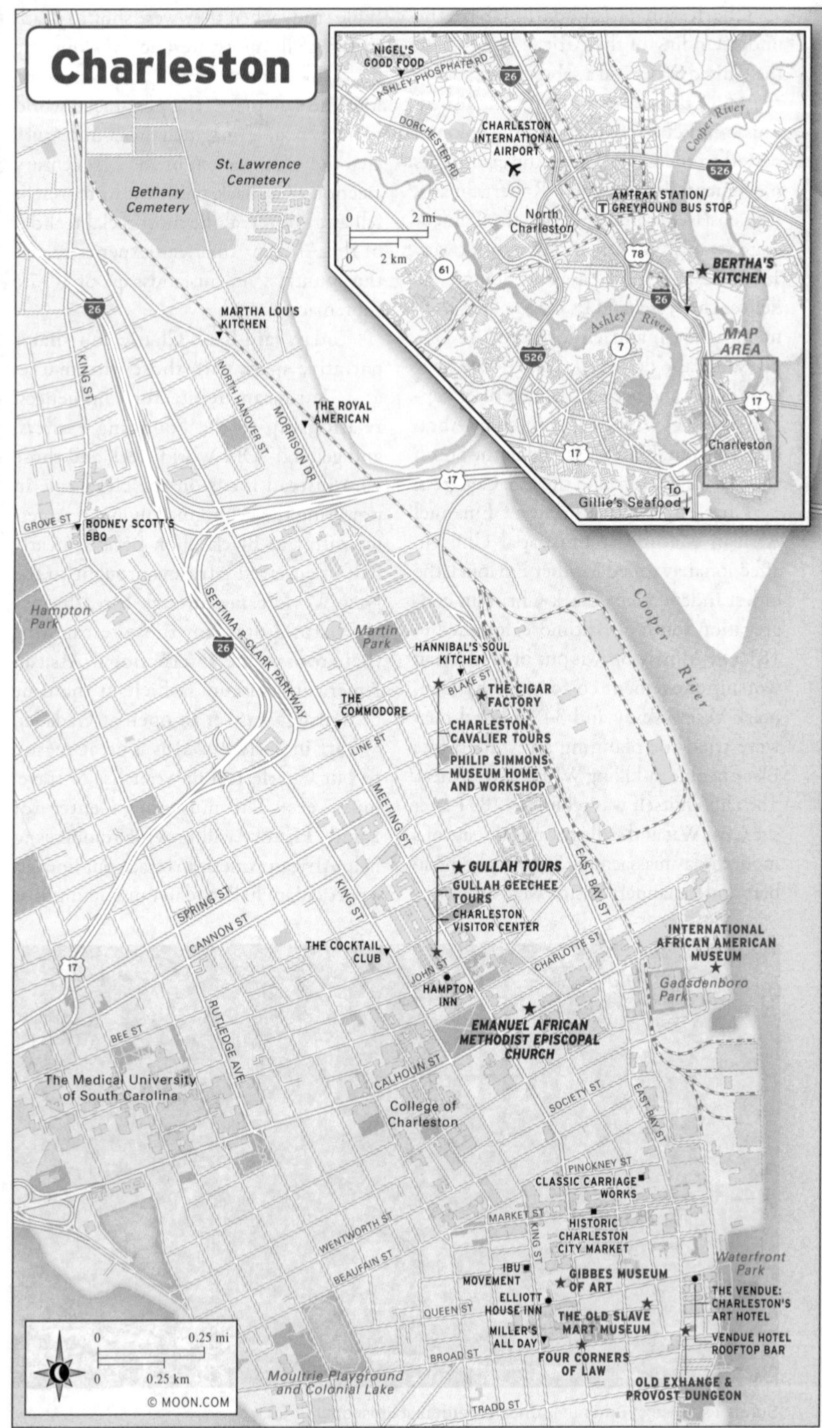
Charleston
NIGEL'S GOOD FOOD
ASHLEY PHOSPHATE RD
DORCHESTER RD
CHARLESTON INTERNATIONAL AIRPORT
Cooper River
AMTRAK STATION/ GREYHOUND BUS STOP
North Charleston
BERTHA'S KITCHEN
Ashley River
MAP AREA
Charleston
To Gillie's Seafood
0 2 mi
0 2 km
St. Lawrence Cemetery
Bethany Cemetery
MARTHA LOU'S KITCHEN
NORTH HANOVER ST
MORRISON DR
THE ROYAL AMERICAN
KING ST
GROVE ST
RODNEY SCOTT'S BBQ
Hampton Park
SEPTIMA P. CLARK PARKWAY
Martin Park
HANNIBAL'S SOUL KITCHEN
BLAKE ST
THE CIGAR FACTORY
THE COMMODORE
CHARLESTON CAVALIER TOURS
PHILIP SIMMONS MUSEUM HOME AND WORKSHOP
LINE ST
MEETING ST
Cooper River
GULLAH TOURS
GULLAH GEECHEE TOURS
CHARLESTON VISITOR CENTER
EAST BAY ST
SPRING ST
CANNON ST
THE COCKTAIL CLUB
JOHN ST
HAMPTON INN
CHARLOTTE ST
INTERNATIONAL AFRICAN AMERICAN MUSEUM
Gadsdenboro Park
EMANUEL AFRICAN METHODIST EPISCOPAL CHURCH
RUTLEDGE AVE
BEE ST
The Medical University of South Carolina
CALHOUN ST
College of Charleston
SOCIETY ST
PINCKNEY ST
CLASSIC CARRIAGE WORKS
MARKET ST
HISTORIC CHARLESTON CITY MARKET
WENTWORTH ST
BEAUFAIN ST
IBU MOVEMENT
GIBBES MUSEUM OF ART
Waterfront Park
ELLIOTT HOUSE INN
QUEEN ST
THE OLD SLAVE MART MUSEUM
THE VENDUE: CHARLESTON'S ART HOTEL
MILLER'S ALL DAY
VENDUE HOTEL ROOFTOP BAR
BROAD ST
FOUR CORNERS OF LAW
OLD EXHANGE & PROVOST DUNGEON
Moultrie Playground and Colonial Lake
TRADD ST
0 0.25 mi
0 0.25 km
© MOON.COM

MOVEMENT TIMELINE

The first Africans—"20 and some odd Negroes"—arrived in Virginia in **August 1619.** Arrivals to Charleston followed.

1800-1865

1816: Emanuel African Methodist Church, the oldest independent Black Christian congregation in the South, is founded by Morris Brown and Denmark Vesey.

July 2, 1822: Vesey is executed by hanging, along with five other enslaved men, for the "crime" of organizing to liberate enslaved Black people and kill White slavers. In all, 131 men were arrested and charged with conspiracy, 67 convicted, and 35 hanged, according to the National Park Service.

1856: The Slave Mart (now a museum) opens after the City of Charleston outlaws the sale of people on open streets.

1862: Robert Smalls, with 12 others, commandeers a Confederate steamboat during the Civil War and offers it to Union forces. He won his family's freedom and served in the state assembly and five terms in the U.S. Congress.

April 15, 1865: The U.S. flag is raised over Fort Sumpter, near Charleston, signaling the end of slavery.

1930s-1960s

1938: Old Slave Mart is converted into a museum—though its "Lost Cause" tone glosses over the horrors of slavery.

October 1, 1945: The Cigar Factory Strike kicks off, including the walkout of 900 Black women workers. The workers eventually win a raise, and the civil rights anthem "We Shall Overcome" emerges from the strike.

1962: Dr. Martin Luther King Jr. speaks to more than 1,500 people at Mother Emanuel as he tours the South urging Black people to register to vote.

2015

June 17: Nine Mother Emanuel members are gunned down by a White supremacist during Wednesday night Bible study.

June 27: Activist Bree Newsome climbs a flagpole at the state capitol in Columbia and pulls down the Confederate flag, which had flown on state grounds since 1961.

1856 illustration of a market in Charleston where enslaved Africans were bought and sold

CHARLESTON

PEOPLE WHO MADE THE MOVEMENT

Denmark Vesey: Born enslaved in St. Thomas (in what is now the Virgin Islands), Vesey purchased his freedom from Charleston lottery winnings. He helped found Emanuel A.M.E. in 1816 and was executed in 1822 for planning a revolt of enslaved Black people.

Robert Smalls: Enslaved man who commandeered a Confederate ship during the Civil War and became the first Black captain of the U.S. Navy. He also became a representative in the U.S. Congress.

Lucille Simmons: Simmons tweaked Charles Albert Tindley's "I Will Overcome" during a tobacco workers' strike in the '40s, by changing "I" to "We."

Septima P. Clark: Civil rights activist who was fired from her teaching job after she joined the NAACP. An expressway near downtown Charleston is named in her honor.

Robert Smalls

Bree Newsome Bass: Activist who reacted to the 2015 murders at Mother Emanuel by scaling a flagpole at the South Carolina State House and pulling the Confederate flag down in an direct-action, nonviolent protest.

ORIENTATION

Charleston Peninsula is bounded by water: the Cooper River to the east and the Ashley River to the west. Most points of interest are clustered **downtown** and north of downtown around **Upper King Street.** Upper King Street is a vibrant area for shopping, restaurants, and nightlife. While visitors are drawn here, more people live outside the peninsula.

In the historic district, Calhoun Street cuts across the peninsula and divides Lower King and Upper King streets. Historically, Upper and Lower had different connotations: Black-owned businesses were above Calhoun Street during segregation (Upper King), and Black residents rarely traversed to Lower King Street. That is definitely not the case today with these two neighborhoods, which are a few square miles combined. Officially, Lower King and Upper King are considered downtown. But if you ask locals with a long memory, they may say Lower King is commonly referred to as "downtown" although the boundaries of that term are expanding northward as far as Spring Street and beyond as gentrification takes hold along King Street.

A few spots (including some recommended restaurants) are located north of downtown and King Street. Take a trolley where available or jump in your car or Uber.

As you explore, you might come across **Septima P. Clark Parkway,** which runs along the western edge of downtown. Originally called Crosstown Expressway, it was renamed in honor of the civil rights activist, who was fired from her teaching job after joining the NAACP. The renaming was a bittersweet tribute as the expressway disrupted Charleston's Black community when built in the 1960s—much like other freeway projects across the nation.

PLANNING YOUR TIME

You can easily spend a good three days in historic downtown Charleston and leave with an air of good feeling, having eaten authentic food from one of the United States' oldest food cultures and learned about the complicated social and political history of this city.

Ask about tours, buy tickets to venues and events, and get advice at the **Charleston Visitor Center** (375 Meeting St.; tel. 843/724-7174; Mon.-Sun. 8:30am-5pm). Located at the old train station, it includes an exhibit hall that highlights Charleston's cultural contributions including its food and history (especially Gullah/Geechee culture). In a market featuring local goods, you can find Lillie's of Charleston hot and barbecue sauces with a South Carolina zing.

CONNECT WITH

Your next closest stops after Charleston are **Raleigh and Durham,** about 2 hours to the north, and **Atlanta,** 4.5 hours to the west.

Three Days in Charleston

Over the next few days, you'll soak up Charleston history and art, while finding plenty of opportunities to buy gifts made with a local flair. And you will eat. If you're up to it, you'll do a lot of walking. The foliage, architecture, and *joie de vivre* kind of invites it. If you tire, app rides and the trolley are good options.

Be sure to book your sightseeing tour with **Gullah Tours** (Day 1) and your tour of **Emanuel A.M.E.** (Day 2) in advance.

DAY 1

1 Grab coffee and an early morning bite to eat at **Historic Charleston City Market,** which opens at 9:30am. While you're there, walk through the long central hallway and feast your eyes on sweetgrass baskets, paintings, locally crafted jewelry, and more.

2 **Hannibal's Soul Kitchen** is just a short drive away, near the Cigar Factory. It's not fancy, but the food is quite tasty, which is the point.

3 Head back over to the **Gibbes Museum of Art** to marvel at many African American masters with roots in the South.

4 Hope you made a reservation with **Gullah Tours,** an engaging and delightful overview of Charleston's Black history. The tour leaves from the bus shed at the Charleston Visitor's Center (375 Meeting St.). The two-hour bus tour includes a couple of stop-offs, such as the Philip Simmons Museum Home and Workshop and a ride by the Cigar Factory. Make notes for places you want to revisit on your own.

5 Make your way to Upper King Street where **The Cocktail Club** opens just in time for Happy Hour.

6 You're in the South, so do what Southerners do: Head over to **Rodney Scott's BBQ**, a couple miles away (so best to drive). Get your hands all sticky with sauce and juicy ribs. Don't worry, plenty of paper towels are on the tables to help you clean up your mess.

DAY 2

You can walk to most of the places on this day up until you reach the **Vendue Rooftop Bar**. Then hop in your car or a taxi to get to **Emanuel A.M.E.** and the Upper King shopping area. Some of these sites pack a heavy emotional weight—anger and sadness are two emotions that come to mind. Pace yourself as you reflect on America's past and present.

1 Start with breakfast at **Miller's All Day**, a happy, well-lit place known for great grits, fried bologna, biscuits and gravy, and pie—plenty of pie.

2 Over at Broad and Meeting or Meeting and Market (aka the **"Four Corners of Law"**) you'll find sweetgrass basket vendors and can see the sweetgrass baskets and other items being made. These tightly coiled creations take several weeks to complete and are highly regarded works of art with high utility.

3 Get grounded in early Charleston history—which is the story of colonial England and the slave trade—by visiting the **Old Exchange & Provost Dungeon**.

4 Walk over to **The Old Slave Mart Museum** for an emotional tour through the site where enslaved Black people were sold.

5 Unwind from those two heavy sights with a light bite (taco, maybe?) at the **Vendue Hotel Rooftop Bar**.

6 Get some shopping done on King Street, which has something for every need and taste. **Ibu Movement** honors women-made crafts and clothing from around the world.

7 Now that you are caught up on how Charles Towne (as Charleston was once known) came to be, you're ready to dive into some serious history of Black self-determination with a tour of **Emanuel African Methodist Episcopal Church**. Be sure to call in advance to book and tour the United States' oldest Black congregation south of Baltimore.

8 Sit down and have an early dinner at **Bertha's Kitchen**. They're waiting on you.

DAY 3

1 Don't leave Charleston without a final feast: **Gillie's Seafood** is open by noon.

2 If you have time left, explore a sight that piqued your interest on the Gullah Tour, such as the **Philip Simmons Museum Home and Workshop.**

Sights

Sights in Charleston touch on enslavement, the civil rights movement, and other aspects of the Black experience in the city. The **International African American Museum,** located on the port through which many enslaved Africans first entered the United States, is scheduled to open in 2022.

It's worth noting that a great deal of the historical narrative downtown, in the area near the Charleston Visitor Center, prioritizes antebellum culture and the "romanticism" of plantation culture. Fortunately, more folks are working on becoming more reliable and inclusive narrators in the evolving conversation about race and place. Tourism officials also report a growing interest by African Americans who are seeking out Charleston to connect with their roots, or at least get a better idea of the origins of Black people in the United States.

DOWNTOWN

The Old Slave Mart Museum

6 Chalmers St.; tel. 843/958-6467; www.oldslavemartmuseum.com; Mon.-Sat. 9am-5pm; adults $8, youth $5

This slave market on the cobblestoned Chalmers Street was the beating heart of the early plantation economy. Here, enslaved Africans were put on display like products, not people. Thousands were sold in the city as part of the domestic trade that

the Old Slave Mart Museum

ensued after the importation of enslaved Black people was banned in 1808.

The market is now a museum that tells a story about the slave trade. Staff here greet visitors with a certain earnestness that sets the tone for your visit. The museum is divided into three zones: The front area is an introduction to both the transatlantic and domestic slave trades. The back area describes how Black people were prepared for enslavement (skin was oiled up, and gray hairs dyed black or plucked); the types of jobs enslaved Black people did; and how and where enslaved people were punished. The museum's upstairs section (currently being updated) provides more information about the transatlantic slave trade.

Artifacts on display have included whips, human restraints, and slave yokes used to tie enslaved people to move around in a line called a coffle. Oversize images outline the slave economy, putting a face to both the enslaved and the people who owned and managed these captives. Records show that an enslaved woman named Lucinda, age 20, was the first to be sold.

The market, a 1,900-square-foot building inside an enclosed yard, opened in 1856, on the very same day the City of Charleston outlawed the sale of enslaved people on open streets. Considered the country's last intact building used to traffic and sell Black bodies, it included both a dead house (morgue) and a "barracoon" (a jail for enslaved Black people). The original stone facade and iron gate remain, providing a glimpse into what enslavers were stepping into.

According to Ruth Miller, a noted Charleston tour guide, the mart was among 40 such establishments situated in a four-block area. The building was turned into a museum in 1938 when Miriam B. Wilson, a Charleston transplant from Ohio and the daughter of a decorated Union general, bought it. White Charlestonians didn't take too kindly to an outsider airing their dirty laundry, and the museum took on a "Lost Cause" tone early on that mollified those folks. The museum is now owned by the City of Charleston and has made great strides in telling a truer story of the horrors of enslavement. The Chalmers Street building also offers a grounding in other aspects of early American history, from which slavery can never be far away.

A visit to this former slave mart can elicit a range of reactions, from anger to discomfort. Some say what it lacks in tangible historical artifacts and ephemera, it makes up for in ghosts. For activist Bree Newsome Bass, whose family lived in South Carolina when the state became the first slave state to leave the Union in 1860, a 2013 visit left a deeply rooted mark. "I'm just thinking about how horrific that could be . . . if you're there with your whole family and when you leave out of there, you might never see them again." Newsome Bass already knew "that is exactly what happened with my ancestors." Still, she says, "something about standing in that actual physical space just made it more real."

Old Exchange & Provost Dungeon

122 E. Bay St.; tel. 843/727-2165; www.oldexchange.org; Mon.-Sat. 9am to 5pm; adults $10, children ages 6-12 $5

In the colonial era, all goods imported into South Carolina had to come through the Old Exchange & Provost Dungeon. Items such as farm equipment were processed here, and the Georgian-style exchange was also a common site for auctioning enslaved Africans. These humans were sold like meat: Leaflets advertised their sale, along with their ages, physical characteristics, and buying terms. The building was also a post office and gathering site.

The building, which features oak-grained floors, a cove ceiling, and, yes, a dungeon, is now privately owned but operated by the City of Charleston as a museum and is listed on the National Register of Historic Places. Guests may peruse the top two floors on their own, while docents escort visits to the dungeon. The dungeon was first used to store goods, but it was eventually turned into a jail that housed 50-60 people in terrible conditions that exposed them to filth, including rats and sewage. During the Revolutionary War, three South Carolina signers of the Declaration of Independence were imprisoned here by the British. Patriots were imprisoned here too, as were enslaved Africans.

The Roman arches that support the building are made of bricks laid by enslaved Africans and other workers. The original brick floor is still there, though a partial wood floor put down during World War II takes up some space.

Two animatronic mannequins help flesh out the narrative. One, "Tom the Teakeeper," helps to animate the story of British tea that was delivered here (and still stains the dungeon floor). In 1773, townspeople and plantation elites started meeting upstairs to talk about the high taxes on British tea. Enslaved Africans would have been at this meeting, being forced to work, of course. In these public talks, the idea of South Carolina was seeded.

Gibbes Museum of Art

135 Meeting St.; tel. 843/722-2706; www.gibbesmuseum.org; Mon.-Sat. 10am-5pm, Sun 1pm-5pm; adults $12, seniors $10, children ages 4-7 $6, children under 4 free

This museum features American art from the colonial to the contemporary era, including a visual story of Charleston, a busy seaport town that is emblematic of America's complex racial relations. Gibbes officials continue to work diligently to diversify the museum's permanent

Photos (top to bottom): a view of the Old Slave Mart Museum; Old Exchange & Provost Dungeon; exhibit the Gibbes Museum of Art

collection, and a number of pieces by African American artists and/or depicting Black themes are on display.

In the Mary Jackson Gallery on the second floor, a stunning, oversized sweetgrass basket showcases the craftsmanship of the gallery's MacArthur Genius namesake, who has appeared at the Gibbes to talk about the Gullah basket-making tradition. Works by Romare Bearden rotate frequently in this gallery. Bearden's work, said to be influenced by the civil rights movement, countered racial stereotypes to depict Black life in full. Also on display is a 1943 charcoal and gouache portrait of Denmark Vesey, the insurrectionist and co-founder of Mother Emanuel, by Charles White.

The third floor is used to rotate special collections.

Traveling exhibitions showcase artists with Southern connections, including African American artists Thornton Dial, Sam Gilliam, Clementine Hunter, Kerry James Marshall, Alma Thomas, and Bill Traylor. One past exhibition, Black Refractions: Highlights from The Studio Museum in Harlem, featured a range of media from the 1920s onward.

International African American Museum

Gadsden Wharf; tel. 843/872-5352; www.iaamuseum.org

A recent addition to the pantheon of museums dedicated to African American history is Charleston's International African American Museum. (At the time of writing, it was scheduled to open in early 2022.) The museum is located at Gadsden Wharf, where many enslaved Africans took their first steps in the New World: It is estimated nearly half of the enslaved disembarked here. Their descendants, however, know next to nothing from whence they came.

A high point of this museum experience will be the Center for Family History. This center will facilitate African Americans in exploring their genealogy from the basics to deeper dives. The Church of Jesus Christ of Latter-day Saints, experts in genealogical resources and research, has dedicated $2 million to this enterprise. This is meaningful given Charleston's foundational role in the development of the United States and role in the slave trade.

The museum's design includes a 42,000-square-foot museum with oversize windows that look out over the water toward Africa and the shore where enslaved Africans arrived in ship holds. The museum embraces a minimalist design that rises from the sacred ground upon which it sits, and gardens and water features will be added to enhance reflection. Designed to place history at your fingertips, the interior will be composed of an orientation theater, interactive galleries and dynamic exhibits, panoramic videos that transport museumgoers through time and space.

An interactive media table called "South Carolina: Power of Place" will feature a color-coded dynamic map of people, places, and events in the state's history. Find spots where civil rights actions took place or locate historical events such as the Stono Rebellion, the largest uprising of enslaved Black people in the British mainland colonies in 1739. The Atlantic Connections gallery will offer a dynamic map of the transatlantic slave trade from the 16th-19th centuries, sure to create some emotional reactions and reflection for those who can imagine their ancestors' as captives in this traumatic trade.

Inside the Gullah Geechee gallery, an exhibit called "Praise House" will honor places of worship in African American communities. Inside this cabin-like structure will be videos depicting aspects of Gullah Geechee culture and traditions, among other activities. An Oral History Booth next to the Center for Family History will allow patrons to record family stories, interviews, and personal reflections.

VOICES OF THE MOVEMENT: ACTIVIST BREE NEWSOME BASS

"I knew my family history of overcoming slavery. I knew the flag was raised in 1961 as a signal of opposition to the civil rights movement. Here we are 50 years later, and I'm stepping into a struggle that started before I came."

—BRITTANY "BREE" NEWSOME BASS, an artist, activist, and filmmaker, climbed into the national consciousness June 27, 2015, the day she donned a helmet and scaled a 30-foot flagpole on the grounds of the South Carolina State House in Columbia, pulling down the Confederate flag. The stars and bars had flown over those grounds since 1961, which was a time of significant civil rights progress. Critics of Confederate symbols say that flags and statues erected well after the Civil War are not memorials but, rather, symbols of White supremacy and racial intimidation.

Newsome Bass's act was a response to the murder of nine parishioners by a White supremacist at Mother Emanuel days prior. (State Sen. Clementa Pinckney, one of the slain members, had lain in state days earlier at the Capitol in Columbia.) The Black Lives Matter movement, along with an ongoing local discussion about the flag among fellow activists, also fueled her zeal.

For this, she was arrested with fellow activist James Tyson. It was worth it. Then-Gov. Nikki Haley, facing immense pressure, signed legislation to permanently remove the flag.

Following Newsome Bass's triumph, several cities, states, and institutions removed Confederate symbols, including New Orleans, Dallas, Austin, Maryland, Louisville, and St. Louis. In Memphis, Tennessee, officials even defied state law to remove statues from taxpayer-funded parks due to unrelenting activist pressure. More of these symbols came down in the wake of mass protests over the police killing of George Floyd, including the removal of a statue of enslaver and Vice President John C. Calhoun from its perch in Charleston's Marion Square.

For Newsome Bass, the Mother Emanuel murders, along with other contemporary examples of racial violence, reframed the idea that the struggle lived in the past. Now, she says more people are working to understand current events in context with history. In Charleston, that means abandoning a romanticized version of a city that celebrates a colonial past and a thriving plantation economy, and understanding that the city we know today was built on the lives and legacy of enslaved Black people.

CHARLESTON

UPPER KING AND VICINITY

★ Emanuel African Methodist Episcopal Church

110 Calhoun St.; tel. 843/722-2561; www.motheremanuel.com; Sun. 9:30am service

Say their names: Rev. and State Senator Clementa Pinckney, Cynthia Hurd, Rev. Sharonda Coleman-Singleton, Tywanza Sanders, Rev. DePayne Middleton-Doctor, Ethel Lance, Susie Jackson, Rev. Daniel Simmons, and Myra Thompson. This church, widely known as "Mother Emanuel," occupies the contemporary imagination because of these nine parishioners, who perished when 21-year-old White supremacist Dylann Roof, whom they had welcomed into the sanctuary, shot them to death during a Wednesday night Bible study on June 17, 2015. But Emanuel African Methodist Episcopal Church has stood for more than 200 years as an emblem of Black self-determination—and continues to do so.

Founded in 1816, Emanuel A.M.E. is the oldest Black church in the Deep South. Denmark Vesey, a formerly enslaved man who also was able to buy his freedom—from winnings in the Charleston lottery—helped found this denomination. Vesey was an early proponent of liberation theology, which employs Bible teachings in addressing social, political, and economic oppression. He was infamously executed by hanging in 1822 for planning a revolt of enslaved Black people that included killing Whites.

Booker T. Washington spoke here in 1909, and W. E. B. DuBois made an appearance here too. The church was also instrumental in the civil rights movement as an amplifier, host, and staging ground. Rev. B. J. Glover, who pastored here from 1953 to 1965, is credited with leading the civil rights charge. Dr. Martin Luther King Jr. spoke in 1962, and Coretta Scott King led a march from the church in 1969 to advocate for better pay and working conditions for Black workers at Medical College Hospital.

Today, the church continues to minister to the Charleston community, providing youth enrichment opportunities and supporting a women's ministry, in the Black church tradition. "This isn't new for us; we've been doing what we have to do," says Willie Glee, who has served as vice chair of the Emanuel board of trustees. The building was damaged by an 1866 earthquake, but officials kept its "bones" and built up around the damage. It's now one of few Charleston churches that retains its original interior, including the altar, pews, and light fixtures. A pipe organ brought in in 1908 is still here. Outside, the Gothic Revival-style white-stucco church stands tall with a steeple perched atop it. With a capacity of more than 1,100 seats, the church is used to being full.

Visitors to the church will be immersed in church history during free, prescheduled 45-minute **tours.** Book tours at tel. 854/444-3856 or email a request to tours@emanuelamechurch.org.

Emanuel A.M.E. is part of the Charleston Historic District and a stop on the official U.S. Civil Rights Trail. It was listed on the National Register of Historic Places in 2018.

Philip Simmons Museum Home and Workshop

30 1/2 Blake St.; tel. 843/723.1259; www.philipsimmons.us; Tues.-Sat. noon-4pm; donation

When you walk into the secluded yard leading to African American master blacksmith Philip Simmons's home and workshop, you're walking into a world. Simmons used the tools you see here, including his forge, hammers, and an anvil, to create his signature ironwork style: a tight curl at the tip of a length of iron that appears on everything from gates, fences, and balconies to window grilles and gardens along the South Carolina coast.

#CHARLESTONSYLLABUS

Dr. Kidada Williams, a historian of African American and American history, had long encouraged her colleagues to start making history more accessible to the public—and the shootings at Mother Emanuel only sharpened that desire. "When Charleston happened," she says, "we saw that a lot of the larger public . . . did not really [have] a framework for understanding exactly how we got here." Enter the #CharlestonSyllabus, a hashtag conceived by Williams and Dr. Chad Williams and curated by Dr. Keisha N. Blain with assistance from Melissa Morrone, Ryan P. Randall, and Cecily Walker.

The goal of the hashtag (which came on the heels of the #FergusonSyllabus, initiated after the police shooting and death of Michael Brown, age 18) was to provide a historical foundation for recent events and serve as a tool for educators as well as the general public. The syllabus includes resources such as texts, songs, films, novels, and scholarly works that magnify the Black experience. "One of the first things I did," says Kidada Williams, "was to share some of Charleston's early records on limiting African Americans' rights and privileges, not only enslaved people but free Black people."

#CharlestonSyllabus went viral.

People were hungry for information about the Black experience in America. Eventually, Williams, Williams, and Blain published a book, *Charleston Syllabus: Readings on Race, Racism, and Racial Violence,* which offers readings to help people understand the United States's history of racial violence and racism. Several resources focus specifically on Charleston's unique history, such as the state's secession declaration.

Visitors often marvel over Simmons's trajectory. Born in 1912 on Daniel Island, he was reared by his grandparents before moving in with his mother in Charleston, where he was consumed by the craft of blacksmithing. Simmons's life embodied the promise of the freedom struggle through creativity, craftsmanship, and a giving spirit. His work was in high demand, but he stayed close to his community and was known for investing in the educations of local youths.

Simmons died peacefully in his sleep in 2009 at age 97. Today, you can hear him talk about craftsmanship at HistoryMakers.org, a vast digital repository of African American oral history. You can also see his work on windows and gates all over Charleston—and once you pick up Simmons's signature style, you can't un-see it (though do note that older ironworks around town also have the tight curl at the end of the scrolls. Usually the iron is wide and heavier than the iron that Simmons used).

Look for Simmons's famous snake gates, which feature a snake motif built into an iron gate, at the historic **Gadsden House** (329 East Bay St.), a private home that's now an events venue. The **Charleston Visitor Center** (375 Meeting St.) has a little island featuring Simmons's work. It's a nice place to sit on a bench under the oak trees and sip on a cup of coffee or tea.

Outside Charleston, Simmons's work is found in the National Museum of American History and the National Museum of African American History

ironwork by Philip Simmons

History and Culture (NMAAHC) in Washington DC, the Museum of International Folk Art in Santa Fe, New Mexico, and on the grounds and the interiors of many homes around the world. In 1982, he was in the first group to be awarded the National Endowment for the Arts National Heritage Fellowship, the highest honor given to traditional artists in the United States.

Tours and Local Guides

Tours of Charleston delve deep into the city's history. Local Gullah guides teach visitors about the Gullah/Geechee people, descended from Africans who were enslaved and brought here against their will to cultivate rice, indigo, and cotton. Or choose a tour that specializes in the slave trade, the civil rights movement, or general Black history.

CARRIAGE TOUR

CLASSIC CARRIAGE WORKS: SLAVERY TO FREEDOM TOUR

tel. 843/853-3747; www.classiccarriage.com

Among several themed horse-and-carriage tours offered by Classic Carriage Works, the **Slavery to Freedom Tour** (1 hour; Fri.-Sat. 1pm; adults $28, children $18) covers the horrors of slavery while recognizing the contributions of West African enslaved people who helped establish the United States. This popular one-hour tour covers Charleston landmarks, including Emanuel African Methodist Episcopal Church, affectionally known as Mother Emanuel. While the journey is deeply grounded in Charleston history, it provides a framework for understanding broader concepts in African American history too, including the journey from West Africa to the West Indies (aka the "Middle Passage"); the September 9, 1739, Stono Rebellion, the largest rebellion of enslaved Africans in the British mainland colonies, which occurred southwest of Charleston; and the Red Summer Riots of 1919, a series of deadly anti-Black attacks across the nation that started in Charleston.

The tour regularly occurs on Friday and Saturday at 1pm, though visitors may book private tours. Reservations are strongly recommended.

WALKING TOURS

In addition to Charleston Cavalier Tours, Godfrey KHill of **Gullah Geechee Tours** offers a **Porgy & Bess Walking Tour,** listed below.

CHARLESTON CAVALIER TOURS: CIVIL, EDUCATIONAL, AND LABOR RIGHTS TOUR

tel. 843/475-7480; www.charlestoncavalier-tours.com

Charleston Cavalier Tours bills itself as a narrative that embraces Charleston's diverse history that includes Black people, Whites, and free persons of color. As such, tours include people and places important in African American history.

The **Civil, Educational, and Labor Rights Tour** (1.5 hours; Tues.-Sun. 9am; $25) focuses on the lives of the laboring class of all races, including African Americans. The tour meets at Philip Simmons Museum Home and Workshop (30 1/2 Blake St.), where guests are guided through the African American blacksmith's home and may also have the opportunity to view a blacksmithing demonstration in Simmons's work area, which contains his original tools and examples of his ironwork. Visitors also walk to the newly renovated Cigar Factory building and dig into the story of the strike, conducted mostly by Black women, that took place here in 1945. The tour also points out Burke High School, founded in 1894, where students and teachers worked to dismantle segregation in the 1950s and '60s.

Throughout the tour, the guide points out architecture and other evidence of the work and lives lived by enslaved and free Black people. For example, you'll learn how some enslaved Black people were "living out," meaning they lived off the premises of the site where they were forced to work.

GULLAH GEECHEE TOURS: PORGY & BESS WALKING TOUR

tel. 843/478-0000; www.gullahgeecheetours.com

Passionate Gullah/Geechee tour guide Godfrey KHill of Gullah Geechee Tours (described in more detail below, under Bus and Car Tours) offers a **Porgy & Bess Walking Tour** (1.5 hours; call to book; $40) that dives into the world depicted by George Gershwin's opera. Charleston is the home of the real people of Catfish Row upon which DuBose Heyward's novel *Porgy* is based. The tour takes guests to 89-91 Church Street, where the Black people who inspired this story lived. The Porgy character, a disabled beggar, is based on Charlestonian Samuel Smalls. While the 1925 story is lauded for putting Black people in a positive light, KHill posits the portrayal wasn't sufficient because Smalls is falsely framed in his incarnation as Porgy. He says Smalls was known as Samuel GOAT Smalls, as in Greatest of All Time. He was not impoverished and had many friends and women admirers. "Perspective is key," KHill says. "We have to tell our own story." KHill goes on to share details about the culture depicted by the book and opera.

The tour also takes visitors to Dock Street Theatre—the original was built in the 1730s as the first building in America dedicated to theater—and to Heyward's two-story house at 76 Church Street, now the wing of another home. You'll absorb KHill's historical insights about the slave market and visit a particularly moving site focused on the Blue Meeting House.

BUS TOURS

GULLAH GEECHEE TOURS

tel. 843/478-0000; www.gullahgeecheetours.com; adults $33-$40, children $22

To hear Godfrey KHill tell it, a bulrush basket saved his life: As a newborn, his mother brought him from New Jersey to South Carolina in such a basket as this. He grew up to honor his full-blooded Gullah Geechee roots as a historian and licensed tour guide. KHill is passionate and intense about this history and takes great pains to engage all the senses in the telling of it.

KHill's hour-long tours meet at Historic Charleston City Market unless otherwise noted. Tours take place in a Mercedes Sprinter van that fits 14 people or a 22-passenger bus. Riding tours integrate video screens with rich narratives about the origins of Charleston and the Gullah community.

Three tours are on offer:

- **Gullah After Dark** (1 hour; 8pm; call to book; $33) offers a raw glimpse of Charleston history, replete with signs and symbols of the Gullah people's early presence in this area. For example, KHill points out a slave auction block at what is now Historic Charleston City Market. KHill challenges the narrative that no enslaved people were sold at the market and interprets the space to make his case: Small fingerprints of enslaved children are found in the bricks used to build the market, and these aren't the only ones found around town. The tour meets at the Charleston Visitor Center Bus Shed, 375 Meeting Street.

- The **Biblical and Historical City of Charleston Tour** (1 hour; call to book; $33) integrates Bible verses with historical facts about Charleston, which is regarded as a spiritual mecca with hundreds of churches. KHill drives to two Black churches, Morris Brown A.M.E. Church and Emanuel A.M.E. Church, and two White churches, St. Phillips Episcopal Church and St. Michael's Episcopal Church (which, incidentally, was where George Washington worshipped during his Charleston tour in 1791.) KHill brings unknown stories to light, noting, for example, three slave auction blocks in front of St. Michael's and one near Atlantic and East Battery streets. There, a concrete structure that looks like a step is actually where the enslaved were put up for sale. He also takes guests to a parking lot that is no ordinary parking lot—it was the site of a church where enslaved worshippers were burned up inside.

- The **Porgy & Bess Walking Tour** is described above, under Walking Tours.

For this option, meet Gullah Geechee Tours at Charleston City Market. Be prepared to question your assumptions about Gullah history, Black history, and the American story in general. Here's a shortcut to one of KHill's opening questions: What is Gullah? A quick Google search shows it is Hebrew for "redemption."

And so it begins.

★ GULLAH TOURS

tel. 843/763-7551; www.gullahtours.com; Mon.-Fri. 11am and 1pm; $20

Alphonso Brown's two-hour bus tour featuring the Black history of Charleston is full of energy and worth every minute. Alphonso slips in and out of English and Gullah as he relates textbook history and Charleston lore, infused with his signature wit and Gullah accent. He'll teach you some Gullah phrases too, like "Where's your frock tail going?" which means "You're wearing your hemline too high." Or "You cam wit cha," which means "You carry it with you."

For the most part, you'll stay on the bus while the gregarious Brown narrates Charleston Black history (though guests are allowed to disembark to spend quality time at the Philip Simmons Museum Home and Workshop). As you ride, Brown points out Underground Railroad stops and the home thought to belong to Denmark Vesey, and he tells the story of the whipping house by the infamous Old Jail (21 Magazine St.), which was in operation from 1802-1932. (The jail is still there; the whipping house isn't.) The tour also goes by the Old Slave Mart, Catfish Row (the area that inspired George Gershwin's opera, *Porgy and Bess*), Mother Emanuel Church, and the home of Richard DeReef, one of the richest Black men in Charleston.

Brown is star of this tour: He's the one who can show you how to determine if an iron work is a Simmons creation, for example. Take his tour to find who actress Lena Horne is related to and hear him crack wise about the Daughters of the American Revolution: "We're all related. I could qualify for the D.A.R.," Brown told one tour group. "I figure, why pay all those dues to frustrate people."

The tour meets at the Charleston Visitor Center (375 Meeting St.) bus shed—look for a bus marked "Gullah Tours." Reservations are required. For last-minute tours, call tel. 843/763-7551.

Shopping

A retail area of the **Charleston Visitor Center** (375 Meeting St.; tel. 843/724-7174; Mon.-Sun. 8:30am-5pm) highlights products native to the area, such as sweetgrass baskets and Jimmy Red corn bourbon, made with heritage grain thought to be extinct a century ago.

For more traditional retail options, your go-to is the **Upper King Street** shopping area.

MARKETS

HISTORIC CHARLESTON CITY MARKET

188 Meeting St.; tel. 843/937-0920; www.thecharlestoncitymarket.com; Mon.-Fri. 9:30am-5pm, Sat.-Sun. 9:30am-10:30pm

This bustling marketplace that spans four blocks offers the best of South Carolina craftsmanship and creativity. The

jewelry maker at Charleston City Market

SWEETGRASS BASKETS

On a table set up at the corner of Chalmers and Broad and Meeting streets (aka the Four Corners of Law), you might see Charleston-born artisan Donald Scott practicing his craft: sewing, repairing, and selling the sweetgrass baskets he learned to make at the direction of this grandmother. (Scott confesses that his 9- or 10-year-old self didn't really want to learn the basket-making craft, "but my grandmother had a way of twisting things and making me get with it," he says.)

sweetgrass basket maker Donald Scott

BACKGROUND

Sweetgrass baskets are made out of bulrush, a type of marsh grass, split oak, and sweetgrass pulled from the root. Their name comes from the scent of the grass, says Scott. It has been described as the smell of freshly cut hay.

These work-baskets have been used along the rice coast from North Carolina to Florida, and on the African continent, for centuries. Enslaved West Africans were expert rice growers, and their technical skills, including basket-making, were leveraged to cultivate the crop that made Charleston wealthy. (Sweetgrass baskets were instrumental in rice cultivation because the tightness of the weave allowed cultivators to separate the grain from the husk through winnowing.)

WHERE TO VIEW OR BUY BASKETS

The sweetgrass technique was elevated by Gullah artists who weave a variety of shapes for practical use or display as high art. Some simpler creations can be crafted in a few hours, but intricate baskets can take weeks to complete. To see a stunning example, head to the **Gibbes Museum of Art** (page 37), where a large basket by MacArthur Genius Mary Jackson is on display.

Looking to buy a basket yourself? Scott is out on the **Four Corners of Law** Tuesday-Sunday. Other sweetgrass artisans vend their creations in this area too. **Charleston City Market** is another place to buy.

Greek Revival-style hall dating back to 1804 is also a living contradiction, with space devoted to Black history as well as the Confederate Museum. (Don't worry: The museum is upstairs, and the shopping action is on the first floor.)

The market houses more than 300 local merchants and offers everything from paintings and jewelry to sweetgrass baskets, books, and clothing. More than 50 Gullah artists can be found here. The market has been called the epicenter of sweetgrass basketry in Charleston, and sweetgrass items on offer range from souvenir-size creations such as coasters and earrings to large baskets. More intricate designs can take months to complete, and sweetgrass artists often weave in a signature that denotes their particular style. Tip: If you're sourcing a sweetgrass basket here, ceramic tiles bearing the words "Certified Authentic Handmade in Charleston" is a sure-fire way to make sure your basket was made by local artisans.

Artists basically set up tables in the market and sell their wares. One vendor to look for is **Corey Alston's Gullah Sweetgrass Basket** table at the market entrance on Meeting Street (on the side below the Confederate Museum). When Alston was a teen, he took sweetgrass basket-making classes with his girlfriend (now longtime wife) "as a way of getting in." Turns out, he was quite adept at producing a clean stitch, and everyone around him was proud to see him express Gullah culture with skill.

THE CIGAR FACTORY

7201 E. Bay St.; tel. 843/723-3685; www.cigarfactorycharleston.com

This historic five-story brick building, which sits on the National Register of Historic Places, was constructed in 1881 and was converted into a cigar factory when it was purchased in 1912 by American Cigar Company. In the 1940s, it was the site of an important strike, when 1,900 workers—more than half of whom were Black women—walked out on the job. The event is considered a triumph of labor organizing.

Today, the building holds about 10 high-end retail shops and restaurants, along with event space and offices. (There's also ample parking.) One cute shop (not Black-owned) is **The COMMUNITY,** a women-owned cooperative where you can browse leatherworks, bespoke home goods, candles, baby clothes, jewelry, and more. A marker on the East Bay side of the building reminds passersby what went on here.

CRAFTS

FOUR CORNERS OF LAW

Find local treasures, such as sweetgrass baskets, at the intersection of Meeting and Market streets or Meeting and Broad Streets, known locally as the Four Corners of Law, in reference to buildings dedicated to city, state, federal and God's law. Artist vendors like **Donald Scott** set up here, handcrafting their goods before your eyes. If you're lucky, Scott might describe his technique to you as he describes the origins of sweetgrass basket-making passed down through the generations.

CLOTHING

IBU MOVEMENT

183 King St.; tel. 843/327-8304; www.ibu-movement.com; Mon.-Sat. noon-6pm

This King Street retail store, not a Black-owned business, features handmade goods by women around the world. For example, you'll find Kantha stitching from India and Bangladesh and beaded cuffs made by Native American craftswomen, woven fans, mirrored pouches, and all kinds of global designs that will break the monotony of your closet. What some might call cultural appropriation, Ibu Movement calls a cultural conversation. Or you can just call it appreciation for everything women are—everywhere.

FOOD PRODUCTS

LILLIE'S OF CHARLESTON

www.lilliesofcharleston.com

In the '80s, when Tracey Richardson and her sister pitched in at their father's Upper King Street restaurant, the Rib Shack, patrons frequently asked for extra sides of barbecue sauce, which was made with a signature mustardy flair. Richardson's dad, Hank Tisdale, not only gave away extras—he'd pop into the kitchen and

WE SHALL OVERCOME:
THE CIGAR FACTORY STRIKE OF 1945

Charleston Cigar Factory

On October 22, 1945, 1,900 workers—including 900 Black women—walked out on their jobs at the Cigar Factory in Charleston (now an upscale retail space).

The factory (which produced 1.5 million cigars a day at its high point) was rife with racism and unequal access to opportunity: White men held the highest-paying skilled jobs; White women held positions higher than that of Black women; and workers were segregated by race to work on different floors. Employees had been promised raises (from 25 cents to 40 cents an hour for Black workers and up to 65 cents an hour for White workers), but after the war ended, officials didn't share any of the $1.3 million they got back from the federal government.

The strike was met with resistance: Although the National Labor Relations Board ruled in the workers' favor, the company wouldn't budge, so the Congress of Industrial Organizations (CIO, which later merged with the American Federation of Labor to make the largest labor union group in the United States) called for a national boycott of American Tobacco Company products. The strike ended after five months with every worker receiving a raise and vow to be treated better.

The Cigar Factory Strike stands out because it fostered a coalition between Black and White workers, especially women working in solidarity for the first time. The civil rights anthem **"We Shall Overcome"** emerged from this strike when Lucille Simmons reworked the song "I Will Overcome One Day" by Black composer Charles Albert Tindley. Simmons changed "I" to "We" so the striking tobacco workers could sing the song on the picket line. Later, Zilphia Horton, cultural director at Highlander Folk School in Tennessee, introduced the song to Pete Seeger, who played it on his banjo in front of Martin Luther King Jr. in 1957. According to officials at the National Museum of African American History and Culture in Washington DC, "We Shall Overcome" became the anthem of the civil rights movement.

GET INTO THE RHYTHM

- **"We Shall Overcome"**: Striking Cigar Factory workers first introduced the idea of tweaking the words of Charles Albert Tindley's song, which became the anthem of the movement. The song has been interpreted by the best in the business, including Mahalia Jackson, the Staple Singers, Joan Baez, and the Freedom Singers.
- **Freedom Singers (SNCC), "Woke Up This Morning"**: It is easy to understand how this reworked gospel song, released in 1964, might have infused the movement with momentum and energy with congregational-style signing. Rutha Mae Harris, an original Freedom Singer, told NPR's "Tell Me More": "Without the songs of the movement, personally I believe there wouldn't have been a movement. . . . We needed those songs to help us not to be fearful when we were doing marches, or doing picket lines. And you needed a calming agent, and that's what those songs were for us."[1]

hand out whole containers full. "Money, walkin' out the door," she recalls. Even when her dad closed the business, people still asked for the sauce. So in 2001, Richardson and her husband, Jamel, a chemistry whiz, unearthed the old family recipes and developed them for mass production.

Today, the Charleston couple runs Lillie's of Charleston, named in honor of Richardson's aunt. A variety of barbecue and hot sauces are available in stores across the nation, including **Gita's Gourmet** (tel. 843/722-8207) and **Edna's Lowcountry** (tel. 843/452-4599), both located in Historic Charleston City Market, and online. The Richardsons are also thought-leaders in the Charleston foodscape. Tracey has Gullah heritage and offers the lowdown on what is good in Gullah-inspired foodways and Charleston yumminess.

Food

Whether on or off the Peninsula, Charleston offers a range of eateries featuring dishes informed by both African and African American foodways. Smoked barbecue is a go-to, as are dishes that reflect the ingenuity of the African diaspora. Rice made Charleston very wealthy early on, so you will frequently see dishes that reflect the contribution of Black people who did the hard work of producing this financial wealth in rice fields, while nurturing a rich cultural heritage that links us to the Motherland.

It's important to note most Black-owned restaurants are not found in tourist areas because Black entrepreneurs can't afford spaces downtown. Black entrepreneurs usually don't own the buildings where they operate, so when they are successful, higher rents can follow, explains

Tracey Richardson, who runs hot sauce and barbecue sauce company Lillie's of Charleston. This structural barrier is addressed by seeking lower rents off the Peninsula and the ability to serve the community up close and personal.

Also true on a visit to Charleston: You will eat, and you will eat well.

DOWNTOWN

Southern and Soul Food

MILLER'S ALL DAY

120 King St.; tel. 843/501-7342; www.millersallday.com; Mon.-Fri. 8am-3pm; Sat.-Sun. 8am-4pm; $6-12

It's right there in the name: Miller's All Day (not Black-owned) serves breakfast all day long, plus lunch if you'd like. This popular spot is run by the folks behind Geechie Boy Mill, which makes small-batch grits, hand-milled grits in several varieties. The menu features everything from frittatas to small stack pancakes to braised okra and tomatoes served over grits and crab fried rice. There's sandwiches, sides, and snacks for sharing. The cocktail menu features a variety of Bloody Mary mixes and mimosas. Bakery offerings include donuts, pie, cookies, and muffins.

UPPER KING AND VICINITY

Gullah and Low Country

HANNIBAL'S SOUL KITCHEN

16 Blake St.; tel. 843/722-2256; www.hannibalkitchen.com; Mon.-Sat. 7am-9pm; $6-11

Hannibal's is sure to come up when asking around for the best soul food in Charleston. You'll find coastal favorites, like Charleston shrimp and grits, grilled or fried whiting filet, okra soup, Hannibal's crab rice, lima beans, smoked turkey . . . the list goes on and on. The restaurant, named for family patriarch Robert Lawrence Huger—whose nickname was Hannibal—is a fixture at community events and causes. The restaurant is right around the corner from the renovated Cigar Factory. The décor has a rustic neighborhood feel.

Barbecue

RODNEY SCOTT'S BBQ

1011 King St.; tel. 843/990-9535; www.rodneyscottsbbq.com; Mon.-Sun. 11am-9pm; $11-28

The thick paper towels found on each table are a clue to the barbecue goodness found at Rodney Scott's BBQ. Pittmaster Scott has been smoking whole hogs since age 11, starting as a boy in Hemingway, South Carolina. His family ran a roadside convenience store that served smoked pork and drew patrons from near and far. Here, you'll find pit-smoked turkey and chicken, spareribs, and fried catfish. Salads skew to the hearty side: Violet's Garden Salad, for example, features mixed greens, pork rinds, bacon, tomato, cucumber, and red onion. Sides include baked beans, hush puppies, greens, potato salad, and more. Rodney Scott's BBQ staff are welcoming and friendly—the food tastes good, and the people here will make you feel good too.

OTHER NEIGHBORHOODS

While a little away from the beaten historical path, the following restaurants are beloved institutions in Charleston that have been recognized widely in the food world.

Gullah and Low Country

MARTHA LOU'S KITCHEN

1068 Morrison Dr.; tel. 843/577-9583; www.marthalouskitchen.com

Sadly, as this book was going to press, the 90-year-old owner of Martha Lou's Kitchen announced plans to close after nearly 40 years in business. Martha Lou's was just the taste of soul you need after taking in

CHARLESTON SPECIALTIES

PERLOO

Hannibal's Soul Kitchen

Rice forms the foundation of a one-pot dish called "perloo" (also spelled pilau, perlou, or purloo): presoaked rice cooked in an aromatic broth, then set aside to soak and finish. Savory perloo can include a range of ingredients, including onions, carrots, celery, bell pepper, pigeon peas or beans, shrimp, and bits of meat. Perloo is cooked in a single pot because that is all enslaved Africans possessed. This takeoff from the West African jollof dish may also include yams.

OKRA SOUP

Gumbo, typically associated with New Orleans, is a word for okra in many West African languages, and it also finds a home in South Carolina. Bertha's Kitchen, Hannibal's Soul Kitchen, and Martha Lou's Kitchen all offer an authentic okra soup. These down-home restaurants are considered soul food joints and feature Black family recipes passed through generations. "Most people here will call it okra stew or okra soup because the dish is so associated with New Orleans," says Tracey Richardson of Lillie's of Charleston.

SEAFOOD

Be sure to enjoy the South Carolina Lowcountry deliciousness of creamy **she-crab soup** made with the orange roe of the crab, and shrimp and grits. Due to the seasonal nature of harvesting the caviar of a female crab, she-crab soup is traditionally served in upscale restaurants: "It's a delicacy," Richardson says.

And oh, do they know how to fry some crispy battered whiting fish in Charleston. Says Richardson: "Whiting's like the top fish here. Some Black people who go to restaurants, if they don't see whiting on the menu, they won't eat fish."

FROGMORE STEW

Named for a community on St. Helena Island, this meal is made of crab, shrimp, sausage, corn, miniature red potatoes, and seasonings that have an Old Bay flavor. Charlestonian's like to mix their own spices, and may add some onions and a bay leaf for good measure. The "stew" is boiled in gallons of water in a big pot, cooled, then eaten on a picnic table covered with paper. "You dump it out, pick up the pieces, and eat it with your fingers. That's it," Richardson says.

Charleston's sights. Inside the tiny seven-table eatery, patrons waited on their meals while sipping on sweet tea and listening to pop and R&B play from the large boombox. The tiny kitchen served up turkey wings, pork chops, fried chicken, rice, lima beans, and even chitterlings (where's gospel great Shirley Caesar when you need her?). The restaurant walls told the story of Martha Lou Gadsden's journey and that of the Black experience. Martha Lou started as a bus girl, then became a waitress, eventually opening her own spot (which is Zagat-rated) at age 53. Her daughters hope to carry on her legacy by reopening the restaurant in a new location.

★ BERTHA'S KITCHEN

2332 Meeting Street Rd.; tel. 843/554-6519; Mon.-Fri. 11am-6pm, Sat. noon-6pm; $8-15

During the lunch and dinner rushes at Bertha's, lines snake from the front door up to the cashier where you place your order. It's worth the wait, and you're even likely to make friends with kind patrons who scoot over to make room for the stream of people coming in and out. This menu of Southern classics and Gullah dishes, first crafted by the late Alberta Grant, covers the gamut, from Hoppin' John peas and smothered chops to oxtails, yams, barbecue pig feet, and cabbage. Patrons can see right inside the open kitchen behind the counter. The carryout business is brisk, but if you chose to eat in, you'll be cooled by air-conditioning plus ceiling fans to deal with the South Carolina heat. This place has always been a family affair: Family photos pepper the entryway, and you can look right into the happy faces of the Grant family glass mural while you're standing in line.

Bertha's is located about five miles north of downtown Charleston, a 10-minute drive along Morrison Drive and US-52 West.

NIGEL'S GOOD FOOD

3760 Ashley Phosphate Rd.; tel. 843/552-0079; www.nigelsgoodfood.com; Tues.-Thurs. 11am-9:30pm, Fri.-Sat. 11am-10pm, Sun. 11am-9pm; $10-16

Nigel's serves up piping-hot regional fare that includes salmon and grits, Nigel's award-winning oyster stew, lima beans and rice, and several pasta dishes such as seafood alfredo and Low Country ravioli tossed in a whiskey cream sauce—yum! Owner Nigel Drayton worked in kitchens throughout Charleston before waking up to his dream of opening a restaurant, and now he has two: The other one, Nigel's, is in nearby Ladson. Be sure to order from the list of "Kool-Aids" served here: fruit punch, peach, and lemonade.

Nigel's Good Food is located about 17 miles north of downtown, a 25-minute drive on I-26 West in North Charleston. Folks say the ride out here is worth the trip.

GILLIE'S SEAFOOD

805 Folly Rd.; tel. 843/297-8615; www.gilliesoulfood.com; Sun.-Sat. 11am-9pm, Sat.-Sun. brunch 11am-2pm; $5-18.50

Gillie's Seafood is off the Peninsula travel path, but it's worth the trip to James Island to enjoy a variety of seafood dishes made from scratch. Appetizers include she-crab soup made with lump crab meat, crab roe, and a touch of sherry. (Sample a cup for $6.) Or try the soul rolls, deep-fried egg rolls stuffed with collard greens, pulled pork, red rice, and pimento cheese. The main event features dishes such as Seafood Purloo, made with seasoned rice, shrimp, crawfish, crab meat, oysters, okra, onions, and smoked sausage, and Granny's Shrimp & Grits, an award-winning dish. Meat-and-threes are on offer here and include fried chicken and meatloaf with sides that run from greens, cabbage, and onion rings to sweet potato fries, hushpuppies, and more.

Photos (top to bottom): Martha Lou's Kitchen; food at Bertha's Kitchen; Rodney Scott's BBQ (left); Miller's All Day (right)

The Richardsons of Lillie's of Charleston like this place, so you know it must be good. Each family member has their own favorite dishes: Jamel loves Gillie's fried pork chops, mac and cheese, and collard greens, and Tracey loves Chef Sean Mendes's shrimp and grits. Her father favors the flounder basket with red rice and lima beans, while her mother always gets okra gumbo with fried chicken and hush puppies.

Nightlife

This might be the Holy City, but it doesn't have to stay that way. Seriously, Charleston is so supremely walkable that the people-watching on the way to your nightlife spot of choice is enjoyable. You'll find plenty of bars around Upper King Street and Market Street, though depending on where you're staying, you might need to book a short taxi to get there.

BARS

VENDUE HOTEL ROOFTOP BAR

19 Vendue Range; tel. 843/577-7970; www.thevendue.com; Sun.-Thurs. 11:30am-10pm, Fri.-Sat. 11:30am-midnight

Atop the Venue Hotel, this rooftop bar (not Black-owned) offers sweeping views of the Holy City. This includes Charleston Harbor, Waterfront Park, and the Arthur Ravenel Jr. Bridge. Folks like to meet here for lunch or to relax after working or sightseeing all day. The drinks menu offers a full complement of specialty cocktails. The fish or shrimp tacos are pretty delicious, but staples like burgers and quesadillas are on offer too. If you have room for dessert, you can't go wrong with either the key lime pie or chocolate cake. One thing though: If you come during the summer, be sure to apply DEET or your mosquito repellent of choice first.

THE COCKTAIL CLUB

479 King St.; tel. 843/724.9411; www.thecocktailclubcharleston.com; Mon.-Sun. 5pm-2am

Located on Upper King right above The Macintosh farm-to-table restaurant, The Cocktail Club (not Black-owned) was renovated into an upscale speakeasy when they decided to rip the plaster to showcase exposed walls with original beams. The custom bar is made from salvaged wood dating back to the late 1800s. This 2,500-square-foot club specializes in house-made infusions, rare liquors, and beverages using fresh-squeezed juices and modern ingredients. For example, the Trapeze Artist blends Old Forrester bourbon, strega, blackberry, fresh lemon, and rhubarb bitters. An extensive list of wine and spirits are on offer. Three seating areas offer the comfort of leather couches, chairs, fireplaces, and sophisticated lighting. There's a rooftop terrace to enjoy the Charleston night sky, and it has a garden from which drink garnishes are picked. The club has its own entrance off King.

CLUBS

THE COMMODORE

504 Meeting St.; www.thecommodorechs.com; Wed.-Sat. 5pm-2am, Sun. 6pm-2am

Forget about calling ahead to ask questions about what to expect at this vintage jazz club; The Commodore doesn't do phones. You'll just have to show up to enjoy distinctive bar offerings, including a range of craft beer and signature cocktails, while listening to a range of music styles, from jazz and funk sets, to DJ sessions that will make you want to hit the dance floor. Live music includes house bands like Lady & The Brass

drinks at The Vendue rooftop hotel bar

and Future Funk, but you can check out The Commodore's online calendar to see who's on deck. This is a grown folks affair—only ages 21 and up are allowed.

THE ROYAL AMERICAN

970 Morrison St.; tel. 843/817-6925; www.theroyalamerican.com; Sun.-Sat. 11am-2am

This downtown venue (not a Black-owned business) serves as a bar, restaurant, and live music venue. Special events include Trappy Hour, featuring independent Charleston hip-hop acts and curated by The Cocktail Bandits, Taneka Reaves and Johnny Caldwell. Live music performed on a small stage showcases local and national acts. It has hosted Cultura, a music festival dedicated to Black R&B and hip-hop artists. The venue has a full restaurant menu too. Atlanta's Slutty Vegan, Pinky Cole, took her show on the road and did a pop-up here as part of her Gettin' Slutty Tour. Located in the Old Charleston Forge, The Royal American retains the rustic feel of iron, sweat, and hard work, accented by stringed lights and band posters.

Accommodations

In addition to the options below, the **Hampton Inn** (345 Meeting St.; tel. 877/214-6725; www.hamptoninncharleston.guestreservations.com; $243), in the Upper King area, is a good choice. The best thing about this midrange hotel (with a pool) is it happens to be right around the corner from Emanuel A.M.E., making a visit there to learn about the history of Black empowerment and self-determination an easy go-to.

DOWNTOWN

$100-200

ELLIOTT HOUSE INN

78 Queen St.; tel. 843/207-2299; www.elliotthouseinn.com; $159

This 26-room coral-colored hotel was a private home for over a century but now welcomes visitors with an inviting breezy courtyard and furnishings that offer shade

Elliot House Inn

from the Southern sun. Breakfast and happy hour in the courtyard allow guests to sit quietly or get to know fellow travelers. Situated on Queen Street, Elliott House Inn is around the corner from The Gibbes Museum and other sights, plus plenty of shopping and restaurants. The inn is a 10-minute walk from the Charleston Historic District.

THE VENDUE: CHARLESTON'S ART HOTEL

19 Vendue Range; tel. 843/577-7970; www.thevendue.com; $189

Routinely rated among the best hotels in Charleston, The Vendue is an exercise in art and luxury. Situated downtown, this boutique art hotel is steps away from sights, shopping, and restaurants. This boutique hotel is actually two buildings: 19 Vendue and 26 Vendue. The older of the two, 19 Vendue is a combination of five warehouses dating to 1780, where you'll get that Old World feel walking down the narrow, twisty hallways lined with artwork. Spacious rooms have tall windows and modern fixtures filled with glorious sunlight. An inviting lobby, called the Drawing Room, offers a full bar. The hotel offers some complimentary breakfast items and an a la carte menu that changes seasonally, and they endeavor to include heirloom ingredients whenever possible.

A short elevator ride takes you to the **Vendue Rooftop** where you can order cocktails and fancy bar food while overlooking Charleston Harbor. Vendue's restaurant, **The Revival,** features Southern fare, including previously extinct ingredients such as Jimmy Red grits or Bradford watermelon. Dishes include beef tartare and Low Country Pirlou and Breast of Duck Au Poivre.

Across the street at 26 Vendue, you will find an art gallery, though both buildings are teeming with hundreds of artworks on the walls. A variety of styles are featured in the rotating displays at The Vendue, which have included Molly Right's beautiful portrait of Maya Angelou made with bottle caps or Will Kurtz's mixed-media sculpture, "Rastafarian."

The Vendue makes bikes available for getting around town, and staff are eager to help guests figure everything out.

The Vendue: Charleston's Art Hotel

Transportation

GETTING THERE

Air

Charleston International Airport (5500 International Blvd.; tel. 843/767-7000; www.iflychs.com) is about 12 miles from downtown. There's a taxi stand outside baggage claim that will run you about $16.

Charleston Regional Transportation Authority's (CARTA) Route 11 Dorchester/Airport goes straight into downtown (dropping off at Meeting Street/Mary Street next to the Charleston Visitor Center) and also serves North Charleston. The X4 express runs every hour but will also get you downtown. The stop is in the passenger pickup area, and another can be found in the rental car lot. A one-way trip costs $3.50.

Train

Charleston's **Amtrak station** (4565 Gaynor Ave., North Charleston; tel. 800/872-7245; www.amtrak.com/stations; Mon.-Sun. 4am-11:45am and 4pm-11:45 pm) is located in the same transit center as Greyhound in North Charleston, about seven miles north of downtown. A one-way fare to Charleston from Durham, North Carolina, costs $65; the trip takes about 8 hours with a transfer in Wilson, North Carolina. To Charleston from downtown Richmond, Virginia, will cost you $78 for a 12-hour 37-minute ride with transfer at Richmond's Staples Mill Station.

Bus

Charleston's **Greyhound station** (4565 Gaynor Ave, North Charleston; tel. 843/744-4247; www.greyhound.com) is located in North Charleston, about seven miles north of downtown. From Atlanta, take an eight-hour ride to Charleston for about $35.

Car

To get to Charleston from:

- **Atlanta:** Take **I-20 East,** then **I-26 East,** for around 300 miles (4.5 hours).

- **Raleigh, North Carolina:** Take **I-95 South,** then **I-26 East,** for around 480 miles (2 hours).

GETTING AROUND

Not only is Charleston walkable, you might very well find yourself walking on historic cobblestones or streets paved with recycled ballast. The DASH Trolley is the best way to get around downtown.

Parking

The City of Charleston operates several parking facilities, including $5 to $7 flat daily rate at several garages. The daily maximum in several locations is $18. On Sundays, metered spots are free.

Public Transit

The **DASH Trolley** (www.ridecarta.com), a hop-on, hop-off shuttle, is a convenient way to get to shops and attractions—and it's free. Pick up a free map at the official **Charleston Area Visitor Center** (375 Meeting St.), or look for one on the CARTA website.

Charleston also has **CARTA buses,** which cost $3.50 per ride. Or save money with a pass, such as a 10-ride pass ($16) or a 40-ride pass ($56). You can buy a pass at **Charleston Visitor Center** (375 Meeting St.; tel. 843/724-7174; Mon.-Sun. 8:30am-5pm).

The trolley is a better option for sightseeing. Buses are generally an option for those who want to leave the peninsula.

Taxi and Ride-Hailing Apps

Uber and **Lyft** are available here. Need a taxi? Call **Charleston Cab Company** (tel. 843/566-5757).

Atlanta

Atlanta was Dr. Martin Luther King Jr.'s Gethsemane, a place of solitude and peace, according to King acolyte Rev. Jesse L. Jackson. Memphis, where King was crucified, was his Calvary.

King's hometown is a vibrant, progressive Southern city and Black mecca, home to several historically Black colleges and universities (HBCUs). Visitors have the opportunity to walk in King's footsteps, eating where he ate and exploring his childhood neighborhood of Sweet Auburn, where he spent his first 12 years in middle-class comfort. Visitors are welcome to walk through Ebenezer Baptist Church, where 19-year-old Martin King gave his first sermon, and where his funeral was held 20 years later. Just across the street, you'll find

ATLANTA'S TOP 3

1. Seeing the room where King was born during a visit to the civil rights luminary's **Birth Home** (page 71).

2. Immersing yourself in a sensory re-creation of the civil rights struggle at the **National Center for Civil and Human Rights** (page 78).

3. Enjoying legendary eats (just as King did) at **Busy Bee Café,** known for their excellent fried chicken (page 88).

Photos (top to bottom): Martin Luther King Jr. Birth Home; National Center for Civil and Human Rights; Busy Bee Café. Previous: John Lewis Mural a still-thriving Ebenezer congregation at 6,000 strong in a newer edifice.

Atlanta is also home to the Southern Christian Leadership Conference (SCLC), the civil rights organization that grew out of the Montgomery Improvement Association (MIA), which successfully led a 381-day boycott to desegregate city buses in Montgomery, Alabama. It was agreed that the SCLC would stand for civil rights for all people and that nonviolent strategies and tactics would be a key method of pressing for desegregation and equal rights. King was chosen as president of the SCLC, Ralph Abernathy was elected financial secretary-treasurer, and Ella Baker was the mastermind of the organization's agenda. The SCLC (320 Auburn Ave NE; tel. 404/522-1420), with chapters and affiliates across the country, is still on the case.

There was a vibrant student movement here too, born in February 1960 when Morehouse College students Lonnie King, Joseph Pierce, and Julian Bond rallied local students into action. Spelman College student Roslyn Pope's "An Appeal for Human Rights" formed a philosophical framework for student actions, and singer Gladys Knight & the Pips sang at Atlanta Student Movement fundraisers.

Thanks not only to King, but also to Atlanta's other early civil rights successes, you might consider Atlanta the spiritual home of the civil rights movement. You can envelop yourself in the story of Black self-determination here by visiting neighborhoods, landmarks, and institutions that have sustained African Americans' sense of belonging, responsibility, and ownership of the democratic experiment.

Today, Atlanta's status as a hub for creative, entrepreneurial people—especially African Americans—is a manifestation of what the movement was all about. Known as the LGBTQ capital of the South, it is generally considered an inclusive city where anyone can find their place. You'll feel this in the city—in the multicultural lines of people waiting patiently for a meal in gentrifying Westview, for example. At museums, where visitors come together to learn about the segregated South and come out on the other side convicted by a shared experience, a type of validation emerges. Still, given the structural inequities built into the U.S. system of work, education, housing, and governance, there is still much more work to be done.

ORIENTATION

Downtown Atlanta is bordered by North Avenue to the north, I-85 to the east, I-20 to the south, and Northside Drive to the west. The **Sweet Auburn Historic District** at Auburn Avenue between Courtland Street and I-75/I-85 is part of downtown Atlanta and is listed on the National Register of Historic Places. Sweet Auburn originally also included the eastern side of Auburn Avenue, where the **Martin Luther King Jr. National Historical Park** is located, but the construction of the highway severed the neighborhood in two. In this book, we've included both the eastern and western ends of Auburn Avenue under the Sweet Auburn Historic District heading.

West of downtown, the **Atlanta University Center** in West End is the world's largest association of historically Black colleges and universities (HBCU): Morehouse College, Spelman College, Clark Atlanta University, and Morehouse School of Medicine.

Westview is a predominately Black neighborhood adjacent to West End with an influx of newer, diverse residents.

Atlanta can be car-centric, but officials are working on making more areas pedestrian friendly. Sweet Auburn is highly walkable.

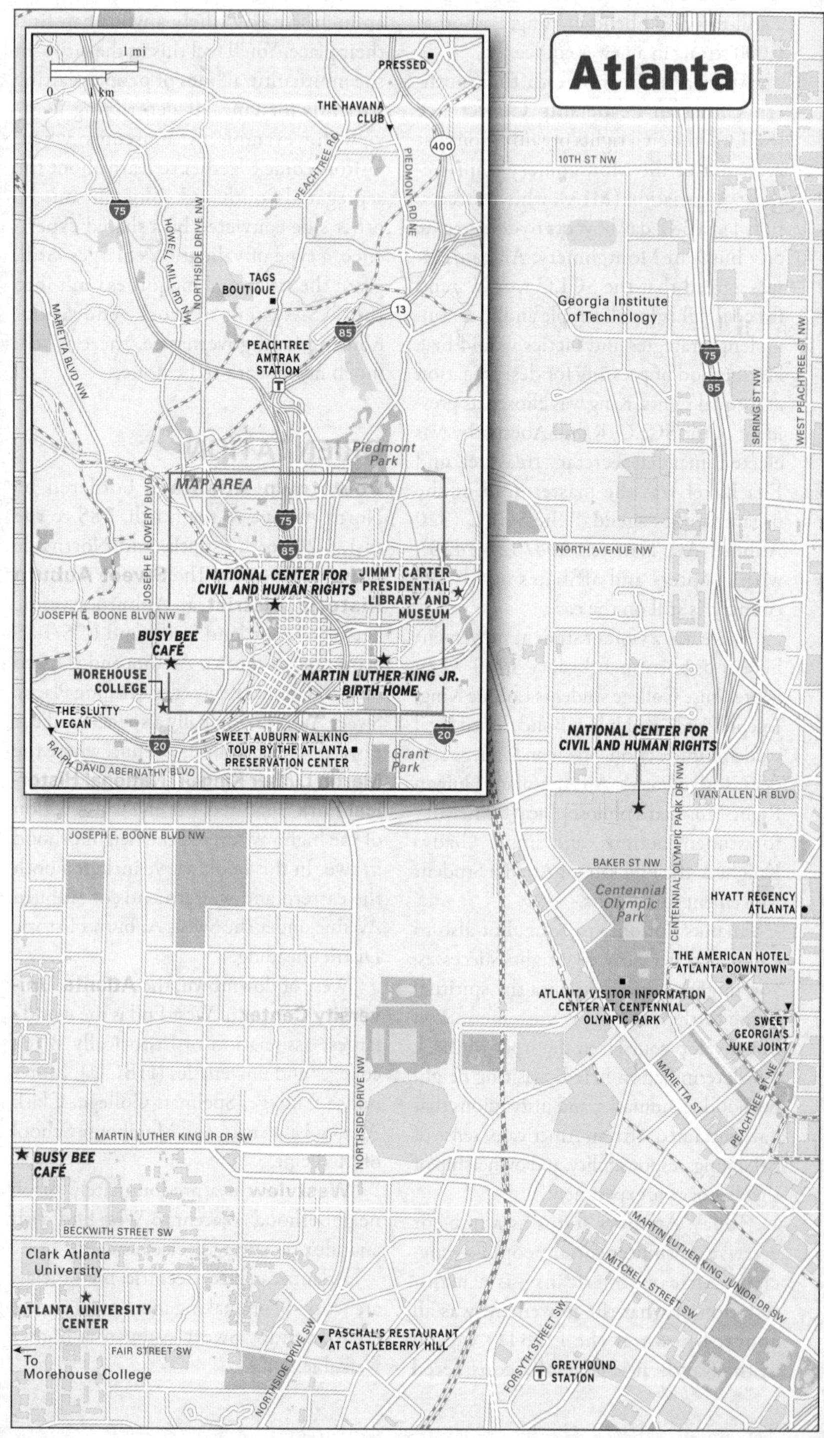
Atlanta
0 1 mi
0 1 km
PRESSED
THE HAVANA CLUB
PEACHTREE RD
PIEDMONT RD NE
75
400
HOWELL MILL RD NW
NORTHSIDE DRIVE NW
TAGS BOUTIQUE
MARIETTA BLVD NW
13
85
PEACHTREE AMTRAK STATION
T
Piedmont Park
MAP AREA
JOSEPH E. LOWERY BLVD
NATIONAL CENTER FOR CIVIL AND HUMAN RIGHTS
JIMMY CARTER PRESIDENTIAL LIBRARY AND MUSEUM
JOSEPH E. BOONE BLVD NW
BUSY BEE CAFÉ
MOREHOUSE COLLEGE
MARTIN LUTHER KING JR. BIRTH HOME
THE SLUTTY VEGAN
20
SWEET AUBURN WALKING TOUR BY THE ATLANTA PRESERVATION CENTER
Grant Park
RALPH DAVID ABERNATHY BLVD
10TH ST NW
Georgia Institute of Technology
SPRING ST NW
WEST PEACHTREE ST NW
NORTH AVENUE NW
NATIONAL CENTER FOR CIVIL AND HUMAN RIGHTS
IVAN ALLEN JR BLVD
CENTENNIAL OLYMPIC PARK DR NW
BAKER ST NW
Centennial Olympic Park
HYATT REGENCY ATLANTA
THE AMERICAN HOTEL ATLANTA DOWNTOWN
ATLANTA VISITOR INFORMATION CENTER AT CENTENNIAL OLYMPIC PARK
SWEET GEORGIA'S JUKE JOINT
MARIETTA ST
PEACHTREE ST NE
NORTHSIDE DRIVE NW
MARTIN LUTHER KING JR DR SW
BUSY BEE CAFÉ
BECKWITH STREET SW
MARTIN LUTHER KING JUNIOR DR SW
MITCHELL STREET SW
Clark Atlanta University
ATLANTA UNIVERSITY CENTER
PASCHAL'S RESTAURANT AT CASTLEBERRY HILL
FORSYTH STREET SW
FAIR STREET SW
To Morehouse College
NORTHSIDE DRIVE SW
GREYHOUND STATION

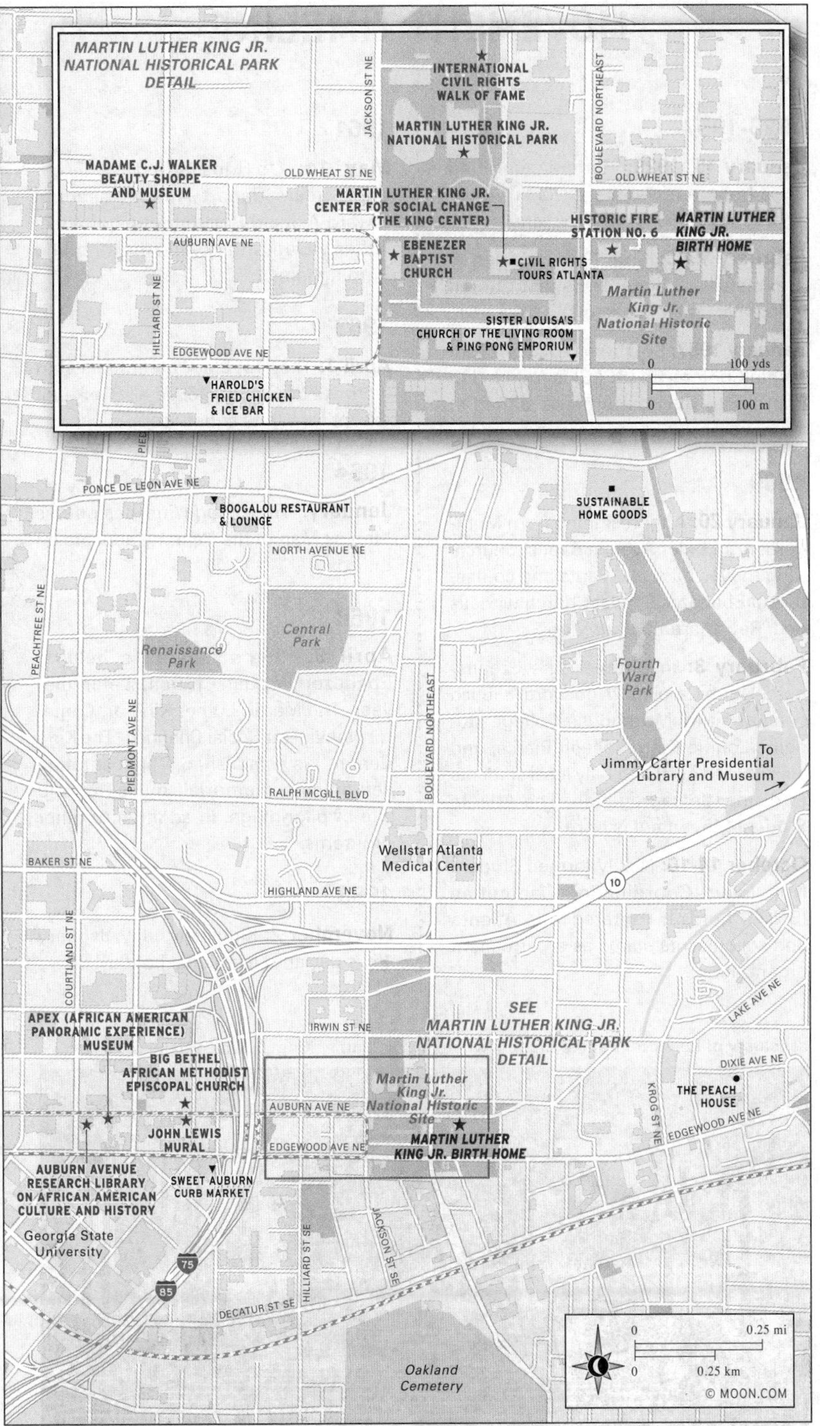
MARTIN LUTHER KING JR. NATIONAL HISTORICAL PARK DETAIL
INTERNATIONAL CIVIL RIGHTS WALK OF FAME
MARTIN LUTHER KING JR. NATIONAL HISTORICAL PARK
MADAME C.J. WALKER BEAUTY SHOPPE AND MUSEUM
OLD WHEAT ST NE
JACKSON ST NE
BOULEVARD NORTHEAST
MARTIN LUTHER KING JR. CENTER FOR SOCIAL CHANGE (THE KING CENTER)
HISTORIC FIRE STATION NO. 6
MARTIN LUTHER KING JR. BIRTH HOME
AUBURN AVE NE
EBENEZER BAPTIST CHURCH
CIVIL RIGHTS TOURS ATLANTA
Martin Luther King Jr. National Historic Site
HILLIARD ST NE
SISTER LOUISA'S CHURCH OF THE LIVING ROOM & PING PONG EMPORIUM
EDGEWOOD AVE NE
HAROLD'S FRIED CHICKEN & ICE BAR
0
100 yds
100 m
PONCE DE LEON AVE NE
BOOGALOU RESTAURANT & LOUNGE
SUSTAINABLE HOME GOODS
NORTH AVENUE NE
PEACHTREE ST NE
Central Park
Renaissance Park
Fourth Ward Park
PIEDMONT AVE NE
To Jimmy Carter Presidential Library and Museum
RALPH MCGILL BLVD
Wellstar Atlanta Medical Center
BAKER ST NE
HIGHLAND AVE NE
10
COURTLAND ST NE
SEE MARTIN LUTHER KING JR. NATIONAL HISTORICAL PARK DETAIL
LAKE AVE NE
APEX (AFRICAN AMERICAN PANORAMIC EXPERIENCE) MUSEUM
IRWIN ST NE
BIG BETHEL AFRICAN METHODIST EPISCOPAL CHURCH
DIXIE AVE NE
KROG ST NE
THE PEACH HOUSE
JOHN LEWIS MURAL
AUBURN AVENUE RESEARCH LIBRARY ON AFRICAN AMERICAN CULTURE AND HISTORY
SWEET AUBURN CURB MARKET
Georgia State University
HILLIARD ST SE
JACKSON ST SE
75
85
DECATUR ST SE
Oakland Cemetery
0.25 mi
0.25 km
© MOON.COM

ATLANTA

MOVEMENT TIMELINE

1929-1957

January 15, 1929: Martin Luther King Jr. is born in a two-story Queen Anne-style home at 501 Auburn Avenue.

February 1948: King, 19, is ordained as a minister at Ebenezer Baptist Church where his father is pastor.

January 1957: Southern Christian Leadership Conference (SCLC) is founded to coordinate regional protests aimed at dismantling racial segregation.

1960

January 20: After resigning from Montgomery's Dexter Avenue Baptist Church, King moves back to Atlanta and co-pastors at Ebenezer Baptist Church with his dad, Rev. Martin Luther King Sr.

February 3: Inspired by the Greensboro, North Carolina, Woolworth's lunch counter sit-in, Morehouse College students Lonnie King, Joseph Pierce, and Julian Bond decide to rally local students to dismantle segregation. The Atlanta Student Movement is born.

October 14-16: Newly formed Student Nonviolent Coordinating Committee (SNCC) holds a conference in Atlanta and solidifies its status as a permanent organization.

1961

May 14: On Mother's Day, Freedom Riders depart Atlanta heading toward Alabama. Both groups of riders suffer violent attacks in Anniston and Birmingham.

1963

April 1: The first Black firefighters start work at Fire Station 16, an all-Black unit except for White supervisors.

1964

January: *Time* magazine designates King as Man of the Year; he appears on the cover.

1968

April 9: King's funeral is held at Ebenezer Baptist Church. Later that year, The Martin Luther King Jr. Center for Nonviolent Social Change ("The King Center") is established. The institution serves as a memorial, museum, and site of pilgrimage, in addition to other programs.

1983

November 2: King's birthday, January 15, is declared a national holiday.

sanctuary of Ebenezer Baptist Church, where Martin Luther King Jr. was ordained

PEOPLE WHO MADE THE MOVEMENT

Dr. Martin Luther King Jr: The civil rights luminary was born and raised in Atlanta. His funeral was held here as well.

John Lewis: Longtime Georgia U.S. congressman; Nashville sit-in movement leader; founding member of the Student Nonviolent Coordinating Committee (SNCC); and a civil rights crusader.

John Lewis in 1964

John Wesley Dobbs: Unofficial mayor of Sweet Auburn Avenue, aka the "richest Negro street in the world." Dobbs also registered 10,000 Black voters in the 1930s and was a co-founder the Atlanta Civic and Political League in 1936 and the Atlanta Negro Voters League in 1946.

Julian Bond: Morehouse College student who launched the Atlanta student movement in 1960 along with two other Black students, Lonnie King and Joseph Pierce. Bond was also a co-founder of SNCC.

Rev. Dr. Bernice King: King's youngest daughter; helms Atlanta's The King Center today.

Rev. Ralph Abernathy: Abernathy and King became fast and enduring friends as they worked in the movement. Abernathy also earned a master's degree at Atlanta University and pastored here. He assumed the helm of the SCLC upon his friend's death.

PLANNING YOUR TIME

It's possible to take in Atlanta's best civil rights sites in two days. Although summer months get pretty hot, the weather is relatively decent year-round, so there's no bad time to visit. Timing your visit to Martin Luther King Jr. Day in January is a great way to feel close to the people and community that nurtured this courageous man; however, it's the busiest day of the year at the King-associated sights. Reserve your spot with Civil Rights Tours Atlanta in advance.

Get maps, directions, and connection to tour guides at the **Atlanta Visitor Information Center at Centennial Olympic Park** (267 Park Ave. W NW; tel. 404/521-6569).

CONNECT WITH

After Atlanta, **Birmingham,** where you can learn about the 1963 Birmingham Campaign, is a logical next stop. Alternatively, now that you've seen where King got his start, you may want to road trip to **Memphis** to contemplate how he came to his end and what that meant for the civil rights movement.

Two Days in Atlanta

ATLANTA

DAY 1

Today, you'll get a broad overview of civil rights at a couple of museums, which are book-ended by two restaurants: one with a historic connection to the movement; the second, a Black woman-owned business, an emblem of modern Atlanta. These sites are fairly spaced out, so you'll probably want to drive.

1 **Busy Bee Café,** near the Atlanta University Center, was a go-to spot for folks in the movement. Grab an early lunch when the café opens at 11 to avoid the long line. Try the in-restaurant platter specials, such as meatloaf, or keep it light with a veggie plate.

2 Start your journey with a bit of quirk and eccentricity at the **Madame C. J. Walker Beauty Shoppe and Museum.**

3 Next, head over to the **National Center for Civil and Human Rights** a couple miles away in downtown Atlanta. Give yourself at least 90 minutes with these stories and exhibits.

4 Finish your day learning about the 39th president and his contributions to humanitarian efforts at the **Jimmy Carter Presidential Library and Museum.** Carter has stressed that the civil rights movement isn't just history; it's about what's happening in real time to create equity and access, regardless of race.

5 A plant-based burger from **The Slutty Vegan,** located across town, is a good look right now. The fanfare of standing in line with other excited diners feels so . . . Atlanta. You can't help but have a good time as the line cooks (seen through the windows) sing, rap, and chant while preparing fresh fries and more.

DAY 2

You'll spend much of your second day in Sweet Auburn, where King grew up, with a few stops downtown later in the day. Map-wise, these places aren't that far apart, but driving (or taking a cab) is still easier than walking, especially if it's a hot summer day.

1 Get to the visitor center of Martin Luther King Jr. National Historical Park early—hopefully you'll secure a spot on the first tour of the **Martin Luther King Jr. Birth Home** at 10am. (Tours are limited to 15 people and must be booked in person.) The tour takes 30 minutes.

2 Afterward, walk over to **Ebenezer Baptist Church,** where King was first ordained, to explore on your own. Rangers are on hand to answer questions.

3 After your tour, stop by privately run **The King Center** and visit exhibits showcasing the life stories of Coretta Scott King, King Jr., Gandhi, and Rosa Parks.

4 You're probably ready for a break, so head over to **Sweet Auburn Curb Market** for lunch.

5 Sweet Auburn Curb Market is right by the stunning **John Lewis Mural,** which you've likely seen from various vantage points during your travels throughout the city. If it's not too hot, take an after-lunch walk over to the mural to take it all in. You might feel some things.

6 Still have time and energy? Head west to the **APEX (African American Panoramic Experience) Museum** to celebrate Black history and achievements with films and exhibits. Note that the museum closes at 5pm.

7 After you finish sightseeing, keep heading west to **SustainAble Home Goods** for some shopping.

8 Dinner at **Paschal's Restaurant at Castleberry Hill,** another historic eatery, is the way to end your day.

Sights

Atlanta is home to several spots on the official U.S. Civil Rights Trail, including The King Center, helmed by King's youngest daughter, Rev. Dr. Bernice King, and King's birth home. But the real treat is the **National Center for Civil and Human Rights,** which follows a through-line of past civil rights battles and conquests of the past to modern-day movements for justice around the globe. It's a visceral museum experience—seen, felt, and heard.

SWEET AUBURN HISTORIC DISTRICT

Though confined by Jim Crow segregation, this area in downtown Atlanta was a middle-class center of Black commerce in the late 19th century and early 20th century. Dubbed "the richest Negro street in the world" by Fortune magazine, Sweet Auburn was once flush with Black businesses, churches, and institutions. The Royal Peacock Club provided live entertainment in an elegant setting. Alonzo Herndon, born enslaved, established Atlanta Life Insurance in 1905 and became Atlanta's first Black millionaire. Ebenezer Baptist Church and Big Bethel A.M.E. have longed grounded the community spiritually and are still going strong.

The area experienced steep decline precisely because the civil rights movement achieved a level of success: Many businesses moved away when they had the freedom to do so. In a familiar pattern of cities featured along the civil rights trail, the Downtown Connector expressway split the community, and disinvestment continued. In the 1970s, Mayor Maynard Jackson attempted to jumpstart improvements, and the establishment of The King Center was expected to foster a rebound. Revitalization efforts formed to turn things around, including restoring historic homes and renewing the commercial area. The district was designated a National Historic Landmark in 1976.

SWEET AUBURN AVENUE

commercial buildings on Auburn Avenue in the 1970s

Racial segregation at the turn of the 20th century offered the ironic opportunity for African Americans to cultivate communities and business districts where residents often worked together to meet their needs and uplift the race. Atlanta's Auburn Avenue, or "Sweet Auburn," as it was called, was one such district. Due to planned segregation that blocked Black people from living wherever they wanted, communities like Sweet Auburn thrived in a spirit of mutuality and purpose.

In early 1900s Atlanta, Auburn Avenue was considered the "richest Negro street in the world." It was run by its unofficial mayor, John Wesley Dobbs, a politician and civic leader who seeded the idea of Black unity by co-founding the Atlanta Civil and Political League in 1936 and the Atlanta Negro Voters League in 1946. This was a solidly middle-class neighborhood when King was growing up in the 1930s and '40s. The community was the first home of *The Atlanta Daily World,* the city's first Black newspaper, and Atlanta Life Insurance, founded by Alonzo Herndon, a formerly enslaved Black barber and businessman, which is still going strong. The SCLC made its home here when it was founded in 1957.

The area was named by Dobbs, according to the National Park Service, and was designated a National Historic Landmark in 1976. Even today, a sense of possibility permeates the community. In some areas of this community that is bisected by the interstate, cosmopolitan residents enjoy hanging back after a day's work at nearby restaurants or grabbing lunch at Sweet Auburn Curb Market.

To learn about the history of Sweet Auburn Avenue, visit **APEX (African American Panoramic Experience) Museum** (page 76), where a short documentary, narrated by the actress Cicely Tyson and SNCC co-founder Julian Bond, covers the story of the neighborhood.

Martin Luther King Jr. National Historical Park

450 Auburn Ave. NE; tel. 404/331-5190 ext. 5046; www.nps.gov/malu; daily 9am-5pm; free

The National Park Service manages several sites as part of the Martin Luther King Jr. National Historical Park, including King's birth home, Historic Fire Station No. 6, and the original Ebenezer Baptist Church, where King first preached and where his funeral was held, just down the street. Both the church and King's birth home, as well as the larger historical park, are stops on the official U.S. Civil Rights Trail. The park encompasses 38 acres in the downtown area; be prepared to spend two to three hours to take it all in. The privately owned King Center is located next door, but National Park tours stop here, too.

Start at the **Visitors Center** (450 Auburn Ave. NE; tel. 404/331-5190 ext. 5046) to get information on how to tour the site, secure a ticket to tour King's birth home, and see a short film about Dr. King and civil rights movement exhibits. Reservations to tour King's birth home are required; you can visit the other sights on your own if you like. A ranger is always inside Ebenezer Baptist Church and may be inside the station too. They can offer insight and nuance you won't get on your own.

The **International Civil Rights Walk of Fame** also begins here at 450 Auburn Avenue NE and continues on to the National Center for Civil and Human Rights (100 Ivan Allen Jr. Blvd.). The walk consists of more than 100 stars commemorating civil rights luminaries, from Rosa Parks to Rev. Ralph David Abernathy, King's right-hand man. Duplicate shoeprints plus tiles for new inductees are located outside the National Center for Civil and Human Rights.

EBENEZER BAPTIST CHURCH

407 Auburn Ave. NE; tel. 404/331-5190 ext. 5046; www.nps.gov/malu; daily 9am-5pm; free

King was a mere seven years old when he felt the call to the fiery grave of baptism after a two-week annual revival. He was later ordained at this church, joining his father in the family business of saving souls. As his spiritual home, Ebenezer took King back into its loving embrace on April 9, 1968, when his funeral was held here.

According to church records, Ebenezer Baptist Church was founded after Reconstruction in 1886, under the leadership of Rev. John A. Parker. In 1894, King's grandfather took over the pastorship with his wife, nurturing and cultivating a congregation of 17 into a powerful institution that promoted Black self-determination in business and civil rights. Throughout this growth period, the congregation worshipped in many locations, outgrowing one after the other. The historic site in Sweet Auburn was completed in 1922. King's father, Martin Luther King Sr. (aka "Daddy King"), was an assistant to Rev. A. D. Williams (Martin Luther King Jr.'s maternal grandfather) until he took over in 1931 upon A. D.'s death. King Jr. co-pastored here with his father from 1960-1968. After King Jr. was assassinated, King's brother, Rev. Alfred Daniel Williams King, took over as co-pastor.

Even if you've never been to Ebenezer, you *know* this church. It was in these pews that Coretta Scott King cradled her young daughter, Bernice, on April 9, 1968, during her husband's homegoing service. Moneta Sleet, the legendary *Ebony* and *Jet* magazine photographer, captured this moment of comfort and intimacy. Sleet won a Pulitzer Prize in 1969 for this iconic image.

The church's architectural style is characterized as late Gothic Revival. The interior has been preserved, featuring stained-glass windows inlaid with the countenances of King Sr. and Williams.

Photos (top to bottom):
Martin Luther King Jr. National Historical Park; Ebenezer Baptist Church; The King Center

Inside, the vintage pulpit, communion chairs, and pews sit eerily frozen in time, and a clock is permanently stopped at 10:30, the time of King's funeral at his home church on April 9, 1968. A baptismal pool is under the pulpit podium floor. This is a must-have for a Baptist church whose beliefs dictate watery immersion is essential for an authentic baptism.

This sacred space nurtured King and his siblings, but it also spiritually and materially fed a community. Think on these things as you journey through the civil rights story in Sweet Auburn and the country at large.

Across the street at 101 Jackson Street NE, the spirit of the old Ebenezer continues to thrive at a newer building with a congregation of 6,000 members still drawn to Sweet Auburn to worship, fellowship, and offer communal support.

★ MARTIN LUTHER KING JR. BIRTH HOME

501 Auburn Ave. NE; tel. 404/526-8900; www.nps.gov/malu; daily 9am-5pm; free

This brown two-story Queen Anne-style home featuring furnishings used by the King family is where Martin Luther King Sr. and his wife, Alberta King, nurtured their family in middle-class comfort. King's parents shared this home with his maternal grandparents, Rev. A. D. Williams and Jennie Parks Williams. King himself suspected he was his grandmother's favorite, noting in his papers, "She was [very] dear to each of us but especially to me."[1] Martin lived in this home until age 12 when, during the summer of 1941, his parents moved the family to 193 Boulevard, about three blocks north of Auburn and Boulevard. (This later home was a yellow brick house, the kind his father always dreamed of having.)

You must visit the Martin Luther King Jr. Birth Home on a National Park Service-led tour; it's not possible to walk through the home on your own. Fortunately, the park rangers are knowledgeable narrators of King family lore.

During the tour, visitors walk past and through several rooms, including the parlor, where Martin Jr.'s maternal grandfather held civil rights movement meetings and the King children took piano lessons. You'll also see the room where the three King children were lovingly coaxed into the world because their parents did not want their babies born in a segregated hospital. The boy's room was said to be always in "great disarray," according to Martin Jr.'s sister, Willie Christine. Not all of the 1930s-era furniture belonged to the family; some of it was installed by the National Park Service. The wallpaper patterns are reprints based on what the family had on the walls when they lived there.

Tours, which last 30 minutes, depart on the hour 10am-4pm daily. Reservations are required and must be made in person at the **visitor center** next door (450 Auburn Ave. NE) on the day of the tour; phone or email reservations are not accepted. Reservations are accepted on a first-come, first-served basis and fill up fast because only 15 people are taken inside at one time. (The **gift shop** is a great place to pass the time and clinch some collectibles until the next tour.) Large groups may not reserve more than three tours totaling 45 people on a given day. Build a little buffer in your schedule to make time to sign up for the tour, then wait if the crowds are brisk that day.

HISTORIC FIRE STATION NO. 6

39 Blvd. NE; tel. 404/331-5190 ext. 5046; www.nps.gov/malu; Mon.-Sat. 9am-5pm; free

On the corner of Boulevard NE and Auburn, this former fire station is emblematic of the opportunities opened by movement wins. Black children like King (who visited this station often) could admire big red fire trucks, like the 1927

American LaFrance fire engine on display, but those same children could never dream of becoming firefighters because the Atlanta Fire Department was segregated. That changed in 1963, when 16 Black firefighters were hired. Women came on board in the '70s.

Operated by the National Park Service, the station serves as a window to yesteryear, which includes the fire department's beginning with horse-drawn carriages to the rescue. Occasionally, a ranger or volunteer can be found inside to answer questions. It's down the street from King's boyhood home.

Martin Luther King Jr. Center for Social Change (The King Center)

449 Auburn Ave. NE; 404/526-8900; www.thekingcenter.org; daily 9am-5pm; free

The King Center is situated on historic "Sweet" Auburn Avenue, next to the original Ebenezer Baptist Church. A pilgrimage destination for travelers from around the world, the center allows visitors to get up close and personal with the King family legacy.

The center was designed to amplify both Martin and Coretta while promoting the philosophy of nonviolent social change. It encompasses both indoor exhibits and artifacts and outdoor monuments and displays. Outdoors, highlights include **Martin Jr. and Coretta Scott King's crypt,** located in the center of a deep-blue reflecting pool; an **Eternal Flame** that symbolizes Dr. King's goals of justice, peace, and equality for everyone; and the **Behold Monument,** sculpted by Patrick Morelli, which features a muscular Black man holding a newborn up to the heaven while saying: "Behold, the only thing greater than yourself." Mrs. King dedicated this to her husband in 1990 as a tribute to his work.

Also outdoors, the **Martin Luther King Jr. World Peace Rose Garden** sits in a plaza near the visitor center. The garden features 185 roses in a variety of colors and is laid out in a starburst designed as a metaphor for the spread of King's values and ideas. Visitors can see the Kings' grave from this vantage point.

From the main parking lot (between Irwin and John Wesley Dobbs) leading to the visitor center on the promenade is the **International Civil Rights Walk of Fame.** The walk features 2 feet by 2 feet granite markers featuring footstep impressions of civil and human rights greats. Among the many footprints, look for one from Rosa Parks; Maya Angelou's pointy-toed shoe; President Lyndon B. Johnson's square-toed outline; and baseball great Henry "Hank" Aaron's sturdy shoe imprint.

Inside, **Freedom Hall** is used for exhibits, special events, and programs. The hall showcases local and global artwork, and in a diasporic nod, the staircase paneling comes from Nigeria's tall sapele tree.

Exhibits dedicated to Mr. and Mrs. King, Gandhi, and Rosa Parks are featured on the second floor. In the King Room, you'll see artifacts, such as fresh-faced childhood photos and stories of the Kings. One eye-opening display shows King's travel kit, including a denim jacket, blue work shirt, gloves, a small suitcase, travel clock, leather boots, and a key to the Lorraine Motel, where he was assassinated on the balcony of Room 306. Other artifacts include Coretta's passport and the black veil she wore to her husband's funeral as she cradled their youngest daughter, Bernice, age five. Another display features red artificial flowers in a vase, which King gave to his wife so they "would last."

The Gandhi Room is dedicated to contributions made by Gandhi, who was assassinated in 1948 but whose ideas stretch with time and caught on with the U.S. movement for civil rights.

The Rosa Parks Room honors the diminutive yet determined former department store seamstress. The walls of this room are lined with images of Parks's life and family, including a photo of her at the Highlander School with educator and activist Septima Clark.

If you dedicate a 90 minutes to this sight, you'll get a lot out of it. Pick up books centered on the movement and freedom struggles in general, among other items, in the first-floor bookstore. The King Center is a stop on the official U.S. Civil Rights Trail.

Madame C. J. Walker Beauty Shoppe and Museum

54 Hilliard St. NE; tel. 404/518-2887; www.madamecjwalkermuseum.com; open by appointment; $5 per person

Hairstylist and preservationist Ricci de Forest knew he had a gem on his hands when he acquired a space in Sweet Auburn in 2004 that housed a Madame C. J. Walker beauty shop in the 1940s and '50s. Walker, nee Sarah Breedlove, became a self-made millionaire and was instrumental in creating beauty care techniques, called the Walker Method. She created products, such as a pomade, that allowed Black women and girls to step out into society with pride and a sense of possibility.

When de Forest moved in, he found original curling and crimping irons, a working vintage blow dryer with a wooden handle, and a stove with a still-working gas line. Today, the space is a tiny 2,000-square-foot museum that is crammed with vintage items from mid-century Black beauty culture, including "pressing combs" from the 1950s, which were used to straighten out natural African American hair textures in an attempt to achieve a look that conformed to White ideals. (Today, some African American women still opt for straightened hair—because it makes them feel good. Others embrace other, more natural, styles, including braids, twists, and locks. What anybody else thinks does not matter one bit.)

In the 1960s, the SCLC offices operated in the same building as the salon—right next door, in fact. And upstairs, WERD, the country's first Black-owned and Black-run radio station, operated from 1949-1968. The station aired jazz and blues during the Jim Crow era and served as a platform for King's Sunday sermons and news about the movement. (King had instant access to the airwaves because he only had to hit the ceiling with a broomstick to have a microphone lowered from a window so he could speak.) De Forest is working to bring back the second-floor radio station with a new series of interactive digital displays. Meanwhile, a display of albums in the museum links to the station's history.

More than just a museum, the salon frequently hosts jazz listening sessions during which de Forest wields his deep knowledge of Black music, noting, for example, how saxophonist Charlie Parker and trumpeter Dizzy Gillespie created the framework for bebop music, or how trumpeter Louis Armstrong taught Cab Calloway (who de Forest credits as a predecessor to hip-hop) and Ella Fitzgerald how to scat. De Forest also curates listening sets for those newer to their jazz journey. Sessions are posted on the website; curious travelers may also call and ask to schedule a session. Music lovers frequently bring a bottle and sit and drink "tea" as they appreciate de Forest's extensive music collection. Look at the website for vintage broadcasts of WERD music shows to feel the connection to this narrative.

Big Bethel African Methodist Episcopal Church

220 Auburn Ave. NE; tel. 404/827-9707; www.bigbethelame.org

If you look up and see a neon cross bearing the words "Jesus Saves" on a steeple in the Atlanta vista, you're looking directly at Big Bethel A.M.E. Church, the Sweet Auburn institution that founded historically Black Morris Brown College in 1881. Dating

ATLANTA

VOICES OF THE MOVEMENT: CONGRESSMAN JOHN LEWIS

"The struggle for civil rights and human rights is bigger than one law, one vote, or one judicial decision. It's beyond one presidential term or act of Congress. Ours is the struggle of a lifetime, and each generation, each citizen, each president and each member of Congress must do his or her part."[2]

—**CONGRESSMAN JOHN LEWIS** always exhorted us to get into "good trouble," knowing that the civil rights movement of the '50s and '60s wasn't even the beginning—and it certainly was not the end.

Lewis was arrested 40 times during the civil rights movement and several times while serving in Congress. He also put his body in harm's way many times in the 1960s and was among the many who were injured in the fight to secure voting rights for African Americans. He has often said he thought he was going to die on Bloody Sunday (March 7, 1965) as he and others tried to cross Selma's Edmund Pettus Bridge on the road to the Montgomery State Capitol to demand voting reforms. White law enforcement offers beat him so badly, they broke his skull. As a Freedom Rider arriving in Montgomery's Greyhound station, Lewis was beaten unconscious by a mob that included White men carrying bats and White women brandishing purses. Even children were invited to lash out.

We owe the passage of landmark 1960s civil rights legislation to fighters like Lewis. What is so exquisite about these laws is their staying

back to 1847, the church was originally named Bethel Tabernacle, founded for Black people who were enslaved by White members of Union Church. The church served as a smallpox hospital during the Civil War and the first school for African Americans during Reconstruction and Morris Brown classes. The basement hosted civil rights activities, and its sermons were broadcast on the Black-owned radio station WERD. Notable speakers have appeared at Big Bethel over the years, including Mary McLeod Bethune, Jimmy Carter, and Nelson Mandela.

Architect J. A. Lankford and builder Alexander Hamilton worked together to create the extraordinary Romanesque Revival edifice you see today on Auburn Avenue. It is the third building in the church's history and was completed in 1924. Inside the hulking stone structure is a light-filled sanctuary surrounded by stained-glass windows and red-cushioned seating. The church features a balcony and a metal-stamped ceiling.

Today, Big Bethel congregation warmly welcomes visitors to worship during Sunday services at 7:30am and 10am. The church has a variety of services and programming geared to various needs and interests. Street parking is free on Sunday, and a church-owned metered lot is in the back on the

power and impact—when left intact. The Civil Rights Act of 1964 banned discrimination based on race, color, religion, sex, or national origin, and required equal access to public places and workplaces. The law didn't change hearts, but it did make it possible for underrepresented people to occupy a bigger space in the American workforce. The law also provided redress to discrimination. And this law is largely responsible for enabling White women to enter the workforce in great numbers, a fact that is often unacknowledged.

Lewis was elected to Atlanta's City Council in 1981, and to Congress in 1986, where he continued fighting for equality and justice. Sadly, even the right to vote without gamesmanship and voting district gerrymandering is not over. The Supreme Court's 2013 *Shelby v. Holder* decision was a serious blow to the Voting Rights Act of 1965. Jurisdictions with past patterns of bad behavior, including vast swaths of the South, are no longer required to seek preclearance to change voting policies. While poll taxes and literacy tests are a relic of the past, voter suppression is not.

Nevertheless, good trouble leads to good lawmaking that withstands the test of time. Contemporary movements and mass protests to demand equity and justice in the workplace, housing, policing, voting, and beyond prove it. In 2020, the strength of the 1964 law proved enough to protect transgender people from workplace discrimination. This watershed decision caused Lewis to remind us of the work that remains:

"It impossible to ignore that deeply rooted structural inequality, xenophobia, and bias continues to permeate our nation, and LGBTQIA+ people of color—especially transgender women—experience violence, discrimination, and socio-economic disparities at alarming rates. As Bayard Rustin, the engineer of the March on Washington reminded us, 'We are all one, and if we don't know, we will learn it the hard way.'"[3]

corner of John Wesley Dobbs Avenue NE and Jessie Hill Drive. Church-owned parking is reserved for church events and services. Big Bethel is believed to be the oldest Black church in metro Atlanta.

John Lewis Mural

219 Auburn Ave. NE (Jesse Hill Jr. Dr. and Auburn Ave.)

A special treat during your visit to Atlanta is seeing the colorful mural of John Lewis peeking out in the distance as Atlanta's epic traffic zips then crawls down the Connector expressway, where I-75, I-85, and I-20 converge. A longtime Georgia U.S. congressman, Lewis was a founding member of SNCC. He was also a leader in the Nashville movement; a Freedom Rider; and a leader in the 1965 voting rights march from Selma to Montgomery.

Like the man himself, the John Lewis Mural looms large over the city, emanating dignity and respect in a most breathtaking manner. The mural by Sean Schwab uses just six colors to depict Lewis's countenance, with the word "hero" affixed above his head. An off-white panel beneath the painting features the words spoken by Lewis at the March on Washington in 1963: "I appeal to all of you to get into this great revolution that is sweeping this

ATLANTA

REVOLUTIONARY ROADS

Whether you're riding on Atlanta's Connector expressway or nearby neighborhoods, streets named for civil rights heroes show how Atlanta takes great care to honor the people who made movement, well, move. See progress in streets named after civil rights workers, including:

- **John Lewis Freedom Parkway,** named for Lewis, who took a beating on the Edmund Pettus Bridge on Bloody Sunday in 1965 and became a longstanding congressman.
- **Donald Lee Hollowell Parkway,** named for the man who forced the integration of the University of Georgia (UGA).
- **Hamilton E. Holmes Drive,** recognizing one of two Black students (the other was Charlayne Hunter Gault) who enrolled at UGA as a result of Hollowell's suit.
- **Ivan Allen Jr. Boulevard** recognizes Atlanta's 52nd mayor, a White man who testified in Congress in support of the Civil Rights Act of 1964.
- **Jesse Hill Jr. Drive** honors the accomplished businessman, who served as CEO of Atlanta Life Insurance Company, publisher of the Atlanta Inquirer, and on The King Center board.
- **John Wesley Dobbs Avenue** honors a man who literally got out the vote—he registered 10,000 Black voters in the 1930s.
- **Andrew Young International Boulevard** is named for a minister and early leader of the Civil Rights Movement who became Atlanta's mayor and served as a congressman, ambassador, and member of the Carter administration.

nation. Get in and stay in the streets of every city, every village and hamlet of this nation until true freedom comes until the revolution of 1776 is complete." At the mural's dedication ceremony, Lewis himself wielded a paint brush to complete his dark-blue signature.

APEX (African American Panoramic Experience) Museum

135 Auburn Ave. NE; tel. 404/523-2739; www.apexmuseum.org; Tues.-Sat. 10am-5pm; adults $7, seniors and students $5

APEX Museum, a stop on the official U.S. Civil Rights Trail, is a great starting point for an understanding of Black history and civil rights. Through displays and film, the museum tells a diasporic story that includes ancient African kingdoms and the perils of the Middle Passage and Black enslavement. Be prepared to spend an hour or two exploring this 200,000-square-foot facility in Sweet Auburn.

Your visit begins with a mini-documentary narrated by actor, playwright, and civil rights activist Ossie Davis. Another short doc, narrated by the actress Cicely

Tyson and SNCC co-founder Julian Bond, covers the story of Atlanta's Sweet Auburn neighborhood. These grounding stories are screened to audiences who sit in a replica of Trolley Car 105, which evokes the streetcars that served as public transportation starting in the late 1800s.

The front portion of the museum addresses African roots, touching on agriculture, architecture, and technology from 5500 BC to 1450 BC. Also on view are images of a slave-trading post in modern-day Ghana, and a replica dungeon shows the degrading environment that captured Africans experienced as they were being brought into enslavement.

Moving on to African American history, another exhibit, a replica drugstore, celebrates Moses Amos, Georgia's first licensed Black pharmacist. The replica display shows Amos's work area, complete with a mannequin, inviting visitors to imagine what it was like serving the Black community's health needs.

APEX is chock-full of information about Black inventors, such as Percy Julian, who invented synthesized cortisone; Lonnie Johnson, inventor of the Super Soaker water gun; and Black hair-care guru and millionaire Madame C. J. Walker. A Hall of Achievements celebrates women in STEM. They are introduced along a long hallway that shows their portraits and success stories.

Auburn Avenue Research Library on African American Culture and History

101 Auburn Ave. NE; tel. 404/730-4001; www.afpls.org/aarl; Sun. 2pm-6pm, Mon. noon-6pm, Tues. 10am-6pm, Wed.-Thurs. noon-8pm, Fri. noon-6pm, Sat. 10am-6pm; free

Photos (top to bottom): Madame C.J. Walker Beauty Shoppe and Museum; APEX (African American Panoramic Experience) Museum; Auburn Avenue Research Library on African American Culture and History

ATLANTA

Standing on the west end of the Sweet Auburn historic district, this library dedicated to the history and study of Blackness is a rich research resource and artistic gem, offering reference and research materials along with culturally specific programming. Electronic kiosks make it easy to navigate this facility, as do friendly library staff and security guards.

A walk through the library reveals inviting rooms infused with history, including a children's gallery on the first floor. In one room, walls are lined with vintage photos of Black family life dating to the early and mid-1900s. These images serve as a powerful counter-narrative to incomplete or twisted stories about the existence and cohesiveness of Black family life and self-determination in the United States. The second-floor research area boasts a sweeping painting of Mary Fields holding a rifle. For the uninitiated, Fields, known as Stagecoach Mary, was born enslaved in Hickman County, Tennessee, and became the first Black female mail carrier, minding a sometimes dangerous Montana-based route from the mid to late 1800s.

Families with school-age children might find this library engaging. It's a few steps from APEX Museum, so it is worth stopping by or calling ahead to see what special programs are offered. Temporary exhibits in a first-floor gallery space are frequently illuminating and always educational.

DOWNTOWN

★ National Center for Civil and Human Rights

100 Ivan Allen Jr. Blvd.; tel. 678/999-8990; www.civilandhumanrights.org; Sun. noon-5pm, Mon.-Thurs. 10am-5pm, Fri.-Sat. 10am-6pm; adults $20, seniors and students $18, children $16

What did it feel like to face the danger of racist forces (people *and* institutions) and to be part of a nonviolent struggle with others who had your back? This all-encompassing museum adjacent to the World of Coca-Cola museum pulls visitors into that experience. Exhibits and stories follow the civil rights through-line into modern-day movements for social justice and human rights. Be prepared to spend at least a solid 90 minutes to get a full appreciation of this experience.

To seed the sensory experience, the front gallery entrance features a white neon sign beaming "Colored" on the right and "White" on the left (taking a page from the Apartheid Museum in Johannesburg). Interactive displays start the story in the 1950s urban South, covering topics from Atlanta's prosperous Auburn Avenue to havens of excellence and propriety like Spelman and Morehouse colleges.

The Freedom Riders exhibit honors the multiracial array of young people, many of them college students, who put their lives on the line in 1961 and beyond by taking interstate buses to desegregate the South. Their black-and-white mugshots show smartly dressed men and women prepared for the work of nonviolent resistance. An interactive push-button display with a black analog telephone receiver tells more about these courageous individuals.

A lunch counter protest simulation lets visitors see how much violence and intimidation they can take. Museumgoers put on earphones while sitting on a lunch counter stool, placing their hands flat on the counter surface. Visitors are encouraged to close their eyes while threats and other forms of racial intimidation play in their ears. Eyes still closed, patrons feel kicking around their seats as the exhibit jumps and bumps to simulate the violence and lack of respect for personal barriers racist resisters employed. The challenge is to stay seated and avoid reacting, because that was the test of nonviolent protest . . . to sit and take it, all the while illustrating the true source of contention and resistance.

A bright hall streams a wall-sized video

Photos: Exhibits at the National Center for Civil and Human Rights. Top to bottom: lunch counter exhibit; international civil rights leaders; sculpture outside the museum (left); Freedom Riders exhibit (right)

ATLANTA

showing scenes from the 1963 March on Washington for Jobs and Freedom where King made his enduring "I Have A Dream" speech. Onlookers view footage from that spirited day at the steps of the Lincoln Memorial when about 250,000 converged on the United States Capitol. Looking back in time at people who crushed the memorial to stand up and bear witness to the particular American truth of inequality of access, it's easy to become overwhelmed with emotion—so much so, museum staff leave tissue boxes throughout the seating area.

The museum invites retrospection, thought, and discussion. Other exhibits honor the children of the movement, like the four little girls murdered in Alabama's 16th Street Baptist Church bombing by the Klan: Addie Mae Collins, Cynthia Wesley, Denise McNair, and Carole Robertson. Some of King's papers and many artifacts and ephemera on loan from the Morehouse College King Collection can be found here, including a wall display showing books King read, if you want to get inside his head, so to speak.

On the human rights front, the center connects the movement to contemporary issues around the globe. One display explains the warning signs of mass killings. An example from Sudan breaks down the language for doing so: Early warning signs include "ghettoization," labeling, defamation, and destruction of cultural artifacts. Exhibits also issue cautions about the price of our technology-driven lifestyles by explaining the violence and educational sacrifices made by global workers, including children. These displays challenge us to consider our ethical footprint when others pay a price to extract minerals to make products such as cell phones and soccer balls.

Outside the center you will find an extension of the International Civil Rights Walk of Fame. Duplicate shoeprints from inductees honored at The King Center can be seen here, and plus ones for new inductees.

The National Center for Civil and Human Rights is a stop on the official U.S. Civil Rights Trail.

OTHER NEIGHBORHOODS

Atlanta University Center

156 Mildred St. SW; tel. 404/523-5148; www.aucenter.edu

The Atlanta U Center Consortium of historically Black colleges and universities includes Morehouse College (covered below), **Clark Atlanta University** (223 James P Brawley Dr. SW; tel. 404/880-8000; www.cau.edu), **Morehouse School of Medicine** (720 Westview Dr. SW; tel. 404/752-1500), and **Spelman College** (350 Spelman Ln. SW; tel. 404/681-3643; www.spelman.edu). These institutions have educated some of the greatest minds in the movement and beyond, from Maxine Smith, a Spelman alum who went on to desegregate Memphis's public schools, to Rev. Ralph Abernathy, King's right-hand man (Atlanta University, master's degree). Morehouse College is where three generations of King men, including King himself, studied.

MOREHOUSE COLLEGE

830 Westview Dr. NW; tel. 470/639-0569; www.morehouse.edu

This liberal arts college for men where King studied promises to provide a space to be one's authentic self without chatter from the outside world.

The campus story is bolstered by the artwork and iconography that celebrates African American striving and accomplishment. In front of the campus's Martin Luther King Jr. International Chapel, a towering bronze statue of King by sculptor Ed Dwight points the way forward. Inside the chapel is a 2,501-seat nave. (Interesting note: 2,500 is the number of students enrolled at any given time. The extra seat is an exercise in Ubuntu, a Nguni Bantu term loosely translated as "I am because we are.")

Also on campus, in the Morehouse plaza, is the Howard Washington Thurman Memorial obelisk and crypt. Thurman, a minister and Morehouse grad who also taught at the campus, introduced the campus to the theory of using nonviolence for confrontation and change. (King has been described as Thurman's spiritual protégé.) Thurman's ashes and those of his wife, Sue Bailey Thurman, are buried beneath an obelisk.

Three Black students, Lonnie King, Joseph Pierce, and Julian Bond, launched the Atlanta Student Movement in 1960 when they rallied fellow students attending the city's HBCUs to stand up to Jim Crow. They formed a coalition called Committee on Appeal for Human Rights and mad their mission clear in a manifesto called "An Appeal for Human Rights." Written by Spelman College Student Government Association President Roslyn Pope, the proclamation was published as a full-page ad in Atlanta newspapers. The document called out inequality in education, jobs, housing, voting, hospitals, movie theaters, concert halls, restaurants, and law enforcement. The manifesto found its way onto the pages of the *New York Times* and *Los Angeles Times,* and entered into the Congressional Record. The coalition was comprised of Morehouse College, Atlanta University, Clark College, Interdenominational Theological Center, Morris Brown College, and Spelman College. The statement was signed by six student government presidents and served as a preamble of demonstrations to come. Days later on March 15, 1960, sit-ins began with scores of students getting arrested.

Tours of the venerable campus showcase the best of Morehouse, including its buildings, leaders, and lore. Arrange a **tour** through the Office of Admissions (tel. 844/512-6672). Individual and family tours are held Mon., Wed., and Fri. at 10am, 11am, and 2pm and Tues. and Thurs. at 10:30am and 2:30pm. Group tours run Mon., Wed., and Fri. at 10am, 11am, and 2pm; and Tues. and Thurs. at 10:30am and 2:30pm. Tours last about 1 hour 15 minutes. Group tours must be arranged at least three weeks in advance and up to four months prior. Each tour starts with a brief presentation led by a carefully selected student tour guide, whose accomplishments and activities will be emblematic of the opportunities to thrive and grow.

Jimmy Carter Presidential Library and Museum

453 John Lewis Freedom Pkwy NE; tel. 404/865-7100; www.jimmycarterlibrary.gov; Mon.-Sat. 9am-4:45pm, Sun. noon-4:45pm; adults $12, seniors and students $10, 16 and under free

In the South, it helps to have good relations with the Black community if you want to move into the White House one day. President Jimmy Carter, elected in 1976, managed to do that. This Georgia Sunday School teacher's impressive civil rights record was informed by the U.S. civil rights movement.

The institution is situated in a bucolic 35-acre wooded area that showcases Carter's lifelong work in government and human rights. Through exhibits, artifacts, images, video, and interactive displays, visitors learn about Carter's humble beginnings growing up without running water and electricity until his teen years, working in fields with Black workers on his family farm. Exhibits spotlight his service in the U.S. Navy and love of photography. The museum also tells the story of the love of his life, Rosalynn, complete with wedding photos of the young couple. Take in the story of his trajectory in local politics and the Georgia governor's mansion to the White House and a life of service, including working with Habitat for Humanity, which helps families access affordable housing they and volunteers

Jimmy Carter Presidential Library and Museum

build and rehab, and other global outreach initiatives. A full-scale replica of his Oval Office is featured, as is a narration of a day in the life of the Carter presidency. Researchers can gain access to presidential library documents and materials on a variety of topics, from Camp David Accords and the president's daily diary to the Iran hostage crisis.

The Jimmy Carter Presidential Library and Museum is a stop on the official U.S. Civil Rights Trail.

Tours and Local Guides

WALKING TOUR

SWEET AUBURN WALKING TOUR BY THE ATLANTA PRESERVATION CENTER

327 St. Paul Ave. SE; tel. 404/688-3353; www.atlantapreservationcenter.com; custom tours start at $75

The Atlanta Preservation Center works to promote the preservation of Atlanta's architectural treasures through education and advocacy. For their Sweet Auburn walking tours, a guide will meet you at 135 Auburn Avenue NE outside the APEX Museum. The tour includes a stop by the still-thriving Big Bethel A.M.E. Church, Atlanta's first Black church, and Ebenezer Baptist Church, King's spiritual home and where he co-pastored with his father. The center has long been a go-to source for historical details.

Tours last 45-90 minutes. Visitors can book tours online, but if no tours are listed, be sure to call. Center staff are friendly and resourceful.

BUS TOURS

CIVIL RIGHTS TOURS ATLANTA

449 Auburn Ave. NE; tel. 404/386-0992; www.civilrightstour.com; Sat. 11am-2pm; $65

Gregarious and funny, civil rights tour guide Tom Houck has a direct connection to the civil rights movement: A White guy, he was expelled from high school for attending the Bloody Sunday march in Selma in 1965. Driven by his youthful conviction, Houck went on to work on voting rights and other issues with the NAACP, SCLC, and other organizations.

Today, Houck and his team of civil rights foot soldiers guide history buffs back in time through video-equipped bus tours of civil rights sites in Atlanta. The three-hour journeys start in the Sweet Auburn community in front of the grave of Dr. Martin Luther King Jr. at The King Center (449 Auburn Ave.). The first stop is 234 Sunset Avenue NW, a four-bedroom brick home where King lived for the final four years of his life. For a long time, King's 1966 navy blue Chevy Impala was still parked it the garage, according to Houck.

Houck points out a spot where Dr. King liked to order pork sandwiches and pig ears, and goes by a club where Coretta and Martin would go to listen to jazz, among more expected stops, such as King's birth home. According to Houck, this is the only tour that includes the South-View Cemetery graves of Martin Luther King Sr. (Daddy King) and John Wesley Dobbs, the unofficial mayor of Auburn Avenue. In the cemetery established by formerly enslaved Black people in 1886, Martin Luther King Sr.'s tomb reads: "I love everyone. Still in business, just moved upstairs."

Houck's tours stand out because he clearly loves this work, but he also has the details. He even served as Dr. King's local driver and assistant for a year.

Tours leave from The King Center gravesite of Coretta and Martin Luther King Jr. at 11am Saturdays. Custom tours are also available.

ROUNDABOUT TOURS ATLANTA BLACK HISTORY & CIVIL RIGHTS TOUR

tel. 404/685-1090; www.roundaboutatlanta.com; Sun.-Sat. 9:30am-1:30pm; $65 per adult, $55 per child 5-12;

Tour guide Omar Akinsika takes a holistic approach to Black history in Atlanta by telling a cross-section of stories about Black leadership, sports, art, and politics, and civil rights is part of this narrative. Roundabout's half-day (4-hour) tours cover Downtown Atlanta, the Historic West End, Vine City, Castleberry Hill, and Sweet Auburn. The Vine City leg includes a stop in front of King's last home at 234 Sunset Avenue, where Akinsika may talk about how Mrs. King conceived of and planned The King Center in this home after her husband's death. Guests often take photos at this four-bedroom home that has been acquired by the National Park Service and will eventually be open to the public.

One of three 20-minute stops on this four-hour journey includes a stop by historic Ebenezer Baptist Church, King's home church and where he co-pastored with his father until his death. A high point of this stop is when Akinsika queries guests about what they think King would say about contemporary civil rights issues: "Would Dr. King approve of a wall?" he asks.

Other civil rights tour high points include a ride by the Atlanta University Center, Martin Luther King Jr. Drive, the new Paschal's and Busy Bee Cafe, SCLC headquarters, and the Madame C. J. Walker Beauty Shoppe and Museum. Guests delight in hopping out and taking photos in front of the King Birth Home.

Black history touchpoints include cruising by Big Bethel A.M.E. Church, Willie Watkins Funeral Home, Atlanta City Hall, Mercedes Benz Dome, CNN Center, and Auburn Curb Market, which doubles as a chance to grab a quick snack. A quick stop by Tyler Perry Studios highlights Black entrepreneurship and creativity.

The tour includes narration and supplemental materials such as photos to help build out the story of each person or place.

Roundabout comes to you, picking guests up at their hotels or at a neutral pickup location. These tours can accommodate two to 200 people with special rates for groups of six or more.

Shopping

Because you're in charming Atlanta, you might as well take a piece of it home—and one way to support the message of the movement is to turn your dollar over in the Black community. You'll need to drive to reach some of the following shops, but it's worth it.

GIFTS

SUSTAINABLE HOME GOODS

675 Ponce De Leon Ave. NE; tel. 770/727-6794; https://yoursustainablehome.com; Mon.-Sat. 10am-9pm, Sun. noon-6pm

SustainAble expresses the passions of its founder, LaToya Tucciarone, who always dreamt of a life of travel and uses her power and exquisite taste for the greater good. The idea behind this home goods store is to celebrate the beauty of the world through products created by global makers from at least 25 countries, while creators achieve financial stability and the dignity that comes from a job well done.

Products sold here include home décor, kitchen supplies (like Tunisian ceramic bowls), textiles (like Malian twig table runners), accessories (like Burundi box drop earrings), and bags (Savannah leather shopper bags made India). SustainAble has a section dedicated to Black makers, featuring products such as Portrait Coffee, roasted in Atlanta. You will also discover organic, vegan beauty products by Atlanta's Ty Jenkins and original paintings by Evan Blackwell.

Located in Ponce City Market inside the historic Sears, Roebuck & Co building, SustainAble is surrounded by other captivating shops and restaurants. This Black- and woman-owned business is a great place to find take-home gifts infused with integrity and goodness.

CLOTHING

TAGS BOUTIQUE

2140 Peachtree Rd. NE, Ste. 225; tel. 404/883-3836; www.tagsatl.com; Sun. noon-5pm, Mon.-Sat. 11am-6pm

If you like the styles seen in Bravo's long-running *Real Housewives of Atlanta* show, take a page from original housewife and serial entrepreneur Kandi Burruss, who owns this boutique in Brockwood Square. Tags offers the latest seasonal fashions for every woman, from skinny to curvy, plus accessories and shoes. This shop is located about three miles north of downtown Atlanta.

PRESSED

3500 Peachtree Rd. NE #2020E; tel. 404/330-8932; www.pressedatl.com; Sun. noon-6pm, Mon.-Sat. 10am-9pm

"Fly" is the operative word at this women's fashion boutique owned by hip-hop artist Rasheeda. Apparel runs the gamut from jumpsuits, bodysuits, and plus-size fashions to cosmetics and the latest shoes and sneakers. This shop is about five miles northeast of downtown in the Buckhead neighborhood. It's the same neck of the woods as Havana nightclub, so keep that in mind if you're here late in the evening.

SustainAble Home Goods sells mugs honoring John Lewis.

Festivals and Events

Can you think of a better place than Atlanta to celebrate Dr. King's birthday in January? Martin Luther King Jr. National Historic Park is a bevy of activity in January during Dr. King's birthday month. The King Center, in connection with the National Park Service, hosts a remembrance April 4-9 with a brief remembrance on the day of King's April 4 assassination.

JANUARY

Dr. King was born on January 15, 1929. All three of the following events take place on the third Monday in January when the nation commemorates his birthday.

KING DAY

Martin Luther King Jr. National Historic Park, 450 Auburn Ave N; tel. 404/331-5190 x5046

Martin Luther King Day is the busiest day of the year for the Martin Luther King Jr. National Historical Park. Up to 25,000 people come from all over the world to engage with Dr. King's ideas and philosophies while celebrating his life.

THE KING CENTER MARTIN LUTHER KING JR. ANNUAL COMMEMORATIVE SERVICE

Ebenezer Baptist Church's Horizon Sanctuary, 101 Jackson St. NE; tel. 404/526-8900; www.thekingcenter.org; free

The annual ecumenical service is held at the new Ebenezer Baptist Church's Horizon Sanctuary on Jackson Street, which seats 1,700. The original Ebenezer church, located nearby at 407 Auburn Avenue NE, was where King was ordained, co-pastored, and was funeralized.

This is a highly anticipated, jam-packed event, and people start lining up around 8am. Seating is first-come, first-served and begins at 10am. Featured keynote speakers exemplify the principles Dr. King lived and died for. Bree Newsome Bass, the millennial woman who scaled the South Carolina state house to pull down the Confederate

ATLANTA

HAPPY BIRTHDAY TO US

The idea to make King's birthday (Jan. 15) a federal holiday was in introduced in 1968 through legislation by Rep. John Conyers of Michigan. It took 11 years for the bill to come up for a vote in the House of Representatives in 1979, but it fell short of the two-thirds of votes necessary to pass. Then folks got busy. Case in point: Stevie Wonder recorded "Happy Birthday" in 1981 to promote the holiday. His version is so resonant, it is the preferred version of singing happy birthday in many Black families.

Before King's birthday became a holiday, some suggested commemorating him on April 4, the date of his assassination.

President Ronald Reagan signed a bill on November 3, 1983, designating the day. The first King Day was celebrated in 1986. King is now one of only three people (including Christopher Columbus and George Washington) who has a dedicated national holiday.

But that's not the end of the story. Even after the bill was signed into law, King's birthday wasn't celebrated everywhere in the country. In fact, it wasn't until 1998, when the New York Stock Exchange (NYSE) Board of Directors, at the suggestion of Rev. Jesse L. Jackson and his son, Jonathan, voted to close the markets on King Day, that things got real. When the markets closed, corporate America took the day off, which in turn allowed people to properly observe the lessons King taught.

flag in 2015, appeared in 2018. Other keynoters have included author and Canadian educator Irshad Manji, best-selling author Dr. Brene Brown, and journalist Jamil Smith. Featured musical performances are part of the program, and popular artists, such as Smokie Norful of "I Need You Now" (2002) fame, always make an appearance.

KING WEEK HOLIDAY MARCH AND RALLY ON AUBURN AVENUE

Auburn Ave. and Peachtree St.; tel. 404/939-5340; www.mlkmarchcommittee.com; free

This annual march and rally on King's federal holiday evoke King's beloved community. The march takes place around 1:30pm, right after the commemorative service at Ebenezer Baptist Church-Horizon Sanctuary (101 Jackson St. NE). The atmosphere of the march is lively and energetic—it's Dr. King's birthday, after all.

Starting at Peachtree Street and Baker Street NE, the march moves down Peachtree and turns on Auburn Avenue NE to head back toward The King Center, about a mile altogether. People flow from the church to either join or observe the march. Young people—from babies to high schoolers, Boy Scouts to Girl Scouts—typically lead, followed by local unions, businesses, activists, and grassroots organizations. Fraternities and sororities bring up the rear, so they don't slow down the movement if they decide to perform stepping routines, which are rhythmic synchronized dance moves particular to Black Greek society culture.

Various groups flow into the mix as the march moves along, and many people choose to chant or sing. Usually, chants link to whatever hot social issue is in the current conversation; one typical shout-out is the classic battle cry, "No Justice! No Peace!"

The march takes about an hour. (If it's cold, the pace is brisk, but if it's a nice day, things move a bit slower.) Either way, things always end up at The King Center for a rally, which also lasts about an hour. The event always includes guest speakers, which, in the past have included Kris Kristofferson, singer Tyrese Gibson, and actor Edward James Olmos. South Africa's Winnie Mandela has appeared as well as political strategist Donna Brazile. King's youngest daughter and The King Center CEO, Rev. Bernice King, always gets the last word. The rally wraps up with a prayer and singing "We Shall Overcome."

APRIL

REMEMBRANCE AT HISTORIC EBENEZER BAPTIST CHURCH

Historic Ebenezer Baptist Church; 407 Auburn Ave NE

Dr. King was assassinated by a sniper's bullet on April 4, 1968, in Memphis's Lorraine Motel. In remembrance of that fateful date, The King Center with the National Park Service and the new Ebenezer Baptist Church hosts a 30-minute remembrance at Historic Ebenezer Baptist Church (407 Auburn Ave NE). Spectators begin to gather around 5:30pm to hear speakers recall King's commitment to dismantling segregation and extending justice to all. The event culminates in a wreath-laying ceremony at 6:01pm (the exact time of King's assassination) on the church's exterior. The wreath is removed on April 9, the day of his homegoing, which occurred at this church. Contact the visitor center at Martin Luther King Jr. National Historic Park (tel. 404/ 331-5190 x5046; www.nps.gov/malu) for other special programming.

Food

As a world-class city, Atlanta has embraced its food future yet honors its past, especially the inventive simplicity of soul food. Situated in a coastal state, signature dishes include several seafood dishes informed by both the Carolinas and New Orleans, in addition to farm-fresh fare.

Atlanta is known as a must-see mecca of Blackness for many African Americans reared on stories of Black business success and a legacy of historically Black colleges and universities (HBCUs). The city has produced so many Black intellectuals, entrepreneurs, educators, politicians, and artists that signal to the diaspora that Black excellence isn't only possible—it is expected. The urban sophisticate style at Sweet Auburn's Seafood, for example, renders that expectation true for new generation. Meanwhile, Atlanta is also home to two beloved historic restaurants frequented by Dr. King and his consorts: Busy Bee Café and Pascale's.

SWEET AUBURN HISTORIC DISTRICT

Hungry after sightseeing in Sweet Auburn? In addition to the options below, a good option is to swing by **Sweet Auburn Curb Market** (209 Edgewood Avenue SW), a neighborhood anchor featuring a variety of eateries, a bookstore, and scrumptious fare like Ms. D's Pralines, which also serves candy apples and a triple mix of caramel, cheese, and butter popcorn. Some businesses in the market are Black-owned; some aren't.

Southern and Soul Food

SWEET AUBURN SEAFOOD

171 Auburn Ave. NE; tel. 678/974-5019; www.sweetauburnseafood.com

The décor and upscale menu at Sweet Auburn Seafood embraced a healthy food future while celebrating the Black culinary past of resourcefulness, creativity, and invention. Menu items included fried catfish, eggplant lasagna, tasty gumbo bowls filled with crawfish, and a shrimp and grits plate featuring chicken sausage, tomatoes, and Low Country cream. Unfortunately, as this book was going to press, Sweet Auburn Seafood reportedly confirmed plans to close, due in part to the devastating financial effects of the coronavirus pandemic. According to *Eater Atlanta,* owner Patrick Williams says he's not ruling out the possibility of opening another restaurant in the historic district in the future, so here's hoping that a new iteration of Sweet Auburn Seafood will grace the neighborhood one day soon.

Sports Bar

HAROLD'S FRIED CHICKEN & ICE BAR

349 Edgewood Ave SE; tel. 404/577-0001; www.haroldschickenatl.com; Sun.-Wed. 11am-10pm, Thurs. 11am-1am, Fri.-Sat. 11am-3am; $10-14

The Black-owned chicken spot is actually a Chicago South Side classic turned upscale. The good word about this delicious yard bird traveled down South to Sweet Auburn, and today it is a go-to spot for quick and easy fried chicken meals served up with a laid-back sports bar feel. Classic Harold's meals are on the menu, such as a quarter dark, one-half white, gizzards, livers, and fish meals that include catfish, perch, and whiting. Buffalo shrimp is served, as are wings, wingettes, and sides such as mozzarella triangles, fried green tomatoes, and pizza puffs. The signature Harold's mild sauce (and hot sauce) is imported from Chicago. All dinners come with a side of fries and coleslaw—it's the Harold's way. The interior offers a traditional sit-down experience with TV screens and a full bar and specialty cocktails. Try the Hennessy margarita, Harold's Wildberry, or The Real Peach.

DOWNTOWN

Southern and Soul Food

SWEET GEORGIA'S JUKE JOINT

200 Peachtree St.; tel. 404/230-5853; www.sweetgeorgiasjukejoint.com; Sun. 11am-10pm, Mon.-Wed. 4pm-10pm, Fri.-Sat. 4pm-midnight; $18-26

If you want to taste what's good about being Southern, you can hit the road or just head over to Sweet Georgia's Juke Joint, which offers the many varied tastes of the South. Starting with coastal fare with shrimp and grits, patrons will find brined baked chicken, smothered pork chops, fried green tomatoes, and gumbo. Sweet Georgia's elevates juke culture to high art and cuisine, featuring colorful artwork that evokes the historic juke experience—but old-school R&B is what you'll hear between these walls. According to Sweet Georgia's, "jook" is Gullah for "disorderly." This establishment is housed in the former Macy's building, which, when opened in 1927, was considered the largest department store south of Philadelphia.

OTHER NEIGHBORHOODS

Southern and Soul Food

★ BUSY BEE CAFÉ

810 M.L.K. Jr Dr. SW; tel. 404/525-9212; www.thebusybeecafe.com; Sun. noon-7pm, Mon.-Sat. 11am-7pm; $11-26

First thing: Dr. King ate here. Established

Photos (top to bottom): food at Busy Bee Café; Sweet Auburn Seafood; a long line at The Slutty Vegan (it's worth the wait)

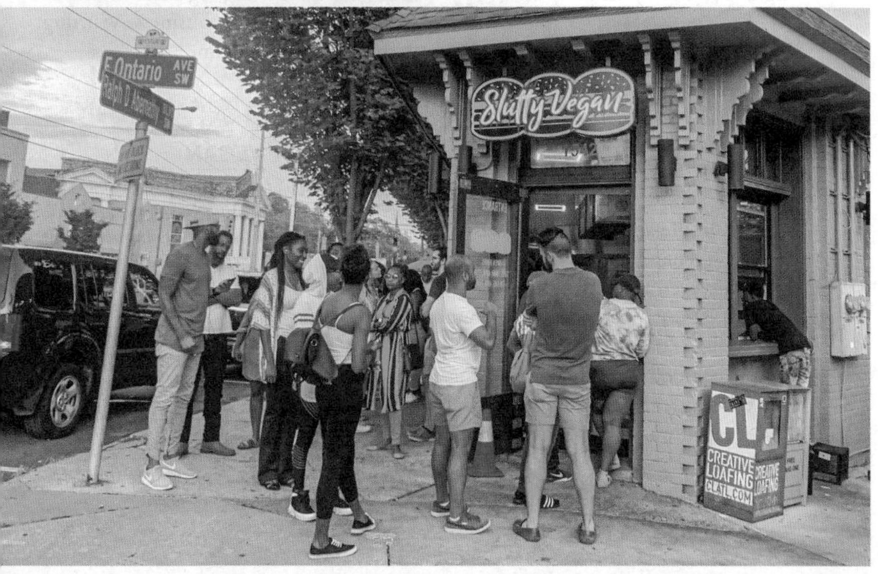

in 1947 by self-taught cook Lucy Jackson, the historic Busy Bee Café near Atlanta University Center really is just that busy. How busy? Try: Folks lined up outside the door, can't wait to scooch inside, can't-wait-till-that-table-over-there-gets-up busy.

Busy Bee is known for its crunchy, moist, well-seasoned fried chicken and lovingly made soul food fare. Corn muffins are served hot and soft, and the baked macaroni 'n' cheese and collard greens evoke Sunday dinner. Feel free to go old-school here because they're still cooking up chitterlings, a delicacy of cleaned and boiled pig intestines that evoke memories of when African Americans were given scraps and created a whole new cuisine.

The walls teem with framed news clippings and photos of celebrities from Jill Scott to Jay Z, and images of civil rights leaders from the likes of Rep. John Lewis to the late Atlanta Mayor Maynard Jackson. Soulful hits like Gladys Knight & the Pips's "Midnight Train to Georgia" are played loud enough to catch a riff but low enough to hear your table mate. The restaurant's website lists current wait times, and the interface allows patrons to sign up to get in line ahead of time. But if you have to wait anyway, lean into it: Have a chat with your neighbor and enjoy the company.

PASCHAL'S RESTAURANT AT CASTLEBERRY HILL

180 Northside Dr. SW; tel. 404/525-2023; www.paschalsatlanta.com; Sun. 11am-4pm, 5pm-9pm, Mon.-Thurs. 11am-9pm, Fri.-Sat. 11am-11pm; $13-41

Brothers in life and business, James and Robert Paschal always had an intense work ethic, even as children. In 1947, they opened a 30-seat luncheonette on Hunter Street, selling sandwiches and sodas, while bringing hot food over from Robert's home by taxi because they had no stove. Their fried chicken was (and still is) a winner, and the brothers expanded and bought more real estate, opening Paschal's Motor Hotel—which became a hub for leaders like King—in 1967. Both Black people and Whites were always welcome at Paschal's, and the brothers' community commitment never wavered: They often posted bond for civil rights protestors and served free meals to them and their families upon release from jail. The Black elite has eaten at Paschal's too, including Aretha Franklin, Andrew Young, Dizzy Gillespie, and Maynard Jackson.

Today, the Paschal's brand operates at Northside Drive SW serving Southern fare in a vast loft-like, brick-walled dining area, with a full bar. If you like fried chicken, you'll love Paschal's: It's so pretty, brown and crispy, you don't know if you should eat it or frame it. The candied yams are bright, fresh, and sweet, and the collard greens, black-eyed peas, and corn muffins taste like memories. Other menu offerings include fried green tomatoes, hot crab and pimento cheese dip, plus West Side Ribs, and jumbo lump crab cakes. A black-and-white posterized print of King hangs high in a corner, while an oversize black-and-white photo features Rev. Ralph Abernathy, arms linked with fellow protestors. And a window to the early world of Paschal's shows vintage photos of the motor hotel and other highlights of the brothers' successful life in business. Warning: There's likely to be a line.

Vegan

THE SLUTTY VEGAN

1542 Ralph David Abernathy Blvd.; tel. 678/732-3525; www.sluttyveganatl.com; Tues.-Fri. 4pm-midnight, Sat. 4pm- 1am; $11-15

There will likely be a line. You will wait. You'll love every minute of it. Slutty Vegan in Westview (a predominately Black yet gentrifying neighborhood) is so much more than a place for health-conscious, meat-free patrons who love a good burger: Slutty Vegan is an experience, and a real sexy one at that.

FREEDOM RIDES: ATLANTA

Following their departure from Washington DC in early May of 1961, the Freedom Riders made several stops in Virginia and North Carolina, including Richmond and Greensboro, encountering violence in South Carolina when they reached Rock Hill, where John Lewis and another Freedom Rider were beaten. Four days later, on May 13, 1961, the Riders arrived in Atlanta, where King apparently warned them about the likelihood of encountering KKK violence if they continued on to Alabama as planned, and suggested that they rethink their plans. The riders continued on anyway.

The Slutty Vegan is the brainchild of Pinky Cole, a young, Black, woman entrepreneur. The vegan burger joint's rep grew virally thanks to Instagram, and new patrons will find the take-out only eatery is a tasty but noisy affair. This is an inviting atmosphere where everyone from the cashier to the line cooks seem to feel they're offering something special. The cooks dance, rap, sing, and lead call-and-response riffs while dropping hot fries and manning an expansive grill filled with vegan patties. Slutty Vegan's philosophy is writ large on its long counter and walls, including mantras like "Kale Yeah," "The Future Is Vegan," and "I've got 99 Problems and Protein Ain't One." Menu items play off the "slutty" vibe with names like Fussy Hussy—an Impossible Burger patty loaded with pickles, vegan cheese, caramelized onions, lettuce, tomato, and a "slutty sauce" on a vegan Hawaiian bun—or the PLT, a jerk plantain sandwich. Other items include the One Night Stand and Ménage à Trois burgers. The Heaux Boy is a vegan shrimp sandwich tossed in New Orleans-style batter. Locals and visitors, carnivores and vegans—it seems everyone is happy to line up here.

Slutty Vegan also runs a highly sought-after food truck called **Big Ol' Slut.** Find out where the big yellow rolling kitchen will be parked by checking Instagram (@sluttyveganatl) daily at 3pm.

Nightlife

Atlanta has something for every taste, whether it is unassuming and intimate, or a fancy night out wearing four-inch heels, requiring a bouncer or two. This area along **Edgewood Avenue** has good hangouts, including Sister Louisa's Church of the Living Room & Ping Pong Emporium, listed below, and the Atlanta Streetcar goes down this street.

BARS

SISTER LOUISA'S CHURCH OF THE LIVING ROOM & PING PONG EMPORIUM

466 Edgewood Ave. SE; tel. 404/522-8276; www.sisterlouisa.com; Mon.-Fri. 5pm-3am, Sat. 1pm-3am, Sun. 1pm-midnight

Start with a pink neon sign over the bar saying, "Come on in Precious!" Right under that are portraits in velvet featuring the three kings: Elvis, Martin Luther King

Sister Louisa's Church of the Living Room & Ping Pong Emporium

Jr., and Jesus Christ. Yes, this place is irreverent, and that's the point. So just get ready for a friendly, whimsical experience, complete with all manner of items hanging from the walls and ceilings, from PeeWee Herman figurines to a whole bicycle mounted from the ceiling. And if you want a laugh, *do* open the wooden box with a White Jesus painting scrawled with "Do Not Open." This is a bar, folks, so leave the children, but bring your sense of humor. The best thing about Sister Louisa's, which is not a Black-owned business, is that all are welcome here—this is a place where you can really be yourself. It's located not far from The King Center in downtown Atlanta.

BOOGALOU RESTAURANT & LOUNGE

239 Ponce de Leon Ave. NE; tel. 404/464-7705; www.boogalouatl.com; Tues. 4pm-1am, Wed.-Thurs. 5pm-1am, Fri. 4pm-3am, Sat. 11am-3am, Sun. 11:30am-1am

The playfulness at Boogalou Restaurant & Lounge takes a sophisticated bent with swinging bar seats, a comfy sofa and chairs, and an array of upscale light figures such as glow chandeliers that make you feel like the investment in a night out was worth it. An extensive bar menu includes the rum-based Boogalou Mudslide and a refreshing-sounding Lemon Tini. Bougaloo's entertainment menu offers a series of themed nights, from karaoke to R&B Thursdays featuring a DJ. The dinner menu features hearty entrees, such as grilled or deep-fried lobster tail and smoked gouda mac and cheese.

CLUBS

THE HAVANA CLUB

3112 Piedmont Rd. NE; tel. 404/941-4847; www.havanaclubatl.com; Fri.-Sat. 9pm-3am; cover ranges from free to $20

DJs spin at this spacious, stylish Buckhead hotspot (north of downtown) featuring Latin sound, House Music, and whatever's popular. Bartenders are creative, so tell 'em what you have a taste for, and they'll think of something. Frequently voted the best nightclub in Atlanta, this dance-the-night-away spot encompasses 15,000 square feet, nine bars, and three rooms: Main, Latin, and cigar lovers will love the onsite humidor. VIP bottle service may be reserved online. The Havana Club is not a Black-owned business.

GET INTO THE RHYTHM

- **Marvin Gaye, "What's Going On"**: Renaldo "Obie" Benson of the Four Tops crafted this song after witnessing police violence in Berkeley, California, in 1969. His group refused to record a protest song, but Gaye had something stirring inside, so he did.
- **Isley Brothers, "Fight the Power, Part 1-2"**: A song of rebellion brought by the Isleys in 1975.
- **Public Enemy, "Fight the Power"**: This anthem debuted in Spike Lee's 1989 film "Do the Right Thing," including references to Black culture and the necessity of revolution. It was released on the 1990 *Fear of a Black Planet* studio album.

Accommodations

DOWNTOWN

$100-200

HYATT REGENCY ATLANTA

265 Peachtree St. NE; tel. 404/577-1234; www.hyatt.com; $112

King and the Southern Christian Leadership Conference were the second-ever customers of what was the new Hyatt in 1967 when he spoke in the Regency Ballroom. Hotels during movement years were loath to welcome Black guests, especially those fighting for civil rights. Hotel officials say Dr. King called this Hyatt location his "hotel of hope." Coretta Scott King was such a loyal customer here, the hotel named a deluxe suite after her.

The Hyatt is in the heart of downtown Atlanta and close to several main attractions, namely the National Center for Civil and Human Rights, The King Center, Martin Luther King Jr. National Historic Site, and Sweet Auburn. This expansive hotel features 1,260 rooms equipped with HDTVs. Deluxe suites offer sleeper sofas and bars, and premium suites featuring a private balcony with city views are also available.

Executive Chef Thomas McKeown makes a point of using locally sourced food and tends an onsite rooftop garden with beehives. **Sway** restaurant is known for Southern specialties, especially the buttermilk fried chicken, which takes 24 hours to prepare. **Twenty-Two Storys Atlanta,** a gastropub in the atrium lobby, offers a full array of beer and wine, burgers, pulled pork sandwiches, and pretzels, plus 17 TVs so patrons won't miss the big game. Just 22 stories up in a glass elevator, overlooking the Atlanta skyline, is **Polaris,** a rotating bar that offers handcrafted cocktails and shared plates.

THE AMERICAN HOTEL ATLANTA DOWNTOWN

160 Ted Turner Dr. NW; tel. 404/688-8600; www.doubletree3.hilton.com; $139

The Peach House

The American Hotel (owned by DoubleTree by Hilton) is as welcoming today as it was when it first opened in 1962. Even then, the hotel welcomed everyone, regardless of race—which was definitely not the case across the Southern hospitality landscape at the time. The hotel has hosted King, James Brown, Jimmy Carter, and others worthy of note. Today, The American is a common reunion hub for African Americans. Situated on a busy downtown corner, the hotel offers 315 rooms featuring pop art retro touches, like halcyon photos of the original hotel, replica Igloo mini fridges, and oversize artwork that evokes an earlier time. The **Cloakroom Kitchen & Bar** offers quick bites and Southern fare, and the bartenders skew friendly and chatty.

OTHER NEIGHBORHOODS

$100-200

THE PEACH HOUSE

88 Spruce St. NE; tel. 404/908-0788; www.the-peach.house; 24-hour coded access; $150-250

If the quiet coziness of a bed-and-breakfast is your style, then The Peach House (located less than a mile east of Martin Luther King Jr. National Historical Park) is as stylish as they come. Built in 1901, The Peach House takes its name from the color of this Victorian home with a sprawling front porch in the Inman Park community. Four well-appointed rooms evoke the Roaring '20s, when Bessie Smith and Duke Ellington made blues and jazz music that spoke to the soul. This being Atlanta, rooms dubbed the Peach Blossom Suite and Peach Pit are also available. Two-night stay required.

Transportation

GETTING THERE

Air

Hartsfield-Jackson Atlanta International Airport (6000 N Terminal Pkwy; tel. 800/897-1910; www.atl.com) is located 10 miles south of downtown Atlanta. A taxi ride into downtown will run about $36. Rideshare apps typically charge about half of what a taxi costs, depending on timing and demand.

The MARTA train station is in the domestic terminal of Hartsfield-Jackson International Airport behind the last baggage claim carousel. The Red and Gold Lines operate from here, but a transfer is available at the Five Points Station for Green and Blue Lines. If traveling after 8:30pm, MARTA officials advise taking the Gold Line to the Lindbergh Center then transferring to the Red Line if that's the stop you need. Google Maps offers transit details if you follow the train icon in the interface. A regular MARTA fare is $2.50 one-way with four transfers allowed within a three-hour period. A $2 Breeze Card allows passengers to reload fare, but a paper ticket costs an additional $1. Senior citizens, disabled riders, and Medicare recipients may ride for $1 through reduced-fare cards that can be purchased 8:30am to 5pm at the Five Points Station, 30 Alabama Street SW, or MARTA Headquarters, 2424 Piedmont Road NE.

Train

Peachtree Amtrak Station (1688 Peachtree St NW; tel. 800/872-7245; www.amtrak.com/stations; 7am-9:30am daily) is located in the Brookwood Hills area between Buckhead and Midtown, a few miles north of downtown. The station is on the Crescent Line, which runs between Penn Station in New York City and New Orleans with stops in Charlotte, North Carolina; Atlanta; and Birmingham, Alabama. If you're coming from Birmingham, the 4-hour ride costs $22.

It is advised to arrive 45 minutes before departure without baggage and 90 minutes ahead of time if you're checking bags. The station doesn't have Wi-Fi, but it is wheelchair accessible with long-term parking across the street in the Best Value Inn on Peachtree Street.

Bus

Atlanta's **Greyhound** station (232 Forsyth St SW; tel. 404/584-1728) is located downtown, less than two miles southwest of the Sweet Auburn Historic District. A round-trip ticket between Atlanta and Birmingham, Alabama, costs about $40, and takes 2.5 hours minimum.

Car

To reach Atlanta from:

- **Birmingham:** Take **I-20 East** about 150 miles (2.5 hours).
- **Montgomery:** Take **I-85 North** about 160 miles (2.5 hours).
- **Nashville:** Take **I-24 East,** then **I-75 South,** about 250 miles (4 hours).
- **Raleigh:** Take **I-85 South** about 400 miles (6 hours).
- **Charleston:** Take **I-20 West** for 300 miles (5 hours).

GETTING AROUND

Generally speaking, Atlanta is a car-centric culture; however, the Atlanta Streetcar works for a civil rights-focused trip, especially because the Sweet Auburn District is highly walkable. Rental cars and rideshare apps are definite options. Rush hour here is like any big city, so consider timing when hitting the road.

Parking

Most parking meters cost around $2 an hour.

Public Transit

MARTA (2424 Piedmont Rd. NE; tel. 404/848-5000; www.itsmarta.com), Atlanta's public transportation system, operates trains, buses, and the Atlanta Streetcar. Locals bemoan MARTA doesn't stretch as far as it needs into the metropolitan area, but the system is clean and efficient for accessing civil rights sights.

One-way fare on buses and trains is $2.50, but most riders must use a Breeze card ($2), which may be used up to three years. Purchase one at any MARTA station vending machine or visit breezecard.com. If you order a card online, you'll have to wait about a week for your card to arrive by snail mail. Passes are available too: Consider a 10-trip pass ($25), a three-day pass ($16), or a seven-day pass ($24).

TRAIN

Trains run every 10-20 minutes, 4:45am-1:15am weekdays and 6am-1am weekends and holidays. Find a train schedule at www.itsmarta.com.

The Martin Luther King Jr. National Historical Park in Sweet Auburn is near the King Memorial MARTA station. The National Civil and Human Rights Center is near MARTA's GWCC/Dome/Philips Arena/CNN station.

BUS

Most MARTA bus routes operate weekdays 5am-midnight. Weekends and holidays, buses start later and are less frequent. Buses arrive in intervals of 15 minutes to an hour, depending on where you're going and time of day. Find a bus schedule at www.martaguide.com.

ATLANTA STREETCAR

The Atlanta Streetcar ($1 per ride) is a solid option for getting to downtown sights and the Martin Luther King Jr. National Historical Park. With 12 stops, it runs in a 2.7-mile loop in downtown Atlanta with a connection to the Peachtree Center MARTA station. Atlanta Streetcar fare does not allow any free transfers from MARTA buses or rail stops. Tickets are valid for two hours.

Taxi and Ride-Hailing Apps

Ridesharing apps like **Lyft** and **Uber** work well in Atlanta. Or call **Atlanta Checker Cab** (tel. 404/351-1111).

Selma

Incorporated in 1820, Selma sits in Alabama's Black Belt, named for the rich soil that produced the cotton that allowed the South to prosper, thanks to labor from enslaved Black people. Just before the end of the Civil War in 1865, Union forces took Selma, burning homes, businesses, and the Confederate naval foundry and arsenal. During Reconstruction when only White and Black men could vote, the state elected its first Black congressman, Benjamin Sterling Turner.

SELMA'S TOP 3

1. Imagining **Brown Chapel A.M.E. Church,** SCLC's headquarters for the Selma campaign, buzzing with civil rights planning (page 107).

2. Learning about the local voting rights movement at the **Selma Interpretive Center** (page 107).

3. Following in the footsteps of voting rights activists who marched across the **Edmund Pettus Bridge** in 1965 (page 109).

Photos (top to bottom): Brown Chapel A.M.E. Church, Selma Interpretive Center; Edmund Pettus Bridge. Previous: participants in the 1965 march from Selma to Montgomery

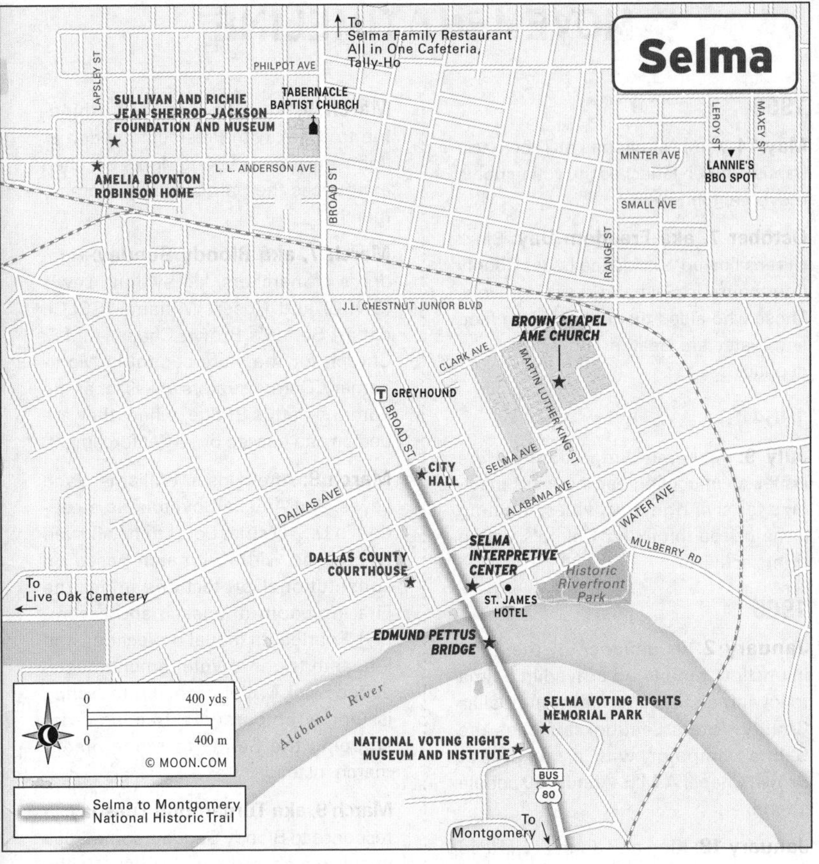

With the institution of Jim Crow, restrictive laws that enforced segregation took root, and Black people were barred from walking through the front door of buildings on Broad Street, the main east-west thoroughfare in Selma. As a result, many Black people here joined the Great Migration northward to pursue greater economic opportunity—and to breathe new air a little less pungent than the stench of Southern racism.

Selma is famous as the site where voting rights protestors heroically marched to the Alabama State Capitol of Montgomery in 1965. The marches are well-known for a reason: By the next year, 11,000 Black people had successfully registered to vote in Selma, and five African Americans ran for public office in Dallas County. And on a national scale, the marches are credited for instigating the passage of the Voting Rights Act of 1965.

It's no coincidence that Selma became a hotbed of voting rights activism in the 1960s: The local Dallas County Voters League had been organizing and educating Black residents about voting and economic justice since the 1920s. In the '30s, a group that would become widely known as the Courageous Eight gave the league momentum and focus. When Alabama Judge James Hare issued an injunction that barred mass meetings for civil rights activities in 1964, the voting rights movement in

MOVEMENT TIMELINE

1963

May 14: A mass meeting at Tabernacle Baptist Church launches the voting rights movement in Selma.

October 7, aka Freedom Day: Black citizens line up outside the Dallas County Courthouse in Selma to register to vote. Those who aided them by bringing food and water are beaten and arrested by deputies.

1964

July 9: Alabama Judge James Hare issues an injunction barring mass meetings for civil rights activities, creating a major roadblock for Selma's voting rights activists.

1965

January 2: In defiance of the 1964 injunction, King (who arrived in Selma following an invitation from the Dallas County Voters League) launches the Selma campaign with a meeting at Brown Chapel A.M.E. About 700 people attend.

January 18: King and John Lewis lead 300 marchers (broken into small groups, per the police chief's regulations) from Brown Chapel to the courthouse to register to vote. Sheriff Jim Clark makes them line up in an alley where nobody sees them and leaves them there.

January 19: Activists return to the courthouse and demand to wait out front. Lewis (SNCC), Hosea Williams (SCLC), and Amelia Boynton (Dallas County Voters League) are arrested. Other marches to the courthouse to demand the right to register are made in January and February. During one, Sherriff Clark pushes marchers down the stairs.

February 18: Jimmie Lee Jackson becomes the first martyr of the Alabama voting rights movement when he is shot and killed by state trooper James Fowler.

March 5: King travels to Washington to speak with President Lyndon B. Johnson about a voting rights bill, then announces the Selma to Montgomery march.

March 7, aka Bloody Sunday: Hundreds of marchers, led by John Lewis (SNCC) and Hosea Williams (SCLC), depart Selma's Brown Chapel A.M.E. Church for the state capitol in Montgomery. Demonstrators get as far as the Edmund Pettus Bridge, where they are beaten and gassed by law enforcement.

March 9: After Hosea Williams, John Lewis, and Amelia Boynton file a petition in U.S. District Court to be allowed to proceed with the march based on constitutional protections under the First (freedom of speech and assembly), Fourteenth (equal protection), and Fifteenth (right to vote) amendments, Judge Frank M. Johnson flips the script, issuing a temporary restraining order stopping the Selma to Montgomery march instead.

March 9, aka Turnaround Tuesday: In response to Bloody Sunday, some 2,000 people march from Brown Chapel to the foot of the Edmund Pettus Bridge, then turn around and head back to Brown A.M.E. (King wasn't so keen on violating Judge Johnson's orders; hence, the turnaround.) Later that night, three White clergymen are assaulted. Rev. James Reeb, a White Unitarian Universalist minister who had heeded King's call to descend on Selma and support the movement, dies of his injuries.

March 17: Judge Johnson gives the go-ahead for the Selma to Montgomery march.

March 20: President Johnson federalizes the Alabama National Guard to supervise and protect marchers as they proceed from Selma to Montgomery.

March 21: King, along with thousands of diverse demonstrators, launches the third march to Montgomery from Selma's Brown Chapel A.M.E. Marchers succeed in crossing the bridge and continue onward toward Montgomery, spending nights at Black-owned farms whose owners bravely opened their lands to marchers.

March 24: The Catholic City of St. Jude allows marchers to camp on its property. A "night under the stars," organized by Harry Belafonte, entertains marchers at the campsite.

March 25: The five-day, 54-mile Selma to Montgomery march concludes at the Alabama State Capitol, where King addresses the crowd, which has grown to 25,000. On this same day, Viola Liuzzo, a White mother of five from Detroit, is murdered by the Ku Klux Klan on Highway 80 while working as a volunteer for the Selma to Montgomery campaign.

August 6: President Johnson signs the Voting Rights Act of 1965, which abolishes literacy tests and establishes federal oversight to boost Black voter registration and evaluate new local voting laws to make sure they don't negatively impact Black people's right to vote.

Participants in the 1965 march from Selma to Montgomery take a rest.

Selma faced a serious challenge. Dr. Martin Luther King Jr. was invited to Selma where Black residents—children included—defied the injunction and doubled down on their commitments to the principle of nonviolent direct action. Spearheaded by King and the Southern Christian Leadership Conference (SCLC), protestors marched to the Dallas County Courthouse to register to vote and engaged in trainings on how to pass the rigged, nonsensical tests they faced when registering.

Local churches provided havens for training in nonviolent tactics, with Brown Chapel A.M.E. Church being the hub of such activity. Meanwhile, leaders of the SCLC set up shop at the home of longtime voting rights activist Amelia Boynton, where they conceived and planned the Selma to Montgomery march. That march resulted in Bloody Sunday, where nearly 500 marchers made it to the Edmund Pettus Bridge where the sheriff, not local police, had jurisdiction. Sheriff Jim Clark was a

PEOPLE WHO MADE THE MOVEMENT

GROUPS AND ORGANIZATIONS

Dallas County Voters League: This league began educating Black residents about voting and economic justice in the 1920s, when it was founded by C. J. Adams. In 1965, under the leadership of F. D. Reese, the league invited King to Selma to boost the momentum for Black people who wanted to vote and have more say-so in their government. The King invitation came courtesy of the league's steering committee, which came to be known as the **Courageous Eight.** They were: Ulysses Blackmon, Amelia Boynton Robinson, Ernest Doyle, Marie Foster, James Gildersleeve, J. D. Hunter, Rev. F. D. Reese, and Rev. Henry Shannon.

Student Nonviolent Coordinating Committee (SNCC): Founded in 1960 after the student sit-in movement took off, this civil rights organization was designed as an independent organization to provide greater voice in leadership on civil rights issues.

MARCH PARTICIPANTS AND ORGANIZERS

John Lewis: SNCC leader who led more than 600 marchers across the Edmund Pettus Bridge on Bloody Sunday and was beaten so badly by police, he suffered a fractured skull. Lewis was a student at American Baptist Theological Seminary (now American Baptist College) when he became active in the Nashville Sit-In Movement, which initiated lunch counter boycotts in 1960. He became a long-serving and beloved congressman in Georgia.

Hosea Williams: Organizer who walked alongside Lewis on Bloody Sunday. Williams also helped enlist mostly White college students to work with local Black activists to register voters in six states. Representing about 100 universities, the initiative succeeded in registering more than 49,000 Black voters.

Dr. Martin Luther King Jr.: King led two marches to the Edmund Pettus Bridge in support of voting rights: Turnaround Tuesday, and the third march, on March 21, 1965, which made it all the way to Montgomery.

Amelia Boynton Robinson: The "matriarch of voting rights" and a member of the Dallas County Voters League, Boynton Robinson turned the 1963 funeral of her husband, Sam Boynton, at Tabernacle Baptist Church into a voting rights mass meeting. Her home was a planning site for the 1965 Selma to Montgomery march. Boynton Robinson was among the protestors on the Edmund Pettus Bridge on Bloody Sunday; she was attacked by state troopers and hospitalized. Boynton Robinson died in 2015 at age 104.

Viola Liuzzo: A White mother of five from Detroit, Liuzzo heeded King's call to come to Alabama and march for voting rights. She used her 1963 Oldsmobile to shuttle activists back and forth between Selma and Montgomery and was in the car with a Black man named Leroy Moton, 19, when Ku Klux Klan members spied her. They murdered her with a bullet to the head.

Rev. James Reeb: A White Unitarian Universalist minister from Massachusetts who came to Selma to support the Turnaround Tuesday ministers march called by King. Along with two other ministers, he was attacked that evening by a mob of angry White men who beat and murdered him. Three White men were tried and acquitted, and no one has ever been held accountable.

Bernard Lafayette: Fresh from the sit-in movement in Nashville, Lafayette and his wife, Colia, came to Selma in 1963 so he could direct SNCC's Alabama voter registration project, including working with the Dallas County Voters League.

OTHER KEY FIGURES

Frank M. Johnson: Federal judge who authorized the 1965 Selma to Montgomery march, citing the constitutional right to assemble with an assurance by President Lyndon B. Johnson the law would be enforced so demonstrators could march peacefully. Johnson faced years of ostracism by White society for his decisions, which included desegregating Alabama schools, getting rid of the poll tax, and allowing Black people to serve on juries.

a marker honoring Rev. James Reeb, who came to Selma to support the Turnaround Tuesday ministers march

staunch segregationist who presided over the beating and gassing of children, women, and men, some of whom were hospitalized and most of whom rebounded back at Brown Chapel A.M.E. Church where the march began.

ORIENTATION

The city of Selma, in Dallas County, sits on the Alabama River, about 100 miles south of Birmingham. Selma has a little more than 17,000 residents and is a small, quiet town that is easy to navigate by car. Montgomery, the endpoint of the 1965 Selma to Montgomery march, is located in Montgomery County fifty miles east of Selma along Highway 80. Lowndes County sits about equidistant between Selma and Montgomery.

The 1965 Selma to Montgomery march occurred along **Highway 80.** Today, that highway is part of the **Selma to Montgomery National Historic Trail** (www.nps.gov/semo), which was established by Congress to preserve the story of the voting rights movement and the 1965 Selma to Montgomery march, which contributed to passage of the Voting Rights Act of 1965. The trail starts at Brown Chapel A.M.E. Church in Selma and ends at the Alabama State Capitol in Montgomery. It's possible to drive it today, stopping at the **Lowndes Interpretive Center,** in Lowndes County, between the two cities.

PLANNING YOUR TIME

Plan to spend at least one day in small-town Selma. If you want to drive along the Selma to Montgomery National Historic Trail, that takes about an hour, not accounting for stops (and you will want to stop at the Lowndes Interpretive Center).

The **Selma Bridge Crossing Jubilee,** held annually in early March, draws massive crowds, so be sure to book your hotel couple of months in advance. Other sights are open by appointment only, including **Tabernacle Baptist Church** and the **Sullivan and Richie Jean Sherrod Jackson Foundation and Museum.**

The **Selma Interpretive Center** (2 Broad St.; tel. 334/872-0509) is a great place to get a foundational understanding of the voting rights movement in Selma and Dallas County. Knowledgeable National Park Service rangers can answer questions and point you to the types of

DRIVING THE SELMA TO MONTGOMERY NATIONAL HISTORIC TRAIL

For travelers interested in the entirety of the Selma to Montgomery march, you can follow (by car) the path of those who trekked 54 miles from Selma to Montgomery. Begin at **Brown Chapel A.M.E. Church,** then head to the **Selma Interpretive Center.** Go across the **Edmund Pettus Bridge** toward the **National Voting Rights Museum and Institute** to get a sense of the people who laid it all on the line to fight for voting rights. Keep driving east to the **Lowndes Interpretive Center,** and watch for signs of the three campsites where the marchers slept and the **Viola Liuzzo Memorial** (situated after the Lowndes Interpretive Center). The trail ends at the **Alabama State Capitol,** down the street from **Dexter Avenue King Memorial Baptist Church.** The drive takes around an hour, not accounting for any stops.

sites and businesses you may be interested in patronizing. The folks at **City Hall** (222 Broad St.; tel. 334/874-2101) can offer useful advice, too.

CONNECT WITH

Montgomery, 50 miles to the east, is your next logical stop.

Two Days in Selma

A good plan is to spend one full day in Selma, then make Montgomery your next destination. In driving between the two cities, you'll be tracing the historic 1965 march route.

Before you head out, make an appointment with the tourism ministry at **Brown Chapel A.M.E. Church** in Selma (Day 1).

DAY 1: SELMA

Your first day in Selma focuses on the voting rights struggle, beginning with the departure point for the 1965 march. All the sights on this day are within a mile or so of each other, so you can walk between them if you wish.

1 It makes sense to begin your visit to Selma at **Brown Chapel A.M.E. Church,** the starting point of voting rights marches in 1965. Advance appointments are required to visit. As you experience the church, imagine it teeming with activists preparing to make the 54-mile march to Montgomery.

2 Grab a bite to eat at **Lannie's BBQ Spot,** where foot soldiers found sustenance during the voting rights movement. Crispy fried pork skins add crunch to sauce-drenched pulled pork sandwiches.

3 Your next stop is the **Selma Interpretive Center.** Located at the foot of the Edmund Pettus Bridge, which marchers crossed en route to Montgomery, it teaches visitors about the voting rights movement in Selma. Oversize photos allow you to look into the faces of locals who faced beatings and death as they pressed their case for the right to vote.

4 Continue walking toward the **Edmund Pettus Bridge,** site of three marches for voting rights in 1965, and walk across and take in the quiet ripples of the Alabama River below.

5 Now that you're on the other side, stop to walk through the **Selma Voting Rights Memorial Park,** on one side of Highway 80. The park offers several interesting visual points of entry.

6 Have dinner at **Tally-Ho** for a fine-dining experience in Selma.

DAY 2: SELMA TO MONTGOMERY

Finish up in Selma in the morning, then cross the **Edmund Pettus Bridge** and drive east toward Montgomery. In doing so, you're tracing the path walked by protestors during the 1965 march.

1 Imagine the energy and intimacy of the movement during a tour of the **Sullivan and Richie Jean Sherrod Jackson Foundation and Museum,** your first stop of the day. This family home served as an organizing hotspot during the movement.

2 Next, walk through **Tabernacle Baptist Church,** where the voting rights movement really kicked off in 1963. It's less than half a mile east of the previous site. If you plan ahead, church ladies will serve you a good Southern lunch.

3 Get in your car, say goodbye to Selma, and drive across the historic **Edmund Pettus Bridge** on your way to Montgomery. As you drive east on Highway 80, try to imagine the feeling shared by the thousands of marchers who marched along this route in support of voting rights in 1965. Keep an eye out for campsite signage along the way and imagine, if you can, being Black and exposed on an open road. The walk from Selma to Montgomery took five days; the drive will take you around an hour.

4 Halfway between Selma and Montgomery, be sure to stop by the **Lowndes Interpretive Center.** The center sits on what was once Tent City, a site where dispossessed Black tenant farmers took refuge. Learn about Tent City, and about the voting rights struggle in Selma, inside.

5 As you leave the Lowndes Center, keep an eye out for the **Viola Liuzzo Memorial,** raised in honor of White Detroit homemaker Viola Liuzzo, a voting rights volunteer who was gunned down on the side of the highway by the KKK for her efforts.

6 When you arrive in Montgomery, drive by the **State Capitol** (page 145) where the march ended. You can barely see it, but a blackened box in the road right in front of the steps is where King delivered a moving speech to a crowd of 25,000.

THE SELMA TO MONTGOMERY MARCH

activists in Harlem marching in solidarity with Selma, 1965

It took voting rights activists a total of three tries to cross Selma's Edmund Pettus Bridge and reach the state capitol of Montgomery, 54 miles to the east, in 1965.

BLOODY SUNDAY

The first march attempt took place on March 7, 1965. On this day, 600 civil rights activists, led by a young John Lewis and Rev. Hosea Williams, began walking along Highway 80 West from Selma to Montgomery, a 54-mile trek. The group didn't get far: State troopers and armed White citizens met marchers as they crossed Edmund Pettus Bridge. When law enforcement ordered the marchers to turn around, Lewis told protestors to pray. As the message was making its way through the crowd, troopers and sheriff's deputies assaulted the activists, beating them, choking them with tear gas, and battering them under horse hooves. Fifty were injured, 17 were hospitalized, and Lewis, who suffered a broken skull, said he thought he might die. Marchers retreated to Brown A.M.E. in Selma to recover. The violent event came to be known as Bloody Sunday.

TURNAROUND TUESDAY

Two days after Bloody Sunday, King led a group of 2,000 (many of them ministers) to the bridge once again. However, to avoid violating a pending court order that Judge Frank M. Johnson had indicated he would issue barring a march to Montgomery, King had the group stop at the site of the attacks, where he asked everyone to kneel in prayer. King then led demonstrators back to their starting point, Brown A.M.E., and the day came to be known as Turnaround Tuesday. Later that evening, three Unitarian Universalist ministers were beaten, and Rev. James Reeb died of his injuries.

THE FINAL MARCH

The third try, on March 21, 1965, worked: King and 8,000 people successfully crossed the Edmund Pettus Bridge and made their way on foot to Montgomery, arriving at the state capitol four days later, where King addressed a crowd that had swelled to 25,000.

Sights

In Selma, you can walk across the Edmund Pettus Bridge and contemplate the violence that occurred here and the victory Selma to Montgomery marches helped produce. Visit civic-minded Black churches that provided safe places to plan, train, and strategize the nonviolent movement. See the homes of residents who made it their business to secure freedom for their neighbors. Alabama takes great pains to document heritage, so you'll see plenty of markers that tell the tale of what happened here during the fight for civil rights. However, not all the signage you'll see around town reflects the same values: A disturbing sign at the historic James Hotel downtown (but not affiliated in any way with the hotel) describes how Alabama's first Black congressman, a formerly enslaved man by the name of Benjamin Sterling Turner, was brought to Selma by his "mistress." ("Enslaver" would be a more accurate term.)

★ Brown Chapel A.M.E. Church

410 Martin Luther King St.; tel. 334/874-7897; by appointment only; $7

Established in 1866, a year after the Civil War ended, this church was the SCLC's headquarters for the Selma campaign to win voting rights for African Americans. Even after a 1964 Alabama court injunction banned mass meetings, paralyzing Selma activists, Brown defiantly persisted as a center of civil rights activity. The church was the starting point for several nonviolent marches, including groups of activists (small groups because of a tendency of Alabama police to arrest Black people for "parading" without a permit) who walked to the Dallas County Courthouse in Selma to demand the right to vote. Many child foot soldiers took part in marches and meetings at Brown.

All three 1965 Selma to Montgomery marches—Bloody Sunday, Turnaround Tuesday, and the third march, which was a success—also started at Brown. On Bloody Sunday (March 7, 1965), the church also served as a place of refuge for the 600 marchers who got as far as Selma's Edmund Pettus Bridge a few blocks away before they were beaten and gassed by law enforcement officers. Malcolm X also spoke here, on February 4, 1965. His speech avoided any references to the differences he and King had on nonviolent, direct action.

Today, the Brown Chapel congregation's Romanesque Revival-style building is recognized as a National Historic Landmark. Architectural details from the red brick building include twin steeples, an oversize stained-glass window that hangs over a portico at the entrance, three balconies, and vaults supported by wooden Ionic columns and a coffered ceiling with several chandeliers. A granite monument in front of the church features a bronze bust of King. It also lists the names of activists who died in the movement in Alabama: Jimmie Lee Jackson (shot by a state trooper as he tried to shield his mother from violence), Viola Liuzzo, and James Reeb.

It's worth making an appointment with the church's tourism ministry for a **tour** that details Brown's role in the push for voting rights that led to the passage of the Voting Rights Act of 1965. The church is a stop on the official U.S. Civil Rights Trail.

★ Selma Interpretive Center

2 Broad St.; tel. 334/872-0509; Mon.-Sat. 9am-4:30pm; free

Located at the beginning of the Selma to Montgomery National Historic Trail, on Selma's main strip at the foot of the Edmund Pettus Bridge, this is the first of three interpretive centers (the other two are in Lowndes County and Montgomery)

that allow visitors to navigate the story of the voting rights movement and get to know the names and faces of its leaders and foot soldiers. The center shows visitors just how much nonviolent defiance and discipline it took to get the ultimate result: passage of the Voting Rights Act of 1965, signed by President Lyndon B. Johnson. The center also affirms that the fight for voting rights in Selma and Dallas County wasn't a new thing: Folks had been organizing and advocating for these rights since the 1930s.

The museum is located inside the three-story former People's Bank and Trust. The first floor features a gift shop and park rangers' desk with interactive exhibits in the back. Rest rooms are on this floor too. The second floor features more interactive exhibits, and the third floor has a room filled with chairs and hanging banners depicting images and names of the Courageous Eight, the Dallas County Voters League steering committee. A window provides a view of the Edmund Pettus Bridge.

Exhibits include oversize photographic displays, and large quotes by activists transport visitors to voting rights marches. Look into the eyes of the Black citizens who bravely took a stand, knowing that danger—in the form of law enforcement or White vigilante action—could strike at any given moment. A quote by SNCC organizer Bernard Lafayette on the first floor exhibition area reads: "A people without a vote is a people without a voice and at the mercy of those in control of the system."

One exhibit, a statue of a White man seated at a desk with a large jar of jelly beans, illustrates one of the "tests" that was devised to thwart Black citizens from registering to vote. (Yes, there were occasions where Black people had to guess how

Photos (top to bottom): inside Brown Chapel A.M.E. Church with Joyce O'Neal, head of the church's tourism ministry; Selma Interpretive Center; the Edmund Pettus Bridge

GET INTO THE RHYTHM

- **"Ain't Gonna Let Nobody Turn Me Around"**: This African American spiritual about persistence was a perfect motivational tool for civil rights marchers as they attempted, multiple times, to cross the Edmund Pettus Bridge in support of voting rights. It's been performed by various artists, including the SNCC Freedom Singers, and in 2011, The Roots performed it for the documentary *Soundtrack for a Revolution*.
- **"Oh, Freedom"**: Performed by Harry Belafonte and Joan Baez, among others, this song throws down the gauntlet: "Before I be a slave, I'll be buried in my grave." Freedom songs like this one gave voting rights marchers the spiritual wherewithal to withstand intimidation and violence. This song was performed on the night of March 24, 1965, during the impromptu star-studded concert at City of St. Jude, the Catholic services complex and last stop before the Montgomery state capitol. Be sure to check out The Golden Gospel Singers' smooth, honeyed rendition that is sure to leave you feeling lifted.
- **Staple Singers, "Freedom Highway"**: This 1965 Staple Singers song in honor of Selma to Montgomery marchers debuted at New Nazareth Church on Chicago's South Side.

many jelly beans were in the jar to qualify to register.) Also on display are three kinds of batons used to beat activists.

Another display shows three types of batons and intimidation tools used by law enforcement officers like Sheriff Jim Clark. Don't be surprised if some of the displays involving audio narratives delivered by phone are inoperable, as they were in need of repair at one point.

On the third floor, a large-screen TV plays oral histories of locals who participated in the voting rights movement in Selma. In this room, educators, tour guides, and foot soldiers, like JoAnne Bland, hold forth about the past and present with a challenge to consider your contribution to the democratic experiment moving forward.

National Park Service rangers who operate the site are on hand for questions and are knowledgeable about the voting rights movement and navigating Selma.

The Selma Interpretive Center is a stop on the official U.S. Civil Rights Trail.

TOP EXPERIENCE

★ Edmund Pettus Bridge

The Edmund Pettus Bridge, a stop on the official U.S. Civil Rights Trail, stretches across the Alabama River. Coming west from Montgomery on Highway 80, it designates the entrance into the city of Selma. When voting rights activists attempted to cross the bridge to leave Selma in a march to Montgomery in 1965, violence ensued.

Today, the bridge is an enduring symbol of the civil rights movement, and a site for the annual commemorative march that takes place every March.

Ironically, the bridge, a powerful symbol for voting rights, is named for a Confederate general and Ku Klux Klan leader. Some have argued the bridge should be renamed for civil rights leader and long-time House Representative John Lewis; others surmise that a landmark representing Black triumph over White supremacy suits the Pettus legacy well.

The bridge, which is nearly 1,250 feet across, is part of the fabric of Selma, crossed by drivers every day, and by some locals seeking to get their steps in. If you're in good shape, it should take about 10-15 minutes to get across the quarter-mile bridge and back. But for many, the bridge with the controversial name will always be a site of pilgrimage and purpose.

National Voting Rights Museum and Institute

6 U.S. Hwy. 80 E; tel. 334/526-4340; www.nvrmi.com; Mon.-Thurs. 10am-4pm; adults $6.50, seniors and students $4.50

This small museum at the foot of the Edmund Pettus Bridge tells the story of the voting rights fight and the local people who participated in the movement though a series of thematic galleries. Timelines, vintage images, stories, quotes, and artifacts help to tell a comprehensive story. One gallery is dedicated to movements in Albany, Georgia; St. Augustine, Florida; Greenwood, Mississippi; and Selma, Alabama, and showcases feature Rev. Jesse L. Jackson, the Selma to Montgomery march, churches, and legal fights. Exhibits and images celebrate the Courageous Eight and the foot soldiers, many of whom still live in the area. They are remembered with a footprint exhibit that runs throughout the facility. The museum is a stop on the official U.S. Civil Rights Trail.

Selma Voting Rights Memorial Park

On Highway 80 as you approach Selma city limits coming from Montgomery, you'll see the Edmund Pettus Bridge jutting into the sky. This small park is off to the right. If you pull over and park, you can view monuments dedicated to the leaders of the voting rights movement, including Amelia Boynton Robinson and Marie Foster, honored as mothers of the civil rights movement "before and beyond the bridge," Congressman John Lewis, Rev. Hosea Williams, and Rev. Joseph Lowery and his wife, Evelyn.

A marker that reads "Never Forget, Never Again" explains how the bridge named for a Klan leader should encourage individuals to cherish the right to vote. Other monuments are scattered throughout, some of them honoring Black history predating the movement. In another area, a towering mound of stones reads: "When your children shall ask you in time to come saying, 'What mean these 12 stones?' Then you shall tell them how you made it over." Joshua 4:21:22. The park also includes trails through wooded areas draped in Spanish moss that lead to breathtaking views of Selma and the Alabama River.

The park is located at the foot of the Edmund Pettus Bridge, which is where you'll find Columbus Mitchell, a local resident who hangs around just being helpful and offer knowledge of civil rights in Selma. The way Mitchell tells it, he has met visitors at the bridge for years to tell the story of the Selma march and of his uncle who participated in the march. Born after the movement, he is intrigued by the story of what happened here and voluntarily describes the monuments and signs to parkgoers, proudly showing his Certificate of Completion from Bernard Lafayette's two-day Kingian Nonviolence Conflict Reconciliation Training course from Healing Waters Retreat Center in 2016. Yes, a guy at the foot of a bridge might seem odd, but it's just the kind of quirky that makes small-town life a treat.

The park is directly in front of the National Voting Rights Museum and Institute.

Dallas County Courthouse

105 Lauderdale St.; tel. 334/874-2500; www.dallas.alacourt.gov; Mon.-Fri. 8:30am-4:30pm; free

This venerable Greek Revival building was a target of marches and altercations during the Selma campaign when voting rights activists kept showing up to register to vote only to be denied. The facility is both a historical artifact and working courthouse, whose leadership now includes Black people.

Back in the day, hateful ol' Sheriff Jim Clark liked to sic his deputies on peaceful protestors. One such occasion was October 7, 1963, called Freedom Day. By 9am there was a line of Black folks waiting to get inside the registrar's office to register to vote. People who brought food and water to those waiting in line were beaten and arrested. Even as Justice Department attorneys looked on from across the street, hostile Sheriff Jim Clark and armed deputies bullied the Black residents. The day before, would-be Black voters met at churches to build themselves up for what they might face. Comedian Dick Gregory encouraged residents at a mass meeting. Also arrested was Annie Lee Cooper who reflexively hit Sheriff Clark after he nudged her with a baton.

All told, hundreds were arrested and locked up on Freedom Day.

Live Oak Cemetery

110 West Dallas Ave.; tel. 334/874-2160; www.selma-al.gov/cemetery-department; Mon.-Thurs. 8am-4pm; free

This historic city-owned cemetery, a burial site of several Confederates who died in the Civil War, provides a necessary antecedent to the civil rights story: It's surrounded by land owned by majority-Black Selma taxpayers, yet it maintains a place of honor for those who insisted on owning other people. A small and controversial private area commemorates the Confederacy, particularly Gen. Nathan Bedford Forrest, the KKK founder who built a fortune selling Black people into enslavement. Vice President William Rufus King is buried here, as is formerly enslaved Benjamin Sterling Turner, Alabama's first Black congressman.

This ugly history, of course, is surrounded by beautiful live oaks, fragrant magnolias, and a blessed peace only found in cemeteries.

Tabernacle Baptist Church

1431 Broad St.; tel. 334/419-6103 or 334/412-4829; tours by appointment; $10 per person or call for group rates

The voting rights movement in Selma kicked off right here at this church on May 14, 1963, when Rev. L. L. Anderson at the behest of SNCC organizer Bernard Lafayette and Amelia Boynton of the Dallas County Voters League, opened the church doors to hundreds of people. The occasion, tragically, was the funeral of Sam Boynton, Amelia's husband, but in a bold organizing move, the gathering also became the first mass meeting for the voting rights movement in Selma.

Today, the Classical Revival church, designed by African American architect David T. West, is listed on the National Register of Historic Places. A dome looming over the pews allows sunlight through windowpanes, and arches hang over the balcony. The church has two identical entrances: a front entrance on Broad Street and side entrance on Minter Avenue. This was because the law prohibited African Americans from owning property on Broad Street (Selma's main thoroughfare), and from entering from there too. The Minter entrance is just as grand as the one on Broad. Architecturally speaking, this was the nicest place in Black Selma for a

Photos (top to bottom): inside the National Voting Rights Museum and Institute; Selma Voting Rights Memorial Park; Tabernacle Baptis Church

THE VOTING RIGHTS MOVEMENT IGNITES

Funeral turned voting-rights rally? Sounds unusual, but that's exactly what happened in 1963, when Amelia Boynton allowed the funeral of her first husband, Sam, her partner in activism, to be a combination homegoing and voting rights rally. Flyers read: "Memorial Service for Mr. Boynton and Voter Registration."

The decision to host this funeral/meeting was a big deal: While other churches (including Boynton's own church, First Baptist) declined to host for fear of White reprisal, Tabernacle, which had been involved in the fight for voting rights since the 1920s, took up the cause. Tabernacle Pastor L. L. Anderson insisted he would hold the mass meeting "on the sidewalk outside and, with a loudspeaker, tell the public the officers were too scared to open the doors."[1]

Still, the congregation was taking a chance in a town rife with intimidation by Whites in day-to-day life. Both the businesslike White Citizens Council and the Ku Klux Klan were organizations to be feared. During the funeral/mass meeting, Dallas County Sheriff Jim Clark had a posse surrounding the church, and these White men documented who was going inside. They even came inside the sanctuary to "supervise" and prevent "insurrection." In addition to their guns, deputies were armed with table legs-cum-nightsticks.

When churchgoers tried to leave, they were met on Broad Street by a White mob and a posse armed with those table legs. Some reports say folks waited until they felt it was safe to leave. Others indicate the Selma High School football coach showed up and ordered current and former players to go home, and that's when the crowd broke up.

Despite the intimidation White segregationists put on display and the violence they wrought on others, African American citizens would get their voting rights, sooner rather than later. And it was all set in motion by a single meeting in the Lord's house.

very long time. When Jim Crow ended, Tabernacle officials changed the church's address to Broad. Amelia Boynton Robinson's homegoing was held here September 5, 2015.

Tabernacle is still going strong and provides tours of the building crafted as an auditorium-style worship space that enhances acoustic excellence, featuring a stained-glass clerestory that allows light to wash over the sanctuary. The basement is where civil rights organizing activity occurred. Today, church ladies will include a home-cooked soul food lunch in group tour packages. Get that old-time religion while you scarf down fried chicken, salad, fresh veggies, and other goodies in the fellowship hall.

Sullivan and Richie Jean Sherrod Jackson Foundation and Museum

1416 Lapsley Ave.; tel. 334/375.3838 and 404/799-1803; www.bcri.org/consortium/sullivan-and-richie-jean-sherrod-jackson-museum; by appointment; $5-15

The home of Mrs. Richie Jean Sherrod Jackson, a teacher, and husband Dr. Sullivan Jackson, a dentist, was an oasis of Black thought and activism during the Selma voting rights movement. And even before the home became a hub for voting rights organizing, it was a guest house for W. E. B. DuBois and Booker T. Washington, who held fire-side chats about economic sustainability, education, and community building. Decades later, the Jacksons welcomed the likes of King and Ralph Bunche, the first African American to be awarded the Nobel Peace Prize, as activists worked feverishly to plan the Selma to Montgomery march.

Forty-five-minute to hour-long tours through this well-kept home feature voting rights movement artifacts, an art collection, and other memorabilia. The Jackson's daughter, Jawana Jackson, grew up amid this activity and fondly remembers "Uncle Martin" (King) staying at the home and reading her stories. He slept in the third bedroom, neatly made up with a wood-framed bed, dresser drawer, and other furnishings. This is where King and other ministers met for a prayer session before going over to Brown Chapel to embark upon would be a successful four-day march to Montgomery on March 21-25, 1965. A beige analog phone is on display in the home; Jawana said President Lyndon B. Johnson would call her parents' home.

One room shows where King sat on March 15, 1965, when Johnson addressed the nation about the Voting Rights Act in what is called his "We Shall Overcome" speech. This seat is marked off with a gold post and a tasseled rope. Here, visitors will see a photo by embedded photographer, Frank Dandridge, who captured King sitting in that chair, wrapped in a blanket while Johnson's visage beamed from the television.

Jawana Jackson, who leads the tours with help from Selma resident A.C. Reeves, maintains her parent's legacy and lessons of the movement by sharing a uniquely homegrown story: "Love will always win over hate," she said. "Even if you are not an activist, you need to be acting."

The home is on the National Register of Historic Places. Call in advance to book a tour.

Amelia Boynton Robinson Home

1315 Lapsley St.; www.ameliaboynton-house.com

Amelia Boynton famously said "A voteless people is a hopeless people." It was from this Craftsman bungalow reportedly built by the Works Progress Administration that she energetically coordinated so much of her voting rights activism on behalf of Selma and surrounding Dallas County. An early draft of the Voting Rights Act of 1965 was crafted in this house. Boynton was an honored White House guest on August 6, 1965, when President Johnson signed the bill into law.

Boynton Robinson's home at the corner of Lapsley and Boynton Streets has fallen into disrepair, but a private organization, The Gateway Educational Foundation & Institute, aims to restore the home to its former glory and use it for educational purposes.

Tours and Local Guides

BUS TOUR

JOURNEYS FOR THE SOUL

tel. 334/412-6604; www.iamjoannebland.com; group of 20 people or less $500 flat rate, group of 21 people or more $25 per person

Tour director JoAnne Bland is history personified: As a veteran of voting rights movement, she participated in Bloody Sunday, Turnaround Tuesday, and the first leg of the successful march from Selma to Montgomery. She had been arrested a total of 13 documented times at the young age of 11. Bland became a member of SNCC in the early 1960s and dutifully trained to leverage nonviolent direct-action techniques on the streets.

VOICES OF THE MOVEMENT:
CHILD FOOT SOLDIER JOANNE BLAND

"Before we could turn to run, it was too late. They came in from both sides, the front and the back. And they were just beating the people. Old, young, Black, White, male, female. People lay everywhere, bleeding, not moving."

—**JOANNE BLAND** was 11 years old on Bloody Sunday—but she was there nonetheless. In fact, before she turned 12, the young civil rights activist had been arrested 13 times. The first time she was arrested, Bland was eight.

"I had never experienced violence [prior to Bloody Sunday]," Bland says. "Marching was fun to me. I liked the spirit of the movement, the songs, the chants, being with my friends . . . not going to school. I liked all of that." Bloody Sunday changed all that. Bland recalls horses running into the crowd, raring then kicking. She saw people get trampled, heard bones breaking. "It seemed like it lasted an eternity," she says.

As a child, Bland had every right to protest. Segregation was so insidious that her mother died in a "White" hospital while waiting for a blood transfusion. (Officials were waiting on "Black" blood for her.)

Bland was not the only child to participate in movement marches. In the 1960s SNCC began organizing local youth and training them in the art of nonviolent direct action. In 1961, Bland attended a meeting where King spoke. She also helped protect White Northerners, ministers, and college students who came to Selma to march. Her grandmother encouraged her and her sister, Linda Blackmon Lowery, to participate, though her father didn't approve.

As an adult, Bland co-founded the **National Voting Rights Museum and Institute,** which now sits at the foot of the Edmund Pettus Bridge, where Bloody Sunday took place. At **Journeys for the Soul,** Bland's tour company, she leads busloads of visitors around Selma, offering a first-person perspective on the city's civil rights history.

Known for her candor, Bland has a straight, no-chaser approach to history. "Every right that African Americans get in the United States is fought for; it's never a given," she says. "To this day, we're still fighting."

SELMA

Bland, who is also a U.S. Army veteran, brings this experience and wisdom to tour groups that travel from all over the world to experience the movement in Selma through her eyes. Bland tells gripping stories of how Black Alabamians were treated when she was young and minces no words about who were the good guys and who was bad. Tours include Brown Chapel A.M.E. Church, where Bland speaks about the Black kids growing up in nearby Carver Homes and of the dueling histories that live in tension with civil rights wins and aspirations. She sometimes takes groups to Live Oak Cemetery, where she talks about Selma's Confederate past and present (but don't you dare take her picture there).

Bland will tease you mercilessly in the kindest way only a natural teacher can. You'll learn a lot of details about the movement and current events as well. (Make sure you pay attention because Bland will definitely quiz you.) Bland's sister, Linda Blackmon Lowery—the youngest person to complete all 54 miles of the Selma to Montgomery march, at the age of 15—also leads some tours.

Tours take 2.5 hours and depart from the Selma Interpretive Center on Broad Street. Tours may also include lunch with a local foot soldier, many of whom still live in the area. (Tourgoers must purchase their own lunch, plus a $50 fee for the honored history maker.)

Festivals and Events

MARCH

SELMA BRIDGE CROSSING JUBILEE

Various locations; http://selma50.com; tel. 334/526-2626; free

Every year, the tiny population of Selma (around 17,000) swells with people from around the globe returning to re-enact the Sunday, March 7, 1965, attempted crossing of the Edmund Pettus Bridge known as Bloody Sunday. This annual commemorative event is billed as the largest civil rights commemoration in the world and takes place the first weekend in March, Friday-Sunday.

Featured Jubilee guests include faith leaders, elected officials, activists, entertainers and global thought leaders. This weekend-long event is staged in venues throughout Selma, including the peaceful, wood-paneled **Healing Waters Retreat Center** (8 Mulberry Road), which looks over rippling waters of the Alabama River at the Pettus Bridge itself. Activities include talks, film screenings, and inductions into the Hall of Resistance, which honors those who fought (and those who continue to fight) for social justice. Sessions in Kingian nonviolence techniques have been taught by Dr. Bernard Lafayette, whose civil rights body of work includes leading in the Nashville Movement and Freedom Rides. Look out for mock trials, a Saturday parade, and space for the hip-hop and younger generations to showcase their talents. The Jubilee Festival & Music features R&B and blues. The gospel is good—all the time—so be prepared to be uplifted.

The big day, however, is Sunday, when the bridge walk reenactment takes place. For the march's 50th anniversary in 2015, 40,000 people, including President Barack Obama, Congressman John Lewis, and Amelia Boynton Robinson, participated. On the morning before the march, folks attend services in several churches that supported the movement, such as Brown Chapel A.M.E., First Baptist Church, and Tabernacle. A pre-march rally always occurs at Brown Chapel A.M.E. Following the original march route, marchers make their way from Brown west to Selma Avenue, then on to Broad Street where the

45th anniversary of the march from Selma to Montgomery in 2010

Pettus Bridge begins. The mass of people hike about 1,200 feet across in a symbolic walk.

Most activities are free of charge. However, events such as the annual golf tournament, gala dinner, and festival ($12 in advance and $17 at the gate) have associated fees. Visit the event website for details.

Past commemorations have been attended by several sitting presidents, including Barack Obama and Bill Clinton, as well as congresspeople and dignitaries. Civil rights heroes, from Rep. John Lewis himself to Amelia Boynton Robinson, have been in attendance as well.

Food

This is Selma, so what you eat here will be food for the soul.

BARBECUE

LANNIE'S BBQ SPOT

2115 Minter Ave.; tel. 334/874-4478; Mon.-Sat. 8am-6:45pm, Sun. 11am-4:30pm; $9-10

Nestled on a neighborhood street, Lannie's has been a family affair since 1944, when Lannie and Will Travis started barbecuing hogs next to their house. Today, Lannie's daughter, Lula Hatcher, presides over the barbecue emporium where she says it's the sauce that makes the difference. The pulled pork sandwiches here just might change your life: They're topped with cracklings (crispy pig skin), so you get a crunch in every moist, juicy bite. Lannie's also serves ribs, barbecue beef, chicken and turkey wings, and fish (catfish and whiting). Sandwiches include pork chop and bologna; sides include potato salad, macaroni 'n' cheese, greens, and cabbage; and dessert includes a range of pies, from pecan to sweet potato.

Lannie's BBQ Spot is notable for its role in feeding foot soldiers the Selma voting rights movement. As Ms. Lula, who was a youth at the time recalls, "The White folks didn't want us downtown.

They didn't want us to go in the courthouse. They would say we were blocking the streets. But we didn't let it stop us." She's a little irked that, after people put their lives on the line to secure the Black vote, "some of the people still won't get up and vote. Every vote counts."

CAFETERIA

SELMA FAMILY RESTAURANT'S ALL IN ONE CAFETERIA

3000 Earl Goodwin Pkwy., Selma; tel. 334/874-7002; www.wccs.edu/business-finance; Mon.-Fri., 10am-2:30pm, Sun. 11am-4:30pm; a la carte starting at $2-7

Yes, this is the school cafeteria at Wallace Community College, but trust that this food is delicious. Why else would there be a line running from the tight cafeteria line into a large dining room if the turkey wings, beef tips, pig feet, pork chops, and fish weren't well-seasoned, served hot, and simply scrumptious? Well, how about a ribeye steak or a hearty chef salad? Community members familiar with the salivating faces lined up here serve up this food with joy. Better get yourself some.

STEAK HOUSE

TALLY-HO

509 Mangum Ave.; tel. 334/872-1390; www.tallyhoselma.com; Mon.-Thurs. 5pm-9pm, Fri.-Sat. 5pm-10pm; a la carte from $8-25

Tally-Ho (not a Black-owned business) brings fine dining to Selma with hearty steaks and entrees from around the globe. Escargots, anyone? In addition to steaks with an array of toppings that include sauteed crab meat, mushrooms, and onions, the menu features salmon, pork chops, and a house burger. Choose from a list of sides: potatoes prepared several ways, angel hair pasta, seasonal vegetables, and more. Start your meal with one of a variety of salads and appetizers, such as fried artichoke hearts or vegetable spring rolls. Tally-Ho offers an extensive wine list and serves dinner-only in a friendly, intimate English-pub-style atmosphere.

Accommodations

Several chain hotels are available in Selma: the **Hampton Inn** (2200 W Highland Ave.; tel. 334/876-9995; www.hilton.com; $119) off Highway 80, about four miles from the National Voting Rights Museum and Institute, is one option. The historic St. James Hotel, under renovation at the time of writing, will provide an opportunity to stay in town in style.

ST. JAMES HOTEL

1200 Water Ave.; tel. 334/872-3234

At the time of writing, this historic riverfront hotel was being redeveloped into a Hilton property that will accommodate throngs of people who return annually to retrace the steps of where the Selma to Montgomery march began at the Pettus bridge. Originally 55 rooms, this full-service hotel in the historic district features a restaurant serving Southern and French cuisine and a full bar. The St. James is a few steps away from the Selma Interpretive Center and the Edmund Pettus Bridge. Other sites are within walking distance or a short car ride away.

Photos (top to bottom): Lannie's BBQ Spot; Selma Family Restaurant's All In One Cafeteria at Wallace Community College; St. James Hotel

Transportation

GETTING THERE

Selma has no public airport, and Amtrak does not stop here.

Bus

Selma's **Greyhound station** (434 Broad St.; tel. 800/231-2222; www.greyhound.com) is easy to find on Selma's main thoroughfare. However, there are no direct Greyhound connections to any of the destinations in this guide, except Montgomery.

Car

To get to Selma from:

- **Montgomery Regional Airport:** Take **Highway 80 West** for 42 miles (40 minutes).
- **Birmingham:** Take **I-65 South** to **AL-22 West** for 90 miles (1 hour 40 minutes).

GETTING AROUND

You're gonna need a car to get around town. **Enterprise** and **Budget** car rental offices are found in Selma. Unless you're visiting during the Selma Bridge Crossing Jubilee, parking in town is pretty effortless.

Taxi and Ride-Hailing Apps

Several taxi companies operate in Selma: Call **Vivian Strong** (tel. 334/875-0694) or **Al Blackmon, Triple A Transportation** (tel. 334/412-4827). **Uber** and **Lyft** are here too.

Selma to Montgomery

With only the clothes on their backs, Black marchers and their White allies struck out from Selma on a five-day walk to demand voting rights, crossing the Edmund Pettus Bridge on the 54-mile trek toward Montgomery. Footage shows marchers with walking sticks or shirts tied around their heads, some wearing sunglasses. Others

In 1965, voting rights activists marched along Highway 80 from Selma to Montgomery.

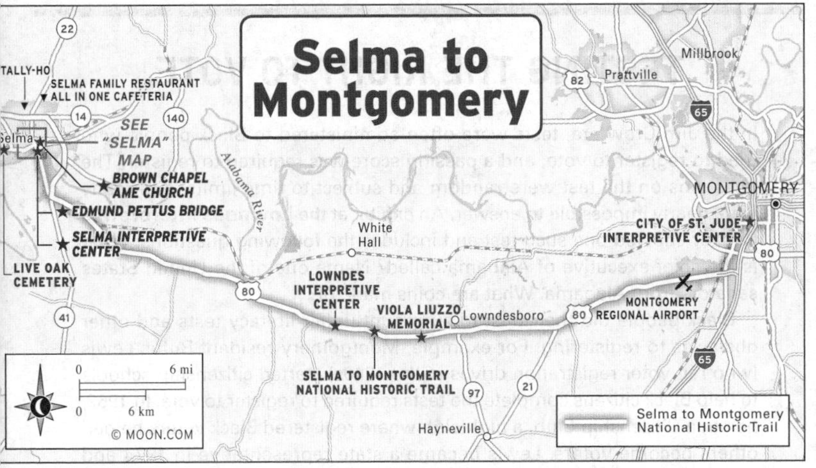

carried the American flag. Clergy of all races joined the march, and somewhere in the scrum, a 15-year-old Black girl, Linda Blackmon Lowery, the youngest marcher, held her own. Also in that crowd was an unidentified young Black man whose face is covered in a chalky white substance with "VOTE" scrawled on his forehead—in the moment but also foreshadowing. Marchers were protected by U.S. Army troops and Alabama National Guard forces under federal control, which meant helicopters flying overhead. The highway narrowed from four lanes to two when they hit Lowndes County, and nonviolent protestors had to keep one lane open to cars.

Marchers carried very little, and the nights were cold and sometimes rainy, so they needed a place to sleep at night. Black-owned farms and the Catholic Church opened up their land, allowing participants a place to eat and rest. The landowners of these farms—David Hall Farm (March 21), Rose Steele Fram (March 22), and Robert Gardner Farm (March 23)—did this at great risk of being abused by surrounding White landowners, among other elements of the White power structure. The City of St. Jude in Montgomery opened its property on March 24; this is where the **Stars for Freedom Rally,** organized by musician and actor Harry Belafonte, was held. On a flatbed trailer turned stage, celebrities—Joan Baez, James Baldwin, Tony Bennett, Leonard Bernstein, Sammy Davis Jr., Billy Eckstein, Dick Gregory, Lena Horne, Mahalia Jackson, Alan King, Johnny Mathis, Nipsey Russell, Pete Seeger, Nina Simone, and Shelley Winters, among others—performed for the marchers. It was an unforgettable event.

By the time the Selma marchers reached Montgomery, their ranks had swelled to 25,000 strong. The march ended with a rally at the Alabama State Capitol on March 25, 1965, where Martin Luther King Jr. delivered a rousing speech.

The road from Montgomery to Selma is wonderfully peaceful and marked by rural scenery. Unless you were there, it's hard to believe African Americans had to take over streets, in this case, a country highway, to make their case. But they did.

As you drive along the highway today, you'll see signage marking the campsites where marchers slept. Rather than stopping, get the full skinny about these campsites inside the Lowndes Interpretive Center.

TESTING THE RIGHT TO VOTE

In the Jim Crow era, tests were often administered to Black people who tried to register to vote, and a passing score was required to register. The questions on the test were random and subject to time limits, and many were nearly impossible to answer. An exhibit at the **Lowndes Interpretive Center** showed one such test and includes the following questions: What is the chief executive of Alabama called? Name one of the United States senators from Alabama. What are coins made of?

Black people did their best to surmount unfair literacy tests and other obstacles to registering. For example, Montgomery resident Rufus Lewis (who ran voter registration drives in the 1940s) started citizenship schools to help Black citizens complete the tests required to register to vote. In 1952, he ran a Citizenship Club, a nightclub where registered Black voters helped others become voters. Lewis became a state representative in 1974 and served in President Jimmy Carter's cabinet.

SIGHTS

Lowndes Interpretive Center

7002 U.S. 80, Hayneville; tel. 334/877-1983; www.civilrightstrail.com/attraction/lowndes-interpretive-center; Mon.-Sat. 9am-4:30pm; free

The Lowndes Interpretive Center, a stop on the official U.S. Civil Rights Trail, is equidistant between Selma and Montgomery on Highway 80 West. Operated by the National Park Service, the center sits on land that held a Tent City, which was erected by SNCC organizers in 1965 to house Black tenant farmers and their families who were thrown out of their homes by White landowners after trying to register to vote. SNCC leaders provided water, heaters, food, and tents while dispossessed farmer looked for a place to live and work. Today, the air around the center is pregnant with memories of oppression and resistance.

Inside the center, visitors can follow the story of the Selma to Montgomery National Historic Trail through a series of galleries and exhibits ranging from newspaper clippings to interactive kiosks. A large map of the 54-mile march along Highway 80 from Selma to Montgomery is featured. The center also tells how Black residents of Lowndes County—including the dispossessed tenant farmers—tried to register to vote and support the movement. Artifacts like washtubs, lanterns, and slop jars underscore the makeshift nature of life in Tent City. A copy of a literacy test that was administered to would-be Black voters when they tried to register, is posted, inviting visitors to see whether they could pass.

Other exhibits narrate the stories of John Myrick Daniels, a White seminarian shot by a White deputy as he stepped in to protect fellow activist Ruby Sales, and Viola Liuzzo, a White mother from Detroit who was shot and killed by the KKK as she transported a Black man between Selma and Montgomery. More than anything, the center brings the high stakes faced by prospective Black voters into focus. An area called A Change Is Gonna Come shares an emotional quote from an unnamed Lowndes County resident: "I figured if I was going to get killed or whatever, I had to stand up for this."

Viola Liuzzo Memorial

Viola Liuzzo was a White mother from Detroit who heeded Dr. King's call to come to Alabama and march for voting rights. Liuzzo used her 1963 Oldsmobile to shuttle activists back and forth between Selma and Montgomery. She was in the car with a Black man named Leroy Moton, 19, when Ku Klux Klan members shot her in the head and murdered her. A memorial on U.S. 80 West, 7.5 miles east of the Lowndes Interpretive Center, marks the spot of Liuzzo's death and calls us to remember her sacrifice. Traffic and other factors mean this isn't the safest place to stop, but do take note of the memorial as you drive by. The Lowndes Intepretive Center takes care to tell her story, as do other sites along the trail.

City of St. Jude Interpretive Center

2048 West Fairview Ave.; tel. 334/265-6791; www.cityofstjude.org; Wed.-Fri. 9am-1pm; $5

The City of St. Jude (a social service organization; not an incorporated city), located about 3.5 miles from the Alabama State Capitol in Montgomery, was the last stop on the Selma to Montgomery march before protestors arrived at the capitol. When founded in 1937 to provide spiritual, educational, and medical assistance, City of St. Jude was the first Catholic social service organization dedicated to serving Black people in central Alabama. (St. Jude is also significant in King family history: St. Jude Catholic Hospital is where Martin and

Photos (top to bottom): a sign along the 1965 march route; Lowndes Interpretive Center, between Selma and Montgomery; memorial to Viola Liuzzo, a White voting rights volunteer who was murdered by the KKK

Coretta King's first two children, Yolanda and Martin Luther King III, were born.) In welcoming the marchers, the City of St. Jude performed an act of courage no other institutions were willing to offer. Here, more than 25,000 people camped on a 36-acre campus as they enjoyed entertainment from a host of stars who had arrived to support the march during the Stars for Freedom Rally.

Today, the interpretive center tells a complex story of the march and features a collection of photos from the era, including people who supported the five-day march and those who didn't. Each wall features a theme, such as Bloody Sunday or the 2,000 demonstrators who camped out during the Stars for Freedom Rally on March 24, 1965. Viola Liuzzo was taken here in a desperate attempt to save her life after she was shot by the Ku Klux Klan while volunteering to transport demonstrators.

The City of St. Jude is a stop on the official U.S. Civil Rights Trail.

Montgomery

Montgomery is Alabama's second-largest city, the first and last capital of the many Alabama has had, and the capital of the traitorous Confederate States of America. Confederate adoration persists here, living in tension with the history of the civil rights movement. In fact, you'll notice that the pristine historical markers in this town commemorate the Confederacy as well as African American history and the civil rights movement. This celebration of White supremacy even has a place at the state capitol, where a statue of J. Marion Sims, a doctor who brutalized Black women in his "research," is symbolically situated high on a hill.

MONTGOMERY'S TOP 3

1. Seeing for yourself how the past informs the present at the **Legacy Museum and the National Memorial for Peace and Justice,** the first-ever memorial to victims of lynching (page 134).

2. Stepping into the first gallery at the **Rosa Parks Museum,** where voice reenactments take you back to the day Parks refused to give up her bus seat (page 138).

3. Partaking in an immersive tour of **Dexter Avenue King Memorial Baptist Church,** a key planning site for the Montgomery Bus Boycott (page 143).

Photos (top to bottom): the Legacy Museum; Rosa Parks Museum; Dexter Avenue Baptist Church sanctuary. Previous: the Rosa Parks statue on Montgomery Plaza by sculptor Clydetta Fulmer

The riverfront is a great place to get grounded in Montgomery's foundations, including the indigenous people who occupied this city and state before White settlers decided to take over. While the transatlantic slave trade was outlawed effective in 1808, Montgomery thrived in the domestic trade of enslaved Black people to power a lucrative cotton industry. The enslaved population grew from 40,000 to 435,000 between 1808-1860 as thousands of Black people were moved from the Upper South to the Lower South. It was common to parade enslaved people up Commerce Street, which sits perpendicular to the river near Riverfront Park and the Legacy Museum, to be auctioned off in numerous markets. By the 1840s, the river (and rails) played a starring role in transporting enslaved Black people moved from the coastal cities of New Orleans and Mobile up the Alabama River to Montgomery. Hundreds of captive Black people flowed into the city daily via river and rail to meet the demand for the highly profitable cotton industry.

Despite this devastating beginning, Montgomery matters because it is central to the civil rights struggle. A decade before it became the end point of the Selma voting rights march, the city was already home to several icons, including Rosa Parks, who tested the efficacy of the '54 *Brown* decision by refusing to move to the back of a city bus in 1955, an act that ignited a bus boycott by Black residents. With this event, Dexter Avenue Baptist Church's hotshot young pastor, Rev. Martin Luther King Jr., was drafted as head of the Montgomery Improvement Association—a call of destiny. On December 21, 1956—after 381 days of protest—Montgomery's buses were integrated. If you think desegregating the city's bus system sounds easy, think again: Passengers risked sniper fire, and one Black woman's legs were shattered by a shooter. The next year, four churches were bombed, as was King's house with his wife and baby Yolanda inside. Fortunately, they were not injured.

While African Americans and their allies beat the streets in protest, they also worked to leverage the power of the courts to seek redress by enforcing U.S. laws and changing those that were mean, cruel, and unjust.

While the stifling presence of a Confederate past continues to hang like a shadow over the city, the wins garnered by the civil rights movement cut through the darkness, shining a light on ongoing efforts to resist injustice. Today, the city of Montgomery is home to thriving institutions crucial to the civil rights movement and its connection to human rights movements throughout the world. The Southern Poverty Law Center, which tracks hate crimes among other activities, hosts the Civil Rights Memorial Center and Wall of Tolerance, where visitors are invited to add their names to a list of those who promise a commitment to justice. Must-sees include the Equal Justice Initiative's Legacy Museum and the National Memorial for Peace and Justice, the nation's first memorial to lynching victims—both transformative sights.

ORIENTATION

Many of Montgomery's sights are clustered **downtown** near the riverfront, within about a mile of Riverfront Park.

Another area of note (though less populated with sights) is **Centennial Hill,** a historic Black neighborhood about half a mile southeast of City Hall. This was a thriving middle-class neighborhood when the King family lived in the Dexter Avenue Baptist Church parsonage. The neighborhood is bounded by Adams Avenue at the north, Carter Hill Road at the south, Decatur Street to the west, and Forest Avenue to the east. I-85 runs through the southern portion, separating Alabama State University from a main residential area.

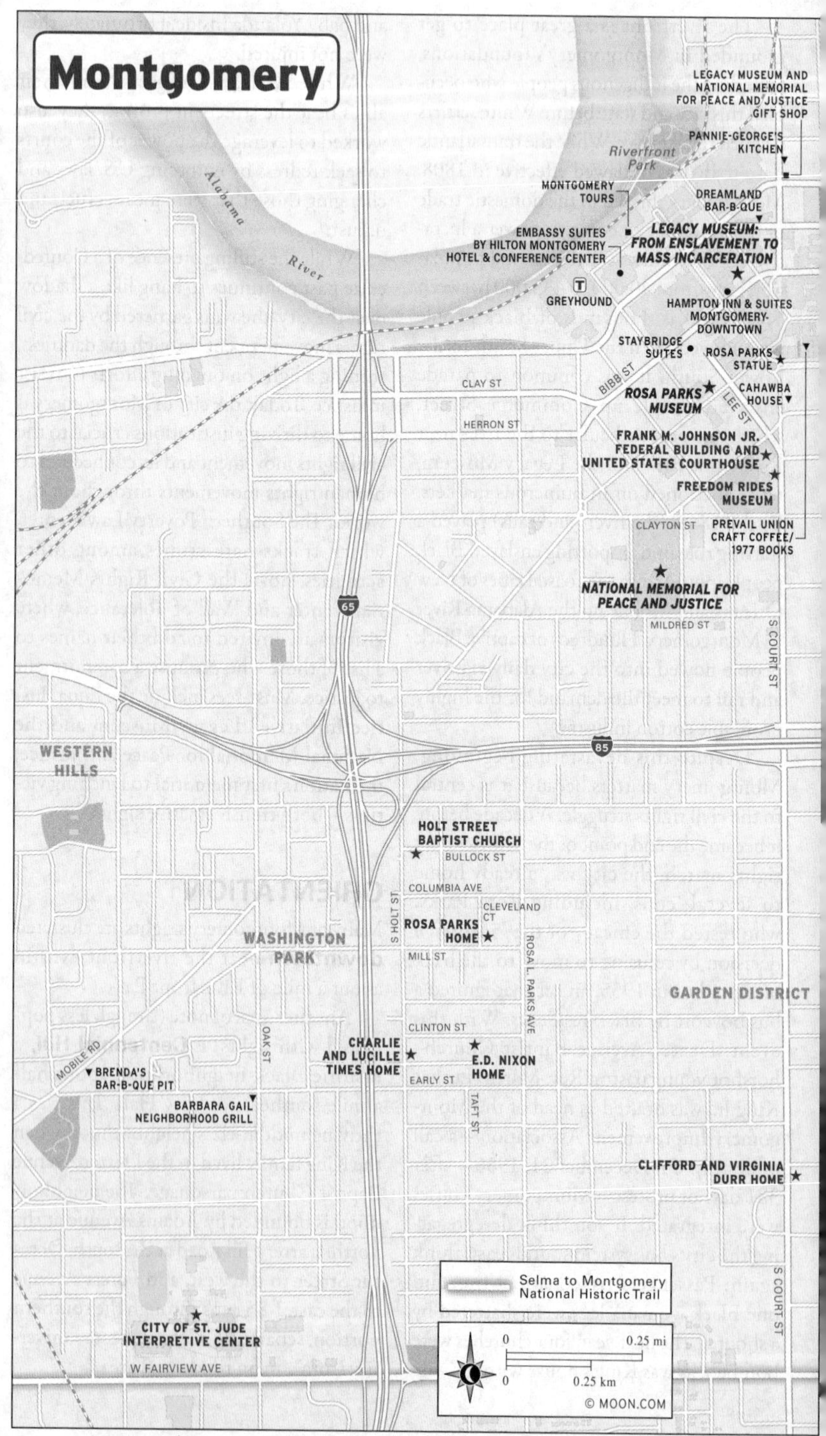
Montgomery
LEGACY MUSEUM AND NATIONAL MEMORIAL FOR PEACE AND JUSTICE GIFT SHOP
PANNIE-GEORGE'S KITCHEN
Riverfront Park
Alabama River
MONTGOMERY TOURS
DREAMLAND BAR-B-QUE
EMBASSY SUITES BY HILTON MONTGOMERY HOTEL & CONFERENCE CENTER
LEGACY MUSEUM: FROM ENSLAVEMENT TO MASS INCARCERATION
GREYHOUND
HAMPTON INN & SUITES MONTGOMERY-DOWNTOWN
STAYBRIDGE SUITES
ROSA PARKS STATUE
CLAY ST
BIBB ST
ROSA PARKS MUSEUM
LEE ST
CAHAWBA HOUSE
HERRON ST
FRANK M. JOHNSON JR. FEDERAL BUILDING AND UNITED STATES COURTHOUSE
FREEDOM RIDES MUSEUM
CLAYTON ST
PREVAIL UNION CRAFT COFFEE/ 1977 BOOKS
NATIONAL MEMORIAL FOR PEACE AND JUSTICE
65
MILDRED ST
S COURT ST
85
WESTERN HILLS
HOLT STREET BAPTIST CHURCH
BULLOCK ST
COLUMBIA AVE
CLEVELAND CT
S HOLT ST
ROSA PARKS HOME
WASHINGTON PARK
MILL ST
ROSA L. PARKS AVE
GARDEN DISTRICT
CLINTON ST
OAK ST
MOBILE RD
CHARLIE AND LUCILLE TIMES HOME
E.D. NIXON HOME
BRENDA'S BAR-B-QUE PIT
EARLY ST
BARBARA GAIL NEIGHBORHOOD GRILL
TAFT ST
CLIFFORD AND VIRGINIA DURR HOME
Selma to Montgomery National Historic Trail
S COURT ST
CITY OF ST. JUDE INTERPRETIVE CENTER
0
0.25 mi
0
0.25 km
W FAIRVIEW AVE
© MOON.COM

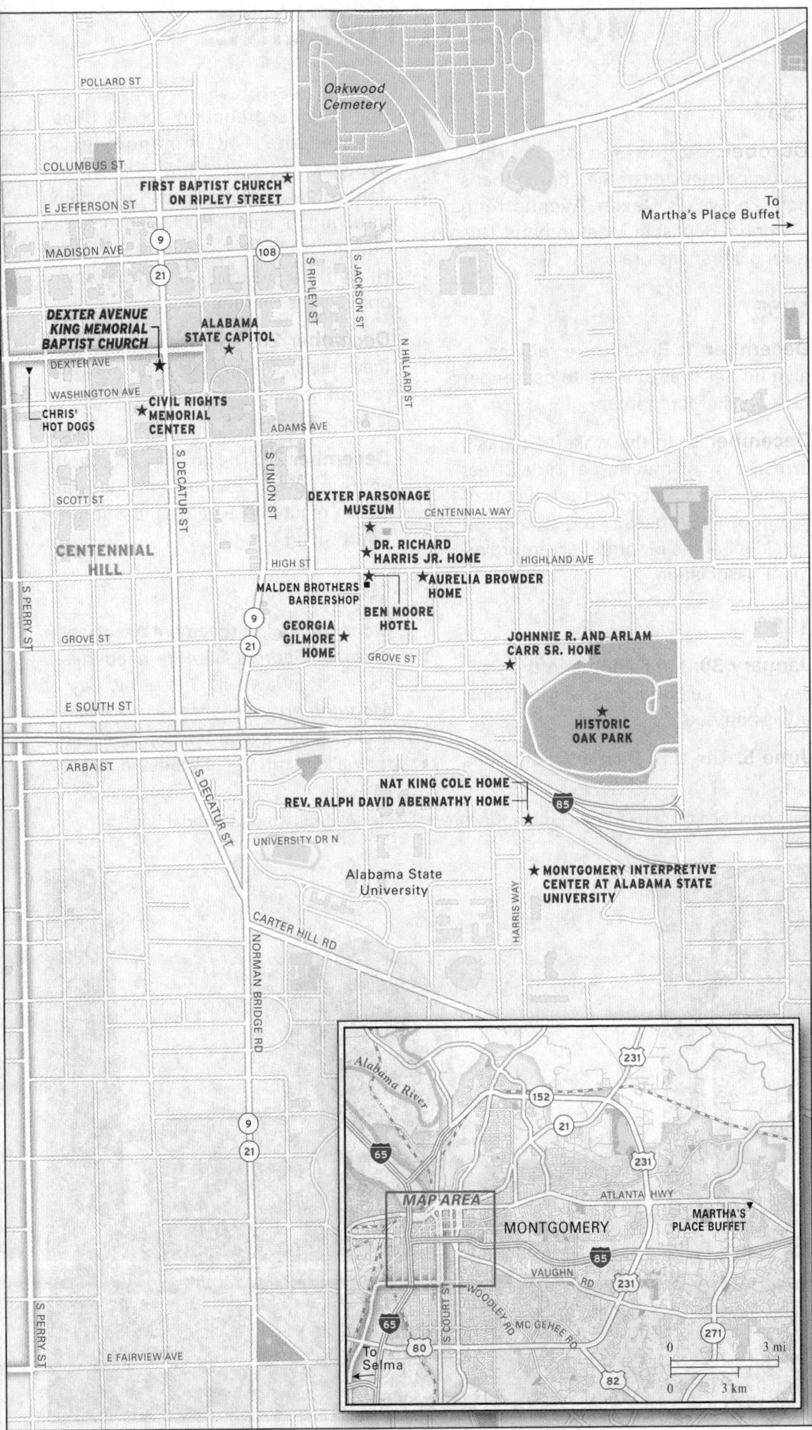
POLLARD ST
Oakwood Cemetery
COLUMBUS ST
FIRST BAPTIST CHURCH ON RIPLEY STREET
E JEFFERSON ST
To Martha's Place Buffet
MADISON AVE
S RIPLEY ST
S JACKSON ST
DEXTER AVENUE KING MEMORIAL BAPTIST CHURCH
ALABAMA STATE CAPITOL
N HILLARD ST
DEXTER AVE
WASHINGTON AVE
CHRIS' HOT DOGS
CIVIL RIGHTS MEMORIAL CENTER
ADAMS AVE
S DECATUR ST
S UNION ST
SCOTT ST
DEXTER PARSONAGE MUSEUM
CENTENNIAL WAY
CENTENNIAL HILL
DR. RICHARD HARRIS JR. HOME
HIGH ST
HIGHLAND AVE
MALDEN BROTHERS BARBERSHOP
AURELIA BROWDER HOME
BEN MOORE HOTEL
S PERRY ST
GEORGIA GILMORE HOME
GROVE ST
JOHNNIE R. AND ARLAM CARR SR. HOME
E SOUTH ST
HISTORIC OAK PARK
ARBA ST
NAT KING COLE HOME
REV. RALPH DAVID ABERNATHY HOME
UNIVERSITY DR N
Alabama State University
MONTGOMERY INTERPRETIVE CENTER AT ALABAMA STATE UNIVERSITY
HARRIS WAY
CARTER HILL RD
NORMAN BRIDGE RD
E FAIRVIEW AVE
Alabama River
MAP AREA
ATLANTA HWY
MONTGOMERY
MARTHA'S PLACE BUFFET
VAUGHN RD
S COURT ST
WOODLEY RD
MC GEHEE RD
To Selma
0 3 mi
0 3 km

MONTGOMERY

MOVEMENT TIMELINE

1954

October: At the age of 25, King becomes minister of the church that's now known as Dexter Avenue King Memorial Baptist in Montgomery. This is King's first pastorate.

1955

December 1: Rosa Parks refuses to give up her seat to a White passenger on a bus in Montgomery.

December 5: In the wake of Parks's arrest, a mass meeting at Holt Street Baptist Church launches a boycott of Montgomery buses. King is elected president of the Montgomery Improvement Association.

1956

January 30: King's home in the Centennial Hill neighborhood of Montgomery is bombed.

June 5: The U.S. District Court rules that racial segregation on city buses violates the 14th Amendment in *Browder v. Gayle*. Judge Frank M. Johnson was a member of the deciding three-judge panel, which also included Judges Richard Rives and Seybourn H. Lynne. The city of Montgomery appeals the finding.

December 20: The city finds out that they are still wrong: The Supreme Court rules that segregation on public buses is unconstitutional.

December 21: The 381-day Montgomery Bus Boycott results in the desegregation of city buses after the Supreme Court ruling.

1958

Montgomery Improvement Association member Georgia Gilmore headlines a class-action lawsuit, *Gilmore v. City of Montgomery,* to challenge segregation in public parks after her son is arrested for walking through a Whites-only park.

seat once occupied by Martin Luther King Jr. at Dexter Avenue King Memorial Baptist Church

1959

King resigns from Montgomery's Dexter Avenue Baptist Church to co-pastor with his father back in Atlanta and to focus on leading the Southern Christian Leadership Conference (SCLC) headquartered there.

1961

May 20: Freedom Riders from Birmingham arrive at Montgomery's downtown Greyhound bus station and meet a violent reception.

May 21: The Freedom Riders who were attacked take refuge in First Baptist Church on Ripley Street, joined by about 1,500 other activists, including King. An angry White mob numbering more than 1,000 attacked the church during this gathering and threatened to bomb it. This event is known as the Siege of First Baptist.

1965

March 25: Marchers from Selma arrive at the Alabama State Capitol in Montgomery where King addresses a crowd of 25,000.

1974

After re-opening the case of *Gilmore v. City of Montgomery* in 1971, the Supreme Court rules in favor of Georgia Gilmore and the other plaintiffs.

1989

November 5: The Civil Rights Memorial in Montgomery is dedicated.

2018

The Legacy Museum: From Enslavement to Mass Incarceration opens in Montgomery.

PLANNING YOUR TIME

Plan to spend at least a couple of days taking in Montgomery, where many important events occurred that are remembered today in a variety of places around town. Most sights are within walking distance of one another.

Note that one of the area's most important sites, the **Legacy Museum and the National Memorial for Peace and Justice** in Montgomery, requires timed-entry reservations and is closed Tuesday. If you're traveling here during the region's busy times, such as the Bridge-Crossing Jubilee that takes place in Selma every March, reserve your pass for the Legacy Museum and the National Memorial for Peace and Justice a few weeks in advance. Otherwise, reserve a week in advance, even though doing so the day before or day-of works fine during less-busy periods.

Pick up maps and brochures at the **Montgomery Convention and Visitors Bureau** (300 Water St.; tel. 334/261-1100, 800/240-9452; https://visitingmontgomery.com; Mon.-Sat. 8:30am-5pm), an ornate red brick Romanesque building on the waterfront that once served as the train station. Note that you're on hallowed ground here. A black and silver marker across from the center commemorates Encanchata Village, a Muscogee village whose inhabitants played a role in the Revolutionary War on the side of the British.

CONNECT WITH

If you didn't come from **Selma,** 50 miles to the west, that's a good place to head next. Otherwise, **Birmingham** (less than two hours away) is the nearest destination.

PEOPLE WHO MADE THE MOVEMENT

GROUPS

Montgomery Improvement Association: Group that formed after the 1955 arrest of Rosa Parks and oversaw the Montgomery Bus Boycott, under the leadership of King. The group led to the formation of the larger Southern Christian Leadership Conference (SCLC) in 1957.

the Rosa Parks statue in Montgomery Plaza by sculptor Clydetta Fulmer

INDIVIDUALS

Dr. Martin Luther King Jr.: In his mid-20s King became minister of the church that's now known as Dexter Avenue King Memorial Baptist in Montgomery. This is King's first pastorate, and it's where he was launched into the limelight. Ten years later, King marched with voting rights activists from Selma to Montgomery, where he addressed a crowd of 25,000 in front of the State Capitol.

John Lewis: The Nashville sit-in movement veteran assumed a leadership position in the Freedom Rides when Congress of Racial Equality (CORE) members were injured and stopped the campaign. When his bus arrived in Montgomery on May 20, 1961, he and other Freedom Riders were attacked by a rabid White mob wielding rocks, bottles, and other weapons.

Rosa Parks: A department store seamstress with Garveyite roots, Parks put a spark in the movement the day she refused to give up her seat for a White passenger and was arrested for quietly asserting her rights.

Jo Anne Robinson: This Alabama State College (now University) English teacher called for a bus boycott after Rosa Parks was arrested. She secretly mimeographed a call to action and had the fliers distributed by the Women's Political Council. This idea wasn't new: Robinson had previously told the mayor a boycott could occur if things didn't change.

E. D. Nixon: A labor and civil rights leader, Nixon bailed Rosa Parks out of jail and helped launch the 381-day Montgomery Bus Boycott that put a young King in the spotlight.

Clifford and Virginia Durr: Clifford was an attorney who supported the civil rights movement and civil liberties of all kinds. He, with E. D. Nixon, bailed Rosa Parks out of jail. Virginia, an activist, worked to end segregation and poll taxes. Her association with Highlander Folk School allowed her to secure a seat for Parks to go to Tennessee and study nonviolent resistance techniques.

Rev. Ralph Abernathy: Confidante to King and Nixon, Abernathy was pastor of First Baptist Church from 1952-1961 where mass meetings for the 1955-1956 Montgomery Bus Boycott were held. King described him as "the best friend that I have in the world."[1] Abernathy presided over the church during the Siege of First Baptist on May 21, 1961.

Georgia Teresa Gilmore: A Montgomery cook and midwife, Gilmore organized a secret kitchen to feed and fund the civil rights movement. She also cooked meals for boycott leaders, including King and Abernathy. In 1958, she headlined a class-action lawsuit, *Gilmore v. City of Montgomery,* to challenge segregation in public parks. The case was reopened in 1971, and on June 17, 1974, the Supreme Court ruled in favor of Gilmore and other plaintiffs.

Two Days in Montgomery

Some advance planning is required for this trip. Make reservations for a 10am tour (not available Sun.) at **Dexter Avenue King Memorial Baptist Church** (Day 1). You'll also need to reserve timed-entry tickets a week before for the Equal Justice Initiative's **Legacy Museum and the National Memorial for Peace and Justice** (Day 2; closed Tues.). Don't dilly-dally; you'll definitely want to see this.

DAY 1

Spend your first day in Montgomery following in the footsteps of Dr. King, seeing where he preached, lived, ate—and even got his hair cut. All of the sights on this day are within walking distance of one another.

1 King got his start as a shepherd here in Montgomery, pastoring what's now called **Dexter Avenue King Memorial Baptist Church.** A visit here lets you see where he preached and learn about the community he served. Call or go online to make reservations for tours that start at 10am Tuesday-Saturday, as walk-ins aren't guaranteed.

2 Visit the family home where Coretta and Martin nurtured their growing family at the **Dexter Parsonage Museum,** which has been preserved as a museum.

3 The Ben Moore Hotel building nearby still houses the **Malden Brothers Barbershop** where King got his hair cut. The shop has a different owner now, but it's worth a glimpse to try to imagine what the shop was like back in the day.

4 Hungry? King liked to grab **Chris' Hot Dogs,** so maybe you should try one too.

5 Round out your day with a visit to the Southern Poverty Law Center's Wall of Tolerance and **Civil Rights Memorial Center** created by Maya Lin. The wall invites you to join others in standing against hate—and for justice for everyone, not just some.

DAY 2

The **Legacy Museum and the National Memorial for Peace and Justice** is the focal point for your second day in Montgomery.

1 Enter the Equal Justice Initiative's **Legacy Museum and the National Memorial for Peace and Justice** with the timed-entry tickets you reserved ahead of time. Expect to spend 2-4 hours at the museum, and another hour at the memorial (easily reached from the museum by a free shuttle). The experience is beyond moving—it's transformative.

2 Lunch at **Pannie-George's Kitchen** is nearby on Court Street in the Legacy Pavilion, where you'll also find the Legacy Museum's gift shop.

3 Hit the **Legacy Museum and the National Memorial for Peace and Justice Gift Shop,** a short walk away, for souvenirs.

4 Now drive over to the **Rosa Parks Museum**. The bus exhibit and engaging narrative will pull you in as you stand in a darkened gallery to see and hear a re-enactment of December 1, 1955, when Parks, like a bridge over troubled water, *would not be moved.*

5 The **Montgomery Interpretive Center at Alabama State University** is a treat and a good place to see a map of the Selma to Montgomery march route.

6 Why not bless Black Montgomery with some of your hard-earned dollars and get some good barbecue at **Brenda's Bar-B-Que Pit?** The little shack is a bastion of deliciousness you'll have to take back to your hotel—or eat in the car if you can't wait.

Sights

DOWNTOWN

★ Legacy Museum and the National Memorial for Peace and Justice

The Legacy Museum and the National Memorial for Peace and Justice offer a justice-minded immersion into the Black presence in America from slavery and lynching to the civil rights movement, the modern-day scourge of mass incarceration and beyond. Together, the museum and memorial, which commemorates U.S. lynching victims, are a physical manifestation of how the past informs the present. Both the museum and the lynching memorial are self-guided: Expect to spend 2-4 hours at the museum and about an hour or more at the lynching memorial. You will be transformed. The museum and memorial require **reserved tickets** for timed-entry, so be sure to plan accordingly and reserve tickets at least a week in advance.

The museum is located in downtown Montgomery; the haunting lynching memorial is about a mile away on six acres that overlook the city. To reach the memorial, hop on one of the free shuttles that depart in front of the museum every 10 minutes, or take a 15-minute walk through historic Montgomery. Shuttle buses circulate in and out of the memorial site, so you won't miss your ride back downtown to the Legacy Museum. It is possible to visit the memorial without visiting the museum ($5).

The museum and memorial, both of which are stops on the official U.S. Civil Rights Trail, are the brainchildren of the **Equal Justice Initiative** (EJI; www.eji.org), a legal nonprofit working to end racial and economic injustice, and its executive director Bryan Stevenson. EJI staff lead talks about the organization's legal work within the criminal justice system and efforts to reform it at **The National Peace and Justice Memorial Center** (414 Caroline St.) at 2:30pm daily except Tuesdays and Sundays. The center, which is located near the Legacy Museum, also features a gift shop. (A more expansive gift shop is found at the Legacy Pavilion on Court Street.)

TOP EXPERIENCE

THE LEGACY MUSEUM: FROM ENSLAVEMENT TO MASS INCARCERATION

115 Coosa St.; tel. 334/386-9100; www.museumandmemorial.eji.org/museum; Sun. 9am-6pm, Mon.-Sat. 9am-7:30pm, closed Tues.; adults $8, seniors and students $5, children 6 and under free

Opened in 2018, the 11,000-square-foot Legacy Museum is housed on the grounds of a former warehouse where Black people were held prisoner. Today, the vintage building is painted a pristine white, with black frames around colorful images hanging on the entrance. Inside, the Legacy Museum unfurls like a timeline, leading visitors chronologically through periods of U.S. history.

An opening exhibit is promisingly ominous, embodying the horrid condition of being sold and enslaved. Patrons walk down a dark hallway where holograms of enslaved Black people dressed in 19th-century garb, held in pens, are on view. Two brown-skinned children wonder where their mother is. In another cell, a woman wearing a head wrap and nightgown talks about her children. The sound of chains clanging and a woman singing a spiritual can be heard distantly in the darkness.

The visit continues into a large open room that takes visitors through the enduring lie of racial inferiority and the policies and customs that reinforce it. One powerful display shows soil samples from cities where people were lynched. You'll learn names of people like Harris Tunstal, lynched July 12, 1885, in Oxford, Mississippi. You'll see soil from Jonesboro, Georgia, where Millie Johnson was lynched on July 29, 1880.

The civil rights movement plays a defining role in the story the museum tells.

Photos (top to bottom): T-shirt from the Legacy Museum gift shop; the National Memorial for Peace and Justice; the Legacy Museum

MONTGOMERY'S HISTORIC HOMES

Alabama's diligence about telling the story of its past pays off generously in Montgomery where a number of activists and other movement participants lived. The following homes are not open for tours, but discreet curbside viewing is an option, and they all have markers providing context.

ROSA PARKS

634 Rosa Parks Ave.

Parks lived with her husband, Raymond, and mother, Leona McCauley, in unit 634 of the Cleveland Court Housing Community. The building that encompasses units 620-638 sits on the National Register of Historic Places and, therefore, cannot be altered, though public housing units surrounding her home are newer. Cleveland Avenue was renamed Rosa Parks Avenue in 1965. A historical marker adorns the front door.

E. D. NIXON HOUSE

647 Clinton Ave.

Nixon was head of the Montgomery branch of the Pullman Porters and president of the local NAACP. When he called to inquire about the December 1, 1955, arrest of Rosa Parks, police refused to talk to him and used racial epithets. He called in attorney Clifford Durr and they secured her release. Nixon was a driving force behind the Montgomery Bus Boycott. His home is on the National Register of Historic Places.

CHARLIE AND LUCILLE TIMES

1265 S Holt St.

When Alabama outlawed the NAACP in the 1950s, Charlie and Lucille Times held meetings in their home. Lucille was boycotting buses several months before Rosa Parks refused to give up her seat: A White driver cut off her car one day, so she stopped riding the bus and started giving rides to others. The couple continued giving rides to Black residents during the Montgomery Bus Boycott.

CLIFFORD AND VIRGINIA DURR

2 Felder Ave.

The home of civil rights attorney Clifford Durr and civil rights activist Virginia Durr, both figures in the Montgomery Bus Boycott, is in The Garden District, a historic area of Montgomery featuring a range of architecture styles, including Queen Anne and Classical Revival.

AURELIA BROWDER

1012 Highland Ave.

Aurelia Browder was lead plaintiff in a federal lawsuit challenging segregated city buses. She was joined by Claudette Colvin, Mary Louise Smith, and Susie McDonald, as they all had been arrested for refusal to give up their seats to White passengers. On June 5, 1956, a three-judge panel ruled in their favor, citing a violation of the 14th Amendment's equal protection clause.

JOHNNIE R. AND ARLAM CARR SR.

780 Hall St.

Filed on behalf of their son, the Carrs were plaintiffs in *Carr v. Montgomery Board of Education*, which resulted in the desegregation of city schools. Active participants in the Montgomery Improvement Association, which oversaw the Montgomery Bus Boycott, they lived here during that time.

REV. RALPH DAVID ABERNATHY

North University Drive and Harris Way

SCLC co-founder Rev. Ralph Abernathy lived in this house, which sits on the Alabama State University campus, when he was pastor of First Baptist Church on Ripley Street. He helped lead the Montgomery Bus Boycott in 1955, and his home and church were bombed in 1957. The home is on the left side at the campus entrance near the Hornets stadium.

NAT KING COLE

North University Drive and Harris Way

In 1956, Montgomery native Nat King Cole was performing at Birmingham's city auditorium when Ku Klux Klan members bumrushed the stage and attacked him. The White Citizens' Council believed certain music to be an NAACP plot to get White youths to integrate. Cole's home was moved from its original location to a spot next to Abernathy's home at the entrance of ASU.

GEORGIA GILMORE

453 Dericote St.

Montgomery Improvement Association member Georgia Gilmore provided food for movement workers and sued the city after her son was arrested for walking through a Whites-only park. She made her home here, in Centennial Hill.

DR. RICHARD HARRIS JR.

333 S Jackson St.

Harris and his wife, Vera, were stalwarts of the civil rights movement. At their home, they sheltered Freedom Riders in 1961 and hosted a makeshift taxi stand during the Montgomery Bus Boycott to transport activists.

Familiar faces (Fannie Lou Hamer, for example) from the movement show up in videos and images. A wall of Jim Crow signs reminds us of how the color line was reinforced in daily movements and interactions. A sign for a laundry reads: We Wash For White People Only.

With timelines, art, video, and audio, the Legacy Museum engages all the senses. Most importantly, the museum draws a critical and irrefutable through-line from Black enslavement to contemporary policies that continue to oppress. Visitors can see for themselves how courts and other civic institutions have long conspired with the beneficiaries of White supremacy to block Black agency and citizenship. For example, the museum takes on the idea that poverty is a crime, since those who are poor remain stuck in jail while those with the money to pay bail can live freely while awaiting trial. The museum also challenges private prisons that generate huge profits that thwart reforms and keep felons and former felons from voting. EJI's work with formerly incarcerated Anthony Ray Hinton is showcased through his haunting and intimate story of freedom, lost and gained. (Hinton spent 30 years on death row and is among scores of people facing the same fate who were proven innocent.) The discussion takes on an American culture that presumes guilt: Research shows that Black girls are punished more harshly at school than White children and are assumed to lack the innocence of girlhood, a dangerous state to behold.

Now, if after visiting the Legacy Museum you feel as if you've walked on sacred ground, it is because you have. The facility was built on land that formerly warehoused enslaved Black people and is blocks away from what once was one of America's most prolific markets for trafficking Black bodies.

NATIONAL MEMORIAL FOR PEACE AND JUSTICE

417 Caroline St.; tel. 334/386-9100; www.museumandmemorial.eji.org/memorial; Wed.-Mon. 9am-5pm; $5, children 6 and under free

This tribute to men and women who perished due to state-sanctioned murder is an emotional journey through an era of lynching from 1877-1950. This is the first-ever memorial to honor the legacy of those terrorized by this revolting act.

Lynching left no one untouched. Fear and weariness of lynching and the mindset behind it urged six million Black people to leave the South and join the Great Migration northward: New York, Chicago, Kansas City, even smaller places like Waterloo, Iowa, to find opportunity and live free of terror. It is a major part of what motivated people to take a stand and join the civil rights movement.

The memorial is comprised of 800 suspended corten steel monuments, which accounts for each county in the United States where racially motivated lynchings occurred. Victims' names—several thousand—are engraved on each column. This stunning display was intended as the beginning of a conversation about truth and reconciliation of America's racist past and present. Interested parties are invited to join the Community Remembrance Project, for example, a collaboration that supports communities across the nation to document their lynching past.

★ Rosa Parks Museum

252 Montgomery St.; tel. 334/241-8615; www.troy.edu/student-life-resources/arts-culture/rosa-parks-museum; Mon.-Fri. 9am-5pm, Sat. 9am-3pm; adults $7.50, children $5.50

This museum at the Montgomery satellite campus of Troy University stands on the very spot where seamstress Rosa Parks was arrested after refusing to give up her bus seat to a White passenger in 1955. Parks wasn't just a tired department store seamstress: She was reared on the ideas of Marcus Garvey and was secretary of the local NAACP. Her refusal to bow to Jim Crow and immediate arrest positioned her to test the Supreme Court's ruling against segregation in public facilities and accommodations.

The roughly 7,000-square-foot museum, a stop on the official U.S. Civil Rights Trail, uses artifacts and other ephemera, including Parks's fingerprint arrest record, to show how Montgomery's Black community came together to demand their rights. The high point is an exhibit that reimagines December 1, 1955: the day Rosa Parks got on the Cleveland Avenue bus in Montgomery and refused to move when ordered to give up her seat to a White passenger. A bus from the 1955 fleet has been situated in a darkened room. Museumgoers can see superimposed faces through the bus windows while a narrator lays out what happened that day, point by point. You'll learn that Parks wasn't even sitting in the so-called White section of the bus: It was so crowded, White passengers pushed into the "Black" area where Parks sat. While the department store seamstress stoically refused to move, three other Black riders did. Hear the bus driver, J. Fred Blake, yelling for Parks to move, and feel the tension when he calls the police who board the bus and decide to arrest her.

Also on view is a restored station wagon that was used to transport residents who were boycotting the segregated bus system. (Often, it was preachers who drove such vehicles to help boycotting Black residents get to and from work, and the cars came to be known as "rolling churches.") Many boycotting residents, of course, walked for as long as they needed to. Just east of the Rosa Parks museum on Montgomery Plaza is the Rosa Parks statue, unveiled on December 1, 2019.

Freedom Rides Museum

210 S Court St.; tel. 334/414-8647; www.freedomridesmuseum.org; www.ahc.alabama.gov/properties/freedomrides/freedomrides.aspx; Tues.-Fri. 11am-4pm, Sat. 10am-4pm; adults $5, college students $4, seniors and children 6-18 $3; discounted admission for groups of 10 or more

As noted on a sign outside Freedom Rides Museum, located in the city's former Greyhound station, the test of interstate travel did not start nor end in Montgomery, but what happened here helped make a difference. Freedom Riders arrived here on May 20, 1961, in the eerie quiet of downtown Montgomery, recalls Bernard Lafayette, who was in charge of a contingent of demonstrators. Soon, an angry White mob, including men, women, and children, attacked the Freedom Riders who arrived that day from Birmingham. These activists had picked up where CORE riders left off after being pressured to stop following attacks in Anniston and Birmingham.

Through a series of exhibits and vintage photos, this one-story museum helps flesh out who the Freedom Riders were when they weren't putting their lives on the line. A display of black-and-white photos of Freedom Riders is arranged by their places of origin—you'll see that these young Black and White activists hailed from all over the country. Learn their ages, what colleges they attended, and their gender distribution—and get a sense of the stakes involved in advocating for equal rights in interstate travel, including segregated trains and airports. You can also get a sense of the Freedom Riders' violent reception in Montgomery; for example, a replica Coca Cola crate like the one that was used to hit John Lewis over the head is on display.

The Greyhound station was segregated in 1961, just like all public buildings in the city. Docents, who provide foundational narratives throughout the museum, explain that the "colored side" wasn't kept consistently clean and was often locked, so Black people could not access a lunch counter on their side of the station. This caused considerable hardship for travelers who were counting on a meal during bus transfers, which is why many packed a lunch. (The contents of those lunches are the subject of Black family lore to this day). Bus stations were the airports of that time, so people

MONTGOMERY

VOICES OF THE MOVEMENT: FREEDOM RIDER BERNARD LAFAYETTE

"When they threw bricks in the window, I thought that the next thing that was going to come was a bomb. We were already in a church that had been bombed. That's what I was worried about."

—**BERNARD LAFAYETTE**, Ph.D., a leader of the Nashville sit-in movement and participant in the Selma voting rights campaign, was also one of a group of six brave students, led by John Lewis, who traveled from Nashville to Alabama to complete the 1961 Freedom Rides after a violent reception in Birmingham caused CORE to pause the campaign to desegregate interstate bus terminals.

FREEDOM RIDERS ARRIVE IN MONTGOMERY

Upon arrival in Montgomery on May 20, 1961, Lafayette and the other Freedom Riders were attacked by an angry White mob who kicked and beat them until they were bloody. Lafayette suffered cracked ribs when vigilantes tried to kick him in his private parts. Lewis was hit over the head with a Coca-Cola crate. Jim Zwerg and William Barbee were knocked unconscious, and Zwerg, a White ally, had to be hospitalized. Catherine Burks-Brooks had declined an offer by Lafayette to be whisked away to safety in a taxi with other women activists and insisted on staying with the group.

Some of the Freedom Riders took refuge in First Baptist Church, where Rev. Ralph Abernathy was the pastor. Thirty-three of them found shelter in the home of the home of Dr. Richard Harris Jr. and his wife, Vera. The violence wasn't over, though: It would continue the next day during what came to be known as the Siege of First Baptist.

SIEGE OF FIRST BAPTIST CHURCH

The day after the Freedom Riders' arrival in Montgomery, the Freedom Riders, along with 1,500 supporters, gathered at First Baptist Church for a mass meeting. Among those inside the church were Lafayette, Lewis, King, Abernathy, Diane Nash, and Fred Shuttlesworth. An angry White mob numbering into the thousands surrounded the church and threw rocks and bricks through the stained-glass windows. Some reports say that tear gas was thrown inside the church as well. "I thought that the next thing that was going to come was a bomb," says Lafayette. "We were already in a church that had been bombed. That's what I was worried about."

Law enforcement officers, armed with warrants to arrest the Freedom Riders, entered the church, brandishing photos of the Freedom Riders and asking folks if anyone had seen them. According to Lafayette, the Nashville group had donned robes and were in the choir singing as this was going on. Their disguise worked: "We'd been singing together for over a year. We probably sounded good, like a real choir," Lafayette says.

THE RIDES CONTINUE

After the Siege of First Baptist, the National Guard and federal marshals saw to it the Freedom Riders got to Jackson, Mississippi. When they arrived, they were arrested. Following the movement's "Jail, No Bail" policy, several hundred Freedom Riders would spend several weeks locked up at Mississippi State Penitentiary, also known as Parchman Farm. Lafayette served 40 days in Parchman, and upon his release, he was re-arrested for successfully recruiting youth to join the ride.

LAFAYETTE ON TRAVELING THE CIVIL RIGHTS TRAIL

What do you gain from traveling to the sites where the rights movement took place? Lafayette explains:

"When people say, why is this happening? Why did that happen? You got to have the background, and you got to have what may sound too intellectual: the contingencies of reinforcement. What are the things that cause things to happen now? Why are people still behaving the way they behave? People don't understand that this is passed on. That's one of the things that people must understand when they go to museums and that sort of thing. It's not that you want to preserve that behavior, but you want to understand the history and where it came from. It is the interpretation of those experiences that really makes the difference."

In Montgomery, Lafayette recommends spending time at the bus station where the Freedom Riders arrived (now the **Freedom Rides Museum**), as well as **Dexter Parsonage Museum,** where Martin Luther King lived. From the parsonage, he says, also make sure you walk down Jackson Street to the **home of Dr. Richard Harris Jr.** and his wife, Vera, where 33 riders took refuge after being attacked. Lafayette remembers sleeping on the couch in the Harris's living room when he could catch a few winks. "We didn't sleep much because we were up all night planning," he says. "We did take naps and stuff like that. People brought food to us." Lafayette recalls the Harris' as "very calm" and hospitable. "They showed a lot of courage," he says. "They didn't seem phased at all about the condition we were in."

Freedom Rides Museum

who wanted to travel didn't have obvious alternatives.

This museum, operated by the Alabama Historical Commission, is an official stop on the U.S. Civil Rights Trail.

Frank M. Johnson Jr. Federal Building and United States Courthouse

15 Lee St.; tel. 334/954-3695; www.thejohnsoninstitute.org; Mon.-Fri. 8am-5pm; $10

Judge Frank M. Johnson Jr., a White man, was the country's youngest federal judge when he was appointed at age 36 in October 1955. When *Browder v. Gayle* landed in his court, he assembled a three-judge panel with Richard T. Rives and Seybourne H. Lynne to decide the case. He believed segregation on city buses violated the equal-protection clause of the 14th Amendment, and in a 2-1 vote, the panel affirmed the Montgomery Bus Boycott by ruling against the segregated seating on city buses. Appeals by the city of Montgomery brought the case to the U.S. Supreme Court, which decided on November 13, 1956, that the practice was unconstitutional.

Johnson is noted for a number of controversial decisions that allowed the civil rights movement to rack up wins. In *Lewis v. Greyhound* (1961), he ordered the desegregation of bus depots. (The plaintiffs in that case were John Lewis, Paul Brooks, Lucretia Collins, Rudolph Graham, Catherine Burks, Matthew Petway, and Ralph D. Abernathy.) Johnson also authorized the Selma to Montgomery march, stating, "The law is clear that the right to petition one's government for the redress of grievances may be exercised in large groups. Indeed, where, as here, minorities have been harassed, coerced and intimidated, group association may be the only realistic way of exercising such rights."[2] Johnson also made decisions about voting rights, affirmative action, humane prison conditions, and upheld the rights of mental patients. Or, as he famously put it, he "did his job"—though White society ostracized him for it. Johnson faced threats, including a firebombing at his mother's home and having a cross burned on his lawn. He had to be protected by U.S. Marshals for 15 years. Governor George Wallace, Johnson's classmate at the University of Alabama School of Law, called him an "integrating, scallawagging, carpetbagging liar."[3]

The Judge Frank M. Johnson Jr. Institute administers brief tours of his courtroom that explain the life and times of the heroic judge. This is a still-functioning courtroom, and a tour (reservations required) is the only way to visit. You'll learn about courtroom moments that produced the best results for those interested in the cause of justice. Guides contextualize Johnson's legal philosophies and aspects of his personal life that help explain how he withstood his critics. If you want to see where Black protest coalesced into law, this might be worth the stop. The courthouse is on the National Register of Historic Places and is a stop on the official U.S. Civil Rights Trail. Note that you'll have to submit to security protocols to enter the courthouse, and not even cell phones are allowed in.

Civil Rights Memorial Center

400 Washington Ave.; tel. 888/414-7752; www.splcenter.org/civil-rights-memorial; Mon.-Fri. 9am-4:30pm, Sat. 10am-4pm; $2

The Civil Rights Memorial Center, a stop on the official U.S. Civil Rights Trail, features a 56-seat theater, classrooms, and exhibits about civil rights movement martyrs, but its most moving aspect is the **Wall of Tolerance,** located in a dark room inside the center. Names of people who have pledged to stand for justice and tolerance are digitally projected high up on the wall. You can add your own name to this timeless scroll by typing on a keyboard. It's a powerful act. It's located across from the Southern Poverty Law Center (403 Washington Ave.), which sponsors this center.

Directly outside the Civil Rights Memorial Center is a **Civil Rights Memorial** (free, accessible 24/7) sponsored by the Southern Poverty Law Center and dedicated in 1989. Water washes over circular, black granite sculpture, which lists 40 people named as victims during the civil rights struggle from 1954-1968. Denise McNair, one of four little girls murdered in the 16th Street Baptist Church bombing, is the youngest. (She was 11 years old at the time of her death.) Other listed names include murdered teen Emmett Till and Viola Liuzzo, a White ally murdered by the KKK while transporting activists between Selma and Montgomery. Touch the cool granite and let the water rush over your hands as you contemplate these lives lost. Think about their courage; about childhoods lost; and about the generational trauma their families endure. The large granite wall that backs the sculpture is engraved with one of King's favorite Bible verses from Amos 5:24: "We will not be satisfied until justice rolls down like waters and righteousness like a mighty stream." The tribute was created by renowned artist Maya Lin, who also designed the Vietnam Veterans Memorial in Washington DC.

TOP EXPERIENCE

★ Dexter Avenue King Memorial Baptist Church

454 Dexter Ave.; tel. 334/263-3970; www.dexterkingmemorial.org; tours Tues.-Fri. 10am, 11am, 1pm, 2pm, and 3pm; Sat. 10am, 11am, noon, and 1pm; adults $7, children $5

Dexter Avenue was born of a breakaway from Brick-a-Day (First Baptist Church) in the late 1800s. First called Second Colored Baptist Church, it was renamed for Montgomery's founder, Andrew Dexter. King's name was added in 1978.

During the civil rights movement, congregants at this church cultivated a consciousness about the meaning and purpose of freedom. Montgomery Bus Boycott organizing activity occurred in the church basement, where King had an office. Even before King arrived in 1954, at the age of 25, Rev. Vernon Johns, a civil rights pioneer in his own right, exhorted church members to challenge Montgomery's repressive segregation laws, including public transportation. In 1959, King resigned from the church to co-pastor with his dad back in Atlanta and to focus on leading the SCLC headquartered there.

A Dexter Avenue church **tour,** led by Tourism Ministry leader Wanda Howard Battle, is an immersive experience—Howard Battle is famous for her energetic, inspiring tours, and you may even be invited to sing to fully appreciate the sanctuary's amazing acoustics.

Upon entering the bottom floor of the red brick building, visitors are greeted by deacon John Feagin's 10-feet-by-47-feet mural, which shows scenes from King's journey from Montgomery to Memphis, including faces of grassroots activists and the people who aimed to thwart their cause. Visitors can walk where King walked and see where he preached in this intimate and spirited guided tour that details the Dexter Avenue church family history. See King's basement office and his high-backed pulpit chair in the upstairs sanctuary, which is awash with sunlight beaming through colored window panes.

This edifice, located at the corner of Dexter Avenue and Decatur Street, was built in the shadow of the state capitol. Today, it is home to a thriving congregation with a range of ministries that characterize Black and Christian traditions, including vacation Bible school, Women's Day, and Brotherhood Day. The church, which contains Gothic Revival and Victorian architectural elements, is on the National Register of Historic Places, and is a stop on the official U.S. Civil Rights Trail. Call or go online for reservations; walk-in tours are available but cannot be guaranteed.

Photos (top to bottom): Frank M. Johnson Jr. Federal Building and United States Courthouse; Civil Rights Memoria created by Maya Lin; Alabama State Capitol, where the Selma tc Montgomery march concluded

GET INTO THE RHYTHM

- **"Which Side Are You On?"**: During a 1931 Kentucky miners' strike, Florence Reece penned the powerful lyrics to this song, declaring neutrality a nonstarter. Singers like Pete Seeger and The Freedom singers picked up a retooled version and put it to good use in the civil rights movement. Well, do you know which side you're on?

Alabama State Capitol

600 Dexter Ave.; tel. 334/242-3188; www.ahc.alabama.gov/alabama-state-capitol.aspx; Mon.-Fri. 8am-4:30pm; free

On March 25, 1965, the 54-mile Selma to Montgomery march concluded here at the Alabama State Capitol, a bold Greek Revival building on a hill. King addressed the 25,000 marchers in front of the capitol as they flowed in from five days of walking: "Last Sunday," he stated, "more than 8,000 of us started on a mighty walk from Selma, Alabama . . . They told us we wouldn't get here. And there were those who said that we would get here only over their dead bodies, but all the world today knows that we are here and we are standing before the forces of power in the state of Alabama saying, 'We ain't goin' let nobody turn us around.'"[4]

Today, a wide black box (easily missed if you don't know what you're looking for) painted on the road in front of the capitol marks the spot where King addressed the crowd. Markers and signage show how thousands traveled on foot to the seat of government to demand full enfranchisement. In a grassy area in front of the capitol stands a modern, rectangular marker featuring a black-and-white photo of demonstrators standing together after their long journey. The marker explains how marchers left St. Jude on Thursday, March 25, 1965, and "continued through the streets of Montgomery, the crowd swelling in numbers as they approached Court Square."

The 1965 march isn't the only historic event that's commemorated here. On the grounds of the capitol, in a place of honor, are statues of a Confederate soldier (whose cornerstone was laid by Confederate President Jefferson Davis himself), and Dr. J. Marion Sims. Considered by some to be the father of modern gynecology, Sims butchered enslaved Black women in his "research." (A statue of him was removed from New York's Central Park in 2018 following repeated demands.) Inside the state house, ornate stairs are the legacy of formerly enslaved architect and bridge builder Horace King.

Listed on the National Register of Historic Places (and a stop on the official U.S. Civil Rights Trail), the capitol offers tours, but civil rights buffs might be more satisfied with a self-guided tour of the grounds so you don't have to hear all the Confederate stuff.

First Baptist Church on Ripley Street

347 N Ripley St.; tel. 334/264-6921; www.firstbaptistchurchmontgomery.com

Pastored for several years by Rev. Ralph Abernathy, First Baptist (aka Brick-a-Day) served as a movement meeting place and haven for Freedom Riders attacked by a White mob on May 21, 1961. On that day, also known as **The Siege of First Baptist,** about 1,500 people, including Freedom Riders Bernard Lafayette and John Lewis, among other Freedom Riders, were inside getting encouragement following the May 20, 1961, Greyhound station attack. More than a thousand angry Whites threw bricks and rocks at the church windows, and the mob threatened to bomb the church. (It wouldn't have been the first time: The church had been bombed before in January 1957.)

Rev. Fred Shuttlesworth, Rev. Wyatt T. Walker, Diane Nash, James Farmer, and King were also present at the church during the siege. King used a basement phone to beseech Attorney General Robert Kennedy for assistance—but instead of blaming the segregationists, Kennedy excoriated the Freedom Riders, reportedly stating they were making "good propaganda for America's enemies."

Kennedy floated the idea of a cooling-off period so Southern Whites could calm down. While King was open to the idea, Freedom Riders Nash and Farmer rejected it. Farmer reportedly said: "Please tell the attorney general that we've been cooling off for 350 years. If we cool off anymore, we will be in a deep freeze. The Freedom Ride will go on."[5]

The mob dispersed when Governor John Malcolm Patterson put Montgomery under "qualified martial rule," which allowed him to call the militia to restore order. Police and state National Guardsmen formed a shield around the church, but people inside still were not allowed out of the church until the next day after officials worked to secure their releases. Twenty-seven Freedom Riders proceeded to Jackson, Mississippi, under the protection of guardsmen and federal marshals. Once there, they were arrested and jailed. The First Baptist congregation was organized in the late 1800s. When their original building burned down, it was rebuilt over several years thanks to a command by its then-pastor to congregants to bring "a brick a day" to contribute to rebuilding the church. (Where those bricks came from is the subject of local lore: Where you got one was your business. Oral history suggests they came from local construction sites, but church officials said people brought bricks in from wherever they could find one.)

If you'd like to tour the church, call in advance of your desired date and leave a message. Tours are free. The church is a stop on the official U.S. Civil Rights Trail.

CENTENNIAL HILL

Dexter Parsonage Museum

303 S Jackson St.; tel. 334/261-3270; www.dexterkingmemorial.org; Tues.-Fri. 10am-4pm, Sat. 10am-2pm; adults $7.50, children under 12 $5.50

Between 1922-1991, 12 ministers and their families lived in this porticoed, clapboard home affiliated with Dexter Avenue King Memorial Baptist Church. King moved here in 1954 when he became shepherd of a flock of 600 members. King was only 25 when he accepted this appointment. He followed in the footsteps of Rev. Vernon Johns, a powerful leader whose philosophies of self-determination and economic empowerment nicely dovetailed into King's principles of social, civic, and economic justice.

To get a look inside, visitors must first meet at an interpretive center next door for an orientation through newspaper clippings, photographs, and video introducing the vibrant Dexter church community. You'll learn details about the 1956 bombing of the King home in the Centennial Hill neighborhood and, through images, meet King family acquaintances like deacon Roscoe Williams and his wife Mary Lucy Williams, a personal friend to Coretta. A wall of pastoral wisdom shows photos of the Dexter members, including civic leaders, entrepreneurs, and ministers involved in the Montgomery Bus Boycott. One photo shows Ralph Abernathy at a weekly mass meeting at First Baptist Church.

You may not notice it at first, but from the outside the windows in front of the parsonage look different from each other, evidence of when a car drove up and threw dynamite at the house when Martin, Coretta, and two of their children lived here. (One window was damaged, but not the other.) Inside, the family home has been frozen in time. You'll see King family mementos, including a rocking chair and other furniture the family used. An ashtray sits on a living room table, as King was a private smoker. (The in-joke is he didn't have a brand because he was always bumming other people's cigs.) A walkthrough includes bedrooms, King's book-lined office, and the dining room and kitchen. Docents help the Kings' day-to-day lives feel present, invoking visitors to imagine, for example, Coretta playing piano while neighbors enjoyed the music as it wafted through an open window. An innocent-looking black hallway telephone could be a source of terror when threatening calls came through.

Call ahead for a reservation for a guided tour, as walk-ins may not be available because officials only allow small groups inside the house. Parking is found in the rear of the interpretive center. The home is listed on the National Register of Historic Places and is a stop on the official U.S. Civil Rights Trail.

Home of Dr. Richard Harris Jr.

333 S Jackson St.

A few steps away from the Dexter Parsonage Museum is the home of Dr. Richard Harris, the pharmacist and Tuskegee Airman who sheltered dozens of Freedom Riders between May 20-24, 1961, after

Photos (top to bottom): First Baptist Church on Ripley Street; Dexter Parsonage Museum; Montgomery Interpretive Center at Alabama State University

they were attacked upon arrival at Montgomery's Greyhound station. A marker out front details the remarkable things that went on in this house. The activists, including King, Abernathy, James Farmer, John Lewis, Diane Nash, and Bernard Lafayette, used this brief respite to continue strategy meetings bent on staying the course, and Montgomery's Black community brought over food to sustain them.

During the Montgomery Bus Boycott in 1955-1956, Harris's pharmacy became a makeshift taxi stand because city officials wouldn't allow pickups on public streets. Harris's wife, Vera, transported many of those boycotters in her own car. Harris also assisted with medical care at St. Jude's Hospital during the 1965 Selma to Montgomery March.

When Vera Harris passed away in 2019, Congressman John Lewis said in a statement: "We slept on couches, in chairs and on the floor, in any nook or cranny we could find. Mrs. Harris made big pots of delicious spaghetti that helped to renew and strengthen us. Her warm and welcoming spirit and the food she fed us encouraged us to stay in the struggle for simple justice in America. Her home was like a safe haven to activists who had to face a hostile world."[6]

Montgomery Interpretive Center at Alabama State University

1521 Harris Way; tel. 334/293-0596; free

The newest of three interpretive centers along the **Selma to Montgomery National Historic Trail,** the Montgomery Interpretive Center is located at the entrance to Alabama State University, next to the ASU Hornets stadium. The facade features an 18-foot-tall limestone sandblasted relief based on a photograph that subtly evokes the march. Architects of this sophisticated, wedge-shaped building integrated cedar wood and dark zinc for contrast.

Inside, the 10,000-square-foot cultural center offers exhibits and educational programming that focuses on events from March 21 to March 25, 1965, when the five-day, 54-mile march from Selma concluded with a mass gathering outside the state capitol in Montgomery. Red dots superimposed on an oversize map indicate the march route. A TV screen shows biographies of local people who supported the voting rights movement, such as Rufus Lewis, who created a social club to help people register to vote. One photo shows a line of girls carrying signs that read: "One man. One vote. Register to vote."

Exhibits cover other aspects of the movement too. Banners featuring civil rights heroes (including local hero Georgia Gilmore, who raised money for the Montgomery Bus Boycott) line the wall of one room. The interpretive center also highlights the role the Centennial Hill neighborhood and the campus played in the civil rights movement. A painting of King's mugshot with his Birmingham jail arrest number hangs here too. Ku Klux Klan regalia is also on view.

OTHER NEIGHBORHOODS

Holt Street Baptist Church

903 Holt St.; tel. 334/263-0522; www.holtstreetmemorialbaptistchurch.net

This church, about 1.5 miles south of downtown, is where the mass meeting that launched the Montgomery Bus Boycott occurred, on December 5, 1955, in the wake of Rosa Parks's arrest for refusing to give up her seat to a White passenger. The 381-day boycott resulted in desegregation of public transportation in Montgomery. Today, Holt Street still thrives in a newer edifice at 1870 Court Street. Tours of the original building aren't available, but a sign out front marks the spot where it all happened. The church is a stop on the official U.S. Civil Rights Trail.

COOKING FOR THE MOVEMENT

Georgia Gilmore, a member of the Montgomery Improvement Association, was a force to be reckoned with. In 1957, after her son was arrested for walking through a Whites-only park, she sued the city of Montgomery—and won.

Her other contribution to the movement was to use her prodigious cooking skills to sell food and raise money to support the Montgomery Bus Boycott. The so-called **Club From Nowhere** that she started served as cover for Black women to cook and sell food to raise money for the boycott too. Black people and Whites alike bought this food.

house of Georgia Gilmore, who sold food to raise money for the Montgomery Bus Boycott

Several months into the boycott, Gilmore testified in court on behalf of boycott leaders who had been arrested and told of a time she was kicked off a Montgomery bus. As a result, she was fired from her cooking job, but King encouraged her to start her own business and gave her start-up funds to make it so. She operated her restaurant out of her Centennial Hill home at 453 Dericote Street. (You can't go inside, but you can walk by today, if you like.) King and Abernathy loved her cooking.

Historic Oak Park

1010 Forest Ave.; tel. 334/625-2300; www.funinmontgomery.com/Home/Components; closes at sundown

In 1957, Black youth Mark Gilmore was taking a shortcut home through Whites-only Oak Park when he was arrested for violating Montgomery's segregation laws. His mother was Georgia Gilmore, a Montgomery Improvement Association member known for feeding the resistance during the Montgomery Bus Boycott. Along with others, and represented by civil rights lawyers Solomon Seay Jr. and Fred Gray, she sued the city for arresting her son—and won.

By 1959, Judge Frank Johnson, a White judge, ruled the city had to integrate recreational facilities. Instead of obeying the law, city officials shut down all parks and filled all the pools with dirt. Later, plaintiffs asked a U.S. District Court to stop Montgomery from giving exclusive access to parks to segregationist academies, which was considered a backhanded way of subsidizing racism with taxpayer dollars. The U.S. Supreme Court upheld part of that order. In essence, *Gilmore v. City of Montgomery* put a stop to that segregated nonsense too.

Historic Oak Park, a couple of miles east of downtown Montgomery, is 40 acres of lush gardens and trees, playgrounds, a pond, picnic tables, and walking trails. Oak Park also has a band shell, a planetarium, and a Wi-Fi hotspot. Be sure to enjoy this lovely place because Black Montgomery residents went through a lot to make sure everyone, regardless of race, color, or creed, can.

Tours and Local Guides

BUS TOUR

MONTGOMERY TOURS

300 Water St., Ste. 301; tel. 334/450-5183; www.mymontgomerytours.com; $300-$450 for groups of 1-14 guests

A studious tour guide with a generous appreciation for all kinds of history, Jake Williams offers a range of tours, including three- and six-hour guided tours to sites that defined the civil rights movement, plus Alabama history. Williams is quite comfortable navigating the complexities of Alabama's dueling histories: Black and White. He knows all the best places to eat too.

Like many residents in this area, Jake Williams *is* civil rights history. He grew up in nearby Lowndes County where he participated in the Selma to Montgomery march. When Williams's mother signed him up to go to an integrated school in the '60s, she got pushback: A White neighbor came by the house and demanded, "Tell your momma I say come here!" and dressed her down right then and there for not "knowing better." Williams also recalls an unoccupied school building that was gifted to White residents for $1 to open the Lowndes Academy, one of the many segregationists academies that sprouted up all over the South as soon as integration was enforced.

Of many tour options Williams's six-hour guided driving tour coordinates stops of at least three of the following: Southern Poverty Law Center Civil Rights Memorial, Rosa Parks Museum, the National Memorial for Peace and Justice, and Dexter Avenue King Memorial Baptist Church and Parsonage Museum. Starting at 9am, stops do not include the price of entry, and allotted time for lunch is at your own expense. On the bus, Williams reveals details and nuances about people and sites it takes a longtime resident and history buff to know. Williams's three-hour guided bus tour offers one or two stops to allow for picture-taking. If you have a big group, such as a school, church, or corporate group, hire Williams as a step-on guide where he can get on your coach bus to navigate and narrate your civil rights tour through Montgomery.

RIDING AND WALKING TOUR

I AM MORE THAN . . . TOURS: SACRED GROUNDS TOUR

tel. 334/296-3024; www.iammorethan7053.com/more-than-tours; 90 minutes; $25

With big red cat-eye glasses perched on her smiling face, Michelle Browder is a force of nature as a tour guide. Her two-hour "Sacred Grounds" tour of Montgomery encompasses Native American, colonial, and civil rights history of Alabama. Browder marches right over to a marker that commemorates the Muscogee Nation's Encanchata Village. Disturbingly, the sign marks the spot denoting the beginning of what would become Montgomery, while saying nothing about the people colonists replaced. She takes a moment of silence in honor and respect for indigenous people.

Browder also takes guests to the riverfront to discuss the domestic slave trade, aka 52 years of human trafficking. At Perry and Monroe streets, she recalls where the Old Montgomery Theatre once stood: African American women, called "slave masons," made the bricks for the building where John Wilkes Booth, the actor who assassinated President Abraham Lincoln, performed. Some of these bricks were found during the renovation of the S. H. Kress building downtown and were donated to the Equal Justice Initiative. This comprehensive tour includes the Dexter Parsonage Museum, the state capitol,

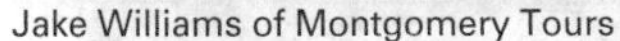
Jake Williams of Montgomery Tours

Michelle Browder of I Am More Than . . . Tours

Court Square Fountain (located near a former slave market), and more.

The joy and wonder of this tour is the nuanced storytelling—and sometimes singing—Browder offers. She knows facts, figures, and personality quirks of historical figures. She relates these tales in a fun, gossipy way, but still respects her elders. (She's Southern bred, after all.) Browder is part of the civil rights DNA: Her auntie, Aurelia S. Browder, was the lead plaintiff in *Browder v. Gayle* (1956), which challenged the treatment of Black women on city buses. Downtown at the Rosa Parks statue on Montgomery Plaza at the Court Street Fountain, inground plates are inscribed with their names: Browder, Mary Louise Smith, Claudette Colvin, and Susie McDonald.

Shopping

GIFTS

LEGACY MUSEUM AND THE NATIONAL MEMORIAL FOR PEACE AND JUSTICE GIFT SHOP

400 N Court St.; tel. 334/386-9100; www.shop.eji.org; Mon.-Sat. 9am-7:30pm, Sun. 9am-6pm; adults $10, seniors and students $7, children 6 and under free

The EJI Legacy Pavilion, which honors local civil rights figures, is a few short blocks away from the Legacy Museum. In addition to the Southern-style eatery, Pannie-George's Kitchen, a gift shop offers a rich array of books about African American history. High-quality products include a memorial hoodie, buttons, and accessories. You'll find EJI's famous T-shirt, emblazoned with this meaningful quote by founder Bryan Stevenson: "The opposite of poverty is not wealth. The opposite of poverty is justice." EJI's racial justice calendar documents challenges and triumphs of the Black experience and reminds us why what happened in the past matters now in policy and practice.

BARBER SHOP

MALDEN BROTHERS BARBERSHOP

407 S Jackson St., tel. 334/262-9249; Tues. 7:30am-5pm, Thurs.-Sat. 7:30am-5pm

THE BEN MOORE HOTEL

The Ben Moore Hotel was the first hotel in Montgomery to serve African Americans.

If you weren't there at the time, everything about the civil rights period may seem filled with paralyzing racial tension. But places like the Ben Moore Hotel (902 High St.) remind us Black people have always made room for joy as they pursued entrepreneurial goals.

The Ben Moore Hotel was the first hotel in Montgomery to serve African Americans. Through the 1960s, it was a site for food, lodging, and entertainment and a safe haven for movement meetings. The ground-floor Majestic Café was a safe meeting place for Black travelers in a city where segregation permeated every corner of life. On the top floor at the Afro Club, entertainers such as B. B. King, Tina Turner, and Clarence Carter of "Patches" (1970) fame performed.

The four-story hotel (located in walking distance to the King parsonage in the next block) is now defunct and vacant—except for Malden Brothers Barbershop, where at least two Kings (Martin Luther and B. B.) got their hair cut. You can still get your hair cut there today.

The Ben Moore Hotel building at S Jackson and High streets still houses the Malden Brothers Barbershop where King got his hair cut by Mr. Nelson Malden. (Tuskegee Airmen came here for cuts as well, as did B. B. King.) This Centennial Hill neighborhood mainstay is still a working barbershop, now under new ownership. The intimate space retains a vintage feel with everything from wood paneling, a tile floor, fluorescent lights, and walls covered with framed photos (including a sepia photo of King). A wall of wood-backed chairs with red and black vinyl-covered seats are perfect spots to sit and wait for a haircut while engaging in the kind of spirited conversations that occur among Black men in the sanctuary of a barbershop. Tours of the shop may be available; call for more information.

BOOKS

1977 BOOKS

39 Dexter Ave., Suite #209; tel. 334/409-1315; www.1977books.com; Tues.-Thurs. 4pm-8pm, Fri. 4pm-6pm, Sat. 10am-6pm

An abolitionist bookstore and community space featuring books focused on social justice and liberation, 1977 Books occupies the second floor of the old S. H. Kress department store buildings. Books emphasize authors who are queer, transgender, indigenous, or people of color and cover history and racial and social justice. Buy a book and head over to Prevail coffee, a similarly welcoming space located in the same building.

The shop, which is not Black-owned, offers monthly memberships at various levels ($5-25 a month) to support their work. One option is the How We Get Free book club, an homage to academic, writer, and activist Keeanga-Yamahtta Taylor's meditation on Black feminism and the Combahee River Collective's 1977 manifesto.

Festivals and Events

JANUARY

MARTIN LUTHER KING DAY CELEBRATION AT DEXTER AVENUE BAPTIST CHURCH

454 Dexter Ave.; tel. 334/263-3970; King day is the third Monday in January; free

The Dexter Avenue King Memorial Legacy Foundation arranges the annual King Day celebration. Previous events have included guest speakers, praise dancers, jazz performances, solos, and singalongs in an uplifting environment that remembers this is King's birthday and, therefore, much to celebrate.

Food

You'll have plenty of opportunities to consume African American foodways during your travels in Montgomery. Soul food, Southern food, American food—whatever you call it, it's all served with a smile and good feeling that reaches all the way down into your belly. And when you want to taste from other traditions, Montgomery, too, is here to serve.

DOWNTOWN

Southern and Soul Food

CAHAWBA HOUSE

31 Court St.; tel. 334/356-1877; www.cahawbahouse.com; Mon.-Fri. 11am-7pm; a la carte $3-5

Choose a meat, then choose two sides, you'll be alright. Selections include a meatloaf topped with a rich, tangy tomato sauce and chicken served many ways. If you want to feel the "bama" in Alabama, try the purple hull peas or collard greens. Taste the South with a pimento cheese sandwich stacked on Texas toast. Other sides include roasted veggies, fried green tomatoes, and green beans, and a range of salads and sandwiches are available. Cahawba House (not a Black-owned business) is near the Freedom Rides Museum, the former S. H. Kress & Co. department store and the Frank Johnson Courthouse, so you can park and walk off everything you're gonna eat.

PANNIE-GEORGE'S KITCHEN

450 N Court St.; tel. 334/386-9116; www.panniegeorgeskitchen.com; Tues.-Sun. 11am-5:30pm; $9-14

In the Legacy Pavilion a few blocks away from the Legacy Museum, the award-winning Pannie-George's Kitchen serves up a taste of home, if that home is downhome and Southern. Cafeteria-style offerings on a range of combo plates include a rotating smorgasbord of delectables, including baked or fried chicken, black-eyed peas, macaroni 'n' cheese, meatloaf, and greens. The Legacy Pavilion honors civil rights figures: Claudette Colvin, Jonathan Daniels,

John Lewis, King, E. D. Nixon, and Jo Ann Robinson. Eat in their honor and enjoy.

Barbecue

DREAMLAND BAR-B-QUE

12 W Jefferson St.; tel. 334/273-7427; www.dreamlandbbq.com; Mon.-Thurs. 10am-9pm, Fri.-Sat. 10am-10pm, Sun. 11am-9pm; $8-15

This local BBQ chain serves hickory-fired ribs, plates, and sandwiches, plus wings and comfort sides. Founded by John "Big Daddy" Bishop, the Dreamland Café opened in 1958 in Jerusalem Heights, south of Tuscaloosa. Bishop started out with hickory-smoked pork spareribs, which are legendary today. The menu features starters, like Big Daddy Nachos and fried okra, sandwiches, and barbecue plates with a choice of two or three meats, plus a full bar and desserts too. Dreamland has locations throughout Alabama and in Georgia and Florida. This branch in Montgomery (which is no longer Black-owned) is located near the Legacy Museum. Eat something you can't live without? (Or, this description make you hungry?) Dreamland will ship a slab, sausages, sauce, and pecan pies to your house.

Hot Dogs

CHRIS' HOT DOGS

138 Dexter Ave.; tel. 334/265-6850; www.chrishotdogs.com; Mon.-Thurs. 10am-7pm, Fri. 10am-8pm, Sat. 10am-7pm; $3-8

Segregation couldn't keep Dr. King from a good hot dog. He liked eating the ones at Chris' Hot Dogs, a mom-and-pop dining institution founded in 1917 by Greek immigrant Christopher Anastasios Katechis aka Mr. Chris. The law wouldn't allow Black people like King to eat inside though. During segregation, Black people

Photos (top to bottom): meatloaf at Cahawba House; Dreamland Bar-B-Que; a welcoming message inside Prevail Union Craft Coffee

could order then take their food out. Other famous Chris' fans include Presidents Franklin D. Roosevelt and Harry S. Truman, and Jimmy Stewart.

Today in the eatery (which is not a Black-owned business), long lines of diverse diners rub shoulders while waiting to put in an order at the register. Eat at the lunch counter, which would have been a no-go during segregation, or sit in the dining room decorated with photographs of Alabama big shots, clippings, and more.

Coffee

PREVAIL UNION CRAFT COFFEE

39 Dexter Ave., Ste. 102; tel. 334/416-8399; www.prevailunionmgm.com; Mon.-Sat. 7am-6pm, Sun. 8am-3pm; $2-6

A powerful message pops from a rustic red brick wall at Prevail Union Craft Coffee: "Together We Prevail." It's a fitting message in a city with so much civil rights history and a hopeful sign for anyone fatigued by all of Montgomery's Confederate symbolism. This craft coffee emporium serves fresh roasted coffee drinks, loose leaf tea, and other beverages in a relaxing, sophisticated atmosphere. People from all walks of life chill here, meeting in groups, working on laptops, or sipping to savor, all prevailing: together. Prevail, which is not Black-owned, is located on the first floor of the former S. H. Kress department store building.

OTHER NEIGHBORHOODS

Southern and Soul Food

BARBARA GAIL NEIGHBORHOOD GRILL

2003 Early St.; tel. 334/269-4142; Mon.-Sat. 7am-noon; $6-13

At the corner of Early and Oak streets (about 1.5 miles southwest of downtown), Barbara Gail's sits on the Selma to Montgomery march route. Opened in 2007, this cozy neighborhood eatery specializes in delicious breakfasts. Owner Larry Bethune Jr. has a pep in his step when he heads back to the kitchen to prepare an order of shrimp and grits. Other family members work there too. When the buttery grits topped with shrimp, cheese, and crumbled bacon arrive, the Bethunes have a gleam in their eyes: like they *know* your tastebuds are about to dance.

The menu also features thick-cut bolonga sandwiches served on a chunky slice of grilled toast. There's also country ham, bacon, patty melts, baked chicken, and links. Fish runs from tilapia and salmon to whiting. The sensation of feeling like you're among family and "play" cousins is made complete with Kool-Aid drinks.

Bethune and his siblings grew up in the restaurant business, working around the corner at Brenda's Bar-B-Cue Pit. He's lived in other places, but Montgomery called him home. He has an entrepreneurial zeal and says he likes the slower pace of life. A red-and-white banner hangs above the front door entrance, celebrating march participants who ate at this west side eatery on the 50th anniversary of the Selma to Montgomery march.

MARTHA'S PLACE BUFFET

7798 Atlanta Hwy.; tel. 334/356-7165; www.marthasplacebuffet.com; Mon.-Sat. 11am-8pm, Sun. 10:30am-3pm; lunch buffet $9, dinner buffet $10

When you walk into Martha's Place Buffet, you'll feel warm and welcome, and you'll leave full. Founder Martha Hawkins, the 10th of 12 children, knows how to feed a family. She was inspired by famed civil rights chef and Montgomery fixture, Georgia Gilmore, who fed people active in the local civil rights movement.

The buffet at Martha's changes daily, but on any given day you'll find baked chicken, Salisbury steak, fried chicken, chicken and dumplings, fried fish, liver and onions, and roast beef. Whew! Vegetables include

FOOD

STORYBOOTH

A phone booth-like structure on the first floor of the historic S. H. Kress department store building is a unique place to learn about civil rights history.

On the first floor of the old S. H. Kress department store building (39 Dexter Ave.; now home to various shops and restaurants), look for a phone booth-like structure located near Prevail Union Craft Coffee. This is the work of **Storybooth** (Storybooth.us), a podcast studio and free online public archive that allows visitors to listen to stories from the civil rights movement. You may also pick up a phone receiver and tell a story of your own.

Dorothy Wright Tillman, a legendary Alabama-born Chicago alderwoman, tells of the time her grandmother took her to Holt Street Baptist Church to hear King speak. She was so inspired, she vowed to "do something." Tillman ended up working under Rev. James Bevel and was arrested in the Kress building in 1964 during a Dexter Avenue Demonstration. Tillman also survived Bloody Sunday.

Built in 1929, the **S. H. Kress building** features restored terrazzo floors and ornate plaster moldings and is now a mixed-used development. During segregation, Black people had to walk through the back door (Monroe St.), Whites in the front (Dexter Ave.). As you enter the Kress building today, go through both: You'll see that the Dexter entrance is definitely grander, though the new development has made both sides quite inviting. Taking care to tell a complete story, the hallway displays original "colored" and "White" drinking fountain signage.

mashed potatoes, candied yams, black-eyed peas, butter beans, steamed carrots, rutabagas, and collard greens. Your meal includes salads and desserts. What's for dessert? Try banana pudding, bread pudding, and coconut, chocolate, and strawberry cakes. Or invest in great-tasting food and take the whole cake home.

Martha's Place is located about 9 miles east of downtown Montgomery on the Atlanta Highway.

Barbecue

BRENDA'S BAR-B-QUE PIT

1457 Mobile Rd.; tel. 334/264-4517; Tues.-Thurs. 10:30am-7pm, Fri.-Sat. 10:30am-11pm; $6-13

Big flavors come out of this tiny brick structure on Early Street, which sits next to a bigger brick building where the magic—and food prep—happens. Standing curbside at dusk, anticipation builds as the cooks chop and pile hickory-, pecan-, and oak-smoked barbecue on sop-worthy white bread. They're big on plates here, so try a pig ear plate, or a pork rib, fish, or chicken plate. It's all good. As a carryout-only place, good luck making it to the car before you rip open your bag. Wishing you the best as you peel back the paper wrapping to get your first taste of well-sauced 'cue to land in your mouth—not on your lap. It happens.

Brenda's is a family-owned business that opened in 1942. Owners Jereline and James Bethune named the place after their daughter, Brenda. Operating during a segregated era, Brenda's was a Black-owned business that was a safe haven for secret NAACP meetings. A concealed courtyard made it possible to talk privately without White interference. Aside from strategy sessions, volunteers taught Black people how to read and write so they could pass the state's poll test, rigged to keep Black people from being able to register to vote.

The pit is a member of the Alabama Barbecue Hall of Fame—quite an accomplishment, considering inductees have to be in business at least 50 years. It's located a couple miles southeast of downtown Montgomery.

Accommodations

DOWNTOWN

Downtown Montgomery has plenty of places to shelter you on your stay. The city has embraced the trend toward revitalized urban downtowns, meaning that venerable old buildings have been made comfortable again.

In addition to the Staybridge Suites, chain hotels located downtown include **Hampton Inn & Suites Montgomery-Downtown** (100 Commerce St., Montgomery; tel. 334/265-1010; www.hilton.com/en; $130) and **Embassy Suites by Hilton Montgomery Hotel & Conference Center** (300 Tallapoosa St., Montgomery; tel. 334/269-5055; www.embassysuites3.hilton.com; $131), which has more than 200 rooms and is located near the Legacy Museum.

$100-200

STAYBRIDGE SUITES

275 Lee St.; tel. 334/532-0700; www.ihg.com/staybridge; $116

This 115-room hotel really does feel like home because suites include a full kitchen with all the equipment you need to prepare a meal, plus traditional hotel room amenities. Staybridge Suites sits on the site of the first White House of the Confederacy. It's an awfully comfortable place with friendly service.

Transportation

MONTGOMERY

GETTING THERE

Air

Montgomery Regional Airport (4445 Selma Hwy.; tel. 334/281-5040; www.flymgm.com; Sun.-Sat. 4am-12:30am), located about 9 miles southwest of downtown; provides flights to Atlanta, Charlotte, Dallas, and Mobile. A cab ride from the airport to downtown costs around $25. Several major car rental companies operate at Montgomery Regional Airport.

Bus

Greyhound buses arrive at **Intermodal Center** (495 Molton St.; tel. 334/286-0658; daily 9am-6:30pm) in downtown Montgomery, a little over a mile west of the capitol building. When you arrive, you can hop right on another bus to take you anywhere in the city. The M, Montgomery's city bus system, also operates out of the Intermodal Center.

Get from Selma to Montgomery in an hour for a $17 bus ticket. From Birmingham, the trip takes 1 hour 40 minutes ($30). From Atlanta, it's a 3-hour ride ($25).

Car

Montgomery is found at the intersection of I-65 and I-85. To get here from:

- **Selma:** Take **U.S. Highway 80 East** to Montgomery for 52 miles. The drive takes about an hour.
- **Birmingham:** Take **I-65 South** for 110 miles (2 hours).
- **Atlanta:** Take **I-85 South** for 185 miles (2.5 hours).

GETTING AROUND

Most sites are in the downtown area and are walkable. You may choose to park and walk to a few spots or jump in the car and drive to a new cluster of activities.

Parking

Metered street parking is 50 cents an hour for up to two hours.

Public Transportation

The M (tel. 334/262-7356; www.montgomerytransit.com) provides fixed-route services within Montgomery city limits; however, a combination of driving and walking is an easier way to get around.

Thirty-four buses serve 14 fixed routes from Monday-Friday 5am-9pm and Saturday 7:30am-6:30pm. Buses do not run on Sundays. A single-ride fixed-route ticket is $2. Riders get one-way transfer free with purchase of any fare. Discounted fares are available for seniors, students, and disabled people with valid ID. Exact change is needed to purchase tickets.

Taxi and Ride-Hailing Apps

If you need a cab, call **Time Taxi** (tel. 334/505-1189; www.ontimetaxi.co). **Uber** and **Lyft** are viable options in Montgomery.

Birmingham

In the early 1960s, Birmingham, Alabama, was 60 percent White and 40 percent Black, and the vast majority of African Americans could not vote. We also couldn't try on clothes in stores, sit at lunch counters, or get hired as clerks or salespeople. In fact, Birmingham was known as the "most segregated city in America."[1]

BIRMINGHAM

BIRMINGHAM'S TOP 3

1. Seeing civil rights artifacts at the **Birmingham Civil Rights Institute**, including the bars of the jail cell where King wrote his famous letter (page 168).

2. Paying respects to movement leaders, and to four little girls who died in a brutal KKK bombing, at **16th Street Baptist Church** (page 168).

3. Walking through **Kelly Ingram Park**, where a series of installations bring the story of the Birmingham Campaign to life (page 172).

Photos (top to bottom): Birmingham Civil Rights Institute; stained glass inside 16th Street Baptist Church; "Three Ministers Kneeling" limestone sculpture by Raymond Kaskey in Kelly Ingram Park. Previous: "Four Spirits" sculpture by Elizabeth MacQueen at Kelly Ingram Park

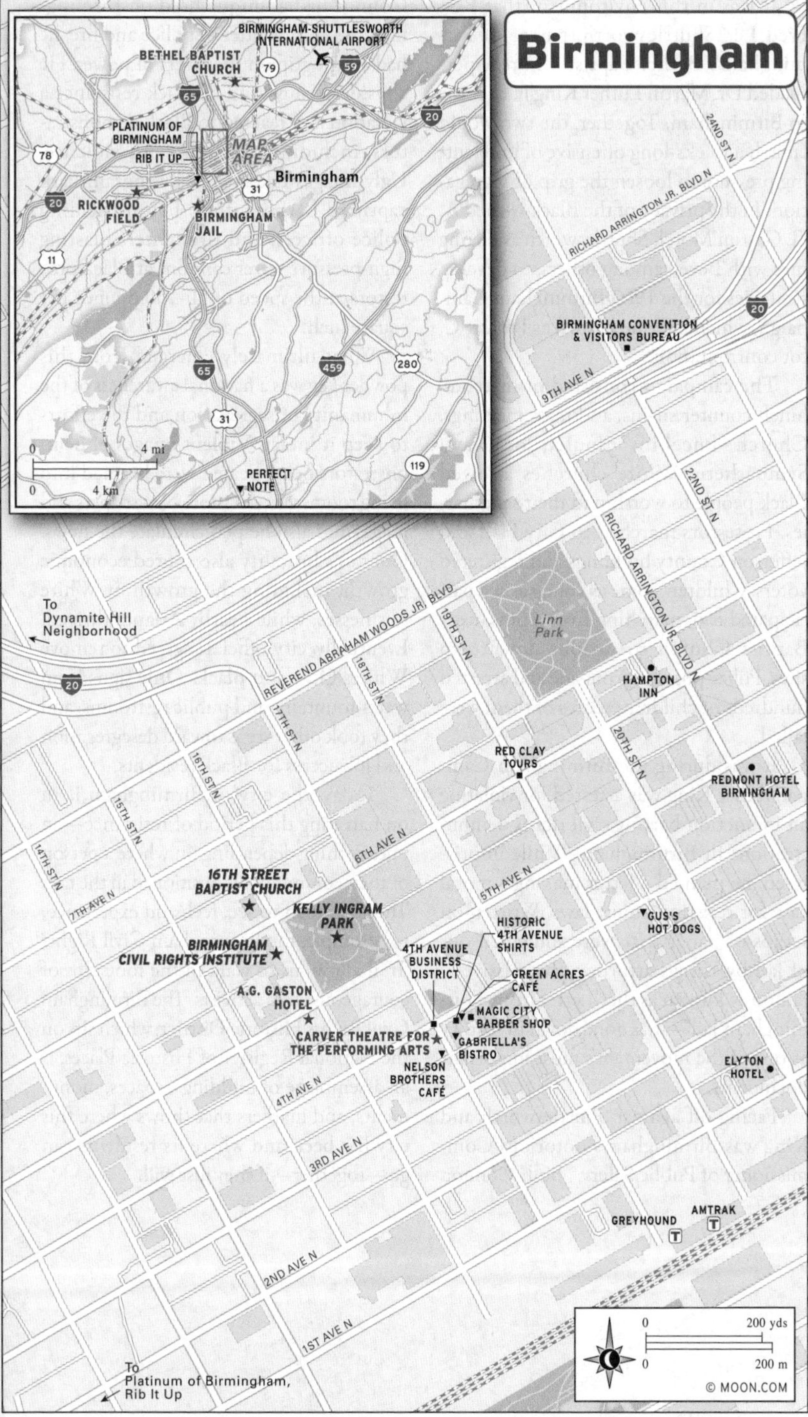
Birmingham
BIRMINGHAM-SHUTTLESWORTH INTERNATIONAL AIRPORT
BETHEL BAPTIST CHURCH
PLATINUM OF BIRMINGHAM
RIB IT UP
MAP AREA
Birmingham
RICKWOOD FIELD
BIRMINGHAM JAIL
PERFECT NOTE
0
4 mi
0
4 km
24TH ST N
RICHARD ARRINGTON JR. BLVD N
BIRMINGHAM CONVENTION & VISITORS BUREAU
9TH AVE N
22ND ST N
To Dynamite Hill Neighborhood
REVEREND ABRAHAM WOODS JR. BLVD
19TH ST N
18TH ST N
17TH ST N
Linn Park
HAMPTON INN
20TH ST N
RED CLAY TOURS
REDMONT HOTEL BIRMINGHAM
16TH ST N
15TH ST N
14TH ST N
7TH AVE N
6TH AVE N
5TH AVE N
16TH STREET BAPTIST CHURCH
KELLY INGRAM PARK
BIRMINGHAM CIVIL RIGHTS INSTITUTE
A.G. GASTON HOTEL
4TH AVENUE BUSINESS DISTRICT
HISTORIC 4TH AVENUE SHIRTS
GREEN ACRES CAFÉ
MAGIC CITY BARBER SHOP
GABRIELLA'S BISTRO
CARVER THEATRE FOR THE PERFORMING ARTS
NELSON BROTHERS CAFÉ
GUS'S HOT DOGS
ELYTON HOTEL
4TH AVE N
3RD AVE N
GREYHOUND
AMTRAK
2ND AVE N
1ST AVE N
To Platinum of Birmingham, Rib It Up
0
200 yds
0
200 m
© MOON.COM

BIRMINGHAM

It was in this environment that Rev. Fred Lee Shuttlesworth, pastor of Birmingham's Bethel Baptist Church, persuaded Dr. Martin Luther King Jr. to come to Birmingham. Together, the two would launch a weeks-long offensive of unrelenting pressure to loosen the grip of segregation. In the privacy of the Black-owned A. G. Gaston Motel, Shuttlesworth and King met with Bevel, among others, to develop strategies for the 1963 Birmingham Campaign, which became known as Project C, for confrontation.

The campaign consisted of marches, lunch counter sit-ins, and mass meetings. Church "kneel-ins" flouted local law: Sympathetic White churches allowed Black people to worship in their sanctuaries. Protestors marched to City Hall and Jefferson County buildings and registered voters. Children, some as young as six, participated too, marching from 16th Street Baptist Church to various downtown sites. Police posted up outside and arrested hundreds of children; scores of them were jailed.

It was during the Birmingham Campaign that King was arrested for violating an injunction barring civil rights demonstrations in Birmingham. While imprisoned, he penned a letter making a moral case for resisting unjust laws. Written on scraps of paper that were smuggled out of jail by King's attorney, the missive—famously known as the "Letter from a Birmingham Jail"—has gone down in history as one of the movement's most important documents.

Facing off against Shuttlesworth and King was Birmingham's notorious Commissioner of Public Safety, "Bull" Connor. Connor had a unique hold on Birmingham: As commander of police and fire, he had a firm grip on the levers of power. He considered any kind of Black resistance a violation and reacted to Black demonstrators, including children, with violence. Ugly images taken at Kelly Ingram Park captured barking dogs, baton-wielding police officers, and firefighters blasting high-pressure water cannons at Black protestors at the speed of 50-100 pounds per square inch.

What ultimately emerged from this powder keg was a national awareness of the inhumanity of segregation and the efforts to keep it intact. Violent images of demonstrators being beaten were beamed into living rooms via television. Newspapers and magazines also helped circulate the news. Connor's brutality also soured economic growth, including the growth of White businesses, while nearby Atlanta thrived. Eventually, city officials agreed to remove Whites Only and Blacks Only signs from water fountains and public restrooms, and they took other steps toward desegregation and job access for Black residents.

Today, the city of Birmingham is in on narrating this period of resistance—an uneasy thing depending on where a person or their community is positioned in the tale. There is much to see, feel, and experience; for example, the Birmingham Civil Rights Trail allows us to walk in the footsteps of courageous child activists. The Birmingham Civil Rights Historic District, which sits on the National Register of Historic Places, is an assemblage of buildings, spaces, monuments, and markers that shows where this city has been and where its residents can go—together—if they just will.

MOVEMENT TIMELINE

The 1950s and 1960s were a violent time in Birmingham, marked by numerous bombings and significant unrest. Things came to a head with the 1963 **Birmingham Campaign,** jointly initiated by Shuttlesworth, Alabama Christian Movement for Human Rights (ACMHR), and King, Southern Christian Leadership Conference (SCLC). The campaign consisted of mass meetings, nonviolent direct action, lunch counter sit-ins, marches on City Hall, and selective buying at downtown stores. It is considered a turning point in the national civil rights movement that contributed to the signing of the Civil Rights Act of 1964, which prohibited discrimination on the basis of race, color, religion, sex, or national origin.

1956

June 1: National Association for the Advancement of Colored People (NAACP) is officially barred from operating in the state of Alabama.

June 5: The ACMHR is born with Rev. Fred Shuttlesworth as its leader. Around 1,000 people (60 percent women) attend the founding meeting.

December 25: Ku Klux Klan bombs Shuttlesworth's home, the parsonage at Bethel Baptist Church, on Christmas Day.

December 26: Shuttlesworth keeps promise to hold protest rides to desegregate city buses.

1958

June 29: Bethel Baptist Church is bombed, the second of three such attacks on the church.

1961

May 17: Freedom Riders arrive in Birmingham and, with permission of the local police, are beaten by an angry mob.

1962

March 15: Anti-Injustice Committee, led by Frank Dukes, initiates a "selective-buying campaign" of White-owned downtown stores.

December 13: Bethel Baptist Church is bombed again.

1963

April 3: The Birmingham Campaign kicks off when 65 demonstrators silently march to Loveman's, Pizitz, Kress, Woolworth's, and Britt's and stage sit-ins at segregated lunch counters. Twenty demonstrators are arrested. ACMHR co-founders, Rev. Abraham Woods Jr., and his brother, Rev. Calvin Woods, lead sit-in groups that day.

April 7: On Palm Sunday, Reverends A. D. King, Nelson Smith, and John Porter direct singing marchers out of St. Paul Methodist Church on 6th Avenue North. Bull Connor is positioned along the route with his officers and calls out police dogs.

April 8: The 16th Street Baptist Church joins the Birmingham Campaign.

April 10: A state judge grants an injunction allowing city officials to ban anti-segregation protest activity in Birmingham. Protestors continue the campaign despite the injunction.

April 12: King, Ralph Abernathy, and 46 others are jailed for violating a state law against mass public demonstrations. The same day, eight White clergymen publish an open letter in *The Birmingham News* called "A Call for Unity," which asked King to delay any further demonstrations and let local people settle local matters.

April 16: King's searing critique of White moderates, now known as the "Letter from a Birmingham Jail," is

Continued on next page

BIRMINGHAM

smuggled out of jail by attorney Clarence Jones.

April 19: King and Abernathy are released on bond.

April 28: Activists participate in kneel-ins at dozens of metropolitan churches.

May 2: The Children's Crusade, brainchild of Rev. James Bevel, begins when more than 1,000 Black children try to march to downtown Birmingham; hundreds are arrested.

May 3: Children head back out for a second day of marching on Demonstration Day, or D-Day, when Connor directs police and firefighters to attack the children with high-pressure fire hoses, batons, and police dogs. Images of these assaults appeared on TV and newspapers everywhere and begin to turn the tide of national opinion in support of civil rights.

May 7: Demonstration is held at Kelly Ingram Park. Shuttlesworth is hosed so badly he must be hospitalized.

May 10: "The Birmingham Truce Agreement" is announced at a press conference at A. G. Gaston Motel, thus ending the Birmingham Campaign. City officials, White business owners, and civil rights leaders agree on the desegregation of downtown stores, removal of Whites Only and Blacks Only signs in restrooms and on drinking fountains, hiring of more Black people, and letting demonstrators out of jail in exchange for the SCLC calling off further protests.

May 11: The home of Rev. A. D. King and A. G. Gaston Motel are bombed.

May 13: President John F. Kennedy sends federal troops to Birmingham to make sure vigilante justice won't take hold in light of the truce.

June 11: Proposing legislation to end discrimination against African Americans, Kennedy calls civil rights a moral issue, "as old as the scriptures and . . . as clear as the American Constitution."[2]

July 23: Birmingham City Council repeals its segregation laws.

September 15: The 16th Street Baptist Church is bombed by the KKK, and four young girls perish. Elsewhere in the city two other Black youth are killed: Virgil Ware is killed by a White teen and Johnny Robinson is shot by police.

The A. G. Gaston Motel was bombed the day after the Birmingham Truce was announced at a press conference held at the hotel.

PEOPLE WHO MADE THE MOVEMENT

LEADERS AND PARTICIPANTS IN THE BIRMINGHAM CAMPAIGN

Fred Shuttlesworth: Along with King, Shuttlesworth was a lead architect of the 1963 Birmingham Campaign. Shuttlesworth was also pastor of Bethel Baptist Church, co-founder of the SCLC, and founder of the ACMHR, which was created when state officials outlawed the NAACP. Shuttlesworth challenged segregated buses, led marches and sit-ins, and persevered through bombings and beatings. During the Birmingham Campaign, he was among those blasted with fire hoses.

Rev. Ralph Abernathy: Leader and strategist of the Birmingham Campaign. On April 12, 1963, SCLC treasurer Abernathy joined King and Shuttlesworth in violating an injunction against marching. King hoped to provoke arrest to boost support for the Birmingham Campaign, and they were indeed arrested. This proved auspicious because this bout of incarceration is when King wrote "Letter from a Birmingham Jail."

Rev. Ralph Abernathy

James Bevel: Architect of the Children's Crusade who got his start in the Nashville Movement.

A. G. Gaston: Millionaire Black businessman, friend of the movement, and owner of the A. G. Gaston Motel, where King and other leaders met to strategize for the Birmingham Campaign.

OTHER FIGURES

Rev. A. D. King: King's younger brother, A. D., was pastor of First Baptist Church of Ensley, a Birmingham suburb. His church was active in civil rights activities of this period. He was arrested several times in service to the cause.

Arthur Shores: Civil rights attorney who successfully fought for Autherine Lucy to be admitted as the first Black student at the University of Alabama in 1956. He also represented King and worked to desegregate public schools, secure voting rights, change racially driven zoning laws, and address police brutality. Many of his cases were on the behalf of the NAACP. Shores was also the first African American to serve on the Birmingham City Council.

Clarence B. Jones: As King's attorney (and also sometime speechwriter), he was the only one who could visit King in solitary confinement after his April 12, 1963, arrest. And it was Jones who helped King smuggle "Letter From a Birmingham Jail" to the outside world in his pockets and under his clothes.

James Peck: Freedom Rider who was beaten by the Ku Klux Klan with pipes, bars, and chains when the group's bus arrived in Birmingham in 1961. A photo of the beating was picked up by the *Associated Press* and published widely.

Frank Dukes: A Miles College student who led the selective-buying campaign in 1962. He formed the Anti-Injustice Committee, which crafted demands for desegregating public accommodations and hiring African Americans. Dukes, an older student who had fought in the Korean War, has said this campaign is what got folks ready for direct action.

Addine "Deenie" Drew: A member of the Black elite known as the Den Mother of the local movement. Drew led voter education classes in her home to help African Americans pass the literacy test. She got the Jefferson County Voters League to support the student-led selective-buying campaign in 1962. She and other society women formed a carpool to drive students from campus to downtown stores to enforce the boycott.

ORIENTATION

Many key events of the civil rights movement took place in downtown Birmingham, in what's now known as the **Birmingham Civil Rights Historic District.** This highly walkable neighborhood bordered by 9th Avenue, Richard Arrington Jr. Boulevard, 1st Avenue, and 14th Street covers several square blocks and encompasses several key sights, including the Birmingham Civil Rights Institute, 16th Street Baptist Church, and Kelly Ingram Park, along with the **Historic 4th Avenue Business District,** where a good number of historic and Black-owned businesses are located.

Outside downtown are other areas worth visiting, such as Bethel Baptist Church (where Shuttlesworth pastored during the movement) in the **Collegeville** neighborhood, a working-class African American neighborhood a few miles north of downtown. The area known as **Dynamite Hill,** which was ravaged by bombs during the Movement, is part of the Smithfield neighborhood in northwest Birmingham.

PLANNING YOUR TIME

Plan on spending a couple of days in Birmingham to take in the civil rights sites—you'll have time left over to relax and enjoy Birmingham's restaurants and shops too.

If you stick to downtown and the Civil Rights Historic District, you're certain to have robust experience exploring the city's history. The downtown area is walkable, but you'll probably want to drive to explore outside of it. Similarly, while it's possible to explore the sights in the Civil Rights Historic District on your own, a guide will add to your experience in areas such as Dynamite Hill.

Pick up city maps and get directions and connections to local tour guides at the **Birmingham Convention & Visitors Bureau** at Vulcan Park and Museum (1701 Valley View Drive; tel. 205/933-1409). The museum gives a good grounding in Birmingham's history and its rise as an industrial powerhouse.

Note that the Birmingham Civil Rights Institute is closed Mondays, and officials request that tour reservations for 16th Street Baptist Church are made at least three weeks in advance.

CONNECT WITH

A trip to Birmingham pairs nicely with visits southward to **Selma** and **Montgomery** if you have a few more days to spare. **Atlanta,** a bit farther away, is another logical connection.

Two Days in Birmingham

Make reservations to tour **16th Street Baptist Church** three weeks in advance. **Bethel Baptist Church** has limited hours but can also be visited by appointment, which is preferred.

DAY 1

Spend your first day in Birmingham in the Civil Rights Historic District and nearby 4th Avenue Business District. It's easy to walk between all the sites covered on this day.

1 Ground yourself during a visit to the **Birmingham Civil Rights Institute** (closed Mon.) to get a comprehensive look at segregation and the Black community's all-hands-on-deck fight for equality. Touch the bars of the Birmingham Jail where King wrote his famous letter. Be ready to commit to at least 90 minutes, but you'll likely want to spend more time in this jam-packed experience.

2 Walk a few blocks or drive over to **Gus's Hot Dogs** for a quick lunch.

3 Backtrack to **16th Street Baptist Church,** right across the street from the Civil Rights Institute, for a tour (schedule a few weeks in advance). King spoke here in support of the movement. The church is also where four young girls perished in a KKK bombing.

4 View the memorial sculptures at **Kelly Ingram Park,** kitty-corner to the church. This park was the site of mass meetings and rallies during the '60s, including during the 1963 Birmingham Campaign, some figures and events from which are depicted in the installations.

5 Join neighborhood regulars for a soul food dinner in the 4th Avenue Historic District at **Green Acres Cafe,** in business since the 1950s.

DAY 2

Jump in the car to explore sights outside the downtown historic district. For more context on **Dynamite Hill** and **Bethel Baptist Church,** book the three-hour **Fight for Rights** bus tour with Red Clay Tours, which departs at 9:45am daily.

1 Before heading out for the day, fuel up with breakfast at historic **Nelson Brothers Café** in the 4th Avenue Historic District.

2 Get in the car and head to **Birmingham Jail** to see where King penned his "Letter from a Birmingham Jail." A marker out front of the jail commemorates the event.

3 Then head north in your car to **Dynamite Hill,** listed on the National Register of Historic Places. You'll see the homes of Arthur Shores, an NAACP attorney, and activist Angela Davis, where she grew up. Signs from the Birmingham Civil Rights Heritage Trail illustrate the experience.

4 Fortify yourself for the journey ahead with a meal from **Rib It Up.**

5 A scheduled tour of **Bethel Baptist Church** on the north side of town gets you up close and personal with the work of Shuttlesworth and churchgoers who demanded more. After visiting the church, follow the signs peppered throughout the Collegeville neighborhood to get the full story.

Sights

DOWNTOWN

Downtown Birmingham includes the highly walkable **Birmingham Civil Rights Historic District**, where most of the following sights are located.

★ Birmingham Civil Rights Institute

520 16th St. N; tel. 205/328-9696; www.bcri.org; Sun. 1pm-5pm, Tues.-Sat. 10am-5pm; adults $15, seniors $5, students $6, youth $5, children under third grade free

This institute, which opened in 1992, is the centerpiece of the Birmingham Civil Rights Historic District and a stop on the offical U.S. Civil Rights Trail. Through photos, video, and narratives, visitors meet courageous Black residents who galvanized Birmingham's Black community—including children—to embrace nonviolent direct-action tactics. While museumgoers will get a good sense of Birmingham's investment in the movement, other events and touchpoints are treated here, such as Rosa Parks and the Montgomery Bus Boycott. Plan on spending 90 minutes to two hours to fully appreciate what the museum has to offer.

The experience begins in dramatic fashion with a film about early Birmingham and why people felt the need to resist. When the film is complete, voila! The screen lifts, and visitors walk right through to begin their experience.

The institute is separated into five themed galleries. "Barriers" covers social norms before the movement kicked off, when segregation seeped into every corner of life and affected everything from water fountains to barbershops. A display here includes marketing messages that show how language and imagery was used to denigrate Black people. In the "Confrontation" gallery, white Ku Klux Klan robes, an emblem of misplaced power, fear, and violence, are on display. The next gallery, "Movement," showcases the Montgomery bus boycott sparked by Rosa Parks. You'll also see original steel bars from the jail cell that held King for 11 days and from which he wrote "Letter from a Birmingham Jail." The bars stand in a moodily lit room that is motion-activated to play King's reading of the famous letter.

Like many civil rights museums, this one links the U.S. civil rights movement to the larger quest for equality and access globally. The "Human Rights" gallery discusses freedom movements and offers interactive exhibits on events such as Tiananmen Square. Here, you're invited to answer questions about how you feel about current social issues and leave a recorded message. A music booth allows listeners to hear songs keyed to modern social movements. The election of the city's first Black mayor, Richard Arrington, in 1979, is still a point of pride in Birmingham, and visitors get to know him and his administration.

In "Resource," the final gallery, you can listen to an oral history collection, including voices of foot soldiers who marched in the 1963 Children's Crusade.

The museum has a constant flow of guests eager to delve into the story of the movement. King's birthday is the biggest day here: The line into the museum is typically wrapped around the corner as thousands of people file in to remember King and the movement.

TOP EXPERIENCE

★ 16th Street Baptist Church

1530 6th Ave. N; tel. 205/251-9402; www.16thstreetbaptist.org; tours available Tues.-Sat. 10am-3pm; adults $10, students $5

THE BIRMINGHAM CIVIL RIGHTS HERITAGE TRAIL

Colorful signs mark sites on the Birmingham Civil Rights Heritage Trail.

Thanks to the Birmingham Civil Rights Heritage Trail (tel. 800/458-8085; www.birminghamal.org), visitors to Birmingham have the amazing opportunity to walk in the footsteps of demonstrators who turned up the heat, culminating in the Birmingham Campaign, which broke the hold segregation had on this city. Large colorful signs mark the spots where Black residents and civil rights leaders marched and demanded their rights, facing dangerous situations as they pressed to make this country live up to its ideals.

Signs for the trail show up in neighborhoods throughout the city, starting at **Kelly Ingram Park** at the corner of 6th Avenue N and 16th Street, and heading to the **Collegeville** community six miles north of the city center. The signs also appear in **Dynamite Hill** area in northwest Birmingham. Some signs show photos while showcasing backstories and movement trivia. Take a self-guided tour, or hire a tour guide to get more nuanced details about each site. Ask the folks at the **Birmingham Convention & Visitors Bureau** at Vulcan Park and Museum (1701 Valley View Drive; tel. 205/933-1409) for tour guide suggestions.

A longtime gathering center for African American Birmingham residents, 16th Street Baptist Church was the site of mass meetings and rallies during the civil rights movement. Toward the end of the Birmingham Campaign, on May 3, 1963, protestors leaving the church were the targets of police dogs and fire hoses, ordered by the notorious Public Saftey Commissioner Bull Connor. The state-sanctioned violence went on for days. Later that year, on September 15, the church was the target of a Ku Klux Klan bombing that killed four young girls. The girls perished while freshening up in a basement bathroom, preparing for a day of youth-focused activities.

From its beginnings, the church was associated with Birmingham's Black professional class. With something to lose, naturally, there was resistance to joining the civil rights movement. When Rev. John Cross became pastor, that changed. Cross had a relationship with King, who persuaded him to let the church be used as a meeting place for the movement. The church was ideal because of its size and location.

VISITING THE CHURCH

Today, travelers can visit the church, which was designed by Black architect Wallace Rayfield, on **tours** led by church members, many of whom have a connection to the movement: Some can even provide first-hand experiences of the day of the bombing and surrounding events. (Note that tours are not available Sundays, which are dedicated to the Christian experience. Visitors are welcome to worship on Sundays, but no tours are given.) Tours cover the sanctuary and the church basement.

The centerpiece of the church is the Wales Window, presented to the church by the people of Wales in memory of the bombing in 1963. The stained-glass piece is situated at the balcony level in the back of the sanctuary. The window features a crucified man resembling a Black Christ—a bold statement that continues to show parishioners that they are the image of God. The figure's right hand image pushes away hatred and justice while the left offers forgiveness. A rainbow above his head represents the covenant between God and His people.

Other historic elements include the 1911 organ that is still used to play the prelude and opening hymn on Sunday mornings. The dozens of stained-glass windows surrounding the church were donated by individuals and societies to help pay for the construction. The east side windows were blown out in the 1963 bombing, but they have been replaced and are secured and protected.

The downstairs is dedicated to the history of the church, the bombing, and thereafter. Visitors are invited to sit in the Experience Room, which contains some of the church's original pews, and contemplate what happened on September 15, 1963. A

Photos (top to bottom): the Birmingham Civil Rights Institute; inside the Birmingham Civil Rights Institute; 16th Street Baptist Church

FOUR LITTLE GIRLS

On September 15, 1963, a bomb planted by the KKK exploded in 16th Street Baptist Church, killing four young girls: Addie May Collins, 14; Carol Denise McNair, 11; Cynthia Wesley, 14; and Carole Rosamond Robertson, 14 were all in the basement bathroom getting ready for a day of activities when the bomb went off. Carole's mother, Alpha Robertson, lovingly recalled how Carole was wearing her first heels on that special day and carried a Bible in her purse. Several other people were injured in the bombing, including Addie Mae's sister, Sarah Collins, who lost an eye.

Not to be forgotten, two Black male youths, Virgil Ware, 13, and Johnny Robinson, 16, were also killed later that day. Virgil was riding on the handlebars of his brother's bike when he was shot by racist teens. A police officer shot Johnnie in the back, alleging that he was throwing rocks at cars. As John Cross, pastor of 16th Street Baptist Church, said at the time: "People everywhere died."

THE WORLD REACTS

King delivered a eulogy for three of the girls at 6th Avenue Baptist Church (Carole Robertson had a private funeral at St. John's A.M.E. Church). Meanwhile, these child murders horrified people all over the world. When Welsh artist John Petts heard about the bombing, he was moved to create a stained-glass window for the church, according to *The Birmingham Times*.[3] The local Wales newspaper mounted a frontpage campaign inviting residents to donate no more than half a crown (about 15 cents), so donations could truly come from "the people." Petts's creation, which features a crucified man resembling a Black Christ, is still visible in the church today.

SEEKING JUSTICE

In 1965, suspects emerged in the 16th Street Baptist Church bombing: Ku Klux Klan members Bobby Frank Cherry, Thomas Blanton, Robert Chambliss, and Herman Frank Cash. Charges were not pressed at the time because witnesses wouldn't talk and there was a lack of physical evidence.

It was not until decades later that three of four suspects in the bombing were convicted. In 1977, Chambliss was convicted of first-degree murder in connection with the bombing and sentenced to life imprisonment. Thomas Blanton was found guilty of first-degree murder and sentenced to four life terms in 2000. Bobby Frank Cherry was found guilty and sentenced to four life terms in 2002.

REMEMBERING THE GIRLS TODAY

The girls are remembered in Spike Lee's 1997 Oscar-winning feature film, "4 Little Girls." Here in Birmingham, visitors are invited to view Petts's stained-glass tribute, and to contemplate the tragic loss of these four girls, on a tour of 16th Street Baptist Church. Nearby, the Four Spirits statue at the entrance to Kelly Ingram Park also depicts the girls as they were the day they died.

15-minute video centers on King's eulogy and features Sarah Collins (Addie Mae's sister, who lost an eye in the bombing) talking about how the bombing affected her. A gift shop offers church mementos, such as baseball caps, golf shirts, water bottles, lithographs, and keychains.

The church is a stop on the offiical U.S. Civil Rights Trail.

★ Kelly Ingram Park

500 17th St. N; tel. 205/458-8000; 8am-8pm daily; free

This historic four-acre park sits in the Birmingham Civil Rights Historic District, across the street from the Birmingham Civil Rights Institute and kitty-corner to 16th Street Baptist Church. During the civil rights movement, Birmingham Campaign (Project C) participants regularly assembled here for rallies, marches, selective-buying campaigns, and sit-ins.

The park was a key location during the Birmingham Campaign. In May of 1963, toward the end of the campaign, city police and firefighters attacked protestors in the streets along this park. On the orders of Public Safety Commissioner Eugene "Bull" Connor, law enforcement officers hosed the protestors, sicced canines on them, beat them with nightsticks, and hauled them off to jail. Lore has it the high-pressure hoses used by law enforcement could blow off a person's hair; Shuttlesworth was hosed so badly he had to be hospitalized. Children were also among those abused and arrested. A series of now-iconic photographs allowed Americans outside Birmingham to witness the violence for themselves, which helped shift the national conversation on desegregation.

Today, park installations show the women, men, and children who fought to dismantle segregation. The Four Spirits sculpture, which greets visitors at the 16th Street entrance, memorializes the four girls who died in the 1963 bombing of 16th Street Baptist Church. It also features six doves taking flight, honoring the girls as well as two Black boys who were murdered elsewhere in Birmingham that day. A statue of King stands behind Four Spirits.

Another installation depicts the high-pressure water cannons aimed at Black protestors, while a sculpture based on a news photo features a White officer and K9 attacking a Black boy. A limestone piece created by artist Raymond Kaskey features three ministers kneeling in prayer. (Ordained ministers, including Revs. Shuttlesworth, Abraham, and Calvin Woods, Edward Gardener, Charles Billups, Nelson Smith, and J. S. Phipher. King and Bevel were responsible for a lot of civil rights organizing, including during the Birmingham campaign.)

Thanks to the Greater Birmingham Convention & Visitors Bureau, the signs at the sculptures are accompanied by a **mobile phone tour:** Dial tel. 205/307-5455, and punch in the sign number when prompted, for additional background on each piece. A link will also be texted to you which provides comprehensive details about the park.

Kelly Ingram Park is a stop on the offiical U.S. Civil Rights Trail.

A. G. Gaston Motel

1510 5th Ave. N; tel. 205/254-2000; www.birminghamal.gov/gaston

This 32-room motel was a meeting place for movement leaders such as Shuttlesworth, King, and Abernathy, and served as headquarters and press conference staging area for the ACMHR during the 1963 Birmingham Campaign (Project C). King held strategy sessions in the motel's best suite: Room 30. The Birmingham Campaign effectively ended at this hotel too, when the Birmingham Truce was announced at a press conference here on May 10. The next day, the motel was bombed, and a big hole was left below the second-floor Room 30 where Project C planning occurred.

This luxury motel was built by A. G. Gaston, a Black serial entrepreneur and

VOICES OF THE MOVEMENT: REV. CALVIN WOODS

"We didn't have any Black policemen. Black people didn't serve in any political positions and were not clerks in the major stores. We couldn't even drive a golf cart."

—**REV. CALVIN WOODS** recalls how little power Black Americans had in Birmingham in the 1950s. He and his brother, Rev. Abraham Woods Jr., were movement stalwarts who led the first sit-ins of the Birmingham Campaign, a joint effort of Alabama Christian Movement of Human Rights (ACMHR) and the SCLC that launched on April 3, 1963.

For Woods, it was the mere mention of the Montgomery Bus Boycott (1955-1956) that put him in the "thick of the movement." He told his congregation at East End Baptist Church, where he was pastor, that "it was wrong for Black people to not be able to sit down wherever there's a vacant seat after paying their fare on the bus." Five church members reported Woods to Public Safety Commissioner Eugene "Bull" Connor. "I didn't know I had spies from the police commissioner in my congregation," he says. Woods was arrested, sentenced to six months of hard labor, and fined $500. During the Birmingham Campaign, he led the lunch counter committee and helped recruit people to stage sit-ins at downtown stores. He was arrested again and spent five days clearing fields.

After the Birmingham Truce, Woods says movement leaders, including King and Shuttlesworth, identified voting rights as the next front. They decided to focus on Selma.

REMEMBERING THE MOVEMENT

Woods credits Birmingham's Black residents, along with a few White ones, for the sacrifices they made to make Birmingham a more equitable place to live. They were beaten and fired from jobs for doing so. Some even lost their lives. As a result of their activism, "more liberal-minded White people were placed in leadership," says Woods. "As time moved on, a Black mayor, Richard Arrington, was placed, and we added Black council people." (Arrington, who took office in 1979 and served the city for 20 years, was Birmingham's first Black mayor.)

Today, a marker in Woods's honor stands in Kelly Ingram Park.

FREEDOM RIDES: BIRMINGHAM

On May 14, 1961, an interracial group of Freedom Riders (activists who boarded buses to test the veracity of *Boynton v. Virginia Supreme Court*, which outlawed segregation in interstate travel) arrived on a corner in Birmingham. The activists were met by KKK members who attacked the bus riders with metal pipes and other weaponry and dragged some of them to a loading dock. The reporters who followed were beaten too, and *Birmingham Post-Herald* photographer Tommy Langston recalls being choked "nearly to death."[4] The Klansmen tried to demolish Langston's film, but he managed to save a roll, which contained what would become the most famous photo of the photographer's career: Klan members beating up Freedom Riders leader James Peck.

A sign marks where Freedom Riders got beaten by Klan members with permission from local police.

After 15 minutes, police finally showed up. Police Commissioner Bull Connor blamed the "outside agitators"[5] rather than the Klansmen and crowed that police were not on the scene immediately because they were celebrating Mother's Day. Big mistake: Thanks to the reporters and photographers who were present, the whole country knew about the brutal event. Soon, the nation would have no appetite for this type of violence.

Today, a marker on the corner of 4th Avenue and 19th Street marks the site of the bus's arrival. Gold-painted lettering reads: "The riders were severely assaulted while the police watched, yet the youth stood their ground."

millionaire who wanted African Americans to have access to high-end sophistication typically reserved for Whites. Gaston was a friend of the movement and spent his life creating jobs and educational opportunities for African Americans. Local laws prohibited free stays for civil rights leaders, so Gaston was forced to charge a fee to these esteemed guests. It's also worth noting that while Gaston allowed the use of his property, he, like other prosperous Black people, was not entirely sold on the campaign's confrontational nature.

The hotel hosted the likes of musician Harry Belafonte, who was a huge supporter of the movement. Actor and director Phylicia Rashad stayed here as a girl, and this is where Alma and Colin Powell honeymooned. The hotel is currently being restored by the City of Birmingham and the National Park Service. Plans for the restored structure are still underway, but will include a museum component, with Room 30, the strategic hub of the Birmingham Campaign, planned as an interpretive center.

OTHER NEIGHBORHOODS

Birmingham Jail

425 6th Ave. S; tel. 205/254-6369

This jail is where King was locked up for eight days in 1963 after he violated an injunction barring civil rights demonstrations in Birmingham. It's also where he penned his resonant **"Letter from a Birmingham Jail,"** which was written in the margins of newspaper and smuggled out in strips by King's attorney Clarence Jones.

King was imprisoned on Good Friday, April 12, 1963. That very day, Alabama's leading White clergymen issued a public statement calling for an end to demonstrations. They also questioned the movement's willingness to defy the law to achieve civil rights and appealed for "law and order and common sense." King's now-famous letter was a response to their demands. Among its many lessons, the letter makes the moral case for resisting unjust laws.

King's attorney, Clarence Jones, secured bail money from New York Gov. Nelson Rockefeller, and King was bailed out of jail on April 20. Meanwhile, Harry Belafonte reportedly raised money to allow the campaign to keep going.

Today, a marker (unveiled in 2013) commemorating King stands outside the jail. The front of the marker recounts how King, Abernathy, and others marched near Kelly Ingram Park in defiance of a law that prohibited anti-segregation marches. The back of the marker recounts several memorable quotes from the letter, such as the following: "One has not only a legal but a moral responsibility to obey just laws. Conversely, one has a moral responsibility to disobey unjust laws."

Other than this sign, there is not much to see here, certainly not the jail itself. You can, however, touch the actual bars of King's cell by visiting the Birmingham Civil Rights Institute.

The jail is located about a mile south of downtown Birmingham.

Bethel Baptist Church

3233 29th Avenue N; tel. 205/324-8489; www.rebuildbethel.org; Mon., Wed., Fri. 10am-3pm or by appointment, which is preferred; $5

During the civil rights movement, Shuttlesworth was the pastor at this church, which served as headquarters for the ACMHR from 1956 to 1961. ACHMR, which effectively replaced the NAACP when it was outlawed in Alabama in a June 1, 1956, injunction, sought to dismantle segregation in Birmingham.

The church and parsonage were bombed several times, including on Christmas Day 1956. Today, the congregation is still thriving in a larger, modern facility around the corner, while the original church has been preserved. Inside the red brick structure, you will find a two-story sanctuary lit by large windows and a choir stand up front. A basement includes space for fellowship, and the eastern façade is noted for its high gable roof. A Rebuild Bethel campaign is raising money for future restoration of the original Bethel.

This Gothic Revival building in the Collegeville neighborhood in north Birmingham (a few miles north of downtown) is listed on the National Register of Historic Places and is stop on the offiical U.S. Civil Rights Trail. Bethel is surrounded by a quiet residential area consisting of one-story houses, bungalows, double shotguns, cottages, and ranch homes.

Dynamite Hill

When Black Birmingham schoolteacher Mary Means Monk bought property on the traditionally White west side of Center Street North, the spot seemed like a fine place to build a brick home for her family in 1949. Unfortunately, Monk's building permit was denied because she was Black. So, Monk became the lead plaintiff in a class-action lawsuit with other African American residents. In 1950, a federal judge ruled it illegal to bar Black people

Photos (top to bottom): Bethel Baptist Church; marker at Birmingham City Jail; the bomb-damaged home of Arthur Shores in the neighborhood known as Dynamite Hill

from areas that had been reserved for Whites, a protection guaranteed by the 14th Amendment. Within days after the decision, dynamite was thrown into Monk's bedroom.

Monk's experience was not unique: Multiple homes were bombed with dynamite in an effort to keep Black people from moving into so-called White neighborhoods. In fact, close to 50 explosions occurred from 1947-1966 (at churches as well as residences). During this period Birmingham became known as "Bombingham," and the phenomenon became so normalized that one local newspaper summed up the events as "Negro-residence bombings." To this day, residents recall the sound of bombs as a "normal" aspect of everyday life.

The residential part of the Smithfield neighborhood that came to be known as Dynamite Hill was particularly hard hit. Center Street (where Monk's home was located) is a main thoroughfare here and also served as an official racial dividing line: Black people were zoned to live in houses on one side of the street; only Whites were allowed to buy property on the other. Bombing picked up when White residents viewed Black people as encroaching on their turf, like when Black insurance company owner John Drew persisted in buying homes on the "wrong" side of the street.

Today, a series of colorful signs in Dynamite Hill commemorates the tragic events that occurred here. This is a quiet residential area largely inhabited by African Americans. You can visit on your own (parking is easy in this neighborhood), but a guide will add richness and context to your experience. Noteworthy sights include:

- The **Monk family home** (950 N Center St.), where onlookers can see the different-colored bricks that show where post-bombing repairs were made.
- The home of civil rights attorney **Arthur Shores** (1021 N Center St.), which was bombed twice in 1963. The red-brick structure shows residual signs of repairs made after bombing.
- The sprawling Queen Anne home (111th Ct. N), just off Center Street, that nurtured philosopher and activist **Angela Davis.** "Some of my very earliest memories," Davis has recalled, "were the sounds of dynamite exploding."[6]
- The family home of **John and Addine Drew** (1108 Center St.), located on the "White side" of Center Street, near the Davis home. King stayed at this house during the Birmingham Campaign because it was a safe haven, thanks to a tall brick wall (which remains to this day) John Drew built in front of the house and the walls constructed between rooms to protect the family from bombs and bullets if they came through the front while they were sleeping. The Drews' son, Jeff, lives here to this day and recalls the White House calling once to ask for King. Movement leaders often met at this house where they sometimes had contentious discussions about what to do next. He remembers King being quite deft at navigating these arguments.

As you tour this community, please remember to be respectful. This is a residential area where people eat, sleep, and care for their families. Smithfield, where Dynamite Hill is located, is a couple miles west of downtown Birmingham.

Rickwood Field

137 2nd Ave. W; www.rickwood.com; tel. 205/999-5742; $5 per person for groups, free to individuals; reserve in advance

America's oldest professional ballpark, Rickwood Field, was home of the minor league (White) Birmingham Coal Barons, which alternated weekends with the Black Barons, a Negro League team. Babe Ruth played here, as did legendary Negro League players like George "Mule" Settles. Satchel Paige was a Black Barons star, and a teen-aged Willie Mays, a future Hall of Fame center fielder, dazzled Rickwood crowds. So important was this American pastime in Birmingham, the city shut down on opening day, August 18, 1910.

What was the difference between White and Black games? Not much. During Black games, Black onlookers were allowed to sit in covered seats normally reserved for Whites. During Black games, Whites could sit anywhere they wanted; they *chose* to sit away from Black fans. (Segregation is exhausting—like musical chairs, but meaner.)

Adding to the absurdity of the racial division, Eugene "Bull" Connor was a popular play-by-play announcer at Rickwood. It was here that the future public safety commissioner built a reputation that helped usher him into elective office. Connor's racism was on full display as he yelled racial epithets aimed at Black players, referring to them as "monkeys" and declaring that foul balls that soared into the open area where Black fans sat were headed for the "coal bin." When segregated parks were deemed illegal, Connor pressured the owner to disband both teams, according to author Larry Colton.

Rickwood Field is situated on the city's west side, west of Smithfield and downtown Birmingham. Great pains have been taken to maintain its vintage feel, so a visit here is like traveling back in time. Both self-guided and guided **tours** are available; call or email ahead for both (tel. 205/999-5742; cwatkins4@charter.net). Tours vary in length: Rickwood's Clarence Watkins says he can talk all day. On your visit, you'll be able to grab a seat in the bleachers or even walk around the bases. A gift shop features vintage gloves, bats, memorabilia, and posters, among other items.

Rickwood Field, where announcer "Bull" Connor (Birmingham's future public safety commissioner) screamed racial epithets at Black players.

Tours and Local Guides

In Birmingham, a knowledgeable tour guide with roots in the community can make the difference between understanding this period in an academic sense and really feeling it in your bones. Guides are especially helpful for understanding sites outside the Birmingham Civil Rights Historic District, such as Dynamite Hill.

BUS TOUR

RED CLAY TOURS: "FIGHT FOR RIGHTS" TOUR

tel. 205/240-3829; www.redclaytourism.com; 9:45am daily; $60

Red Clay Tours' Fight for Rights Tour provides a deep dive into the local civil rights movement and other progressive causes. Stops include Kelly Ingram Park, 4th Avenue Business District, 16th Street Baptist Church, Phillips High School, where Shuttlesworth was beaten by the KKK in 1957 for trying to register his two daughters, and the Freedom Riders attack site. You may be able to enter some, but not all, of the sights visited. On a drive through the downtown business district, your guide will discuss the small indignities of shopping in segregated stores, such as not being able to try on clothes with a no-return policy and no ability to try on shoes. (Black people were required to take a cardboard cutout to stores to insert into shoes for fitting.)

The tour also includes Dynamite Hill, where your guide will discuss the phenomenon known as Bombingham and the Collegeville neighborhood, home of Bethel Baptist Church, which was the headquarters of Rev. Shuttlesworth's Alabama Christian Movement for Human Rights and the site of several bombing attempts. Guides cover the history of the church and also update the story with information about environmental and economic issues that affect the community to this day. Visitors also learn about Klan member and antisemite J. B. Stoner, whose group was involved in the second bombing at Bethel.

The tour takes three hours. Participants meet at the Shuttlesworth statue in front of the Birmingham Civil Rights Institute. Red Clay provides a comfy, air-conditioned vehicle for transportation. A ride-only version (May-Sept. only; 1:45pm daily; 2 hours; $45) allows travelers to get the narrative from the comfort of the tour bus.

Shopping

In the early 1960s, shopping in Birmingham was political: The 1962 selective-buying campaign was intended to force the integration of retail stores and hiring of Black clerks and salespeople while paving the way for hiring in government jobs. The campaign was patterned after the Montgomery Bus Boycott and took place March-June 1962, just before the Birmingham Campaign kicked off for Easter season. It was supported by Shuttlesworth and the American Christian Movement for Human Rights.

The '62 campaign did cause sales to drop. Retailers made token efforts by removing Whites Only/Blacks Only signs from water fountains and restrooms. But participation in and excitement about it diminished before headway could be made in negotiations. Bull Connor did his part to crush the campaign by arresting picketers.

The selective-buying campaign is immortalized in the documentary

HISTORIC 4TH AVENUE BUSINESS DISTRICT

Throughout the South, Black business districts formed out of necessity due to racial divisions wrought by Jim Crow. In Birmingham, 4th Avenue from 15th to 18th Streets North served the needs of Black residents from the early 1900s.

The district, which has been compared with Harlem and Memphis's Beale Street, was a cultural, social, and retail mecca. Black institutions were planted and nurtured here, including movie theaters, nightclubs, funeral homes, cleaners, barbershops, and professional offices. Historic 4th Avenue Business District was home to **Carver Theatre for the Performing Arts** (1631 4th Ave. N), the last remaining Black theater in town today. The theater, which is under renovation by the City of Birmingham, is also home to the **Alabama Jazz Hall of Fame.**

Carver Theatre for the Performing Arts

The multistory Renaissance Revival **Colored Masonic Temple** (1630 4th Ave. N), which housed the NAACP's legal team, Black professional offices, a ballroom, and a library, also thrived here. The temple sheltered the Freedom Riders in 1961 and is where Shuttlesworth organized demonstrations. The building has fallen into disrepair and is no longer functioning.

Today, you will find restaurants in this revived district, plus a T-shirt and ice cream shop. You can also meet aging foot soldiers at the offices of the **Civil Rights Committee** (1701 4th Ave. N). Businesses that were in operation in 1963 when the Birmingham Campaign took off are **Green Acres Cafe** (which first launched in 1958 at 16th and 6th), **Magic City Barber Shop,** and **Nelson Brothers Café.**

"STAND: Untold Stories from the Civil Rights Movement." Frank Dukes has said the campaign got Birmingham ready for what would come in 1963. And his daughter, Donna Dukes, has written that the campaign gets special credit for being inclusive: Black women were instrumental, and Whites were fully welcome to join.

Today, shoppers in Birmingham have the opportunity to patronize Black-owned businesses in the **Historic 4th Avenue Business District** (1500-1900 4th Ave. N), which sits on the National Register of Historic Places and is a part of the highly walkable Birmingham Civil Rights Historic District.

DOWNTOWN

Clothing

HISTORIC 4TH AVENUE SHIRTS

1703 4th Ave. N; tel. 205/613-7145; Mon.-Sat. 9am-5pm

This T-shirt shop is about so much more than clothing; it's about pride and positivity about the Black experience. Operated by Peggy, Albert, and Al Jr. Logan, this storefront serves as a welcoming community and retail space. Featuring T-shirts emblazoned with empowerment messages such as "HBCU Pride," the store offers a book swap where young people can take a book for free. A bar in the rear serves up jars of candy, snacks, ice cream ($1 cups and pints for $2.60), and sodas. One T-shirt gives a shout-out to Birmingham's historic Black communities, which include Sherman Heights, Ensley, Dolomite, Smithfield, and Norwood.

Barber Shop

MAGIC CITY BARBER SHOP

1711 4th Ave. N; tel. 205/254-9038; Mon. 8am-5pm, Tues.-Sat. 7am-6pm

Barber and beauty shops have always been about so much more than a haircut or new 'do: Historically, barbershops function as community centers where lively debates and vulnerable conversations could be held. They have been so central to African American culture that public health campaigns frequently target these trusted spaces for healthful messages. As such a key part of the cultural fabric of Black life, barber, and beauty shops, they frequently serve as scene setters in TV shows and movies, such as "Coming To America" starring Eddie Murphy and "Barbershop" starring Ice Cube. But you don't have to wait for movies because Magic City Barber Shop is right here.

Festivals and Events

The Birmingham Civil Rights Institute is a hub of activity, including programming and live performances. In addition to the two events listed below, the museum hosts music and games on Martin Luther King Jr. Day, Black History Month activities, and a fundraiser gala for the Fred L. Shuttlesworth Human Rights Award in November (ticket $100-200).

MAY

ANNIVERSARY CHILDREN'S MARCH

520 16th St. N; tel. 205/703-0212; www.bcri.org/bcrievents; free

The spirit of the May 2, 1963, Children's Crusade lives on every May, thanks to this commemorative event hosted by the Birmingham Civil Rights Institute. This annual march, held on a Friday during the first week of May, honors a generation of young activists who changed the world for the better. Today's participants get to walk in the footsteps of these original foot soldiers as they take stock of the violence they faced in their efforts to end segregation.

Participants meet at St. Paul United Methodist Church (1500 6th Ave. N), where youth activists were trained in nonviolent resistance in the 1960s. From here, the children march to sites such as City Hall and Kelly Ingram Park. As they march, students are led in singing freedom songs that Freedom Riders sang, such as "Ain't Let Nobody Turn Me Around." The children who participate in this event are given the same instructions young people received during the Children's Crusade, including walking two by two, staying on

VOICES OF THE MOVEMENT:

CHILDREN'S CRUSADE PARTICIPANT PAULETTE ROBY

"I remember that morning Shelley the Playboy was announcing on the radio, 'Today is D-Day.' And that was our signal."

—**PAULETTE ROBY** was a teenager when she heard this call and became a foot soldier in the Birmingham Campaign.

By late April 1963, the Birmingham Campaign needed an injection of energy and volunteers if it were to continue. King called a meeting with the Central Committee of the Alabama Christian Movement for Human Rights and the Southern Christian Leadership Conference to strategize.

Rev. James Bevel made what some considerd a radical suggestion: that the campaign would benefit by inviting children. Students had previously participated in pickets and sit-ins, but some thought this idea went too far. Still, a call was sent for children to join the movement in earnest. Roby recalls hearing the call to participate from local disc jockeys Shelley the Playboy and Tall Paul. Roby's mother didn't want her teenage daughter to participate in D-Day, but Roby was undeterred: Students defied orders to stay in school and headed to 16th Street Baptist Church to get involved.

On May 2, hundreds of youngsters left the church bound for various destinations, including City Hall and the downtown shopping area. As they marched, the children sang freedom songs and held picket signs. Bull Connor ordered the arrest of many of the young participants. Despite concerns about involving children, the 16th Street mass meeting that night was full.

On May 3 (aka D-Day), more than 1,000 children showed up ready to demonstrate, but Connor and his police and fire troops were ready for them. Shouting orders to disperse, they turned hoses and police-trained attack dogs on the young demonstrators. Unaffiliated Black onlookers threw bricks and bottles at the firefighters, but the children heeded their training in nonviolence and did not leave. Many of them were jailed.

The result of the Children's Crusade was that Birmingham was exposed: Images of what happened to the children here were seen everywhere.

Even President John F. Kennedy was horrified. He sent a representative down to ask that the demonstrations end. He soon called for a civil rights bill to protect African Americans from discrimination. After Kennedy's assassination, President Lyndon B. Johnson signed the Civil Rights Act of 1964, which prohibited discrimination on the basis of race, color, religion, sex, or national origin.

Children's Crusade participant Paulette Roby with fellow foot soldier Raymond Goolsby

the sidewalk, obeying all laws, and avoiding carrying anything that could be construed as being a weapon, such as pocket knives, hair picks, or fingernail clippers.

During the reenactments, streets are blocked off where appropriate. When the marchers arrive at their designated spot, they are met by original foot soldiers from the movement. "The whole idea of the reenactment is to bring the kids from 1963 together with the kids of today," says historian, tour guide, and teacher Barry McNealy.

Participants traditionally include students from the Jefferson County area, and the first reenactment drew 2,000 people. Register in advance to participate as an individual or a group.

JUNE

JUNETEENTH

520 16th St. N; tel. 205/703-0212; www.bcri.org/bcrievents; free

Juneteenth celebrates the end of enslavement: Some enslaved Black people did not get news that President Lincoln had emancipated them until two years later on June 19, 1865. The date, known as "Juneteenth," is now celebrated around the country. Here in Birmingham, the **Civil Rights Institute** commemorates the event on the Saturday closest to June 19. Access to the Civil Rights Institute is free on this date, and galleries come alive with spoken word poetry and music. Outside, **Kelly Ingram Park** is the site of an outdoor festival featuring live entertainment that includes African drumming, dance, and music.

Food

If you are hungry and on foot in the Civil Rights District in downtown Birmingham, the nearby Historic 4th Avenue Business District is a great place to go for family-owned restaurants: a couple have been in operation since the 1960s. Businesses serve up the best soul food traditions and more, with dishes ranging from baked chicken to bean pie. Other popular restaurants can sate your taste for food that's quick 'n' easy or regional in flavor.

DOWNTOWN

Southern and Soul Food

GREEN ACRES CAFE

705 4th Ave. N; tel. 205/251-3875; www.greenacres-cafe.com; Mon.-Wed. 9am-9:45pm, Tues.-Sat. 9am-10:45pm; $3-7

Be prepared for long lines and tasty food at this venerable restaurant in the heart of the 4th Avenue Historic District. Green Acres has operated since 1958, when Charles Gratton opened a location across from 16th Street Baptist Church before moving here. The restaurant is known for its fried chicken wings, pork chop sandwiches, gizzards, and more. You will find neighborhood regulars waiting for their orders to be served up piping hot. Green Acres also has several other locations in the area.

GABRIELLA'S BISTRO

317 17th St. N; Sun. 11am-9pm; $18

Nestled in the Birmingham Civil Rights Historic District, Gabriella's sits just off 4th Avenue and is open only on Sunday. This restaurant is a family affair, where patrons are greeted at the main entrance with a dramatic buffet. You'll find baked chicken, dressing, greens, sweet potatoes, and a variety of desserts. You'll get a lot for your money and exceptional service too. Grab a seat in the intimate dining room or at one of the tables outside.

NELSON BROTHERS CAFÉ

312 17th St. N; tel. 205/254-9098; Mon.-Fri. 7:30am-5pm, Sat. 7:30am-3pm, Sun. 7:30am-5pm; $2-7

Daniel Nelson opened this café in 1943 right by the Carver Theater in the 4th Avenue Historic District. Since then, several generations have helmed this institution, which has served the community through triumphs and trials that include the 16th Street Baptist Church bombing in 1963. During the Birmingham Campaign, Nelson fed civil rights foot soldiers based on what they could afford to pay. The café also fed the professional class who worked out of the nearby Masonic Temple, where the NAACP had offices and a ballroom showcasing the greatest jazz performers of the time.

Today, the café offers breakfast all day (try the fluffy scrambled eggs and grits). It's also a go-to for pork chops, rice and gravy, and sweet potato pie. The eatery has a cozy feel fit for friendly conversation.

Barbecue

RIB IT UP

830 1st Ave. N; tel. 205/328-7427; www.ribitup.com; Tues.-Sat. 10:30am-7pm; $6-13

You're likely to find cars lined up for drive-thru orders at this sit-down restaurant that specializes in barbecue, plus everything else tasty and Southern. Look for barbecue ribs, rib tips, pulled or sliced pork, smothered pork chops, and chicken in addition to fish and an array of sides that include greens, both turnip and collard, fried okra, and crackling muffins. The drive-thru is always hopping, but you can order takeout at the counter or step inside the dining room for full service. There's a full bar in this cozy space.

Photos (top to bottom): Nelson Brothers Café; a hearty meal at Rib It Up; Perfect Note in Hoover

GET INTO THE RHYTHM

- **Carlton Reese, "We've Got A Job"**: A leader of the ACMHR Choir, Reese was known for his ability to craft catchy and easy-to-learn freedom songs from the Black Christian songbook. He wrote this song while languishing in Birmingham Jail where he was arrested for protesting inequality.
- **John Coltrane, "Alabama"**: Coltrane—who was not considered overtly political—composed this song in response to the KKK bombing of 16th Street Baptist Church in 1963.

Hot Dogs

GUS'S HOT DOGS

1915 4th Ave. N; tel. 205/251-4540; www.gusshotdogs.com; Mon.-Fri. 8am-5pm, Sat. 10am-4pm; $3

Serving hot dogs since the late '40s, this is downtown Birmingham's longest surviving Greek-owned hot dog stand. It's tucked into a narrow shotgun-style building next to the parking garage on Fourth Avenue North.

Nightlife

Need to blow off some steam? Birmingham has a few nightlife options, including one suburban venue that is recommended for newer construction, plentiful parking, and a progressive, open outlook that makes you feel welcome.

DOWNTOWN

Bar

PLATINUM OF BIRMINGHAM

821 2nd Ave. N; tel. 205/324-0791; www.platinumbham.com; Tues. noon-3am, Wed. 6pm-midnight, Fri.-Sat. noon-3am

Platinum of Birmingham is where the grown 'n' sexy crowd goes for live entertainment and deejayed music from soul to hip hop in a lounge and bar atmosphere. The club features regular drink specials and dinner buffets. Get ready for theme nights that include Tasty Tuesdays or Mardi Gras. VIP seating is available, and reservations are accepted for special occasions. On weekends, this club stays open later than most. The club is about a five-minute drive from the Birmingham Civil Rights Historic District.

OUTSIDE BIRMINGHAM

Live Music

PERFECT NOTE

1845 Montgomery Hwy. #201, Hoover; tel. 205/986-7280; www.perfectnotelive.com; Wed. 11am-2pm, Thurs.-Sat. 5pm-11pm, Sun. noon-5pm

In suburban Hoover, Perfect Note is just that: This place hosts live music and fine dining that caters to several generations and across racial difference. This place is a labor of love for owners Karen and Tremayne Thompson, who serve up a comprehensive menu ($5-20) that includes Soulful Sundays, meat and three, crab cakes, pecan pie,

Hampton Inn & Suites Birmingham Downtown Tutwiler

turkey burgers, and creamy chicken pasta, to name a few dishes. A full bar offers a range of creative cocktails. Musical acts in this intimate space include jazz and R&B. Show ticket prices vary depending on the act.

Perfect Note is a 15-minute drive from downtown Birmingham, but it's worth the trip. The acts are fresh; space is new, inviting, and intimate; and the service is friendly. This venue draws a multiracial, multigenerational group of patrons seeking to enjoy a night of entertainment in a sophisticated environment.

Accommodations

Birmingham has loads of hotels close to the Birmingham Civil Rights Historic District, including the **Hampton Inn & Suites Birmingham Downtown Tutwiler** (2021 Park Pl.; tel. 205/322-2100; www.hilton.com; $125), the **Elyton Hotel, Autograph Collection** (1928 1st Ave. N; tel. 205/731-3600; www.marriott.com), and the **Redmont Hotel Birmingham, Curio Collection** (2101 5th Ave. N; tel. 205/957-6828; www.curiocollection3.hilton.com).

Transportation

GETTING THERE

Air

Birmingham-Shuttlesworth International Airport (5900 Messer Airport Hwy.; tel. 205/322-2100; www.flybirmingham.com) is located about seven miles from the Birmingham Civil Rights Historic District. A taxi to downtown costs around $12-15 and takes about eight minutes.

Train

Amtrak (1801 Morris Ave.; tel. 800/872-7245; www.amtrak.com; 8:30am-5pm daily) is located downtown, less than half a mile east of the Civil Rights Historic District. Amtrak offers daily service to New Orleans, Atlanta, and New York. If you're coming from Atlanta, the 4.5-hour ride costs about $22.

Bus

Birmingham's **Greyhound station** (1801 Morris Ave.; tel. 205/252-7190; open 24/7) is located in the same downtown transit center where Amtrak is located. Coming from Nashville? Get to Birmingham in a little over 4 hours on a $38 ticket. From Montgomery, get to Birmingham on a $32 ticket and 1-hour-40-minute trip.

Car

To reach Birmingham from:

- **Jackson:** Take **I-20 East** for about 240 miles (3.5 hours).
- **Nashville:** Take **I-65 South** for about 195 miles (3 hours).
- **Atlanta:** Take **I-20 West** for about 145 miles (2.5 hours).
- **Montgomery:** Take **I-65 North** for about 90 miles (1.5 hours).

GETTING AROUND

The Birmingham Civil Rights Historic District is invitingly walkable, but outside this, your best bet for getting around town is by car or taxi. If you're driving or walking through Collegeville to the north of downtown, beware that the neighborhood is known for lots of train tracks.

Parking

Downtown, parking garages are plentiful and cheap (often free for the first hour and $1 for each additional hour with a daily maximum of $9). The Birmingham Civil Rights Institute has two parking lots. Downtown metered parking is also available for $1 an hour, and it's possible to download and use the Park Mobile app to reserve and pay for a space.

The area around Dynamite Hill is residential, so it's easy to park here if you want to look at a house or sign from a sidewalk view.

Public Transportation

Max Transit (1735 Morris Ave.; tel. 205/521-0101; www.maxtransit.org; Mon.-Fri. 5:30am-9pm, Sat. 6am-8pm; adults $1.50, students $1, children five and under free) offers a series of bus routes throughout the city, but most agree that it's not a very helpful way to get around. Find routes online and track buses in real-time with the MyStop Mobile App.

Taxi and Ride-Hailing Apps

Uber and **Lyft** operate in Birmingham. If you need a taxi, call **Birmingham Yellow Cab** (tel. 205/222-2222; www.birminghamyellowcab.com).

Jackson, Mississippi

Mississippi has given America many gifts, including music, food, and cotton when it was king. But it's also left an unforgettable record of racist atrocities whose effects show up in social and economic indicators to this day. The state has been known as ground zero of the civil rights movement due to horrific acts of violence that catalyzed African Americans throughout the nation to mobilize in a sustained, coordinated effort—and Jackson, as the state capitol, is central to that story.

JACKSON'S TOP 3

1. Standing under "This Little Light of Mine" at the **Mississippi Civil Rights Museum:** This 30-foot sculpture of mood lighting gets brighter as more people stand under it—a metaphor to the power of collective change (page 198).

2. Honoring the civil rights leader at the **Medgar Evers Home Museum,** where Medgar and Myrlie Evers lived with their three children and where Medgar was gunned down by a sniper hiding in the vines across the street (page 201).

3. Visiting the **Canton Freedom House** (now a museum), where civil rights leaders stopped on the March Against Fear before continuing on to Jackson (page 217).

Photos (top to bottom): "This Little Light of Mine" in the Mississippi Civil Rights Museum; Medgar Evers Home Museum. Previous: "This Little Light of Mine" in the Mississippi Civil Rights Museum

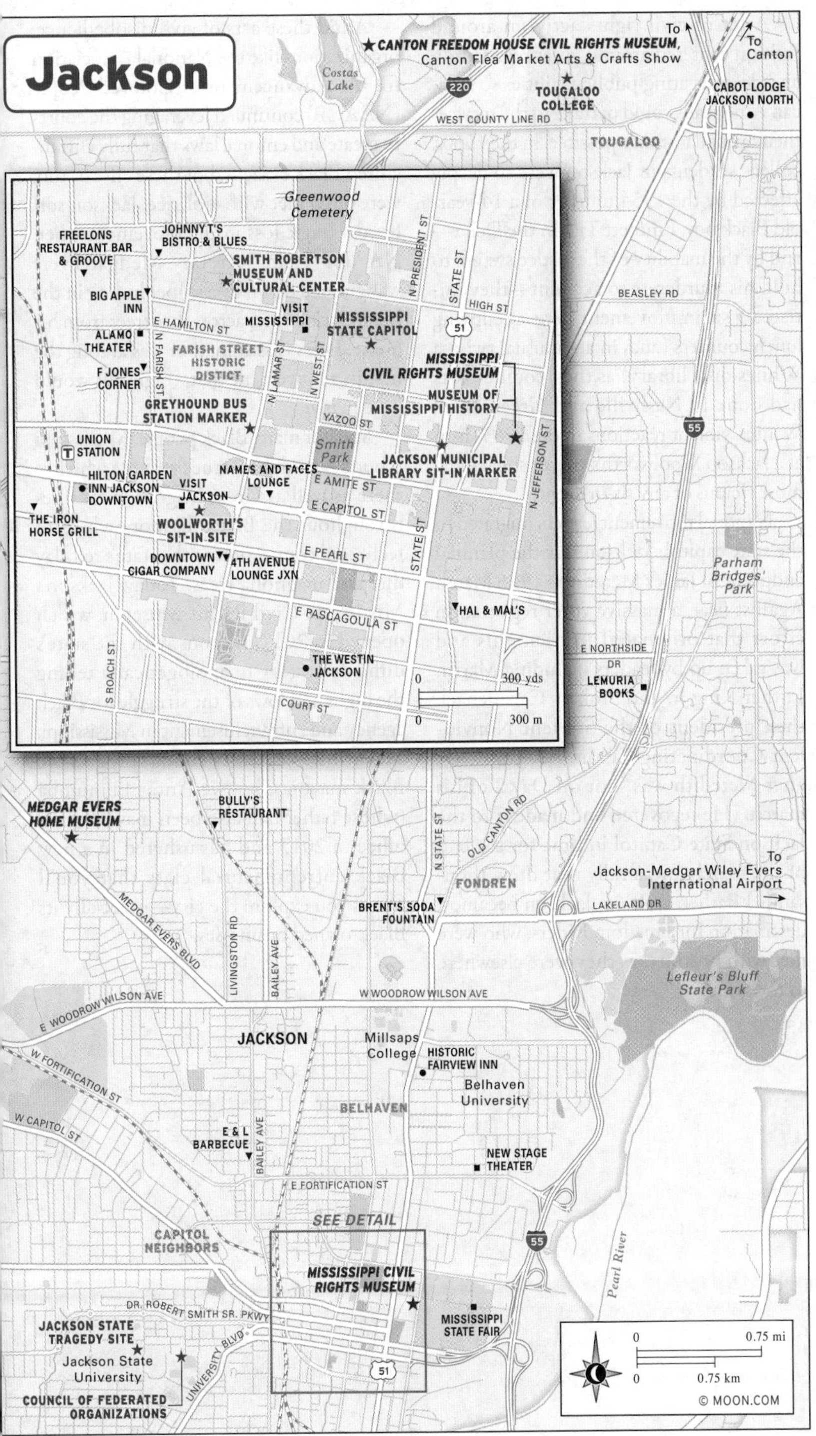

Jackson
CANTON FREEDOM HOUSE CIVIL RIGHTS MUSEUM,
Canton Flea Market Arts & Crafts Show
To
To Canton
Costas Lake
220
TOUGALOO COLLEGE
CABOT LODGE JACKSON NORTH
WEST COUNTY LINE RD
TOUGALOO
Greenwood Cemetery
FREELONS RESTAURANT BAR & GROOVE
JOHNNY T'S BISTRO & BLUES
SMITH ROBERTSON MUSEUM AND CULTURAL CENTER
N PRESIDENT ST
STATE ST
BIG APPLE INN
VISIT MISSISSIPPI
MISSISSIPPI STATE CAPITOL
HIGH ST
51
E HAMILTON ST
ALAMO THEATER
N FARISH ST
FARISH STREET HISTORIC DISTICT
N LAMAR ST
N WEST ST
F JONES CORNER
MISSISSIPPI CIVIL RIGHTS MUSEUM
MUSEUM OF MISSISSIPPI HISTORY
GREYHOUND BUS STATION MARKER
YAZOO ST
UNION STATION
Smith Park
JACKSON MUNICIPAL LIBRARY SIT-IN MARKER
N JEFFERSON ST
NAMES AND FACES LOUNGE
HILTON GARDEN INN JACKSON DOWNTOWN
VISIT JACKSON
E AMITE ST
E CAPITOL ST
THE IRON HORSE GRILL
WOOLWORTH'S SIT-IN SITE
STATE ST
DOWNTOWN CIGAR COMPANY
4TH AVENUE LOUNGE JXN
E PEARL ST
HAL & MAL'S
E PASCAGOULA ST
S ROACH ST
THE WESTIN JACKSON
0
300 yds
COURT ST
0
300 m
BEASLEY RD
55
Parham Bridges' Park
E NORTHSIDE DR
LEMURIA BOOKS
MEDGAR EVERS HOME MUSEUM
BULLY'S RESTAURANT
OLD CANTON RD
N STATE ST
To
Jackson-Medgar Wiley Evers International Airport
FONDREN
LAKELAND DR
BRENT'S SODA FOUNTAIN
MEDGAR EVERS BLVD
LIVINGSTON RD
BAILEY AVE
Lefleur's Bluff State Park
W WOODROW WILSON AVE
E WOODROW WILSON AVE
JACKSON
Millsaps College
HISTORIC FAIRVIEW INN
W FORTIFICATION ST
Belhaven University
BELHAVEN
W CAPITOL ST
E & L BARBECUE
BAILEY AVE
NEW STAGE THEATER
E FORTIFICATION ST
SEE DETAIL
CAPITOL NEIGHBORS
55
Pearl River
MISSISSIPPI CIVIL RIGHTS MUSEUM
DR. ROBERT SMITH SR. PKWY
MISSISSIPPI STATE FAIR
JACKSON STATE TRAGEDY SITE
UNIVERSITY BLVD
Jackson State University
51
COUNCIL OF FEDERATED ORGANIZATIONS
0
0.75 mi
0
0.75 km
© MOON.COM

A lot of civil rights activism around Jackson centered around voter registration and desegregating public facilities so African Americans could partake in the services their tax dollars made possible. In the 1960s, college students in Jackson were so deeply affected by the 1954 murder of a 14-year-old Black boy, Emmett Till, in the Delta—and by the inability of the justice system to hold his murderers to account—they initiated a sit-in movement here, occupying lunch counters (and, in an unusual twist, a Whites-only library) as their counterparts had done in Nashville and Greensboro. Whites' violent reactions to the 1963 sit-in at a Jackson Woolworth's are considered the most vicious of any sit-in event.

National movement leaders migrated to the state capitol: Jackson was the planned endpoint of James Meredith's 1966 March Against Fear, a massive voter registration effort that originated in Memphis and was taken up by leaders including Martin Luther King Jr. and Stokely Carmichael, then president of the Student Nonviolent Coordinating Committee (SNCC), after Meredith was shot on Day 2 of his march. (He recovered and made it to the Jackson State Capitol in time for the end of the march and a rally that drew thousands.) Earlier, in 1961, Jackson became a destination for Freedom Riders, who were met with hostility, as they were elsewhere in the South.

Amid these acts of civil disobedience, organizations like the National Association for the Advancement of Colored People (NAACP) continued leveraging the courts to create and enforce laws that fully enfranchised Black citizens, but these efforts, too, were often met with violence. Jackson suffered a tragic loss in the movement when NAACP Field Secretary Medgar Evers was gunned down by a sniper hiding in the honeysuckle vines across the street from his home. Evers's assassination was among the first in a movement that, tragically, would have many.

Still, for many Black people, Mississippi is home—and that's true for those who live there as well as Great Migration families throughout the Black diaspora who still feel a soul connection to the state's red clay dirt and magnolia trees. Today, Jackson's Mississippi Civil Rights Museum, which opened in 2017, reckons with the state's difficult past by unapologetically telling the highs and lows of the struggle for Black agency and enfranchisement in Mississippi. Meanwhile, Jackson's young, progressive Black mayor, Chokwe Antar Lumumba (whose father had also been mayor), took office in 2017 and has ushered in a new Black entrepreneurial class that you'll feel as you explore the city—especially its Black-owned businesses.

MOVEMENT TIMELINE

1961

March 27: Nine university students, who came to be known as the Tougaloo Nine, hold a read-in to desegregate in the Whites-only Jackson Municipal Library. They are arrested and held for 32 hours.

April 20: Jackson State students George Washington, Doris Bracey, and Walter Jones sit in a Whites-only section of a city bus. They are charged with breach of peace and fined $1,000 when they refuse to move to the "Colored Section." The charges are suspended later.

May 23: James Farmer, John Lewis (still wearing bandages from a racially motivated beating), Martin Luther King Jr., and Ralph Abernathy announce the Freedom Rides would continue from Montgomery to Jackson.

May 24: Twenty-seven Freedom Riders are arrested when they arrive at a Jackson bus station.

May 28: Tougaloo College students stage a sit-in at Woolworth's lunch counter. An angry White mob hurls insults, pours condiments on them, and slaps them. One student, Memphis Norman, is kicked in the head.

July 12: Students from Campbell and Tougaloo colleges stage a sit-in at the Walgreens on East Capitol Street. Two days later, four students from the Tougaloo Nonviolent Action Group join in.

1962

October 1: James Meredith successfully enters the University of Mississippi in Oxford, becoming the first Black student to attend.

1963

May 12: NAACP Field Secretary Medgar Evers sends letters to city officials to let them know the organization's goal is integration. Mayor Allen Thompson responds with a tired segregationist refrain, calling the NAACP outside agitators.

May 20: Evers replies to the mayor on WLBT TV: "What then does the Negro want? He wants to get rid of racial segregation in Mississippi life . . . The Negro citizen wants to register and vote without special handicaps imposed on him alone . . . The Negro Mississippian wants more jobs above the menial level in stores where he spends his money."

May 28: Students sit-in at Woolworth's lunch counter and are met with violence. This event, which is regarded as the most violently attacked sit-in of the '60s, receives national attention.

May 30: Lanier High School students walk out in response to the Woolworth's sit-in.

May 31: Students march down Farish Street in response to other nonviolent actions.

June 12: Medgar Evers is assassinated in the driveway of his Jackson home.

1966: MEREDITH MARCH AGAINST FEAR

June 5: James Meredith departs Memphis on foot for a 220-mile March Against Fear, intended to encourage Black people to register to vote. Jackson, the Mississippi State Capitol, is his destination.

June 6: On the second day of the march, Meredith is shot in the chest by a White man named Aubrey Norvell. He is taken to a hospital in Memphis.

June 7: Leaders, including King, and organizations step in to complete the march with Meredith's blessing. Those organizations were: Student Nonviolent Coordinating Committee (SNCC), the Southern Christian Leadership Conference (SCLC), the Mississippi Freedom

Continued on next page

Democratic Party (MFDP), the Congress of Racial Equality (CORE), and the Medical Committee for Human Rights (MCHR).

June 16: March Against Fear participant Stokely Carmichael is arrested in Greenwood, Mississippi. Upon his release, he asks a roused crowd at a rally what they want. Their response—"Black Power!"—sparks controversy among movement stalwarts.

June 22: Local Whites attack marchers in Philadelphia, Mississippi.

June 24: Marchers set up camp at a school in Canton, just outside Jackson. State troopers attack them with tear gas and rifle butts. Several people are injured.

June 26: The March Against Fear (which Meredith had been able to rejoin) concludes with a rally in Jackson. A crowd of 15,000 attends, making it the largest civil rights demonstration in state history.

1968

Flonzie Brown Wright runs for county election commissioner in Madison County, north of Jackson, winning and becoming the first Black woman elected to office in Mississippi since Reconstruction.

1994-PRESENT

1994: Evers's murderer, KKK member Byron De La Beckwith, is finally convicted thanks to reporting efforts by local journalist Jerry Mitchell.

2013: Jackson elects a young Black mayor, Chokwe Lumumba.

2017: The Mississippi Civil Rights Museum—the state's first-ever state-sponsored civil rights museum—opens.

2020: Mississippi's governor signs a law to remove the state flag, the last in the nation to incorporate the Confederate flag in its design.

James Meredith walks onto the campus of the University of Mississippi, accompanied by U.S. marshals, in 1962.

PEOPLE WHO MADE THE MOVEMENT

Medgar Evers: Mississippi native and the first-ever state field secretary for the NAACP, Evers worked hard to register Black voters, among his other civil rights work. He was assassinated in his driveway in 1963.

James Meredith: The first Black student to attend the University of Mississippi in 1962, Meredith also embarked on a March Against Fear from Memphis to Jackson in 1966 to encourage Black people to attempt to register to vote. Meredith was shot on the way but ultimately completed the march.

Stokely Carmichael: SNCC chairman who caused controversy by shouting "Black Power!" during James Meredith's March Against Fear, a sentiment that was deemed too radical by some.

Medgar insisted the childrens' beds be low just in case bullets came through the window, according to docent Minnie White Watson.

ORIENTATION

Downtown Jackson is roughly delineated by I-55 to the east, George Street to the north, and Silas Brown Street to the south. The western edge of this small downtown district of 65 blocks is near the railroad tracks or two blocks past Gallatin Street, depending on whom you ask. Trending toward mid-rise structures, downtown buildings feature a mixture of neoclassical and beaux-arts-inspired buildings, with some mid-20th-century Brutalist architecture featured.

In the northwest corner of downtown, running north to south, is **Farish Street,** a former Black business mecca that began to decline in the mid-1960s. Though it doesn't bustle like it once did, you'll find a few original restaurants along with some newer ones launched by progressive-minded Jacksonians.

Other Jackson neighborhoods include the area around **Jackson State University,** west of downtown; **Fondren,** a restaurant and shopping district a few miles north of downtown; and the **Tougaloo College** area even farther north (about 10 miles from downtown).

The town of **Canton,** the Madison County seat, and the site of a civil rights museum (along with a lot of history) is about 25 miles north of Jackson.

PLANNING YOUR TIME

It's possible to see Jackson's main sights, including its top two draws, the Mississippi Civil Rights Museum and the Museum of Mississippi History (both closed Mon. and free the third Sat. of each month), plus the Woodworth Chapel at Tougaloo College and Canton Freedom House Civil Rights Museum, in two days. Tours of the Medgar Evers Home Museum are required in advance.

Find tourist information at **Visit**

Mississippi (501 N West St., Ste. 500) or **Visit Jackson** (111 E Capitol St. #102; tel. 601/960-1891; Mon.-Fri. 8:30am-5am). Another resource for Jackson visitors is the **Mississippi Civil Rights Project** website (www.mscivilrightsproject.org). The site offers an extensive map showing where other civil rights protests and events took place throughout the state—and who was involved.

Winters are mild, but **summer heat** in Mississippi can be sweltering and oppressive, so be sure to stay hydrated and pace yourself when walking outdoors. (Buildings here do tend to be air-conditioned.)

CONNECT WITH

Memphis and **Birmingham** are both within a few hours' drive of Jackson and are logical places to stop next. The **Delta** is another logical next stop, especially if you're including Canton in your Jackson trip, as it's already on the way to the Delta.

Two Days in Jackson

DAY 1

You'll see two of Jackson's major sights on this first day and end by getting a taste of historic Farish Street. Be sure to make a reservation in advance to tour the **Medgar Evers Home Museum,** covered here after lunch.

1 Don't waste any time getting to the **Mississippi Civil Rights Museum** so you have plenty of time to see and experience displays in several galleries documenting the movement in the state from 1945-1976. Be sure to stand in the center under the "This Little Light of Mine" 30-foot sculpture of mood lighting that gets brighter the more people stand under it—a metaphor to the power of collective change.

2 Drive over to **Bully's Restaurant** for lunch, featuring soul food fare made with love. This place is relatively tiny, tight, and cluttered, but if you focus your eyes on the art and artifacts hanging from the walls, you'll see expressions of community.

3 Head over to **Medgar Evers Home Museum** for a 45-minute tour (advance reservations required) to see where the movement martyr lived with his family, and was shot and killed in his driveway.

4 Head over to the Jackson State campus to see if you can sneak a peek at the **Jackson State University Marching Band** practice—the public is free to attend evening practices that start around 7:30pm, on the corner of Pondexter street and Terry Road or J R Lynch Street, when the band is not traveling to away games.

5 Have some dinner at **Iron Horse Grill** downtown . . . some Soul Train wings, maybe?

DAY 2

1 Have breakfast on the first-floor bakery and café of Banner Hall, then head upstairs to **Lemuria Books** to get lost in stacks and stacks of books, including a section about African American culture and history topics and books by Black authors.

2 Keep heading north to **Tougaloo College** where you can visit Woodworth Chapel, a civil rights organizing site.

3 Now drive on up into Madison County to Canton, about 25 miles away. Participants in James Meredith's March Against Fear stopped here in 1966 before arriving at the state capitol in Jackson. Today, you can browse civil rights memorabilia and artifacts at the **Canton Freedom House Civil Rights Museum.** (Note that it's closed Sundays and open Saturdays only by appointment.)

4 If you plan to head up into the Delta, continue in that direction from Canton. If not, come on back down to Jackson and visit **Smith Robertson Museum and Cultural Center,** which covers Black history and includes an exhibit on historic Farish Street.

5 Hungry? Pick up some barbecue-sauce-drenched rib tips on a couple slices of white bread from **E & L Barbecue** and take it back to your hotel.

6 Not tired? If you want to dance, a young-adult crowd hangs out at **Freelons Restaurant Bar & Groove.**

Sights

Many historic sites in Jackson, including the Medgar Evers Home Museum and Tougaloo College, are stops on the **Mississippi Freedom Trail** (www.mississippimarkers.com/civil-rights), a series of markers that commemorates people and events that were pivotal in the civil rights movement. These brown-and-orange markers were first unveiled in 2011 as part of the 50th commemoration of the 1961 Freedom Riders. (Some older historical markers, which are green, are also included.) The Mississippi Freedom Trail is an official part of the U.S. Civil Rights Trail.

Some markers, such as those at the Medgar Evers Home Museum, are accompanied by a museum or other information source. Others stand on their own on sites where there may be little other than the marker to evoke the important events that happened there. (This is the case at the Woolworth's Sit-In Site and the Read-In Site at Jackson Municipal Library.) Markers are spread out, so it's best to drive between them.

You can find the full list of markers on the Freedom Trail website. In addition to those listed below, other Freedom Trail stops in Jackson include the **Jackson State Tragedy Site** near the entrance to Jackson State University (1400 John R. Lynch St.), where Black students Phillip Lafayette Gibbs and James Earl Green were killed by law enforcement officers on May 15, 1970. Along with other students, Gibbs and Green were protesting against police intimidation, harassment by Whites driving through campus, and the Kent State University killings of unarmed students by the Ohio National Guard on May 4, 1970. Law enforcement had come to campus to quell this student unrest.

DOWNTOWN

Two Mississippi Museums

The big draw for Jackson, Mississippi, is Two Mississippi Museums, the shared name of both the Mississippi Civil Rights Museum and the Museum of Mississippi History, which covers state history dating back to its indigenous inhabitants. The two museums are housed in the same modernist structure with a shared lobby and courtyard. It's possible to fully experience both of these museums (which, together, comprise eight galleries and 700,000 square feet) in one day. Dual admission ($15, seniors $13, children ages 4-18 $8, under 3 free) is available. If you're choosing just one, the Civil Rights Museum, which is full of interactive displays and sensory experiences, is the more engaging of the two.

TOP EXPERIENCE

★ MISSISSIPPI CIVIL RIGHTS MUSEUM

222 North St., Ste. 2205; tel. 601/576-6800; www.mcrm.mdah.ms.gov; Tues.-Sat. 9am-4pm; adults $15, seniors $13, children ages 4-18 $8, children under 3 free

Opened in 2017, the Mississippi Civil Rights Museum honors the state's role "as ground zero in the U.S. Civil Rights Movement" with interactive and sensory experiences that illustrate African American courage and resistance to the White racial hierarchy from 1945-1976.

This museum offers many ways to transport yourself back into the not-too-distant past through sound, film, and touchable displays. Exhibits include the wooden door of Bryant's Grocery & Meat Market. A 14-year-old Black child, Emmett Till, walked through this door in the Mississippi Delta in 1955, not knowing that the action would be among his last as a false accusation against him and his brutal murder soon followed. Also on view is a story quilt by Hystercine Rankin that illustrates her move to the home of her formerly enslaved grandfather after the racially motivated murder of her father.

The displays don't mince words about the terror of living in the Jim Crow South. One installation features an endless list of lynching victims of all races and genders—mostly Black, though. You'll see mugshots of Freedom Riders who defied the odds to end segregation. The museum's **"This Little Light of Mine" gallery** features a light display that functions as a moving metaphor for racial healing: Starting at a dim purplish color, the more visitors move to the center of the room underneath the display, the brighter it gets. And that's just a sneak peek. The museum is a stop on the official U.S. Civil Rights Trail.

MUSEUM OF MISSISSIPPI HISTORY

222 North St.; tel. 601/576-6800; www.mmh.mdah.ms.gov; Tues.-Sat. 9am-4pm; adults $15, seniors $13, children ages 4-18 $6, children under 3 free

The Museum of Mississippi History provides a broad view of the state's background. Your visit begins with a film that offers context. Next, several galleries proceed from the Native American experience (focusing on the local Chickasaw and Choctaw tribes) to the advent of European exploration and trade to statehood and the enslavement of Africans whose bodies and skill produced the booming cotton economy. Galleries also feature modern-day highlights and accomplishments. But you know what sticks out? Observing artifacts and examples of historic women's clothing and soldiers' uniforms, you're left thinking how *tiny* people were back in the old days.

This museum does justice by Mississippi's Native American citizens through a rich telling (and showing) of indigenous history and customs, and by offering translations into Choctaw and Chickasaw languages. The exhibits were created with expertise from native populations who still call the state home.

Admission to the Museum of Mississippi History is free on the third Saturday of every month.

Mississippi State Capitol

400 High St; tel. 601/359-3114; www.legislature.ms.gov; Mon.-Fri. 8am-5pm; free

This National Historic Landmark is the seat of government, a 171,000-square-foot building with a beaux-arts edifice built on the grounds of the former state penitentiary. It's significant to our story as the site where James Meredith's March Against Fear concluded in June of 1966. A crowd of 15,000 gathered here the day the march ended, making it the largest civil rights demonstration in state history.

The building's first floor features portraits in the Hall of Governors dating back to 1798 when Mississippi was a territory. A central rotunda on the second floor depicts the face of Lady Justice, paintings, and hundreds of light fixtures. An 8-foot-tall, 15-foot-wide eagle tops the exterior dome, which is gilded in gold leaf. The Legislature is on the third floor with other state offices, including the governor's. Guided tours are available Mon.-Fri. 9:30am, 11am, 1 pm and 2:30 pm. Reserve by contacting 601/359-3114 or tours@house.ms.gov. Self-guided tours may be taken while the building is open. Pick up a tour sheet at the visitors desk on the first floor, north side.

Woolworth's Sit-in Site

On May 28, 1963, three Black Tougaloo College students (Memphis Norman, Pearleana Lewis, and Anne Moody, who later wrote a memoir called *Coming of Age in Mississippi*) bravely took seats at an all-White Woolworth's lunch counter—much like their passionate, justice-seeking counterparts had done at lunch counters in Greensboro, North Carolina, and Nashville in 1960. The nonviolent protestors were attacked by an angry mob of White thugs who threw stuff at them, including dumping seasonings on them. In fact, the sit-in at the Jackson Woolworth's is considered the most violent of the 1960s sit-ins. After Norman was attacked by a crowd member, then arrested, White Touglaoo student Joan Trumpauer took a seat, along with Lois Chafee, a White faculty member. Professor John Salter, a White ally and mentor, was punched, and White segregationists dumped a container of sugar on Trumpauer's head.

A Mississippi Freedom Trail marker on Capitol Street across from The Elite Restaurant (141 E Capitol St.) memorializes this violent and pivotal movement. You can learn more about the sit-in at the Smith Robertson Museum and Cultural Center here in Jackson and at the National Center for Civil and Human Rights in Atlanta, which contains an interactive lunch counter simulation that allows visitors to see just how much violence and intimidation they can stand.

FARISH STREET HISTORIC DISTRICT

Smith Robertson Museum and Cultural Center

528 Bloom St.; tel. 601/960-1457; Mon.-Fri. 9am-5pm, Sat. 10am-1pm; adults $7, seniors $5, children $4. Only cash and checks accepted

This museum may be overshadowed by the shiny, new civil rights museum, but you should see this locally produced venue for yourself. Erected in 1894 as the first school for African Americans in Jackson

VOICES OF THE MOVEMENT: MARCH AGAINST FEAR LEADER JAMES MEREDITH

"[The march] was about revealing the all-pervasive fear that kept Blacks in their place. And the main objective was to challenge that fear."

—JAMES MEREDITH, who embarked on a 220-mile trek from Memphis to Jackson, Mississippi in early June of 1966.

The purpose of the march was to persuade African Americans to register to vote, despite White supremacist pressure to stay away from the ballot box. For Black people, the risks of registering to vote ranged from violence to loss of livelihoods. (When Black Delta resident Fannie Lou Hamer persisted in registering, she and her husband were kicked off the land they worked and put out of their home.) The march started at Memphis's famed Peabody Hotel, and Meredith, who was 32 at the time and accompanied by a few companions, donned a white pith helmet and carried a walking stick.

On the second day of the march, Aubrey James Norvell, a middle-aged White man from Memphis, shot Meredith in the chest with a 16-gauge shotgun just south of Hernando, Mississippi. From a gully, Norvell screamed, "James Meredith! James Meredith—I only want Meredith!" the Congressional Record from June 13, 1966, shows. Upon hearing the scream, the men walking with Meredith "hit the dirt," reported Claude Sterrett, 21, of New York. "When I was shot, I was by myself," Meredith recalls today. "There were other people walking with me, they moved out of the way. I don't blame them. I was trying to get out of the way, too."

Meredith was hospitalized in Memphis. Major civil rights organizations (the Southern Christian Leadership Conference, NAACP, and Con-

(aka the "Mother School," as it was commonly known), this museum and cultural center contains an expansive view of Black history, beginning with a Middle Passage installation. The Memories On Farish Street vintage photo exhibit documents Jackson's bustling Black community, which was established before the end of the Civil War and became a center for Black business and political activity. The elementary school was named for Smith Robertson, Jackson's first Black alderman, and author Richard Wright is among is notable graduates. The school shuttered in 1971, but a community effort helmed by Jessie Mosley and Alferdteen Harrison led to the establishment of a museum in 1984.

Interactive exhibits and filmography showcase Mississippi's role in the civil rights movement, with special emphasis

gress of Racial Equality) and leaders (including Dr. Martin Luther King Jr., Rev. James Lawson, Floyd McKissick, and Stokely Carmichael) stepped in to complete the march.

There were allies along the way—Minnie Lou Chinn, whose husband was an enforcer for CORE, recounted how she fed King, Hosea Williams, and Ralph Abernathy "baloney sammiches" when they came to her Canton home—but the march was not easy. Marchers received death threats, and state police lobbed tear gas at them as they tried to set up tents at a local school in Canton, just outside Jackson. Meanwhile, internal tensions seeped into the mission when SNCC's Carmichael and field organizer Willie Ricks let out a cry for "Black Power," according to SNCC records. The phrase had previously been used in Alabama but was deemed too radical by more conservative elements of the movement and the greater Black community. King reportedly felt the phrase would be perceived as a rejection of the movement's nonviolent stance.

More than 4,000 African Americans registered to vote along the march route as they defied White violence and intimidation to secure their constitutionally protected right. Meredith was able to join the completion of the march, which ended with a rally at the state capitol grounds in Jackson. With a crowd estimate of about 15,000, it was the largest civil rights demonstration in state history. Today, a **Mississippi Freedom Trail marker** on the capitol grounds (400 High St.) marks the site. Another marker in North Mississippi in Hernando recognizes the spot where Meredith was shot.

Meredith makes his home in Jackson today. An Air Force veteran who grew up in Attala County, Mississippi, near Kosciusko where Oprah Winfrey grew up much later, he was no stranger to activism when he embarked on the march: In 1962, he fought (successfully) to become the first Black student to enter the University of Mississippi. Still, Meredith says the March Against Fear was "the most important thing I ever did." In clarifying the aim of his campaign, he says, "James Meredith started a *Walk* Against Fear. A walk is an exercise of U.S. citizens' right and privilege to use the highways and byways to move from one point to another."

on the background and work of NAACP field secretary Medgar Evers. A Woolworth's luncheonette counter exhibit tells the story of the May 28, 1963, sit-in, which is regarded as the most violently attacked sit-in of the '60s. Life-size mannequins represent the resisting Tougaloo students, while life-size photos of angry, intimidating White protestors help transport visitors to a tense time and space.

OTHER NEIGHBORHOODS

★ Medgar Evers Home Museum

2332 Margaret W Alexander Dr.; tel. 601/977-7839, tel. 601/979-3935, tel. 601/977-7706, or tel. 601/977-7935; https://civilrightstrail.com/attraction/medgar-evers-home/; guided tours by appt.; free, but donations are accepted

The home of Medgar and Myrlie Evers,

MEDGAR EVERS

For more than a decade, Mississippi native Medgar Wiley Evers threw his life and passion into making Mississippi a better place for Black people. Evers was born in Decatur, Mississippi, and went into the segregated U.S. Army where he fought in the Battle of Normandy in 1944. The GI Bill paved the way for Evers to attend Alcorn Agricultural and Mechanical College (now Alcorn State University) where he met and married Myrlie, and they eventually had three children. Evers wanted to attend law school at the University of Mississippi in Oxford and made an attempt to do so in 1954, the same year *Brown v. Board of Education* desegregated public schools; however, he was unsuccessful. (Integration did not occur at the university until 1962, when James Meredith was escorted onto campus by federal forces.)

In 1952, the couple moved to the Delta where Evers sold insurance—an experience that exposed him and Myrlie to a crushing poverty that made them want to do more. In 1954, Medgar became the first state NAACP field secretary where he investigated civil rights violations, registered people to vote, and organized protests and economic boycotts.

Evers was assassinated at his ranch home in Jackson, Mississippi, in 1963, by Byron De La Beckwith, a Ku Klux Klan member who hid in the bushes across the street and shot Evers with a rifle. Evers is buried in Arlington National Cemetery and received full military honors at his funeral. White Mississippi juries failed—twice—to reach a verdict to convict De La Beckwith, though he was finally tried and sentenced to life in prison in 1994, thanks to dogged reporting efforts by local journalist Jerry Mitchell and to state prosecutors who were willing to take up the case yet again.

Myrlie, who eventually remarried, continued her activism and public service work in a variety of capacities. She retired from public life in 2018, continuing to serve as chair of the **Medgar and Myrlie Evers Institute** (www.eversinstitute.org), a Jackson-based organization that preserves Medgar Evers's legacy, promotes justice through social and economic change, and engages youth.

The **SNCC Digital Gateway** website (www.snccdigital.org), maintained in partnership with Duke University, is a great place to learn more about Evers's work as an NAACP field secretary.

now known as the Medgar and Myrlie Evers Home National Monument, sits in a quiet Jackson neighborhood. An early martyr in a movement that would create many, Evers, a civil rights leader, was gunned down in this driveway in 1963, steps away from his wife and three children: Darrell, Reena, and James. After Evers's murder, the family moved to California and deeded the home to Tougaloo College to serve as a museum. The Medgar and Myrlie Evers Institute, however, is headquartered in Jackson.

Working tirelessly for civil rights, Evers traveled the state investigating acts of racial terror, and he and his wife were always aware of the danger associated with his work, according to curator Minnie White Watson. Medgar Evers designed the three-bedroom family home with defense in mind, insisting on a side—not

GET INTO THE RHYTHM

- **Phil Ochs, "Ballad of Medgar Evers"**: This tune and its melancholy guitar strum captured the sadness of losing Medgar Evers and the miscarriage of justice when two all-White juries failed to convict his assassin. Matthew Jones and the SNCC Freedom Singers performed this song in tribute to Evers. The group toured and sang this song and others to help raise money for the movement.
- **Nina Simone, "Mississippi Goddamn"**: Released in 1964, after the 1963 murders of Medgar Evers and four girls in the 16th Street Baptist Church bombing in Birmingham, Alabama, this raw, damning anthem is what Simone called her first civil rights song. In 2019, the song was admitted to the Library of Congress's National Recording Registry for its relevance.

front—door, and placing the children's mattresses on the floor and raising window heights to avoid the spray of bullets. Today, the home is frozen in time, and loving touches of family life are found throughout, including faded family photos and children's toys. Peek through the living room window and you'll see the spot across the way where his assassin—who escaped conviction until 1994—lay in wait.

The home is now a National Historic Landmark, and a stop on the official U.S. Civil Rights Trail. It's also a stop on the Mississippi Freedom Trail, and a Freedom Trail marker outside shows family photos, including the iconic *Life* magazine cover of Myrlie comforting her weeping son, Darrell, at Medgar Evers's funeral. Guided **tours** of the home, available only by appointment, last 45 minutes.

Tougaloo College

500 County Line Rd.; tel. 601/977-7870; www.tougaloo.edu

Tougaloo College, a tiny liberal arts campus and a historically Black institution, was founded by the American Missionary Association in 1869 to train teachers and provide industrial education. It was formerly the Boddie Plantation. During the civil rights movement, the college served as a sanctuary for movement workers in the Jackson area—a risky decision, it turns out: Though Tougaloo is a private institution, sheltering activists put their charter in jeopardy of revocation. In 1961, nine students from this school made history when they held a read-in to force the desegregation of the Jackson Municipal Library.

Woodworth Chapel, a 3,250-square-foot Queen Anne-style church at the center of campus, is where civil rights leaders openly exhorted and secretly strategized the gospel of peaceful resistance and social change. Inside, warm wood paneling and high beams evoke the greats who have come through these doors, including Evers, King, Fannie Lou Hamer, Malcolm X, Carmichael, Julian Bond, Ralph Bunche, Roy Wilkins, and Robert F. Kennedy. April 1964 generated the most integrated

THE TOUGALOO NINE READ-IN

photos of the Tougaloo Nine at the Mississippi Civil Rights Museum

In 1961, a group of African American students from Tougaloo College, seeking books from the all-White Jackson Municipal Library, were told, "There's a colored library on Mill Street. You are welcome there." The books weren't available in the city's Black library, though, so the nine students took action, staging a "read-in" to force the desegregation of the Whites-only library.

As NAACP Youth Council members, the nine students (four women and five men) had been trained by Medgar Evers in using nonviolent resistance techniques, and when police ordered them to retreat to the coloreds-only Carver library, they simply refused. Police arrested the students, who were jailed for two days and convicted of breach of peace, fined, and given a 30-day suspended sentence. When the Black community (including Medgar Evers) came to support the students at court, police sicced dogs on them and advanced on them with batons, an action Evers said only fostered greater unity in the Black community and elevated the power of the NAACP. Evers was among those injured at the hands of police.

The students' sentence was suspended after they agreed to forego further demonstrations. However, after the read-in, protests at Jackson State College (now JSU) and the city jail ensued. Ultimately, the read-in sparked other youth actions across the state to desegregate public accommodations such as swimming pools, parks, stores, and theaters. Because their actions mattered, we will today know the Tougaloo Nine by their names: Meredith Anding Jr., James "Sammy" Bradford, Alfred Cook, Geraldine Edwards Hollis, Janice Jackson, Joseph Jackson Jr., Albert Lassiter, Evelyn Pierce, and Ethel Sawyer.

Today, a Mississippi Freedom Trail marker at the corner of State Street and Yazoo Street in downtown Jackson commemorates the activists. Learn more details about the read-in at the **Mississippi Civil Rights Project** website (www.mscivilrightsproject.org).

Photos (top to bottom): Minnie White Watson, docent at the Medgar Evers Home Museum; family photos at the Medgar Evers Home Museum; inside Tougaloo College's Woodworth Chapel, a venue for civil rights activists in the '60s (left); commemorative sign outside Tougaloo College (right)

audience the chapel had ever seen when folk singer Joan Baez performed.

Today, a well-worn footpath, now painted red, leads from the college entrance to the chapel. Call 601/977-7871 to arrange a free guided tour of the chapel. A Mississippi Freedom Trail marker in front of the chapel honors the entire Tougaloo community—students, faculty, and staff—who made the campus an oasis of safety during the movement.

Tougaloo College is a stop on the official U.S. Civil Rights Trail.

Council of Federated Organizations at Jackson State University

1017 John R Lynch St.; tel. 601/979-4348; www.jsums.edu/cofo; tours by appointment; free

Jackson State University is home to the Council of Federated Organizations (COFO) office, which was the state headquarters for the Mississippi Civil Rights movement. The umbrella organization, designed to enhance solidarity between civil rights groups, was envisioned by Bob Moses, SNCC field secretary, and sanctioned by Dr. Aaron Henry and Medgar Evers. Officially organized in 1962, COFO focused on voter education and registration and was instrumental in organizing the 1963 Freedom Vote, the Mississippi Freedom Democratic Party (MFDP), co-founded by SNCC community organizer Fannie Lou Hamer, and the 1964 Mississippi Summer Project, also known as Freedom Summer.

Hamer notably ran for Congress in 1964 on the MFDP ticket against Democrat Jamie Whitten. She spoke at the Democratic National Convention that year in an effort to get her party recognized; her appearance came after Rita Schwerner, wife of Michael Schwerner, one of three civil rights workers murdered by the Klan near Philadelphia. During a campaign speech, Hamer said: "My opponent has done nothing to help the Negro in the Second Congressional District. If I'm elected as congresswoman, things will be different. We are sick and tired of being sick and tired. For so many years, the Negroes have suffered in the state of Mississippi. We are tired of people saying we are satisfied, because we are anything but satisfied."

The COFO office now functions as a museum run by Jackson State's Margaret Walker Center. Inside, photographs and interpretive exhibits walk visitors through these movement activities that showcase a time when Black Mississippians took freedom into their own hands. A Mississippi Freedom Trail marker pays tribute to COFO volunteers.

Tours and Local Guides

SELF-GUIDED TOUR

JACKSON CIVIL RIGHTS MOVEMENT DRIVING TOUR

308 E Pearl St., Ste. 301; tel. 800/354-7695; www.visitjackson.com; Mon.-Fri. 8:30am-5pm

The City of Jackson offers a free self-guided driving tour map of four neighborhoods featuring 81 sites critical to the Jackson movement, what city officials call "the greatest grassroots upsurge in Mississippi history" over four decades. The Jackson movement describes an early 1960s period of nonviolent, direct action protests to end racial discrimination in public accommodations. The period also encompassed Freedom Riders, who rode into Jackson in 1961 to demonstrate against segregated interstate transportation facilities. James Meredith's March Against Fear is counted as well.

Covered sites are located in four

neighborhoods: downtown Jackson, the Jackson State University area, Medgar Evers's neighborhood, and the Tougaloo College community. Stops include homes, churches, businesses, and public buildings. You'll drive by the former site of the state's first student-led lunch counter sit-in, which occurred at Walgreens drug store July 12, 1961, the former Jackson Municipal Public Library (where the Tougaloo Nine held a read-in), and Soul Scissors Barbershop (1104 J. R. Lynch St.), the former office of the Jackson Nonviolent Movement. The drive takes about an hour.

Shopping

Jackson's Fondren neighborhood, about five miles north of downtown, is a walkable area and a good place to shop, with cute boutiques and a variety of eateries. Shopping includes art, designer duds, and consignment finds. **Banner Hall** is located here and houses a variety of merchants, from stationery to baked goods to books at Lemuria Books, one of the city's can't-miss experiences.

BOOKS

LEMURIA BOOKS

4465 I-55 N; tel. 601/366-7619; www.lemuriabooks.com; Mon.-Sat 8am-7pm, Sun. 10:30am-3pm

A stream of sunshine warms Lemuria's second-floor haven, where rooms are lined with tall shelves of books. Mississippi is known for producing some of the nation's most talented writers, many of whom have appeared here, including Jesmyn Ward and Kiese Laymon. Lemuria, not a Black-owned business, has everything a good bookstore has, including vintage furniture, savvy staff, and the most important and latest books about the civil rights movement. The store is also a major sponsor of the Mississippi Book Festival held every August.

Lemuria Books

Arts and Culture

THEATER

NEW STAGE THEATER

1100 Carlisle St.; tel. 601/948-3533; www.newstagetheatre.com; tickets $25-35

This hidden gem, the only professional regional theater in Mississippi, was founded in 1965 to create a space for both integrated casting and audiences. Nestled on a quiet street in Jackson's Belhaven area, the theater offers plays and programs for children and adults. Some plays, such as *Not Us, Then Who? Freedom Rides to Freedom Summer,* written by Sharon Miles to coincide with the 2017 opening of the Mississippi Civil Rights Museum, aim to tell hard truths about Mississippi's past; others evoke tears and laughter and may be accompanied by song. Every year, a history-themed play is offered. Past themes have included the Underground Railroad and the Montgomery bus boycott. The theater also features classics like "A Christmas Carol" and the Mississippi New Play Series. Shows run September through mid-July.

ALAMO THEATER

333 N Farish St.; tel. 601/352-3365

This historic 750-seat theater was once an icon on historic Farish Street. Today, a refurbished sign marks the theater (the third Alamo in Jackson) that served the Black community with Westerns and other movies and live acts like B. B. King and Nat King Cole when it opened in 1949. The venue closed in 1983 and fell into disrepair. It has since been refurbished and hosts a variety of art, dance, music, and theater events.

Festivals and Events

Mississippians possess strong pride of place, and the festivals and events serve to express the state's unique brand of Southern culture.

AUGUST

MISSISSIPPI BOOK FESTIVAL

400 High St.; www.msbookfestival.com; 9am-5pm on a Saturday in August; free admission

Billed as a literary lawn party, this festival features national, regional, and local authors, panels, and booksellers. Situated on and around the Mississippi State Capitol, the festival extends to Galloway United Methodist Church (305 N Congress) and surrounding streets. As many as 10,000 people have attended past events. Featured authors have included National Book Award Winner Angie Thomas, a Jackson native and author of the post-Ferguson young-adult novel *The Hate U Give;* Gulfport-born former U.S. Poet Laureate Natasha Trethewey; Jabari Asim; and W. Ralph Eubanks.

OCTOBER

MISSISSIPPI STATE FAIR

1207 Mississippi St.; tel. 601/961-4000; www.mdac.ms.gov; $5

In 1962, protesters boycotted and picketed the segregated Mississippi State Fair, which had Whites-only and Blacks-only days. Today the fair is open and welcoming to all—regardless of the day. The annual Mississippi State Fair begins the first Wednesday in October each year and runs for 12 days. See the pig races, but first, stop by the Biscuit Booth for a free Southern-style biscuit baked by employees at the Mississippi Department of Agriculture &

JACKSON STATE UNIVERSITY MARCHING BAND

Football culture is palpable in the South, but the marching band culture of historically Black colleges and universities takes halftime showmanship to a whole other level. Dubbed the **Sonic Boom of the South**, Jackson State University's marching band expertly performs traditional marches like "Rolling Thunder" and spirit tunes like "Get Ready," plus popular tunes such as Beyonce's "Crazy In Love" and Frankie Beverly's "Before I Let Go." This is all done while doing elaborately choreographed dance routines.

members of the Jackson State University Marching Band

Find a **game schedule** at www.gojsutigers.com/sports, and buy tickets at ticketmaster.com or call tel. 601/979-2420. A real treat is watching the band practice during fall semester outside practices. If you're lucky, you can catch an outdoor practice at the corner of Poindexter Street and Terry Road or the corner of J R Lynch Street and Poindexter Street around 7:30pm or 8pm until 10pm on weekdays August-December.

Commerce: Holding one drenched with syrup while watching the pigs "fly" totally completes the experience. Visit the petting zoo, livestock shows, or the antique and classic car show. Musical performances celebrate independent music with Mississippi and Southern roots. Ride tickets are just $1.25.

Food

Be fancy if you want to, but in Jackson the focus is on homestyle eateries that emphasize flavor, freshness, and memories of home. The Black-owned restaurants included here are cherished because of their consistency and the kindness of their owners and staff.

FARISH STREET HISTORIC DISTRICT

Sandwiches

BIG APPLE INN

509 N Farish St.; tel. 601/354-9371; Tues.-Fri. 7:30am-8pm, Sat. 8am-8pm; $2

Big Apple Inn

On Farish since the 1930s, Big Apple Inn is known for its sandwiches—namely pig ears—which bring patrons blazing through the door daily. The pig ears are cut into three pieces (so they fit the diminutive buns Big Apple Inn cooks use for everything), then slathered in mustard sauce, slaw, and hot sauce. Other sandwiches, such as bologna, and the usual hamburgers and hot dogs are also available. The quick bites served in this humble storefront debuted at 10 cents apiece and now cost a whole $1.66. The restaurant owner is Mexican American. Ordering tamales is like asking for a secret weapon: Big Apple Inn staffers quietly disappear to the back, only to emerge with a steaming hot package of six or a dozen.

Southern and Soul Food

IRON HORSE GRILL

320 W Pearl St.; tel. 601/398-0151; www.theironhorsegrill.com; Mon.-Wed. 11am-9pm, Thurs. 11am-10pm, Fri.-Sat. 11am-midnight, Sun. 10:30am-3pm; $11-19

Iron Horse Grill (not a Black-owned business) serves Southern-style pub fare, think: fried chicken Cobb salad, Soul Train hot wings, stuffed Delta catfish, and hot tamales, with a Mississippi blues museum upstairs. Displays tell the story of Mississippi's contribution to the musical landscape, starting in the 1800s until now, from spirituals and the blues to rock 'n' roll. Life-size models of musicians from this state are on exhibit; take a selfie with drummer Jaimoe or Grammy Award-winning blues pianist Joe Willie "Pinetop" Perkins, sitting at a piano. Iron Horse is an early American term for locomotive, which is fitting for this welcoming place that has survived two major fires and is back in operation because community members championed its return.

Bistro

JOHNNY T'S BISTRO & BLUES

538 N Farish St.; tel. 601/954-1323; www.johnnytsbistroandblues.com; Tues.-Fri. 4:30pm-midnight, Sat.-Sun. 6pm-2am; $12-33

This venue was known as Crystal Palace Night Club and featured entertainers like

Duke Ellington, Lionel Hampton, and Louis Armstrong. H. C. Speir, a talent scout who owned a music and furniture store on Farish Street in the 1920 and '30s, recorded Mississippi blues records here. Today, Johnny T's Bistro & Blues aims for a progressive-minded crowd vibing off sophisticated Southern fare in a blues-filled ambiance. The bistro owner is not Black, but Chef Bryan Myrick is. Johnny T's serves small plates, like homemade cheese balls and crab claws. Entrees include chicken or shrimp alfredo, an Atlantic seafood platter, and shrimp 'n' grits.

Upstairs, the **Renaissance Room** is known for bringing in national comedy acts and infusing the air with blues, which takes a late-night twist into R&B and hip-hop. The venue features an extensive bar and wall-to-wall mirrors for a laid-back, sexy feel. And the **540 Ultra Lounge** is open Fri.-Sat. 9pm-2am.

OTHER NEIGHBORHOODS

Southern and Soul Food

BULLY'S RESTAURANT

3118 Livingston Rd.; tel. 601/362-0484; Mon.-Sat. 11am-6:30pm; $7-9

Bully's, which opened several decades ago, was envisioned as a short-order place catering to factory workers and other working-class folks. This is some soul food hall-of-fame-style cooking: baked chicken, greens, sweet potatoes, oxtails, neckbones, chitterlings, meatloaf, macaroni 'n' cheese, turkey wings, okra, and the list goes on. The vegetables are well seasoned, and the meat, be it oxtails or baked chicken, falls off the bone. The modest roadside eatery features a dining room with walls plastered with historical ephemera, family and community photos, and framed newspaper profiles. Two paintings on opposite walls stand out: a proud Medgar Evers on a vibrant blue background, and a classic oil painting of Rev. Jesse L. Jackson, hung at patrons' eye level.

Working people still come here today, including city council members and state legislators. When the Freedom Riders had a 50th reunion, they made sure they ate here too. Bully's has been recognized by the James Beard Foundation as an American classic. The restaurant is located a few miles north of downtown, in the same direction as the Medgar Evers Home Museum.

Barbecue

E & L BARBECUE

1111 Bailey Ave., tel. 601/355-5035; Mon.-Thurs. 11am-9pm and Fri.-Sat 11am-11pm; $5-14

E & L, located about half a mile north of downtown, is a simple-looking place, but it's the rib tips, chicken, baked beans, and beyond that count: Everything here tastes great. There are plenty of seats in the dining room, or take your order to go. The restaurant was the brainchild of the late Eddie Hilliard, who cooked these recipes in Chicago until moving back home to Mississippi. Today, his daughter, Gladys Wilson, runs it along with her son and daughter-in-law.

Diner

BRENT'S SODA FOUNTAIN

655 Duling Ave; tel. 601/366-3427; brentsdrugs.com; Tues.-Fri. 7am-7:30pm, Sat. 8am-7:30pm, Sun. 10am-2pm; $7-11

This '40s-style diner in Fondren (not a Black-owned business) offers tasty milkshakes and malts, burgers, and BLTs. It is also the old-style drugstore that was featured in the movie *The Help*, a source of controversy: Actress Viola Davis has expressed regret for starring in the story that centered on White characters, not the Black maids. Still, it's fascinating to imagine the Jackson that was during Jim Crow with the city it has become.

FARISH STREET

Established during Reconstruction, Farish Street grew into Mississippi's largest Black business mecca where professionals, tradesmen, and entrepreneurs could exercise their agency in pursuit of the American Dream. By post-World War II, the street was a magnet for Black Jacksonians and country folk who rode in from surrounding rural areas. Proud to commune with kith and kind, they packed sidewalks as they stocked up on dry goods, bought furniture, visited cafes, and clinched the latest tune at the local record store.

Big Apple Inn, in operation since the 1930s, is the only business from Farish Street's heyday that's still in operation.

Today, although it is listed on the National Register of Historic Places, Farish Street is but a shadow of its former self. Ironically, the decline began with the passage of the Civil Rights Act of 1964, which ensured that public facilities like stores, schools, and other businesses across Jackson—not just on Farish Street—were open to everyone, regardless of race. When African Americans were free to come and go as they pleased, many left Farish Street to experience the posh downtown stores. (As Big Apple Inn's Geno Lee says, "Integration was great for the Black race but terrible for the Black business owner.")

Officials have preserved what they could of Farish Street icons, like the **Alamo Theater** (page 208), placing markers as breadcrumbs leading to a new future. There's also one business that has withstood the test of time: **Big Apple Inn** (page 209) is still here, serving juicy pig ear sandwiches. Meanwhile, some progressive-minded residents have taken ownership of this rich, if troubled, narrative. Businesses like **F Jones Corner** (page 213) and **Johnny T's Bistro & Blues** (page 210) welcome like-minded folks regardless of race to work, play, and thrive. Both venues offer entertainment (which, at Johnny T's, is upstairs at 540 Ultra Lounge), but a way to enjoy both is to start with a meal at Johnny T's, then leave your car parked and walk on over to F Jones to hear some of the most authentic blues music around.

The best strategy, though, is to take in Farish Street during daylight hours when you can walk down the street and see historical markers and imagine a time when the street teemed with Black joy.

Nightlife

If you are a true night owl or simply like to prowl, **F Jones Corner** is your best bet in Jackson for a night that won't get started until around midnight and end at 4am. The **Fondren** area, while great for shopping and restaurants, also features some excellent nightlife.

BARS

NAMES & FACES LOUNGE

224 E. Capitol St.; tel. 601/955-5285; Mon.-Fri 11am-midnight, Sat. 6pm-midnight

Locals congregate in this small downtown haunt for an after-work drink with a little dinner (think: Taco Tuesday), and sometimes they wear their best nightlife gear to celebrate milestone birthdays and events. The atmosphere is fueled by the sounds of Floetry and Erykah Badu playing overhead and Black-themed TV shows on BET and MTV2 behind the bar. The menu features everything from shrimp and grits, wings, hamburgers, and cheesesteaks to quesadillas and the aforementioned tacos. Friendly bartenders are keen to make drink recommendations from a full-service bar.

4TH AVENUE LOUNGE JXN

209 S Lamar St.; tel. 601-259-5825; www.4thavenuejxn.com; Tues.-Wed. 4pm-10pm, Thurs.-Fri. 4pm-midnight, Sat. 4pm-2am

This downtown restaurant and cocktail lounge is a go-to place for Jackson's progressive-minded urbanists. The menu features shareable dishes like hummus and wings and a range of bowls, sliders, salads, and pizzas. Leather couches, small tables, and sliding glass doors complete the after-hours ambiance. The TVs in the bar are shut off after 8pm unless folks are bonding over a headliner event.

CIGAR BAR

DOWNTOWN CIGAR COMPANY

159 E Pearl St.; tel. 769/572-5889; Mon.-Thurs. 11am-10pm, Fri.-Sat. 11am-midnight, Sun. noon-6pm

Relaxation with sophistication is the goal at this cigar bar that features two humidors and prides itself on creating a "clean smoke" for patrons. This roomy venue also includes a speakeasy lounge, full bar, and patio for mellowing out alone or with friends. Cigar-wise, the bar features 110 faces or varieties ranging from $7-25. The bar is located next door to 4th Avenue Lounge JXN.

LIVE MUSIC

F JONES CORNER

303 N Farish St.; tel. 601/983-1148; www.fjonescorner.com; Thurs.-Sat. 10pm-4am; $3-7

When you see the blindingly bright blue wall at the corner of Farish and Griffith, you'll know you have arrived at the intimate, diverse late-night hotspot that is F Jones Corner. Get your fill of cheap eats while enjoying local and regional blues music. Originally a filling station, the building is listed on the National Register of Historic Places and now pays homage to a noted Farish Street businessman in what was Jackson's Black business hub for several decades. F Jones Corner is not a Black-owned business. What's the vibe here? Just read the sign inside: "No Black. No White. Just the Blues."

FREELONS RESTAURANT BAR & GROOVE

440 N Mill St.; tel. 601/832-6856; www.freelons.com; Fri.-Sat. 10pm-4am

It's always party time at Freelons near the historic Farish Street area where young adults like to hit the dance floor, mingle on the patio, get spoiled in the VIP seating area, and, of course, eat. The biggest names in Dirty South, hip-hop, and R&B have been featured here, including David Banner, Lil Wayne, Yo Gotti, and Eric Benet. Boasting three bars and frequent drink specials, Freelons has themed parties aimed at young adults looking to blow off steam after a hard day's work or for milestone events like homecoming.

HAL & MAL'S

200 Commerce St.; tel. 601/948-0888; www.halandmals.com; Mon. 11am-2:30pm, Tues.-Thurs. 11am-9pm, Fri. 11am-10:30pm, Sat. 6pm-10:30pm

If you've never had a deep fried dill pickle, this is the place to experience your first time in a friendly, welcoming atmosphere with good food and live music that tends toward jazz, bluegrass, folk, classic country, and rock. Decor-wise, there's a high quirk factor in this restaurant situated in an old train depot, and it's worked quite well for locals for a long time.

Hal & Mal's is closed on Monday—but that's the night **Central Mississippi Blues Society, Inc.** (www.centralmississippibluessociety.com) takes over, and a mix of music veterans and up-and-coming artists jam the night away.

Hal & Mal's is not a Black-owned business.

Accommodations

Accommodations in the Jackson area tend toward chain hotels. A good option downtown, conveniently located near the Mississippi Civil Rights Museum and nightlife venues, is **The Westin Jackson** (407 S Congress St.; tel. 601/968-8200; www.marriott.com; $157). In the Farish Street Historic District is the 186-room **Hilton Garden Inn Jackson Downtown** (235 W Capitol St.; tel. 601/353-5464; www.hiltongardeninn3.hilton.com; $114).

OTHER NEIGHBORHOODS

$100-200

HISTORIC FAIRVIEW INN

734 Fairview St.; tel. 888/948-1908; www.fairviewinn.com; from $199

The Fairview Inn is housed in an early 1900s Colonial Revival mansion for a truly Southern boutique hotel experience. The inn offers 18 rooms featuring four-poster beds, working fireplaces, and whirlpools. A spa features massages, facials, and all sorts of body treatments. The Library Lounge, with cushy leather chairs in a relaxing environment, serves lunch and has a happy hour featuring wine flights, small plates, and farm-to-table fare.

The hotel is located north of downtown, less than two miles from the Civil Rights Museum.

FREEDOM RIDES: JACKSON

Mugshots of every Freedom Rider line the walls in a gallery in the Mississippi Civil Rights Museum.

On May 24, 1961, 27 Freedom Riders continued, with the help of a police escort, from Montgomery (where they suffered beating at the hands of a White mob) to Jackson. The Riders were greeted with supportive cheers—but also arrested when Black Freedom Riders tried to enter Whites-only areas. Attorney General Robert F. Kennedy asked for a cooling off period that same day: "In this confused situation, there is increasingly possibility that innocent persons may be injured. A mob asks no questions. The Alabama and Mississippi law enforcement officials are meeting the test today, but their job is becoming increasingly difficult. A cooling off period is needed."[1]

The arrested Freedom Riders choose **"Jail, No Bail,"** a movement strategy adopted in 1960 at a SNCC conference in Atlanta. Acceptance of bail would mean validating a corrupt system. Besides, being locked up amplified and intensified their struggle, which was indeed difficult. Ten activists were locked up in cells designed for four. Several were tried and sentenced to serve time in Mississippi State Penitentiary, aka Parchman Farm, where they were served inedible food, given ill-fitting clothing, and kept locked up with no exercise.

Today, a **Mississippi Freedom Trail marker** located at 219 North Lamar Street outside the Greyhound station commemorates the activists.

ACCOMMODATIONS

Transportation

GETTING THERE

Air

Jackson-Medgar Wiley Evers International Airport (JAN; 100 International Dr.; tel. 601/939-5631; www.jmaa.com) is located six miles east of Jackson. A cab ride to downtown Jackson takes about 15 minutes and will run $35-42.

Train

Amtrak's **Union Station** (300 West Capitol St.; tel. 601/355-6350; www.amtrak.com) is located in the Farish Street Historic District in a renovated Georgian Revival building. It's operated by the Jackson Transit System and serves Amtrak's City of New Orleans rail line. Adult coach fares range from $32-$84 each way between Jackson and **Memphis.**

Bus

Greyhound (tel. 601/353-6342; www.locations.greyhound.com) also operates out of Union Station in the Farish Street Historic District. Bus tickets from **Memphis** to Jackson range from $28-$70.

Car

To reach Jackson from:

- **Memphis:** Take **I-55 South** for about 220 miles (3 hours).
- **Birmingham:** Take **I-20 West** for 240 miles (3.5 hours).

GETTING AROUND

Jackson is synonymous with car culture and not entirely walkable given the distance of venues and the scorching heat in summer and early fall. The major car rental companies have agents at Jackson-Evers International Airport.

Parking

Parking in Jackson is pretty easy to find. Metered parking is 50 cents an hour.

Public Transit

The city does have a bus system—**JATRAN** (www.jatran.com)—with extremely limited service every hour or 30 minutes.

Taxi and Ride-Hailing Apps

Uber and **Lyft** ridesharing are available, or call **Jackson Taxi** (tel. 601/292-1100).

Canton, Mississippi

Canton, Mississippi, located about 30 minutes north of Jackson, was the final stop along the 1966 March Against Fear before activists arrived at the state capitol in Jackson. Marchers—200 of them—stopped here for a rally and rest, meeting with 1,000 rallygoers uptown at the courthouse. When the marchers tried to set up camp at a local elementary school, state troopers, defying a promise by the state to the federal government to leave the marchers unmolested, shot tear gas at them and beat the ones who wouldn't move. According to local sources, many marchers ran to the CORE's Freedom House in Canton where they washed their faces and tried to recoup.

Madison County, where Canton is located, had long been a tough place for Black people. In the 1950s, 300 African American Canton residents went to the courthouse to register to vote; only 40 succeeded. In 1964, Canton participated

Canton Freedom House curators Alderman Tim Taylor and Wesley Rushing in front of the museum

in three planned Freedom Days, which involved marching to the courthouse to register to vote. In response, White supremacists shot at the Freedom House, the organizing center of the Madison County movement, and tried to bomb it. Second-class treatment of Black people was manifest in everyday acts too, such as being forced to allow Whites to go first in a grocery store line.

The majority-Black population of Madison County wasn't happy with this rigid racial hierarchy that placed Whites at the top; as a result, the Madison County movement, which sought to secure a fair share of power and decision-making in civic affairs, took hold. Today, you can experience some of that movement at the Freedom House, which has been turned into a tiny home-bound museum.

SIGHTS

★ Canton Freedom House Civil Rights Museum

838 George Washington Ave.; tel. 601/317-2557; www.freedomhousecanton.org; Mon.-Fri. 9am-4pm, Sat. by appt.; free admission, donations encouraged

This home, owned by local Black grocers George and Rember Washington, was frequently visited by movement leaders during the civil rights movement, including Evers and Meredith. King visited during the March Against Fear, which stopped in Canton for a rally and rest. In 1963, the Washingtons rented the home to George Raymond, CORE's Canton director and the Madison County Project's first staffer, who came to Canton after participating in the 1961 Freedom Rides. The White power structure had warned George against renting the home to Raymond, but he did so anyway. And for that, White segregationists tried to destroy George's grocery business by taking away his gas pumps and blocking the delivery of goods. Friends and allies found other ways to get goods into the store under the cover of night, according to Glen Cotton, the Washingtons' grandson.

Today, Cotton owns the home, which now functions as the Canton Freedom House Museum. Against a backdrop of red walls, the tiny museum features historic photographs, civil rights memorabilia, and artifacts such as cotton sacks and wood-burning stoves that illustrate the life Black Mississippians were trying to leave

CANTON'S LOCAL HEROES

In Madison County, and the town of Canton specifically, a core of spirited resisters rose in opposition to the vicious White power structure. Local figures included:

- **Grocery store owners George and Rember Washington,** who risked White backlash and economic destruction when they rented their house to CORE director George Raymond. The Washingtons' store was a gathering place, with two chairs situated inside just so folks could come and sit and talk. Their home (now a museum run by their grandson) was frequently visited by movement leaders, including Evers.
- **Educator Annie Devine,** who sold insurance for the Black-owned Security Life Insurance Company and became part of the insurgent Mississippi Freedom Democratic Party's delegation to the 1964 Democratic National Convention.
- **Businessman, farmer, and bootlegger C. O. Chinn,** a tough-minded enforcer for CORE. Chinn provided armed protection for Freedom Movement workers throughout the '60s, and folks looked for him in a crowd during certain actions because his presence—and gun—made them feel safe.
- **NAACP leader and organizer Flonzie Brown Wright,** who (at Annie Devine's insistence) ran for county election commissioner and in 1968 became the first Black woman elected to office in Mississippi since Reconstruction. Brown Wright brought to office her own history of facing down voter discrimination: She recalls trying to register in the mid-1960s, only to "fail" a 20-question test administered only to Black people when she couldn't define habeas corpus, a concept that was not taught in segregated schools.

behind as they sought better opportunities, full citizenship, and equal rights.

FESTIVALS AND EVENTS

CANTON FLEA MARKET ARTS & CRAFTS SHOW

tel. 601/859-8055; www.cantonmsfleamarket.com; free

Canton's outdoor arts and crafts fair, held the second Thursday of May and October (7am-4pm) on the town square, showcases Southern creativity and ingenuity. Find quirky items like handmade bubble gum dispensers, handcrafted lawn ornaments, and everything in between. Food stalls offer the best of Southern cooking, from fried pickles to shrimp and grits. Several Black vendors sell their wares at the fair.

GETTING THERE

Canton is about 27 miles north of **Jackson.** From I-55, take Canton exit #119 (Hwy. 22) and travel east on Hwy. 22 (Peace Street) to reach the town.

The Delta

Mississippi is notable for its racially charged dark side. This is where Emmett Till, 14, was tortured and murdered in 1955, after being accused of whistling at a White woman, Carolyn Bryant, at Bryant's Grocery & Meat Market in rural Money. (This type of violence against Black people was not unusual in the Delta: Other Black bodies were tossed into the river for any number of "infractions" during the Jim Crow era.)

THE DELTA

THE DELTA'S TOP 3

1. Feeling a range of emotions as you stand outside the ruins of **Bryant's Grocery & Meat Market** and consider how the workaday business of slicing bologna and selling penny candy escalated to the murder of a child (page 227).

2. Hearing the call to action at the **Emmett Till Intrepid Center** in Glendora, a raw museum that pays homage to a brutally murdered child (page 227).

3. Celebrating a man and his music at **B. B. King Museum & Delta Interpretive Center** in Indianola, where you will learn how the legendary blues guitarist supported the movement with his talents (page 232).

Photos (top to bottom): Emmett Till Intrepid Center; B.B. King Museum & Delta Interpretive Center. Previous: statue of Fannie Lou Hamer by sculptor Brian Hanlon

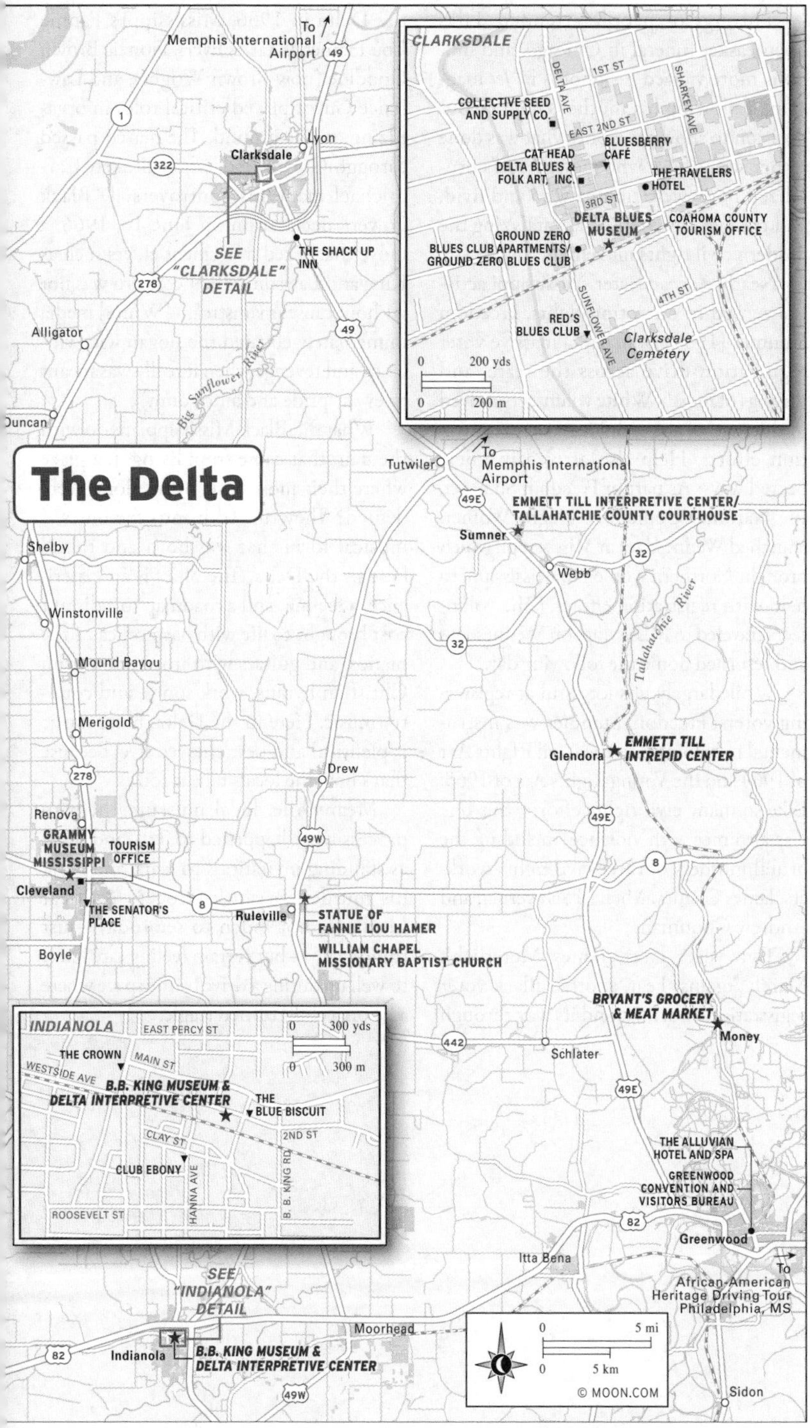

The Delta
To Memphis International Airport
Clarksdale
Lyon
SEE "CLARKSDALE" DETAIL
THE SHACK UP INN
Alligator
Big Sunflower River
Duncan
Tutwiler
To Memphis International Airport
EMMETT TILL INTERPRETIVE CENTER/ TALLAHATCHIE COUNTY COURTHOUSE
Sumner
Webb
Shelby
Winstonville
Mound Bayou
Tallahatchie River
Merigold
Glendora
EMMETT TILL INTREPID CENTER
Drew
Renova
GRAMMY MUSEUM MISSISSIPPI
TOURISM OFFICE
Cleveland
THE SENATOR'S PLACE
Ruleville
STATUE OF FANNIE LOU HAMER
WILLIAM CHAPEL MISSIONARY BAPTIST CHURCH
Boyle
BRYANT'S GROCERY & MEAT MARKET
Money
Schlater
THE ALLUVIAN HOTEL AND SPA
GREENWOOD CONVENTION AND VISITORS BUREAU
Greenwood
Itta Bena
To African-American Heritage Driving Tour Philadelphia, MS
SEE "INDIANOLA" DETAIL
Moorhead
Indianola
B.B. KING MUSEUM & DELTA INTERPRETIVE CENTER
Sidon
0 5 mi
0 5 km
© MOON.COM
CLARKSDALE
1ST ST
DELTA AVE
SHARKEY AVE
COLLECTIVE SEED AND SUPPLY CO.
EAST 2ND ST
BLUESBERRY CAFÉ
CAT HEAD DELTA BLUES & FOLK ART, INC.
THE TRAVELERS HOTEL
3RD ST
DELTA BLUES MUSEUM
COAHOMA COUNTY TOURISM OFFICE
GROUND ZERO BLUES CLUB APARTMENTS/ GROUND ZERO BLUES CLUB
4TH ST
SUNFLOWER AVE
RED'S BLUES CLUB
Clarksdale Cemetery
0 200 yds
0 200 m
INDIANOLA
EAST PERCY ST
0 300 yds
0 300 m
THE CROWN
MAIN ST
WESTSIDE AVE
B.B. KING MUSEUM & DELTA INTERPRETIVE CENTER
THE BLUE BISCUIT
CLAY ST
2ND ST
CLUB EBONY
HANNA AVE
B. B. KING RD
ROOSEVELT ST

Throngs of people attended Till's open-casket funeral in Chicago, and millions more viewed his photos in *Jet* magazine following his mother's courageous decision to show the world what was done to her son. Those who viewed Till's brutalized body were traumatized and livid, and the event is credited as catalyzing the modern civil rights movement.

Nearly a decade later, Mississippi activists zeroed in on voting rights. Freedom Summer (1964) launched a massive voter registration drive across the state, and throngs of mostly White volunteers arrived in the state to aid with local voter registration efforts. Help also arrived in unexpected ways: As part of Freedom Summer, the National Council of Negro Women launched Wednesdays in Mississippi, which brought Northern women to Mississippi to help with registration efforts. (The volunteers traveled to Mississippi on Wednesdays and returned home the following day.)

While largely unsuccessful at registering voters, Freedom Summer was instrumental in helping pass the Civil Rights Act of 1964 and the Voting Rights Act of 1965. Like so many civil rights efforts, this one was also met with violence, including the brutal murders of three civil rights workers, James Chaney, Michael Schwerner, and Andrew Goodman.

Two years later, James Meredith's March Against Fear, another Black voter registration effort, wound its way through the Delta in 1966. Mississippi's Fannie Lou Hamer, Charles Evers, Flonzie Brown Goodloe (now Brown Wright), and Lawrence Guyot played critical roles in organizing on the ground. The march passed through Greenwood, where Stokely Carmichael made his controversial "Black Power" declaration on June 16, 1966, a move that vexed movement elders such as King and Lawson. (Their concern was not without cause: mainstream [White] media immediately equated the slogan with violence and revenge when it really was meant to evoke pride and autonomy.)

What did Black Mississippians do with the pain that came from living in a place where their most basic of freedoms were denied? They turned it into the blues, a musical form that was born and raised here in the Delta. The blues is an experience, a feeling, and a roadmap to a distant past brought to life with harmonicas, fifes, pianos, and guitars with inspiration from Christian hymns, work songs, and country music. Here in the Delta, blues music is plentiful and best enjoyed live, because that's how the locals take it too.

Meanwhile, local museums help to process what happened to Till, and serve as standing invitations to learn and from his murder. Bryant's Grocery & Meat Market is not much to see today—just ruins, really—but certain feelings are likely to well up during a drive by the space where a lie on a child turned tragic.

MOVEMENT TIMELINE

1955

August 28: Fourteen-year-old Emmett Till is brutally murdered after a White woman accuses him of whistling at her.

September 3: Emmett Till's funeral is held in Chicago. Till's mother decides to leave the casket open, stating, "I think everybody needed to know what had happened to Emmett Till."

September 23: Till's murderers, J. W. Milam and Roy Bryant, are acquitted by an all-White male jury.

1962

August: Student Nonviolent Coordinating Committee (SNCC) organizers visit William Chapel Missionary Baptist Church in Ruleville, inspiring sharecropper Fannie Lou Hamer to register to vote.

1964

April: Mississippi Freedom Democratic Party is founded to encourage Black political participation and challenge the regular Democratic Party, which was dominated by White segregationists.

June 15: Freedom Summer kicks off as the first 300 (mostly White) volunteers arrive in Mississippi to register Black voters.

June 21: Three Freedom Summer workers—James Chaney (Black), Michael Schwerner, and Andrew Goodman (both White)—are abducted after investigating the burning of a church in Philadelphia, Mississippi.

August 4: The bodies of Chaney, Schwerner, and Goodman are found.

August 22: Delta native Fannie Lou Hamer speaks at the Democratic National Convention in Atlantic City, New Jersey, about trying to register to vote in Mississippi.

1966

June 16: While participating in Meredith's March Against Fear, Stokely Carmichael is arrested in Greenwood. Upon his release from jail a few hours later, he addresses the crowd: "We been saying freedom for six years and we ain't got nothin. What we got to start saying now is Black Power! We want Black Power."[1]

1985

David Jordan becomes the first Black city council member in Greenwood, Mississippi. As a result, his life is threatened and his home is shot at.

2005

June 21: A state court convicts Klan leader and minister Edgar Ray Killen of manslaughter in the 1963 deaths of Freedom Summer volunteers Schwerner, Chaney, and Goodman.

2006

December 15: President George Bush awards B. B. King the Presidential Medical of Freedom for his contributions to American music

Emmett Till's mother, Mamie Till-Mobley, center, at her son's funeral

PEOPLE WHO MADE THE MOVEMENT

GROUPS

Mississippi Freedom Democratic Party (MFDP): Party that attempted to unseat the segregationist Democratic delegation in 1964.

INDIVIDUALS

Emmett Till: Fourteen-year-old boy who was murdered in 1955 after he allegedly whistled at a White woman.

James Chaney, Andrew Goodman, and Michael Schwerner: Freedom Summer workers who were kidnapped and murdered by the KKK in 1964. Chaney was Black; Goodman and Schwerner were White.

Fannie Lou Hamer: Local activist who fought for Black people's right to vote. Hamer also co-founded the Mississippi Freedom Democratic Party and ran for Congress in 1964.

Stokley Carmichael: SNCC chairman who sparked controversy by promoting Black Power at a speech in Greenwood, Mississippi, during the March Against Fear (1966).

Fannie Lou Hamer

B. B. King: Delta-bred musician who raised money to support the movement.

ORIENTATION

This is a region of small towns and a lot of space in between. Reconciling the quaintness of town squares and genteel Southern manners can pose a mental challenge during a journey such as this. There are plenty of places to eat and sleep; you just might have to drive a bit farther out than if you were in a more populated place, depending on where you decide to bunk.

Several Delta towns are strung along or near **U.S. 49**: From south to north, **Greenwood, Money, Glendora, Sumner,** and **Clarksdale** are all roughly 10-15 miles apart. U.S. 49 is called Money Road at the spot where what's left of Bryant's Grocery & Meat Market stands. State Senator David Jordan says Emmett was staying with his uncle about a mile and a half from the store. This area is where Till's murder took place, and most of these towns have at least one sight relating to that horrific event.

Of these towns, Clarksdale is a nice music and food oasis from the weight of the region's civil rights sights and a good place to spend the night. (Greenwood also has good accommodations.) From these key Delta cities, several sites on the U.S. Civil Rights Trail are clustered together and easily accessed by car.

From U.S. 49, turn west on Highway 8 to reach **Ruleville,** home of Fannie Lou Hamer (13 miles) and **Cleveland** (10 miles from Ruleville). **Indianola,** home to the **B. B. King Museum & Delta Interpretive Center,** plus blues clubs and restaurants, is 30 miles west of Greenwood on Highway 82.

PLANNING YOUR TIME

Take two or three days to take in civil rights sites and enjoy Delta food and music. Note that the **Emmett Till Interpretive Center** is open by appointment only. Call the center before you leave home to insure a call back and a spot.

The Emmett Till-related sights are strung between the towns of **Greenwood** and **Clarksdale.** If you're interested in the blues, Clarksdale and **Indianola** are your best bets for informative museums as well as clubs.

For travel-related questions, contact the **Mississippi Delta Tourism Association** (P.O. Box 1770, Clarksdale; tel. 662/627-6149); the **Coahoma County Tourism Office** in Clarksdale (326 Blues Alley; tel. 662/627-6149; Mon.-Fri. 9am-5pm, Sat. 9am-noon); the **Greenwood Convention and Visitors Bureau** (225 Howard St.; tel. 662/453-9197); or Cleveland, Mississippi's **Tourism Office** (101 S. Bayou; tel. 662/843-2712).

CONNECT WITH

Jackson (about 100 miles south) and **Memphis** (about 80 miles north) are logical places to pair with a trip to the Delta.

Two Days in the Delta

Base yourself in **Clarksdale** for a trip that takes in the Till tragedy along with the best of the blues.

DAY 1

Brace yourself for an emotional first day in the Delta as you visit sights associated with Emmett Till's murder. Get an early start so you can make it back to Clarksdale before 1:30pm, when the **Bluesberry Café** closes every day but Monday, when it's open into the evening.

1 Make your way to **Bryant's Grocery & Meat Market** in Money, which is 10 miles north of Greenwood, where a false accusation on a child turned deadly. There isn't much to see, but it's worth pausing by the roadside to absorb what happened here.

2 Drive north to the **Emmett Till Intrepid Center,** which provides an unvarnished assessment of local race relations. (It's a powerful space, and you may feel a call to action.)

3 Head next to Sumner, where you can drop into the **Emmett Till Interpretive Center** (if you've scheduled in advance—it's by appointment only), which evokes the environment of the 1955 trial of Till's murderers through photos, news headlines, and other media coverage.

4 Cross the street to visit the **Tallahatchie County Courthouse,** where the trial took place.

5 Drive next to Clarksdale, where you'll spend the rest of your day. Begin by enjoying a meal at the **Bluesberry Café**.

6 Unwind by exploring some of Clarksdale's shops, like **Cat Head Delta Blues & Folk Art, Inc.**

7 You've earned a night out at one of Clarkdale's blues clubs. If it's a Friday or Saturday, look for live music at **Red's Blues Club**. (There's a barbecue pit out front for when you get hungry.)

DAY 2

Sink into the blues on your second day in the Delta.

1 Spend the morning at the **Delta Blues Museum** in Clarksdale, learning about small-town artists who became blues legends.

2 Drive south on U.S. 278 West/U.S. 61 South to Cleveland, where you can take in some buffet-style soul food at **The Senator's Place**.

3 Continue south on U.S. 278 West/U.S. 61 South, turning on MS 448 East toward Indianola. Park your car and beeline to the **B. B. King Museum & Delta Interpretive Center**. Learn about King's music as well as his role in the civil rights movement.

4 End your day with a stop by **The Blue Biscuit**, right across the street from the museum, for live jazz and blues music, along with the 72-hour pulled pork that the restaurant is known for.

Sights

REMEMBERING EMMETT TILL

In 1955, 14-year old Emmett Till left for Bryant's Grocery & Meat Market to get some candy with his cousin, Curtis Jones, and some other boys. There, when Carolyn Bryant, who ran the store with her husband Roy, accused him of flirting with her, she stirred up a deadly cauldron resulting in Emmett being kidnapped from his great-uncle Mose Wright's home, beaten, tortured, mutilated, and weighted down with a 75-pound cotton gin fan and tossed in the Tallahatchie River.

Wright testified at the trial of Emmett's murderers, Roy and J. W. Milam, his half-brother. The moment when he pointed his finger from the witness stand to identify one of the child's killers, famously saying, "Dar he," was captured in film by Black photographer Ernest Withers. This statement identifying Emmett's killers took monumental courage because Wright, also called "Preacher," risked his own life in speaking against the White murderers. Some say he might have been the only Black man up to that point to accuse a White man (two in this case) and survive.

Still, Milam and Bryant were acquitted after a five-day trial. The all-White male jurors said they didn't think White men should be held accountable for killing Black people.

Emmett's mother, Mamie Till-Mobley, didn't give up, and pressed for a federal investigation into the murder of her child. Her decision to display Emmett's mutilated, swollen body in an open casket back home in Chicago at Roberts Temple Church of God is considered the spark for the modern civil rights movement.

Till's murder and the series of events that followed took place in Money, where Bryant's Grocery is located; Glendora, where the cotton gin fan and wire was taken to weigh down Emmett's body; and Sumner, where the trial of his murderers was held. Visiting these sights from south to north, as they are listed below, allows you to follow the chronological trajectory that was set in place by Bryant's lie.

TOP EXPERIENCE

★ Bryant's Grocery & Meat Market

Leflore County Road 518, Money, 10 miles north of Greenwood

The grocery store where Emmett Till, 14, was accused of whistling at a White woman still stands off Money Road 10 miles north of downtown Greenwood. In front of the store, a state marker bears witness to the crime against Emmett. Onlookers often veer off the road for a closer look at the marker, which outlines the events leading up to Till's murder, as well as its aftermath.

Today, Bryant's Grocery is a stop on the official U.S. Civil Rights Trail. The store has largely decayed from disrepair, but Ben Roy's Service Station, located next to it, provides a glimpse back to the 1950s. Peering through the window of the service station, visitors can see wooden shelves, a scale, and an empty red Toms potato chip holder, among other retail artifacts. Behind mesh wire on the front door is a rectangle sign emblazoned with cigarette packs with an invitation to "PUSH." The dusty Delta landscape is placid, with only the occasional car rumbling down Money Road, and the quietness seems to belie the fact that this is the site where a vicious lie on a child turned merciless and brutal.

★ Emmett Till Intrepid Center

33 Thomas St., Glendora; tel. 662/375-4360; www.glendorams.com; Mon. by appt., Tues.-Fri. 10am-5pm, Sat. 10am-2pm; $5, youths under 18 $3

Situated in Glendora (pop. 151), 18 miles north of Money, this museum is housed in the same cotton gin where Emmett's murderers pulled down the 75-pound fan that weighed his body down after he was thrown in the Tallahatchie River. Erected as a Main Street-style walk down memory lane, the center doesn't mince words when portraying the state of race relations and small-town life in historic Glendora. It features a replica of Bryant's Grocery & Meat Market and describes the economy of rural Mississippi, from plantation commissaries to general stores often run by poor Whites and Chinese merchants (who came to the Delta after being recruited during the Civil War to replace the Black workers plantation owners suspected would leave). The immersion ends with a replica of Emmett lying in his casket. This is not played for thrills but to throw down a challenge: A photo of Emmett's eyes accompanies signage that implores onlookers to remember his legacy and commit to being a healing agent for human rights.

Glendora Mayor Johnny B. Thomas established this museum in 2005. He said he believes his father, Henry Lee Loggins, who worked for Milam, was forced to help the White men with the abduction. The cotton-gin-turned-museum was owned by Milam.

The Emmett Hill Intrepid Center is a stop on the official U.S. Civil Rights Trail.

Emmett Till Interpretive Center

120 N Court St., Sumner; tel. 662/483-0048; www.emmett-till.org; by appointment; $5 suggested donation

This sparse museum in Sumner, 13 miles north of Glendora, features photos, vintage news accounts, and magazine coverage of the trial of Emmett Till's murderers, J. W. Milam and Roy Bryant. It is a good point of entry for visiting the Tallahatchie County Courthouse, where the trial took place in September 1955, across the street.

Inside the center, visitors can view a news account featuring the headline: "These Are The Jurors Who Will Decide In Slaying of Emmett L. Till." An accompanying photo shows the all-White male jury. A framed news report describes how Emmett's great-uncle, Mose Wright, planned to take the stand, unprecedented for being the first time in state history a Black man was allowed to accuse White men of murder.

The center also holds a purple sign that was posted as a memorial to Till in nearby Glendora, by the Tallahatchie River, where his body was removed from the water. The sign tells how Till's body was taken to nearby Greenwood for transport back to Chicago on Mrs. Till's orders. This memorial sign, which is pockmarked with bullet holes, is actually one of several that were posted: The first memorial, posted in 2007, was stolen a year later. Another sign was shot up. In August of 2018, a third sign was riddled with bullets 35 days after it was erected. In July 2019, a photo surfaced of three White fraternity brothers from the University of Mississippi posing with guns in front of the memorial sign. A report by Jerry Mitchell of Mississippi Center for Investigative Reporting said it was unclear if the students were responsible for the damaged sign.

The images within this center, which is a stop on the official U.S. Civil Rights Trail, offer a glimpse into the horror that gripped the country after Till's murder. The subsequent trial was a turning point for many African Americans, solidifying the need to stand and fight for full inclusion into American civic, social, and political life.

Tallahatchie County Courthouse

401 W Court St., Sumner; tel. 662/483-0048; www.emmett-till.org; Mon.-Fri. 8am-5pm; free

The Tallahatchie County Courthouse where the trial of Emmett's murderers took place still stands on the Sumner town square. It's open to visit for those who want to stand in the courtroom where, in an extraordinary miscarriage of justice, an all-White male jury failed to render a guilty verdict for Roy Bryant and J. W. Milam.

Today, the courthouse is listed on the National Register of Historic Places. Friendly courthouse workers wave visitors down the hall to the upstairs courtroom, where the sun streams through tall windows. The wooden seats you see today are the same ones courtroom watchers sat in during the fall of 1955, during Bryant and Milam's trial. Until 2020 when the legislature finally agreed to retire the state flag, the judge's bench was flanked by the U.S. flag and Mississippi's controversy-riddled one featuring Confederate symbolism. The record shows that when not in court, Emmett's mom, Mamie Till-Mobley, was ensconced in the safety of the all-Black town of Mound Bayou at Dr. T. R. M. Howard's home. Historic photos show how poised she was when asked about the not-guilty verdict the jury rendered after only deliberating for an hour and a half.

The courthouse is a stop on the official U.S. Civil Rights Trail. The courtroom is still functions as such, and cases are still heard here today.

Photos (top to bottom): long-closed Bryant's Grocery & Meat Market; Ashley Haywood (daughter of museum founder and Glendora mayor Johnny B. Thomas) at the Emmett Till Intrepid Center; Tallahatchie County Courthouse

GET INTO THE RHYTHM

- **"Go Tell It On the Mountain"**: This spiritual traditionally heralded the birth of the savior and was a go-to song at Christmas time: "Go tell it on the mountain, over the hills and everywhere. Go tell it on the mountain, Jesus Christ is born." During the movement, the song was remixed and reused to announce the arrival of the civil rights resistance. Fannie Lou Hamer famously sang this song, frequently leading gatherings in an uplifting, congregational-style sing-along: "Go tell it on the mountain, over the hills and everywhere. Go tell it on the mountain to let my people go!"
- **Sam Cooke,"This Little Light of Mine"**: Folklorist, musician, and activist Zilphia Horton at Highlander Folk School is responsible for introducing the children's gospel song, "This Little Light of Mine," as a movement anthem. In his characteristically smooth, upbeat manner, Cooke brought this song, embraced by grassroots activists, to New York's Copacabana in 1964.

CELEBRATING THE BLUES

A trio of museums spread out across the Delta commemorates blues music, which originated here. The **Blues Highway** (Highway 61) inspired many blues musicians who have made the roadway the subject of their music. Originally, the road started in downtown New Orleans and made its way to Baton Rouge, Natchez, and Vicksburg, and on the through the Delta to Memphis northward to the Canadian border. The highway was a way out for Black people who hit the road northward during the Great Migration and is now a way in for those who want to return home to where it all began.

Delta Blues Museum

1 Blues Alley, Clarksdale; tel. 662/627-6820; www.deltabluesmuseum.org; Mar.-Oct. Mon.-Sat. 9am-5pm, Nov.-Feb. Mon.-Sat. 10am-5pm; $10, children $8, under six free, group rate $8 per person

The Delta Blues Museum in Clarksdale celebrates the men and women who found meaning from growing up in the sharecropping economy, surfacing a unique kind of expression that comes from a particular racially inscribed pain. At this museum, learn about the trajectory of artists like Muddy Waters, aka McKinley Morganfield, who was raised by his grandmother on Stovall Plantation outside Clarksdale, where the family worked as sharecroppers, and came to be known as a father of Chicago blues. The sequined shirt of singer and guitarist Little Milton (of "Grits Ain't Groceries" fame) is on display, along with his alligator shoes and signature hat. Posters celebrating Bobby Rush, Denise LaSalle, and Charlie Musselwhite hang here. Bronze busts behold the glory of the great men of blues, including Mississippi John Hurt, Nehemiah Curtis "Skip" James, Chester Arthur Burnett "Howlin' Wolf," and Furry Lewis.

Located across from the Ground Zero Blues Club, the museum includes the Delta Blues Museum Stage, which hosts a year-round music education program and a venue for local festivals such as the Sunflower River Blues and Gospel Festival in August and the Juke Joint Festival in April.

Grammy Museum Mississippi

800 W Sunflower Rd., Cleveland; tel. 662/441-0100; www.grammymuseumms.org; Tues.-Sat. 11am-5pm, Sun. 1pm-5:30pm; groups of 10 or more by request; $14, seniors $12, children $8

Mississippi has produced so many Grammy-winning musicians, an interactive museum devoted to the Grammys is a no-brainer. Nestled on the campus of Delta State University, it's also one of the state's top attractions. The 28,000-square-foot museum pays tribute to the state's Grammy winners, from John Lee Hooker to Honeyboy Edwards. This museum exists to educate the public about the significance of American musical forms. It features a 130-seat soundstage and exhibits that explore several genres, from R&B and jazz to rock, country, Latin, and hip-hop. In The Roland Room, folks can play musical instruments and consider the complexity of music creation. Learn about artists' backgrounds in the Mississippi Gallery, an interactive discovery experience that introduces songs, photos, and awards. See instruments played by major artists, like B. B. King and Bruno Mars, and visit a red-carpet exhibit featuring the duds worn by artists on the biggest night in the music business. Public programs, films, and lectures are hosted here.

Photos (top to bottom): Delta Blues Museum; B.B. King Museum & Delta Interpretive Center; Club Ebony

FANNIE LOU HAMER

An earthy-but-eloquent farm laborer, Fannie Lou Hamer risked her life to fight for full enfranchisement for Black Mississippians. She started the back-breaking work of picking cotton at age 6, eventually dropping out of school. Hamer was a natural leader in the fields where she worked. She was barred from registering to vote many times, by poll taxes and literacy tests, but this only fueled her activism. She eventually joined SNCC, and when she and her husband were thrown off the land they sharecropped for a Black landowner, she regarded it as a sort of freedom. In addition to her work with voter registration, Hamer was involved on the most granular levels in getting food assistance to hungry families.

In 1964, Hamer ran for Congress, and helped found the **Mississippi Freedom Democratic Party** (MFDP), which registered new voters. The MFDP aimed to challenge the state Democratic Party on its exclusion of Black people from the state political processes; lack of loyalty to the national Democratic Party; and its "fanatical determination" to maintain the status quo. MFDP, an integrated coalition, fielded 68 delegates at the 1964 Democratic National Convention in Atlantic City, New Jersey, seeking to challenge the seating of the "regular" state Democratic Party, which was rife with White segregationists called Dixiecrats. Hamer was among the MFDP's delegates, and word on the street was President Lyndon B. Johnson was afraid of her. The Democrats offered the MFDP two seats with the stipulation that Hamer would not be given one of them. The MFDP unanimously voted to decline the offer.

Racism took a toll on Hamer in more ways than one. In 1961, Sunflower County medical staff removed her uterus in what was supposed to be a minor surgery on a uterine tumor. This kind of forced sterilization, known colloquially as a "Mississippi Appendectomy," was common as a way of reducing the Black population, ironically, after centuries of forcing Black

★ B. B. King Museum & Delta Interpretive Center

400 2nd St., Indianola; tel. 662/887-9539; www.bbkingmuseum.org; Apr.-Oct. Tues.-Sat. 10am-5pm, Sun.-Mon. noon-5pm; Nov.-Mar. closed on Mon.; $15, seniors $12, children $19, five and under free

Mississippi native B. B. King (born 1925) was dedicated to his music—and his guitar "Lucille"—but he never forgot where he came from, nor what was at stake for African Americans throughout the South. This museum clarifies his role in civil rights as much as it celebrates King's unique way of bending the notes of his electric guitar to create his signature sound. His success as a bluesman allowed him to raise money to play a role in funding the civil rights movement. One museum display shows a quote from the artist: "I couldn't have did them much good just marching and marching only. I could do better by helping them raise money to get them out of jail, and I did a lot of that."

Museumgoers will see guitars on display, King's larger-than-life suit, and a tour-bus-like exhibit that superimposes video stories. The man, whose music

women to bear children to serve as an unpaid workforce. Hamer and her husband, Pap, went on to adopt two daughters.

Hamer was a gifted singer and quite the wordsmith. She's famous for many enduring sayings, including: "Whether you have a PhD, or no D, we're in this bag together. And whether you're from Morehouse or Nohouse, we're still in this bag together"; "Nobody's free until everybody's free"; and, famously, "I'm sick and tired of being sick and tired." Hamer, who died in 1977, has been awarded several honorary PhDs, including one from Howard University.

Mississippi Freedom Democratic Party supporters outside the 1964 convention

REMEMBERING HAMER

Hamer and Pap are buried next to each other at the **Fannie Lou Hamer Memorial Garden** (726 Byron St.) in Ruleville, Hamer's hometown. Nearby, a bronze **statue** depicts her elevated on a pedestal, clasping a microphone that will allow her words to reverberate forever.

Down the street is the **William Chapel Missionary Baptist Church** (915 Byron St., Ruleville), the spiritual center where Hamer was encouraged to register to vote during a mass meeting of SNCC and SCLC in 1962. Hamer was also funeralized at William Chapel where then-United Nations delegate Andrew Young gave her eulogy.

Both the statue and church are sights on the Mississippi Freedom Trail.

went from the sharecropping field where he also drove a tractor, to street corners and juke joints to the world stage, also earned several honorary degrees, including one from Yale University. King's electric, big-band style once competed with Black church music, but it also withstood changing tastes to be brought back to the forefront when imitated by British bands, like The Beatles and Rolling Stones. A black granite slab protected by a wrought iron gate outside the museum denotes King's resting place.

CLUB EBONY

404 Hannah Ave., Indianola; tel. 662/887-9539; www.bbkingmuseum.org; Apr.-Oct. Tues.-Sat. 10am-5pm, Sun.-Mon. noon-5pm

A Mississippi Blues Trail sign marks the spot where Club Ebony was born at the end of World War II. Throughout its storied history, the club featured the greatest names in blues, including Little Milton, Ray Charles, Bobby "Blue" Bland, and B. B. King, who eventually purchased it to preserve the history that happened here.

Club Ebony no longer functions as a traditional blues club. Instead, travelers

FREEDOM SUMMER

Freedom Summer, also known as the **Mississippi Summer Project,** was a massive voter registration drive that kicked off in June 1964, as hundreds of volunteers arrived in Mississippi, a state where only a small minority of Black people were able to register to vote.

Upon the suggestion of Council of Federated Organizations (COFO) Director Bob Moses, the campaign actively recruited White student volunteers based on their successful participation in past projects with the Mississippi Freedom Democratic Party (MFDP). "We know what [the White volunteers] bring with them are the eyes of the country," Moses told journalist Nikole Hannah-Jones in 2014. "The country is able to see through their eyes what they weren't able to see through ours."[2]

The volunteers had to get a Mississippi driver's licenses and state car tags. They were asked to prepare by educating themselves through books, including King's Montgomery Bus Boycott memoir, *Stride Toward Freedom.* They were also made aware of the risk of arrest and the need for bail money, according to the King Institute at Stanford.[3]

All the students had to be committed to nonviolence, and training sessions covered how to register Black voters at Freedom Schools, where they would also teach literacy and civics and promote the MFDP. According to Hannah-Jones, the students needed to register enough disenfranchised Black voters so the biracial MFDP could mount a formidable challenge the state Democratic Party at the National Democratic Convention in Atlantic City in August 1964.[4]

The volunteers were met with violence at the hands of local law enforcement as well as the Ku Klux Klan. Three Freedom Summer workers—James

should request in advance a tour of the club at the B. B. King Museum (which owns the club) around the corner. The museum package for tour groups (the only way to see the club) includes lunch and live music at Club Ebony ($28-$34 per person). What's to eat? Most groups request the Southern delicacies meal, which includes fried catfish and chicken, hushpuppies, salad, dessert, and drinks.

Shopping

Clarksdale is artistic, quirky, and fun, with plenty of live music to boot. Take a piece of this Delta town home by shopping for blues-related items or Mississippi-made products that make perfect gifts. Neither of the below businesses are Black-owned.

MUSIC

CAT HEAD DELTA BLUES & FOLK ART, INC.

252 Delta Ave., Clarksdale; tel. 662/624-5992; www.cathead.biz; Mon.-Sat. 10am-5pm

Chaney (Black), Michael Schwerner (White), and Andrew Goodman (White) —were even abducted about a week after the first volunteers arrived. Weeks after their abductions, the three volunteers' bodies were found. They'd been murdered by the KKK with assistance from local law enforcement.

Adding to the tragedy, in spite of the volunteers' efforts, many Black Mississippians still found themselves unable to register by the summer's end. (Of 17,000 Black people who tried to register, only 1,600 applications were accepted by local registrars, according to the King Institute at Stanford University.[5]) However, the campaign did succeed in raising awareness, and it's been credited for helping pass two important bills: The Civil Rights Act of 1964 and the Voting Rights Act of 1965.

If you're interested in seeing where these events took place, Neshoba County offers an **African American Heritage Driving Tour** map that covers nine sights in Philadelphia, Mississippi, and surrounding Neshoba County, including Neshoba County Jail, where Schwerner, Goodman, and Chaney were detained, the Council of Federated Organizations office, a staging area for movement efforts, and Road 515 "Rock Cut Road," the murder site. Contact the Community Development Partnership (256 W Beacon St., Philadelphia; tel. 601/656-1000; www.neshoba.org; free) to receive a map. The partnership will also connect tourists with a resident volunteer guide if they desire.

The **Andrew Goodman Foundation** (www.andrewgoodman.org), started by the volunteer's parents, cultivates young leaders and focuses on voting accessibility and social justice initiatives, necessary efforts despite the passage of the Voting Rights Act of 1965. As a student, Goodman had noted how Northern apathy played a critical role in racial oppression and disenfranchisement in the South. He was murdered on his first day of work.

Midwest-born shop owner Roger Stolle was drawn to Clarksdale by the blues. Now, he invites visitors to stop into his shop to get their bearings to the town, find great blues performances, or stock up on their favorite tunes from his curated blues collections. With an encyclopedic knowledge of blues music and culture, Stolle takes time to chat with customers from near and far, field queries about blues esoterica, and listen to personal anecdotes of close calls with musical greatness. Hear some of that great live music during intimate late-night concerts right here at the eclectic store decked out in folk art, portraits of blues greats, Highway 61 signage, and blues-themed DVDs, videos, and books. Rustic, peeling walls and the vintage wooden ceiling create the perfect backdrop for discovering the soundtrack to a bygone era that might fit your mood right now.

Cat Head has free music festivals in front of the store on the porch/sidewalk/ street several times a year: April (Juke Joint Festival), May (Clarksdale Caravan Music Fest), August (Cat Head Store Anniversary), early October (Cat Head Mini Blues Fest), and mid-October (Deep Blues Fest Busking Stage). Sporadic single-act performances occur randomly every month or

two. Everything is listed on the Cat Head Music Calendar at www.cathead.biz.

GENERAL STORE

COLLECTIVE SEED AND SUPPLY CO.

145 Delta Ave., Clarksdale; tel. 662/624-2381; Tues.-Sat. 9am-5pm

Ann Williams's sunny, welcoming general store is complete with a resident green-eyed cat, gifts, garden supplies, and local food items. All kinds of seeds are available, from lima beans and collards to purple hull peas and speckled butter beans. The store prides itself on sourcing Mississippi-born products, so you'll find locally grown rice and Sweet Magnolia gelato (a local brand) too. Quirky greeting cards stand on a twirling rack: An inky print of Shirley Chisolm features her famous quote: "If they don't give you a seat at the table, bring a folding chair." Straw hats, metal watering cans, pottery, organic oils, and soy candles complete the countrified experience. Lest anyone forget, a small red-and-white sign in the front window invites all who enter to "Be Nice!"

Williams is also executive director of the Coahoma Collective, an arts and community development nonprofit dedicated to seeing Clarksdale thrive.

Photos (top to bottom): Roger Stolle, the owner, in Cat Head Delta Blues & Folk Art, Inc.; Collective Seed and Supply Co.; inside Collective Seed and Supply Co.

Festivals and Events

Mississippi Delta blues is an American musical treasure you can thankfully revel in during signature festivals held annually in the region. In Clarksdale, blues lovers like to share the wealth, which is why you can enjoy live blues music seven nights a week stretched over a variety of venues. The Sunflower River Blues and Gospel Festival also celebrates another quintessential Black music form—gospel. Between the two, you will get a feel for the rhythms and songs that bear witness to the Black experience and decode how we got over.

CLARKSDALE

SUNFLOWER RIVER BLUES AND GOSPEL FESTIVAL

127 Martin Luther King Blvd., Clarksdale; tel. 866-733-6477; www.sunflowerfest.org; second week in August Fri.-Sun. 8am-5pm; free

Some of the biggest acts in blues and gospel have performed at this free festival, held annually the second week of August, which draws tens of thousands from across the globe and features loads of local and regional talent. USA Weekend named this festival one of America's Top 10 Places to hear authentic music. Performers have included Jelly Roll Kings, Jessie Mae Hemphill, Boogaloo Ames, and James "Son" Thomas. Count Vickie Winans, Clarksdale Mass Choir, Diane and the Spiritual Angels, the Jackson Southernairs, and the Myles Family among other gospel performers who've felt the spirit here.

The Gospel Stage is inside the air-conditioned Civic Auditorium, which might come in handy on a sweltering August day. Adjacent to the Delta Blues Museum, you'll find seven acoustic stages and a main stage (air-conditioned, of course) for Delta blues.

The festival generally attracts 25,000-30,000 attendees and features food vendors at the downtown festival site. In all this is a laid-back atmosphere that is hospitable and accessible for visiting with the musicians.

JUKE JOINT FESTIVAL

Clarksdale; tel. 662/624-5992; www.jukejoint-festival.com; April

Downtown Clarksdale is the site of the annual Juke Joint Festival, which bills itself as a half blues festival, half small-town fair. More than 100 blues acts appear live to perform the music on 13 stages that celebrates Mississippi's blues past. Most daytime street vendors and musical stages operate 10am-6pm. At night, you can use your preordered wristband to access and carouse area juke joints and blues clubs from around 7pm-1am. More than 30 acts perform at 20-plus wristband venues on over 20 stages.

GREENVILLE

MISSISSIPPI DELTA BLUES AND HERITAGE FESTIVAL

119 S Theobald St., Greenville; tel. 662/335-3523 or tel. 662/645-7045; www.deltabluesms.org; gates open 10am, festival starts at noon and runs until 10pm or 11pm; $25 in advance

Held annually in September, this signature blues festival aims to celebrate the blues in the place that it was born (rather than in academic centers and high-brow institutions away from the people whose lived experiences created the form). It's considered the oldest blues festival in the world, and the biggest names in blues have been featured here, including B. B. King, Muddy Waters, John Lee Hooker, Denise LaSalle, Son Thomas, and Bobby Rush. The late Unita Blackwell, the first Black woman mayor in Mississippi and a MacArthur Foundation genius, is a founding member of the festival. The event is held on the grounds of the Washington County Convention Center, where food vendors are also onsite.

Food

According to chef and Mississippi native **Nick Wallace** (www.nickwallaceculinary.com), winner of The Food Network's *Chopped,* Mississippi cuisine is marked by the freshness of ingredients and a slow cooking method that allows flavors to develop. Mississippi cooks also love scratch cooking, says Wallace, who grew up in a rural area where his family raised animals, including heirloom pigs, and cultivated their own produce, growing crookneck squash, onions, corn, okra, rosemary, basil, sweet potatoes, and more. The produce was often grown from heirloom seeds used over many generations.

Cornbread and greens are probably the two items that scream "Mississippi," according to Wallace. Cornbread is "supposed to flake and break down a different way when you stick your fork in it," he says. It should also have a buttery taste and natural sweetness that is released when you bite into a slice. Greens, Wallace says, "should be nice and crisp, and the leaves should be soft but still have a great texture" that can stand up to whatever protein you're eating. Greens should also have a slight acidity. A little vinegar will help that along, as well as some pepper and onions.

Now that you have Chef Wallace's philosophy of Mississippi cuisine, you know what to look for as you eat your way through the Delta. Wallace also notes the Delta's love of tamales (which, here, are influenced by African American as well as Mexican cooking styles), and that this region's focus on catfish-farming makes that a go-to in a state where fishing culture is fully embraced.

CLARKSDALE

Here in Clarksdale, you can grab dinner at **Ground Zero Blues Club** or from the barbecue pit at **Red's.**

BLUESBERRY CAFÉ

235 Yazoo Ave.; tel. 662/627-7008; Tues.-Sun. 8am-1:30pm, Mon. 6am-11:30pm; $9

Monday night is when Bluesberry Café (not a Black-owned business) stays open late to feature live blues and jazz music. The rest of the time, it's a great place to get breakfast, like ham that's been sourced locally by the chef-owner, Art Crivaro, who'll cook your eggs any way you like. If you don't clean your plate, he'll ask why. You've been warned (smile). They grind the coffee on site, and if you're a coffee fiend, you can tell: It's bottomless and good.

CLEVELAND

THE SENATOR'S PLACE

1028 S Davis Ave.; tel. 662/846-7434; www.thesenatorsplace.com; Mon.-Wed. 11am-2pm, Thurs. 11am-8pm, Fri. 11am-2pm and 5pm-9pm, Sat. 7:30am-10:30am and 11am-3pm, Sun. 11am-5pm; buffet $10-12

The Senator's Place serves buffet-style soul food cooking in a large but laidback dining room that's frequented by locals and anybody considered a VIP around these parts. Owned by State Sen. Willie Simmons and his wife, Rosie, it's been featured on national TV food shows. You will leave full because The Senator's Place lets diners get their fill of ribs, fried fish, and fried or baked chicken with all the fixins at a decent price. Those include macaroni 'n' cheese, sweet potatoes, greens, corn muffins, green beans (we need Shirley Caesar to sing this for us), and so much more. Attentive staff keeps your glass full, whether that is sweet tea (just called tea around here) or a glass of water. Folks are friendly in here and make eye contact; they're likely to strike up a conversation. Advice? Just go with it.

The Blue Biscuit in Indianola

INDIANOLA

THE CROWN

112 Front St.; tel. 800/833-7731; www.thecrownrestaurant.com; Tues.-Sat. 11am-2pm; $10-12

This sit-down restaurant with an old-style Southern ambiance is located a few blocks from the B.B. King Museum. The Crown, not a Black-owned business, offers classics like catfish po'boys, homemade chicken salad, and Delta fudge pie. Enter through the front or the back; you'll pass through a combination art gallery and gift shop to get to a room emblazoned with framed artwork and dining tables set off with tablecloths and cloth napkins.

THE BLUE BISCUIT

501-503 Second St.; tel. 662/645-0258; www.thebluebiscuit.com; Fri. 11am-2pm and 5pm-midnight, Sat. 11am-2pm and 5pm-1am, Sun. 5pm-11pm, Mon. 11am-2pm

There it is, right there across the street from the B. B. King museum, beckoning you with a monster Bloody Mary skewered with all manner of things (hamburgers, onion rings) and stuck in tall glass. The 72-hour pulled pork is what this place is known for, but perhaps you'd like a nice salad or Gulf Coast shrimp because that's available too, along with live jazz and blues music, featuring mostly local and regional musicians. Like much of the Delta blues decor, this place is packed with quirky ephemera. The Blue Biscuit is not a Black-owned business.

Nightlife

In another time, the virtues of Black church culture stood juxtaposed against juke joints—transgressive jerry-built sanctuaries of Blackness peppered throughout the Southern countryside. Here, folks who spent their days working in the dirt or with hands dipped in bleach-filled water doing other folks' laundry could let loose and drink, gamble, and dance to Devil's music, like ragtime and the blues. (According to Sweet Georgia's in Atlanta, "jook" is Gullah for "disorderly.") Juke joints aren't as plentiful as they once were in the Delta, but there are still good places to find good blues music. Several venues in the area do double-duty: restaurants by day, blues clubs by night.

CLARKSDALE

Clarkdale club owners' spirit of cooperation means Monday night live blues and jazz music at **Bluesberry Café.**

Blues Clubs

GROUND ZERO BLUES CLUB

387 Delta Ave.; tel. 662/621-9009; www.groundzerobluesclub.com; Tues. 11am-2pm, Wed.-Thurs. 11am-11pm, Fri.-Sat. 11am-midnight; $5-25 cover depending on who's performing

Co-owned by former Clarksdale Mayor Bill Luckett, actor Morgan Freeman, and others, Ground Zero aims to showcase the best of today's blues right here in downtown Clarksdale. Come nightfall, this place is jumping with live blues and a diverse, all-ages crowd just vibing together and blowing off steam while enjoying great music. This performing arts-blues restaurant has a bar that runs the length of the club, pool tables, and a pit with plenty of tables and dancing room as acts take center stage up front. The happenings inside the white-painted brick building with the blue-and-red neon sign are chill in all the best ways.

The kitchen specializes in down-home cooking like fried catfish, a Home Wrecker Chicken Sammich, and fried pickles or grits. Folks gather to smoke and chat on the club's front porch, where old castoff chairs and couches complete the country vibe. The Delta Blues Museum is across the way.

RED'S BLUES CLUB

398 Sunflower Ave.; tel. 662/627-3166; www.facebook.com/pages/Reds-Blues-Club/163702543685722; Fri.-Sat; $10 cover, cash only

With an intimate juke joint feel, there's nothing fancy here, except the way you'll feel hearing real blues music. This is not that touristy homogenized stuff; this is down and dirty feels-so-bad-it's-good blues. Red's serves cold beer, but patrons are welcome to BYOB. Hungry? There's a barbecue pit on wheels out front, so you can buy a moist, pulled-pork sandwich to soak up all that beer.

INDIANOLA

The Blue Biscuit (also a restaurant) features live jazz and blues music, focusing mainly on local and regional musicians.

Accommodations

Greenwood has particularly nice accommodations, as does Clarksdale about an hour north where there's plenty to do, entertainment-wise. The Delta also features the usual national chain hotels.

GREENWOOD

THE ALLUVIAN HOTEL AND SPA

318 Howard St.; tel. 662/453-2114; www.thealluvian.com; $220-235

Small-town hospitality meets big-city accommodations at the Alluvian, which functions as a well-appointed hotel and spa, while offering cooking lessons at its Viking Cooking School across the street. The 45 rooms, five suites, and four lofts are spacious with high beds, chairs comfy enough to read or nap in, and a minibar hidden inside a modern chifforobe that comes with a special key to get the goodies inside. Bathrooms scream "new" with marble and granite showers, granite countertops, and plenty of towels and toiletries.

There's a fourth-floor dining and lounging area for breakfast, which also has an accessible porch. Happy hour with piano music, free nuts, and a cash bar is on the first floor. You can eat at the **Giardina Restaurant** bar on site, or better yet, make a reservation and have a nice, quiet dinner dressed in Delta casual in one of the restaurant's 14 private booths or dining room that opens onto a courtyard.

CLARKSDALE

THE SHACK UP INN

001 Commissary Circle Rd.; tel. 662/624-8329; www.shackupinn.com; Sun.-Thurs. $65-80, Sat-Sun $75-95

Black farm workers helped keep Hopson Plantation productive until automation moved in, and the farm became the first to be planted, harvested, and baled by machine in 1944. Today, the shacks where Black sharecroppers once lived are now the stuff of rustic, shotgun house-style hotel accommodations. Wood-sided with tin roofs, the shacks have been upgraded with plumbing, electricity, air-conditioning, and Wi-Fi, of course. Of 50 units, one is as small as 300 square feet, and the Cadillac can hold four people. There's a 10-room sister location on the same grounds called the Cotton Gin Inn, crafted from old cotton bins. Tour buses and loud fraternity types are decidedly not welcome here; the management proudly says so. The main building features musical events and workshops. It doesn't have a bar, but there is a Happy Hour. Of course, you can have your own Happy Hour on the porch of your very own shack too. Rates increase during festivals.

Now, some of you might be thinking: Why would you want to sleep where enslaved Black people and, later, Black farmhands worked their fingers to the bone? The White-owned Shack Up Inn is part of an ongoing conversation cultural tourism. On one hand, it's admittedly cute and quirky; on another, this land represents the kind of economic exploitation that fueled growth of the American economy. Ultimately, this land worked and coaxed and nurtured by Black people is sacred, but it's up to each visitor to decide whether it's a space they'll enjoy staying.

GROUND ZERO BLUES CLUB APARTMENTS

387 Delta Ave.; tel. 662/645-9366; www.deltacottoncompany.com; $150

Folks come from all over the world to Ground Zero Blues Club, but they don't have to go around the world to get a good night's rest. After a long day of taking in sights scattered throughout the Delta, this is a great place to drop your bags and head downstairs for drink and a snack while a live blues band plays on the stage. Upon check-in, you get a door code that will allow you to walk up the creaky (in a good way) wooden stairs flanked by walls that have been scrawled with messages from past visitors. (Drawing on the hotel hallway walls is actually encouraged.) Apartment entryways have an old farm industry motif, riffing off quality measures for freshly picked cotton: strict middling, good middling, and strict good ordinary. The seven apartments above the club, in what was once a cotton-grading warehouse, are not fancy, but they are clean and have plenty of towels, toiletries, a kitchen, and a living room. Don't forget to ask for the Wi-Fi code. Note that if a band is playing downstairs, the noise does travel, but that's part of the charm—unless you're exhausted, then you should head to the Travelers Hotel for a quieter experience. The club closes at 2am, and then you can get some serious shut-eye. It's all part of the experience, you know? Guests do have to pay cover at the club, but you'll be happy to do so because it all goes to the band.

THE TRAVELERS HOTEL

212 3rd St.; tel. 662/483-0693; www.stayattravelers.com; $120-180

Photos (top to bottom): a live performance at Ground Zero Blues Club; night out at Ground Zero Blue Club; The Travelers Hotel

A combination of sleek sophistication and country comfort, this renovated 20-room, artist-run hotel is a welcoming oasis in what used to be an overnight stopover for railroad workers in the early 1900s. A lobby bar features regional beer and overlooks an expansive lobby suitable for chilling out or hanging out. A fancy coffee maker is just around the corner of the open, airy first floor in the kitchen where patrons can enjoy a cup of Meraki Roasting Co.'s locally hand-roasted organic coffee. Local art is featured on hotel walls, much of it giving homage to Delta residents who created the culture folks are flocking to Clarksdale to enjoy. Creative types will marvel at the sunbathed rooms with high ceilings, rustic brick walls, writing desks, and handcrafted quilts made by ladies over in Tutweiler, a neighboring town. Folks love these quilts so much, they often buy them right off the bed for about $400, a steal when you think about what goes into piecing a quilt's symphony of color. Bunk beds are available too, but not in-room TVs. Wi-Fi is good.

INDIANOLA

THE BLUE BISCUIT

501-503 Second St.; tel. 662/645-0258; www.thebluebiscuit.com; $125

Next door from the restaurant, The Blue Biscuit has two bungalows, featuring either full beds or queen, a kitchen, and dining and work area. A large walk-in shower has a glass roof that lets you feel like you're showering outdoors. The bungalows have porches (overlooking either a pool or the B. B. King Museum), which are a good place to relax after driving or walking into town (a few blocks) to have a bite to eat or shop.

Transportation

GETTING THERE

The best and only way to get around the Delta is by car. Please make sure you have put some freon in for your air-conditioner and enough windshield-wiper fluid so you can clear off the bug juice that will surely hit your front windows while whizzing down the road.

Air

Memphis International Airport (2491 Winchester Rd.; tel. 901/922-8000; www.flymemphis.com) is a tad closer to the Delta than Jackson's **Jackson-Evers International Airport** is, and your ticket will likely be cheaper as well. Major car rental companies are available at both airports.

Train

AMTRAK

The 900-mile **City of New Orleans** Amtrak line (www.amtrak.com/city-of-new-orleans-train) from Chicago to New Orleans runs through the Delta with several stops, including Greenwood and Jackson. A ticket from New Orleans to Jackson costs $22 (coach). From New Orleans to Greenwood, a coach ticket is $42.

Bus

GREYHOUND

There are Greyhound bus stops in **Cleveland** (4 hours from Jackson, $33-38, 2.5 hours from Memphis, $39-44)**, Indianola** (2 hours from Jackson, $26-30, 17 hours—with two extremely long layovers—from Memphis, $52-59) and **Clarksdale** (4 hours, 20 minutes from Jackson, $48-47, 1.5 hours from Memphis, $26-30). Buses

VOICES OF THE MOVEMENT:
INCARCERATED FREEDOM RIDERS, MISSISSIPPI STATE PENITENTIARY

Throughout the course of the Freedom Rides, hundreds of riders were arrested in Mississippi, with many, including John Lewis and Bernard Lafayette, sent to notorious Mississippi State Penitentiary (aka Parchman Farm) in the Delta's Sunflower County, midway between Jackson and Memphis and about 30 minutes south of Clarksdale. At Parchman Farm, the Freedom Riders were served inedible food, given ill-fitting clothing, and kept locked up with no exercise. They also endured abuse at the hands of prison guards. Freedom Riders recount their time at Parchman:

LEW ZUCHMAN

"[The guards] hated us. The kind of hate I experienced there I never experienced in my life. It was visceral."

The day after seeing his hero, baseball great Jackie Robinson, standing up for the Freedom Riders on the *The David Susskind Show*, 19-year-old Lew Zuchman decided to volunteer for the Freedom Rides himself. He received a call to join a ride just a couple weeks later.

Zuchman was arrested in Jackson and taken to Parchman. As a White man, he was segregated from the Black Freedom Riders and held in a barrack with about 50 other White Freedom Riders.

Zuchman says he wasn't afraid in the early days of imprisonment. He was scared, however, when he and other Freedom Riders were moved to Death Row. He recalls that there were two people assigned to a six-by-nine cell where they were confined 24/7.

"I got very anxious and very crazy," says Zuchman. "You couldn't do anything with the anxiety. You couldn't listen to music or walk away." Zuchman also recalls that "there was a lot of tension in prison, unfortunately, between some of the White and Black Freedom Riders, and the Black reverends who were pacifists and the young African Americans from up North like Stokely Carmichael, who was a good friend of mine."

None of the Freedom Riders really knew when they were going to get out. Zuchman guesses it was around Day 42 or 43 when his name was called, and he was told to leave without saying a word—an order he ignored. "I started saying goodbye to everyone, and they threw me in this back room me and started to really scare me." He says that the White guards threatened to take him out into the woods so the Klan could kill him. He sat there for hours before being released and dumped somewhere outside Jackson.

FRED CLARK

"We prayed every day. Most of the day when we weren't delusional and could read, that's what we did."

Fred Clark grew up in Jackson and got involved in the movement as a teen, receiving SCLC training on nonviolent resistance in Georgia. In 1961, he became a Freedom Rider but never rode: Instead, he was arrested in Jackson after the police chief told him and other riders to exit the Trailways bus station. "If you didn't move you were under arrest for breach of peace and inciting a riot. That's what we went to Parchman for. They put us on maximum security: Death Row."

Once, the prison staff cut the Freedom Riders' food in half, Clark says. So all night, they sang freedom songs and spirituals whose sound carried 'round the prison. When they were asked to be quiet, "we kept singing and getting louder since we knew we were being effective," says Clark. The guards then opened all the cell doors and told the Freedom Riders to throw everything out in the hallway. Other inmates came and hauled everything off, including mattresses. The Freedom Riders were put in a tiny vault with a hole in the floor, and the guards turned the air off, Clark says.

"We were suffocating," he recalls. "All of my associates, fellow freedom fighters, were passing out." Clark noticed a crack at the bottom of the door and got air through that, sharing the source with other Freedom Riders.

It was a long time being cooped up. When the guards finally allowed the prisoners to return to their cells, they found them empty. "We didn't have any toilet tissue, and they turned the air on us at night. That's how I got pneumonia," remembers Clark.

Clark ended up serving 38 days at Parchman.

REV. JAMES LAWSON

"You didn't just go to jail and become a jail person. You went to jail and you tried to educate yourself about nonviolence; about the struggle."

Prisoners sentenced to time in Parchman followed the movement's **"Jail. No Bail"** policy, which held that paying bail only validated a corrupt system. Prisoners responded to the experience at Parchman by turning the prison into a "university," according to Rev. James Lawson, a Freedom Riders who served time at Parchman. "This is how the movement developed a sense that we've never done this before; we have to do it together," says Lawson.

leave daily from Jackson and Memphis, and schedules are subject to change without notice.

DELTA BUS LINES

The **Delta Bus Lines** tour bus (P.O. Box 5998; 662/335-2144; www.deltabuslines.net) includes scheduled regular route service between Memphis and Baton Rouge via U.S. 61 and 82, and Memphis and Jackson, Mississippi, via U.S. 61 and U.S. 49 W. Charters for groups are available.

Buy a ticket at stations throughout the Delta, including **Clarksdale** (1604 State St., tel. 662/627-7893; Mon.-Sat. 7am-5:30pm, 7:30pm-8:30pm; Sun. 4:00pm-5:30pm and 7:30pm-8:30pm), **Cleveland** (800 Davis St., tel. 662/846-5112; Mon.-Fri. 8am-5pm), and **Indianola** (106 Martin Luther King Blvd., tel. 662/887-2716; Mon.-Sat. 8am-11:59am, 1pm-5pm, Sun. 2pm-3pm).

Car

- To reach **Greenwood** from **Jackson,** take **I-55 North** for around 100 miles (2 hours).
- To reach **Clarksdale** from **Memphis,** take **U.S. 61 South** for around 80 miles (1.5 hours).

GETTING AROUND

A car is the only way to efficiently get around the Delta. Rent one with good air-conditioning.

Little Rock

In 1957, the nation held its collective breath as nine Black high school students risked violence to desegregate the all-White Little Rock Central High School. Three years earlier, the U.S. Supreme Court in *Brown v. Board of Education* had ruled that public schools must be desegregated, but Arkansas Governor Orval Faubus couldn't stand the thought of Black kids going to school with White kids and refused to implement the order. This earned the attention of President Dwight D. Eisenhower, who ultimately sent the U.S. Army and federalized the National Guard to escort the nine Black students into the school.

LITTLE ROCK'S TOP 3

1. Conjuring the bravery of the nine Black students who desegregated all-White **Little Rock Central High School** in 1957 (page 255).

2. Admiring the **Little Rock Nine Memorial at the Arkansas State Capitol**, the South's first monument on state capitol grounds (page 260).

3. Learning about West 9th Street, a historic Black neighborhood, and other aspects of the Black experience in Little Rock at **Mosaic Templars Cultural Center** (page 262).

Photos (top to bottom): Little Rock Central High School; Little Rock Nine Memorial at the State Capitol by scupltor John Deering. Previous: Little Rock Nine Memorial at the State Capitol by John Deering

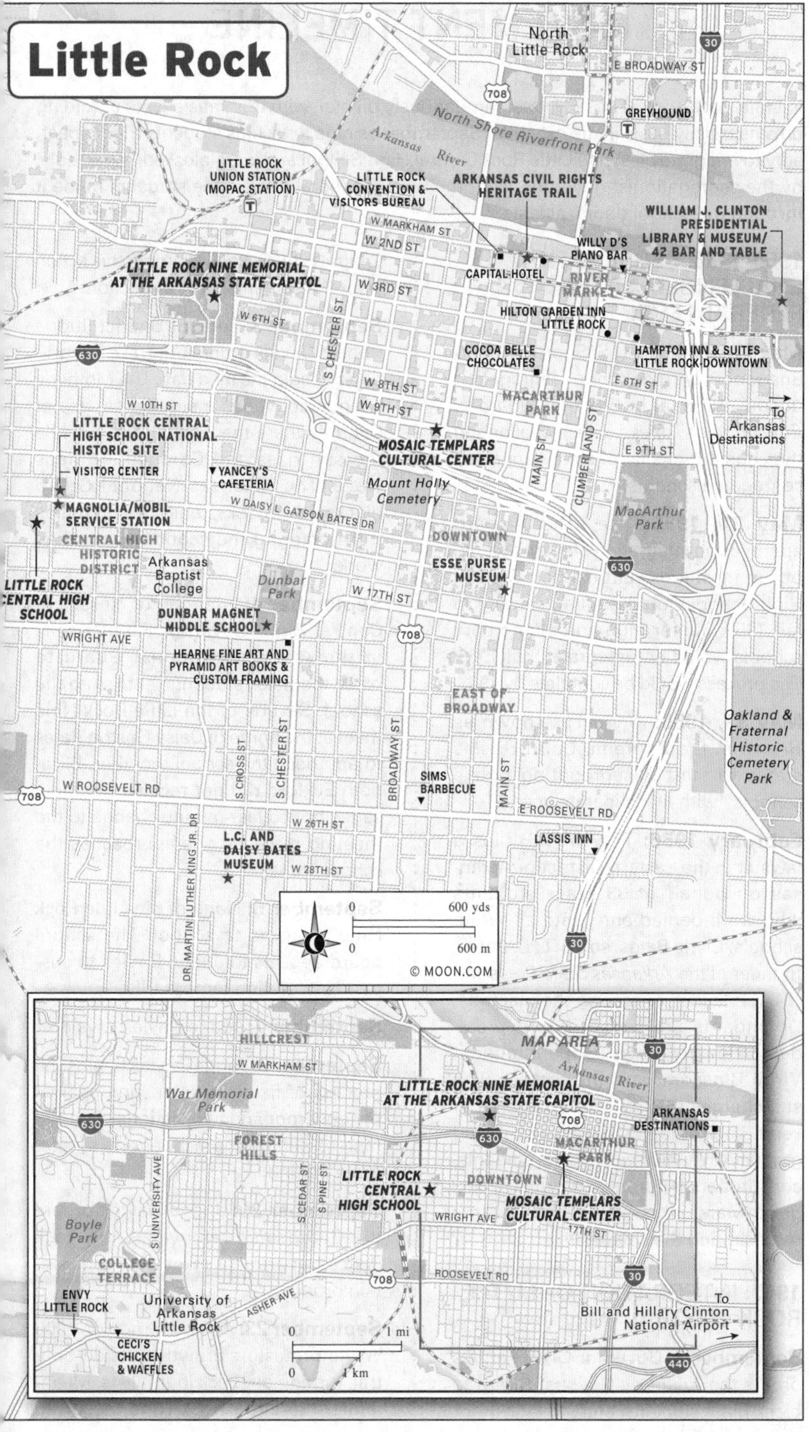

Little Rock
North Little Rock
E BROADWAY ST
GREYHOUND
North Shore Riverfront Park
Arkansas River
LITTLE ROCK UNION STATION (MOPAC STATION)
LITTLE ROCK CONVENTION & VISITORS BUREAU
ARKANSAS CIVIL RIGHTS HERITAGE TRAIL
WILLIAM J. CLINTON PRESIDENTIAL LIBRARY & MUSEUM/ 42 BAR AND TABLE
W MARKHAM ST
W 2ND ST
WILLY D'S PIANO BAR
CAPITAL HOTEL
RIVER MARKET
LITTLE ROCK NINE MEMORIAL AT THE ARKANSAS STATE CAPITOL
W 3RD ST
W 6TH ST
HILTON GARDEN INN LITTLE ROCK
HAMPTON INN & SUITES LITTLE ROCK-DOWNTOWN
COCOA BELLE CHOCOLATES
S CHESTER ST
E 6TH ST
W 8TH ST
W 9TH ST
MACARTHUR PARK
To Arkansas Destinations
W 10TH ST
LITTLE ROCK CENTRAL HIGH SCHOOL NATIONAL HISTORIC SITE
VISITOR CENTER
YANCEY'S CAFETERIA
MOSAIC TEMPLARS CULTURAL CENTER
MAIN ST
CUMBERLAND ST
E 9TH ST
Mount Holly Cemetery
MAGNOLIA/MOBIL SERVICE STATION
W DAISY L GATSON BATES DR
MacArthur Park
CENTRAL HIGH HISTORIC DISTRICT
DOWNTOWN
Arkansas Baptist College
ESSE PURSE MUSEUM
LITTLE ROCK CENTRAL HIGH SCHOOL
Dunbar Park
W 17TH ST
DUNBAR MAGNET MIDDLE SCHOOL
WRIGHT AVE
HEARNE FINE ART AND PYRAMID ART BOOKS & CUSTOM FRAMING
EAST OF BROADWAY
Oakland & Fraternal Historic Cemetery Park
S CROSS ST
S CHESTER ST
BROADWAY ST
SIMS BARBECUE
MAIN ST
W ROOSEVELT RD
E ROOSEVELT RD
W 26TH ST
LASSIS INN
DR. MARTIN LUTHER KING JR. DR
L.C. AND DAISY BATES MUSEUM
W 28TH ST
0 600 yds
0 600 m
© MOON.COM
HILLCREST
MAP AREA
W MARKHAM ST
Arkansas River
War Memorial Park
LITTLE ROCK NINE MEMORIAL AT THE ARKANSAS STATE CAPITOL
ARKANSAS DESTINATIONS
FOREST HILLS
MACARTHUR PARK
DOWNTOWN
LITTLE ROCK CENTRAL HIGH SCHOOL
S UNIVERSITY AVE
S CEDAR ST
S PINE ST
MOSAIC TEMPLARS CULTURAL CENTER
WRIGHT AVE
17TH ST
Boyle Park
COLLEGE TERRACE
ROOSEVELT RD
ENVY LITTLE ROCK
University of Arkansas Little Rock
ASHER AVE
To Bill and Hillary Clinton National Airport
CECI'S CHICKEN & WAFFLES
0 1 mi
0 1 km

MOVEMENT TIMELINE

In Little Rock, the fall of 1957 was tremendously pivotal, with dramatic events unfolding on a near daily basis in the month of September as nine tenacious students tried repeatedly to integrate all-White Little Rock Central High School and were blocked, repeatedly, by the segregationist governor. With the help of federal troops, the students made it through the school doors, at last.

1954-1956: SEGREGATION CHALLENGED AT THE FEDERAL LEVEL

May 17, 1954: The U.S. Supreme Court unanimously rules school segregation unconstitutional in *Brown v. Board of Education of Topeka,* which challenged the constitutionality of state-supported segregated schools.

May 24, 1955: The school board approves an integration plan that would occur in stages. Little Rock Central High School would go first, starting in fall 1957. Junior high and elementary schools would not integrate until 1960. The process would be complete by 1963.

May 31, 1955: In what is known as *Brown II,* the Supreme Court directs states to start desegregating public schools "with all deliberate speed."

February 1956: The NAACP files a lawsuit in the Eastern District of Arkansas on behalf of 33 Black students who were denied entry into all-White schools. Clyde Bates, son of L. C. Bates, founder of the *Arkansas State Press* and NAACP leader, is among the plaintiffs. Defendants are school board president William Cooper, Superintendent Virgil Blossom, and the district. The suit charges that officials conspired to keep Black students out by embracing gradualism, which violates the students' constitutionally protected rights. Thurgood Marshall is one of the lawyers representing the children.

1957: INTEGRATION OF LITTLE ROCK CENTRAL

September 2: Governor Orval Faubus orders the Arkansas National Guard to block Black students' entry to Little Rock Central High School, claiming this action is for the students' own protection.

September 3: Federal District Judge Ronald Davies orders Central's integration to begin the next day. The Mother's League convenes a sunrise service at Central where they sing "Dixie," while the sun rises and Confederate flags wave. The Arkansas National Guard blocks Black cooks, janitors, and maids from entering the school where they work.

September 4: First day of classes at Central High. Governor Faubus calls in the Arkansas National Guard to block the Black students' entry into the school. Several of the Little Rock Nine meet at the home of Daisy Gaston Bates to approach the school together. Elizabeth Eckford did not receive the message about a last-minute change to the meeting place, so she approaches the school alone.

September 5: None of the Little Rock Nine try to go to school. The school board appeals to Judge Davies to suspend integration temporarily.

September 7: Judge Davies says no.

September 9: Judge Davies begins the process of fixing an injunction against the governor and two National Guardsmen for interfering with efforts to integrate Central.

September 20: Judge Davies orders the Guardsmen removed. Little Rock Police Department takes over to maintain order.

September 23: An angry mob of 1,000 White protestors crowds outside Central, turning on Black journalists. Meanwhile, the Little Rock Nine, escorted into school by police, slip into school through a side door.

September 24: President Eisenhower sends in 1,200 members of the U.S. Army's 101st Airborne Division and places them in charge of the 10,000 National Guardsmen on duty.

September 25: Escorted by the troops, the Little Rock Nine attend their first full day of classes.

October 1: The 101st Airborne relinquish duties back to the federalized Arkansas National Guard. The nine students are left to deal with racial hostility and physical assaults inside the hallways and classrooms of Central High.

AFTER 1957

May 1958: Ernest Gideon Green, the only senior among the Little Rock Nine, graduates, becoming the first African American graduate of Central High. Dr. Martin Luther King Jr. attends the ceremony.

August 1958: In protest of integration, Faubus closes all Little Rock high schools. The schools remain closed for an entire year.

June 1959: A federal district court rules the closure of Little Rock high schools unconstitutional.

August 12, 1959: All four Little Rock public high schools reopen—almost a month early.

1999: Arkansas native President Bill Clinton awards each member of the Little Rock Nine the Congressional Gold Medal.

2009: The Little Rock Nine receive special invitations to attend the first inauguration of President Barack Obama, America's first Black president.

So important were the Little Rock Nine to the national movement, Dr. Martin Luther King Jr. attended the 1958 graduation of Ernest Green, the first Black student to graduate from Central. Today, a breathtaking bronze statue called *Testament* honors those students on the grounds of the state capitol.

The movement touched other aspects of life in Little Rock, including efforts to desegregate downtown facilities, a sit-in at the downtown F. W. Woolworth's in 1960, and voter registration efforts, fueled by local college students and activists working for the Student Nonviolent Coordinating Committee (SNCC) and the Congress of Racial Equality (CORE). Local organizations, such as Council on Community Affairs, were founded to take on these issues; segregationists formed their own groups too.

The 1950s and '60s were a heady time, both locally and nationally. But the roots of the African American quest for equality run much deeper and extend far beyond this period. Long before the national media put Little Rock on blast, Black people were striving for equal access and the right to live, learn, build, and create. Mosaic Templars Cultural Center captures the narrative arc of Black Little Rock in this respect. Meanwhile, many Black residents cherish the communal memories created when attending churches and segregated schools like Dunbar that seeded their values and nurtured their dreams. Integrating schools was about accessing resources, which would open the door to future opportunity. And it did.

PEOPLE WHO MADE THE MOVEMENT

GROUPS

Little Rock Nine: The nine Black students who integrated Little Rock Central High School in 1957. Their names: Minnijean Brown Trickey, Elizabeth Eckford, Ernest Green, Thelma Mothershed-Wair, Melba Pattillo Beals, Carlotta Walls LaNier, Terrence Roberts, Jefferson Thomas, and Gloria Ray Karlmark. Several students who had expressed interest in attending Central were subject to vetting by school officials. The school board narrowed the list, but some students decided to stick with the Black high school, Horace Mann.

INDIVIDUALS

Daisy Gaston Bates: Newspaper publisher and NAACP leader who supported and mentored the Little Rock Nine.

New York City Mayor Robert Wagner greets the Little Rock Nine in 1958.

Lucious Christopher (L. C.) Bates: Daisy's husband; also a newspaper publisher and NAACP leader.

Christopher Columbus Mercer Jr.: NAACP field secretary who drove the Little Rock Nine to school.

ORIENTATION

Most points of interest are located in Little Rock's **downtown,** which stretches from the Arkansas River south to West Roosevelt Road and is bordered (loosely) by I-30 to the east and by Dr. Martin Luther King Drive to the west.

Downtown Little Rock encompasses several distinctive neighborhoods. Its centerpiece is the **River Market District,** which features an array of restaurants, events, and hangouts along the Arkansas River. South of the River Market District, **West 9th Street** runs parallel to I-630. Before construction of the interstate system, this street was a hub of Black shopping and nightlife. Today, that area is a mostly vacant commercial district, but it is notably a historical district because of the presence of the Mosaic Templars Cultural Center (which tells the story of the neighborhood) and Taborian Hall/ Dreamland Ballroom. On the western edge of downtown is the **Dunbar** neighborhood, where Dunbar Magnet Middle School (originally an all-Black school built after Central was constructed) thrives.

Another noteworthy neighborhood, just to the west of downtown, is the **Central High School Historic District,** where the (now famous) high school of the same name is located. This is a quiet area lined with homes that sit across from the stately school. On the corner, the Magnolia gas station has been preserved as part of the historical narrative; a modern visitor center sits kitty-corner to the school.

Downtown (especially the River Market District) is invitingly walkable and includes many opportunities to interface with the civil rights story while walking down Markham Street. Download the

Arkansas Civil Rights History Tour app to locate more than 35 sites linked to the struggle for equality.

PLANNING YOUR TIME

Over two days, you can have a thorough experience of Little Rock's civil rights sites and get a feel for the city's hospitality.

Some tickets should be booked in advance—even before you leave home. Notably, tours of the **Little Rock Central High School National Historic Site** should be booked 48 hours (ideally, one month) in advance to secure a spot. If you visit during summer, your tour may include entry into the school cafeteria (not accessible to visitors) for a history lesson. Note that weekend tours do not enter the school campus at all; you'll just see the school from the outside.

The **L. C. and Daisy Bates Museum** is run by a dedicated group of Bates's fans. Be sure to call ahead for reservations if you want to see inside.

When you arrive, check out the **Little Rock Convention & Visitors Bureau** (101 S Spring St; tel. 501/376-4781) for maps and information.

CONNECT WITH

Little Rock connects well with **Memphis,** which is a straight shot east on I-40, about a two-hour drive. The **Mississippi Delta** is about five hours away.

Two Days in Little Rock

DAY 1

Your first day in Little Rock is dedicated to the Little Rock Nine. Jump in the car to hit all these places in the course of a day. Make reservations to tour **Little Rock Central High School National Historic Site** at least 48 hours (and ideally a month) in advance. If you want to see inside the **L. C. and Daisy Bates Museum,** make reservations as early as possible.

1 Follow in the footsteps of segregationist protestors, national media, law enforcement, but, most of all, the Little Rock Nine students themselves on a 1-2-hour walking tour of **Little Rock Central High School National Historic Site.** Tours begin at 9am.

2 Now that you've seen Little Rock Central, take a one-mile detour over to Wright Avenue to stand in front of **Dunbar Magnet Middle School,** which functioned as Dunbar High School and Junior College when it opened in 1929. The campus was constructed with philanthropist money for all-Black students after all the taxpayer funds were spent on state-of-the-art Central.

3 Around noon, head over to **Lassis Inn** where you can enjoy the buffalo ribs and hush puppies while you sit in the same bright blue booths Daisy Bates and other residents sat in as they plotted the next steps in their civil rights quest. The beer is cold, but if it's early, maybe stick with the sweet tea.

4 Backtrack a bit to the **L. C. and Daisy Bates Museum** for a tour of the home that was a meeting spot before and after school for the Little Rock Nine.

5 Drive over to view the **Little Rock Nine Memorial at the Arkansas State Capitol** called *Testament*. What happened together and individually to these students and their families was a lot to endure; take your time to take it all in.

6 Get ready to blow off some steam with a night out in downtown Little Rock. **Willy D's Piano Bar** has a full restaurant, plus live music on the first floor. This venue draws a mixed crowd that is laid back and friendly.

DAY 2

The highlight of your second day in Little Rock is the **Mosaic Templars Cultural Center,** which tells the story of the West 9th Street Historic District, a thriving commercial neighborhood before the interstate system was constructed around it.

1 To start the day, the biscuits at One Eleven at the **Capital Hotel** are to die for.

2 Once you've had your fill of breakfast, burn off a few calories with a little walk. Just head out the Capital's front door and cross the street. Now, look down to see several markers embedded in the sidewalk courtesy of the **Arkansas Civil Rights Heritage Trail.** The markers recognize the people who powered the civil rights movement. Look for markers commemorating Freedom Riders who stopped in this city, along with the Little Rock Nine.

3 OK, you can look up now! Drive to **Mosaic Templars Cultural Center** to see and hear the story of Black Little Rock, with special focus on the once-thriving West 9th Street District.

4 Hungry? Ride on over to **Sims Barbecue** and get your fingers sticky in the sauce.

Sights

CENTRAL HIGH SCHOOL HISTORIC DISTRICT

Little Rock Central High School National Historic Site

The high school that was famously integrated by the Little Rock Nine in 1957 is still a functioning high school today, but it also works overtime as part of a national historic site that includes a combination museum/visitor center (the next block over from the high school) and the Magnolia gas station (across the street from Central) where the national press called in reports about the integration crisis in 1957. The national historic site is also an official part of the U.S. Civil Rights Trail.

Walking tours of the site (1-2 hours; free), led by knowledgeable National Park Service rangers, will engage your senses as you follow the footsteps of the Little Rock Nine students. Tours begin at the visitor center before heading to the gas station and high school. On weekdays, you'll see the outside and inside of the campus. On weekends, you'll see the exterior only. It is possible to check out the gas station and the visitor center on your own, if you like, but access to the high school campus is only via ranger-led tour.

Tours are available daily at 9am and again at 1pm. Call tel. 501/374-1957 for reservations. Tour space is limited: It's advised to reserve at least 48 hours in advance, and your best bet is calling a month in advance. When booking a tour, be prepared with the number of people you'll be bringing and whether you need ADA access or have other special needs. Precautions surrounding the coronavirus pandemic might dictate crowds of 10 or fewer people, so if you know you want to visit here, be sure to call ahead.

VISITOR CENTER

2120 W Daisy L Gatson Bates Dr.; tel. 501/374-1957; www.nps.gov/chsc; 9am-4pm daily; free

Your first stop on the Little Rock Central High School National Historic Site tour is this one-story visitor center, located on W. Daisy L. Gatson Bates Drive, named for the NAACP leader who mentored the Little Rock Nine. Inside, a small museum showcases the local players who made an outsize impact on the national civil rights movement.

The center contains a gallery as well as an education space. Short films, such as one showcasing the enduring impact the Little Rock Nine made on students across the nation, are screened in the education space. In the gallery, photos, artifacts, and interactive audio-and-video kiosks tell the story of integration in Little Rock and beyond. One interactive kiosk features the Little Rock Nine answering the question, "Why step forward?" Another exhibit is a photo showing Little Rock Schools Superintendent Virgil Blossom, whose stance on integration in a city that dragged its feet in complying with the law was this: "Our purpose is to comply with the law in a manner that would be accepted locally."

Perhaps the most fascinating artifact in this space is a pair of white saddle shoes that resemble those worn by Little Rock Nine student Melba Pattillo Beals. Beals has written that she shined her shoes up every morning as if going to war.

TOP EXPERIENCE

★ LITTLE ROCK CENTRAL HIGH SCHOOL

1500 S Park St.

Picture this: It's the morning of September 4, 1957. Elizabeth Eckford, one of the nine Black students selected to integrate Little Rock Central High School, showed up for school, looking for eight other Black students, only to find that they were nowhere to be seen. At the last minute, the meetup spot had changed to the home of NAACP president Daisy Bates for safety reasons, but the Eckford family didn't have a phone and didn't receive the message. That is why iconic photos of that day depict a stoic Eckford all alone, wearing dark shades and clutching a loose-leaf binder as she maneuvered through a crowd that spat on her and shouted for her to leave. The National Guard had pushed everyone off the walkway in front of the school, so Eckford was forced into the angry White crowd gathered in the street.

As you approach the majestic Gothic Revival structure, try to imagine Eckford's experience. Picture the area packed with angry White people, all of whom have their attention trained on you. They yell filthy names, telling you to "Go back to Africa" when all you want to do is go to school. Onsite guards must be there to protect you, right? Wrong. At least on September 4, 1957, when Elizabeth Eckford tried to make her way into school, she had no protection as she walked the gauntlet. She says she's glad she wore shades on that fateful day.

Your park tour starts on the sidewalk in front of the same school, where National Park Service rangers invite crowds to

VOICES OF THE MOVEMENT: ELIZABETH ECKFORD OF THE LITTLE ROCK NINE

"I thought I would be accepted after people got to know me. But when it became apparent that I wasn't even a human being to a lot of people, and there was an organized group trying to drive us away, part of the reason I stayed was just plain stubbornness."

—**ELIZABETH ECKFORD** is the student in iconic photos of the Little Rock integration crisis wearing dark shades and a white collared dress, holding a binder in one arm as White students shout and glare at her. It wasn't intended for Eckford to enter the school alone, but her family didn't have a phone, so she didn't receive a message to meet at NAACP president Daisy Bates's home so local Black ministers could escort the Little Rock Nine to school together. During Eckford's solo entry, an angry White mob shouted racial epithets at her, soaking her new dress in spit.

THE INTEGRATION PROCESS

Eckford had to apply to be one of the Black students who would integrate Central. "We had individual motives for wanting to go to school there," says Eckford, noting that Superintendent Blossom made the final decision on who was allowed in. "He wanted a very, very small number of students. And he did not want anybody associated with the NAACP. I had not met anybody from the NAACP before I actually tried to go to Central."

imagine throngs of people gathered to demand the school stay Whites-only. They point to where police and National Guardsmen stood and describe how they controlled the crowd. Across the street, the private homes that were present in 1957 still remain. Because this is a historic area, they have been preserved and are largely untouched.

The tour enters the auditorium, where rangers discuss the Black student experience at Central. Guests are directed to be very quiet and stay with the group, as this is a still-functioning high school.

The rest of the school is generally off limits, but during summer rangers may take guests to the cafeteria, where Little Rock Nine student Minnijean Brown dropped a tray of chili on a White student who blocked her path. A deafening silence ensued . . . until Black workers in the cafeteria began to clap. Minnijean was suspended for the incident. (Later, she was expelled after calling a group of White girls "White

INSIDE LITTLE ROCK CENTRAL HIGH

Eckford points out that, contrary to what Little Rock officials may have stated, "integration was not intended at all." The handful of Black students who integrated Central only served to show "a few dark faces" who could prove compliance with the law while the system carried on as usual.

Little Rock Central was an aggressive environment for the nine Black students, each of whom managed managed hostility from White students and teachers in their own ways. Eckford says her own stubbornness motivated her to stay, but certain behaviors really got to her. When White students saw she was being bullied and failed to react, it felt like they either "approved of what was happening . . . or what was happening to us didn't matter to them at all. The people who said nothing but looked away—that was very, very hurtful to me," says Eckford.

Eckford, who had previously attended Dunbar, an all-Black school, also remembers an American history teacher at Central who taught that the Civil War wasn't about slavery at all, and that enslaved persons were treated well. Sadly, she says, "There was no reaction from the students whatsoever."

LIFE AFTER HIGH SCHOOL

During The Lost Year (1958), when Little Rock high schools closed, Eckford took correspondence courses. When school resumed in 1959, she skipped high school and went straight to Knox College in Galesburg, Illinois, where she studied for a year. College opened up new opportunities for Eckford, who worked on theater sets and played a minor role in the play *Little Foxes*. Eckford enlisted in the U.S. Army and became a member of the Women's Army Corps, serving five years. She earned a degree in history at Central State University in Wilberforce, Ohio. In 2018, she published a children's book, *The Worst First Day: Bullied While Desegregating Little Rock Central High,* with Eurydice and Grace Stanley about her courageous effort as a teen.

trash" after they attacked her. Minnijean Brown completed her education at New Lincoln High School in New York, where she was warmly welcomed.)

Little Rock Central has changed since the 1950s. Today, the student body at Little Rock Central is majority (55 percent) Black and 35 percent White. At one count, the student body represented 24 countries, and more than 31 languages were recently reported as being spoken inside the school.

ELIZABETH ECKFORD COMMEMORATIVE BENCH

An emotional photo captures a distraught Eckford sitting on a city bus bench across from the Little Rock Central High School, surrounded by White onlookers as she waited for a ride so she could retreat to the safety of her mother. Next to her wearing a checkered dress is Grace Lorch, who comforted Eckford on that trying day. A replica bench, named for Eckford and modeled on the one that sat here in 1957, now sits in

VOICES OF THE MOVEMENT:
LITTLE ROCK CENTRAL STUDENT SYBIL JORDAN HAMPTON

"There are still many opportunities to be first, which means you don't fit someplace very comfortably."

—SYBIL JORDAN HAMPTON, NEE JORDAN, was a 15-year-old sophomore bookworm who loved English when she entered Little Rock Central High School in 1959, two years after the Little Rock Nine integrated the school. She was one of three more Black students who had been psychologically vetted and interviewed by the all-White school board before being cleared to attend Central. She would be the first to attend the high school, a three-year institution, all three years. And as the only Black 10th grader, she would have a singular experience of ostracism and racial tension all those years.

LITTLE ROCK CENTRAL AFTER INTEGRATION

To hear Hampton tell it, nobody knows what happened at Little Rock Central after the Little Rock Nine officially integrated the school in 1957. "It fell off the radar screen," she says. After TV news crews and print reporters packed up and went home, federal troops marched to their next assignments, and local cops went back to their respective beats. For all the world knew the trouble in Little Rock was solved—except nothing was, Hampton says.

Little Rock Central remained a toxic dish of racial tension and resentment aimed at the school's Black students. No one spoke to Hampton the entire time she attended Central, she recounts. Sure, her teachers called on her in class, but there was no engagement or after-class mentoring. Students only spoke to her if a teacher directed them to do so. "It was a very odd thing," says Hampton, who went on to earn a doctorate at the University of Chicago and eventually became president of the Winthrop Rockefeller Foundation. "They didn't interact with me personally. What they did is respect me as a student and made sure that I was involved. I think my teachers respected me because they loved learning."

REFLECTING ON INTEGRATION

How did Hampton have the wherewithal to stick it out at Central? Growing up in Little Rock's Bethel A.M.E. set the tone. She knew the circumstances of enslavement, including how Black people were abused on forced labor camps, denied their agency, and how her ancestors still believed the promise of democracy could be realized in Arkansas. "I felt I was a part of that wonderful thing that has happened to our people, the belief that you keep your shoulder to the plow and press on," Hampton explains.

Looking back, Hampton has empathy for her teachers and sees them as victims too. No one prepared them to lead the kind of massive social change that integration represented. Civic leadership was "so anxious to implement whatever they were doing, they didn't set expectations," she says. Unfortunately, nobody took the time to facilitate the inclusion of Black students in their midst.

LOOKING FORWARD

Decades later, when Hampton was invited to her 20th class reunion, she brought her parents, Leslie Sr. and Lorraine Jordan, because they were not allowed to come to the school when she was in high school: "I wanted my parents to have some sense of what my brother and I had experienced." Sadly, White former classmates were still uncomfortable with her presence, and Hampton's family sat alone at their table with the one classmate who was instrumental in making sure Hampton was invited.

While desegregating schools worked to address the equity question, inclusion is still an issue. Years after her own high school experience had ended, a high school student introduced herself to Hampton as the only Black student in her Advanced Placement classes, relating that she often felt excluded and misunderstood, but seeing Hampton and hearing her story lifted her spirits and gave her the confidence to go on. Hampton reflects, "There's still many opportunities to be first, which means you don't fit someplace very comfortably."

that spot as a commemoration of Eckford's courage.

MAGNOLIA/MOBIL SERVICE STATION

2125 W Daisy L Gatson Bates Dr.; tel. 501/374-1957; www.nps.gov/chsc; 9am-4pm daily; free

This gas station, located at the southeast corner of Daisy Gaston Bates Drive and Park Street, will go down in history because it had something every reporter needed: a phone.

In 1957, journalists descended on the area around Little Rock Central High School (along with angry White residents and law enforcement) to report on the integration crisis. They came from everywhere: The *New York Times*, *Life* and *Look* magazines, the *Arkansas Gazette*, *Arkansas Democrat*, *Chicago Defender*, *Baltimore Afro-American*, *Der Spiegel* (Germany), and the *Arkansas State Press*, to name a few. Television was still entering the American mainstream, and TV reporters from major networks followed the story here,

capturing live footage of the Arkansas National Guard troops blocking the students' entrance into school.

These journalists desperately needed to stay in contact with editors and producers to file stories and updates, and they relied on this station to make their calls. Today, tours gather here, and you can try to imagine the desperation of really needing a phone when every other reporter needed the same thing at the same time.

The gleaming white station with reddish accents was built around the same time as Little Rock Central High School. It's been restored to evoke 1957, down to the signage, paint, and vintage gas pumps. The station operated through the 1980s and opened as part of the historic site in 1997, the 40th anniversary of the integration event.

Of the reporting on the school's integration, Little Rock Nine student Minnijean Brown Trickey recalled, "... the world media took a moral stand on Little Rock, and they were horrified. There was so much media coverage, even though we knew [the people in the crowd] were crazy, we also knew that they would have to be really crazy to kill one of us in public."

DOWNTOWN AND THE RIVER MARKET DISTRICT

★ Little Rock Nine Memorial at the Arkansas State Capitol

500 Woodlane St.; tel. 501/682-1010; www.sos.arkansas.gov/state-capitol

As the civil rights movement gained steam, the Arkansas State Capitol was emblematic of entrenched racism that gripped the state: Black people could only work

Photos (top to bottom): Ranger Randy Dotson in front of Little Rock Central High School; Elizabeth Eckford commemorative bench (replica); Magnolia/Mobil Service Station

1958-1959: THE LOST YEAR

Arkansas Gov. Orval Faubus lost the battle to preserve segregation on September 25, 1957, when the Little Rock Nine were successfully escorted into Central High School, but he was determined not to lose the war.

a girl being educated via TV in September 1958, when Little Rock schools were closed

FAUBUS CLOSES SCHOOLS

Shortly before school was to start in August 1958, Faubus orchestrated the passage of 16 bills that would allow the closure of all Little Rock high schools and thwart further efforts to integrate. The bills also sought to identify Black activists and sympathizers who worked in state government and punish them for standing up for the constitutionally protected rights. All four Little Rock high schools were closed, disrupting the education of nearly 4,000 students. Oddly, the governor ordered high school football games to continue.[1]

PARENTS REACT

Private schools sprouted up to educate White students. Black people, meanwhile, worked communally to keep children caught up on their lessons. (Some students of both races also attended Catholic schools, which existed for both Black people and Whites.) Families throughout Little Rock engaged a patchwork of options to educate their children, including sending them to schools in nearby towns or moving in with relatives in other states. Some students entered college early, and others never finished high school. Others worked during The Lost Year and graduated later.

Not surprisingly, Faubus's actions further inflamed racial tensions. White residents took sides and formed groups to push for or against integration.

On May 25, 1959, a school board election recalled three segregationist members: Ed I. McKinley Jr., Robert W. Laster, and Ben D. Rowland Sr. The *New York Times* reported heavy voter turnout on this sunny day, where emotions ran high. And in an about-face, local newspapers editorialized against the governor, according to the *Times.*

SCHOOLS REOPEN, ENDING THE LOST YEAR

In June 1959, a federal district court declared the schools' closing unconstitutional. The four high schools reopened on August 12, 1959, after being closed for the entire school year.

But the story didn't end there. In 1971, federal courts encouraged busing with hopes of achieving full integration in school districts across the nation. As a result, White flight took off, and more private schools—known throughout the South as segregation academies—were opened.

Today, Central's student body of 2,500 or so students is racially and ethnically diverse. About half (51 percent) are African American, and 30 percent of the student body is White.

certain positions, such as janitorial staff or cooks, and were forced to eat lunch outside away from White state employees. Thus, John Deering's aptly named tribute sculpture, *Testament*, is just that. Situated on the north side of the Capitol grounds, *Testament* is a series of nine life-size bronze statues honoring the Little Rock Nine.

Unveiled August 30, 2005, *Testament* is the South's first monument on state capitol grounds. The monument faces the governor's office window, serving as a constant reminder to sitting governors of their responsibility to all residents; just think of how segregationist Gov. Faubus would have responded to that.

The memorial, a stop on the official U.S. Civil Rights Trail, stands triumphantly alight at nighttime, which is a great time to drive by and contemplate its meaning. It is also perfectly OK to park and view the monument up close. The installation features lots of details that provide insight into the hearts and minds of the Little Rock Nine, such as quotes from the students that are engraved in its base.

Several other monuments are found on these grounds, many of them seemingly in tension with desegregation goals, such as those honoring the Confederacy. Other worthy monuments include a Vietnam Veterans Memorial, memorials for law enforcement officers and firefighters, and the Medal of Honor Memorial featuring a majestic bronze eagle that recognizes Arkansas's Congressional Medal of Honor holders.

Arkansas Civil Rights Heritage Trail

300 W Markham St.; www.arkansascivilrightsheritage.org

As you walk up and down Markham Street, a busy downtown street with places to grab coffee, shop, club, or engage with history and culture, look down to see a series of bronze markers embedded in the sidewalk. The markers, which are the brainchild of the Anderson Institute on Race and Ethnicity (2801 S University Ave.; tel. 501/569-8932), honor the achievements of people who fought to secure racial and ethnic justice in this state. The medallions fall into several categories, including sit-ins and Freedom Rides; desegregation of Central High School; and Gov. Winthrop Rockefeller, whose policies supported Black empowerment and inclusion. You may see familiar names and learn new ones, and if you take some time to read about them after viewing the medallions, you'll leave Little Rock smarter, for sure.

The trail starts at 300 W Markham Street, outside the Old State House Museum (the oldest standing state capitol west of the Mississippi River) and ends up less than a mile eastward by the William J. Clinton Presidential Library and Museum. The institute expects to continue announcing new markers in the future.

★ Mosaic Templars Cultural Center

501 W 9th St.; tel. 501/683-3593; www.mosaictemplarscenter.com; Tues.-Sat. 9am-5pm; free

A whole lot went on before African Americans reached a point of no return and demanded their rights by organizing, protesting, and risking their lives to do things like have a soda at a lunch-counter or get a quality education. The Mosaic Templars Cultural Center, which is a stop on the official U.S. Civil Rights Trail, tells that story.

The center became the state's first African American history museum in 2008, but its history goes back to the 1880s. John E. Bush and Chester W. Keatts, both formerly enslaved, learned of a woman who couldn't bury her son for lack of money. They found this unconscionable, so they decided to do something about it, founding the Mosaic Templars of America as a fraternal organization offering mutual aid along with life and death insurance to

FREEDOM RIDES: LITTLE ROCK

As part of a summer campaign organized by The Freedom Ride Coordinating Committee, five Freedom Riders arrived in Little Rock from St. Louis on July 10, 1961. They were led by Rev. Benjamin Elton Cox and included Bliss Ann Malone, Annie Lumpkin, pastor John Curtis Raines, and Janet Reinitz.

The riders were arrested after they arrived at a Midwest Trailways station at Markham and Louisiana Streets. (Technically, the waiting room had been integrated, but police made the arrests after the passengers refused to leave.) A crowd of more than 300 people assembled at the station watched. These Freedom Riders were convicted on July 12, 1961, fined, and sentenced to six months in prison. The judge agreed to let them go if they left the state. They did.

Bus terminals in Little Rock were desegregated in November 1961, thanks to the work of the CORE Freedom Riders and sit-in participants. Today, the series of markers that comprise the **Arkansas Civil Rights Trail** on Markham Street include markers honoring the riders arrested here.

African Americans in 1882. In 1913, the organization's headquarters, situated in the historic hub of Little Rock's Black community on West 9th Street, opened, and the fraternal organization grew in worldwide influence. By 1930, the organization went into receivership and stopped operations in Arkansas, though they are still functioning in Barbados.

The original Mosaic Templars building, erected in 1911, burned in a 2005 fire. Founding documents were discovered in a cornerstone that was rescued from the debris and are on display inside the new building. Today, this 35,000-square-foot museum features four permanent exhibits on the first floor, the Arkansas Black Hall of Fame on the third floor, and the Bush-Remmel genealogical research center, which provides access to Ancestry.com so people can trace their roots, on the second floor. At the time of writing in 2020, the museum was in the process of revamping several displays and adding new ones, along with interpretive theater and children's interactive space.

Exhibits in the museum depict the life and times of Black Little Rock residents, with a special focus on historic West 9th Street, a social hub and commercial district where Black business thrived in the late 19th century and early 20th century. Among the museum's high points is an interactive grid of this street. The exhibit has an audio element, so you can listen to re-enactments of residents' interactions in shops—hearing, for example, a cash register ringing up a sale in a pharmacy as a screen projects names of businesses and people involved in the health care of the community. Jazz music introduces nightlife and people who enjoyed entertainment in places like the Gem Theatre. Videos feature residents talking about nightlife on 9th Street. This museum experience is a fascinating way to spend a couple of hours.

The museum covers early Black resistance efforts, such as the Separate Coach Law of 1891, which was the state's first step into legalized segregation. It also celebrates Black entrepreneurial spirit; explains who the Mosaic Templars were and why the

Photos (top to bottom): the Little Rock Nine Memorial at the Arkansa State Capitol; a marker on the Arkansas Civil Rights Heritage Trail William J. Clinton Presidential Libra and Museum

organization was founded; and honors the role of Little Rock's Black churches in civil rights activities. Learn the names of churches where organizing meetings took place and the ministers, such as Rev. Joseph C. Crenchaw, who promoted membership in the NAACP. Other exhibits include a mellophone brass band instrument that was used by marching bands sponsored by Black fraternal organizations.

On the third floor, The Arkansas Black Hall of Fame seeks to correct the erasure of Black people from the American narrative. Each year, the Hall of Fame celebrates the accomplishments of at least six African American Arkansans at an induction ceremony. Past inductees have included Ernest Green, the first African American graduate of Little Rock Central High School; local heroine Daisy Gaston Bates; poet Maya Angelou; Lottie Shackleford, the first woman mayor of Little Rock; and gospel singer W. R. Smokie Norful, among many others. The Hall of Fame includes photos and biographies of the inductees.

Planned additions to the center include an interpretive gallery and a children's gallery intended to encourage youth ages 3-9 to have conversations about race with adults.

William J. Clinton Presidential Library and Museum

1200 President Clinton Ave.; tel. 501/374-4242; www.clintonlibrary.gov; Sun. 1pm-5pm, Mon.-Sat. 9am-5pm; adults $10, seniors and college students $8, youth 6-17 $6, children 0-5 free

Arkansas is one of just a handful of states that feature a presidential library, that of native Bill Clinton, who lived in Little Rock for 16 years while he was governor of the state. Housed in a modernist, LEED-certified building, the William J. Clinton Presidential Library and Museum includes exhibits, artifacts, and archives from Clinton's two terms as president. Exhibits include full-scale replicas of Clinton's Oval Office and Cabinet Room and an oversize timeline of the Clinton administration. And oh, Bill and First Lady Hillary have a private residence here, but nope—you can't go in there.

Elected president in 1992, Clinton spoke on a frequency understood by Southern African Americans based on years of living, liaising, and governing here. Toni Morrison once called him "our first Black president" in a nod to the scrutiny under which he often found himself. (In 2020, he brought it on himself with a critique of Stokely Carmichael and the Black Power movement at John Lewis's funeral.)

On the second floor of the museum, African Americans can find their places in this presidential narrative. Here, a permanent exhibit on the Little Rock Nine includes a display of their Congressional Gold Medals awarded by Clinton in 1999 during a special White House ceremony. This medal is considered the highest civilian honor given by Congress: George Washington was the first recipient. The Little Rock Nine donated theirs to the library. Video segments include a September 24, 1957, TV address by President Eisenhower, and footage of the ceremony where the Little Rock Nine received their medals decades later.

The William J. Clinton Presidential Library and Museum is a stop on the official U.S. Civil Rights Trail.

Dunbar Magnet Middle School

1100 Wright Ave.; tel. 501/447-2600; www.lrsd.org

Dunbar High School and Junior College (now a middle school called Dunbar Magnet Middle School) opened in 1929. Dunbar was built in response to Black residents who sought a new facility after Little Rock Central was constructed for White students.

"THE LINE": LITTLE ROCK'S WEST 9TH STREET HISTORIC DISTRICT

The six blocks of West 9th Street between Broadway and West Chester were once the site of Black-owned barber and beauty shops, churches, entertainment venues, restaurants, and medical and lawyers' offices. Time was when you asked young folks where they were going Saturday night, they said they were going to "The Line," as the area came to be known.

There isn't much left of it today, but the story of the area's heyday—and its subsequent decline—is well worth knowing.

FORMATION OF THE LINE

Originally called West Hazel Street, West 9th Street grew out of an area where Union soldiers built log cabins for freed Black people in 1863, at the beginning of Reconstruction. During Jim Crow, as states started passing laws to restrict Black movement and keep Black and White people separated, Black residents around West 9th Street started calling the area "The Line," in reference to the color line that separated Black Little Rock from White Little Rock.

Like we have with so many things, Black people took a negative and turned it into a positive, and from the late 19th century to the early 20th century, West 9th Street established itself as the commercial and social hub of the Black community. The 1920s were good to the area as businesses continued to grow. The area declined during the Depression, when many businesses and fraternal groups were forced to close up shop. Clubs were social centers, hosting the likes of B. B. King, Ella Fitzgerald, Billie Holiday, and Cab Calloway, to name a few. During World War II, Black soldiers liked the downtown feel of West 9th Street clubs over other areas where they could be entertained.

Little Rock Central was called the "most beautiful high school in America" when it was completed in 1927. The campus had everything, from an auditorium that seated 2,000 to a gym, an electrical and plumbing shop, homemaking rooms, and a space to take junior college classes. The facility came at a cost of $1.5 million in taxpayer money, both White and Black. That money had been earmarked to build a Black school too, but the school board spent all of it on the White students.

At the request of school board member G. DeMatt Henderson, Sears, Roebuck & Co. executive and philanthropist Julius Rosenwald financed the all-Black Dunbar, which cost $400,000 to build. (The Julius Rosenwald Fund built nearly 5,000 schools for African Americans in the South.) Originally called the Negro School of Industrial Arts, Dunbar housed a high school as well as a junior college. Its blueprint was, in fact, taken from the Central High plan—just a corner of it.

The school and surrounding neighborhood are named for the Ohio-born literary giant Paul Laurence Dunbar, whose body of work addresses the African American struggle for equality. Today, the campus is not open for tours, but a marker standing out front lets readers know that the Black community here didn't stop living just

THE NEIGHBORHOOD DECLINES

The joy and striving embedded in this district began to unravel with the introduction of urban renewal. The Federal Housing Act of 1949 set out to upgrade "blighted areas." Black residents were told to move or be removed from their homes.

Like many Black communities across the country, West 9th Street became a target of "improvement" efforts that required the expansion of freeways. Here in Little Rock, the construction of I-630 divided people south of the interstate. Overpasses were built, but they functioned more as barriers than access points, according to Bryan McDade of the Mosaic Templars Cultural Center. The plan to build I-630 worked its way through the courts, ultimately succeeding, and many Black residents were displaced.

Redlining also played a role in the fate of this community. The West 9th Street area shows up prominently on maps created by the Home Owner's Loan Corporation between 1935 and 1940 to determine the creditworthiness of communities. As in cities across the country, the area was shaded red, signaling a low grade.

The effects of redlining linger to this day, in Little Rock and in cities across the country.

THE LINE TODAY

Today, the West 9th Street area is a mostly vacant commercial area, and many Black residents wistfully recall the sense of pride and cohesiveness of the district. The **Taborian Hall/Dreamland Ballroom** (800 W. 9th St.) is the only original building left from its heyday. But the area remains culturally relevant thanks to the **Mosaic Templars Cultural Center** (page 262), which tells the story of the once prosperous neighborhood.

because of the integration crisis around the way. Residents are proud of their community roots, however segregated they were.

ESSE Purse Museum

1510 Main St.; tel. 501/916-9022; www.essepursemuseum.com; Tues.-Sat. 11am-4pm, Sun. 11am-3pm; adults $10, students, seniors, and military $8

This sublime museum is dedicated to the life and times of—wait for it—purses! The museum tells the story of 20th century women and their work, aspirations, and wins through the handbags they carried, and this narrative includes Black women too. Permanent exhibits showcase bags, totes, and clutches in every size, shape, color, and purpose alongside photos and paintings that offer context and set the mood. Purses are cataloged by decade so your imagination can shift with time as you maneuver through.

The gift shop sells a variety of finely crafted purses of varying prices, among an array of other items including scarves and jewelry.

OTHER NEIGHBORHOODS

L. C. and Daisy Bates Museum

1207 W 28th St.; tel. 501/375-1957; free

This home, where NAACP president Daisy Bates lived with her husband, was the last-minute staging area for the Black students who set out to integrate Little Rock Central High School on September 4, 1957. (An earlier plan had them meeting near the school but was changed the night before for safety reasons.) The students met here so they could arrive at Central together. Elizabeth Eckford didn't get the call about the venue change because her family didn't have a phone. Bates had arranged for a multiracial group of ministers to escort the students to school that morning.

The Bates home was a meeting place and haven for members of the Little Rock Nine. For one thing, it was the students' official daily pickup and drop-off spot. (NAACP attorney Christopher Columbus Mercer Jr. took five of the kids to and from school during their first semester.) Bates also served as a liaison between the school board and the students and their families, and frequently provided the Black press with access to the students at her home. Sybil Jordan Hampton, among the second group of Black students to enter Central in 1959, recalls meeting here with her cohort for an interview and photoshoot with *Jet* magazine.

Segregationists vandalized the property and home, which was a target of a bombing after high schools were closed in 1958-59. People burned crosses here twice, and bullets were fired through the windows. Bates and her husband needed nightly guards.

Today, the 1950s-style ranch home serves as a museum. Interior furnishings, including a faux brick fireplace and a built-in sideboard in the dining room, have been restored to evoke the 1950s. Portraits of Bates, as well as images of the

Photos (top to bottom): historical marker outside Dunbar Magnet Middle School; Crystal Mercer, daughter of Christopher Columbus Mercer, lawyer for Little Rock Nine, at ESSE Purse Museum; Daisy Bates's house

DAISY BATES

When people hear about a Black woman who mentored the Little Rock Nine, a type of nurturing ideal often springs to mind. But Daisy Bates was more than that: The NAACP president was about the business of securing a place for Black children in Little Rock. She was very much on the front line of negotiation and confrontations to accomplish this goal.

Before she and her husband opened their home as a command post to the nine tenacious students, Bates was involved in the pre-trial proceedings of *Aaron v. Cooper* (which later changed to *Cooper v. Aaron*) in 1956, which charged that officials conspired keep Black students out by embracing gradualism and set the stage for the Little Rock desegregation fight.

Bates frequently clashed with segregationists who tried to intimidate her. When a Little Rock school board attorney addressed her by her first name, which is how Whites typically addressed Black people at the time, Bates told him it was inappropriate. Her act of resistance landed her on the front page of the state newspaper the *Arkansas Gazette* the next day.

In 1957 she was named Woman of the Year by the *Associated Press*. Bates's many accomplishments include being the only woman to speak at the 1963 March on Washington at the Lincoln Memorial, where she proclaimed, "We will kneel-in; we will sit-in until we can eat in any corner in the United States. We will walk until we are free, until we can walk to any school and take our children to any school in the United States. And we will sit-in and we will kneel-in and we will lie-in if necessary until every Negro in America can vote. This we pledge to the women of America."[2]

Bates and her husband published the *Arkansas State Press*, a weekly newspaper that advocated for civil rights until it shut down in 1959. Bates says she ran the paper "on the conviction that a newspaper was needed to carry on the fight for Negro rights as nothing else can." One campaign led by the paper in 1942 resulted in the appointment of Little Rock's first Black police officers to patrol the Black neighborhood around the West 9th Street area.

Bates's courage and leadership are celebrated every President's Day in February, which in Arkansas is also known as Daisy Gaston Bates Day.

---

students, adorn the walls. Vintage copies of the Bates' *Arkansas State Press* newspapers and others provide clues and context to that heady time. True to the era, an original built-in electric oven and refrigerator are harvest gold, and there is a rotary-style telephone. One of the bedrooms has a built-in wall safe in a closet.

The home, located a couple blocks south of West Roosevelt Road, just south of downtown, sits on the National Register of Historic Places and is accessible only on tours. **Tours** are by appointment only, free, and must be scheduled two weeks in advance. Leave a message if there's no answer. While free of charge, the Daisy Bates Museum Foundation will accept donations.

Even if you don't tour inside the house, feel free to drive by stand in the carport to pay homage to Bates and the risks she and her husband took. (And don't worry about the neighbors; they're quite used to this.) A plaque out front highlights its importance to the civil rights movement.

Tours and Local Guides

BUS TOUR

ARKANSAS DESTINATIONS: AFRICAN AMERICAN HISTORY TOUR

301 Pepper Ave.; tel. 501/603-0113; www.ardestinations.com; private tours $50 per hour with two-hour minimum

Because they are deeply rooted in Little Rock, Arkansas, Destinations guides are well-equipped to share special nuances of the civil rights story here. (Tour guide and Little Rock native Felicia Moore once turned up a photograph of her dad with his childhood baseball team at the Mosaic Templars Cultural Center.) Arkansas Destinations crafts private tours for individuals and groups (two-hour minimum; $50/hour) on a range of themes, including an African American History Tour. The level of depth and detail makes this totally worth the investment.

Shopping

Downtown Little Rock is filled with plenty of places to shop, eat, drink, and find little pieces of Arkansas, such as handcrafted jewelry and locally made food items, to take home with you.

BOOKS

HEARNE FINE ART AND PYRAMID ART, BOOKS & CUSTOM FRAMING

1001 Wright Ave.; tel. 501/372-6822; www.hearnefineart.com; Mon.-Fri. 9am-5pm, Sat. 10am-6pm

This bookstore and gallery is chock full of books by Black authors and about Black themes. There's a full gallery next door, but art pieces, like the emotionally laden fired-clay works featuring Black women created by the artist Chukes, are scattered throughout the bookstore too. Located in the historic Dunbar neighborhood, this bookstore/gallery also serves as a community space that includes exhibitions, book signings, and other cultural programming.

CHOCOLATE

COCOA BELLE CHOCOLATES AT BELLA VITA JEWELRY

108 W 6th St., Ste. A; tel. 501/943-7570; www.cocoabellechocolates.com; Tues.-Fri. 11am-5:30pm, Sat. 10am-4pm

After studying chocolate-making in Europe, Chef Carmen Portillo created a gourmet brand that is the talk of the town. Portillo offers an array of products, including milk chocolate salted caramel sauce, ambrosia bark, pecan pie bark, and colorful boxed truffle sets. These chocolate masterpieces make great gifts. **Bella Vita Jewelry** in downtown Little Rock is your local place to stock up.

Cocoa Belle Chocolates

Festivals and Events

JANUARY

DR. MARTIN LUTHER KING JR. MARADE

33rd St. & MLK Boulevard to the Arkansas State Capitol; tel. 501/773-1824; free

The Little Rock NAACP hosts a "marade" every year to celebrate King's birthday. What's a marade, you ask? The word is a mashup of "march" and "parade," but the event feels just like the latter, complete with fire trucks and cruising cars. The marade begins at 33rd Street and ends at the Arkansas State Capitol. Look out for the likes of the high school dance team, the Central Steppers, or the Dunbar marching band, plus members of the Divine Nine Black Greek-letter fraternities and sororities. Parade marshals have included the Little Rock Central High School youth NAACP chapter, and the marade always concludes with a speech at the capitol, given by celebrties and dignitaries.

A much-anticipated local affair, the marade takes place at 10am on the third Monday in January on the federal King Day holiday.

Food

Little Rock is famously known as the city where cheese dip was invented in 1935 and where the World Cheese Dip Festival is held annually. But a few local restaurants are appreciated for their connection to the Black experience, whether they're dishing up culturally held recipes like barbecue or holding the memory of being a safe space for Black people to gather and strategize next steps in the fight for civil rights.

CENTRAL HIGH SCHOOL HISTORIC DISTRICT

Southern and Soul Food

YANCEY'S CAFETERIA

1510 Wright Ave; tel. 501/372-9292; Tues.-Sat. 11:30am-6pm; $10

The front door of this humble eatery, located in the Central High district, swings open and closed as residents stream in to get a bite of home-cooked food. Yancey's is about as old-school as you can get. For those of you still eating chitterlings, they serve 'em up here right along with cornbread muffins, cabbage yams, baked chicken, Salisbury steak, and more. Patrons delight in posting photos of their chitterlings on social media. This restaurant, near Dunbar Magnet Middle School, is a community staple and treasure of a bygone past.

DOWNTOWN AND THE RIVER MARKET DISTRICT

Barbecue

SIMS BARBECUE

2415 Broadway St., tel. 501/224-2057; www.simsbbqar.com; Mon.-Thurs. 11am-9pm, Fri.-Sat. 11am-10pm; $7-15

A Little Rock tradition since 1937, Sims has three locations and serves up every kind of barbecue you can imagine: chopped pork, rib tips, smoked bologna, BBQ ribs, combo plates—you name it. Sides include barbecue beans, potato salad, and coleslaw. The sauce is so in demand, Sims serves it by the gallon.

Bistro

42 BAR AND TABLE

1200 President Clinton Ave.; tel. 501/748-0454; www.42barandtable.org; lunch Mon.-Sat. 11am-2pm, dinner Thurs.-Sat. 5pm-10pm, brunch Sun. 11am-2pm; $6-35

This light and open restaurant (not a Black-owned business) inside the William J. Clinton Presidential Library and Museum is the perfect place for a light lunch or delicious dinner that celebrates local fare while bringing international flavors into the mix. Dinner options run from herb Provencal pan-seared salmon and Clinton's Curry to pepper grilled beef tenderloin with garlic mashed potatoes and asparagus and chicken pot pie.

The center sits on the eastern edge of the downtown River Market District where you can also enjoy views of the natural beauty of the Arkansas River and Clinton Presidential Park Bridge while you eat.

Seafood

LASSIS INN

518 E 27th St.; tel. 501/372-8714; Tues.-Thurs. 11am-6pm, Fri.-Sat. 11am-9:30pm; $6-18

Guess you could say fish and freedom is Lassis Inn's claim to fame. Opened in 1905, this is one of Arkansas's oldest restaurants. The eatery, which sits in the breezy shadow of I-30 and a couple blocks south of downtown, was a safe haven for African Americans during the school integration crisis of the late '50s. Daisy Gaston Bates, the mentor to the Little Rock Nine, often met other civil rights leaders here to talk shop. Today, patrons can slide in a cozy blue booth and enjoy a variety of fish, from catfish fillets and steaks to Lassis Inn's famous buffalo ribs, which is big-boned buffalo fish cut into the shape of a rib. Go figure. The fish is made to order, hot and fresh with sides that include crispy hush puppies, slaw, fries, tomato relish, and peppers.

The famous Lassis jukebox is still there. When it was first put in, folks danced so much up and down the narrow aisles of this tiny space, repairs had to be made once a week. Some customers complained. Years later, signs posted here still ask patrons to avoid dancing as Lassis never did get over that time some folks got carried away.

OTHER NEIGHBORHOODS

Southern and Soul Food

CECI'S CHICKEN & WAFFLES

4700 S University Ave.; tel. 501/448-5076; www.cecischickenwaffles.com; Tues.-Sat. 11am-7pm. Sun. 11am-3pm; $9-19

This food truck planted in a diverse commercial area belongs to Ciceley "Ceci"

Photos (top to bottom): Lassis Inn; Sims Barbecue rib tips; Ceci's Chicken & Waffles

McDowell, who happens to be the niece of Little Rock's first woman mayor, Lottie Shackleford. McDowell cherishes Little Rock's civil rights history and recognizes her role in that through line by being a business owner and employing local residents. A serial entrepreneur, McDowell is also a single mom who frequently talks about the importance of supporting locally owned and Black-owned businesses. Her restaurant focuses on a sweet and savory array of chicken and waffle dishes, among other soul food-inspired fare. Ceci's well-seasoned, crispy chicken wings are something else, with options including country fried, sweet and chili, or mango habanero. The fluffy waffles they're served over come in range of flavors too, from red velvet and chocolate chip to the Baconator. Ceci's also serves hearty salads; Southern favorites like gizzards; and pork chop, fish, or chicken dinners with sides that include greens, candied yams, purple hull peas, and macaroni and cheese.

Ceci's Chicken & Waffles is located seven miles west of downtown Little Rock (about a 15-minute drive).

Nightlife

There's a little something for everyone in the Little Rock nightlife scene, and visitors need not travel far to enjoy live music, dancing, or sports bars. Note that in Arkansas, **smoking** is allowed in bars, though some venues choose to prohibit it.

CLUBS

ENVY LITTLE ROCK

7200 Colonel Glenn Rd.; tel. 501/569-9113; Sun.-Sat. 9pm-5am; $10 cover

This lounge, dance, and nightclub features a variety of theme nights, including grown folks to Ladies' Night. DJs set the mood with music trending toward R&B and hip-hop. Join the locals and plate up at the soul food buffet, kick back and relax, then hit the dance floor when the feeling moves you. Plenty of security staff and a VIP section.

Envy Little Rock is located four miles west of downtown Little Rock (about a 10-minute drive). The vibe here is grown folks: Nothing wild is going to happen, and you can just kick it and have a good time.

WILLY D'S PIANO BAR

322 President Clinton Ave.; tel. 501/244-9550; www.willydspianobar.com; Tues.-Sat. 7pm-2am; $10 cover

There's a lot going on at Willy D's, which is actually three venues: **Prost,** featuring beer pong, big screen TVs, and local brews; **Deep Ultra Lounge,** a smoke-free venue downstairs where you'll find a full bar and a dance floor complete with a DJ playing the latest in R&B and hip-hop; and Willy's D's itself. Willy D's is known for its piano show and featured live musical acts. There's a full kitchen on-site. Prost is in back of Willy D's, and on weekends you can pay the cover at their door at 120 Ottenheimer Plaza and walk on through. Tuesday night at Prost is karaoke night with free admission. Locals like to come and vibe out with drinks and song. Willy D's is not a Black-owned business.

LIVE MUSIC

STICKYZ ROCK N' ROLL CHICKEN SHACK

107 River Market Ave.; tel. 501/372-7707; www.stickyz.com; Sun. 11am-midnight, Tues.-Fri. 11am-2am, Sat. 11am-1am; $0-30 cover

GET INTO THE RHYTHM

- **Sam Cooke, "A Change is Gonna Come"**: Cooke captured the the collective mood of African Americans with this song released in 1964. It burrows itself into your heart and your head so you can't help but feel—everything.
- **The Impressions, "People Get Ready"**: This Gospel-infused, Grammy-winning song by Curtis Mayfield is tinged with social commentary. It was released in 1965, at a time of great civil unrest.

Both a restaurant and live music venue, Stickyz (not a Black-owned business) is situated in the River Market District and showcases a wide range of national and international musical acts that include blues, rock reggae, soul, and more. Pinetop Perkins, Shuggie Otis, Killer Mike, and Run the Jewels have performed here. Stickyz serves as an extensive menu of bar food including the Smokey Robinson Sandwich, made with house-smoked chicken, swiss cheese, parmesan cheese, horseradish sauce, and side of au jus and a variety of hamburgers, from pimento-bacon to queso bacon to the Backporch, a classic burger served with lettuce, tomato, creole mustard, pickle, red onion, and your choice of cheese. Nachos and quesadillas are on the menu too. Watch out for Taco Tuesday and open mic nights.

Willy D's Piano Bar

Accommodations

Little Rock has just shy of 8,000 hotel rooms with about 2,000 of them downtown. Downtown hotels include full-service, convention, and boutique hotels in a range of price points from upscale to comfy cool. As is the case in most cities, budget accommodations can be found outside downtown.

DOWNTOWN AND THE RIVER MARKET DISTRICT

In addition to the Capital Hotel below, two more good options in (or near) the River Market District are **Hampton Inn & Suites Little Rock-Downtown** (320 River Market Ave.; tel. 501/244-0600; www.hilton.com; $229) and **Hilton Garden Inn Little Rock** (322 Rock St.; tel. 501/244-0044; www.hilton.com; $329).

$100-200

CAPITAL HOTEL

111 W Markham St.; tel. 501/374-7474; www.capitalhotel.com; $195

Featuring a novel prefabricated cast-iron facade with white marble lobby walls, this storied hotel (President Ulysses S. Grant slept here) on the National Register of Historic Places is a downtown treasure that first opened in 1870. It is right near the Old State House and a short walk to the Clinton Presidential Library. It's been said that the large elevator was built to accommodate Grant's horse because he couldn't trust Confederate sympathizers in this Southern city. This hotel features high-end bedding and linens and a welcoming snack of spiced pecans, which you can order by phone if you get a hankering for some once you go home.

The 94 rooms have been preserved in their Victorian splendor. Two restaurants offer fine dining options: **One Eleven** (6:30am-2pm) offers bistro-style fare, including fluffy, soft biscuits and other divine breakfast items. The **Capital Bar & Grill** tends toward upscale comfort food with dishes that range from ribeye and frog leg poutine to fried black-eyed peas and pimento grilled cheese.

Capital Hotel

Transportation

GETTING THERE

Air

Bill and Hillary Clinton National Airport/Adams Field (1 Airport Rd.; tel. 501/372-3439; www.clintonairport.com), the state's largest airport, is served by six airlines with nonstop service to 14 destinations.

The airport is about five miles east of downtown Little Rock. Find a taxi outside of Exit H on the west side of baggage claim, near carousel 1. Taxi fare to downtown costs about $16. Ride-sharing is found at Exit D near the carousel. For shuttles and buses, follow the crosswalk at Exit D near carousel 3. You'll find the Rock Region METRO bus stop adjacent to the shuttle area. Bus fare is $1.35 one-way and takes about a half-hour to get downtown. Take bus #12 or #20.

Train

Located at Markham and Victory streets, **Little Rock Union Station** (Mopac Station; 1400 W Markham St.; tel. 800/872-7245; www.amtrak.com) serves as Amtrak's Texas Eagle Line that runs from Chicago to St. Louis, Dallas, San Antonio, and Los Angeles. There's no direct way to get to the two nearest destinations in this book, Memphis or Mississippi, on Amtrak.

Bus

Little Rock's **Greyhound station** (118 E Washington Ave., N. Little Rock; tel. 501/372-3007; www.locations.greyhound.com; Sun.-Sat. midnight-8pm) is an unassuming terminal across the bridge over the Arkansas River. A one-way fare from **Memphis** to Little Rock is $9-$20 and can take about 2.5 hours. A one-way fare from Little Rock to **Clarksdale** runs $31-$55 and stops in Memphis. This journey takes about five hours.

Car

Little Rock is served by **I-630,** an eight-mile-long east-west freeway connecting I-30 on the east and I-430 on the west.

To get to Little Rock from:

- **The Delta:** From **Clarksdale, Mississippi,** take **US-49 North,** then **I-40 West** for 150 miles (2.5 hours). From **Indianola,** take **US-65 North** and **I-530 North** for 175 miles (3 hours).
- **Memphis:** Take **I-40 West** for approximately 140 miles (2 hours).
- **Jackson, Mississippi:** Take **US-65 North** for approximately 265 miles (4.5 hours).

GETTING AROUND

Little Rock is definitely car-centric, but the city offers reliable buses if you're interested in lowering your carbon footprint while riding around with the locals. A streetcar system with savvy conductor tour guides are also available to get you to downtown destinations.

While Little Rock is an urban area, Arkansas prides itself on its great outdoors, so folks don't mind walking; it's just another way to get outside. Downtown is walkable, and the Little Rock Central High School National Historic Site is best walked to get a full sense of this space and time.

Parking

Downtown in the River Market District public parking is available at Second Street and River Market Avenue for $2 per hour or $12 per consecutive 12-hour period. Throughout this area, you'll find parking at surface lots and street parking spaces.

Public Transit

Rock Region METRO (301 E Capitol; tel. 501/375-6717; bus passes: adult one-way $1.35; children 5-11 $0.60, day pass $3.75) serves Little Rock and the surrounding area. Buy passes at the River Cities Travel Center (310 E Capitol Ave.) or the Rock Region METRO Administration Office, which both accept cash, check, and debit or credit cards. Exact change is strongly suggested if paying on a bus. The MetroTRACK app provides bus and streetcar schedules and alerts.

STREETCAR

The Rock Region METRO Streetcar system uses three replica historic trolleys traveling along a 3.4-mile route to sights around Little Rock, including the River Market District and the Clinton Presidential Library. Savvy conductors tell the story of Little Rock and provide delightful nuance about the people and events that built this city and contribute to its culture.

The **Green Line** stays in Little Rock and stops running at 5:35pm daily, and the **Blue Line** crosses the Arkansas River into North Little Rock. Embark at posted spots found on the streetcar system map. Download the MetroTRACK app for schedules and alerts. Check the system or streetcar signs for trolley fees. Round-trip fares are 50 cents and 25 cents for kids. A day pass is $2. However, at the time of writing, the Rock Region METRO was free to ride and seemed relatively likely to remain so. The service was suspended entirely during the coronavirus pandemic.

Taxi and Ride-Hailing Apps

If you need a cab, call **Little Rock Yellow Cab** (tel. 501/222-2222; www.yellowcablr.com; Mon.-Fri 8am-4pm, Sat. 8am-noon). Uber and Lyft operate here too.

Memphis

Memphis, Tennessee, is called

Bluff City for several bluffs along the Mississippi River. The river fueled the city's growth, thanks to the lucrative cotton trade powered by the sweat and muscle of enslaved Black people, then sharecroppers who frequently worked for subsistence pay. Before that, Memphis was home to Native Americans—Choctaw, Chickasaw, Quapaw, and Cherokee.

MEMPHIS'S TOP 3

1. Walking in King's footsteps at the **National Civil Rights Museum at the Lorraine Motel.** Room 306, where King stayed before being assassinated on the balcony, has been frozen in time (page 286).

2. Contemplating where Memphis has been—as well as where it's headed now—at **I Am A Man Plaza,** where sanitation workers went on strike for better pay and working conditions in 1968 (page 290).

3. Getting yourself some gospel-inflected funk/soul "Oooh!" at the **Stax Museum of American Soul Music** in the Soulsville community (page 295).

Photos (top to bottom): National Civil Rights Museum at the Lorraine Motel; I Am A Man plaza and sculpture by Cliff Garten; Stax Museum of American Soul Music. Previous: a wreath hangs outside Room 306 of the Lorraine Motel

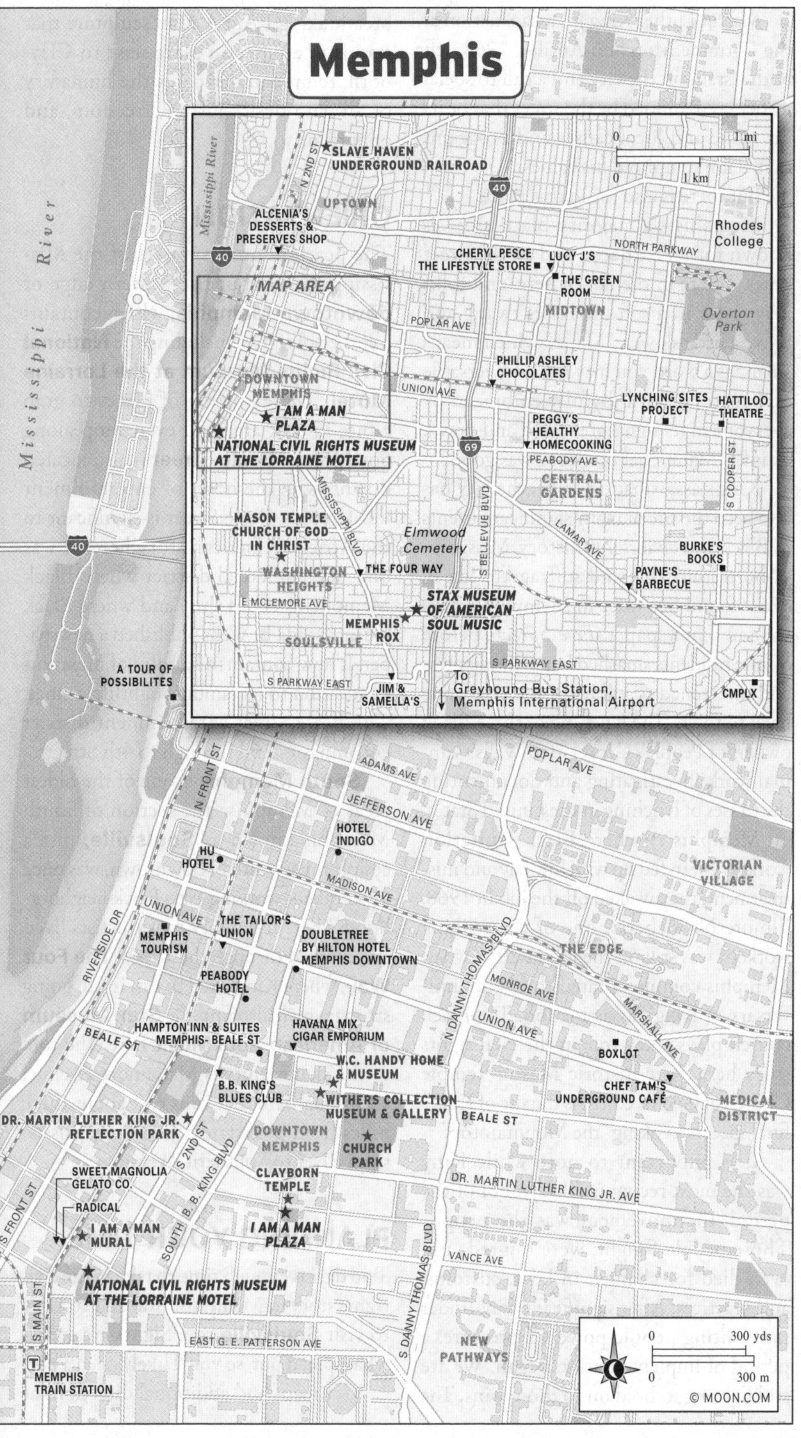
Memphis
Mississippi River
SLAVE HAVEN UNDERGROUND RAILROAD
N 2ND ST
UPTOWN
ALCENIA'S DESSERTS & PRESERVES SHOP
40
CHERYL PESCE THE LIFESTYLE STORE
LUCY J'S
THE GREEN ROOM
NORTH PARKWAY
Rhodes College
MAP AREA
MIDTOWN
Overton Park
POPLAR AVE
PHILLIP ASHLEY CHOCOLATES
DOWNTOWN MEMPHIS
UNION AVE
I AM A MAN PLAZA
NATIONAL CIVIL RIGHTS MUSEUM AT THE LORRAINE MOTEL
LYNCHING SITES PROJECT
HATTILOO THEATRE
PEGGY'S HEALTHY HOMECOOKING
PEABODY AVE
69
CENTRAL GARDENS
S COOPER ST
S BELLEVUE BLVD
MISSISSIPPI BLVD
MASON TEMPLE CHURCH OF GOD IN CHRIST
Elmwood Cemetery
LAMAR AVE
BURKE'S BOOKS
WASHINGTON HEIGHTS
THE FOUR WAY
PAYNE'S BARBECUE
E MCLEMORE AVE
STAX MUSEUM OF AMERICAN SOUL MUSIC
MEMPHIS ROX
SOULSVILLE
S PARKWAY EAST
JIM & SAMELLA'S
To Greyhound Bus Station, Memphis International Airport
CMPLX
0
1 mi
1 km
A TOUR OF POSSIBILITES
N FRONT ST
ADAMS AVE
POPLAR AVE
JEFFERSON AVE
HOTEL INDIGO
HU HOTEL
MADISON AVE
VICTORIAN VILLAGE
UNION AVE
THE TAILOR'S UNION
MEMPHIS TOURISM
DOUBLETREE BY HILTON HOTEL MEMPHIS DOWNTOWN
N DANNY THOMAS BLVD
THE EDGE
RIVERSIDE DR
PEABODY HOTEL
MONROE AVE
MARSHALL AVE
UNION AVE
HAMPTON INN & SUITES MEMPHIS- BEALE ST
HAVANA MIX CIGAR EMPORIUM
BEALE ST
BOXLOT
W.C. HANDY HOME & MUSEUM
CHEF TAM'S UNDERGROUND CAFÉ
B.B. KING'S BLUES CLUB
WITHERS COLLECTION MUSEUM & GALLERY
MEDICAL DISTRICT
BEALE ST
DR. MARTIN LUTHER KING JR. REFLECTION PARK
S 2ND ST
DOWNTOWN MEMPHIS
CHURCH PARK
SWEET MAGNOLIA GELATO CO.
SOUTH B.B. KING BLVD
CLAYBORN TEMPLE
DR. MARTIN LUTHER KING JR. AVE
S FRONT ST
RADICAL
I AM A MAN MURAL
I AM A MAN PLAZA
VANCE AVE
NATIONAL CIVIL RIGHTS MUSEUM AT THE LORRAINE MOTEL
S DANNY THOMAS BLVD
S MAIN ST
EAST G. E. PATTERSON AVE
NEW PATHWAYS
MEMPHIS TRAIN STATION
300 yds
300 m
© MOON.COM

Martin Luther King Jr.'s assassination at the Lorraine Motel on April 4, 1968, left both a stain on the city and a call to social justice, as reminded by the street that bears his name and local causes and programs that claim to uphold his values.

But there is also joy in this place.

Memphis—a majority-Black city—is known for its barbecue and Beale Street blues. You're in the South here, and folks may speak in a soft, molasses twang and move a little slower. "Mane," which means "man," is a word you may hear—a versatile exclamatory word joyfully embraced by everyone in its signature sound and drawl. Think: "Mane, that barbecue was good."

King's assassination aside, the city has also been the site of many significant events in Black and civil rights history. Mississippi-born journalist and suffragette Ida B. Wells found her voice in Memphis, where she ran a newspaper, *Free Speech,* before White residents smashed her printing press and threatened to kill her if she ever came back to town. The lynching of three Black owners of People's Grocery fed Wells's seminal work investigating and documenting the causes of lynching in the United States.

Memphis is where Black sanitation workers got so fed up with low pay and mistreatment, they walked off the job in 1968. Elmore Nickleberry, one of the striking workers, was still on the job in 2018 when Memphis commemorated the 50th anniversary of King's assassination. The Black church plays a key role in the civil rights story here: The historic Mason Temple Church of God in Christ is the site of King's final speech, evoking "the Mountaintop."

It is important to note while King was the most recognizable symbol of the period, the movement was the people. Those people fought, were injured, and even died for changes in laws, customs, and practices. After significant wins under unrelenting people-powered pressure, a period of implementation began. We are still fighting to hold on to those wins. The breathtaking I Am A Man sculpture that stands in a peaceful plaza next to Clayborn Temple underscores the humanity of all who desire justice, freedom, and opportunity.

ORIENTATION

The peaceful brown waters of the Mississippi River abut the western edge of **downtown Memphis,** which contains a cluster of sights, including the **National Civil Rights Museum at the Lorraine Motel**. There's plenty of places to grab a bite in that area and even shop along South Main. **Beale Street** is also located downtown. The heart of entertainment in Memphis, Beale Street is significant to the African American story here: It was once a commercial district where Black Memphians could shop and where Black journalist Ida B. Wells published a newspaper. It now contains a handful of museums in addition to its famous nightlife venues. The Beale Street entertainment district encompasses 2nd through to 4th Streets.

South Memphis is one of the oldest areas of Memphis. The section of South Memphis known as **Soulsville,** just a couple miles south of downtown, was once a prominent working-class Black neighborhood where legendary music artists lived and worked through the 1960s. **The Four Way,** where King liked to eat, is still going strong; you'll also find the **Stax Museum of American Soul Music** here. The core of this community is McLemore Avenue, a thoroughfare that runs east about three miles from Interstate 55 near the Mississippi River to Southern Avenue.

PLANNING YOUR TIME

Two days is enough time to take in the civil rights story in Memphis. Add an extra day to visit **Soulsville** too. Sights are somewhat spread out, so you'll likely need a **car.**

Get maps and additional directions at

MOVEMENT TIMELINE

The fight for equal rights in Memphis stretches back to at least 1961, when the Memphis 13 desegregated four all-White elementary schools. Long before that, in 1892, journalist Ida B. Wells bravely investigated the lynching of three Black men whose grocery store competed with a nearby White-owned grocery. But things really came to a boil in 1968, when a strike by Black sanitation workers drew King to the city in support.

1961-1966

1961: Thirteen African American first-graders, aka the Memphis 13, desegregate four all-White elementary schools in Memphis.

1962: James Meredith becomes the first Black student at the University of Mississippi.

June, 1966: Meredith departs Memphis bound for Jackson on his March Against Fear (page 200), intended to promote voter registration and defy racism. He is shot and wounded on the way.

1968

February 1: Black sanitation workers Echol Cole and Robert Walker are crushed to death while on the job.

February 12: 1,300 Black sanitation workers walk off the job to demand better pay and working conditions.

April 3: King, who was in town to support the striking sanitation workers, delivers his prophetic "Mountaintop" speech at Mason Temple Church of God in Christ.

April 4: King is assassinated on the balcony of Room 306 at the Lorraine Motel.

April 16: Memphis City Council votes 12-1 to recognize the sanitation workers' union. Sanitation workers vote to accept an agreement with the city, and the strike ends.

1990s TO TODAY

September 28, 1991: The National Civil Rights Museum at the Lorraine Motel opens.

October 3, 1991: Willie Herenton becomes the first Black person elected mayor of Memphis.

April 4, 2018: Memphis commemorates the 50th anniversary of King's assassination, with participation from King's children, Revs. Jesse L. Jackson and James Lawson, Diane Nash, Congressman John Lewis, and Tamika Mallory of Black Lives Matter.

James Meredith, center, walks onto campus at the University of Mississippi, 1962

PEOPLE WHO MADE THE MOVEMENT

GROUPS

Memphis 13: Group of 13 first-graders who desegregated four all-White Memphis schools in 1961. Their names were Dwania Kyles, Jacqueline Moore Christion, Sheila Malone Conway, Pamela Mayes Evans, E. C. Freeman Fentress, Menelik Fombi (Michael Willis), Alvin Freeman, Deborah Ann Holt, Sharon Malone, Joyce Bell White, Leandrew Wiggins, Clarence Williams, and Harry Williams.

1960s MOVERS AND SHAKERS

Dr. Martin Luther King Jr.: The civil rights leader came to Memphis to support striking sanitation workers and was assassinated in this city.

Rev. James Lawson: Leading movement theorist and strategist on nonviolence who invited King to Memphis to amplify the Black sanitation workers' cause in 1968.

Maxine Smith: Activist who helped escort the Memphis 13 to school. The following year, she became the local NAACP's first executive secretary.

Ida B. Wells

EARLIER ACTIVISTS

Ida B. Wells: Journalist who investigated lynchings around Memphis in the 1890s; publisher of the *Memphis Free Speech and Headlight*; and co-founder of the NAACP.

Memphis Tourism (47 Union Ave.; tel. 888/633-9099). Note that the biggest civil rights attraction in Memphis, the **National Civil Rights Museum at the Lorraine Motel,** is closed Tuesdays.

Memphis does swelter in the summer: Wear sunscreen and cover appropriately to avoid sunburn.

CONNECT WITH

The Delta is the nearest destination (1.5-2 hours away), and from there, you can continue south to **Jackson** (3 hours from Memphis). **Little Rock** is about two hours to the west, and **Nashville** around three hours to the northeast.

Three Days in Memphis

Spend your first couple days in downtown Memphis to fortify your hunger for the civil rights story and to visit **Beale Street,** which is bursting with energy all day and night. On Day 3, hop in the car and head over to the **Stax Museum of American Soul Music** in Soulsville.

Call ahead to schedule your tour with **A Tour of Possibilities** on the morning of Day 2. Note that the **National Civil Rights Museum at the Lorraine Motel,** covered here on Day 1, is closed Tuesdays.

DAY 1

1 A big red curved sign on Main Street announces you've arrived at the **National Civil Rights Museum at the Lorraine Motel.** Make your way to a view from King's room, where he spent some of the last moments of his life, and end by going across the street to the building where James Earl Ray lay in wait and made his final shot. The museum may leave you with strong emotions, whether joy, sadness, relief, or all three. Be prepared to spend two to three hours at this museum to get the full effect.

2 Have lunch at locavore restaurant **Radical** in Puck Food Hall on Main Street, followed by a gelato at Sweet Magnolia Gelato Co. in the same building.

3 Feel free to window shop on Main, but whatever you do, don't miss artist Marcellous Lovelace's powerful **I Am A Man mural** just a few steps from Huling and Main, kitty-corner to Puck Food Hall.

4 Visit the **Withers Collection Museum & Gallery** on Beale. (Don't worry, you'll have plenty of time to carouse on Beale later.) The gallery offers a sneak peek into the civil rights photographer's vast collection of images made over a 60-year career.

5 Beale Street isn't going anywhere, so let's spend the night nearby at **Havana Mix Cigar Emporium,** where you can get a quality cigar from the cedar humidor, order chicken wings, and listen to hometown talent sing and dance R&B and pop tunes.

DAY 2

1 **A Tour of Possibilities** offers two-hour to all-day tours of Black history sites and Memphis history that will knock your socks off. Try to schedule a two-hour tour in advance (and feel free to circle back to your favorite spots later today to spend more time on your own).

2 Next, head to **Chef Tam's Underground Café** on Union Avenue for great portions served up with a lot of whimsy and even more texture and flavor.

3 After your meal, visit the **I Am A Man Plaza,** where a sculpture and wall featuring the inscribed names of 1,300 Black sanitation workers commemorate the 1968 strikers. This site, about a mile from your previous stop at Chef Tam's, is great for photos.

4 Beale Street beckons. Head on over for people-watching or to listen to some classic blues, R&B, or rock 'n' roll. **B. B. King's Blues Club** is a good place to start getting your groove on (and you can eat here too). The thrill ain't gone: It's right here.

DAY 3

Pack some workout gear for this day so you can go rock climbing at **Memphis Rox** in Soulsville.

1 Hop in the car today to get yourself an education in Black music at the **Stax Museum of American Soul Music** in the Soulsville community.

2 Exercise and engage with the local community at **Memphis Rox,** a climbing gym across from the Stax Museum. The facility is a pay-what-you-can, so anybody (especially neighborhood kids) who wants to learn rock climbing can do so. Juice Almighty, a snack bar located inside, follows the same pay-it-forward ethos.

3 Oh, bless your heart! You must be hungry after all that climbing. **The Four Way** isn't too far from here, so hop a ride and grab a soul food meal. King loved eating here, so it must be good.

Sights

Travelers to Memphis can walk in King's footsteps, visiting churches where he preached in support of the 1968 sanitation workers' strike, along with the Lorraine Motel, where King was assassinated; it's now a moving museum devoted to civil rights history that draws visitors in pilgrimage fashion from around the world.

Less somber sights include a cluster of museums around Beale Street, the epicenter of Memphis nightlife and a street with deep roots in the Back community. South of downtown, the aptly named Soulsville neighborhood is home to the Stax Museum of American Soul Music.

DOWNTOWN

TOP EXPERIENCE

★ National Civil Rights Museum at the Lorraine Motel

450 Mulberry St.; tel. 901/521-9699; www.civilrightsmuseum.org; daily 9am-5pm; adults $17, seniors and students with ID $15, children 5-17 $14, four and under free

King traveled to Memphis in 1968 to support striking Black sanitation workers, checking into Room 306 of the Lorraine Motel. Soon after, the civil rights leader was assassinated on his balcony by a White gunman, James Earl Ray, perched in a building across the street. The world has seen the iconic photo of King's lifeless body, as aides, including confidant Rev. Andrew Young, pointing in the direction of the fatal bullet.

The museum experience takes place in two buildings, starting with the original Lorraine Motel structure, which has been turned into a museum dedicated to King's legacy and the civil rights movement. Here, visitors can stand right outside King's glass-encased room and peer across Mulberry Street where the assassin posted up. The journey continues across the street at the boarding house where Ray holed up as he lay in wait in a tiny bathroom to take the fatal shot. From a window here, you can see the balcony outside Room 306 and the wreath that hangs in King's memory.

A meaningful tour of the National Civil Rights Museum at the Lorraine Motel will take about two to three hours. It will engage all your senses with pictures, sound, and contextual narratives about the people, including children, who took risks to make democracy real. Several galleries are designed to be touched to unlock your imagination and deepen your understanding of not only the years marked off as the civil rights movement, but the foundation of resistance that came before and the influence the period had on subsequent movements for social and economic justice and equality. Photographs are encouraged throughout the museum.

Among the highlights is an exhibit on the 1968 sanitation workers' strike in Memphis. Life-size statues of the workers hold brilliant white signs with red lettering that read: "I Am A Man"—a phrase coined by strike organizer Bill Lucy. A day after police used mace and tear gas on nonviolent demonstrators, Rev. James Lawson

Photos: exhibits at the National Civil Rights Museum at the Lorraine Motel

MEMPHIS

THE SANITATION WORKERS STRIKE

The death of two Black sanitation workers in Memphis on February 1, 1968, kicked off a strike that would become one of the most significant events in the city's civil rights history. Within the span of a few months, the more than 1,000 striking workers managed to get their union—but only after many of them were arrested, beaten, or sprayed with pepper spray. Meanwhile, King, who had traveled to Memphis to support the workers, was assassinated at the Lorraine Motel.

The strike had lasting repercussions, both locally and nationally. Here's how it unfolded:

WORKING CONDITIONS

In the 1960s, Black sanitation workers in Memphis labored under unsafe and unfair conditions: Many worked beyond a 40-hour work week and still couldn't make ends meet; a significant number received food stamps. White bosses called these men "boy," and they were forced to work in filth, exposed to maggots, for example. When segregationist Mayor Henry Loeb took office in 1968, working conditions became worse.

THE STRIKE BEGINS

On February 1, 1968, Black sanitation workers Echol Cole and Robert Walker perished when they were crushed by a faulty truck while seeking shelter from the rain. The day before their deaths, Black workers had been sent home without pay due to rain, but White workers were allowed to wait it out, then return to work.

Black sanitation workers had tried to strike before, but they couldn't get support from the city's religious community or middle-class residents. Now, Cole's and Walker's deaths were the last straw. Two weeks later, as many as 1,300 workers walked off the job to demand better pay, treatment, and the right to unionize. The strikers began marching daily at noon and were beaten by police who sprayed them with pepper spray. As the strike progressed, more than 100 strikers were arrested at City Hall. Clayborn Temple was an organizing base for striking sanitation workers, and they staged daily marches from there to City Hall.

declared it so on February 24, 1968, during meeting establishing Community on the Move for Equality. The phrase became a consistent echo. A film detailing the strike story is superimposed on an orange garbage truck inside the museum.

In another area of the museum, a bus holds a plaster statue of a seated Rosa Parks. Climb inside and sit next to her, and try to imagine the courage it took for this department store seamstress to defy the law and refuse to give her seat up to a White patron in 1955. An overhead speaker blares threatening statements ("Please move to the back of the bus!" "Get up from there!").

Visitors can also stand behind bars in a re-creation of the Alabama cell where King was held when he wrote "Letter from a Birmingham Jail" in 1963. Hear his voice as King reads a portion of the letter, a missive addressed to clergymen.

A civil rights movement timeline

KING ARRIVES

King arrived in Memphis in March to support the workers. On March 18, he spoke to an overflow crowd—25,000 people—at Mason Temple Church of God in Christ, urging support for the strike and vowing to come back to town to support the effort.

King's arrival stirred racial tensions in the city, and on March 28 local teen Larry Payne was shot and killed by a White cop intent on tracking down looters. Police arrested hundreds of mostly Black people, and the legislature authorized a 7pm curfew, with the National Guard moving in.

The next day, about 300 sanitation workers and ministers marched silently from Clayborn Temple to City Hall, with a National Guard escort, including military trucks and bayonets. President Lyndon B. Johnson and AFL-CIO president George Meany offered help to resolve things, but Loeb refused.

On April 2, Larry Payne's funeral was held at Clayborn Temple, and the National Guard withdrew from the city.

On April 3, King gave his prophetic "Mountaintop" speech during a mass rally at Mason Temple Church of God in Christ. The next day, he was assassinated on the balcony of his Memphis hotel room. Several cities nationwide erupted in violence and anger.

RESOLUTION

On April 16, 1968, Memphis City Council voted 12-1 to recognize the sanitation workers' union and pay better wages. Sanitation workers accepted and ended the strike. A few months later, the unionists had to threaten another walkout to make the city really do it.

LEGACY

Today, a two-sided marker on Colonial Street reads "Tragic Accident Sparks Sanitation Strike." Just a block away, at Colonial and Verne streets, is the site where the faulty truck took these men from their families.

In 2017, the City of Memphis awarded tax-free grants of $50,000 to several surviving sanitation workers from the '68 strike. One of them, Elmore Nickleberry, was still working on his route in 2017 at age 85.

illustrates how events unfolded and the movement grew stronger through methods such as proper leadership training. A multitouch interactive map illustrates how desegregation unfolded across the nation.

Included in the museum's storytelling elements are chilling and violent reactions from the White power structure. (For example, an exhibit relating to the Little Rock Nine features the lyrics to "Nine Little N------" sung by Little Rock's Central High School students.) Touchable displays query museumgoers on positions taken during the movement, including nonviolence.

The National Civil Rights Museum weaves a comprehensive tale that reverberates till this day. A particularly poignant wall display describes King's last request when he asked tenor saxophonist Ben Branch, a close friend of Rev. Jesse L. Jackson, to play "Precious Lord, Take My Hand" at that night's rally. King reportedly said: "I want you to play it real pretty." Branch said: "You know I will, Doc."

The museum is a stop on the official U.S. Civil Rights Trail.

I Am A Man Mural

400 S Main St.

This graffiti-style tribute to the 1968 sanitation workers and their rallying cry, "I Am A Man," was created by rap artist Marcellous Lovelace, who based it on Richard Copley's photograph of the sanitation workers' march on March 28, 1968. The colorful modernist-style mural sits proudly and loudly on South Main Street near Hueling Street, not far from the National Civil Rights Museum, where you can walk by it and be inspired any time. Walk right up to the mural and take a selfie. It's so vibrant, you might want to walk across the street and take some photos from that vantage point too.

Memphis is a city of murals, and this piece is part of the **South Main Mosaic ArtWalk,** a collection of public art installations in a square-mile neighborhood near Beale Street.

Clayborn Temple

294 Hernando St.; tel. 901/907-0532; www.clayborn-temple.org

Standing tall in a residential area near historic Beale Street and downtown Memphis, this Romanesque Revival church was originally a Presbyterian church opened in 1843. In 1949, the church sold to a Black congregation that renamed it Clayborn African Methodist Episcopal Church.

During the civil rights movement, the temple carried a spirit of resistance. In particular, it was a hub of organizing activity during the 1968 sanitation workers' strike and the site where nearly 1,000 workers gathered twice daily to march together to the courthouse. In the evening, strikers and their families and supporters streamed into the sanctuary to hear inspirational speeches. After King's assassination, a silent memorial march of 10,000 people, led by Coretta Scott King and her four children, began here and proceeded to City Hall. And when the strike ended on April 16, 1968, it was at Clayborn Temple where sanitation workers met to accept the terms.

The church was shuttered for much-needed renovation at the time of writing, but travelers can still visit I Am A Man Plaza, a contemplative outdoor spot that honors sanitation workers, which sits in the yard behind the church. That yard is a frequent site of community gatherings around sacred events and prayerful protests. For example, a group of people gathered at the I Am A Man installation after the police shooting of 28-year-old Atatiana Jefferson in Fort Worth, Texas in 2019.

The National Trust and the Clayborn Reborn organization aims to reinterpret the church as a safe place to have difficult conversations. Though worn, the interior is quite stunning: An eight-sided nave radiates from a dome in a suspended ceiling. Pews emanate in a curved-like fashion with a second level of pews formed by a balcony. Stained glass windows make way for a warm light to fill the sanctuary.

Clayborn Temple is a stop on the official U.S. Civil Rights Trail.

TOP EXPERIENCE

★ I Am A Man Plaza

Hernando St.; tel. 901/454-0474; www.memphistravel.com/i-am-man-plaza; open 24/7; free

This contemplative plaza sits next to the historic Clayborn Temple, where striking sanitation workers and their supporters organized and met daily in 1968. The centerpiece is an award-winning work of art by Cliff Garten that honors the striking workers. Fifteen-foot-tall bronze-and-steel letters form the sanitation workers' rallying cry: I Am A Man. The plaza, shaped

THE "I AM A MAN" LEGACY

I Am A Man sculpture by Cliff Garten

In 1968, nearly 1,000 striking sanitation workers marched twice a day from Clayborn Temple to City Hall, carrying signs emblazoned with the words: I Am A Man. Labor organizer Bill Lucy is credited with coining the phrase, and Lawson underscored this sentiment, stating: "For at the heart of racism is the idea that a man is not a man, that a person is not a person. You are human beings. You are men. You deserve dignity."

"I Am A Man" became a rallying cry for the strike, and Clayborn Temple's pastor, Rev. Malcolm Blackburn, a White Canadian who owned a small printing press, had the words printed on placards (along with other phrases that didn't stick like this one did).

The I Am A Man slogan was powerful and has since been adopted and remixed by other movements, including:

- **Arab Spring (2011)**: A sign was spotted at a demonstration reading "Ana Rajul," which translates from Arabic to "I am a man."
- **Black Lives Matter (2014)**: Following the police shooting and subsequent death of 18-year-old African American Michael Brown Jr. in Ferguson, Missouri, St. Louis artists have asserted the humanity of themselves and the Black community at large with the implicit message: "I am a human being."
- **Immigration Rights (2018)**: In 2018, the National Civil Rights Museum featured an exhibit called I AM A CHILD to raise awareness of the inhumane practice of separating immigrant children from their parents at the United States-Mexico border.

by landscape architect John Jackson, also features a wall with the names of all 1,300 sanitation workers, along with text by poet Steve Fox.

The plaza was dedicated in April 2018, 50 years after King's assassination. Lawson, the movement theorist and strategist, and who originally invited King to Memphis to amplify the strikers' cause, was present to cut the ribbon.

The plaza is open 24 hours a day and is free to visit. It serves as a meeting place for vigils and reflection about the people who made the movement and more. The sculpture's letters are lit up at night, creating an ethereal, transcendent effect.

Dr. Martin Luther King Jr. Reflection Park

Northwest corner of Dr. Martin Luther King Jr. Blvd. and S Second St.

The City of Memphis established this memorial park in 2018, 50 years after King was assassinated. The park is now home to Richard Hunt's 1977 "I Have Been to the Mountaintop," a low-slung work of public art made of weathering steel, featuring abstract forms and curves that suggest a mountain with a man reaching its peak.

The park, lined with red-and-white signs describing King's mission and the civil rights movement, features mounted photos taken by noted civil rights photojournalist Ernest Withers. It is within blocks of the Lorraine Motel, Clayborn Temple, and Beale Street.

Take a walk through the park, taking in the signs and images scattered throughout. The red metal benches are a good place for peaceful contemplation about the meaning of the messages therein.

BEALE STREET

Beale Street is considered the heartbeat of downtown Memphis and the official home of the blues, but it also has a lot of history, and is included on the official U.S. Civil Rights Trail.

In the late 1800s, Memphis was a segregated society, and Beale Street was a commercial district where Black Memphians could get whatever they needed, including food, clothing, and funeral services. It drew blues musicians and thought leaders and was where Wells published her newspaper, *Memphis Free Speech and Headlight.*

After the 1870s yellow fever epidemic, property values tanked, and Robert Reed Church, the South's first Black millionaire, purchased land around the area. Thanks to Church's influence, by the 1900s more Black entrepreneurs opened clubs, restaurants, and shops. Around the same time, another side of Black life flourished on Beale Street too, in the form of drinking, gambling, sex work, and voodoo. Jazz made its way here, and a style of music called Memphis Blues was born on Beale: All the greats—W. C. Handy, Muddy Waters, B. B. King, Louis Armstrong, and Memphis Minnie—performed here.

The street eventually fell into disrepair in the '60s and was revitalized by city officials in the '90s. Today, Beale Street is a global mecca calling blues lovers home. The area is also home to a couple of museums that commemorate Memphis culture, including the street's connection to Black history in Memphis.

Withers Collection Museum & Gallery

333 Beale St.; tel. 901/523-2344; www.thewitherscollection.com; Tues.-Wed. 10am-6pm, Thurs.-Sat. 10am-9pm, Sun. 11am-6pm; free

Situated on historic Beale Street, this 7,000-square-foot gallery showcases a fraction of the 1.8 million photos taken by Ernest Withers, an independent photojournalist who was close to many civil rights greats, including King, Medgar Evers, James Meredith, and striking local sanitation workers. This is the man behind

Photos (top to bottom): Dr. Martin Luther King Jr. Reflection Park; shoppers on Beale Street in the late 1930s; Withers Collection Museum & Gallery (left); W.C. Handy Home & Museum (right)

well-known images such as Black sanitation workers standing shoulder to shoulder carrying "I Am A Man" signs and who documented the entire trial of 14-year-old Emmett Till's murderers in 1955 in Tallahatchie County, Mississippi, about 100 miles south.

Not only did the late Withers document the movement, he captured the joy and pain of Black life, such as nightlife; entertainers like B. B. King, Aretha Franklin, and Ike and Tina Turner; and even funerals. He once caught the sun beaming on first-grader Dwania Kyles's face as she sat in the back of a car on her way to Bruce Elementary School, which she helped integrate as one of the Memphis 13. And Withers took a big risk (for a Black man) in the courthouse when he snapped a forbidden photo of Moses Wright, Emmett Till's great-uncle, as the man pointed his finger from the witness stand to identify one of the child's killers, famously saying, "Dar he."

Withers's daughter, Rosalind Withers, runs the gallery and welcomes visitors with a smile and stories about her father's passion for photography, sparked during his childhood and developed further while serving in the U.S. Army. The Withers Family Trust offers prints and books for sale and will ship them so you don't have to worry about being bogged down while enjoying the gallery and rest of Beale Street. The venue features programs and discussions on the themes Withers documented in pictures, including social and economic justice. Docent-led tours for students include a film about Withers, known as the Original Civil Rights Photographer. The staff is happy to narrate the story of his museum and the life of Withers. Just ask if they don't come to you first.

W. C. Handy Home & Museum

352 Beale St.; tel. 901/527-3427; www.wchandymemphis.org; Tues.-Sat. 10am-5pm; adults $8, students $5

W. C. Handy, aka the "Father of Blues," lived in this two-room shotgun house, which was originally located on the city's Jeanette Street. Handy grew up in Alabama and traveled performing the blues, landing in Memphis in 1905. It was here he composed "Memphis Blues," the first commercially successful blues song, which helped popularized this Black folk music form.

Today, the home has been moved to the bottom of Beale Street and serves as an interpretive center. The blue house features examples of sheet music published by the company he established, because, as a Black man, he couldn't get his music published by other companies. Evidence of 40 songs he classified as the blues are on display. The iconic "Memphis Blues" was "swindled away from him in 1912," says Elaine Turner, museum director. "But he was able to regain his author's rights." Because Handy rose to the challenge of publishing his own works, his family continues to benefit financially from his creations to this day.

The museum also features family photos, and pictures also document Handy's time in Memphis. The home was moved from South Memphis near the Stax Museum in 1985 when Beale Street was being revitalized.

You'll find another tribute to Handy halfway down the strip: a bronze **statue** of a distinguished-looking man holding a trumpet midway down the strip, standing in a park named for Handy. Handy Park hosts local musical acts throughout the year.

Church Park

In addition to opening the door for Black businesses on Beale, Black millionaire Robert Reed Church paid the city to create Church Park at 4th and Beale, which became a draw for blues musicians to play. You can cross the noisy threshold of the Beale Street entertainment district and see that park for yourself. This vacant space is dotted with commemorative signage that celebrates Black history and Black people, such as Mary Church Terrell, a charter member of the NAACP and suffragette who pushed for passage of the 19th Amendment, and Sara Roberta Church, the first Black woman in Memphis to be elected in public office (1952).

SOUTH MEMPHIS AND SOULSVILLE

Soulsville, about six miles from downtown, is the community where the Stax Museum of American Soul Music is found and where the noted Stax Music Academy, an afterschool and summer music academy, is cultivating the next generation of music makers. The late, great Aretha Franklin was born here, at 406 Lucy Street, and you can stop by and take a photo in front of the fenced-off home that appears to be under renovation. (City officials don't have details about what is planned for this site.) More recently, Bruno Mars recorded "Uptown Funk" at Willie Mitchell's Royal Studios in this neighborhood.

Mason Temple Church of God in Christ

938 Mason St.; tel. 901/947-9300; www.cogic.org; Mon.-Fri. 8am-4pm; donations accepted

This spiritual center of the Church of God in Christ (COGIC), located in South Memphis not far from Soulsville, was named for Bishop Charles H. Mason, who was born enslaved and established the denomination in 1897. COGIC eventually grew into a worldwide Pentecostal congregation with the temple serving as a haven of civil rights activities in the 1950s and '60s. This was the site where King delivered his iconic and prophetic "Mountaintop" speech, which would tragically be his last. Thousands looked on in awe and uplift that night, April 3, 1968, the day before King was assassinated. Rev. Ralph Abernathy, King's right hand, was slated to talk that night, but the crowd demanded to hear from King.

Others figures in the temple's history include actor and activist Paul Robeson, who came to rally for the Progressive Party in 1948. King himself first spoke at the temple during a get-out-the-vote rally featuring iconic gospel singer Mahalia Jackson in 1959. (The ticket he supported failed to elect any Black people, but the effort did boost the number of Black voters.) And striking sanitation workers met here regularly to organize for higher pay and better working conditions.

Employing early 20th-century architectural styles, the two-story structure has a basement and includes elements of Art Moderne and Beaux Arts touches. (Imagine how it must have looked when a crowd of 25,000 gathered to hear from King the night he delivered the "Mountaintop" speech.) This fully functioning world headquarters was placed on the National Register of Historic Places in 1992 and is open to the public for viewing. Mason is entombed inside the temple. The church is a stop on the official U.S. Civil Rights Trail.

★ Stax Museum of American Soul Music

926 E McLemore Ave.; tel. 901/942-7685; www.staxmuseum.com; Tues.-Sun. 10am-5pm; adults $13, seniors and students $12, children 9-12 $10

On the site of the storied Stax Records, this 17,000-square-foot museum celebrates the company founded in 1957 by Jim Stewart with Estelle Axton, who mortgaged her home to invest in what would become an integrated powerhouse of the American music landscape: "Stax" is a mashup of their names. The now-defunct Stax presided over an era of soul music which brought us the gift of The Staple Singers, The Bar-Kays, blues great Albert King, and Isaac Hayes, who delivered the iconic "Hot Buttered Soul" album in 1969. The beauty of Stax

GET INTO THE RHYTHM

After King's assassination, a tension born of self-determination, resistance, and pride permeated the air. Memphis-based **Stax Records** responded with a characteristic grittiness that spoke with authenticity and truth, unlike Motown, which smoothed its edges for crossover appeal. Legendary producer Al Bell actually worked in the movement as a youth but was asked to leave when he responded to violence by defending himself. Bell may have stopped working in the movement directly but always supported it. The tension and power being generated at this time couldn't help but permeate the music. Here are some of the studio's most moving hits:

- **The Staple Singers, "Why? (Am I Treated So Bad):"** According to Mavis Staples of The Staple Singers, this song was a favorite of King's.
- **The Staple Singers, "Respect Yourself" and "I'll Take You There"**: These 1970s hits helped set the tone for an era of Black pride in the '70s with these hits.

In 1939, long before the Staple Singers recorded these hits, Billie Holiday recorded **"Strange Fruit,"** which originated as a poem written by Jewish-American writer Abel Meeropol to protest the lynching of Black people. Numerous others have covered the song, including Nina Simone.

Records is when an artist said "Oooh!" producers left it right there in your face, instead of smoothing it out. The studio's first hit was a duet between Rufus and Carla Thomas called "Cause I Love You." Otis Redding (of "Sitting on the Dock of the Bay" and "Try a Little Tenderness" fame) was signed early on.

The museum covers the origins of Black musical forms, starting in the Mississippi Delta, where the people created a sound (and a message) that has resonated through generations. You'll know you've arrived by the inviting neon marquee perched proudly in the Soulsville community. Inside, the more than 2,000 artifacts, memorabilia, video footage, and exhibits on display include Isaac Hayes's gold-plated Cadillac Eldorado and walls of album covers.

Memphis Rox

879 E McLemore Ave.; tel. 901/401-6104; www.memphisrox.org; Sun. noon-8pm, Mon. 9am-9:30pm, Tues. 10am-5pm, Wed.-Thurs. 7am-9:30pm, Fri. 9am-9:30pm, Sat. 10am-8pm; day use for adults $12, students $10 (or pay what you can)

Soulsville was a thriving working-class Black neighborhood starting in the 1900s, but, sadly, the place fell on hard times with only a handful of businesses in operation by 1990. Fortunately, the neighborhood is on the comeback because of people in and around the community who understand the treasure it is.

Enter Memphis Rox, a rock-climbing gym located kitty-corner from the Stax Museum of American Soul Music. The facility was founded by film director Tom Shadyac, whose father helped found St. Jude Children's Research Hospital. Shadyac has noted that rock-climbing gyms are typically built in high-end ZIP codes with fees that are out of reach for many working folks—and certainly for the children of Soulsville, which has a higher poverty rate and lower life expectancy than other areas around Memphis. For this reason, the gym has a "pay what you can" policy. It also employs local youth and gives them unfettered access to climbs in exchange for volunteering here or at local charities.

You'll get a sense for the vibe when you step in the front door of the building where Memphis Rox is located and see a vibrant portrait of King to the left. You'll likely be greeted by energetic local teens working the front desk or leading climbing sessions. **Juice Almighty,** inside Memphis Rox, offers healthy food options.

OTHER NEIGHBORHOODS

Slave Haven Underground Railroad

826 N 2nd St.; tel. 901/527-3427; www.slavehavenmemphis.com; Mon.-Sat. 10am-4pm; adults $12, seniors and students $11

The cotton economy fueled the desire for Black bodies to work the fields, but, apparently, German immigrant and stockyard owner Jacob Burkle, who lived in this home, disagreed with the whole nasty enterprise. According to Burkle family

Photos (top to bottom): First Beale Street Baptist Church; Stax Museum of American Soul Music in Memphis's Soulsville neighborhood; climber at Memphis Rox

IDA B. WELLS

Journalist, educator, and activist Wells called out lynching for what it was—racial terrorism—and not the late 19th-century crime control tool it was purported to be. As a result, she was the target of racial and gendered attacks on her character for documenting the truth and telling it out loud and often. She did not wither under the social expectation of public shaming.

Wells's advocacy took on several forms, including:

Activist: Wells "won" a $500 settlement from Chesapeake, Ohio, and Southwestern Railroad after she sued them for asking her to move to the colored car. In 1883, she was a 20-year-old teacher traveling from Memphis to nearby Woodstock when she refused the conductor's request. She testified: "I resisted him—holding on to my seat when he called for help, and two White passengers helped him to carry me out. I resisted all the time and never consented to go. My dress was torn in the struggle, one sleeve was almost torn off. Everybody in the car seemed to sympathize with the conductor and were against me."[1] The decision was later overturned in 1887 by the Supreme Court of Tennessee.

Publisher: Wells ran a Black newspaper, *The Free Speech and Headlight*, out of First Baptist Beale Street Church—before White residents smashed her printing press and threatened to kill her if she ever came back to town. (She never did.)

Investigative journalist: In 1892, a White mob in Memphis lynched three Black men—Thomas Moss, Will Stewart, and Calvin McDowell—who ran a grocery store that was starting to rival a nearby White-owned grocery. Wells investigated their deaths. Her reporting using statistic and quantitative data on lynching and debunked accepted notions of the cause of lynching, establishing that the cruel practice was indeed a tool of economic terrorism and disenfranchisement.

Civil rights leader: In 1909, Wells helped found the National Association for the Advancement of Colored People (NAACP) in New York with an

lore, Jacob harbored escaped enslaved Black people here as part of the Underground Railroad from 1855 through the end of slavery.

Today, docents lead groups through this small, white-framed house in the Uptown neighborhood (north of downtown). During a 45-minute tour of the house, visitors learn how Burkle initially purchased a Black man and woman to establish a pro-slavery cover. He secretly freed the initial "purchases," then went about his business hiding and shipping more runaways to the nearest taste of freedom—Cairo, Illinois. Burkle's activities were dangerous—lynching dangerous—so they were only documented through oral family history.

From room to room, visitors learn the untold story of Black resistance, as revealed in quilt patterns, artifacts, artwork, vintage furniture, and other details. The docent-led tour includes a walk down into a damp brick cellar with crawl spaces leading to a wall on the side of the house. This is where runaways waited in the dark, the rain, and the cold before taking their next risk to pursue freedom.

interracial group of men and women, including Archibald Grimké and W. E. B. DuBois. The NAACP was founded to abolish segregation and its storied ability to use the courts to accomplish its goals. *Brown v. Board of Education* (1955) is its most notable win. The organization's legal defense fund was a source of support during the civil rights movement and frequently used to bail out demonstrators.

investigative journalist and anti-lynching activist Ida B. Wells

Wells had opinions on economic inequality too. Musing on what might have happened if Black businesses were allowed to thrive after the Civil War, Michelle Duster, Wells's great-granddaughter, says: "[My great-grandmother] was very clear about how there was an effort to disenfranchise African Americans who were doing well, or at least on their way to doing well . . . people who were enterprising and considered leaders," Duster says.

It took more than 100 years since Wells's revelations for Congress to seek to outlaw lynching. In February 2020, Emmett Till Antilynching Act passed the House of Representatives by a vote of 410-4. A similar bill passed unanimously in the Senate; at the time of writing, a Republican senator was blocking the reconciliation of both bills. The process will likely have to start over in the next session of Congress.

In 2020, Wells was awarded a posthumous Pulitzer Prize. Her work continues to inspire. Says noted journalist Nikole Hannah-Jones: "If there was ever a kick-ass woman journalist, it was Wells. She lived her whole life in spaces where people did not think she belonged. And she did not give a single damn what people thought about that."

Tours and Local Guides

SELF-GUIDED TOUR

LYNCHING SITES PROJECT

1900 Union Ave.; tel. 731/277-9352; www.lynchingsitesmem.org; free

Rev. Randall Mullins; his wife, Sharon Pavelda; and others launched the Lynching Sites Project with the aim to find and memorialize every lynching in Shelby County since the Civil War. A comprehensive website lists the names and other details about lynching victims, along with associated police or newspaper reports. An online map plots the site where each victim was lynched: Click the map pin for directions to the lynching site, where a marker commemorates the victim. (Some sites are found in fields where snakes live and thrive, so if you choose to visit, be careful wandering around.)

Inspired by Bryan Stevenson and the Equal Justice Initiative in Montgomery, the Lynching Sites Project was made with the goal of creating a new legacy of racial equality and justice grounded in truth. Listed victims include Ell Persons, a Black woodcutter accused of killing and decapitating a White teenage girl. Persons was captured by a mob, beaten, burned, and decapitated as thousands of White onlookers partook in a carnival-like atmosphere, complete with vendors selling snacks. A marker honoring Persons has been placed at 5404 Summer Avenue, near where Persons was killed.

BUS TOUR

A TOUR OF POSSIBILITIES

tel. 901/326-3736; www.atopmemphis.com; daily; $44, $55-175/hour for individuals, depending on the tour

A Tour of Possibilities was founded by Carolyn Michael-Banks, aka "Queen," an East Coast transplant who moved to Memphis for love, then fell in love with the city itself. Queen's tours focus on African American history in Memphis, with visits to civil rights landmarks and Black history touchpoints, such as historic Mason Temple, the National Civil Rights Museum, Beale Street, and Stax Museum of American Soul Music. The secret sauce in these tours are guides with deep knowledge of Black history who grab your attention before you can barely click your seat belt shut. Queen herself leads tours with a booming voice and sense of humor; other guides are knowledgeable and entertaining in their own rights. While focusing on Black history, tours may touch on other historical events. For example, guides may point out the place where indigenous people were forced to trek down a path toward the Mississippi River into Arkansas on the Trail of Tears.

Tours require reservations. A variety of options, from two-hour to full-day tours, are available, including an audio driving tour. The Grand Tour is a good bet for a comprehensive experience. Visit the website to find a tour that fits your interests and schedule. Some tours involve driving by select sites; others allow guests to stop and enter featured venues. All tours meet at the Tennessee Welcome Center (119 Riverside Drive; tel. 901/543-6757).

Shopping

Like any big city, the Memphis area offers the requisite malls, big-box stores, and discount outlets. But if you want a touch of whimsy, try shopping at homegrown retailers, some of which are located a bit outside downtown.

Among Memphis's local entrepreneurs is South Memphis youth Moziah Bridges, who started making bowties in his grandmother's kitchen in South Memphis when he needed a way to look sharp and is now the pride of his community. **Mo's Bows** (www.mosbowsmemphis.com) are now available at Cheryl Pesce: The Lifestyle Store. At the time of writing, Mo's Bows had popup space in BoxLot too. You can also purchase through the Mo's Bows website. Bow ties run $50 each ($20 for the youth version), and pocket squares and face masks are now available too.

GIFTS

CHERYL PESCE: THE LIFESTYLE STORE

1350 Concourse Ave., Ste. 125; tel. 901/308-6017; www.cherylpesce.com; Sun.-Fri. 11am-6pm, Sat. 10am-9pm

This captivating boutique serves up owner/designer Cheryl Pesce's signature quirk and flair for lifestyle goods and jewelry. Pesce makes just a few of her own edgy yet

Photos (top to bottom): a selelction of Mo's Bows at Cheryl Pesce: The Lifestyle Store; Carolyn Michael-Banks, aka "Queen," of Tour of Possibilities, leads a tour through Memphis; gifts for sale at Cheryl Pesce: The Lifestyle Store

sophisticated jewelry creations at a time. Her materials or those she sources from other artisans range from sea glass and stone to leather and freshwater pearls. Other items include colorful, stackable bowls, customized serving utensils, feminist T-shirts, dolls, and a vibrant array of Mo's Bows.

Cheryl Pesce: The Lifestyle Store is located in the mixed-use Crosstown Concourse building about three miles east of downtown.

FOOD PRODUCTS

PHILLIP ASHLEY CHOCOLATES

1200 Madison Ave.; tel. 901/572-1011; www.phillipashleychocolates.com; Sat. 10am-6pm, weekdays by appointment only; $25-89

Award-winning confectioner Phillip Ashley Rix (a "real-life Willy Wonka," according to Forbes magazine) uses superior fair-trade chocolate in handmade creations such as whiskey cherry cordials, giant turtles, and truffles. Signature flavors include bourbon and fig, sweet potato, and French blue cheese. So unique in their sophistication, these chocolates are a sought-after gift item. Rix's shop also features local artwork and other food items, like popcorn sold by local Black entrepreneurs. The storefront, located a few miles east of downtown, is open only on Saturdays, but you can make an appointment to come in weekdays and build a box of chocolates or order online. Coffee or tea are served, so sip and savor away.

POPUP SHOP

BOXLOT

607 Monroe Ave.; www.boxlotmemphis.com; Thurs.-Fri. 4pm-8pm, Sat.-Sun. 1pm-6pm

Crafted from vibrant blue shipping containers accented with red, yellow, aqua, and green, the BoxLot is a micro-retail and music venue designed to incubate ideas. The project sits in the Edge District of downtown, near Sun Studios, where Elvis Presley got his start (but not before musicians like Howling Wolf and Rufus Thomas put some funk upon that place with their signature sounds). It's meant to be a welcoming communal space, and when furniture is set out, anyone can sit and enjoy.

BoxLot businesses are popups, so they don't stay forever. However, you're sure to be surprised and delighted at whatever you find. At the time of writing, one gem was musician and producer Tonya Dyson's **KickSpins** (www.kickspinsmemphis.com), a sneaker-and-vinyl shop with a hip-hop flair where you can shop for Memphis Soul apparel or comb through vintage album covers (think: the cover of Marvin Gaye's "What's Goin' On," 1971; poet Nikki Giovanni's "Like a Ripple in a Pond: And the New York Community Choir," or "Enter the Wu Tang (36 Chambers)," the eponymous group's 1993 debut hip-hop album.)

BOOKS

BURKE'S BOOKS

936 Cooper St.; tel. 901/278-7484; www.burkesbooks.com; Mon.-Wed. 10am-6pm, Thurs.-Sat. 10am-9pm, Sun. 11am-6pm

If you needed a reason to head over to the hip Cooper-Young neighborhood, Burke's Books (not a Black-owned business) is as good as any. Get lost in the stacks of books, including those that delve into African American history and literature. Burke's specializes in new, used, and rare books. Vintage typewriters sitting on wooden chairs line the main aisle, which will make word nerds giddy, for sure.

While you're in Cooper-Young, grab your new book and have a bite or cup of artisanal coffee at one of the neighborhood's coffee spots. An architecturally interesting working-class area, Cooper-Young is named for an intersection of streets, and features bungalows and Craftsman homes surrounded by restaurants, bars, and shops.

THEATER

HATTILOO THEATRE

37 Cooper St.; tel. 901/525-0009; www.hattiloo.org; general admission $35, seniors and students $30

Founded in 2006, Hattiloo is the only freestanding Black repertory theater in the mid-South. In addition to producing original material, the playhouse amplifies Black cultural expression by bringing diverse Black artistic talent to Memphis while creating original productions that resonate with a local audience and leveraging the talents of Memphis-based actors, musicians, and playwrights. Featured productions have included Suzan-Lori Parks's Pulitzer Prize-winning "Topdog/Underdog," Endesha Ida Mae Holland's "From the Mississippi Delta," and "Take 'Em Down 901," a one-act play about the grassroots movement to remove Memphis's Confederate monuments.

The theater, in a sleek, modern steel and glass building, offers youth programs and hosts panel discussions. The wall art here is breathtaking, featuring Black literary/theater royalty, like an expressive painting of Zora Neale Hurston painting by Memphis's own Carl E. Moore, plus portraits of James Baldwin, August Wilson, Suzan-Lori Parks, and Ruben Santiago Hudson. The theater sits in the trendy Overton Square area (about four miles east of downtown), which is full of shops and restaurants and public art displays.

CONCERTS

THE GREEN ROOM

1350 Concourse Ave., Ste. 280; tel. 901/507-4227; www.crosstownarts.org/music/green-room; tickets $5-15

With a max capacity of 150, this lounge-like listening space creates an intimate venue for musical acts, including Americana, jazz, hip-hop, and even poetry. Located at the mixed-used Crosstown Concourse building, The Green Room is a prime showcase for local acts, including members of the Memphis Symphony Orchestra to funk, soul, and R&B performers. For those who are purely into music (rather than a bar scene), The Green Room is the place to go. While performers come from everywhere, this venue cherishes local talent of which there is plenty. Don Bryant has performed here; he is the husband of Ann Peebles, the legendary soul singer who croons classics like "I Can't Stand the Rain" (1973) and co-wrote the song with her and Bernard Miller. IMAKEMADBEATS and Black Cream have also performed at The Green Room. There are usually two to four shows per week.

GALLERY

CMPLX

2234 Lamar Ave.; tel. 901/421-6476; www.thecltv.org/the-space; Tues.-Sun. 4pm-8pm

The CMPLX is a nonprofit Black arts hub featuring works by local artists. Memphis's young and beautiful come here to show up and show out. The 5,300-square-foot space features two galleries that aim to elevate Black artists and unleash Black genius. Past exhibitions have included the Thug Exhibition, which explored Black masculinity through identity. Among Black arts and activist circles nationwide, the notion of "safe space" is often evoked. Here, a clear glass sign greets visitors with the words "Welcome Home." A safe space for a new generation is found.

CMPLX is located about four miles southeast of downtown Memphis in the Orange Mound neighborhood, which was founded in 1890 as the nation's first planned community for African Americans. Orange Mound started out with

VOICES OF THE MOVEMENT:
FIRST-GRADE STUDENT DWANIA KYLES

"I remember going to school with my mom and my dad, and that there were a lot of policemen. And for me, not having ever gone to school before, I kind of thought, 'Well, aren't I special? Isn't this a special day?'"

—**DWANIA KYLES'S** first day of first grade in 1961 was a memorable one. Escorted by her parents and policemen, the five-year-old became one of the first Black students to attend all-White Bruce Elementary School in Memphis. (Activist Maxine Smith, known locally as the Mother of the Civil Rights Movement, also participated in escorting students to their respective schools.) Kyles's parents, Rev. Billy Kyles and his wife Aurelia, were so committed to the movement that they had moved in a reverse migration from Chicago to Memphis to participate.

Kyles doesn't remember the specific actions her parents took to prepare her for the day. What she does recall are kids, especially older ones, insisting on seeing if she had a tail when she went to the girls' bathroom: "Those were myths circulating in communities about Black people having tails," says Kyles, who always struggled to hold the door shut. White children refused to play with her, and she was called the N-word. This also was the first time she heard the word "cooties," as in "She's got cooties." Kyles looked forward to recess when she could see two other Black boys who were part of the Memphis 13, the 13 Black first-graders who bravely desegregated Memphis's all-White elementary schools in 1961.

Kyles stayed within the system, but by the time she got to high school, she'd had enough of mostly White learning environments and insisted on attending a historically Black college where she could revel in the Black experience. She attended Spelman College for two years, then Howard University.

Looking back, Kyles says the experiences she had at age five defined her as a person. Her trauma stayed with her and led to traumas later in life "that were rooted in that that I did not understand—until I decided to understand." As a wellness coach, Kyles spends her days showing adults and children how to focus their breath to reduce stress. For her, breathwork and mindfulness are the front line to optimal health: "The way I got to it was I had to not want to hate people," Kyles says.

For more information on the Memphis 13, look for *The Memphis 13,* law professor Daniel Kiel's 2011 documentary. "It can be a scary thing, first grade, even without the burden of making history," notes the film's narrator.

about 900 shotgun houses that went for a deal: $100. Though the original homes built on a former plantation were not up to the standards of White homes, this community has long provided pride of place for Black families living there, making lasting family and community.

Festivals and Events

A pair of events at the National Civil Rights Museum honors King: a commemoration of his death on April 4 and a celebration of birth in January. Other events celebrate the city's vibrant music culture.

JANUARY

KING DAY

National Civil Rights Museum, 450 Mulberry St.; tel. 901/521-9699; www.civilrightsmuseum.org

On the third Monday of January (King's officially observed birthday), the National Civil Rights Museum honors the life and legacy of the civil rights leader. The museum is open extended hours and admission is reduced or sometimes free of charge. The day is packed with day-long performances, such as music and song, dance, and activities for children and families in the museum courtyard. Past commemorations have included a blood drive and zoo coupons for those who bring a canned good to donate to the local food bank.

INTERNATIONAL BLUES CHALLENGE

tel. 901/527-2583; www.blues.org/international-blues-challenge; $100 pp for the entire week with finals upgrades available for an additional $25

The B. B. King Blues Club is just one of the many venues along Beale Street that hosts acts every January during the International Blues Challenge. Vetted by regional blues societies, featured musicians, including singers and musicians, range from "very good" to "give-'em-a-contract great." Awards are given for Band, Solo/Duo, Best Band Guitarist, Best Solo/Duo Guitarist, and Best Harmonica Player, and musicians are marked for qualities such as stage presence, originality, and blues content. A youth showcase is held at age-appropriate hours. The event runs Tuesday-Saturday sometime each January. Find a schedule and ticket details at the Blues Foundation website.

APRIL

DR. MARTIN LUTHER KING JR. COMMEMORATIVE CEREMONY AT THE NATIONAL CIVIL RIGHTS MUSEUM

National Civil Rights Museum, 450 Mulberry St.; tel. 901/521-9699; www.civilrightsmuseum.org; free

At the National Civil Rights Museum, April 4 is a day of remembrance in commemoration of King's death. At 6:01pm, when King was fatally shot, crowds outside the museum grow silent as a bell tolls in his memory. A brief ceremonial changing of the wreath on the balcony of Room 306 takes place. The commemoration, which takes place in the museum courtyard, is free and open to the public. If you're in the Mulberry Street area, stopping in your tracks to contemplate, pray, meditate, or whatever your practice is a good thing to do at this moment.

MAY

BEALE STREET MUSIC FESTIVAL

tel. 901/525-4611; www.memphisinmay.org; $89 single-day tickets, $145 three-day passes, discounts for buying early

The Beale Street Music Festival, held Friday-Sunday the first week of May, kicks off the month-long Memphis In May International Festival. The three-day, four-stage music festival is part of a wider celebration that includes the World Championship Barbecue Cooking Contest and Great American River Run 5K and 10K. The festival takes place downtown by the Mississippi River in Tom Lee Park, where Beale Street begins. (The park is named for a heroic Black man who rescued 30 people from the river in 1925.) Acts like John Legend, Snoop Dogg, and Neil Young have performed at the festival. Purchase passes on the Memphis In May site or at the entrance.

JUNE

NIGHT AT THE LORRAINE

National Civil Rights Museum, 450 Mulberry St.; tel. 901/521-9699; www.civilrightsmuseum.org; $100 per person

The Lorraine Motel was regarded as a safe haven for Black people during the Jim Crow era. The motel was listed in the *Negro Motorists Green Book,* which listed safe places for African Americans to eat, lodge, and get other services before passage of the Civil Rights Act of 1964. Musicians from Stax came to the motel to swim and relax unencumbered. Booker T. and the M.G.'s came here, as did Aretha Franklin.

For one night every June, the storied history of this popular gathering spot is celebrated with a party that features live music and dancing to 1960s music. Local chefs and restaurants provide a taste of Memphis, and patrons have the opportunity to view special exhibits such as Soulsville versus Hitsville, which compared Memphis's iconically gritty sound with Detroit's smoother rhythms.

Food

Eating in one of Memphis's Black-owned restaurants is not just about sating one's hunger: It's about celebrating Black creativity and food-ways that fuel economic empowerment for a new day. An added treat is one of those restaurants, The Four Way, allows diners to take a seat at the table where civil rights royalty like Rosa Parks and King supped in the comfort of a safe, communal space.

DOWNTOWN

Southern and Soul Food

CHEF TAM'S UNDERGROUND CAFÉ

668 Union Ave.; tel. 901/207-6182; www.thecheftam.com; Tues.-Sat. 11am-8pm; $5-18

The inventive dishes created and served by Chef Tamra Patterson suggests a person who really likes her job. Her peach cobbler nachos are a marvel in dessert deconstruction, and her deep-fried ribs are otherworldly in their outside crunchiness and inside tenderness. Chef Tam calls her food "Southern-bred and soul-infused," and many of her dishes, such as fried green tomatoes, will be familiar. Others illustrate the fancifulness and fun of her approach, including Kiss My Grits (cheese grits), Grown Folks Chicken & Waffles, and Dorian's Hijacked Fries, topped with bacon, sour cream, and green onions. Community youth and young adults serve as attentive waitstaff, ready and willing to bring another glass of Kool-Aid to your table if you wish.

Locally Sourced

RADICAL

409 S Main St.; tel. 901/264-8359; www.puckfoodhall.com; Tues.-Fri. 7am-10pm; $6-13

Clean eating and seasons mean something at Radical, where wholesome salads and other delectables are built using locally sourced produce from within 100 miles and protein items whenever possible. Think: a salad with red and green cabbage, pickled carrots, rice noodles, green onions, peanuts, herbs, and Thai dressing. Aside from the economic and climate-change argument for locally sourced food, "it just tastes so much better," says general manager Yolanda Manning.

Radical, located on the first floor of Puck Market Hall, is a part of the 275 Food Project, which aims to shift 20 percent of food spending to local farmers and producers by working with restaurants, neighborhoods, and institutions. The eatery relies on a demographically diverse grower network, including women, Black, brown, and LGBTQ farmers. For example, the Produce Tribe of African American farmers is a main source of tomatoes and kale.

Sweets

SWEET MAGNOLIA GELATO CO.

409 S Main St.; tel. 901/264-8359; www.puckfoodhall.com; Tues.-Fri. 7am-10pm

Hugh Balthrop was living the big-city life in DC, making ice cream for his wife and children, when the family decided to move to Mississippi, where his wife's family is from. There, he got really serious about his creations and founded Sweet Magnolia Gelato Co. Today, Sweet Magnolia confections can be found all over the South, with several locations in Mississippi, Alabama, Memphis, Nashville, and Atlanta. Find this branch on the first floor of Puck Food Hall on Main Street, just down the street from the National Civil Rights Museum and near the I Am A Man mural. Sweet Magnolia gelato comes in more than 300 flavors that are constantly changing. Think: strawberry champagne, brown sugar and bourbon, peppermint bark, and blueberry cheesecake. Ingredients are locally sourced—Balthrop's team even knows the name of the cow who made the milk!

SOUTH MEMPHIS AND SOULSVILLE

Southern and Soul Food

THE FOUR WAY

998 Mississippi Blvd.; tel. 901/507-1519; www.fourwaymemphis.com; Tues.-Sat. 11am-7pm, Sun. 10am-5pm; $10

This venerable restaurant has been feeding Memphis, particularly the Soulsville community, since 1946. During the civil rights movement, the tiny business was a safe place for activists to meet and a favorite of King, who loved the fried catfish, chicken, and peach cobbler lovingly made by Irene Cleaves, who opened this place with husband Clint. Civil rights greats have frequented The Four Way, including Rosa Parks, Rev. Jesse L. Jackson, Martin Luther King III, and Rev. Samuel "Billy" Kyles—artists and celebrities too, including Aretha Franklin, Tina Turner, Alex Haley, and Isaac Hayes. After the 50th commemoration of King's assassination, Jackson made a beeline here to enjoy a hearty dinner of short ribs after giving a sermon to remember his fallen comrade and mentor.

The Four Way, now under new ownership and expanded to accommodate hungry customers, offers the full complement of soul food deliciousness, from neck bones, liver and onions, pot roast, and boiled okra to macaroni and cheese, yams, fried green tomatoes, and corn muffins. And, yes, fried chicken is on the menu, as are peach and apple cobbler, sweet tea, and so much more. Inside is spacious with an upstairs dining room.

Photos (top to bottom): Yolanda Manning, general manager of Rad cal; locally made ice cream at Swe Magnolia; fried chicken at The Fou Way

JIM & SAMELLA'S

841 Bullington Ave.; tel. 901/265-8761; Tues.-Thurs. 7am-4pm, Fri. 7am-7pm, Sat. 7am-noon, Sun. 10am-4pm; $6-12

You're likely to make friends in this restaurant set up in a small house in South Memphis with tables in four rooms, including a community table by the kitchen. Owners and siblings Talbert and Sheldon Fleming named this place for their parents, Jim and Samella, and designed it to feel and taste like home. Try the chicken and waffles for breakfast, and bring an appetite for oxtails and grits, crispy fried catfish, lamb chops, and collard greens. The bread pudding is sublime; get yourself some. The restaurant is about five miles from downtown Memphis.

OTHER NEIGHBORHOODS

Southern and Soul Food

PEGGY'S HEALTHY HOMECOOKING

326 S Cleveland St.; tel. 901/474-4938; Tues.-Thurs. 11am-7pm, Fri. 11am-9pm, Sun. noon-6pm; $9-13

The grandmotherly Ms. Peggy Brown frequently holds court in a tight corner at the entrance of her restaurant as staff serve up home-cooked fare with speed and smiles. Here, you'll find daily and Blue Plate specials and feel perfectly comfortable skipping the hard work of cooking Sunday dinner because you can get your fill of baked chicken and dressing, smothered/grilled/fried pork chops, fish, black-eyed peas, greens, yams, okra, and more right here. Entire families flock to Peggy's to taste well-seasoned, hot-buttered memories and to create new ones. Peggy's is a six-minute drive from downtown Memphis along I-40 in the Annesdale Park area.

Barbecue

PAYNE'S BARBECUE

1762 Lamar Ave.; tel. 901/272-1523; Tues.-Fri. 11am-6pm, Sat. 11am-4pm; $6-16

The word-of-mouth on this family-owned barbecue restaurant is fierce, including social media shout-outs for their barbecue bologna sandwiches and smoked sausage sandwiches topped with mustard-based slaw. Of course, chopped pork is the 'cue of choice around these parts, and Payne's sandwiches are piled high with a perfect mixture of smoky meat flavor, fat, and spicy-vinegary sauce. Flora Payne and her son, Ron, maintain high standards for barbecue smoked in a recessed pit over hickory coals. This family business was founded in 1972 by Flora's late husband, Horton Payne, and his mother, Emily. It's located in a straightforward cinderblock building at the corner of Lamar and S. McLean Boulevard, five miles west of downtown Memphis.

Sweets

ALCENIA'S DESSERTS & PRESERVES SHOP

317 N Main St.; tel. 901/523-0200; Tues.-Thurs. 11am-5pm, Sat. 9am-3pm

Folks describe Alcenia's as a taste of home. You can get a snack of chicken wings, sweet potato fries, or grilled cheese sandwiches here, but the highlight is dessert. Offerings include pound cake, peach cobbler, and an impressive array of pies, including buttermilk, sweet potato, and egg custard. Oh, and they sell homemade cha cha—a type of relish made of green tomatoes, cabbage, onions, and peppers by the pint. This southern delicacy may be hot or mild. Try Alcenia's tea cakes, shortbread-like cookies, for a taste of the past. Alcenia's is in Uptown, north of downtown; it's an area that's on the comeback.

MEMPHIS

LUCY J'S

1350 Concourse Ave., Ste. 151; tel. 901/257-9206; Mon.-Fri. 7am-7pm, Sat. 9am-7pm

Located at Crosstown Concourse, which features other retail shops and businesses, the bakery is open, bright, and inviting. The menu includes croissants, Danishes, muffins, cakes, cookies, pies, and breads, and in an open, well-lit space, patrons can peer through a clear barrier to see cupcakes being iced, beckoning to be bought and eaten. Lucy J's is a labor of love for founders Tracy and Josh Burgess, who embody the values King preached by paying workers a living wage, providing job training, and selling coffee on a pay-what-you-can scale. Proceeds benefit Dorothy Day House, a transitional shelter for families experiencing homelessness.

Nightlife

A rainbow of neon lights heralds the three-block blues mecca that is Beale Street. Before stepping inside dozens of blues clubs, plus restaurants and shops, this is some of the best people-watching you can find anywhere. Credit street performers like the **Beale Street Flippers,** athletically jumping and flipping their way to tips for the electricity that fills the strip. Whatever workaday burdens people come with, they're cast aside once they cross the threshold and a lightness takes over. You'll find the Flippers during the evenings in the middle of the street on Beale on any given day.

A few rules about Beale Street: At 9pm on Friday and Saturday, a security checkpoint ensures guests are ages 21 and up. Minors accompanied by an adult who are already there can stay until 11pm. After 11 on Friday and Saturday, it's grown folks time, and Beale is strictly 21 and up.

Beale Street is fun and full of energy, which can be a lot after a while. If you're on a more relaxed frame of mind, walk a few blocks to some off-Beale venues to chill.

BEALE STREET CLUBS

B. B. KING'S BLUES CLUB

143 Beale St.; tel. 901/524-5464; www.bbkings.com/memphis; Mon.-Thurs. 11am-midnight, Fri.-Sat. 11am-1am, Sun. 11am-11:30pm; $5 cover

All lights lead to this neon glory of Beale Street, the reborn mecca of African American music forms. Named for the blues great, B. B. King's Blues Club is situated at the top of Beale's three-block strip. The venue has everything you want for an authentic experience on this historic street: food, drinks, and live music that not only celebrates the blues but classic soul and rock and roll too. They specialize in ribs here, but you can get other Southern goodies, like catfish bites and street tacos, pulled pork, and a variety of po' boys, plus signature drinks, like Delta Blues, a mixture of rum, blue curacao and pineapple.

Go ahead and be entertained by uniquely Black music stylings that draw aficionados from around the globe: But remember, the sorrow, joy, and angst rendered through B. B. King's guitar and lyrics came from a shared experience marked by poverty and disenfranchisement that moved the movement to take risks and make demands. And while King, who died in 2015 at age 89, focused on his passion and purpose in making music, he did not forget the struggle: The world's pre-eminent blues guitarist supported the civil rights movement behind the scenes, giving money to bail out civil rights protestors, for example.

B.B. King's Blues Club

NIGHTLIFE OFF BEALE STREET

HAVANA MIX CIGAR EMPORIUM

250 Peabody Pl., Ste. 105; tel. 901/522-2909; Sun. noon-10pm; Mon.-Thurs. 11am-11pm, Fri.-Sat. 11am-1am; no cover

This father-son labor of love features cigars and pipes from around the world, along with live music. Inside a cedar walk-in humidor, you'll find a range of cigars (over 50,000), including a Rocky Patel exclusive, the Beale St. Cigar. Even if you're not a smoker, there's something for anyone looking for a grown 'n' sexy night on the town, including leather chairs and flat-screen TVs. Both locals and tourists frequent this mellow place that's super friendly. Hungry? Try the wings and fries, featuring owner Rhobb Hunter's "sweet heat," pizza, or a plate of sausage and cheese, which is kind of a thing around these parts.

Located near Clayborn Temple, Memphis Rock 'n' Soul Museum, and the Beale Street entertainment district, the emporium validates parking for patrons who park in the garage next door.

THE TAILOR'S UNION

115 Union Ave.; 901/623-8567; www.tailorsunionmemphis.com; Wed.-Thurs. 5pm-11pm, Fri.-Sat. 5pm-1pm; no cover

Two blocks north of Beale Street, The Tailor's Union is a great place for lunch or dinner (the restaurant offers small plates), or just quick and easy drinks. The business looks unassuming from its storefront. Inside, you'll find the accoutrements of a tailor, from an old-fashioned sewing machine and dress patterns to a big mirror. Elegant white couches and white leather booths punctuate the chic look, and a photo booth allows patrons to memorialize the moment. You'll want to dress up a bit for this bar. Bathrooms are unisex.

Downstairs is a dimly lit speakeasy called **The Pocket** where jazz is played; it's members-only though.

Accommodations

Travelers in Memphis may want to stay close to downtown and Beale Street for easy access to the city's main sights and nightlife. In addition to the choices below, other reliable options include **DoubleTree by Hilton Hotel Memphis Downtown** (185 Union St.; tel. 901/528-1800; hilton.com), just two blocks from Beale Street, and the **Hampton Inn & Suites Memphis-Beale St.** (175 Peabody Pl.; tel. 901/260-4000; hamptoninn3.hilton.com), also located near Beale Street.

DOWNTOWN

$100-200

HOTEL INDIGO

22 N B. B. King Blvd.; tel. 901/529-4000; www.ihg.com

This downtown boutique hotel takes its design inspiration from Memphis music, with a focus on regional blues, rock and soul legends, and local artwork. And to put a bow on it, guests receive complimentary tickets to the Stax Museum of American Soul Music. Hotel Indigo sits between Beale Street and Memphis Cook Convention Center and has a rooftop pool. The 119 rooms here have spa-like showers and hardwood floors with high-end toiletries and amenities. The onsite restaurant specializes on locally sourced, seasonal fare. Most sites are a short car ride away.

HU HOTEL

79 Madison Ave.; tel. 866/446-3674; www.huhotelmemphis.com

Named for the grandson of one of Memphis's founders, this boutique hotel features an upscale restaurant, Hu Diner, and a rooftop bar with a beautiful view of the Hernando De Soto bridge, especially at night when it is lit with a range of colors. The light and airy lobby has a café and plenty of space to either lounge or plug in a laptop and surf courtesy of free Wi-Fi. The hotel is next to the Memphis Area Transit Authority trolley, which will get you within walking distance of Beale Street and the Orpheum Theatre. Situated downtown, most civil rights sites are a short ride by car. Hu Hotel has 110 rooms decorated in peaceful palates.

Over $200

PEABODY HOTEL

118 S 2nd St.; tel. 901/529-4000; www.peabodymemphis.com

The Peabody is known for the brace of ducks who march from the glass and marble Royal Duck Palace on the roof to the hotel's foundation that features a bronze duck spitting water. This affair takes place daily at 11am and 5pm, and it's best to arrive 30 minutes early if you want to take in the spectacle. The bustling downtown hotel features 464 rooms, including suites, private concierge service, and the full-service Feathers Spa. The Mississippi River inspires the color palette, which includes calming neutral hues and artwork that evokes Memphis, blues music, the storied river, and those beloved ducks. Breakfast, evening hors d'oeuvres, and late-evening pastries are complimentary.

Transportation

GETTING THERE

Air

Memphis International Airport (2491 Winchester Rd.; tel. 901/922-8000; www.flymemphis.com) is about 11 miles south of downtown Memphis, off I-240.

The airport is serviced by local taxis outside arrivals near luggage claim, and app rides are upstairs on the departures deck, clearly marked by hard-to-miss signs. A rental car hub is a little walk away in the ground transportation center. The cab ride downtown takes about 15 minutes and costs $21-26.

Train

Amtrak's City of New Orleans line serves **Memphis Central Station** (545 S Main St.; tel. 800/872-7245; www.amtrak.com/stations; open 24/7) which includes an enclosed waiting area, wheelchair accessibility, and parking. The station, which is connected to the Central Station Hotel, is within walking distance of the National Civil Rights Museum. The lobby hotel is a great place to hang out because they have more than 2,500 vinyl albums with a DJ who plays music authentic to this area—the Memphis Sound, like Al Green and Rufus Thomas.

Southbound, adult fares to Memphis from Greenwood (2.5 hours) start at $30; from Jackson, Mississippi (4.5 hours), $43.

Bus

Memphis's **Greyhound Station** (3033 Airways Blvd.; tel. 901/395-8770; www.greyhound.com; open 24/7) is located at the 30,000-square-foot Airways Transit Center, which also serves as a hub and customer service center for city buses. Downtown Memphis is about 10 miles to the west.

This station offers 24 outbound and 23 inbound schedules daily, with rides to the Mississippi Delta—Clarksdale, specifically (1.5 hours)—for $26. You can also

Trolleys operate in downtown Memphis.

connect with Jackson, Mississippi (6 hours; $19-26); Nashville (4 hours; $27-44), and Little Rock (2.5 hours; $9-16).

Car

To reach Memphis from:

- **Little Rock:** Take **I-40 East** for about 140 miles (2 hours).
- **The Delta:** From **Clarksdale, Mississippi,** take **US-61 North** for about 80 miles (1.5 hours). From **Greenwood, Mississippi,** take **I-55 North** for about 130 miles (2 hours).
- **Jackson:** Take **I-55 North** for about 210 miles (3 hours).
- **Nashville:** Take **I-40 West** for about 210 miles (3 hours).

GETTING AROUND

Most people in Memphis get around in cars, then park and walk once they've reached the neighborhood they want to explore.

Parking

It costs $10 or less per day to park in Memphis with a $2 minimum. Meters are primarily downtown, and they cost about $1.50 per hour.

Public Transit

MEMPHIS AREA TRANSIT AUTHORITY

444 N Main St., Ste. 1; tel. 901/274-6282; www.matatransit.com

Downtown trolleys ($1 each way; day pass $3.50; 3-day pass $9) operate along three lines. The **Riverfront Shuttle Line,** with a nice view of the Mississippi River, runs about every 20 minutes, Mon.-Fri. 9am-9pm, Sat. 8:30am-10:30pm, Sun. 10:30am-6pm. **Main Street Rail Line** (which takes you from City Hall south to the National Civil Rights Museum) runs every 12 minutes, Mon.-Fri 6:45am-12:15am, Sat. 8am-12:10am, Sun. 10am-6:10pm, and costs $1 each way. **Madison Avenue Shuttle Line,** which provides access to the Midtown area, runs every 15 minutes, Mon.-Fri. 6:45am-6pm, Sat. 8:15am-6:30pm.

Bus services is not generally regarded as convenient here, but if you want to contribute to a lower carbon footprint and try the bus, find a map and schedules at matatransit.com. Fare is $1.75 for adults.

Taxi and Ride-Hailing Apps

Uber and **Lyft** operate in Memphis. If you need a cab, call **Bluff City Taxi** (tel. 901/566-9000; www.bluffcitytaxi.com).

Nashville

The sit-in movement began in Greensboro, North Carolina, but Nashville is where it really gained momentum. Here, students at the city's numerous historically Black colleges and universities (HBCUs) formed the core of the Nashville sit-in movement. For months, the students trained in nonviolent protest using training tactics, such as role-playing, and set their sights on desegregating lunch counters, department stores, and bus terminals. When they were ready, the students bravely claimed seats at segregated lunch counters in Nashville in a peaceful demand for equal rights.

NASHVILLE'S TOP 3

1. Watching the documentary *NBC White Paper: Sit-In,* which chronicled the Nashville Student Movement on December 20, 1960, inside the **Civil Rights Room at the Nashville Public Library** (page 325).

2. Vibing out at the **Jefferson Street Jazz & Blues Festival,** a phenomenal way to celebrate Black music and joy in Nashville, during Juneteenth weekend (page 336).

3. Enjoying a meal in a diverse, welcoming environment at **Woolworth on Fifth,** where nonviolent protestors were met with violence and arrests during the sit-in movement (page 337).

Photos (top to bottom): the Civil Rights Room at the Nashville Public Library; Woolworth on 5th. Previous: the Nashville Public Library

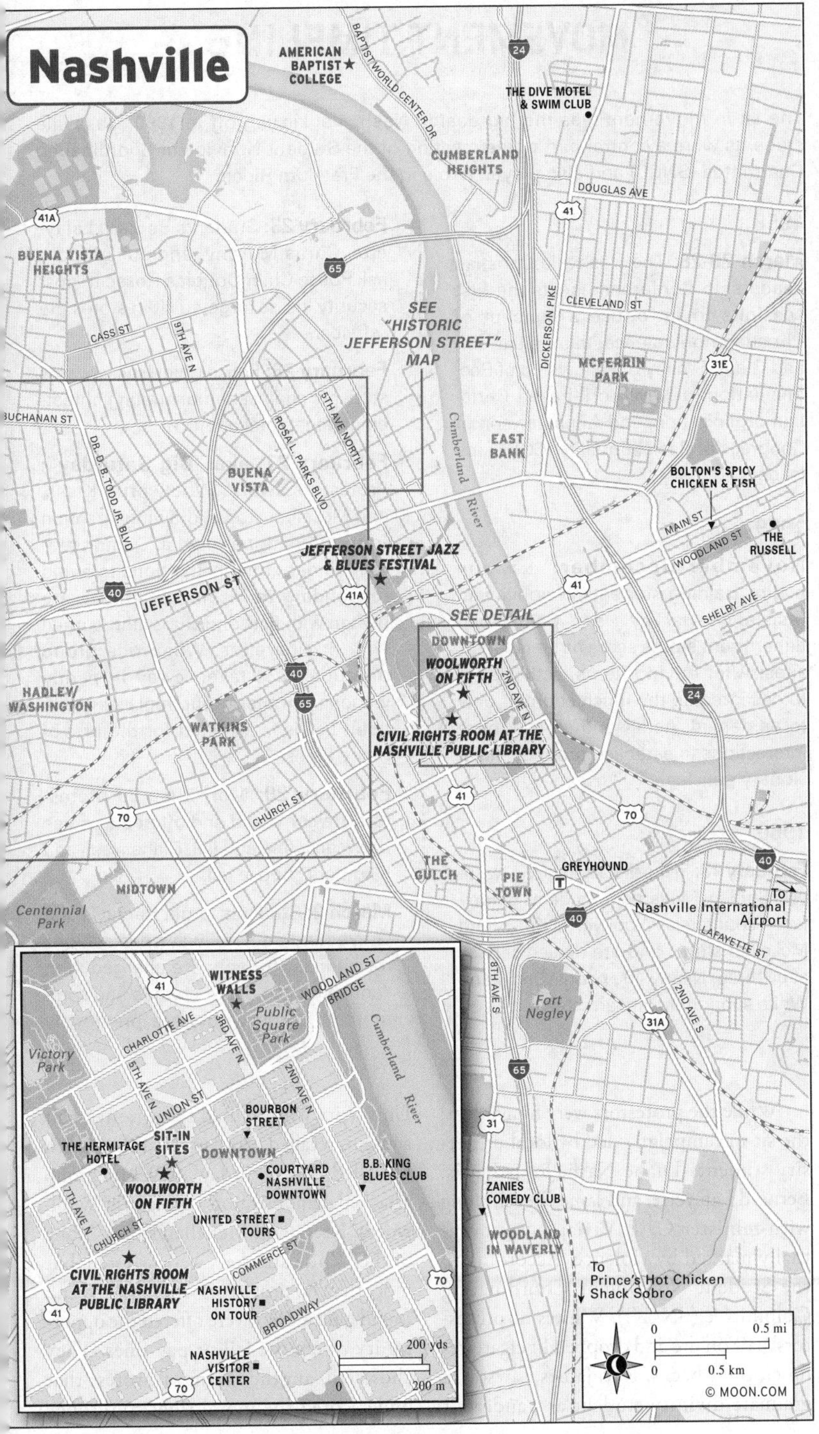

Nashville
AMERICAN BAPTIST COLLEGE
BAPTIST WORLD CENTER DR
THE DIVE MOTEL & SWIM CLUB
CUMBERLAND HEIGHTS
DOUGLAS AVE
BUENA VISTA HEIGHTS
SEE "HISTORIC JEFFERSON STREET" MAP
CLEVELAND ST
DICKERSON PIKE
CASS ST
9TH AVE N
MCFERRIN PARK
BUCHANAN ST
DR. D. B. TODD JR. BLVD
ROSA L. PARKS BLVD
5TH AVE NORTH
BUENA VISTA
Cumberland River
EAST BANK
BOLTON'S SPICY CHICKEN & FISH
MAIN ST
WOODLAND ST
THE RUSSELL
JEFFERSON STREET JAZZ & BLUES FESTIVAL
JEFFERSON ST
SHELBY AVE
SEE DETAIL
DOWNTOWN
WOOLWORTH ON FIFTH
2ND AVE N
HADLEY/ WASHINGTON
WATKINS PARK
CIVIL RIGHTS ROOM AT THE NASHVILLE PUBLIC LIBRARY
CHURCH ST
THE GULCH
PIE TOWN
GREYHOUND
MIDTOWN
Centennial Park
To Nashville International Airport
LAFAYETTE ST
8TH AVE S
Fort Negley
2ND AVE S
WITNESS WALLS
WOODLAND ST BRIDGE
Public Square Park
CHARLOTTE AVE
3RD AVE N
Victory Park
6TH AVE N
2ND AVE N
UNION ST
BOURBON STREET
THE HERMITAGE HOTEL
SIT-IN SITES
DOWNTOWN
COURTYARD NASHVILLE DOWNTOWN
B.B. KING BLUES CLUB
WOOLWORTH ON FIFTH
7TH AVE N
UNITED STREET TOURS
CHURCH ST
COMMERCE ST
CIVIL RIGHTS ROOM AT THE NASHVILLE PUBLIC LIBRARY
NASHVILLE HISTORY ON TOUR
BROADWAY
NASHVILLE VISITOR CENTER
0 200 yds
0 200 m
ZANIES COMEDY CLUB
WOODLAND IN WAVERLY
To Prince's Hot Chicken Shack Sobro
0 0.5 mi
0 0.5 km
© MOON.COM

NASHVILLE

MOVEMENT TIMELINE

NASHVILLE

The sit-in movement was the big deal in Nashville, kicking off in 1960. Nashville students were a central part of the creation of the Student Nonviolent Coordinating Committee (SNCC) and also played a role in the Freedom Rides.

1958

March 26-28: The Nashville Christian Leadership Conference hosts the first sessions to introduce a concept of Christian nonviolence. James Lawson and Glenn Smiley of Fellowship of Reconciliation, a New York-based Christian organization, and Anna Lawson of Congress of Racial Equality (CORE) are leaders.

1959

November-December: Lawson begins training students in nonviolent resistance. Harvey's and Cain Sloan department stores serve as sit-in "test" sites: After buying items, activists try to desegregate the lunch counter, only to be denied. Activists then use these interactions to establish proof of exclusionary policies.

1960

February 13: In the first sit-in of the Nashville Student Movement, students occupy lunch counters at Woolworth, Kress, and McLellan stores and are denied service at all three. Nearly 100 people, including White supporters, are arrested.

February 23: Students Bernard Lafayette, Curtis Murphy, and Julia Moore ask Police Chief Douglas Hosse to post security inside targeted sit-in stores. He refuses.

February 26: Police Chief Hosse warns students against demonstrating, threatening legal retaliation.

February 27, aka "Big Saturday": Protestors swarm Woolworth, Kress, and McLellan stores, drawing attention from the national media. Demonstrators, under strict instructions to avoid responding to insults or attacks, are beaten with fists and clubs, and burned with lit cigarettes. When one group of students is taken away in paddy wagons, another group replaces them. John Lewis is arrested for the first of many times.

February 29: More than 80 protestors are convicted and offered a choice between a fine and jail. Diane Nash and 59 others choose jail.

March 2: Students target Harvey's and Greyhound and Trailways bus stations for sit-ins. Students are charged with "conspiracy to obstruct trade and commerce"; some who were previously

While the protestors were nonviolent, the sit-in campaign—led by local university students Diane Nash, John Lewis, Bernard Lafayette, and James Bevel, along with minister C. T. Vivian—was eventually marked by violence. According to the Student Nonviolent Coordinating Committee (SNCC), Whites lit protestors' hair on fire and dropped lit cigarettes down their backs. Rev. James Lawson, a graduate divinity student at Vanderbilt University who trained these nonviolent activists, recalled February 27, 1960, which he called "Big Saturday." A White group attacked demonstrators sitting in at Woolworth, Kress, and McLellan stores. None of the White attackers were arrested, but more than 80 protestors were arrested and found guilty. They were offered the opportunity to choose jail or pay fines. They chose jail, another form of protest that underscored the moral right to disobey

arrested are arrested again and decline offers for bond money.

April 17-19: SNCC is founded after Southern Christian Leadership Conference (SCLC) acting executive director Ella Baker, inspired by student participation in the sit-in movement, calls for a meeting of student activists in Raleigh, North Carolina. Students from Nashville (including John Lewis, Diane Nash, Bernard Lafayette, and Marion Barry) represent the largest contingent of students in attendance and become founding members of SNCC.

April 19: The Nashville home of civil rights lawyer Z. Alexander Looby is dynamited by segregationists. Thousands of protestors march from Fisk University to the Davidson County Courthouse, where Diane Nash confronts Nashville's mayor.

April 20: Dr. Martin Luther King Jr. speaks at the Fisk gym: "I came to Nashville not to bring inspiration, but to gain inspiration from the great movement that has taken place in this community."[1]

May 10: Nashville becomes the first major Southern city to integrate lunch counters.

1961

May 17: Diane Nash leads a group of Nashville students to Birmingham to continue the Freedom Ride, which was abandoned by CORE due to violence. The students are arrested and taken back to the Tennessee state line.

2017

Davidson Country Courthouse and the Witness Walls are dedicated.

A sign marks the home of civil rights lawyer Z. Alexander Looby, which was bombed in 1960.

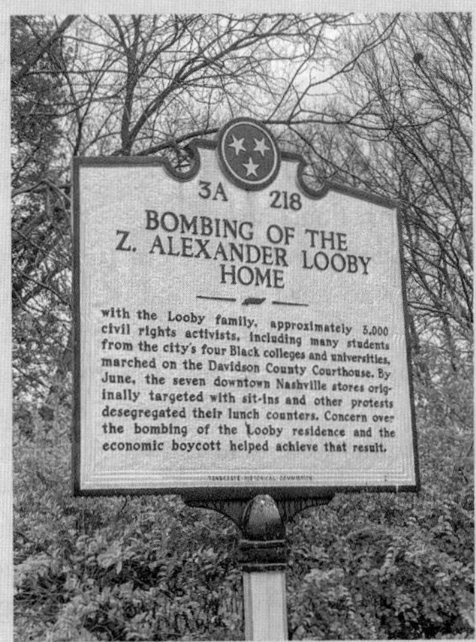

the "law" when local customs were actually unconstitutional.

Eventually, the protests paid off, and the students' efforts clinched one of the early successes of the civil rights movement when Nashville became the first Southern city to desegregate lunch counters in 1960.

While Nashville is known widely as Music City USA, its other nickname, Athens of the South—versions of which have existed since 1824—reveals a deeply rooted investment in higher education. African Americans cherish this identity because of the several HBCUs that have long existed here. Legions of Black middle-class professionals were educated at Fisk University, established after the Civil War, Meharry Medical College, Tennessee A&I (now Tennessee State University), and American Baptist Theological Seminary (now American Baptist College). During the Nashville Movement, students from these same institutions found the courage to lead the nation into a better version of itself.

Today, Nashville is best known for its music scene, especially country. What many people don't know is that country music was heavily influenced by African instruments, such as the banjo, and song styles brought to this land by enslaved Africans. The city is also a hub for gospel music, another uniquely American music style created and nurtured by African Americans, rivaling Chicago as a center of this art form. The National Museum of African American Music, which opened in 2020, dedicates 56,000 feet to the role Black people played in creating American music forms. Clubs offering live music, such as B. B. King's Blues Club, are another way to enjoy the rhythms of Black music, and the annual Jefferson Street Jazz & Blues Festival celebrates Black music and the history of a street where Black entertainers and clubs once flourished.

Modern Nashville is bursting at the seams with newcomers and natives who seek to make the most of opportunities to prosper in work, business, and social networks. In this environment of progress, equity and inclusion issues endure. For example, in June 2020, six teens—Jade Fuller, Nya Collins, Zee Thomas, Kennedy Green, Emma Rose Smith, and Mikayla Smith—organized the area's biggest demonstration against police brutality and racism in recent history.

ORIENTATION

Downtown Nashville, bordered to the east by the Cumberland River, to the south and west by I-40, and to the north by Jefferson Street, is a highly walkable area. Most sights are located here and on historic **Jefferson Street.** (Jefferson Street is the northern border of downtown, but most relevant sights are located on the western portion of the street.)

Jefferson Street was once the heart of Nashville's Black community, where a vibrant music scene drew world-class performers. But like so many Black communities across the country, the community suffered with the construction of the interstate system, as construction on I-40 began in the late 1960s. A good amount of civil rights organizing took place on Jefferson Street, including an impactful march that originated here and ended at the courthouse downtown. There are still sights worth seeing on Jefferson Street, along with shops and restaurants. Three of Nashville's HBCUs are located off this street: **Fisk, Meharry Medical College,** and **Tennessee State University.** Some stops on the street are close enough to walk between, while others are best accessed by vehicle.

PLANNING YOUR TIME

Nashville's climate is typically pleasant; only a few days of the year are very hot or cold. Most rain falls in spring, although showers are possible year-round.

sit-in exhibit at the Tennessee State Museum

Though there are compelling sights in Nashville, experiencing the civil rights movement here may take a bit more imagination than it does in other cities: The movement just doesn't feel as present as it does in, say, Birmingham or Little Rock. A good sightseeing strategy is to make quick stops at **Davidson County Courthouse** and the **Witness Walls,** the **Civil Rights Room at Nashville Public Library,** and **Fisk University,** but really dedicate some time to the **Tennessee State Museum,** which tells the story of the struggle for the entire state.

A good couple of days will give you a firm grasp of the city's civil rights story while leaving time to enjoy Nashville-flavored food and fun. Pick up maps and brochures and ask for advice to enhance your travel experience at the **Nashville Visitor Center** (501 Broadway; tel. 501/657-6910). Note that the **Jefferson Street Sound Museum** is only open on Saturdays. The Tennessee State Museum is closed Mondays.

CONNECT WITH

This trip pairs well with a drive southwest on I-40 to **Memphis**, just a little over three hours. Keep going west on I-40 from Memphis and you'll land in **Little Rock,** a battleground city for the desegregation of public schools.

Two Days in Nashville

DAY 1

Spend your first day in downtown Nashville, the site of lunch-counter sit-ins at **Woolworth on Fifth** and the end point of an important protest march. Downtown Nashville is compact, so it's easy to walk between all the day's sights. (You'll be leaving downtown for dinner.) Be sure to book your customized **Nashville History On Tour,** your first activity on Day 1, in advance.

1 Your day begins with a two-hour **Nashville History On Tour: Civil Rights and Song.** The tour starts at the Ryman Auditorium (116 5th Ave. N) downtown, where legendary musicians, including Black musicians, have performed.

2 Next, spend some quality time at the **Civil Rights Room at the Nashville Public Library.** A timeline display in the center of the room evokes a lunch counter, which was a famous target for Nashville's nonviolent sit-in actions. Spend an hour here perusing books about the movement, Black history, and resistance, studying historic photos, and asking helpful library staff to flesh out details. View *NBC White Paper: Sit-In,* a 1960 documentary on the sit-in movement.

3 Hungry? Lunch is served at **Woolworth on Fifth**—the very site of several lunch-counter sit-ins in 1960. The space has been reworked into a restaurant, complete with a replica lunch counter. Take a seat and order up a "counter classic."

4 Look out for historic markers as you walk over to the Davidson County Courthouse and **Witness Walls.** The Witness Walls are situated on the site where Diane Nash, flanked by Rev. C. T. Vivian and Bernard Lafayette, confronted Nashville's mayor on segregation on April 19, 1960.

5 Leaving downtown, head east across the Cumberland River to grab a Nashville hot chicken sandwich at **Bolton's Spicy Chicken & Fish.**

DAY 2

Your second day is centered on Jefferson Street, which was the heart of historic Black Nashville, and a hotbed of civil rights planning activity. It's about a 1.5-mile walk down Jefferson Street from the first stop of the day to the pair of shops in Stops 5 and 6. From there, take a taxi to **Slim & Husky's Pizza Beeria.**

1 If it's a weekend, start with brunch at the **Silver Sands Cafe,** a family- and Black-owned authentic soul food eatery. On Sundays, there's a line, but it's worth the wait.

2 The **Tennessee State Museum** is your first stop after breakfast. (Do note that it's closed Mondays, and not open until 1pm Sundays.) Here, you can get a firm grounding in Tennessee history overall and various cities' and regions' roles in the civil rights movement specifically.

3 As you continue along Jefferson Street, take a detour to your left to stroll through **Fisk University.** As you walk through campus, you're walking through history: Fisk was where students like Diane Nash, John Lewis, and Marion Barry were inspired to fight for civil rights. Take note of historical markers as you stroll through campus.

4 For a peek at Black artistic prowess (among other pieces of stunning art) drop into **Carl Van Vechten Gallery at Fisk University.**

5 Back on Jefferson Street, head over to **College Crib** at Price Plaza. If you're in a Black sorority or fraternity, this shop has all the organization-specific gear you'll ever need, including outerwear, jewelry, stoles, and more.

6 **Alkebu-Lan Images Bookstore & Gifts** is on the corner, so pop in for books, jewelry, or shea butter: because it's all here. Both Alkebu-Lan and College Crib are Black-owned, so spending here is a tangible step toward investing in the Black community.

7 You must be hungry, eh? How about some artisanal pizza served with a hip-hop flair? The energetic team at **Slim & Husky's Pizza Beeria** on Buchanan in North Nashville are waiting. Order a locally sourced beer while you wait for your pizza to come out of the oven piping hot.

8 **Minerva Avenue Bar,** a craft cocktail lounge, is located right by Slim & Husky's. Duck in here if you're in the mood for a nightcap.

PEOPLE WHO MADE THE MOVEMENT

ORGANIZATIONS

Student Nonviolent Coordinating Committee (SNCC): Student-centered activist group born in Raleigh, North Carolina in 1960, after the sit-in movement took hold. The largest contingent of students came from Nashville, where nonviolence was a key aspect of the student movement.

RELIGIOUS LEADERS

Rev. James Lawson: A minister who came to Nashville at the behest of King, Lawson enrolled in Vanderbilt University for the 1958-1959 school year and trained Nashville protestors in nonviolent direct-action techniques inspired by Gandhi.

C. T. Vivian: Minister who co-founded the Nashville Christian Leadership Council and mentored the Nashville Student Movement. Vivian joined the Freedom Rides in 1961 when Congress of Racial Equality (CORE) members were injured.

Kelly Miller Smith Sr.: Founding president of the Nashville Christian Leadership Council, an affiliate of the Southern Christian Leadership Conference.

STUDENT ACTIVISTS

College students were the heart and soul of the nonviolent protest movement in Nashville. The five leaders below were founding members of **SNCC** and active participants in the **Nashville Student Movement,** including marches and lunch-counter sit-ins.

John Lewis: Before he took a leading role in the voting rights protests in Selma in 1965, Lewis (who was also a Freedom Rider) was a student who participated in the Nashville lunch-counter sit-ins. In fact, it was during the lunch-counter protests when Lewis was arrested for the first time (of many).

Diane Nash: A Chicago native and Fisk English major, Nash trained in nonviolent techniques and worked with CORE to coordinate the Freedom Rides into Mississippi. In 1960, Nash famously demanded of Nashville's mayor, "Do you feel it is wrong to discriminate against a person solely on the basis of their race or color?" His "yes" reply was a turning point for the movement.

James Bevel: Mississippi Delta-born Baptist minister who joined the Nashville sit-in movement in February 1960. Helped direct the 1961 Freedom Rides with Diane Nash, when CORE members were injured. (He and Nash married but later divorced.)

Marion Barry: Mississippi-born, Memphis-reared Barry, a Fisk chemistry student, participated in the Nashville Student Movement and became the first president of SNCC at its April 1960 founding meeting at Shaw University in Raleigh, North Carolina.

Marion Barry

Bernard Lafayette: American Baptist Theological Seminary student who participated in the 1960 sit-in campaign. Lafayette was also a Freedom Rider who served 40 days in Mississippi's Parchman Prison.

OTHER KEY FIGURES

Z. Alexander Looby: Civil rights attorney whose Nashville home was bombed on April 19, 1960. The act of violence inspired a silent march to the Davidson County Courthouse, where a confrontation between Diane Nash and Nashville Mayor Ben West was a turning point in the downtown desegregation campaign.

DOWNTOWN

Sit-In Sites

5th Avenue

In downtown Nashville, 5th Avenue was the epicenter of the city's lunch-counter sit-in movement in the 1960s. Today, 5th Avenue features a mix of retail, office, and residential space. **Woolworth's on Fifth** (221 5th Ave. N)—site of John Lewis's first arrest—has been reimagined as a restaurant with a replica lunch counter that allows patrons to engage with the events that occurred here. You can dine here, and also head up to the mezzanine to see original lunch counter seats.

On this same block is the terra cotta façade of the old **S. H. Kress** five-and dime (239 5th Ave. N), another sit-in site. The art deco building was built in 1935, and, like many Kress stores, features the brass lettering associated with the chain. The building now known as Kress Lofts (237-239 5th Ave. N) is a condo complex that holds an art gallery, Tinney Contemporary, on the first floor.

Any vestiges of **McLellan** (229-33 5th Ave. N), another sit-in target, are long gone. However, The Rymer Art Gallery (233 5th Ave. N), is found here, and is where John Lewis spoke in 2013 when original panels from his award-winning civil rights co-authored graphic memoir, *March: Book One-Three,* were on view.

A city alley called The Arcade was originally developed in the early 1900s in a Greek revival style to be Nashville's first indoor shopping area and features shops, restaurants, galleries, and more. Beyond the Palladian facades between 4th and 5th Avenues is another sit-in site, **Walgreens** (218 5th Ave. N), which doesn't have any markers of what happened in this store, pre-renovation.

The street also features a marker dedicated to the Nashville Student Movement, located near Woolworth on Fifth.

Witness Walls

1 Public Square, Public Square Park; tel. 615/862-6732; free

Dedicated in 2017, this public artwork installation next to the **Davidson County Courthouse** (also known as Metropolitan Courthouse) features a series of sculptural concrete walls embedded with images of people powering Nashville's role in the movement. The images show a variety of events: sit-ins, bus rides, meetings, economic boycotts, and marches. Rather than highlighting specific people, the images, which do not appear in any sort of chronological order, suggest a general sense of collective action. The effect is an invitation to not only remember, but to also imagine where you might fit in such a narrative.

The Witness Walls monument, a stop on the official U.S. Civil Rights Trail, is located on a significant site: This was where Diane Nash, flanked by fellow leaders C. T. Vivian and Bernard Lafayette, led 3,000 students and community members to confront Mayor Ben West on the steps of City Hall after the home of civil rights attorney Z. Alexander Looby was bombed on April 19, 1960. Nash famously asked West, "Do *you* feel it is wrong to discriminate against a person solely on the basis of their race or color?" He courageously said, "Yes." Shortly thereafter, Nashville desegregated its lunch counters, becoming the first Southern city to do so.

At the very top of the courthouse is the jail that held students arrested during the sit-in campaign. The building's architecture mixes art deco and Greek classical styles. It is listed on the National Register of Historic Places.

FREEDOM RIDES: NASHVILLE

The Freedom Riders didn't come to Nashville: Nashville students went to them.

During their 1961 journey from Washington DC, through the South headed for New Orleans, this interracial group of demonstrators faced terrifying violence: One Klansman firebombed a bus; another climbed aboard and beat riders. CORE stopped the campaign after riders were met with more violence in Birmingham. That's when SNCC members from the Nashville Student Movement decided to take up the cause. Nashville student leader Diane Nash declared, "The [Nashville] students have decided that we can't let violence overcome. We are coming into Birmingham to continue the Freedom Ride."[2]

Organized by Nash, a group in Birmingham was taken back to the Tennessee state line by police. Three days later, a group in Montgomery, which included John Lewis and Bernard Lafayette, was beaten by the Ku Klux Klan after police disappeared when the Freedom Riders arrived.

★ Civil Rights Room at the Nashville Public Library

615 Church St.; tel. 615/862-5782 or tel. 615/862-5800; www.library.nashville.org; Mon.-Fri. 9am-6pm, Sat. 9am-5pm, Sun. 2pm-5pm; free

The Civil Rights Room, located on the second floor of the Nashville Public Library, looks out over the intersection of Church Street and Seventh Avenue N, the site of nonviolent protests against segregation. Exhibits show how Nashville became a standard bearer among those seeking the right to full enfranchisement across the South.

In the center of the room, a timeline wrapped around a symbolic lunch counter takes visitors through decades of resistance. Many people associate the civil rights movement with the 1960s, but the timeline makes it clear the resistance to segregation and disenfranchisement started much sooner in Nashville and throughout Tennessee. A display shows the Ten Rules of Conduct (which includes being friendly and courteous) Nashville Student Movement protestors had to follow during sit-ins and other protests.

Black-and-white photos displayed around the room—including a mug shot of John Lewis—illustrate movement events. See children dressed in their best clothing as their parents lead them through an angry gauntlet to desegregate a school. See Diane Nash speak truth to power when she pressed Mayor Ben West on what his heart told him about segregation. Interactive displays allow visitors to learn more.

The room is filled with books that chronicle the Black experience, especially movements and philosophies that undergirded the civil rights movement. Guests can either schedule a guided experience of the space or explore on their own (though reservations are required for groups).

Among films you may watch here is *NBC White Paper: Sit-In* (1960), an hour-long documentary that centers Nashville in its exploration of the Southern sit-in movement. A voiceover of one White

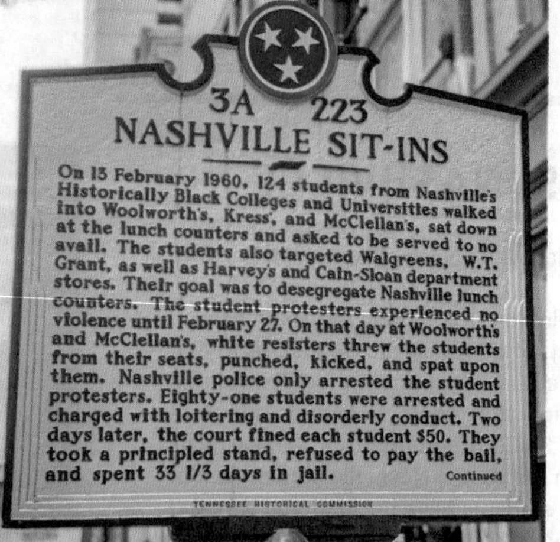

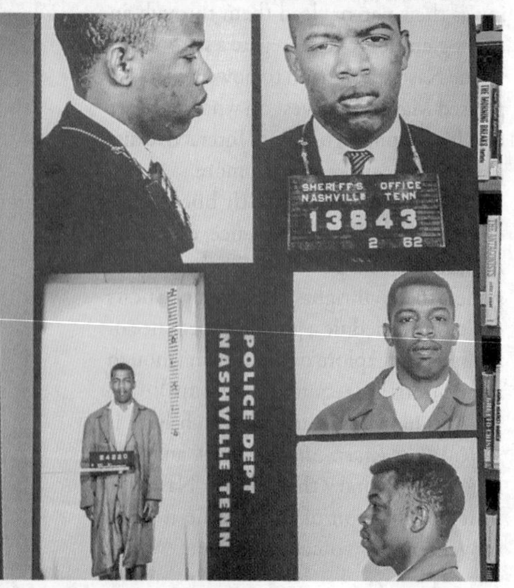

observer says: "I saw a bunch of Coloreds sitting on the stools; they looked like a bunch of idiots sitting up there waiting for people to try and throw 'em off. They just look like they're trying to egg on a fight." A Black demonstrator recounted: "None of us looked back, but we yet could see everything that was going on through the long mirror."

Ask a librarian for help accessing the film.

The Civil Rights Room is a stop on the official U.S. Civil Rights Trail.

JEFFERSON STREET AND VICINITY

During the antebellum era, what is now Jefferson Street was a footpath from a plantation belonging to a man named John Hadley that led east toward the Cumberland River. That footpath eventually became a wagon road, according to Professor Reavis Mitchell, and eventually the street grew to become the heart of Black Nashville before the civil rights movement and I-40 construction.

A great deal of organizing during the civil rights movement occurred here on Jefferson Street. The Nashville Student Movement office was located on this street, near Fisk University, and served as a training ground for student protestors. And on April 19, 1960, following the bombing of civil rights attorney Z. Alexander Looby's home, thousands of students gathered at Tennessee A&I (now TSU) and marched silently along Jefferson Street and up 4th Avenue toward the Davidson County Courthouse in protest. Today, a marker at 21st Avenue N and Jefferson Street shows

Photos (top to bottom): a sign outside Woolworth on Fifth commemorating the sit-in movement; the Witness Walls next the Davidson County Courthouse; photos of John Lewis at the Civil Rights Room at the Nashville Public Library

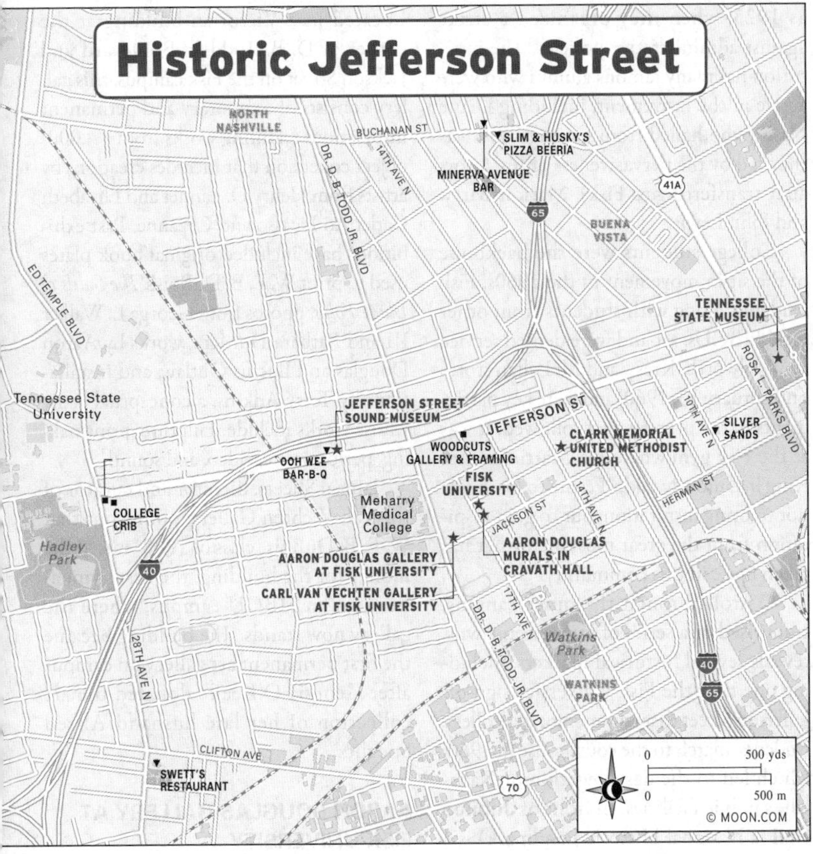

where the protestors organized—look for it near a Smoothie King.

Jefferson Street thrived as a nightlife district from the 1940s-1960s, but that scene was crushed by the construction of I-40 in Nashville. Today, Jefferson Street is a busy thoroughfare dotted with small businesses and shopping plazas. The Jefferson Street area is home to three historically Black schools: Fisk, Meharry, and Tennessee State University.

Fisk University

1000 17th Ave. N; tel. 615/329-8500; www.fisk.edu

Fisk University, one of several historically Black colleges and universities (HBCUs) in Nashville and a stop on the official U.S. Civil Rights Trail, was founded in 1866, after the Civil War. The campus actually sits on what was a Civil War refugee camp called Fort Gilliam. Freed Black women and children were sent to such camps, while freed Black men were assigned to support the Union army or serve as soldiers. Fisk was named for Union General C. B. Fisk.

As one of the first U.S. colleges to educate formerly enslaved individuals, Fisk attracted Black students and faculty from around the nation, providing a ready environment for the discussion of race relations in Nashville and America. Students here were politically active as early as 1925, when they organized a strike against administrative policies. The institution has many famous alumni who were active in the movement, including Diane Nash (who hailed from Chicago and was shocked by the pervasiveness of Jim Crow after transferring to Fisk), Marion Barry, and John Lewis.

College students were the backbone of the sit-in movement in the 1960s. Fisk students, along with students from other local HBCUs, sat and were denied service at Woolworth, Kress, and McLellan stores on February 13, 1960, and were key participants in the protests that followed. It was at the Fisk gym where Dr. Martin Luther King Jr. famously said, "I came to Nashville not to bring inspiration, but to gain inspiration from the great movement that has taken place in this community."

A stroll through the quiet campus, comprised of a series of lush green lawns, reveals several historical markers, including one near the Fisk University sign off Jefferson Street that commemorates college students' march to the courthouse in 1960, which led to the desegregation of Nashville's public facilities. In front of **Jubilee Hall** (a National Historic Landmark) is a marker honoring the **Fisk Jubilee Singers,** who traveled far and wide raising money for the school. In 1873, the singers even performed for Queen Victoria. They are still singing to this day.

Free access to Fisk galleries are available to tours and classes who schedule ahead by contacting tel. 615/329-8720 or emailing galleries@fisk.edu. It's easy enough to walk through campus on your own, but touring Fisk with a quality guide can really help you fill in the blanks about what happened here, which isn't always visible.

CARL VAN VECHTEN GALLERY AT FISK UNIVERSITY

1000 17th Ave. N; tel. 615/329-8720; www.fiskuniversitygalleries.org; Mon.-Sat. 10am-4pm; $10

Located in a Victorian building at the corner of D. B. Todd Jr. Boulevard and Jackson Street on the Fisk campus, this gallery consists of temporary and permanent installations featuring works from a 4,000-object collection that includes creations by artists from Henry O. Tanner and Elizabeth Catlett to Picasso and Cezanne. Past exhibitions have included original book plates used to print W. E. B. DuBois's *The Souls of Black Folks,* photos from George L. Walker III and Barbara DuMetz, works by Aaron Douglas and Lucius Outlaw, and installations by Terry Adkins, a conceptual artist whose works include sculpture, printmaking, performance, video, and sound.

Jamaal Sheets, director and curator of the Van Vechten Gallery, points out that W. E. B. DuBois (class of 1888) raised the money for the building, the first gymnasium on an HBCU campus, where the gallery now stands. The building became the first permanent art gallery on campus after Georgia O'Keeffe donated the art collection of her late husband Alfred Stieglitz.

AARON DOUGLAS GALLERY AT FISK UNIVERSITY

1000 17th Ave. N; tel. 615/329-8720; www.fiskuniversitygalleries.org; Sun. 2pm-10pm, Mon.-Fri. 7:45am-10pm, Sat. 1pm-5pm; free

This gallery is named for Harlem Renaissance stalwart Aaron Douglas, who was the first African American art professor at Fisk and eventually became department chairman. Called the "father of Black American art," Topeka-born Douglas was an illustrator and painter who infused his cubist-inspired works with social commentary around race and segregation. This gallery inside the John Hope and Aurelia Elizabeth Franklin Library houses a collection of African, African American, and folk-art works, including pieces by Douglas himself that were painted in the 1930s.

GET INTO THE RHYTHM

- **James Weldon Johnson, "Lift Ev'ry Voice and Sing":** This song, written by lawyer, novelist, poet, diplomat, and civil rights activist James Weldon Johnson, is largely regarded as the Black national anthem. Johnson's home, at the intersection of Dr. D. B. Todd Jr. Boulevard and Hermosa Street, south of Fisk in Nashville, is where Johnson lived from 1931-1938 when he was the Adam K. Spence chair of Creative Literature and Writing. The home stills stands, and historical signage marks the spot.

AARON DOUGLAS MURALS IN CRAVATH HALL

1000 17th Ave. N; tel. 615/329-8720; www.fiskuniversitygalleries.org; Mon.-Fri. 9am-5pm; free

Inside Fisk's **Cravath Hall,** the administration building, you'll find the famous Douglas murals, oil paintings on canvas that are mounted on the walls. While the second-floor Rotunda, boardroom, and admissions office all hold paintings, the Rotunda is open and most easily accessible to the public. A series called the *Negro Mural Cycle* in the Rotunda "depicts seven phases," according to Van Vechten director and curator Jamaal Sheets. "You start with Diana, the huntress of night, and then it ends with Apollo. It talks about music, theater, poetry, dance—all the different aspects of what we would hope that are students would be doing on campus. I would argue that's one of his greatest contributions to the campus. I highly recommend for visitors to go see."

Other murals are not always accessible, but Sheets invites guests to ask for a gallery ambassador who may be able to provide access. Among the murals are a set called *The Pageant of the Negro* that takes onlookers from Africa and across the Atlantic Ocean, through enslavement to the Negro spiritual. Douglas held Black women in high esteem, a fact that is evident in the sensitive depiction of Black enslaved women chained together on a slave ship in this piece.

Jefferson Street Sound Museum

2004 Jefferson St.; tel. 615/414-6675; www.jeffersonstreetsound.com/museum; Sat. 11am-4pm; donations only

This quirky little nonprofit museum highlights the African American musical legacy of historic Jefferson Street, which was a hub of jazz, blues, and R&B, mainly from 1935-1965. The award-winning museum is a labor of love by Lorenzo Washington, a jack of all trades who has been in proximity to musicians all his life. This space is packed with instruments, artwork, clothing, and ephemera that pays tributes to decades of Black Nashville music makers. A poster featuring the Jefferson Street entertainment family tree delineates the acts and the clubs that thrived on Jefferson Street through the '70s and contributed to the sounds of their respective eras here and everywhere. Nashville's Queen of the Blues, Marion James of "That's My Man" fame, also has several artifacts on display. Note that this museum is only open Saturdays unless you make a special appointment.

Photos (top to bottom): Fisk Memorial Chapel; Jubilee Hall, a National Historic Landmark; Carl Van Vechten Gallery at Fisk University (left); Lorenzo Washington of Jefferson Street Sound Museum (right)

Citizens Bank (2013 Jefferson St.), located across the street from Jefferson Street Sound Museum, is a landmark in and of itself: The Black-owned bank is said to be the oldest continually operating minority-owned bank in the country.

Clark Memorial United Methodist Church

1014 14th Ave. N; tel. 615/329-4464; www.clarkumcnashville.org; Sun. fellowship/breakfast 8:30am, Sunday school 8:45am-9:45am, worship service 10am, fellowship meal noon

A still-thriving institution and a stop on the official U.S. Civil Rights Trail, this church hosted nonviolent training workshops led by Rev. James Lawson in 1958. Lawson was invited to Nashville by King, and by fall of 1959 he was introducing student leaders and clergy to Gandhi-inspired nonviolent philosophies and tactics he learned about while traveling in India years before. In 1961, Clark Memorial hosted the annual meeting of the SCLC, which aimed to coordinate nonviolent resistance of protest groups across the South. Founded 1957, the organization was led by King until his death in 1968.

As you walk by the church today, take a moment to contemplate the courageousness of those who adopted civil disobedience in service of the greater good.

Tennessee State Museum

1000 Rosa L Parks Blvd.; tel. 615/741-2692; www.tnmuseum.org; Sun. 1pm-5pm, Tues.-Wed. and Fri.-Sat. 10am-5pm, Thurs. 10am-8pm; free

This gorgeous 137,000-square-foot museum at the northwest corner of Bicentennial Capitol Mall State Park captures everything from the First Peoples through modern day movements to secure rights for African Americans and women. The museum contains seven permanent exhibitions, several of which relate directly to Black history in Tennessee.

First, the Civil War collection is a necessary visit. Rest assured that the African American quest for full enfranchisement is depicted in the telling of a war that was fought over whether Black people would be considered capital or people. Next, the Change and Challenge gallery (1870-1645) highlights Black people's resistance to segregation and disenfranchisement.

Finally, Tennessee Transforms (1945 to present) breaks down the civil rights struggle by city and regions throughout the state. Oversize photos and artifacts from the Nashville Student Movement underscore the risks HBCU students took during sit-ins and other protests. One photo at the zoo in Memphis depicts a sign saying "No White People in Zoo Today," a telling reminder of segregated times. A gleaming silver fire hose nozzle used by Chattanooga police in 1960 is a potent reminder of the danger protestors faced. (The water from hoses like this and those used in Birmingham, Alabama, are said to be strong enough to blow the hair off one's head.) Favorite son Alex Haley is celebrated for his seminal work *Roots,* which traced his Tennessee enslavement roots back to West Africa.

Museum officials make room for students and other visitors to process heavy events (such as King's assassination in Memphis) by writing on notecards their ideas of what the future might hold.

OTHER NEIGHBORHOODS

American Baptist College

1800 Baptist World Center Dr.; tel. 615/256-1463; www.abcnash.edu

Leaders for social change were cultivated at American Baptist Theological Seminary (now American Baptist College). Heavy hitters who set the tone for nonviolent resistance studied and trained in **Griggs Hall,** the first building to be erected on this campus in 1923. They include Rev.

Photos (top to bottom): Tennessee State Museum; inside the Tennesse State Museum; Chakita Patterson of United Street Tours

C. T. Vivian; Rev. Kelly Miller Smith, pastor of First Baptist Church, Capitol Hill; and Professor J. F. Grimmett, who coached young men in nonviolent protest. Notable student leaders who came out of this institution include John Lewis (who also earned a degree at Fisk), Bernard Lafayette (who became president), and James Bevel. Griggs Hall is a stop on the official U.S. Civil Rights Trail.

American Baptist College is on the National Register of Historic Places. On guided **campus tours** (by appointment only; contact officeofthepresident@abc-nash.edu for more information), which are best for students and families considering an HBCU experience, student ambassadors explain the college's role in the movement.

Tours and Local Guides

Judging from the historical markers that dot the Nashville landscape, residents know a compelling story when they hear one. But because the civil rights story isn't broadcast as loudly here as it is in other cities, joining a tour can help bring the past to life.

WALKING TOURS

NASHVILLE HISTORY ON TOUR: CIVIL RIGHTS AND SONG

tel. 615/ 615 838 4507; www.nashvillehistory-ontour.com; $250 for up to four guests

Historian, attorney, and tour guide David Steele Ewing is a ninth-generation Nashvillian—and he's got the goods. Ewing's Civil Rights and Song tour starts at the **Ryman Auditorium** (116 5th Ave. N), a place where Marion Anderson, Louis Armstrong, and Nat King Cole performed. For country music, this 2,362-seat auditorium is sacred ground and, like anything quintessentially American, Black people share a piece of that history.

Next, guests walk to the Civil Rights Room at the Nashville Public Library to learn about the nonviolent lunch-counter sit-ins led by John Lewis and Diane Nash. Woolworth on Fifth, the once segregated five-and-dime (now a restaurant), is the next stop to see where John Lewis was arrested for the first time while protesting segregation at the lunch counters in 1960.

The knowledgeable Ewing shares deeply sourced, contextual details that will surprise, delight, and make you crave a more nuanced understanding of local history. He comes by this authentically as a ninth-generation Nashville resident related to Prince Albert Ewing, the first Black lawyer allowed to practice in Tennessee. Ewing's family traces their lineage to being enslaved by President Andrew Jackson.

Ewing specializes in upscale, private tours that cover everything from civil rights to women's suffrage, politics, sports, and business. In 2016, he discovered the lost mugshots of John Lewis's early arrest in Nashville and helped restore Frederick Douglass's proper name to a city park in 2017. (In the 1930s, White park officials had named the site Fred Douglas Park—so disrespectful. Thankfully, it's fixed now.)

These are private tours that can last as long or short as your interests allow. Ewing will come to your hotel or a mutually agreed upon spot to discuss your wishes and craft a tour based on that.

UNITED STREET TOURS

150 4th Ave. N, Floor 20; tel. 615/447-8107; www.unitedstreettours.com; one-hour tour $27, two-hour tour $53

United Street tours (a proudly Black-owned, woman-owned business) was founded by Memphis native Chakita

Patterson, a first-generation college graduate and schoolteacher who found that educating young people and adults through heritage tours provided the kind of transformation she always dreamed of.

Patterson's tours focus exclusively on Black history in Nashville. The range of available tours includes the **Slavery to Freedom Walking Tour, Secret Network of Women in Civil Rights,** and a **Local Food and History Experience.** Passionate guides detail the stakes involved in standing up for the right to vote, eat at lunch counter, and attend well-funded schools without regard to race. Tours also connect the past to modern-day movements.

Tours visit a range of sites, including Public Square, a five-acre park in front of the Davidson County Courthouse where enslaved Black people were once sold. A walk down 5th Avenue introduces tourgoers to the Nashville Student Movement and the sit-ins movement leaders organized. During the walk, Patterson, with assistance from her husband, Ogden, intermingle stories of other places and events, such as the founding of Fisk and the Fisk Jubilee Singers.

These brisk walking tours take one hour or two, and take place rain or shine. They depart from the downtown Nashville Visitor Center (501 Broadway). Tours take place daily, except Sunday.

SELF-GUIDED TOUR

NASHVILLE SITES: DOWNTOWN CIVIL RIGHTS SIT-INS TOUR

tel. 615/669-4503; www.nashvillesites.org

This free self-guided audio tour (1.2 hour, one mile) covers 10 sites connected to Nashville's civil rights story, including the 5th Avenue sit-in sites and Davidson County Courthouse and Witness Walls. Written by historian Linda Wynn, a scholar of the Nashville Student Movement, the tour begins at Harvey's, site of a "test" sit-in in 1959. Visit the website to take a tour (a virtual tour is also available.) Historic images depicting protests and pickets, courtesy of the Nashville Public Library, complement your journey. These tours take care to ensure accessibility.

Shopping

Jefferson Street isn't what it once was, but the street features some retailers, including some compelling Black-owned businesses.

ART

WOODCUTS GALLERY & FRAMING

1613 Jefferson St.; tel. 615/321-5357; www.woodcutsfineartgallery.com; Mon.-Fri. 10am-6pm

Engineer-turned-artist Nate Harris runs this frame shop and gallery that specializes in African American art, both prints and original pieces. He has sold work by Jacob Lawrence, Romare Bearden, and Jamaal Sheets, a painter and repousse artist who helms the galleries at Fisk. The shop features several examples of Black folk art, such as handmade dolls by octogenarian Ludie Amos that perfectly capture the essence, postures, and gestures of Black church women. The shop carries "a combination of what I found in my travels," says Harris. It's located not far from Fisk.

CLOTHING

COLLEGE CRIB

2719 Jefferson St., Price Plaza, Ste. D; tel. 615/329-3885; www.collegecrib.com; Mon.-Sat. 11am-6pm

Membership in Black fraternities and sororities lives on beyond college and become lifelong investments in community. So whether you're partial to the pink and green marker of an AKA or a red-and-white Kappa man and everything in between, you can represent your abiding connection to your Greek-letter organization with a full array of sorority and fraternity apparel and products available here. The Black-owned College Crib occupies 4,000 square feet of Price Plaza and has been in business since 1966. In addition to Divine 9 gear, College Crib creates screen-printed and monogrammed items for choirs, churches, athletic teams, and family reunions.

BOOKS

ALKEBU-LAN IMAGES BOOKSTORE & GIFTS

2721 Jefferson St.; tel. 615/321-4111; Mon.-Fri. 10am-7pm

Are you thinking Black thoughts and doing Black things? Well, you can do that here too. Alkebu-Lan offers an array of Black-themed books or books by Black authors, plus educational materials, T-shirts, jewelry, gifts, and Afrocentric apparel. The shop is located on the corner of Jefferson and 28th Avenue N, in front of Price Plaza.

Photos (top to bottom): Nate Harris, owner of Woodcuts Gallery & Framing; art by Ludie Amos at Woodcuts Gallery & Framing; Deborah Stewart of Alkebu-Lan Images Bookstore & Gifts

Festivals and Events

NASHVILLE

Given its status as Music City USA, there's something big and musical going on in Nashville pretty much every month—including an event that pays homage to historic Jefferson Street. It's also a foodie city, and a festival focused on hot chicken, the local specialty, only makes sense.

JUNE

★ JEFFERSON STREET JAZZ & BLUES FESTIVAL

www.nashvillejazzandbluesfest.com; $5-20

Before the I-40 expansion ripped through the community, Nashville's Jefferson Street hosted a vibrant club scene with performances by musical greats such as Otis Redding, Little Richard, Marion James, Billy Cox, Etta James, Aretha Franklin, and James Brown. Jimi Hendrix and his band, The King Kasuals, played at Club Del Morocco, next door to his house. This annual two-day festival, which takes place over Juneteenth (June 19) weekend, celebrates that bygone era, showcasing blues, jazz, R&B, and hip-hop music.

Friday night's activities, known as the **SoBro Block Party,** are centered around 5th Avenue and Demonbreun Street in downtown Nashville between Omni Nashville Hotel (250 5th Ave. S) and Music City Center (201 5th Ave. S). Food trucks line the street while local R&B artists grace the stage. The night begins around 5pm and ends at midnight, concluding with a nationally recognized DJ who sets the party atmosphere.

On Saturday, festivities move to the amphitheater at **Bicentennial Capitol Mall State Park** (600 James Robertson Pkwy.). Saturday's events start at 4pm and go on till 11pm.

Food vendors are on site, and performances take place both days. Past performers include After 7, Rose Royce (of "Car Wash" and "I Wanna Get Next to You" fame), Shirley Murdock, DJ Kid Capri, DJ Chubb Rock, and Valerie Simpson of Ashford & Simpson. In the past, entry fees have run from $5 for the SoBro Block Party and range from $20 for the Saturday event.

JULY

NASHVILLE HOT CHICKEN FESTIVAL

East Park, 700 Woodland St.; www.hot-chicken.com/festival; free

The Nashville Hot Chicken Festival brings the community together for a hot 'n' spicy good time in honor of this homegrown culinary invention. The free festival takes place every July 4 at East Park (700 Woodland St.), about a mile east of downtown, across the Cumberland River. A fire truck parade kicks it off at 10:30am, then hot chicken sandwiches are passed out to the first 500 people in line. Get there early to get one. Festival gates open at 11am, and guests are free to peruse vendors selling the best Nashville has to offer, hot chicken-wise and more. The event features live music and an amateur cooking contest. Find Black-owned hot chicken purveyors—Prince's Hot Chicken Shack and Bolton's Spicy Chicken & Fish—here.

Food

Nashville's famous **hot chicken**—fried right, drenched with hot sauce, and typically served sandwich-style—is just one delicious thing about dining in this city, known for its burgeoning, chef-driven food scene. Nashville offers a mouthwatering range of down-home, upscale, and casual dining fare. You won't go hungry at all. One good option is to seek a taste of the culinary genius of our ancestors' wildest dreams at Slim & Husky's Pizza Beeria, founded by three fellow Tennessee State University graduates.

Tennessee's capitol city is also home to the **meat-and-three** phenomenon of cafeteria-style, affordable goodness. The custom is just what it sounds like: Choose one main meat item, such as chicken or pork chops, then three sides. Tack on some sweet tea and dessert and you have yourself some good eating.

This bustling city also provides a dining experience with a side of historical context: One of the original lunch-counter sit-in sites, Woolworth on Fifth, is now a restaurant, complete with a rebuilt lunch counter. If reading about all the abuse student protestors faced for the privilege of eating a hamburger at a retail store lunch counter makes you feel some kind of way, dining here may be the place to confront those feelings. On the other hand, if learning about the type of change peaceful acts of civil disobedience can produce leaves you feeling inspired, this is also a place to celebrate.

DOWNTOWN

Lunch Counter

★ WOOLWORTH ON FIFTH

221 5th Ave. N; tel. 615/891-1361; www.woolworthonfifth.com; Mon.-Thurs. 11am-9pm, Fri. 11am-10pm, Sat. 9:30am-10pm, Sun. 9:30am-10pm; $13-17

In 1960, the three-story Woolworth building, part of the larger UK-based Woolworth chain, was a five-and-dime retail space, selling everything from

lunch at Woolworth on Fifth

VOICES OF THE MOVEMENT: REV. JAMES MORRIS LAWSON

"I have been teaching for years that the 21st century must have nonviolent campaigns that make our movements of the 20th century pale in comparison."

—**REV. JAMES LAWSON** was part of the Nashville Christian Leadership Conference, which was dedicated to the understanding and activation of Christian nonviolence and civil disobedience. The workshops he taught in Black churches throughout the city led to the creation of a student movement that challenged segregation through sit-ins.

Lawson was also instrumental in organizing (along with Ella Baker and Martin Luther King Jr.) the student meeting that birthed SNCC in 1960. He was a Freedom Rider who served time at Mississippi State Penitentiary. In 1968, while pastoring in Memphis, he became chairman of the sanitation workers' strike committee.

TRAINING FOR SIT-INS

Lawson, who had studied principles of civil disobedience while living in India, was inspired by the nonviolent teachings of Mohandas Gandhi. He went on to teach these principles to students and other activists in preparation for the Nashville Sit-in Movement. "The people of Nashville recognized that our direct action had to be carefully strategized and choreographed," says Lawson."We did five or six months of [trainings] one night a week to prepare for the first stage of the campaign, which was the use of the sit-ins."

Lawson's trainings were "life-changing," according to student participant Diane Nash. Bernard Lafayette, who started attending Lawson's trainings at the behest of fellow student John Lewis, was similarly moved. At first, "I wasn't interested because I was working," says Lafay-

toothpaste and kitchen towels to greeting cards and toys, with a lunch counter in the dining room.

As Nashville historian David Steele Ewing tells it, going downtown to Woolworth's on the weekend was a traditional activity for Nashvillians. White residents would shop, grab a cheap meal at the store's lunch counter, then go to one of several downtown theaters to watch the latest movies in the best seats in the house. African Americans, meanwhile, were perfectly free to spend their money in the store, but they couldn't eat at the lunch counter at Woolworth or elsewhere. (Black people in Greensboro, where the sit-in movement kicked off, could order takeout and stand to the side while waiting for their order, but even this was not permitted in Nashville.) In 1960, Black students famously staged a

ette. "I had several jobs. I was very busy. John insisted, so I went so I could stop hearing him talk. I got exposed to this workshop, the first one, and I said, 'This is for me.' I had to manage my work and quit some other jobs in order to go."

Nash, Lafayette, and Lewis all grew into movement leaders, and the sit-in movement orchestrated by Lawson resulted in Nashville becoming the first Southern city to desegregate lunch counters in 1960.

VOTING RIGHTS IN RURAL TENNESSEE

Lawson's activism was not limited to Nashville. It also led him to Fayette County, Tennessee—"the only place I know I was shot at," he recalls.

In the early 1960s, Lawson, along with civil rights attorneys Russell Sugarmon, Benjamin Hooks, and A. W. Willis, made a pastoral call to John McFerren. McFerren was a founder of the Fayette County Civic and Welfare League, Inc., which was formed with the purpose of registering Black voters—no easy task in Fayette County, where White poll workers barred Black people from of voting in an "all-White primary" and White citizens circulated a blacklist of African Americans who tried to vote. McFerren, along with his wife, Viola, and others, also created Fayette County's Freedom Village, a "tent city" on Black-owned land, after Black sharecroppers were evicted for attempting to vote.

Driving back to Memphis after visiting McFerren, Lawson and his companions were trailed by White vigilantes in trucks. When shots were fired, "we all tried to get as low in our seats as we could," Lawson remembers. "We never got hit. Ben Hooks gunned it to the best of his ability."

ON MODERN ACTIVISM AND BLACK LIVES MATTER

"I have been teaching for years that the 21st century must have nonviolent campaigns that make our movements of the 20th century pale in comparison," says Lawson. He has good things to say about activism today: "We have to give the Black Lives Matter founders and their network credit that this moment has arrived and that these massive marches are taking place. And we have to give them credit for the fact that it's intergenerational."

series of sit-ins to protest for equal rights at this iconic retail establishment—and the rest is history.

In 2018, the three-story building reopened featuring original architectural features, including gilded handrails and wall accents and hand-laid terrazzo floor tiles. It's been reimagined as a restaurant and music venue that resembles the classic Woolworth, complete with a rebuilt lunch counter. (A dining room provides additional restaurant seating.) The business is not Black-owned, but diverse diners flock to the eatery to enjoy "Counter Classics": original dishes that include pot roast and meatloaf. The food is decent and the service is top-notch, but dining here is more about the experience.

The mezzanine level displays several sit-in photos of civil rights activists, including King, Rev. Kelly Miller Smith of the Nashville Christian Leadership Council, and John Lewis, who faced the first of more than 40 lifetime arrests on behalf of civil rights and social justice here. A long, padded bench sits where the mezzanine-level lunch counter once stood, and you'll also see patched holes in the floor where Whites-only lunch-counter stools used to be.

Two original stools from the 1960 sit-in campaign greet visitors at the top of the stairs leading to the mezzanine. Lewis sat in one of these stools before being arrested on the first floor. White segregationists threw activists down these very stairs, as depicted in the *NBC White Papers: Sit-In* documentary, according to Ewing. The mezzanine level looks down upon the dining room, and you can eat in here if the area is not closed off for special events.

"It's important for people to go to these neighborhoods and go the streets where people used to work and live," Ewing said in June 2020, days after Lewis passed away (on the same day as C. T. Vivian, another leader in the Nashville movement). "You have to tell the story. We're a very visual society—it's like Instagram—where we want to see things, we want to experience things, and so if you go to walk into this Woolworth's where John Lewis was arrested, that is important."

This 30,000-square-foot building, a working tribute erected in 1930, is on the National Register of Historic Places. It's also a stop on the official U.S. Civil Rights Trail.

Hot Chicken

PRINCE'S HOT CHICKEN SHACK SOBRO

5814 Nolensville Pike #110; tel. 615/810-9388; $6-13

Now, about that hot chicken: Part of the charm of this dish is its origin story. Heretell, Thornton Prince III, a pig farmer in the late 1800s, came home one night a little too late for his girlfriend's taste. When she fixed his favorite dish, fried chicken, the next day, she used a lot of cayenne pepper and other spices to fix him up but good—but it turned out, he liked it. The family of Thornton Prince III continues the delicious legacy at this restaurant.

JEFFERSON STREET AND VICINITY

Meat-and-Three

SWETT'S RESTAURANT

2725 Clifton Ave.; tel. 615/329-4418; www.swettsrestaurant.com; 11am-8pm daily; $15

A classic meat-and-three eatery less than a mile southwest of Fisk University, Swett's has been in operation since 1954. For three generations, this family-owned restaurant has provided a taste of home for students attending Nashville's HBCUs, and a diverse array of residents, celebrities, and local politicians also leave feeling quite satisfied. The extensive menu includes Southern classics, like turnip greens, pinto beans, macaroni and cheese, beef tips, country fried steak, fried chicken, pork shoulder, and rib tips. Like traditional cafeteria-style restaurants, Swett's hits you with the dessert when you first line up with a tray and utensils, making future choices delightfully difficult.

SILVER SANDS CAFE

937 Locklayer St.; tel. 615/780-9900; www.silversandsnashville.com; Tues.-Fri. 6:30am-2:30pm, Sun. 11am-3pm; from $3-7

Hearing Sophia Vaughn say, "Hey baby, how you doing?" is enough to make you feel warm and welcomed all over. Vaughn is the latest family member in a 50-year period to helm this Black-owned business that serves breakfast takeout and lunch meat-and-threes. Silver Sands prides itself on using only the freshest ingredients to produce its soul food creations served cafeteria-style. This includes everything

VOICES OF THE MOVEMENT:
NASHVILLE STUDENT LEADER DIANE NASH

"To be part of the group where I was willing to put my body between someone and harm, and have confidence that they would put their bodies between me and harm, was a unique and wonderful experience."

—**DIANE NASH** was a college student in Nashville who trained with Rev. James Lawson in nonviolent tactics and went on to become a movement leader herself, and a founding member of SNCC.

The movement in Nashville was unique not only because it was largely student-led, but also for its full embrace of nonviolent tactics. "Rev. James Lawson was educating anyone who wanted to come to his workshops in the philosophy and strategy of nonviolence," says Nash. "It was life-changing information for me." The students' training included simulated verbal and physical attacks and humiliation that was designed to push them to their limits.

During the sit-ins students were struck, stomped on, and verbally abused. Some had lit cigarettes pushed into their backs. The documentary *NBC White Paper: Sit-In,* broadcast on December 20, 1960, shows an interracial group of Nashville sit-in movement activists preparing for abuse. (View the film while in Nashville in the Civil Rights Room at the Nashville Public Library.)

Nash describes the experience of training for and participating in sit-ins: "We worked with a leadership group of about 30 people who were representatives from each of the universities and colleges that were participating in the movement: the Nashville Student Central Committee. We developed such a bond that we would put our bodies between another member of the group who had been harmed. One of the ways that we could defend ourselves and still practice nonviolence is if someone was getting beat severely . . . one person could step between that person and whoever was attacking them. Or several people could step between the attacker and the person being attacked and distribute the violence rather than let it be on one person."

Painful though they were, the sit-ins in Nashville, and the principles of nonviolence they employed, worked. "Nashville was the first Southern city to desegregate lunch counters, and a pacesetter for the rest of the civil rights movement," says Nash. "We achieved the desegregation of lunch counters using nonviolence and therefore proved that nonviolence worked and could make social change. And that is the reason that the rest of the Southern cities where lunch counter sit-ins were taking place adopted nonviolence as their means of acting."

from beef tips, salmon croquettes, catfish, stewed oxtails, and fried chicken. Sides run the gamut from shoepeg corn to mac and cheese, green beans, spinach, squash, and okra. The breakfast menu features hot, buttery grits, pancakes, bacon, eggs, bologna, Polish sausage, rice, apples, and more.

Barbecue

OOH WEE BAR-B-Q

2008 Jefferson St.; tel. 615/200-7191; www.orderoohweebarbq.com; Mon.-Sat. 11am-8pm; $2-13

The drive-thru-only barbecue stand located next to the Jefferson Street Sound Museum lures you in with the promise of a leg quarter for $1. But that's just the hook. Frederick Waller admits that the set-up, which includes a full-works barbecue pit, "is not a good-looking place," but the food is delicious, and judging from the line cruising in, nobody cares much about the appearance. The smoky aroma of chicken leg quarters, rib slabs, turkey legs, and more is enough to keep you coming back, and the restaurant also serves wings, spaghetti, smoked sausage, gizzards, hot dogs, and sandwiches.

Nashville residents know the drill: Give your order on one side of the food prep trailer; pick it up on the other. The savviest know to call ahead and cruise on around to the pickup side of this operation. The whole experience is a lot of tasty fun. Waller has an interesting story too: Having spent time in prison, he says his wife, Sharon, grounded him, and this business saved his life. He saw the set-up was up for lease in 2013 and told Sharon he was going to "get that place." "Didn't have no money," Waller deadpanned. "I made it happen." The rest is history. "To be able to be your own boss," Waller muses today, "that within itself is a valuable thing."

OTHER NEIGHBORHOODS

Pizza

SLIM & HUSKY'S PIZZA BEERIA

911 Buchanan St.; tel. 615/647-7017; www.slimandhuskys.com; Mon.-Sat. 10:30am-10pm, Sun. 11am-7pm; $12-15

A specialty pizza emporium with a hip-hop feel, Slim & Husky's was founded by Tennessee State University graduates Emmanuel Reed, Clint Gray, and Derrick Moore. This branch in North Nashville, about a mile north of Jefferson Street, is the original locale, but additional locations show how much the world has taken to the place.

"Slim" and "husky" refers to the size of the artisanal pizzas. Diners can either choose their own toppings or pick from a range of fast-casual, hip-hop- and R&B-inspired creations, including Rony, Roni, Rone!, California Love, and the Nothin But a "V" Thang, a vegan cheese pizza with bean ragu, roasted peppers, and oven-roasted corn and spinach. They specialize in cinnamon rolls here too: Be sure to try a Cookie Monsta. Alcohol selections include locally brewed beer in constant rotation.

Hot Chicken

BOLTON'S SPICY CHICKEN & FISH

624 Main St.; tel. 615/524-8015; www.boltonsspicy; Tues.-Sun. 11am-7pm; $6-18

A labor of love between husband-and-wife Dollye Graham-Matthews and Bolton Matthews, Bolton's Spicy Chicken thrives on a famous family recipe created by Matthews' uncle Bolton Polk. Think: Dry rub spices that hurt so good going down your throat. Also look for the chicken on a stick, spicy or hot, the ultimate portable food. Plates centering chicken, fish, and pork (pulled, pork chop, or half slab) come with two sides, which include, but are not limited to, turnip greens, white beans, or corn on the cob. The restaurant was featured on chef David Chang's Netflix show, *Ugly Delicious.*

Slim & Husky's Pizza Beeria

Nightlife

Some visitors will like to skip sightseeing and just eat/drink in this city, and that's just fine. After all, this is Nashville, where people work hard and party harder.

In decades past, before the construction of I-40 in the city, Jefferson Street was a hub for Black music, including R&B and rock and roll. You could see music greats like Otis Redding, Jimi Hendrix, and Little Richard perform in clubs like the Del Morocco (which was destroyed by the construction of the highway), and Club Baron, now an Elks Club at 2614 Jefferson Street.

Today, there's a lot going on downtown, but other parts of town are just as fun. It's the South, so you can vibe on the blues, or go out for a night of creative cocktails with an upscale hip-hop vibe. Or maybe you just want a hearty belly laugh; there's comedy too, because Nashville has it all. Black Nashvillians tend to look out for themed nights that feature Black acts or Black themes.

DOWNTOWN

Live Music

B. B. KING'S BLUES CLUB

152 2nd Ave. N; tel. 615/256-2727; www.bbkings.com/nashville; Sun. 10am-10:30pm, Mon.-Thurs. 11am-11pm, Fri.-Sat. 11am-1am; no cover

This club might be a chain, but this is Music City USA, so this location is gonna be extra good. Live musical acts perform on two stages, including the house band, the B. B. King's Blues Club All-Star Band, comprised of talent from throughout the mid-South. Other featured homegrown artists include award-winning guitarist Carl Stewart and Memphis native Ping Rose, leader of the band called the Anti-Heroes. The signature B. B. King's menu includes starters like loaded tater tots, hummus, and Memphis-inspired sausage and cheese platters. You'll find ribs, fried fish, burgers, and po' boys. A range of signature drinks, shooters, and whiskey is available too.

Bar

BOURBON STREET

220 Printers Alley; tel. 615/242-5837; www.bourbonstreetbluesandboogiebar.com; daily 11am- late night; $5-$10 cover

Follow the neon sign for New Orleans-style good times in downtown Nashville. Bourbon Street is not Black-owned, but legendary acts such as James Brown and B. B. King have performed here. This intimate space is built for all-night dancing powered by live entertainment from bands like Bizz & Everyday People, who infuse fun and energy into our favorite covers. (You should hear their rendition of the Jackson 5's "One More Chance.") Other performers have included Freddie T Holt and the After 5 Tux Band. (Holt, a trumpeter and educator, has played with or opened for some of the world's greatest acts, including Mary J. Blige, Bobby Womack, and Stevie Wonder.) Local fave Tyrone T is featured here, as is indie guitarist Ping Rose. Foodwise, Creole and Cajun dishes are on the menu, including Voodoo Wings. Or try hand-breaded alligator bites with remoulade sauce, a blackened, grilled, or fried shrimp basket, sliders, gumbo, and more. Full bar, plus a fascinating range of hurricanes—Easy Easy, Satsuma, and Southern Comfort. The New Orleans-themed décor is complete with twinkling lights and wrought-iron balconies.

OTHER NEIGHBORHOODS

Cocktail Bar

MINERVA AVENUE BAR

1002 Buchanan St.; tel. 615/499-4369; www.minervaavenue.com; Sun. 5pm-midnight, Wed.-Thurs. 5pm-midnight, Sat. 5pm-2pm; no cover

Food, art, and culture converge at this craft cocktail '80s and '90s throwback lounge that makes for the perfect evening out for grown-and-sexy types. Located near Slim & Husky's in North Nashville's Buchanan Arts District, Minerva Avenue conjures community and family of owner Robert Higgins Jr., which includes his parents, siblings, and foster siblings. Outdoor seating includes semi-private cabanas. Inside, the cozy interior is set off by dark wood. Minerva Avenue implores guests to "Sip local. Think global. Be social." Cocktail names (Mackin and Hangin and Don't Let the Margarita Make You) and shots (Bye Felicia and Wanna See a Dead Body) are full of attitude. There are also gourmet popcorns and snacks like the Ludacris, which is a chicken hotdog and waffle on a stick.

Comedy

ZANIES COMEDY CLUB

2025 8th Ave. S; tel. 615/269-0221; www.nashville.zanies.com; Sun. 7:30pm, Wed.-Thurs. 7:30pm, Fri. 7:30pm and 9:45pm, Sat. 7pm and 9:15pm, sometimes 11:30pm; tickets $5-$50

This comedy franchise, not a Black-owned business, is a go-to for national acts like Nicole Byer, Tommy Davidson, and Jay Pharoah, and local comedians who give you a taste of the local flavor of what's funny. There's a two-food or drink minimum. The menu features typical bar fare, such as wings, tacos, and chicken fingers among other items. This club is located about two miles south of downtown Nashville.

Accommodations

Nashville is a popular city to visit, and hotel prices reflect that.

DOWNTOWN

Over $200

For a reliable spot that's centrally located in downtown Nashville, close to the Witness Walls and other sights, try the **Courtyard Nashville Downtown** (140 4th Ave.; tel. 615/275-1675; www.marriott.com; $239).

THE HERMITAGE HOTEL

321 6th Ave. N; tel. 615/244-3121; www.thehermitagehotel; $400+

This 122-room hotel is the oldest hotel in Nashville and is a great place for a luxury stay in the downtown business district. There's a great bar here, called the Oak Bar.

OTHER NEIGHBORHOODS

$100-200

THE RUSSELL

819 Russell St.; tel. 615/861-9535; www.russellnashville.com; $115-145

Nestled in East Nashville, The Russell features 23 guest rooms in a century-old converted church founded in 1904. The building, which sold because of damage from a 1998 storm that was too expensive for the church to repair, retains some of the original features, including brick walls, stained glass windows, and repurposed pews. The spirit of community outreach and social justice remains too: The Russell donates a portion of their proceeds to help house people experiencing homelessness.

THE DIVE MOTEL & SWIM CLUB

1414 Dickerson Pike; tel. 615/650-9103; www.thedivemotel.com; $179-269

This updated 1960s/1970s throwback hotel features 23 rooms, each decked out with a party switch and disco ball. Groovy! As the name suggests, it also has a pool. (Day passes are available, so everyone is invited to jump right on in.) The motel features a vintage dive bar complete with vinyl seating that takes you back in time.

Transportation

GETTING THERE

Nashville does not have an Amtrak station.

Air

Nashville International Airport (1 Terminal Dr.; tel. 615/275-1675; www.flynashville.com) is located about 6.5 miles east of downtown Nashville. A cab ride from the airport to downtown takes around 15 minutes and has a set rate of $25 to downtown. The No. 18 bus also runs between Nashville International Airport and downtown.

WeGo Transit (430 Myatt Dr.; tel. 615/862-5950; www.nashvillemta.org) provides hourly service between downtown and the airport seven days a week (adults $2 one-way, youth $1 one-way). Midday express trips downtown on the No. 18 bus run at 3:35pm, 4:05pm, and 4:35pm and take only 20 minutes; local service takes 45 minutes. As you exit Baggage Claim, turn right and walk to the end of the terminal to catch a WeGo bus.

Bus

Nashville's **Greyhound station** (709 5th Ave. S; tel. 615/255-3556; www.greyhound.com) is located downtown, near restaurants, shops, and other entertainment. A one-way ticket from **Memphis** (about 4 hours) is as low as $49 one-way. Travel from **Atlanta** (close to 5 hours) starts at $32.

Car

To get to Nashville from:

- **Atlanta:** Take **I-75 North** and **I-24 West** for about 250 miles (4 hours).
- **Memphis:** Take **I-40 East** for about 215 miles (3.5 hours).
- **Richmond, Virginia:** Take **I-81 South** and **I-40 West** for about 615 miles (9 hours).

GETTING AROUND

Downtown Nashville is highly walkable, but you'll need a vehicle to get around other parts of town. Nashville has a robust public bus system that covers 50 routes, but (as several intersecting interstates suggest) this city is a car culture right down to the tight downtown parking gauntlet. Because this is a town built for entertainment, there are plenty of car services, taxis, and the requisite app rides too.

Parking

Parking in downtown Nashville depends on the lot, and hourly rates can range from $4 to $16 per hour. The website www.parkitdowntown.com/maps/parking-options is a helpful guide. On Jefferson Street, you may find free street parking depending on your timing and exact location. There should be parking available on side streets off Jefferson too.

Public Transit

WeGo Transit (430 Myatt Dr.; tel. 615/862-5950; www.nashvillemta.org) operates area buses. **Route 29** covers most of what travelers are looking for, and **Route 64** is the downtown route. All-day passes run $4 for adults and $2 for youth.

Ride-Hailing Apps

Uber and **Lyft** operate in Nashville. Need a taxi? Call **Checker Cab** (tel. 615/256-7000).

Greensboro, Raleigh, and Durham

On February 1, 1960, four Black college students (David Richmond, Franklin McCain, Ezell Blair Jr., who later changed his name to Jibreel Khazan, and Joe McNeil) defied segregation laws by taking seats at the Woolworth's lunch counter in Greensboro and refusing to leave until closing time. The students, who came to be known as the Greensboro

GREENSBORO, RALEIGH, AND DURHAM'S TOP 3

1. Stepping back in time at the **International Civil Rights Center & Museum,** which is situated in the same Woolworth's where the Greensboro Four staged their courageous sit-in (page 356).

2. Engaging with the programming at the **Pauli Murray Center for History and Social Justice,** which is located inside Murray's childhood home (page 369).

3. Digging into Durham's rich Black history, including Pauli Murray's life story, on a walking tour with **Whistle Stop Tours** (page 371).

Photos (top to bottom): the original lunch counter from a 1960 sit-in at the International Civil Rights Center & Museum; Aya Shabu leads Whistle Stop Tours in Durham. Previous: the Durham Civil Rights Mural, titled "We Must Remember and Continue to Tell" by Brenda Miller Holmes

Four, had no way of knowing that their actions would have a nationwide impact, but that's exactly what happened. The day these students took their seats and refused to budge, the sit-in campaign was born.

The courageous Greensboro Four were supported by other students, including those from Bennett women's college, who served as spotters when the young men entered the Woolworth's. The Bennett students joined the sit-in as well (and many others), as they had discussed taking action, too. A lunch counter sit-in in Durham followed a week later. From there, the sit-in trend spread like wildfire, with sit-ins taking place in Raleigh, Charlotte, Winston-Salem, and elsewhere in the state, and outside of North Carolina in Richmond, Baltimore, Nashville, and Montgomery. In Charlotte, Black student demonstrators stood in the doorway of Belk's Department Store yelling "freedom" and were arrested. In New Bern, North Carolina, high school students participated in protests. By April 1960, sit-in demonstrations had taken place in more than 60 cities.

Demonstrators faced hecklers and threats and weathered arrests for trespassing, disturbing the peace, and disorderly conduct. In subsequent years, they described the fear they felt, but the demonstrators bravely held their own, adhering to principles of nonviolence. So impressed was Dr. Martin Luther King Jr. by the Durham sit-in and the subsequent demonstrations it inspired that he publicly endorsed sit-ins, which became a hallmark of the civil rights movement, for the first time. By July 1960, Woolworth's management agreed to desegregate lunch counters in Greensboro, a gesture replicated elsewhere. However, some five-and-dime store lunch counters stayed segregated until passage of the Civil Rights Act of 1964. The Greensboro Woolworth's lost about $200,000 from boycotts, an estimated $1.7 million in current value.

As a wave of sit-ins swept the South, they also inspired the formation of the Student Nonviolent Coordinating Committee (SNCC) at Shaw University in Raleigh, a little over an hour from where the Greensboro sit-in took place. SNCC's work and accomplishments loom large over the civil rights landscape. They focused their efforts throughout the Deep South, helping Black people take charge of their political lives through voter registration and education, demonstrations, and more.

Durham, located between the two cities, experienced its own sit-ins. This is also where the four-block stretch that was famously known as Black Wall Street is located and where the ever-inspiring Pauli Murray came of age. Today, the city commemorates its Black history with a series of vibrant murals.

ORIENTATION

These three cities are strung along **I-40,** with Greensboro being the farthest west, Durham in between, and Raleigh the farthest east (about 80 miles from Greensboro). The area is served by two airports: **Piedmont Triad International** west of Greensboro, and **Raleigh-Durham International Airport,** located between Raleigh and Durham.

PLANNING YOUR TIME

You can hit all the civil rights high points in Raleigh and Durham, which are about 30 minutes apart by car, in a day. Plan to spend another day in Greensboro, which is about an hour drive west of Durham.

Whistle Stop Tours in Durham and the **Grassroots History Tour** in Greensboro both require advance booking. Note that Greensboro's **International Civil Rights Center & Museum** is closed Sundays.

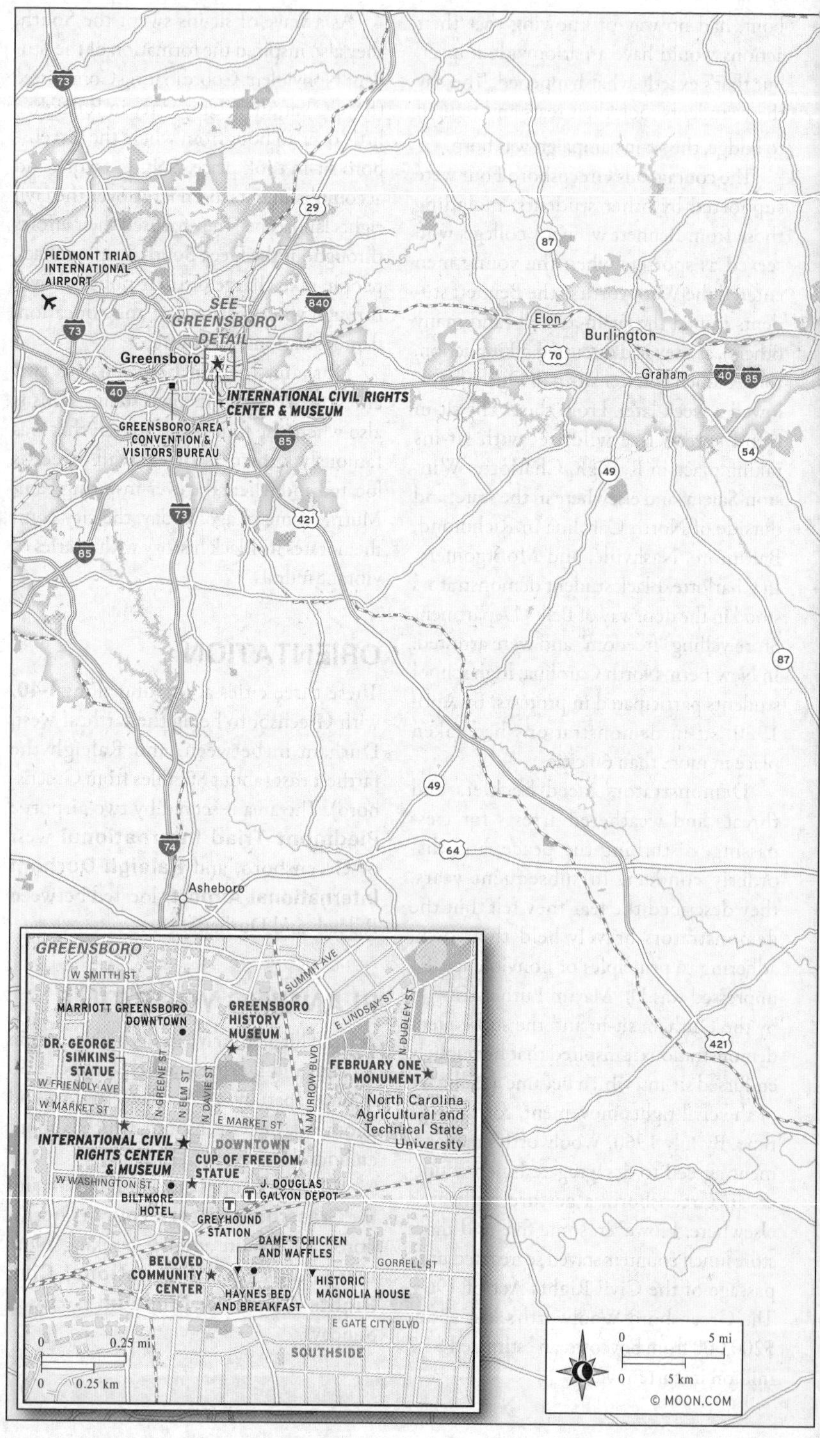
PIEDMONT TRIAD
INTERNATIONAL
AIRPORT
SEE "GREENSBORO" DETAIL
Greensboro
INTERNATIONAL CIVIL RIGHTS
CENTER & MUSEUM
GREENSBORO AREA
CONVENTION &
VISITORS BUREAU
Elon
Burlington
Graham
Asheboro
73
29
840
40
85
421
74
87
70
49
54
64
GREENSBORO
W SMITH ST
SUMMIT AVE
MARRIOTT GREENSBORO
DOWNTOWN
GREENSBORO
HISTORY
MUSEUM
E LINDSAY ST
N DUDLEY ST
DR. GEORGE
SIMKINS
STATUE
FEBRUARY ONE
MONUMENT
W FRIENDLY AVE
W MARKET ST
N GREENE ST
N ELM ST
N DAVIE ST
N MURROW BLVD
North Carolina
Agricultural and
Technical State
University
E MARKET ST
INTERNATIONAL CIVIL
RIGHTS CENTER
& MUSEUM
DOWNTOWN
CUP OF FREEDOM
STATUE
W WASHINGTON ST
J. DOUGLAS
GALYON DEPOT
BILTMORE
HOTEL
GREYHOUND
STATION
DAME'S CHICKEN
AND WAFFLES
BELOVED
COMMUNITY
CENTER
GORRELL ST
HISTORIC
MAGNOLIA HOUSE
HAYNES BED
AND BREAKFAST
E GATE CITY BLVD
SOUTHSIDE
0 0.25 mi
0 0.25 km
0 5 mi
0 5 km
© MOON.COM

Greensboro, Raleigh, and Durham

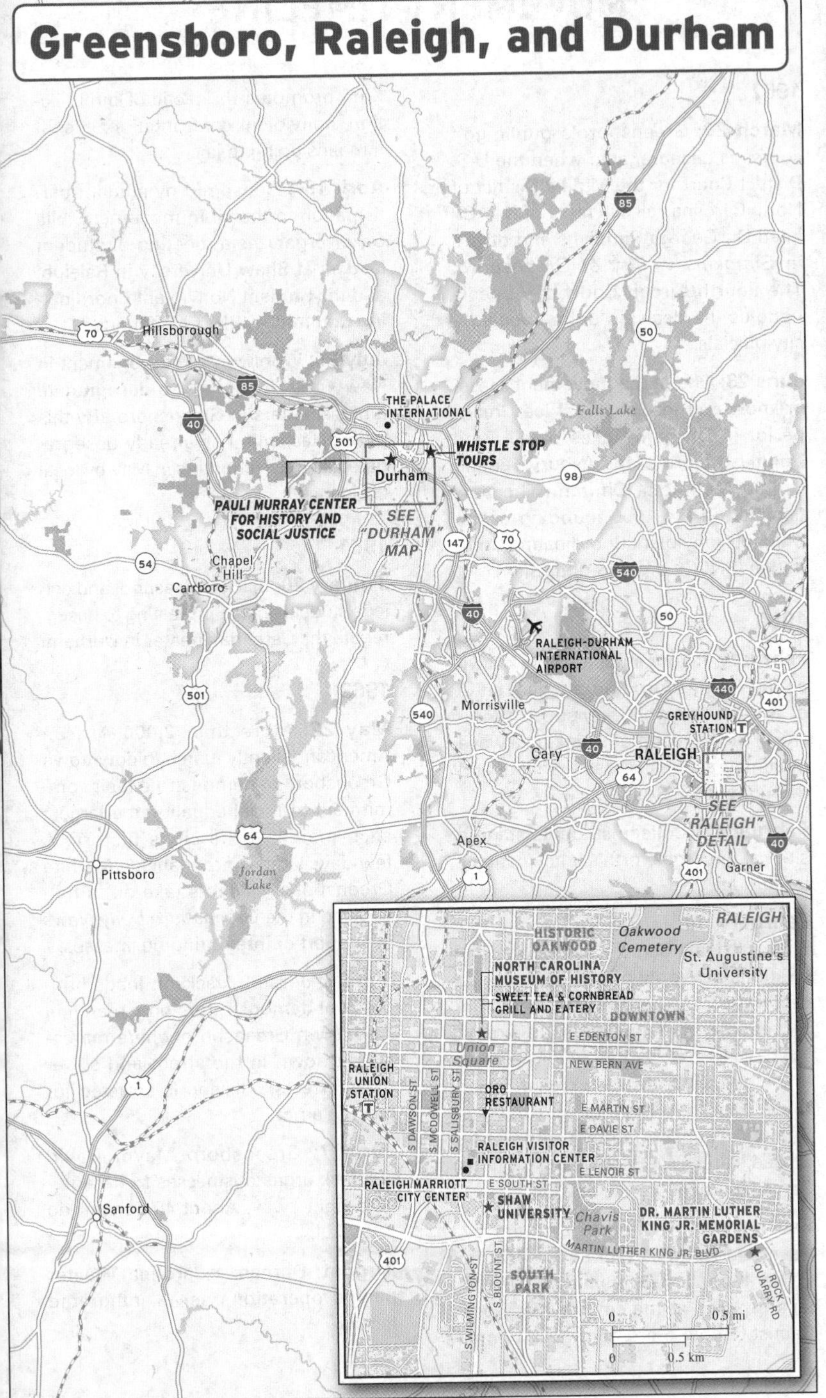

MOVEMENT TIMELINE

1957

March 20: Greensboro's public golf course is desegregated when the U.S. District Court for the Middle District of North Carolina rules in favor of NAACP head Dr. George Simpkins and others in *Simpkins v. City of Greensboro.* The Fourth Circuit Court of Appeals upholds the decision upon appeal by city officials.

June 23: One of the movement's lesser-known sit-ins, at Royal Ice Cream parlor in Durham, takes place. Rev. Douglas Moore of the Asbury Temple United Methodist Church, who participated in the 1960 founding of the Student Nonviolent Coordinating Committee (SNCC), organized the sit-in.

1960

February 1: Four students now known as the Greensboro Four stage a sit-in at the downtown Greensboro Woolworth's lunch counter, sparking a wave of similar actions across the state and throughout the South.

February 8: College students stage a sit-in at the Woolworth's lunch counter in Durham.

February 10: In Raleigh, about 150 Black students begin a day of demonstrations at Woolworth's, stopping at other sites around the city including McLellan's, Hudson-Belk, and Kress. Everywhere the demonstrators go, the lunch counters abruptly close. Signs read: "Closed in the Interest of Public Safety," "Luncheonette Temporarily Closed," and "We Reserve the Right to Serve the Public As We See Fit."

February 16: Invited to Durham by Reverend Douglas Moore, Dr. Martin Luther King Jr. delivers his "fill up the jails" speech at the city's White Rock Baptist Church. Here, for the first time, King promotes the tactic of direct-action, nonviolent confrontation, even if it means going to jail.

April 15-17: Inspired by student participation in the sit-in movement, Ella Baker organizes a meeting of student leaders at Shaw University in Raleigh, and the Student Nonviolent Coordinating Committee (SNCC) is founded.

July 25: Woolworth's management in New York City agrees to desegregate lunch counters in Greensboro. (By this point, Nashville has already desegregated its lunch counters in May by local ordinance.)

1961

January 20: Black high school and college students begin protesting to desegregate the Carolina Theater in Durham.

1963

May 22: More than 2,000 African Americans silently march to downtown Greensboro to demonstrate their commitment to racial equality, the largest such march in the city's history. A few days later, more than 1,600 White Greensboro residents take out a full-page ad in the *Greensboro Daily News* in support of integrating businesses.

June 6: Jesse L. Jackson leads hundreds of demonstrators on a march in downtown Greensboro where marchers sit down in the street and suffer mass arrests. Jackson is arrested for inciting a riot.

June 7: Greensboro Mayor David Schenck urges businesses to desegregate right away. About 40 percent do so by fall.

August: Durham's Carolina Theater begins operations as an integrated facility.

Visitors Centers

- **Durham Visitor Info Center:** 212 W Main St. #101; tel. 919/687-0288; www. discoverdurham.com
- **Greensboro Area Convention & Visitors Bureau:** 2411 W Gate City Blvd.; tel. 336/274-2282; www. visitgreensboronc.com
- **Raleigh Visitor Information Center:** 500 Fayetteville St. tel. 919/834-5900; www.visitraleigh.com

CONNECT WITH

Logical next stops are **Richmond** and **Farmville,** Virginia, to the north; **Charleston** to the south; or **Atlanta** or **Nashville** to the west.

Two Days in Greensboro, Raleigh, and Durham

For this itinerary, be sure to schedule your tour with **Whistle Stop Tours** in Durham (Day 2) in advance. Note that Greensboro's **International Civil Rights Center & Museum** (Day 1) is closed Sundays.

DAY 1: GREENSBORO AND DURHAM

1 Start your day at the Greensboro branch of **Dame's Chicken and Waffles.**

2 From your breakfast spot, the **International Civil Rights Center & Museum,** located in the old F. W. Woolworth's building where the seminal February 1, 1960, sit-in took place, is less than half a mile away. Contemplate the courage of the Greensboro Four as you view the very lunch counter where they sat, which has been preserved in the museum. Dedicate at least 90 minutes to get solid insight into the local civil rights story.

3 Before leaving Greensboro, have a look at the **Cup of Freedom statue,** located near the museum, for a creative depiction of the Greensboro Four.

4 Hit the road and drive east for an hour until you reach Durham. When you arrive, pop into the **Beyu Caffe** for a late lunch.

5 Right by the café is the **Durham Civil Rights Mural,** a colorful depiction of Black Durham residents, including those who participated in the movement. Take a quick drive over to the West End neighborhood, where Pauli Murray was raised. Drive around town to see murals dedicated to Murray's life.

6 Back downtown, the **Durham Food Hall** has all the options you'd want for an early dinner.

PEOPLE WHO MADE THE MOVEMENT

GROUPS AND ORGANIZATIONS

The Greensboro Four: Four North Carolina A&T students who staged a sit-in on February 1, 1960, in Greensboro, when they decided they'd had enough with second-class treatment under Jim Crow. Their sit-in set off a wave of other similar demonstrations across the South. The names of the Greensboro Four are David Richmond, Franklin McCain, Ezell Blair Jr. (Jibreel Khazan), and Joe McNeil.

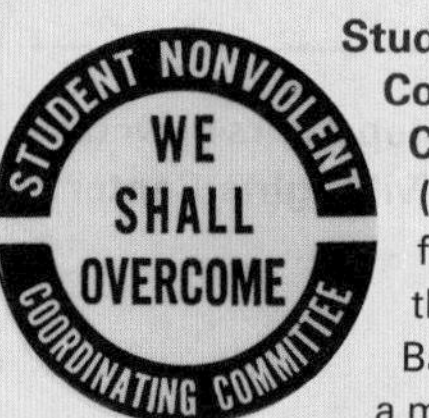

Student Nonviolent Coordinating Committee (SNCC): Group formed in 1960 at the behest of Ella Baker, who called a meeting of student leaders after noticing how active students were in the sit-in movement. The student group participated in voter registration, the Freedom Rides, and more.

INDIVIDUALS

Louis E. Austin: Austin purchased a newspaper in 1927 and turned it into the *Carolina Times,* which became the voice of the Black experience and the civil rights movement. He championed Black political participation in the Democratic Party, challenged segregation in higher education, and published the names of stores that failed to hire African Americans in the 1960s, among other issues.

Ella Baker: The "Mother of the Civil Rights Movement" was a field secretary and director at the NAACP in the 1940s. In 1960, she convened student leaders on the campus of her alma mater, Shaw University, where they created the Student Nonviolent Coordinating Committee (SNCC). She was a major player in three influential civil rights organizations: National Association for the Advancement of Colored People (NAACP), Southern Christian Leadership Conference (SCLC), and SNCC.

Rev. Jesse L. Jackson: The future presidential candidate was a student at North Carolina A&T in the '60s when he became involved with the civil rights movement. His first arrest of many would take place July 17, 1960, when he and seven other college students challenged the "no coloreds" policy of Greenville's main library. In 1963, Jackson was arrested and charged with inciting a riot in Greensboro.

Douglas Moore: The mastermind behind the Royal Ice Cream parlor sit-in, which challenged laws allowing segregated public accommodations. He later moved to Washington DC, where he advocated for the majority-Black district to become the 51st state and served on the City Council.

Rev. Pauli Murray: An attorney and civil rights and women's rights activist who became the first Black female Episcopal priest in the United States. Murray's Howard Law School paper undergirded the winning argument for *Brown v. Board of Education* in 1954.

George Simpkins: A Greensboro dentist and NAACP chapter president who spearheaded several successful civil rights fights, including a lawsuit that resulted in desegregating the city golf course, a Wachovia Bank picket that forced the bank to hire Black tellers, and a successful NAACP lawsuit to desegregate Greensboro hospitals.

DAY 2: DURHAM AND RALEIGH

1 Hopefully, you've made arrangements to take the **Whistle Stop Tour** of your choice. These 75-minute tours celebrate Durham's Black history, covering topics such as Black Wall Street, the life of Pauli Murray, and Hayti, a historic Black neighborhood.

2 Before leaving for Raleigh, make a detour down to the **Chicken Hut** (closed weekends) on Fayetteville Street, which was the center of Hayti, Durham's historic Black community. After your meal, drive back up Fayetteville Street to get on the Durham Freeway (NC 147) toward Raleigh. As you approach the highway, note that the area it covers was the site of White Rock Baptist Church, where King endorsed nonviolent confrontation after the sit-in movement ignited. Sadly, this freeway displaced thousands of Hayti residents and businesses when it was constructed later in the 1960s.

3 Upon arrival in Raleigh (after about a 30-minute drive), pay a visit to the **North Carolina Museum of History,** where some compelling exhibits touch on Black history and the civil rights movement.

4 On your way from the museum to the Martin Luther King Jr. Memorial Gardens, you'll pass **Shaw University,** where SNCC was founded.

5 Keep driving to the **Dr. Martin Luther King Jr. Memorial Gardens,** which are at their most beautiful and peaceful at dawn and dusk.

6 Have a taste of the diaspora back in Durham at **Boricua Soul,** the locally famous food truck that has expanded to a storefront on the American Tobacco Campus. The golden delicious maduros will melt in your mouth.

Greensboro

In Greensboro, as in many other places, Black people striving for equality was happening long before the 1960s: Black soldiers returning home from World War II, having fought Nazis to save Jewish and other marginalized people, wanted full access to the American promise and underscored the need to dismantle segregation. Returning soldiers in Greensboro were ready to roll up their sleeves to get African Americans registered to vote and swelled the ranks of the NAACP, according to V. O. Key in *Southern Politics: In State and Nation.* The city saw its first Black elected city council member, Dr. William Hampton, in 1951. In 1955, the NAACP leader helped to file lawsuits demanding for the right to play next to Whites at the city's golf course. That same year, Edward Edmonds, a sociology professor at Bennett College, led parents in protesting inferior educational facilities for Black students.

But it's the February 1, 1960, Woolworth's sit-in that put Greensboro on the map, as far as civil rights were concerned. This event, staged by four students at North Carolina Agricultural & Technical University, ignited a movement of direct action in the form of nonviolent demonstrations throughout the South. Rev. Jesse

L. Jackson also makes an appearance here: On June 6, 1963, he was arrested and charged with "inciting to riot and disturb the peace and dignity of the state" after leading hundreds of demonstrators through downtown Greensboro, chanting. The demonstration made national news, an early glimmer of how Jackson could come to dominate the news cycle and impact the public conversation.

Today, the city has more than 280,000 residents, of which 43 percent are White, 42 percent Black, 5 percent Asian, and 7 percent Hispanic. Greensboro is home to several colleges and universities, and close to 50,000 students study here.

ORIENTATION

Most points of interest are located **downtown,** which is bordered by East Gate City Boulevard to the south, Spring Street to the west, Smith Street to the north, and Morrow Boulevard to the east, an area of roughly one square mile by one square mile.

SIGHTS

You'll want to go straight to the International Civil Rights Center & Museum because standing there on the grounds of the 1960 sit-in is enough to make you feel things. Inside, you'll get a comprehensive telling of the local, regional, and even national civil rights struggle. The Greensboro History Museum tells a more expansive story of local history, but displays give credit where it is due when it comes to local players and civil rights efforts.

★ International Civil Rights Center & Museum

134 S Elm St.; tel. 336/274-9199; www.sitinmovement.org; Mon.-Sat. 10am-6pm; adults $15, seniors $12, students $10, youth 6-12 $8, children 5 and under free

The International Civil Rights Center & Museum building, a site on the official U.S. Civil Rights Trail, occupies the former F. W. Woolworth's building where the trailblazing sit-in of February 1960 took place. The original full-scale lunch counter is still here—other parts added on at later dates have been donated to other museums, including the National Museum of African American History and Culture in Washington DC. When four students took their seats on these red-topped stools and refused to move—instead of standing at the end of the counter and waiting for their orders, which would be consumed elsewhere, as African Americans were permitted to do—history was made.

The room containing the lunch counter still has an open, department store feel, and the display, which includes scene-setting details like vintage signs and table settings at each seat, offers a window into the segregated world demonstrators set to destroy, one defiant act at a time. Along the counter's back wall are screens showing reenactments of the day the sit-in took place.

Other exhibits relating to the Greensboro Four include a replica of a room in Scott Hall Dormitory, where the four students lived on the campus of North Carolina Agriculture & Technical State University. (On the campus itself, the dorm was demolished to build a set of dorms named in honor of the Greensboro Four.) An interactive map shows how far the sit-in movement spread, with yellow dots representing campaigns started by students at historically Black colleges and universities. Points include Shaw University in Raleigh, where SNCC was founded.

In another area of the museum, near the entry, is a glass wall onto which images and statements about what it means to be American are projected. Then more ominous messages come into view, such as Jim Crow signs emblazoned with Confederate flags that read "Colored Entrance" or "Zoned for a White Community." The narrative point here is that exclusion has been as much a part of the American experience as the high ideals linked to the mythology of the United States. Next up is a Hall of Shame, a collection of jagged frames that features superimposed images depicting violence against Black people, including images of children in Birmingham being attacked.

The museum's signature exhibition, called The Battlegrounds, delves further into the lived experience of segregation. See photos of public buses with barriers marked "Colored Passengers" to corral Black riders in the back. The bright red Coca Cola machine that's on display could be used as a tool of racial division: With an opening on each side, when placed in the middle of a Whites- and Blacks-only public space, the soda dispensary emphasized segregation. Giving context to oversize photos of beaches, docents explain how chain link fences stretched hundreds of feet into the ocean as a method of dividing Black and White swimmers. The fence also served to enforce false notions of inferiority or superiority.

The museum occupies 30,000 square feet of exhibition space. You can walk through at your own pace, but **tours,** led by knowledgeable docents known for the passion they bring to narrating civil rights history, are also available as part of your museum admission fee. At the time of writing, museum officials were in the process of reimagining the visitor experience, so check ahead if you're interested in one exhibit in particular.

Greensboro Coffee Cup Collaborative Walk

When the Greensboro Four sat down at the segregated lunch counter at Woolworth's in 1960, they each asked for a cup of coffee. Sipping coffee was the most natural thing to do at the busy downtown lunch counter that buzzed with activity—unless you were Black. That polite request for coffee that didn't come was the inspiration behind the Coffee Cup Collaborative's sit-in public art commemoration, a collaboration between local groups including the International Civil Rights Center & Museum and ArtsGreensboro. The installation comprises seven bronze coffee cup sculptures that are displayed downtown and at the Greensboro Coliseum. Each cup is 20 square inches and mounted on a pedestal.

Charles Jenkins's interpretation of the Greensboro Four, called **A Cup of Freedom** (132 S Elm St.), is located next to the International Civil Rights Center & Museum. The sculpture depicts Ezell Blair Jr. (Jibreel Khazan), David Richmond, Franklin McCain, and Joe McNeil sitting around a cup whose rim is also a lunch counter.

Jay Rotberg's **A Cup of Coffee Please,** situated outside the coliseum (1921 W. Lee St.), uses dividing walls to question how much more work needs to be done to bring the races together. Rodney Bennett's **Overcome** is found on Melvin Municipal Building lawn (300 West Washington St.). It features a quote by Ambrose Redmoon: "Courage is not the absence of fear, but rather the judgment that something else is more important than fear." The **Spoons** cup outside the Carolina Theater (310 S. Green St.) features spoon handles hanging outside a coffee cup, representing the collective of people who powered the sit-in movement. Timothy Daniel's **The Pearl of Equity** (345 South Elm St.) is shaped like a flower, symbolizing rebirth. Kurt Gabriel's **Awake** coffee cup in front of the J. Douglas Galyon Depot (236 East Washington St.) is the artist's call to wake up from indifference. Derrick Monk's **In the Face of Strange Fruit** (200 North Davie St.) was inspired by Billie Holiday's haunting critique of lynching and depicts faces of people who fought for freedom and equality.

Greensboro History Museum

130 Summit Ave.; tel. 336/373-2043; www.greensborohistory.org; Tues.-Sat. 10am-5pm, Sun. 2pm-5pm; free

Photos (top to bottom): the International Civil Rights Center & Museum; the February One Monument by James Barnhill; a lunch counter exhibit in the Greensboro History Museum

This 17,000-square-foot Smithsonian affiliate museum interprets the entire history of Greensboro, including segregation and the civil rights movement. Exhibits show and tell what it was like to live in segregated Greensboro, and cover the period after the movement as well. You'll get a different take on what it has meant to be a member of Greensboro's Black community and discover some of its civil rights pioneers.

A core exhibit called Voices of a City includes photos of people involved in the movement, accompanied by quotes and audio reenactments. The Changing Times exhibit highlights the lunch counter sit-in campaign, addressing what was happening in Greensboro before and after the 1960 sit-ins. For example, displays highlight Josephine Boyd, the first Black student to enter Greensboro Senior High School on September 4, 1957 and Dr. George Simkins, a dentist who was president of the Greensboro NAACP for more than two decades. This exhibit celebrates many firsts: Willa Player, first Black woman college president in the United States, who hosted an influential speech King gave at Bennett College in 1958; Elreta Alexander, first Black woman appointed Superior Court Judge; and Henry Frye, first African American elected to North Carolina General Assembly in the 20th century and first Black chief justice of the North Carolina Supreme Court.

A section of the Woolworth's counter where the original sit-in took place (donated by ICRCM) is also on display here. You'll also learn about the Freedman's neighborhood and the city's link to the Underground Railroad.

Dr. George Simpkins Statue

Eugene and W Market Streets

A bronze commemorative statue of civil rights leader Dr. George Simpkins honors the local dentist who helmed the NAACP Greensboro chapter from 1959-84. The statue stands on the lawn of the Old Guilford County Courthouse. Simpkins worked to register Black voters, desegregate public housing, banking and city services, and change how Greensboro residents elected their city council. His first big win was a 1955 lawsuit that desegregated the city's Whites-only Gillespie Golf Course, which was better maintained than the Black people-only course in Nocho Park. The city opted to close the course, and when it reopened, it had nine instead of 18 holes.

February One Monument

1601 E Market St.; tel. 336/334-7500

On the campus of North Carolina Agricultural & Technical University, students can look up to four alumni for examples of courage in the quest for justice: Ezell Blair Jr. (Jibreel Khazan), Franklin McCain, Joseph McNeil, and David Richmond, aka the Greensboro Four who ignited a sit-in movement on February 1, 1960, when they sat down at the downtown Woolworth's lunch counter and refused to budge until close. This 15-foot-tall monument, which is a stop on the official U.S. Civil Rights Trail, stands on an island in University Circle in front of the Dudley Building. What these students did was a big deal, so a drive by and take note.

TOURS AND LOCAL GUIDES

Walking Tour

GRASSROOTS HISTORY TOUR

tel. 336/230-0001; www.belovedcommunitycenter.org; from $100 per group

Greensboro's **Beloved Community Center** (417 Arlington St.; Mon.-Fri. 10am-5pm; free) offers this tour of Greensboro for those who want to know more about the city's civil rights history, according to Lewis Brandon III, a veteran of the 1960 sit-in campaign, who leads the tour. There's no set schedule for the tour, but the center will make arrangements for dates and times for groups who call in advance. Depending on the size of the group, tour costs can start at $100 for a group. Tours may include trips to North Carolina A&T University, where the February One Monument stands, Bennett College for Women, and the International Civil Rights Center & Museum.

The center is a hub of activity that continues the work of the civil rights movement by promoting social, gender, economic, and racial justice. A multigenerational formation organized in 1991, the center emerged out of a countywide, grassroots initiative to address problems of health care, homelessness, and police accountability. Beloved is perhaps most noted for organizing a citizen-led, citywide truth and community reconciliation process in response to the tragic killing of five members of the Communist Workers Party and the wounding of 10 others by Klan and Nazi members during the 1979 Greensboro Massacre. The Greensboro TRC process, the first of its kind in the United States, was organized to seek justice, equity, and racial healing. It continues to stand as a model for the country, as calls for national truth initiatives emerge.

The organization has enthusiastically supported Moral Mondays, an initiative led by Rev. Dr. William Barber, who rebooted King's agenda by launching the Poor People's Campaign: A National Call for Moral Revival. Moral Mondays consist of protests by a racially diverse coalition to challenge racism, poverty, climate change, and the war economy by pressing public officials to make moral choices. Get involved with the organization by visiting www.poorpeoplescampaign.org, where you can also donate to the cause. The website details upcoming actions and fact sheets on everything from the cost of poverty to health and environment and disparate impacts caused by the coronavirus.

FOOD

A worthy dining option is the local branch of **Dame's Chicken and Waffles** (301 Martin Luther King Jr Dr.; tel. 336/275-7333; www.dameschickenwaffles.com; Mon. 10am-3pm; Tues.-Thurs. 11am-8pm, Fri.-Sat. 10am-9pm, Sun. 10am-4pm; $4-7) here in Greensboro. There's a branch in Durham, though the Greensboro location is their first.

HISTORIC MAGNOLIA HOUSE

442 Gorrell St.; tel. 336/617-3382; www.thehistoricmagnoliahouse.com; brunch Sun. 11am-3pm

Magnolia House, formally known as the Daniel D. Debutts House, was listed in *The Negro Motorist Green Book,* which served as a roadmap to safe havens for Black people on the road during the Jim Crow era. During segregation, notable individuals who slept in this six-room bed and breakfast included Jackie Robinson, Carter G. Woodson, Satchel Paige, Ray Charles, James Brown, Ruth Brown, and Tina Turner. It was the only place African Americans could stay between Atlanta and Richmond, Virginia.

Today, the Italianate Victorian-style home is a special events space that hosts Sunday jazz brunches and ticketed events. The Miles Davis Jazz Band from the University of North Carolina at Greensboro are features players at brunches. (Davis met the hotel's original owner, Arthur "Buddy" Gist, at New York's famed Birdland, and gifted Gist his trumpet, which Gist in turn gifted to the university.)

A real treat for civil rights trail travelers is Historic Magnolia House's shoebox lunches, in keeping with its *Green Book* theme. These lunches—shoeboxes packed with fried chicken, cake, cornbread, and fruit—are the stuff of Black family lore. They were carried by Black travelers to the South to ensure they would have something to eat because segregation barred them from eating in roadside restaurants. These

Historic Magnolia House

lunches staved off hunger and instilled dignity through sustenance, while African Americans avoided the "disappointment and humiliation of being turned away," says managing partner Natalie Pass Miller. Local students may visit and have a shoebox lunch and a lesson as part of the house's educational mission.

The **Magnolia African American History Museum,** scheduled to open in 2022, will narrate untold stories of the Black experience in North Carolina. The spotlight will turn to people like Dr. George Simpkins, the dentist and longtime NAACP president who desegregated Greensboro's Whites-only Gillespie Golf Course and local hospitals, among other civil rights wins.

Historic Magnolia House is on the National Register of Historic Places.

ACCOMMODATIONS

In addition to the Haynes Bed and Breakfast, the **Marriott Greensboro Downtown** (304 Greene St.; tel. 336/379-8000; marriott.com) and the **Biltmore Hotel** (111 W Washington St.; tel. 336/272-3474; www.thebiltmoregreensboro.com), a former apartment complex, are within walking distance of the International Civil Rights Center & Museum.

HAYNES BED AND BREAKFAST

320 Gorrell St.; tel. 866/223-9445; www.haynesbedandbreakfast.com; $119

Haynes Bed and Breakfast offers two rooms with a private bath and queen-size bed. The B&B is a five-minute walk to downtown Greensboro, where you can find the International Civil Rights Museum, and the train and bus stations are a 10-minute walk from here. This vintage gem is near Bennett College and North Carolina A&T University, whose students played a key role in the civil rights movement.

GETTING THERE

Air

Greensboro is 12 miles east of **Piedmont Triad International Airport** (1000 Ted Johnson Pkwy.; tel. 336/665-5600; www.flyfrompti.com). From the airport, a cab ride into downtown Greensboro takes around 15 minutes.

Train

The **J. Douglas Galyon Depot** (236 E Washington St.; tel. 800/872-7245), also known as Greensboro station, is the hub for city buses and also serves **Amtrak**. It's located in downtown Durham.

Bus

Greensboro has a **Greyhound station** (234 E Washington St.; tel. 800/231-2222; daily 7am-11pm) downtown.

Car

To reach Greensboro from:

- **Raleigh**: Take **I-40 West** for around 80 miles (1.5 hours).
- **Atlanta:** Take **I-85 North** for around 335 miles (5 hours).
- **Nashville:** Take **I-40 East** for around 465 miles (7 hours).

GETTING AROUND

Downtown Greensboro is walkable with plenty of parking. For longer distances, car are the best way to travel, though the city does have public transit, ride-share services, and scooter/bike rentals.

Durham

College students in Durham, inspired by their counterparts in Greensboro, staged their own Woolworth's lunch counter protest just a week later. (Though, with all due respect to Greensboro, the first notable restaurant sit-in actually happened at Durham's Royal Ice Cream parlor on June 23, 1957, at Roxboro and Dowd streets. Rev. Douglas Moore and six others participated in the sit-in and were arrested and fined. Angela Lee, executive director of the Hayti Heritage Center, says the Greensboro sit-in campaign tends to get the limelight because Durham residents didn't want the world to know that that kind of discrimination was going on here.)

Taking note of the movement, King traveled to Durham after the sit-in and delivered a speech at White Rock Baptist Church, which no longer stands. Eight years later, King was also due to make another visit to the city, but he diverted to support striking sanitation workers in Memphis, where his tragic assassination occurred.

Durham was a place of unrestrained Black striving long before the sit-in movement, as evidenced by the "construction" of Brush Arbor, an outdoor worship space located in the historic Black neighborhood of Hayti, during Reconstruction. Segregation did not stop Durham's Black residents from thinking big and working harder. After all, this is the home of Black Wall Street, a thriving commercial district along Parrish Street in the 1800s and early 1900s.

Today, Durham cherishes the entirety of its Black history through murals found throughout the city, including a vibrant one downtown that honors those who fought for civil rights locally and provided a foundation of Black institutions steeped in excellence. Meanwhile, the Hayti Heritage Center, a beacon of the neighborhood's Black heritage, stands on the site where Brush Arbor was once located.

ORIENTATION

Downtown Durham is bordered by NC 147 to the west, Elizabeth Street to the south, and North Buchanan Boulevard (roughly) to the north. Main Street runs through the center of downtown, and the neighborhood's jagged eastern boundary is roughly half a mile east of this main road.

On the other side of NC 147 is Fayetteville Road, where the historic Black community of **Hayti** developed after the Civil War. Also on this side of NC 147, above Fayetteville Road, is the **West End,** where civil rights leader Pauli Murray came of age. The neighborhood is now peppered with murals celebrating Murray's life.

SIGHTS

Downtown

DURHAM CIVIL RIGHTS MURAL

120 Morris St.; www.muraldurham.com/durham-civil-rights-mural-2015

This inspiring 2,400-square-foot mural, titled "We Must Remember and Continued to Tell," next to the Durham Arts Council honors the talent and intellect of Black Durham residents, including those who fought for equality. In 2013, Brenda Miller Holmes, an artist and collaborative community muralist, facilitated Durham residents from ages 15-65 in sharing stories of the civil rights movement to inform the creation of this vast artwork bursting with color and meaning. A core group of 30 residents, mostly African American, developed the mural concept. "All of the decisions that went into what images went into the mural were completely collective decisions," Miller Holmes says.

Everyone featured is a Durham-specific figure, with the exception of Dr. Martin Luther King Jr. and Philadelphia architect Julian Francis Abele. Here's a tour of the cast of characters:

On the far left on the short wall next to a water tower is **Stanford L. Warren,** a co-founder of North Carolina Mutual Life Insurance who donated the $4,000 necessary to build a library named for him (1201 Fayetteville St.) in 1940. Not only did the library provide access to books and boost community literacy, it was considered a safe haven for Black people. Today, the library is considered a cultural treasure.

Next to him is **William Gaston Pearson,** a Shaw University graduate and local principal who paved the way for Black educational access, including helping to found North Carolina Central University.

Highlighted in the upper left of the tall wall is **Julian Francis Abele,** the Philadelphia architect who designed most of Duke University's original neo-Gothic-style buildings, including the chapel, even though the campus was segregated until 1961. He's the man wearing a brown suit at the top left standing next to a rendering of Duke Chapel (above the Howard Johnson's sign). According to Miller Holmes, the addition of Duke Chapel was controversial, and the only way to get it in was to add Abele, a case successfully argued by a youth design corps member.

The sky-blue portion at the top of the mural depicts several men key to the creation of Black Wall Street: **John Merrick** co-founded North Carolina Mutual Life Insurance Co. with **Richard Fitzgerald,** who is to his right. Fitzgerald, great uncle to activist Rev. Pauli Murray, was Durham's leading brickmaker. Also in blue is **Dr. Aaron Moore,** founder of Lincoln Hospital, the first for African Americans and a North Carolina Mutual Life co-founder.

Draped with a Remember banner in the center is **Louis Austin,** *Carolina Times* publisher and civil rights activist. To the right of him in monochromatic blue is **James Shepard,** a conservative leader who founded North Carolina Central University, and **Charles Clinton Spaulding,** who became president of North Carolina Mutual Life, founded by his uncle Moore, and who led the Mechanics and Farmers Bank, an offshoot.

Martin Luther King Jr. is shown standing in front of White Rock Baptist Church where, on February 16, 1960, the Southern Christian Leadership Conference (SCLC) leader gave his "fill up the jails" speech. To the bottom left of King is St. Joseph's African Episcopal Methodist

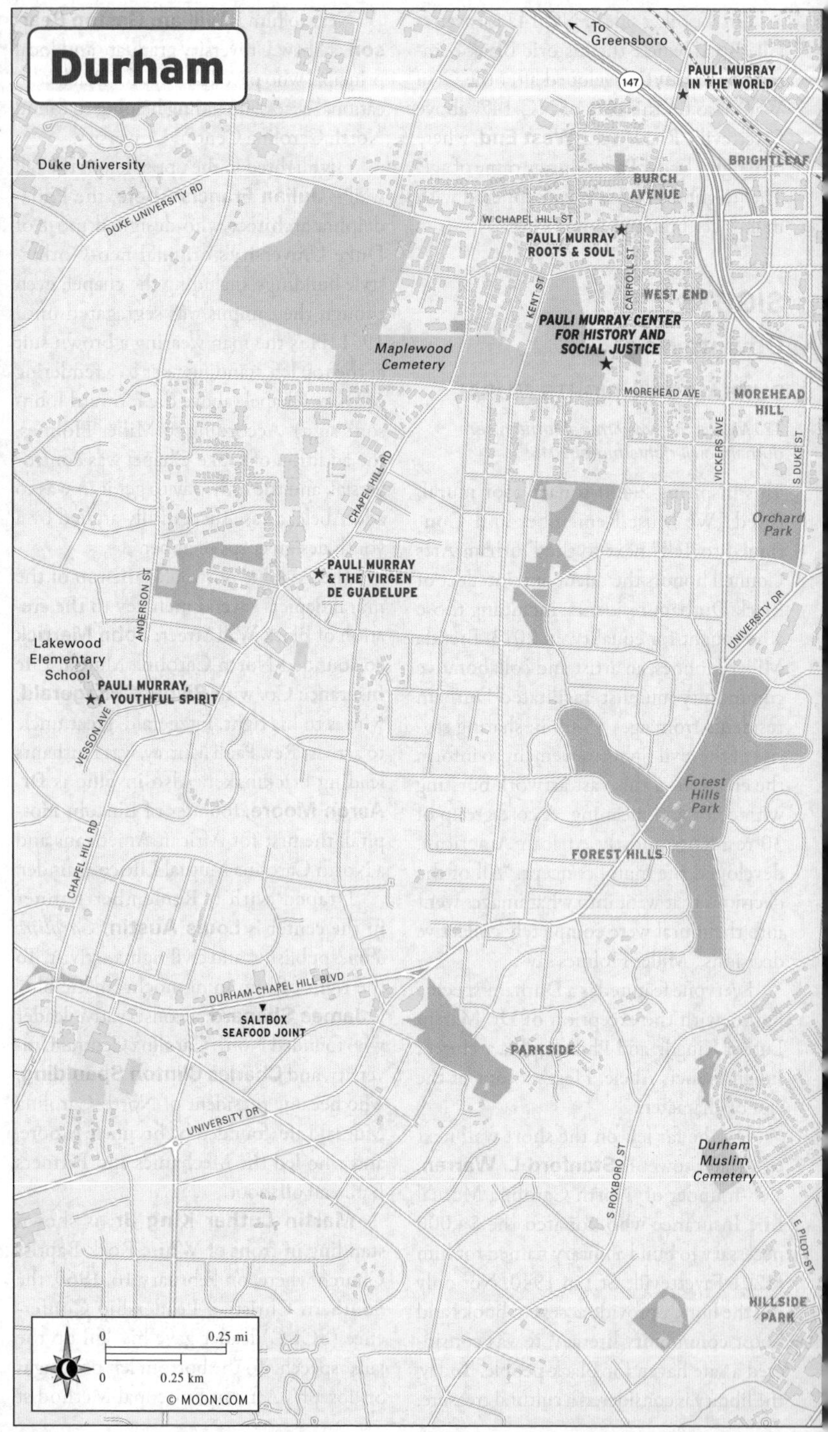
Durham
To Greensboro
147
PAULI MURRAY IN THE WORLD
BRIGHTLEAF
Duke University
DUKE UNIVERSITY RD
BURCH AVENUE
W CHAPEL HILL ST
PAULI MURRAY ROOTS & SOUL
CARROLL ST
KENT ST
WEST END
PAULI MURRAY CENTER FOR HISTORY AND SOCIAL JUSTICE
Maplewood Cemetery
MOREHEAD AVE
MOREHEAD HILL
VICKERS AVE
S DUKE ST
CHAPEL HILL RD
Orchard Park
PAULI MURRAY & THE VIRGEN DE GUADELUPE
ANDERSON ST
UNIVERSITY DR
Lakewood Elementary School
PAULI MURRAY, A YOUTHFUL SPIRIT
VESSON AVE
Forest Hills Park
FOREST HILLS
CHAPEL HILL RD
DURHAM-CHAPEL HILL BLVD
SALTBOX SEAFOOD JOINT
PARKSIDE
UNIVERSITY DR
S ROXBORO ST
Durham Muslim Cemetery
E PILOT ST
HILLSIDE PARK
0
0.25 mi
0
0.25 km
© MOON.COM

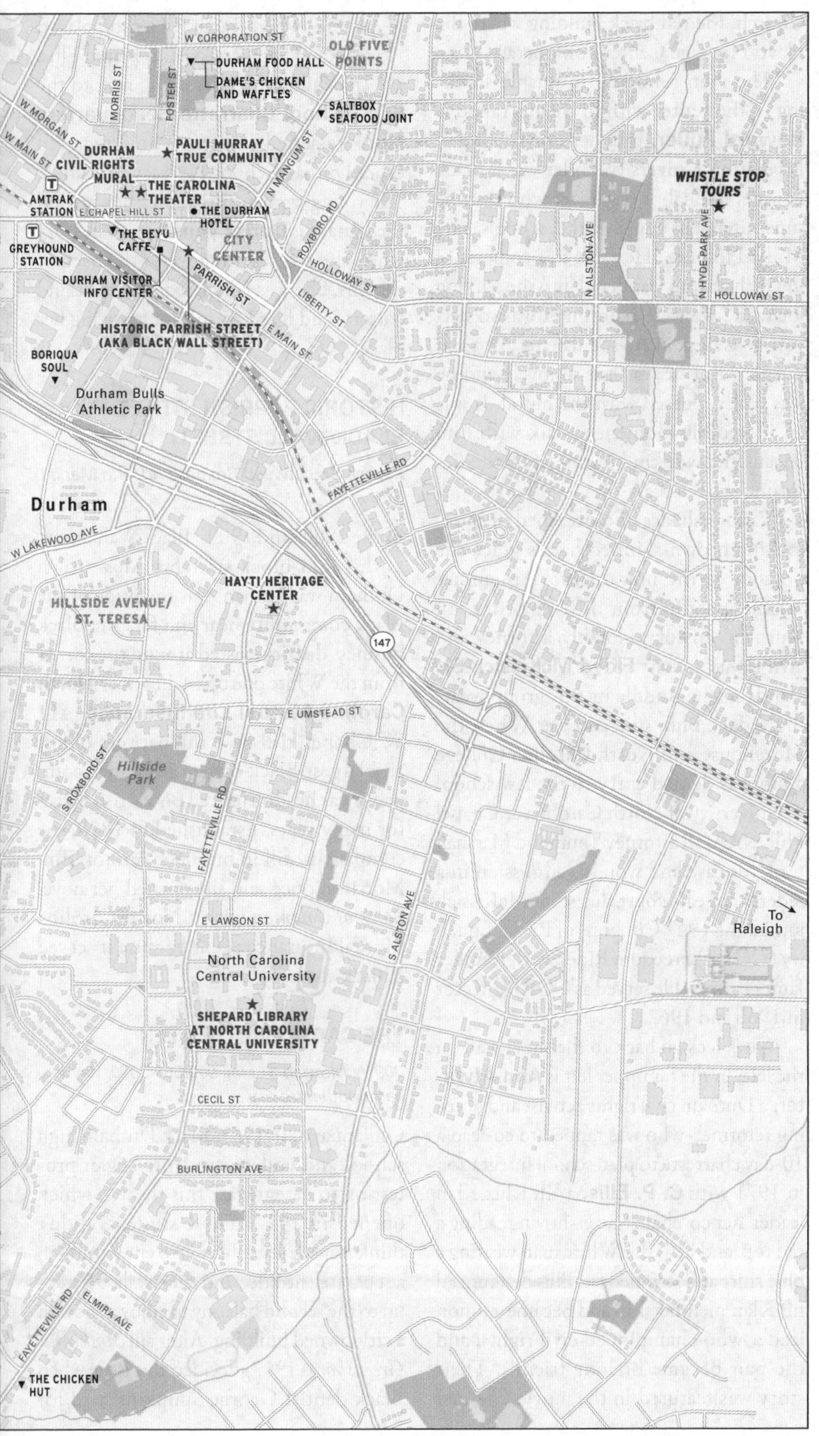
W CORPORATION ST
OLD FIVE POINTS
DURHAM FOOD HALL
DAME'S CHICKEN AND WAFFLES
SALTBOX SEAFOOD JOINT
MORRIS ST
FOSTER ST
W MORGAN ST
W MAIN ST
N MANGUM ST
PAULI MURRAY TRUE COMMUNITY
DURHAM CIVIL RIGHTS MURAL
THE CAROLINA THEATER
AMTRAK STATION
E CHAPEL HILL ST
THE DURHAM HOTEL
GREYHOUND STATION
THE BEYU CAFFE
CITY CENTER
DURHAM VISITOR INFO CENTER
PARRISH ST
ROXBORO RD
HOLLOWAY ST
LIBERTY ST
E MAIN ST
HISTORIC PARRISH STREET (AKA BLACK WALL STREET)
BORIQUA SOUL
Durham Bulls Athletic Park
WHISTLE STOP TOURS
N ALSTON AVE
N HYDE PARK AVE
HOLLOWAY ST
FAYETTEVILLE RD
Durham
W LAKEWOOD AVE
HAYTI HERITAGE CENTER
HILLSIDE AVENUE/ ST. TERESA
147
E UMSTEAD ST
Hillside Park
S ROXBORO ST
FAYETTEVILLE RD
S ALSTON AVE
To Raleigh
E LAWSON ST
North Carolina Central University
SHEPARD LIBRARY AT NORTH CAROLINA CENTRAL UNIVERSITY
CECIL ST
BURLINGTON AVE
FAYETTEVILLE RD
ELMIRA AVE
THE CHICKEN HUT

Church, the red brick building where the Hayti Heritage Center now operates.

The man rendered in purple standing in the center with his hands raised is **Howard Fuller,** founder of Malcolm X Liberation University. Fuller was a Black Panther and labor organizer who became superintendent of Milwaukee schools. Says Miller Holmes: "He came to a conference in Durham and wandered into the parking lot while we were painting. I was so nervous—'Is he going to mind being giant and purple?' But he was just so lovely and he was really pleased with the mural. It was an incredible moment to talk with him because he was kind of one of my heroes through the process."

Various shades of outreached or interlocking brown-skinned hands grace the bottom of the mural. Above them are various people from different times in Durham's history. Notably, attorney and civil rights activist **Floyd McKissick Sr.** stands in the middle of this group wearing a dark blue suit and tie. When the Morehouse and North Carolina College alum was denied entry to the law school at University of North Carolina at Chapel Hill, NAACP attorney Thurgood Marshall took his case and won his admission in a federal appeals court decision. McKissick joined the 1947 Congress of Racial Equality (CORE) Freedom Rides, with founder James Farmer. He served as CORE director in 1966 and 1967.

Now, let's go back to the short wall on the left: In the far upper left is **Ann Atwater,** a Durham civil rights activist and housing reformer, who was tapped to co-lead a 10-day charrette to plan school integration in 1971 with **C. P. Ellis,** a Ku Klux Klan leader, her co-chair. She is shown reading a red top, and he is the White man wearing a blue shirt and stripped tie. Ellis denounced his Klan membership and became a union leader who championed civil rights, and the pair became lifelong friends. Their story was featured in the movie *The Best of Enemies,* where Taraji P. Henson played Atwater and Sam Rockwell depicted Ellis.

The children seen walking next to the **SOS School Charrette Headquarters sign** are actual children who integrated other Durham schools several years earlier. The young woman sitting on a bus behind the signage is **Doris Lyons,** age 16 in 1943 when she refused to move to the back of the bus. She was convicted of assault and battery, and fined $5 for not knowing her place.

HISTORIC PARRISH STREET (AKA BLACK WALL STREET)

Parrish St. between Roxboro Rd. and Market St.

In the 1800s and 1900s, Black Wall Street, as this four-block stretch of downtown Durham was known, was the pride of the Black community near and far. The Black business district existed around the corner from the White one on Main Street. **North Carolina Mutual Life Insurance** (411 W Chapel Hill St.), the nation's oldest and largest Black-owned insurance company, was headquartered on Parrish Street for many years. Established in 1898, the company is still in business. Author Toni Morrison once said she opened her novel *Song of Solomon* with a North Carolina Mutual insurance agent because it served a Black clientele.

THE CAROLINA THEATER

309 W Morgan St.; tel. 919/560-3030; www.carolinatheatre.org

On January 20, 1961, Black Durham high school and college students began protesting to desegregate this theater, which opened in 1927. These students didn't think it made sense having to enter through a separate entrance and then walk 97 steps up to the second balcony to enjoy a show in a city-owned building. After all, *Simkins v. Greensboro* (1957) decided this issue when Black dentist George Simpkins sued for use of a public golf course: The court ruled Black people should have access to public facilities.

Attorney Floyd McKissick directed local NAACP efforts to help the students protest the theater's segregation policies. Newly elected Mayor Wense Grabarek worked to get theater officials to negotiate. In August 1963, days before King spoke at the March on Washington for Jobs and Freedom, the theater began operations as an integrated facility.

Today, a permanent civil rights exhibit outside the second-floor balcony includes an oversize photo of the student protestors. The lobby exhibit also features the old box office Black patrons were forced to use when buying tickets. Another photo display is found on the balcony level.

Along Fayetteville Street

After the Civil War, Black people migrated to this area on the southwest edge of modern-day Durham, which came to be known as **Hayti** (hey-TIE), to work in nearby tobacco warehouses. Although it started out as a labor pool, the Hayti community became a bustling residential and commercial area. Jazz greats Cab Calloway and Louis Armstrong performed here. Booker T. Washington called the area "shining examples of what a colored man may become."

St. Joseph Church (now Hayti Heritage Center) and **White Rock Baptist Church** were central to the Hayti community. The latter, located at the corner of Mobile Avenue and Fayetteville (now underneath the Durham Freeway, aka NC 147), has been demolished, but it looms large in civil rights history: This was where, on February 16, 1960, King delivered his "fill up the jails" speech, in which he promoted the

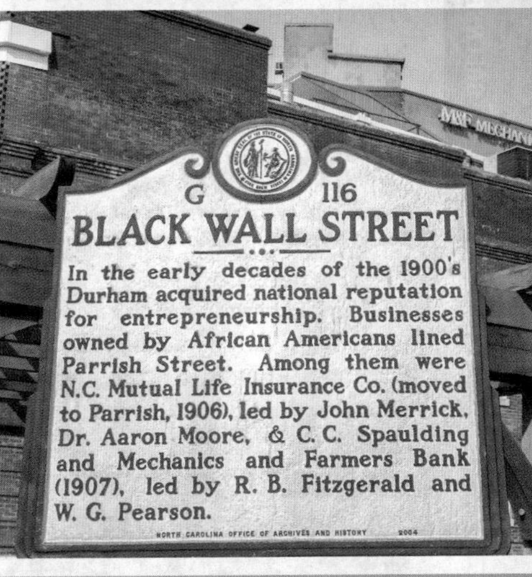

Photos (top to bottom): the Durham Civil Rights Mural, titled "We Must Remember and Continue to Tell" by Brenda Miller Holmes; a marker on Historic Parrish Street, aka Black Wall Street; the Carolina Theater

tactic of nonviolent confrontation against segregationists for the first time in the South. This is something to think about as you drive along Fayetteville Street en route to the Hayti Heritage Center.

Like so many Black enclaves across the country, urban renewal and interstate construction decimated Hayti. In the 1960s, the construction of the Durham Freeway displaced thousands of Hayti residents and hundreds of businesses. So far, the renewal part of "urban renewal" hasn't materialized, though there have been discussions about Hayti becoming better connected to the rest of Durham.

HAYTI HERITAGE CENTER

804 Old Fayetteville St.; tel. 919/683-1709; www.hayti.org; Mon.-Fri. 10am-5pm, Sat. 10am-3pm, evening and weekend hours based on programs and events; prices vary by event

The Hayti Heritage Center is a living monument to the early days of Black people in Durham, who migrated to this area on the southwest edge of modern-day Durham after the Civil War.

A central part of the Hayti community was the St. Joseph's A.M.E. Church, whose congregation came together in 1868 in a most humble manner: Formerly enslaved missionary Edian Markham sunk four posts in the ground and used boards and branches to make a roof, deeming the structure a church. Those who came to worship brought their own seats, including boxes and stools. In 1891, members decided to build a brick structure on the land and call it St. Joseph Church. Today, that former church is the Hayti Heritage Center, a cultural arts and arts education space that celebrates Black heritage.

The structure itself has notable features. Exterior bricks were crafted by Richard and Robert Fitzgerald who built a brick empire in Durham and helped establish Black Wall Street (Parrish Street). So well-made were Fitzgerald bricks that the Fitzgeralds were the preferred brickmaker of the monied class, including the Duke family of Duke University. Inside the center, a tin ceiling is painted turquoise with gold accents, and an Art Nouveau chandelier hangs over the center aisles. There are also several memorial stained-glass windows, including those that honor Edian Markham. Atop the old

the performance hall in Hayti Heritage Center

church steeple is a vèvè, a Haitian religious symbol. Hayti, of course, is named in honor of Haiti and its successful fight for independence, making this a fitting tribute to Black self-determination through the diaspora.

The center presents core programming in visual and performing arts, including an annual film festival, artist exhibitions, a music concert series and a spoken word/poetry slam team. Author talks have included civil rights icons such as the late Congressman John Lewis. Come December, the Hayti Heritage Center is where you'll find Black Santa.

SHEPARD LIBRARY AT NORTH CAROLINA CENTRAL UNIVERSITY

1801 Fayetteville St.; tel. 919/530-7310; www.nccu.edu; Mon.-Thurs. 7:30am-11pm, Fri. 7:30am-5pm, Sat. 10am-6pm, Sun. 2pm-11pm; free

Just a week after the Greensboro sit-in, three student members of the North Carolina College (now North Carolina Central University) NAACP chapter—Lacy Streeter, Callis Brown, and Robert Kornegay—orchestrated their own sit-in at the downtown Durham Woolworth's lunch counter. The Durham protestors were refused service, but they kept sitting. Over the next several days, the sit-in grew to more than 300 students and expanded to nearby businesses. Their act of courage drew the attention of King and Rev. Ralph Abernathy, who came to visit on February 16, 1960, on a tour of downtown lunch counters that had closed in the wake of demonstrations.

The Durham Woolworth's building was demolished in 2003, but what's left of the lunch counter is on display behind a main staircase in this library: two bright orange plastic seats, the steel-gray spokes that formed the seat backs, and a Formica countertop. It's a simple display that invites a time-bound contemplation of what it took to defy established power.

The library is located on the university campus, about a half a mile down Fayetteville Street from the Hayti Heritage Center.

West End

★ PAULI MURRAY CENTER FOR HISTORY AND SOCIAL JUSTICE

906 Carroll St.; tel. 919/796-1728; www.paulimurrayproject.org

The family home that nurtured Pauli Murray as a child is the site of the Pauli Murray Center for History and Social Justice and a National Historic Landmark. At the time of writing, the center was being restored and was scheduled to open to the public by the end of 2020. The center seeks to amplify the inclusive principles Murray pursued over her lifetime and which informed her work.

The restored blue-and-white wood framed house was built by Murray's grandfather, Robert Fitzgerald, a Union Civil War veteran and esteemed brickmaker with his brother Richard Fitzgerald. Murray's parents died young, and she was the only one of six siblings sent from Baltimore, Maryland, to Durham to live with her mother's family. Murray's aunt, Pauline Fitzgerald Dame, raised her in this home. "There is definitely a sense of Pauli Murray in the house," says Executive Director Barbara Lau. "I think this was a place that Pauli . . . found a sense of belonging and was incredibly surrounded by love. There's a way that this house is really Pauli's touchstone." A plaque commemorating Murray and her family stands outside the home.

The center coordinates **walking tours** of the historic neighborhood. The center also develops programming around her birthday on November 20. In the past, folks have met at Lyon Park Elementary School (1309 Halley St.) where Murray's Aunt Pauline taught. There, the center offers awards for a youth poetry contest, poetry readings, interactive exhibits about

PAULI MURRAY

Black, queer, and feminist, Pauli Murray, who grew up here in Durham, played many roles during her lifetime: legal theorist, civil rights activist, and the first ordained African American woman Episcopal priest in 1977. She was also a co-founder of the National Organization for Women.

It was Murray, while a student at Howard Law School, who posited the idea of challenging the "separate" part of the separate but equal doctrine established by *Plessy v. Ferguson.* It was a wild idea at the time, but Murray was firm in her belief that segregation was a violation of the 13th and 14th amendments. When Thurgood Marshall and the NAACP argued *Brown v. Board of Education,* Murray's contribution undergirded their winning argument.

During Murray's lifetime, her work and activism paralleled civil and human rights movements. She faced racism and gender bias throughout her life, first when she applied to graduate school at the University of North Carolina at Chapel Hill and was rejected because of her race. She was first in her Howard Law School graduating class where she was the lone woman. Being first meant access to a fellowship at Harvard University, which denied her entrance because the school did not allow women. Even Harvard alum President Franklin D. Roosevelt wrote on her behalf, but they still wouldn't let her in. In 1952, she became a victim of McCarthyism based on her associations with progressive-minded people: First Lady Eleanor Roosevelt, Thurgood Marshall, and union leader A. Philip Randolph.

She co-authored with Mary O. Eastwood *Jane Crow and the Law: Sex Discrimination and Title VII* in 1965, which was critical in keeping "sex" in Title VII of the Civil Rights Act of 1964. Her activist bonafides include old-school protests against segregation, such as her 1940 arrest for refusing to sit on broken seats at the back of a bus headed to Durham. While studying law at Howard in the early '40s, she participated in restaurant sit-ins in Washington DC—well before the sit-in movement sparked in Greensboro in 1960.

Murray eventually came to believe the legal issues she spent so much of her life understanding and advocating for were moral issues. She left a tenured professorship at Brandeis University and went to divinity school, which led to her ultimate ordination.

As an Episcopal saint, **St. Titus Episcopal Church** (400 Moline St.; tel. 919/682-5504) dedicates a service to her human and civil rights legacy every July.

Durham activists, opportunities for 'zine making, music, and other activities.

Other Neighborhoods

PAULI MURRAY MURALS

Several murals of Pauli Murray are found in southwest Durham on exterior walls of schools, businesses, and other public places. Depicting Murray at different ages, the murals are a part of the **Face Up: Telling Stories of Community Life** project. See the murals at the following addresses:

- **Pauli Murray, A Youthful Spirit** (2520 Vesson Ave.)
- **Pauli Murray Roots & Soul** (1101 W Chapel Hill St.)
- **Pauli Murray & the Virgen de Guadelupe** (2009 Chapel Hill Rd.)
- **Pauli Murray True Community** (313 Foster St.)
- **Pauli Murray in the World** (117 S Buchanan Blvd.)

TOURS AND LOCAL GUIDES

Walking Tour

★ WHISTLE STOP TOURS

1114 N Hyde Park Ave.; tel. 617/959-2076; www.whistle-stoptours.com

Tour guide Aya Shabu celebrates the fullness of Black history in Durham, including the success of Black Wall Street downtown, Hayti, and the West End, where Pauli Murray grew up. With a background in dance, theater, and storytelling, Shabu bills her 75-minute walking tours as performances that educate and entertain guests who will leave knowing much more about the journey of Black Durham residents from enslavement to freedom to prosperity. Whistle Stop Tours offers several experiences, including **Pauli's Durham: History of Racial Segregation in the West End, Hayti: Free Soil Haven,** and **Black Wall Street: The Price of Progress,** all of which are $450 for 25 participants. Shabu can also design an experience according to your interests.

On all her tours, Shabu details the proud history of Durham, the Capital of the Black Middle Class, as scholar E. Franklin Frazier called it. Though hemmed in by segregation, African Americans in Durham managed to build institutions that were the envy of the Black elite. Shabu describes the walking journey as such: "The words that I write and the gestures my body make are my libation—a pouring out of names, an invocation of the men and women who gave life to Durham's African American neighborhoods."

Book a tour directly with Shabu or coordinate with the **Pauli Murray Center for History and Social Justice** or the **Hayti Heritage Center.**

FOOD

Downtown

BORICUA SOUL

705 Willard St.; tel. 919/902-0520; www.boricuasoulnc.com; Tues.-Thurs. 4:30pm-7pm, Fri. 4:30pm-7:30pm, Sat. 3:30pm-7:30pm; $8.50-12.50

Toriano and Serena Fredericks's Boricua Soul started out as a popular food truck, and they have expanded to a storefront on the American Tobacco Campus. Puerto Rican and soul food dishes include the Boricua Soul Bowl, slow-roasted pork topped with pickled red onions and served with arroz con gandules (rice and peas), collard greens, macaroni and cheese, and tostones. Golden sweet fried maduros (plantains) are on the menu.

THE BEYU CAFFE

341 W Main St.; tel. 919/683-1058; www.beyucaffe.com; Mon.-Fri. 8am-5pm, Sat. 9am-6pm, Sun. 9am-4pm; from $2

The Beyu Caffe is a stylish hotspot for coffee and spirits, whether you crave an Oprah Mocha, Dirty Chai, or Bull City Punch made with Bacardi and Malibu rums with pineapple juice, grenadine, and fresh lemon juice. The food menu features a variety of omelets, along with French toast made with challah and sweet potato bread in a variety of flavors. Lunch and dinner includes cornbread collard bites and the triple decker Sock-It-To-Me Grilled Cheese, along with sandwiches, soups, salads, and desserts.

DAME'S CHICKEN AND WAFFLES

530 Foster St., Ste. 130; tel. 919/682-9235; www.dameschickenwaffles.com; Mon. 10am-3pm, Tues.-Thurs. 11am-8pm, Sat. 10am-9pm, Sun. 10am-4pm; $12-14

Dame's Chicken and Waffle owners Randy Wadsworth and Damion "Dame" Moore became best friends as college roommates studying business at the University of North Carolina-Greensboro, where they pledged the same fraternity, Omega Psi Phi. For a while, they did the corporate thing. The entrepreneurial Moore was catering and Wadsworth co-owned a bar when they decided to open a restaurant in 2010. "Back in 2010, there was nothing really in downtown Durham that was giving us something cultural, something off the beaten path," Wadsworth said of their dream to make something special. Today, "everybody comes to Dame's," including celebrities, though the general mood is relaxed, friendly, and open to all: "We're probably one of the most diverse restaurants."

As the name suggests, the menu centers on chicken and waffles. The dish, Wadsworth explains, harkens back to the jazz age: "Back in the day, [musicians] would finish their sets, then basically get what was leftover in the kitchen. So, they had chicken, but one day they put a waffle with that bad boy, and it was on from that point on."

A sample of the Dame's Chicken and Waffles's menu turns up: Dame's Daily Dish allows you to choose your chicken and pair it with a classic waffle and shmear; Light Brown Leghorns features four drumsticks, a waffle drizzled with caramel and cashews, and chocolate hazelnut shmear; and A Hot Mess comes with two eggs with cheese, turkey bacon or sausage, and grits drizzled with ketchup and hot sauce (no exceptions). Sides include mean (spicy) greens, Southern potato salad, and more. Portions are large. The Jazz Age also informs the vibe, with photos of jazz musicians decorating the walls.

There are three Dame's locations, including a branch in Greensboro.

SALTBOX SEAFOOD JOINT

2637 Durham-Chapel Hill Blvd. and 608 N Mangum St.; tel. 919/237-3499; www.saltboxseafoodjoint.com; Tues-Sat. 11am-8pm; from $14

Don't leave Raleigh without tasting what Chef Ricky Moore's got cooking at two Saltbox locations. Moore sources his menu from North Carolina fishermen, which is why the menu changes daily and dishes are served simply prepared. Offerings include mahi mahi, Southern flounder, grey trout, gag grouper, bay scallops, shrimp, oysters, and catfish. Journalist, historian, and bon vivant Cynthia Greenlee says Saltbox has the "freshest catch in town" and "oyster po' boys that are ridiculous!"

THE PALACE INTERNATIONAL

1104 Broad St.; tel. 919/416-4922; www.thepalaceinternational.com; Tues.-Sat. 11am-9pm; $14-19

The family-owned downtown restaurant is a Durham institution that serves up dishes from the Motherland. Dishes include whole fried fish, Jollof rice, curry goat served with rice and collard greens, samosas (beef, veggies, and special), and dengu na chapati (green lentils cooked with curry and coconut milk and served with rice, cabbage, and chapati).

DURHAM FOOD HALL

530 Foster St., Suite. 1; tel. 919/908-9339; www.durhamfoodhall.com; Sun.-Fri. noon-7pm, Sat. 9am-7pm

This food hall a few steps away from Dame's Chicken and Waffles is an incubator for local chefs. It's a communal and casual dining environment where small plates feature the freshest ingredients from a variety of cuisines: Munch on wood-fired Neapolitan-style pizza or artisanal gelato at **Napoli Pizzeria & Gelateria,** or try **Lula & Sadie's** eggnog-pecan French toast, tomato salad, or chicken pot pie. Other options includeing everything from bagels and coffee to seafood. The **Auctioneer Bar,** in the center, features locally brewed beer, craft cocktails, and wine.

Along Fayetteville Street

THE CHICKEN HUT

3019 Fayetteville St.; tel. 919/682-5697; www.chickenhutnc.weebly.com; Mon.-Fri. 11:30am-3:30pm; $9

This neighborhood institution has served homecooked meals to several generations of Durham families. The menu changes daily, but you can always get fried chicken. Other options include baked spaghetti, pig feet, fried shrimp and fish, neckbones, and more. Desserts go from peach and apple cobblers to red velvet cake, banana pudding, and pound cake.

Photos (top to bottom): brunch at Dame's Chicken and Waffles; french toast at Lula & Sadie's in Durham Food Hall; the Durham Hotel

ACCOMMODATIONS

Downtown

THE DURHAM HOTEL

315 E Chapel Hill St.; tel. 919/768-8830; https://thedurham.com; $189

The Durham Hotel offers 53 rooms with a modern touch in downtown Durham. It's also a hotspot for rooftop jazz on Thursday nights and Sundays during brunch. Other rooftop events include yoga and story time.

GETTING THERE

Air

Raleigh-Durham International Airport (tel. 919/840-2123; www.rdu.com) is about 15 miles south of Durham. A cab into Durham from the airport costs about $43 and takes around 30 minutes.

Train

Durham's **Amtrak** Station (601 W Main St.; tel. 800/872-7245; Sun.-Sat. 8am-11am and 4:30pm-7:30pm), located downtown, is served by the Piedmont and The Carolinian lines.

Bus

Durham **Greyhound** station (515 W Pettigrew St.; tel. 919/687-4800; Mon.-Sat. 7am-4pm and 7am-11pm) is located downtown.

Car

To get to Durham from:

- **Greensboro:** Take **I-40 East** for around 50 miles (1 hour).
- **Raleigh:** Take **I-40 West** and **NC 147 North** for a total of around 25 miles (30 minutes).

Raleigh

Raleigh's biggest contribution to the movement was the creation of SNCC in 1960, spearheaded by Ella Baker. Shaw University, Baker's alma mater, is also home to Estey Hall, the first building ever constructed for the higher education of Black women, built in 1873. The city's Black Main Street on E. Hargett is where black entrepreneurs and professionals thrived in the 1910s and '20s. Buildings from that era still standing include the Grand United Order of Odd Fellows (117 E. Hargett St.) and Raleigh Furniture Building (119 E. Hargett St.). The Delaney Building (133 E. Hargett St.) stands erect as a testament to its builder, Dr. Lemuel T. Delaney, the first practicing Black surgeon at St. Agnes Hospital, the first state nursing school for Black people on the campus of St. Augustine's University.

Raleigh is also the capital of North Carolina. Like many cities in the South, it shares an uncomfortable space with both civil rights and Confederate history.

ORIENTATION

Most points of interest are located **downtown,** which is bordered by U.S. 401 to the west, Raleigh Boulevard to the east, and Brookside Street and Glascock Drive to the north. The neighborhood stretches just beyond Martin Luther King Boulevard in the south.

SIGHTS

Dr. Martin Luther King Jr. Memorial Gardens

1215 Martin Luther King Jr. Blvd.; tel. 919/996-4115; www.raleighnc.gov/places/

THE GREEN BOOK

1956 edition of The Green Book

During the Jim Crow era, the United States was full of sundown towns where Black people, Jews, Native Americans, Mexican Americans, and Chinese Americans were expected to be out of the city limits once the sun went down at the risk of bodily harm. For Black travelers, traveling by car could be a life-or-death affair if they met with Ku Klux Klan members or other White segregationists. Other obstacles were presented for Black people when their cars broke down and they were denied service, or when they needed a bite to eat or a place to stay, since Whites-only hotels and restaurants obviously did not welcome Black people.

Published from 1936-67, *The Negro Travelers' Green Book* helped Black travelers navigate this unwelcoming national landscape, especially the Jim Crow South. Victor Hugo Green's travel guide, organized by states and cities, listed businesses and homes where it was safe to eat, sleep, and secure services, such as service stations. The book initially cost 25 cents and up to $1.95 for later editions. A go-to for Black travelers concerned about safety, the book sold about 15,000 copies annually and was sold at churches and gas stations, among other places.

In Raleigh, you can see a 1959 edition of the *Green Book* at the **North Carolina Museum of History**. The **Historic Magnolia House** (page 360) in Greensboro was listed as a safe stop in the *Green Book.* Today, you can enjoy Sunday brunch here.

dr-martin-luther-king-jr-memorial-gardens; daily sunrise-sunset; free

These gardens, located on the eastern edge of downtown, are devoted to King's legacy and pursuit of equality, dignity, justice, and peace. King is depicted standing tall, wearing his doctoral robes, hands gesturing, in a 6'2" bronze statue. The King Memorial Wall, composed of 2,500 bricks with the names of people, churches, businesses, and organizations that helped make this space possible, surrounds the statue. The statue is also accompanied by a 12-ton granite monument featuring flowing water that honors local people who powered the movement.

This is the first U.S. park dedicated to King and the civil rights movement, and King's birthday has been celebrated here with a wreath-laying ceremony. The memorial debuted in 1989, and the King statue was dedicated in 1997. Find the installation in the southwest quadrant of Martin Luther King Boulevard and Rock Quarry Road.

Your best bet is to visit at dawn or dusk: There's a stillness embedded in the golden hour that enhances peace and

Photos (top to bottom): North Carolina Museum of History; Dr. Martin Luther King Jr. Memorial Gardens; sign in front of Estey Hall at Shaw University

contemplation. The landscape includes a variety of trees, shrubs, and flowering plants. Benches are available, as is a picnic shelter with a grill and 17 tables that can accommodate up to 133 people for $15 an hour. Parking is limited to 30 cars.

North Carolina Museum of History

5 E Edenton St.; tel. 919/814-7000; www.ncmuseumofhistory.org; Mon.-Sat. 9am-5pm, Sun. noon-5pm; free

This 55,000-square-foot museum focuses on general North Carolina history with a few exhibits that relate to Black history specifically.

In "The Story of North Carolina" exhibit on the first floor is an original Woolworth lunch counter and upholstered stools where the Salisbury, North Carolina, sit-in took place, following the seminal February 1, 1960, sit-in in Greensboro. Accompanying the counter is an inviting "Visit Woolworth's Luncheonette" sign, along with a smaller "Lunch Dept. Temporarily Closed" sign, the likes of which was used to deter Black patrons intent on making a statement by sitting in.

The museum also features an encased 1959 edition of *The Negro Travelers' Green Book,* the annual guide created by postal carrier Victor Hugo Green, and a baseball jersey belonging to Negro league first base legend Walter "Buck" Leonard of the Homestead Grays. A cabin from Martin County, east of Raleigh, that was inhabited by seven enslaved African Americans in 1860, is also featured.

What this museum lacks in permanent physical exhibits, it makes up for in programming and an online civil rights exhibit.

Shaw University

721 S Wilmington St.; tel. 919/546-8200; www.shawu.edu

Shaw University was founded in 1865 as part of robust, church-based movement to provide educational opportunities for freedmen after the war. Women soon followed. **Estey Hall** (tel. 919/546-8275; Mon.-Fri. 9am-4pm; free), the oldest building on campus, was built in 1874 to serve these women with classes in home economics, music, art, and religion. (They had an option to take courses offered to male students.) Estey Hall is the first higher education edifice built for African American women. The four-story building was constructed with bricks that were made on the grounds. Located on the 100 block of E South Street on the Shaw campus, Estey Hall served as a women's dormitory for a time and is now used for meetings and events. The building is listed on the National Register of Historic Places.

Shaw is also famous as the location where the **Student Nonviolent Coordinatng Committee (SNCC)** was founded in 1960. The building where the founding took place is no longer there, but a sign marks the occasion.

Ella Baker, who was instrumental in the founding of SNCC, was herself a student at Shaw, where she challenged university policies she considered unfair and graduated as valedictorian. Other notable Shaw graduates include Dorothy Cotton, an SCLC executive staffer and close King confidante who spent several years as education director, and Rita Walters, a civil rights advocate who became the first Black woman elected to the Los Angeles City Council. Formerly enslaved William Henry Steward graduated from Shaw and went on to become a civil rights activist and first appointed Black letter carrier in Kentucky. He founded the *American Baptist* newspaper.

Shaw has established the Center for Racial and Social Justice to feature lectures, research activities, and academic programs that build on the institution's social justice foundation. The center's Ella Baker Institute aims to ground students in leadership and

SNCC IS BORN

Ella Baker saw that the February 1, 1960, Greensboro sit-in ignited a spark in Black student communities. She considered this as an opportunity to harness youthful energy and ideas. According to SNCC records, she convinced SCLC head King to invest $800 to host a conference at Shaw where student leaders could meet and strategize for something beyond local activism. The meeting included about 200 student leaders from several states, including many from the Nashville sit-in movement who hashed out the goals and agreed on a commitment to nonviolent direct action.

"It was a very heady meeting," says Dr. David Forbes, a retired Shaw divinity school dean and pastor who was a sophomore at Shaw when he helped plan the event, and who had been arrested while participating in a Woolworth sit-in in Raleigh. "By Easter 1960, hundreds of us had already been arrested and gone to jail. . . . We talked about what it was like to go to jail, how were we processed, what kind of violence did we meet, how were we able to mobilize local communities."

Rev. James Lawson recalls that the meeting took place with "a great deal of unity," and that "a lot of White students in the North, the East, and the West supported that campaign."

King hoped a student wing of the SCLC would emerge from the meeting. Baker had other ideas. (She and King didn't always see eye to eye because she didn't believe his male-centric, charismatic leadership that relied on a single personality was good for the movement.) She championed autonomy from existing civil rights organizations and group-centered leadership. Student leaders agreed the group would be temporary and function as its own entity.

Right after the weekend meeting, on April 16, 1960, King addressed a crowd at Raleigh Memorial Auditorium, according to the King Institute at Stanford. He described the exciting new organization as "a revolt against those Negroes in the middle class who have indulged themselves in big cars and ranch-style homes rather than in joining a movement for freedom."[1]

SNCC, which would remain separate from the SCLC, would go on to organize Freedom Rides and play a role in the 1963 March on Washington for Jobs and Freedom. They directed Black voter registration drives and participated in Freedom Summer 1964. Stokely Carmichael and other SNCC members helped Lowndes County, Alabama, residents launch the Lowndes County Freedom Organization that later became known as the Black Panther Party.

"As a sophomore, I recognized it was a historical moment, but I was too young at the time to fully appreciate what the implications would be down the years," says Forbes. "Had there not been a SNCC there would not be a civil rights act, voting rights act—we would not know the name Barack Obama. . . . The modern marches and movements take great inspiration from what we did."

critical-thinking skills through training, workshops, and opportunities to put their learning into practice at local organizations. Other projects include a Black Church Initiative to train change agents in church and society; the Griot Storytelling Project, to harness the West Africa tradition of storytelling; and Legacies of Slavery Project to address commemoration and memory by leveraging the resources and archives of sister HBCUs in the mid-Atlantic region. Prospective students interested in the HBCU experience should contact admissions to set up a tour led by a peer guide.

FOOD

SWEET TEA & CORNBREAD GRILL AND EATERY

5 E Edenton St.; www.ncmuseumofhistory.org/sweet-tea-and-cornbread; Mon.-Sat. 11am-3pm; $3-9

The granddaughter of the beloved Mildred "Mama Dip" Council, Tonya Council runs this eatery inside the North Carolina Museum of History that features Southern favorites and more. The menu includes a chicken-fried-steak sandwich and chicken salad croissant, burgers, hot dogs, salad, and soups. The elder Council, who passed away in 2018, ran Mama Dip's in Chapel Hill and was a fixture on "best of" lists. The legacy continues.

ORO RESTAURANT

18 E Martin St.; tel. 919/239-4010; www.oro-raleigh.com; Tues-Thurs. 5pm-9pm; $9-$35

The dinner menu specializes in platters that are meant to be shared or small plates that invite a curious palate. "Center of the Table Features" include Chilean sea bass served with miso butter and filet mignon served with potato gratin. Other items include wok-fried brussels, smoky ribs, and mini baked brie. Desserts are housemade and feature banana bread pudding and The Campfire (smores for the table). The atmosphere at the restaurant inside the PNC Building is chic and casual, with a nine-foot fireplace on the mezzanine and a full bar.

ACCOMMODATIONS

The **Raleigh Marriott City Center** (500 Fayetteville St.; tel. 919/833-1120; www.marriott.com) is a downtown hotel that features 391 rooms, 10 suites on 17 floors. The **Rye Bar** offers a soft place to land and have a drink, and **Southern Kitchen** offers dishes enhanced by local ingredients.

GETTING THERE

Air

Raleigh-Durham International Airport (tel. 919/840-2123; www.rdu.com) is about 16 miles northwest of Raleigh. A cab into Raleigh from the airport costs about $40 and takes around 30 minutes.

Train

Amtrak arrives at **Raleigh Union Station** (510 W Martin St.; tel. 800/872-7245; Sun.-Sat. 7am-noon and 4pm-10:30pm). The city is served by the following Amtrak lines: The Carolinian, from Charlotte to Cary to Raleigh to New York; The Piedmont, from Charlotte to Cary to Raleigh; and The Silver Star, from Florida to Raleigh to New York.

Bus

Raleigh's **Greyhound** station (2210 Capital Blvd.; tel. 919/834-8275), located a couple miles northwest of downtown, is open 24 hours daily.

Car

To reach Raleigh from:

- **Durham:** Take **NC 147 South** and **I-40 East** for a total of around 25 miles (30 minutes).

- **Richmond, Virginia:** Take **I-95 South** for around 175 miles (2.5 hours).

GETTING AROUND

The best way to get around Raleigh is by car, whether it's your own, taxi, or ride share. Once downtown, visitors can take the Raleigh Transit Authority's free circulator bus, the **R-Line,** to get around the core of downtown. It goes past Shaw University for those headed to see Estey Hall. It runs every 15 minutes daily: Mon.-Wed. 7am-11pm, Thurs.-Sat. 7am-2:15am, and Sun. 1pm-8pm. Go to https://goraleigh.org for details. In 2020, during the coronavirus pandemic, buses stopped running at 6pm.

Richmond and Farmville

Many of Virginia's civil rights contributions are tied to the pursuit of legal remedies: The Supreme Court ruled in *Morgan v. Virginia* (1946) that racial segregation on commercial interstate buses violated the constitution's commerce clause. *Johnson v. Virginia* (1963) led to the desegregation of Southern juries. *Loving v. Virginia* (1967) famously ruled that laws banning interracial marriage violated constitutionally protected rights to equal protection and due process.

RICHMOND AND FARMVILLE'S TOP 3

1. Celebrating the courage and ingenuity of Barbara Johns, the 16-year-old student who staged a walkout at her all-Black high school in 1951. The school has been reimagined as the **Robert Russa Moton Museum** (page 389).

2. Reflecting on the Emancipation Oak, a replica of a tree at Hampton University that's significant in Black history, at the **Black History Museum & Cultural Center of Virginia** (page 394).

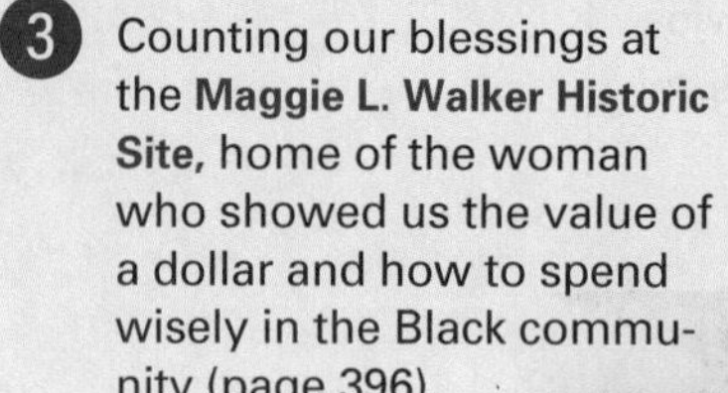

3. Counting our blessings at the **Maggie L. Walker Historic Site,** home of the woman who showed us the value of a dollar and how to spend wisely in the Black community (page 396).

Photos (top to bottom): the main building of the Robert Russa Moton Museum; the Emancipation Oak in the Black History Museum & Cultural Center of Virginia; Maggie L. Walker Historic Site. Previous: the Virginia Civil Rights Memorial by sculptor Stanley Bleifeld

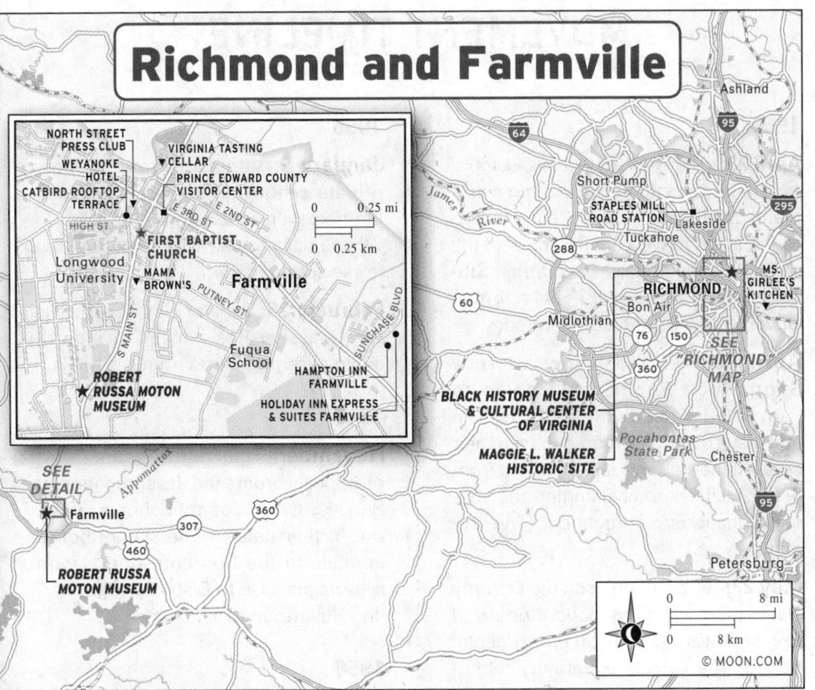

Another famous landmark case, *Brown v. Board of Education* (1954), also sprung, in part, from actions in Virginia. In 1951, a fed-up 16-year-old, Barbara Johns, led a walkout at her all-Black high school, Robert Russa Moton High, in Farmville, Virginia, to protest the school's poor conditions. The ensuing case, *Davis v. County School Board of Prince Edward County,* was added to the four other cases that formed *Brown v. Board of Education.*

The movement in Virginia also produced the Richmond 34, a group of Virginia Union University students who were convicted of trespassing when they refused to leave Thalhimers' Richmond Room restaurant in 1960. The students were inspired by the Greensboro sit-ins launched by four students at North Carolina Agricultural & Technical University (now North Carolina A&T University). In Richmond, demonstrators kept up the pressure, and several businesses quietly desegregated their lunch counters. But it took an appeal all the way up to the U.S. Supreme Court to get those 34 convictions vacated. In 2018, they discovered the charges still on their records and had them expunged.

Today, the school where Johns led a walkout is now the Robert Russa Moton Museum, where classrooms have been reimagined as galleries that tell the story of Johns and her classmates. The courageous student is also commemorated annually statewide every April 23 (the anniversary of the walkout) on Barbara Rose Johns Day.

The state capitol of Richmond, meanwhile, is home to the historic Black neighborhood of Jackson Ward, a Black history museum, and a bronze-and-granite monument on the grounds of the Virginia State Capitol that honors Johns. Etched into the marble is a quote by Johns: "It seemed like reaching for the moon."

MOVEMENT TIMELINE

1951

April 23: In Farmville, 16-year-old sophomore Barbara Johns incites her classmates at all-Black Robert Russa Moton High School to walk out in protest of the school's substandard conditions. Students reach out to civil rights attorney Oliver W. Hill Sr. the very same day.

April 25: Hill and fellow attorney Spottswood Robinson III come to Farmville to meet with students. The attorneys eventually agree to take their case—if the students shift their ask from better facilities to challenging the constitutionality of segregation. (The students agree.)

May 23: Hill and Robinson file *Dorothy Davis et al. v. County School Board of Prince Edward County* on the students' behalf. The case is eventually folded into four others that comprised *Brown v. Board of Education.*

1954

May 17: The U.S. Supreme Court decides *Brown v. Board of Education,* ruling that racial segregation in public schools violates the 14th Amendment's equal-protection clause.

June 25: Virginia Governor Thomas B. Stanley states: "I shall use every legal means at my command to continue segregated schools in Virginia."[1]

1955

May 31: U.S. Supreme Court issues *Brown II,* which mandates that public schools desegregate "with all deliberate speed"—a vague timeline that allows slow movement by segregationists.

June 26: The Board of Supervisors in Prince Edward County (where Farmville is located) votes to stop funding public schools—the only county in the nation to do so.

1956

January 9: Virginians vote to allow private school tuition grants, allowing taxpayer dollars to be funneled to Whites-only private schools committed to racial segregation.

February 25: Senator Harry Byrd calls for "Massive Resistance," a plan to avoid desegregating Virginia schools.

1957

November: The Fourth Circuit Court of Appeals orders the desegregation of Prince Edward County Schools "without further delay." The school board appeals to the Supreme Court, who returns the case to District Judge Sterling Hutcheson to set a timeline.

1958

August 4: Judge Hutcheson determines that "all deliberate speed" means "continued delays."

September 15-17: Governor J. Lindsay Almond Jr. closes schools in Norfolk, Charlottesville, and Front Royal, and threatens to close others that try to desegregate.

1959

May 5: The U.S. Fourth Circuit Court of Appeals orders Prince Edward County to desegregate its schools by September 1, 1959.

June 26: Rather than desegregate, Prince Edward County Board of Supervisors decides to stop funding public schools for the 1959-1960 school year, thereby shutting them down.

September 10: All Prince Edward County public schools close. White students shift to the private Prince Edward Academy. Many Black students, meanwhile, miss out on an education.

1960

February 20: About 200 students stage sit-ins at segregated Richmond department store lunch counters.

February 22: Thirty-four Virginia Union University (VUU) students are arrested and convicted of trespassing during a sit-in at Thalhimer's Richmond Room restaurant.

1961

May 4: Thirteen Freedom Riders, fresh from training in Washington DC, stop in Richmond on their way down South.

1963

February 28: President John F. Kennedy speaks out against the slow pace of desegregation in schools and invokes Congress to take action.

June 10: The Supreme Court overturns the convictions of the Richmond 34.

Sept. 16: Kennedy spearheads the Free School Association to provide a year of school for Prince Edward County students regardless of race.

1964

May 25: The Supreme Court orders the Prince Edward County Board of Supervisors to reopen schools.

September 8: Prince Edward County schools reopen after five years of closure. Of 1,500 students who show up, all except eight are Black.

1967

June 12: *Loving v. Virginia results* in the striking down of laws prohibiting interracial marriage. (Today, the date is unofficially commemorated as "Loving Day.")

2003

June 15: Prince Edward County holds a graduation ceremony for the "Lost Generation," as the Black students affected by the five-year school closure came to be known.

2008

July 8: The Prince Edward Board of Supervisors approves a resolution apologizing for closing the schools from 1959-1964.

July 21: The Virginia Civil Rights Memorial honoring Barbara Johns is unveiled on the Capitol grounds.

2017

The state of Virginia declares April 23 Barbara Johns Day.

Farmville students entering Mary E. Branch School, a "Free School," in September 1963

PEOPLE WHO MADE THE MOVEMENT

GROUPS

Richmond 34: Virginia Union University students who staged a sit-in Thalhimers' Richmond Room restaurant in 1960 and were subsequently convicted of trespassing. Their names are: Leroy M. Bray Jr., Gordon Coleman Jr., Gloria C. Collins, Robert B. Dalton, Marise L. Ellison, Joseph E. Ellison, Wendell T. Foster Jr., Anderson J. Franklin, Donald Vincent Goode, Woodrow B. Grant, Albert Van Graves Jr., George Wendall Harris, Thalma Y. Hickman, Joanna Hinton, Carolyn Ann Horne, Richard C. Jackson, Elizabeth Patricia Johnson, Ford Tucker Johnson Jr., Milton Johnson, Celia E. Jones, Clarence A. Jones, John J. McCall, Frank George Pinkston, Larry Pridgen, Ceotis L. Pryor, Raymond B. Randolph Jr., Samuel F. Shaw, Charles Melvin Sherrod, Virginia G. Simms, Ronald B. Smith, Barbara A. Thornton, Randolf A. Tobias, Patricia A. Washington, and Lois B. White.

CIVIL RIGHTS FIGURES

Barbara Johns: Sixteen-year-old sophomore who led a walkout at her high school in 1951.

John Arthur Stokes: Classmate of Johns who helped organize the strike by creating a diversion that pulled the school principal off campus.

Rev. L. Francis Griffin: Pastor of First Baptist Church in Farmville who supported the students' efforts to protest for a better school and connected them with the NAACP attorneys who took the case.

Oliver Hill and Spottswood Robinson III: Richmond-based NAACP attorneys who took the case of Moton High School students. They persuaded the students to shift their demand for a new school to pursue integration instead. Robinson filed *Dorothy Davis et al. v. County School Board of Prince Edward County,* then consolidated the case into *Brown v. Board of Education* with several others.

Rev. L. Francis Griffin in 1963

Mildred and Richard Loving: The couple who defied the state's ban on interracial marriage when Mildred, a Black woman with Native American and European blood, and Richard, a White man, married in Washington DC, then went back home to Virginia's Caroline County. They were accused of violating the state's Racial Integrity Act of 1924, sent to jail—while Mildred was pregnant—and told to leave the state and not to come back together for 25 years. Their case, *Loving v. Virginia,* reached the Supreme Court, which outlawed the prohibition against interracial marriage in 1967.

Rev. Wyatt Tee Walker: Minister who organized prayer pilgrimages in Virginia to protest segregation in public accommodations. He also helped circulate King's "Letter From a Birmingham Jail" and organized the March on Washington for Jobs and Freedom.

EARLIER FIGURES

Maggie L. Walker: A resident of Richmond's Jackson Ward and the first Black woman in the nation to found a bank.

ORIENTATION

Richmond, Virginia, is a midsize city that is located about halfway between Washington DC and Raleigh, North Carolina, on I-95. **Farmville,** a rural town that's home to two colleges, is about 65 miles west of Richmond, a 1.5-hour drive.

On this leg of your trip, plan on driving and availing yourself of street parking.

Find the **Richmond Visitors Center** at 405 N. 3rd Street, open daily 9am-5pm. Call tel. 804/783-7450 or visit www.visitrichmondva.com. The **Prince Edward County Visitor Center** is at 121 E. 3rd Street in Farmville (tel. 434/392-1482; https://visitfarmville.com).

PLANNING YOUR TIME

You can cover significant portions of Virginia's civil rights story in a couple of days, with stops in Richmond and in Farmville. Note that several important sights in Richmond and Farmville are closed on Sundays.

CONNECT WITH

Logical next stops are **Washington DC** to the north or **Raleigh** and **Durham,** North Carolina, to the south.

Two Days in Richmond and Farmville

DAY 1: RICHMOND

Spend most of your time on this day in Richmond's historic **Jackson Ward.** Note that both the **Maggie L. Walker Historic Site** and the **Black History Museum & Cultural Center of Virginia** are closed Sunday and Monday, so if you're in Richmond on these days of the week you'll have to make other plans.

1 Head over to the **Maggie L. Walker Historic Site** when it opens at 9am to see the bespoke home owned by the first Black woman in the country to found a bank.

2 Stop for lunch nearby at family-owned **Mama J's Kitchen.**

3 How about a little shopping? **Little Nomad** and Barky's Spiritual Stores are two Black-owned businesses on the western edge of Jackson Ward.

4 Your last big stop of the day is the **Black History Museum & Cultural Center of Virginia,** where you can see an impressive replica of the Emancipation Oak, an important landmark in the state's Black history.

5 Black-owned **Speakeasy Grill** is back near the Maggie L. Walker Historic Site, in Jackson Ward's historic Hippodrome Theater. It's a great place for dinner and a drink.

DAY 2: FARMVILLE

This day is devoted to brave student Barbara Johns. You'll visit the school where she staged her protest, even visiting the auditorium where she implored her classmates to join her. Note that the big site of the day, **Robert Russa Moton Museum,** is closed Sundays.

1 Before leaving Richmond, make a stop at the **Virginia Civil Rights Memorial** on the State Capitol grounds. The commemorative two-sided sculpture of Barbara Johns and other students who participated in her walkout, along with their lawyers, Oliver W. Hill Sr. and Spottswood Robinson III, will set the tone for the rest of the day.

2 When you arrive in Farmville, stop for breakfast or lunch at **Mama Brown's.**

3 Your big stop of the day is the **Robert Russa Moton Museum** (closed Sun., opens at noon Mon.-Sat.), where a brave Barbara Johns incited a massively influential walkout in 1951. Plan to spend around an hour to 90 minutes walking through the classrooms (now galleries) at this former high school.

4 Before leaving Farmville, make a point to walk by **First Baptist Church,** where Rev. L. Francis Griffin was pastor in the early 1950s. Griffin encouraged the students' protest and connected them to NAACP attorneys who would elevate their cause to a national level.

Farmville

When 16-year-old sophomore Barbara Johns looked around her all-Black high school in Farmville, Virginia, 1951, she saw inequality: 450 Black students squeezed into a one-story brick building constructed to hold 180; hand-me-down furniture and textbooks; no gym, no science lab, no cafeteria. Previous requests for a new school had resulted, disappointingly, in the construction of two "god-awful tarpaper shacks" as the students called them—"adult sized chicken coops," according to Cameron Patterson, the managing director of the Robert Mussa Moton Museum, which now occupies the school's main building—meant to handle student overflow. The nearby school for Whites, meanwhile, was amply resourced, with lots of classrooms, a gymnasium, and other necessities. Johns complained to a teacher, whose straightforward reply—"Why don't you do something about it?"—became a catalyst for change on a national scale.

Seeking a forum to address her fellow students, Johns orchestrated a plan to gather the entire student body into the auditorium by forging notes to teachers announcing a school assembly. Meanwhile, classmate Arthur Stokes called the school and asked for Principal Jones in a disguised voice. Stokes told the principal that a few of his students were causing a disturbance downtown at the train station, and he ought to come down and handle it, which the principal did.

When the teachers and students arrived in the auditorium, the teachers were asked to leave. It was suggested that leaving was for their own good so they would not be implicated in what was to come, Patterson says. With football players guarding the auditorium doors, Johns took to the stage and made an impassioned plea for a walkout to demand a new school. Fellow students were afraid they would get in trouble at school—or worse, arrested. But walk they did. They picketed the school until told they were trespassing and stayed on strike for two weeks.

The students' petition eventually reached the NAACP. The ensuing case, *Davis v. County School Board of Prince*

GET INTO THE RHYTHM

- **Marvin Gaye, "Save The Children"**: In a spoken-word style, Gaye asked, who really cares? This single appears on *What's Goin' On* (1971), a contemplative protest album that pierced the public conversation.
- **Gil Scott-Heron, "The Revolution Will Not Be Televised"**: A timeless social critique about the disconnect between protests in the streets and consumerism, this urgent spoken-word masterpiece was first released on Heron's debut album, *Small Talk at 125th and Lenox,* and is part of the National Recording Registry at the Library of Congress.

Edward County, was added to the four other cases that formed the landmark *Brown v. Board of Education.* Of all five cases, this was the only one spearheaded by students. In May 1954, the Supreme Court affirmed what the students always knew: Separate is *not* equal.

As a quiet and reserved girl, Johns proved to be a sleeping giant. Between her parents, grandparents, and uncle, Rev. Vernon Johns (the pioneering activist pastor at Dexter Avenue Baptist Church in Montgomery who preceded Dr. Martin Luther King Jr. at the helm), she had family support to bolster her purpose. As an early standard-bearer, she showed what it looks like to get organized, speak up, and take a chance on change.

Today, visitors looking for inspiration can visit Robert Russa Moton High, where Johns took a stand back in 1951. The school, which now functions as a museum, is considered by many as the birthplace of the modern, student-led civil rights movement.

SIGHTS

★ Robert Russa Moton Museum

900 Griffin Blvd.; tel. 434/315-8775; www.motonmuseum.org; Mon.-Sat. noon-4pm; free

This museum is located in the main building of the former Robert Russa Moton High School, an all-Black school during the Jim Crow era. This is where, on April 23, 1951, sophomore Barbara Johns gave an impassioned speech to her fellow classmates on the auditorium stage, catalyzing a walk-out in protest of the school's inferior facilities.

Your museum visit begins in Gallery I, the auditorium where Johns spoke, which retains its original floors and fixtures. Here, a 20-minute film featuring the late Johns and other students who took part in the strike sets the tone for the museum experience.

The galleries that follow (there are six in all) are housed in former classrooms and tell a chronological story, beginning with life in a "separate but equal" society and ending with the final gallery, called Rebirth, which evokes the feeling of success and completion students must have had when the school became accessible. Throughout, images, interactive displays, and first-person accounts narrate the students' journey. Exhibits introduce local players, such as Rev. L. Francis Griffin, a Baptist minister who connected the students to the Richmond branch of the NAACP. Exhibits also cover the 1902 Virginia constitution, which codifies Jim

Photos (top to bottom): Galleries 6 (Rebirth), 1 (Studio Ammons—the original auditorium where Johns spoke to classmates), and 5 (Prince Edward County Says No) in the Robert Russa Moton Museum

Crow policies and explicitly states that Black and White children would not be educated in the same environment. Visitors can see indentations from desks and chairs in the walls, evoking the former classroom space. In the museum bookstore is a copy of the letter students wrote to NAACP civil rights attorneys that turned out to be massively influential, prompting the filing of a lawsuit that later joined *Brown v. Board of Education*.

It's possible to explore this sight at your own pace, but groups of five or more who prefer a guided **tour** should reserve at least 10 business days in advance by emailing info@motonmuseum.org or calling 434/315-8775, ext. 6. Plan to spend around an hour to 90 minutes on a self-guided tour of this sight.

The museum is a National Historic Landmark designed to maintain historic views and plantings of the period. It is also a stop on the official U.S. Civil Rights Trail.

First Baptist Church

100 S Main St.; tel. 434/391-1279

Rev. L. Francis Griffin, aka "The Fighting Preacher," was pastor of this church at the time of Johns's walkout, and he is heralded for supporting the Black students in their protest. He connected the students to the Richmond NAACP, which took their case all the way to the Supreme Court. Griffin's work stretches back earlier than this. In the 1940s, he worked with the Black parent-teacher association to petition county officials to improve learning conditions for Black students. Later, in 1962, Griffin was elected president of the Virginia State Conference of the NAACP.

Listed on the National Register of Historic Places, First Baptist Church is a historic Black church built in the late 1800s. The Gothic Revival building is one story with pointed arch windows with stained-glass and milk panes. The sanctuary features original pews and bead board wainscoting. In the '50s and '60s, First Baptist hosted several meetings to discuss desegregation.

First Baptist Church is still thriving years after Griffin helped the striking students with their cause. Make a point to walk by the church while you are in Farmville and reflect on what it means to sustain a community generation after generation.

FOOD

MAMA BROWN'S

308 D S Main St.; tel. 434/315-5688; Fri.-Sat. 11am-9pm, Sun. 1pm-8pm, Mon. 11am-8pm; $5-15

Mama Brown's promises to serve you Sunday cooking every day, starting with breakfast platters (biscuits and gravy, salmon cakes, fried ham) and ending with burgers, rice bowls, sandwiches, and a range of dinners: chicken, pork chops, and seafood. Got a taste for chitterlings? Well, Mama Brown's got that too.

NORTH STREET PRESS CLUB

127 North St., tel. 434/392-9444; www.facebook.com/northstreetpressclub; Mon.-Wed. 11am-1:30pm, Thurs.-Sat. 11am-2am, Sun. 11am-2pm; $9-13

Featuring a printing and old-school newspaper theme, North Street Press Club (not a Black-owned business) is a great place to grab a bite, sit on the patio, and even hear live music. Appetizers (found on the "Above the Fold" section of the menu) include treats such as Havarti flatbread topped with chorizo and candied peppers, hummus, and ahi tuna tartar. Other menu items include a variety of tacos and a selection of burgers named for famous newspaper columnists, including Clarence Page, the longtime Washington columnist for the *Chicago Tribune*.

AFTER THE WALK-OUT

Barbara Johns managed to convince her classmates to join her in protest, but what happened after that? Here's how the case made it all the way to the Supreme Court, and what happened in Virginia in the aftermath of *Brown v. Board of Education.*

FROM THE NAACP TO THE SUPREME COURT: 1951-1954

At the behest of Baptist minister Rev. L. Francis Griffin, on the day of the walkout, the students called and then wrote a letter to Oliver Hill and Spottswood Robinson III, civil rights attorneys in Richmond. Hill and Robinson took the students' case and persuaded them to shift their cause away from demanding a new school and toward integration. The day after the walkout, the students also walked to the Farmville courthouse to meet with the White superintendent, T. J. McIlwaine, who tried to gaslight them by insisting their school was just as good as any other in Prince Edward County and that students would get a larger building. The students initially agreed to return to school on May 7, but the situation changed significantly thereafter.

On May 23, 1957, the attorneys filed *Dorothy Davis et al. v. County School Board of Prince Edward County.* (Davis was a 14-year-old ninth-grader and named plaintiff in an NAACP lawsuit filed on behalf of 116 students at Moten High.) The case was eventually added to *Brown v. Board of Education,* the 1954 case in which the Supreme Court ruled that racial segregation of public schools was unconstitutional.

On a local level, Moton Principal M. Boyd Jones was fired, sadly, when county school officials declined to renew his contract in light of a walkout, whose planning he knew nothing about. A Moton teacher, Vera Allen, also lost her job because her daughter participated in the strike. The students' mentor, Rev. Griffin, faced retaliation: His credit was pulled from local stores, and his bills suddenly became due. Similar things happened to other Black Farmville residents too.

NIGHTLIFE

CATBIRD ROOFTOP TERRACE

202 High St.; tel. 434/658-1144; www.hotelweyanoke.com; Thurs.-Fri. 4pm-11pm, Sat. 2pm-11pm

The rooftop terrace of the Weyanoke Hotel offers panoramic views of downtown Farmville. It's not a Black-owned business, but is still a lovely way to spend your evening.

VIRGINIA TASTING CELLAR

201 C Mill St.; tel. 434/392-7255; www.thevatastingcellar.com; Fri. 4pm-7pm, Sat.-Sun. noon-4pm

Enjoy Virginia-made wine, cider, and craft beer served with small plates at this tasting room inside Charley's Waterfront Cafe. Craft beer is quite a thing in Virginia, and this place leans into it with an extensive menu. Start with the "young and effervescent" Amuse-Bouche cider, which is aged in neutral wine barrels and then aged a second time with Viognier skins from a Charlottesville vineyard. Or try The Rosemont Virginia White, which has a crisp flavor like a Pinot Grigio, plus more. The Virginia Tasting Cellar is not a Black-owned business.

"MASSIVE RESISTANCE": 1956-1964

In 1956, Virginia leaders detonated an official policy called Massive Resistance to block school desegregation. The phrase was coined by U.S. senator Harry F. Byrd Sr., a conservative Democrat and former governor. White Prince Edward County officials refused to fund any school that fought segregation. As part of that strategy, Governor Thomas Stanley announced a plan to close any schools under a federal desegregation order.

Even after the watershed *Brown* decision, White resistance to Black progress increased: In 1959, the Prince Edward County Board of Supervisors stopped funding schools for the 1959-1960 school year and forced the closure of county schools. While White students transitioned to a segregation academy, Black students had to leave the county or the state for schooling—or not go at all. The American Friends Committee stepped into to arrange for some students to obtain an education elsewhere by recruiting Black and White host families in several states. Meanwhile, all-White private schools received funding from the state and county in the form of tax credits and donations.

A Supreme Court decision in 1964 forced Prince Edward County schools back open. In sum, 1,500 Black students in Prince Edward County lost out on a formal education during the shutdown. They became known as the Lost Generation.

SCHOOLS REOPEN: 1964

On May 25, 1964, the Supreme Court ruled the Prince Edward County Board of Supervisors was in violation of the 14th Amendment. Prince Edward County schools reopened the following September. Five years since the start of the closure, students, overwhelmingly Black, filed back to class on September 8. It took until the Supreme Court's 1968 *Green et al. v. County School Board of New Kent County* decision for Virginia to get real about desegregating schools. It took forced busing in the 1970s to make school districts across the country comply.

ACCOMMODATIONS

In Farmville, historic **Weyanoke Hotel** (202 High St.; www.hotelweyanoke.com; tel. 434/658-7500; $140) has upscale accommodations with a small-town feel, with a total of 70 guest rooms and suites.

Good accommodations options on the road to Farmville include **Hampton Inn Farmville** (300 Sunchase Blvd.; tel. 434/392-8826; www.hilton.com) or **Holiday Inn Express & Suites Farmville** (300 Sunchase Blvd.; tel. 434/392-8826; www.ihg.com/holidayinnexpress), both located five minutes from Farmville in the direction of Richmond off U.S. 460. The latter has free hot breakfast and an outdoor pool.

GETTING THERE

Farmville is 65 miles west of **Richmond** on U.S. 360 W, about a 1-1.5-hour drive. It's about 135 miles north of **Greensboro, North Carolina** (a 2.5-hour drive via U.S. 20 N and U.S. 360 E), and 115 miles north of **Durham** (2-hour drive via I-85 N and U.S. 15 N). There's also a **Greyhound** (www.greyhound.com) station in town (204 E 3rd St.; tel. 434/392-5153; daily 6am-11pm).

Richmond

Virginia's state capital, Richmond, has the country's oldest elected legislative body. During the civil rights movement, the original Freedom Riders stopped here, sharing a meal at Virginia Union University before continuing deeper into the South.

Notable sites in Richmond include a memorial to Barbara Johns at the state capitol and a Black history museum with a replica oak that holds a prominent place in the state's Black history. It's also worth visiting to experience Jackson Ward, a historically Black neighborhood located in Richmond's downtown that is a National Historic Landmark District. Visitors to Richmond can enjoy a rebirth of the Jackson Ward area by eating in Black-owned restaurants like the Speakeasy Grill (located in the historic Hippodrome Theater) and shopping for just-right gifts in local shops. The neighborhood is populated by two- to three-story brick row houses or buildings with common party walls.

ORIENTATION

Downtown Richmond is roughly bordered by North Belvidere Street to the west, I-95 to the east, the James River to the south, and I-64 to the north (where 64 and 95 overlap). **Jackson Ward** takes up the northwestern portion of downtown, running North Belvidere Street to Third Street and north from West Broad Street to I-95. You'll want to head to 2nd Street for historical sites in the highly walkable Jackson Ward area, where there's ample free parking.

SIGHTS

Jackson Ward

After the Civil War, free Black people and African American soldiers from the North migrated to Jackson Ward, which was originally populated by Germans and European Jews who moved away as African Americans moved in. Here, Black residents created institutions and systems of mutual support despite segregation, and by the early 20th century, Jackson Ward had become a vital Black community known as "Harlem of the South." It was here that Maggie Walker became the first Black woman in the United States to charter a bank in addition to her other enterprises, which included a newspaper. Second Street, known as "The Deuce," was a particular hotspot, where jazz entertainers, including Ella Fitzgerald, Louis Armstrong, Duke Ellington, and Cab Calloway appeared in clubs like the Hippodrome Theater, which opened in 1914 as a Vaudeville venue and served the Chitlin' Circuit.

For more information on the storied neighborhood, check out the **podcast tour** (www.nps.gov/mawa/learn/photosmultimedia) offered by the National Park Service, which touches on Maggie L. Walker and other local characters.

★ BLACK HISTORY MUSEUM & CULTURAL CENTER OF VIRGINIA

122 W Leigh St.; tel. 804/780-9093; www.blackhistorymuseum.org; Tues.-Sat. 10am-5pm; $10 adults, $8 seniors and students, $6 children 4-12

Housed in the old Leigh Street Armory for Black residents in the heart of Jackson Ward, this museum takes visitors on a journey from emancipation, reconstruction, and Jim Crow to desegregation, resistance, and the civil rights era, including the story of local heroes, the Richmond 34. This two-floor museum contains permanent exhibitions on the first floor and temporary exhibitions on the second floor. Throughout, artifacts, photos, videos, and interactive displays enhance the experience.

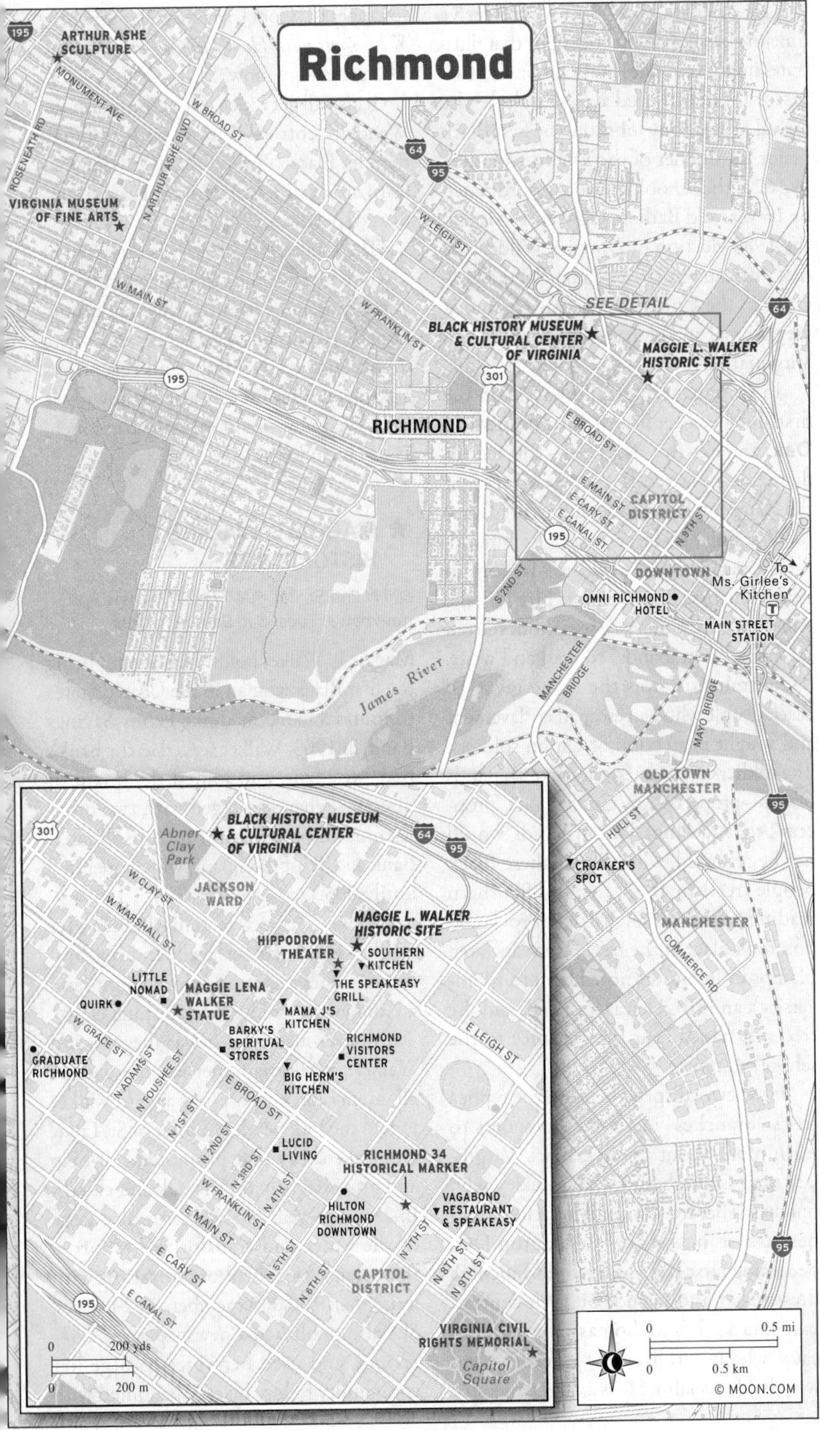
Richmond
ARTHUR ASHE SCULPTURE
MONUMENT AVE
ROSENEATH RD
W BROAD ST
N ARTHUR ASHE BLVD
VIRGINIA MUSEUM OF FINE ARTS
W LEIGH ST
W MAIN ST
W FRANKLIN ST
SEE DETAIL
BLACK HISTORY MUSEUM & CULTURAL CENTER OF VIRGINIA
MAGGIE L. WALKER HISTORIC SITE
RICHMOND
E BROAD ST
E MAIN ST
E CARY ST
E CANAL ST
CAPITOL DISTRICT
N 9TH ST
DOWNTOWN
S 2ND ST
OMNI RICHMOND HOTEL
To Ms. Girlee's Kitchen
MAIN STREET STATION
James River
MANCHESTER BRIDGE
MAYO BRIDGE
OLD TOWN MANCHESTER
HULL ST
CROAKER'S SPOT
MANCHESTER
COMMERCE RD
Abner Clay Park
JACKSON WARD
W CLAY ST
W MARSHALL ST
HIPPODROME THEATER
SOUTHERN KITCHEN
THE SPEAKEASY GRILL
LITTLE NOMAD
MAGGIE LENA WALKER STATUE
QUIRK
MAMA J'S KITCHEN
W GRACE ST
BARKY'S SPIRITUAL STORES
RICHMOND VISITORS CENTER
E LEIGH ST
GRADUATE RICHMOND
N ADAMS ST
N FOUSHEE ST
BIG HERM'S KITCHEN
N 1ST ST
N 2ND ST
N 3RD ST
N 4TH ST
LUCID LIVING
RICHMOND 34 HISTORICAL MARKER
W FRANKLIN ST
HILTON RICHMOND DOWNTOWN
VAGABOND RESTAURANT & SPEAKEASY
N 5TH ST
N 6TH ST
N 7TH ST
N 8TH ST
CAPITOL DISTRICT
VIRGINIA CIVIL RIGHTS MEMORIAL
Capitol Square
0
200 yds
200 m
0.5 mi
0.5 km
© MOON.COM

Get oriented at a 35-foot interactive timeline located on the first floor that illustrates important dates in Richmond's Black history. Highlighted dates include the arrival of Anthony Johnson, the first Black major landholder of the English colonies, in 1621; the school walk-out coordinated by 16-year-old Barbara Johns in 1951; and the 1985 election of Douglas Wilder, the first African American to be elected governor in the United States. Also included are national and global events that inform Virginia's history.

In Commanding Gallery One on the first floor is a replica of **Emancipation Oak,** the massive oak tree—100 feet in diameter—located near the entrance of the Hampton University campus in Hampton, Virginia, 1.5 hours east of Richmond. Emancipation Oak was where Mary Smith Peake, the first Black teacher hired by the American Missionary Association, started teaching "contrabands" to read and write. ("Contrabands" was the name given to Black people who had escaped enslavement and sought protection of Union soldiers. The soldiers considered them contrabands of war—property. Any Confederate "property" that fell into Union hands would not be returned, which made these Black people free.) In 1863, the first Southern reading of the Emancipation Proclamation took place at the tree. Five years later, Hampton Institute (now Hampton University), an HBCU, was founded, and the tree still stands near the entrance to the school's campus.

Interactive displays beneath the replica tree's "branches" invite museumgoers to learn more about notable Black Virginians such as Elizabeth Hobbs Keckley, who purchased her freedom and went into business as a seamstress in Washington DC, becoming First Lady Mary Todd Lincoln's dressmaker and friend; or 19th century bare-knuckle boxer Thomas "Tom" Molineaux, who boxed his way to freedom and worldwide acclaim. He is a direct ancestor to rapper LL Cool J, as revealed on *Finding Your Roots with Henry Louis Gates, Jr.*, the PBS genealogy show.

Kids will get a kick out of the first-floor Wendell Scott exhibition, which honors the first Black NASCAR driver. They can learn about him while "driving" on a simulated speedway.

The Richmond 34 story is rendered in a Woolworth replica dining room found at the museum entrance. This space functions as a community gathering area where events such as weddings and receptions are staged. Or you can just sit down—it is allowed now—and eat your bag lunch, Wi-Fi included.

★ MAGGIE L. WALKER HISTORIC SITE

600 N 2nd St.; tel. 804/771-2017; www.nps.gov/mawa; Tues.-Sat. 9am-5pm; free

Maggie L. Walker holds the honor of being the first Black woman in the United States to found a bank, St. Luke Penny Savings Bank, in 1903. Walker served as the bank's first president, and joined the board of directors when it merged with two other Richmond banks to form Consolidated Bank and Trust Company, which operated until 2005.

Walker's rise was remarkable. Her mother was born enslaved, and her biological father was an Irish immigrant (and a Confederate soldier and hospital clerk). They never married—it was illegal—and Walker's Black stepfather was her dad for all intents and purposes. As a teen, Walker joined the Independent Order of St. Luke, a burial society that promoted self-help and provided help for the sick and elderly. In 1899, 35-year-old Walker took charge of the order and transformed it into a financially successful organization with more than 100,000 members in 24 states. She also published a newspaper, *St. Luke Herald*, and used her voice to urge her community to buy Black. She joined with

The Richmond Planet in 1904 to support a two-year boycott of the city's segregated streetcar system. (The campaign ended in the summer of 1906 when Virginia passed a law mandating the separation of Black and White people on streetcars.) Walker worked to register Black women to vote, and became the first Black woman to run for statewide office in Virginia in 1921. In 1932, she also helped found what was likely the South's first Black Girl Scout troop.

Walker moved into this Jackson Ward row house with her family in 1905. The home, built in 1883, sat on "Quality Row," a residential block where the Black elite—lawyers, doctors, ministers, and bankers—lived during the Jim Crow era. The home had nine rooms when Walker moved in but was expanded into a 28-room Victorian mansion over time. Walker had diabetes, and an elevator with a rope-and-pulley system accommodated her wheelchair later in life. (Walker's elevator was even larger than the one at President Franklin D. Roosevelt's home in Hyde Park.) The family also installed central heating and electricity.

The home takes up two floors with an unfinished basement. More than 90 percent of Walker's things, including books, a porcelain bidet, a baby grand piano, and that giant elevator, are still found inside as she left them. The home also includes a Colonial Revival front porch with a tiled floor and sunroom. While Walker was alive, she welcomed Black thought leaders here, including W. E. B. DuBois, Booker T. Washington, and Mary McLeod Bethune. Poets Langston Hughes and Countee Cullen hung out in the kitchen around the same table and chairs you'll see today. While touring this home, imagine being a fly on the wall with these luminaries of Black excellence coming and going.

Photos (top to bottom): a house in Jackson Ward; the Black history timeline in the Black History Museum & Cultural Center of Virginia; Maggie Lena Walker statue by sculptor Tony Mendez

The home stayed in the family after Walker's passing and accommodated guests until it was taken over by the National Park Service. Today, NPS rangers lead **guided tours** (limit 15 people) every hour from 10am-4pm Tuesday-Saturday. A 20-minute introductory film kicks off the tour in the visitor center (600 N. 2nd Street). From there, an NPS ranger walks groups around the corner to the house, which is on Leigh Street. All in all, the film plus the tour take about an hour. Reservations are required for groups of 10 or more, but it never hurts for solo travelers to call in advance. The Visitor Center store offers a variety of books and other items. When she was alive, Walker had a black-and-white photo display of *101 Prominent Colored People*; this has been reprinted as a poster and is a much sought-after purchase. Half a mile to the west, the **Maggie Lena Walker statue** (Broad St. and Adams St.) was dedicated in 2017 on what would have been Walker's 153rd birthday.

HIPPODROME THEATER

528 N. Second St.; tel. 804/308-2913; www.hippodromerichmond.com

Opened in 1914, the Hippodrome Theater was a welcoming spot on the Chitlin' Circuit that allowed Black performers to showcase their talents during the Jim Crow era. Stars such as Moms Mabley, Ella Fitzgerald, and Bill "Bojangles" Robinson performed at this Jackson Ward venue. After a fire in 1945, it was rebuilt and repurposed as a movie theater serving Richmond's Black community. The venue opened and closed many times over the decades, and even served as a church at one point.

Today, the renovated venue serves as an event space where weddings, birthday parties, and other events are celebrated. It also houses the Speakeasy Grill and a stunning art deco-style theater that features high ceilings, a mahogany bar, a vast eight-foot-wide chandelier, and a balcony.

Downtown

VIRGINIA CIVIL RIGHTS MEMORIAL

Bank and 14th Streets, Capitol Square; http://vacivilrightsmemorial.org

Unveiled in 2008, the Virginia Civil Rights Memorial commemorates the students, led by sophomore Barbara Johns, who staged a walkout in 1951 at Robert Russa Moton High School in Farmville to protest poor conditions in their segregated school. The bronze-and-granite monument, situated on the Virginia State Capitol grounds, is two-sided. On one side, Johns stands with her arm raised in the foreground, flanked by other students who walked out with her. With them stands Rev. L. Francis Griffin, the Prince Edward County civil rights activist who backed the students' effort. The other side features NAACP attorneys Oliver W. Hill Sr. and Spottswood Robinson III. The monument joins several others at Virginia's Capitol Square that commemorate revolutionary leaders and, until recently, Civil War figures.

RICHMOND 34 HISTORICAL MARKER

E Broad St. between 6th and 7th

At the site of the old Thalhimers department store, now Thalhimers Richmond CenterStage, a historical marker commemorates the courage of the Richmond 34, the group of university students who staged a sit-in at the store's Richmond Room restaurant in 1960 and were subsequently arrested. When the marker was unveiled in 2016, Elizabeth Johnson Rice of the Richmond 34 spoke at the ceremony, declaring, "Today is a monumental day."[2]

Other Neighborhoods

VIRGINIA MUSEUM OF FINE ARTS

200 N Arthur Ashe Blvd.; tel. 804/340-1400; www.vmfa.museum; daily 10am-5pm; free

Photos (top to bottom): the Hippodrome Theater; an exhibit at the Black History Museum & Cultural Center of Virginia; the terrace at the Virginia Museum of Fine Arts

This flagship museum is located a couple miles north of downtown Richmond. It contains nearly 50,000 pieces of art spread over three floors, with pieces from around the world, including a number of works by African American artists. Notable pieces include Jacob Lawrence's "Catfish Row," a colorful depiction of the abundance of life, featured in the American Galleries on the second floor. The painting was created in 1947, when Lawrence was commissioned by *Fortune* magazine to portray African American life in the area of the South known as the Black Belt. Robert Pruitt's stunning "Steeped," located in the Lewis Contemporary Galleries on the second floor, depicts a dark-skinned Black woman dressed in green with a large, pyramid-like Afro on a pink background. The museum also features pieces by Kehinde Wiley, who painted the portrait of Barack Obama that hangs in the National Portrait Gallery in Washington DC.

ARTHUR ASHE SCULPTURE

Rose Neath St. and Monument Ave.

Richmond served as the capitol of the Confederacy, which partially explains Monument Avenue, which, until the 2020 nationwide protest over police brutality, was a cozy home for Confederate memorials. Thankfully, a monument to native son Arthur Ashe, the tennis great who became the first Black man to win Wimbledon, is here to celebrate Black excellence as well. (The irony is that Ashe would not have been allowed to visit this place as a child because of segregation.) The bronze statue was dedicated in 1996.

Until mid-2020, Monument Avenue was lined with statues commemorating Confederates who fought in the Civil War. In 2020, the city of Richmond voted to remove them all, including the six-ton statue of Stonewall Jackson and a monument to J. E. B. Stuart. (The *Richmond Times* reported that 1,000 people showed up to watch Jackson go.) At the time of writing, a 12-ton equestrian statue of Confederate General Robert E. Lee remained because of an ongoing lawsuit.

Meanwhile, the people of Richmond have reclaimed the space around the monument, spray-painting "Black Lives Matter" and other progressive messaging and projecting images of John Lewis, Harriet Tubman, and George Floyd. This delicious reimagination of space and place has also featured a drum circle and a basketball court.

SHOPPING

Clothing and Gifts

LITTLE NOMAD

104 W Broad St.; www.littlenomadshop.com; tel. 804/447-9135; Mon. 11am-5pm, Tues.-Wed. 10am-5:30pm, Thurs.-Fri. 10am-6pm, Sat. 11am-6pm, Sun. 1pm-5pm

This adorable shop on the western edge of Jackson Ward features clothing for kids and women, books, jewelry, toys, bath items, and more. The "There Is Magic in Melanin" T-shirt is #blackgirlmagic personified. Find kid-size cotton face masks and flexible sunglasses, among other items.

Music

BARKY'S SPIRITUAL STORES

18 E Broad St.; tel. 804/643-1987

Barksdale "Barky" Haggins, in business in several locations around Richmond since 1956, started out selling all kinds of music, but that changed one day in the early '70s, when he pulled into a filling station and heard a car radio blaring something that wasn't to his taste. Now, it's all gospel all the time for Haggins, who supplies local churches and other music lovers with religious items that include CDs, hymnals, robes, sheet music, and music lesson books. Barky's is centrally located downtown, five blocks from the convention center. If you meet him, you just might understand why Haggins loves the assuring, meditative, motivating sounds of gospel, because the

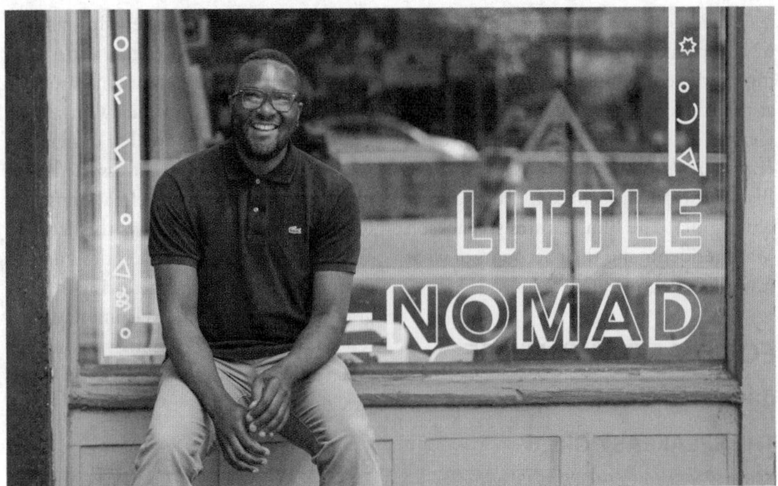

Anthony Bryant of Little Nomad

joy just pours out of him. As he likes to say: "Life is too short to be anything but happy. Falling down is a part of life. Getting back up is living." The shop is located on the western edge of Jackson Ward.

Wellness

LUCID LIVING

300 E Grace St.; tel. 804/592-0747; www.lucidlivingrva.com; Mon.-Thurs. 10am-8pm; Fri. 10am-6pm, Sat. 9am-5pm

If you want to treat yourself to healing touch, book a session at Lucid Living. Natasha Freeman's holistic healing wellness center offers a variety of healing sessions, including Thai bodywork, Reiki, sound healing, and spiritual grounding, tailored to individual needs. The vast menu of services cost $89 for 60 minutes to $129 for an hour. The space is centrally located downtown.

TOURS AND LOCAL GUIDES

Walking Tour

WALKING THE WARD

www.walkingtheward.com; Wed. and Fri. noon-3pm, Sat. and Sun. 10am-3pm; $20 per adult, $10 per child under age 10

Gary Flowers, a community historian, radio host, and tour guide, grew up visiting historic Jackson Ward: His great-grandparents lived across the street from Maggie L. Walker's corporate headquarters at 900 N. St. James Street. "My mother vividly recalls seeing the entourage—Mrs. Walker, her limousine, and all of the activity—across the street," he says. "Hearing these stories, I felt a sense of historic pride that their neighborhood was once called the Harlem of the South and referred to as Black Wall Street before Tulsa, Oklahoma."

Flowers's 2.5-hour tours cover 20 historic sites, including Historic Ebenezer Baptist Church, Lee Street Armory, the William "Bojangles" Robinson statue, Historic Sixth Mount Zion Baptist Church, the Southern Aid Life Insurance Co. building, and the Maggie L. Walker statue and plaza. As a tour guide, Flowers overflows with facts about Black Richmond; for example, he'll tell you that Virginia led the nation in Black-owned banks and was home to several Black-owned insurance companies based in Jackson Ward. His favorite site is Walker's installation. "She may well be the embodiment of the ideals and virtues of historic Jackson Ward: self-reliance, dignity, entrepreneurship, collectivism, and defiance to unjust laws," he says.

Schedule a tour by calling tel. 804/614-6208 or emailing Doretha@IAMMeetingsAndEvents.com. Tours usually begin at the Black History Museum & Cultural Center of Virginia. Flowers's film *Celebrating Jackson Ward* can be viewed at the Black History Museum & Cultural Center of Virginia. The film features six Jackson Ward residents and their accounts of what it was like to grow up here.

FOOD AND NIGHTLIFE

Jackson Ward

THE SPEAKEASY GRILL

526 N 2nd St.; tel. 804/308-2913; www.hippodromerichmond.com; Wed.-Fri. 11:30am-2pm and 5pm-9pm, Sat. 5pm-9pm, Sun. 11am-3pm; dinner $10-26

Situated in historic Jackson Ward, in the also historic Hippodrome Theater, The Speakeasy Grill serves offers lunch, brunch, and dinner. The lunch menu offers selections such as the Yardbird & Waffle Jr., which is seasoned fried chicken on a buttered waffle triangle, and the Louisiana Gumbo Cup, made with chicken, shrimp, sausage, and okra in Creole gravy. Dinner menu offerings include Grilled Atlantic Salmon, grilled with Cajun seasoning and garlic ginger sauce, with chef's sides of the day. The vibe? The layout flows like an early 20th-century home and features a cast-iron fence at the entrance and white brick walls. In the back of the grill is a space with a high ceiling and dark wood designed to evoke Richmond's heyday and a speakeasy feeling. There's a full bar back here, so grab a seat and have a cocktail.

MAMA J'S KITCHEN

415 N 1st St.; http://mamajskitchen.com; tel. 804/225-7449; Sun.-Thurs. 11am-9pm; Fri.-Sat. 11am-10pm; $9-15

This family-owned restaurant features Southern fare in a casual environment. Go for the fried chicken or consider other entrees, such as beef brisket with mashed potatoes, savory crab cakes, and trout. Mouthwatering sides feature macaroni 'n' cheese, collard greens, candied yams, string beans, cabbage, and more. For dessert, try peach cobbler, ice cream, and assorted cakes made pretty. Co-owner Velma Johnson, a former sheriff's deputy, says this Jackson Ward sit-down restaurant is designed so customers feel like they're eating in their grandmother's kitchen: welcome and well-fed on delicious food. Look for the sage green and beige storefront with the Mama J's sign out front.

BIG HERM'S KITCHEN

315 N Second St.; tel. 804/643-0202; www.bighermsrva.com/5175; Mon.-Fri. 11am-5:30pm, Sat. 11:30am-6pm; $7-9

Popular items at this take-out spot include Big Herm's wings and the Philly cheese sandwich with beef or chicken. Salads range from Cobb and Buffalo chicken to roasted asparagus. Desserts are homemade: Try the peach bread pudding or Michelle's pound cake. Born and raised in Fredericksburg, Herman Baskerville's spot in the heart of Jackson Ward is a Richmond staple. "We have a hell of a product and we try to execute well," says Big Herm, who is a regular featured chef on local TV.

SOUTHERN KITCHEN

541 N 2nd St.; 804/729-4141; www.southernkitchenrva.net; Tues.-Sat. noon-9pm, Fri. noon-10pm, Sun. noon-7pm; $17-32

Fish, chicken, and everything Southern is featured on this menu. The Southern Fried Fish is whiting served on Texas toast, and Big Mamas Fried Chicken may be served fried, barbecued, or honey-dipped: you choose. Need a drink? Try the Kitchen Sink, made with rum, tequila, vodka, and gin, topped with orange juice, cranberry juice, and a splash of grenadine with a brandy floater garnished with mixed fruit. Or just drink some Hennessy 'cause they've got that too.

Downtown

VAGABOND RESTAURANT & SPEAKEASY

700 E Broad St.; http://vagabondrva.com; tel. 804/643-2632; Sun.-Wed. 4:30pm-9pm, Thurs. 4:30pm-midnight, Fri.-Sat. 4:30pm-1am; entrees $14-19; covers free-$5

Treat yourself to some good ol' Southern comfort food served with an air of urban sophistication. The Vagabond menu includes blackened Alfredo pasta, grilled pork chops, catfish sandwiches, and portabella mushroom burgers and fries. Sides? Try cheese grits, collard greens, and sautéed string beans. The dessert menu has an intriguing Virginia distilled apple brandy bread pudding. When you're done with dinner, head downstairs to Vagabond's Rabbit Hole Entertainment to enjoy jazz, blues, and R&B in the intimacy of 1920s-style speakeasy environment brought to you by the folks at Mama J's.

Other Neighborhoods

MS. GIRLEE'S KITCHEN

4809 Parker St., #1520; tel. 804/562-3501; www.msgirleeskitchen.com; Tues.-Sat. 11am-6:30pm; $15

Ms. Girlee's owners, Helen Holmes and Trey Bradby, both come from rural Charles City County about 30 minutes outside Richmond, where it is natural to pick up great cooking techniques and offer hospitality. That informs the vibe in this intimate eatery, where, according to Bradby, The Chicken Sandwich is your go-to—so good it has been featured in *Richmond* magazine. The Seafood Combo comes with a crab cake, a piece of fried whiting, three fried shrimp, two sides, and cornbread. Popular sides are the macaroni 'n' cheese, which pairs well with the yams, in Bradby's opinion. The collard greens have no pork.

Photos (top to bottom): Vagabond Restaurant & Speakeasy; Hilton Richmond Downtown; Quirk, an arty hotel in downtown Richmond

The interior is painted a vibrant green with splashes of purple. Ms. Girlee's Kitchen also proudly represents Richmond's Fulton neighborhood, in which the restaurant is located, with photos of community landmarks and a map of the area on the walls.

CROAKER'S SPOT

1020 Hull St.; tel. 804/269-0464; www.croakersspot.com; Mon.-Thurs. 11am-9pm, Fri. 11am-10pm, Sat. noon-10pm, Sun. noon-9pm; $17-30

The menu at Croaker's Spot features seafood by the count, such as butterfly fried shrimp, fried oysters, and steamed mussels. Appetizers include twin crab cake medallions and hot buttered soul wedges, cornbread drizzled in hot butter, and a shrimp sampler. Soups and salads are available too. This restaurant is apparently named for a Richmond-born man who ran a Harlem restaurant that was frequented by jazz musicians and affectionately called "Croaker's Spot."

ACCOMMODATIONS

Good accommodations options in Richmond include the 359-room **Omni Richmond Hotel** (100 S 12th St.; tel. 804/344-7000; www.omnihotels.com; $169); **Quirk** (201 W Broad St.; tel. 804/340-6040; www.destinationhotels.com/quirk-hotel; $179) an artful and totally cute Hyatt hotel in downtown Richmond; **Hilton Richmond Downtown** (501 E Broad St.; tel. 804/344-4300; www.hilton.com; $173), located in the historic former Miller & Rhoads department store; and **Graduate Richmond** (301 W. Franklin St.; tel. 804/644-9871), part of a chain of boutique hotels located in college towns that bills itself as the "smartest place to stay." It's near Virginia Union University.

TRANSPORTATION

Getting There

AIR

Richmond International Airport (tel. 804/226-3000; www.flyrichmond.com) is located about seven miles southeast of downtown Richmond. A 20-minute taxi ride downtown will cost about $35.

TRAIN

Amtrak (www.amtrak.com) arrives and departs from Richmond's historic **Main Street Station** (1500 E Main St.; Mon.-Fri. 6am-7pm, Sat.-Sun. 9am-8:30pm). **Staples Mill Road Station** (7519 Staples Mill Rd.; Sun.-Sat. 5:30am-10:30pm) is located in Henrico County, five miles north of downtown Richmond. Get to Washington DC for as low as $22 for a trip that takes about 3 hours.

BUS

Richmond's **Greyhound** (www.greyhound.com) bus station (2910 N Arthur Ashe Blvd.; 804/254-5910; open 24/7) is located a few miles north of downtown.

CAR

To reach Richmond from:

- **Washington DC:** Take **I-95 South** for around 110 miles (2 hours).
- **Raleigh, North Carolina:** Take either **I-85 North** (155 miles; 3 hours) or **I-95 North** (170 miles; 3 hours).

Getting Around

You will need a car to get around Richmond. Once you park, it's all walkable, and parking is generally free in Jackson Ward. Be prepared to pay for metered parking spots or garages. Hourly rates for city parking depends on the site and max out for the day at $20-25. Sometimes, folks park free in nearby neighborhoods and walk.

Washington DC

Whether daring to register to vote or insisting on the right to a fair and equitable education through integration, citizens' personal acts of courage in cities, towns, and counties across the country eventually found a hearing in the nation's capital. The Supreme Court played a starring role, desegregating public schools in the 1954 *Brown v. Board of Education* decision and upholding desegregation in public transportation in 1956 after Rosa Parks refused to give her seat to a White Montgomery bus patron.

WASHINGTON DC'S TOP 5

1. Considering the preeminent civil rights leader's many powerful words at the **Martin Luther King, Jr. Memorial** (page 416).

2. Making a pilgrimage home at the **National Museum of African American History and Culture,** which tells a comprehensive story of Black history in America (page 416).

3. Viewing portraits of the nation's first Black president and first lady at the **National Portrait Gallery** (page 423).

4. Delving into 19th-century civil rights at the **Frederick Douglass National Historic Site** (page 437).

5. Kicking it at **Howard Homecoming** as you soak up loads of Black joy, excellence, and progress (page 450).

Photos (top to bottom): Martin Luther King, Jr. Memorial; National Museum of African American History and Culture; National Portrait Gallery; a reconstruction of the "growlery" cabin where Frederick Douglass retreated to read and write at the Frederick Douglass National Historic Site. Previous: the 1963 March on Washington for Jobs and Freedom

Congress, buoyed by President Lyndon B. Johnson, father of the Great Society, passed the Civil Rights Act of 1964, the Voting Rights Act of 1965, and the Civil Rights Act of 1968 (aka the Fair Housing Act). It cannot be left unsaid that the 2008 and 2012 elections of America's first Black president, Barack Hussein Obama, were seeded by the small and big wins accomplished during the civil rights era.

However, the roots of inequality were also planted and nurtured here. Enslaved and free Black people built the White House, and those in bondage were pressed into service keeping it running. Several presidents were human traffickers, starting with George Washington himself. Those men could credit their wealth to the inherent value of Black bodies. It's something to consider as you explore the District (and the White House, should you choose to do so) as well as the country at-large.

In spite of the oppression, Black Washingtonians throughout history have mounted impressive efforts to support one another and access the promise of a free society. In one poignant example, when the historic U Street corridor erupted in violence and looting the night Dr. Martin Luther King Jr. was assassinated, Ben's Chili Bowl was left untouched. After all, this place, known for its famous half-smokes, fed those who attended the 1963 March on Washington for Jobs and Freedom.

The District was once majority Black, reaching peak Blackness at 71 percent in 1970, but that's changed in recent decades, with the Black population dropping to 53 percent in 2009 and 46 percent in 2019. Still, longtime Black residents retain the joy and spirit of "Chocolate City," a reflection of pride in being a mostly Black city. You'll feel this in the Black-owned shops in U Street and Anacostia and during festivals, like Howard Homecoming and the annual Funk Parade. Seeing the Obama portraits hanging in the National Portrait Gallery is a moving experience for many, as is a journey "home" to the National Museum of African American History and Culture. The idea of NMAAHC was seeded long ago when Black Civil War veterans suggested a memorial for African Americans as early as 1915. In 1929, Congress authorized a study into the idea of erecting a moment honoring African American contributions, but it took President George W. Bush to put the idea into action. It opened in 2016 to great fanfare at an auspicious time: when Barack Obama was in office.

ORIENTATION

DC is comprised of a logical grid of streets and avenues that connect its distinct neighborhoods. The U.S. Capitol is the center point where "The District" divides into four unequally sized quadrants. Visitors typically spend the majority of their time in the northwest (NW) quadrant, home to the White House, many of the Smithsonian museums, Howard University, tony Dupont Circle, and more.

From the Capitol, the **National Mall** stretches a little over two miles west to

the 1963 March on Washington for Jobs and Freedom

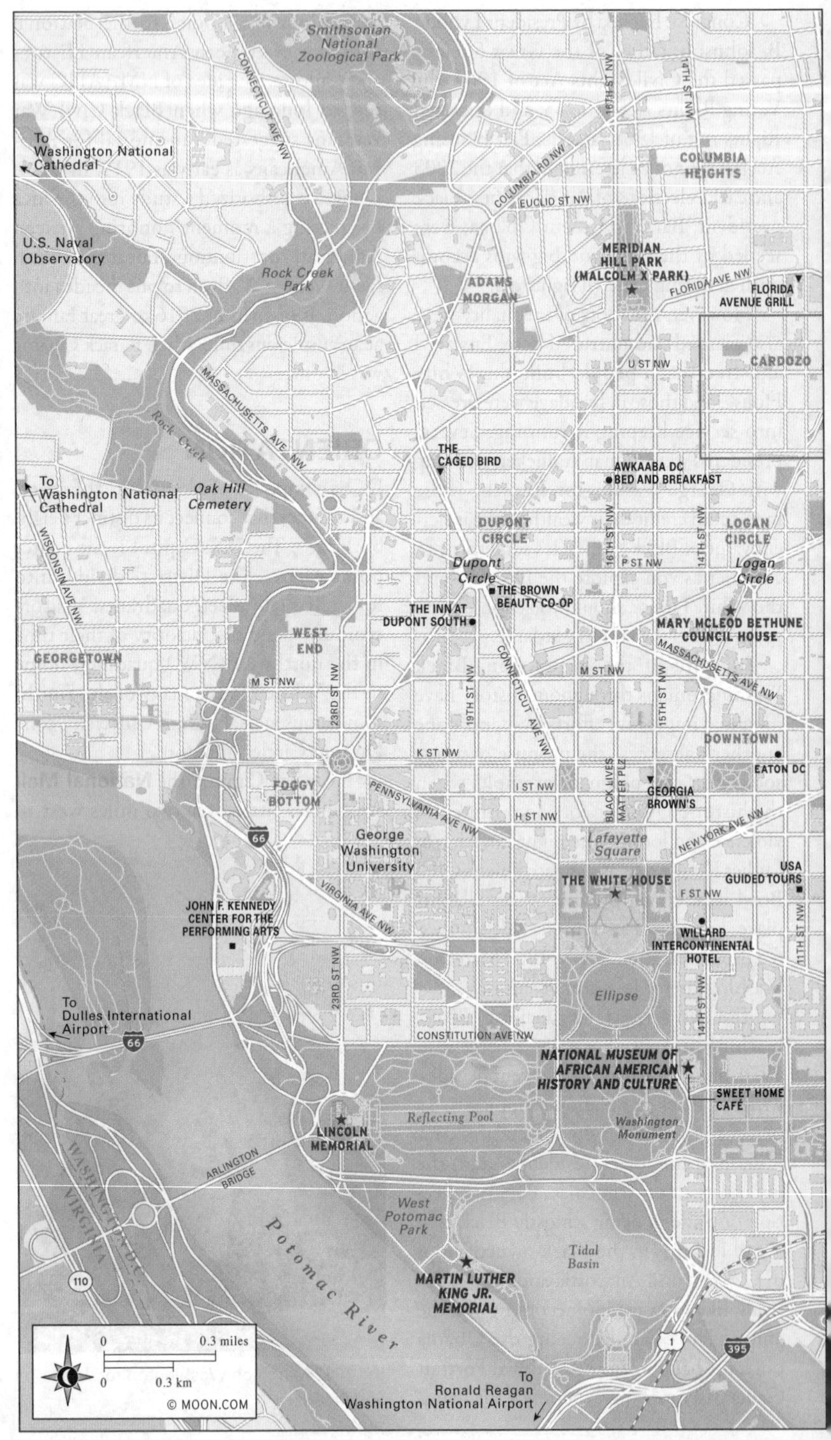

Smithsonian National Zoological Park
CONNECTICUT AVE NW
16TH ST NW
14TH ST NW
To Washington National Cathedral
COLUMBIA RD NW
COLUMBIA HEIGHTS
EUCLID ST NW
U.S. Naval Observatory
MERIDIAN HILL PARK (MALCOLM X PARK)
Rock Creek Park
ADAMS MORGAN
FLORIDA AVE NW
FLORIDA AVENUE GRILL
U ST NW
CARDOZO
MASSACHUSETTS AVE NW
Rock Creek
THE CAGED BIRD
AWKAABA DC BED AND BREAKFAST
To Washington National Cathedral
Oak Hill Cemetery
DUPONT CIRCLE
LOGAN CIRCLE
WISCONSIN AVE NW
P ST NW
Dupont Circle
Logan Circle
THE BROWN BEAUTY CO-OP
THE INN AT DUPONT SOUTH
MARY MCLEOD BETHUNE COUNCIL HOUSE
WEST END
GEORGETOWN
CONNECTICUT AVE NW
M ST NW
M ST NW
23RD ST NW
19TH ST NW
15TH ST NW
DOWNTOWN
K ST NW
EATON DC
FOGGY BOTTOM
PENNSYLVANIA AVE NW
I ST NW
BLACK LIVES MATTER PLZ
GEORGIA BROWN'S
H ST NW
66
George Washington University
Lafayette Square
NEW YORK AVE NW
USA GUIDED TOURS
THE WHITE HOUSE
F ST NW
VIRGINIA AVE NW
JOHN F. KENNEDY CENTER FOR THE PERFORMING ARTS
WILLARD INTERCONTINENTAL HOTEL
11TH ST NW
23RD ST NW
Ellipse
14TH ST NW
To Dulles International Airport
66
CONSTITUTION AVE NW
NATIONAL MUSEUM OF AFRICAN AMERICAN HISTORY AND CULTURE
SWEET HOME CAFÉ
Reflecting Pool
LINCOLN MEMORIAL
Washington Monument
ARLINGTON BRIDGE
WASHINGTON D.C.
VIRGINIA
West Potomac Park
Potomac River
Tidal Basin
110
MARTIN LUTHER KING JR. MEMORIAL
1
395
0
0.3 miles
0
0.3 km
© MOON.COM
To Ronald Reagan Washington National Airport

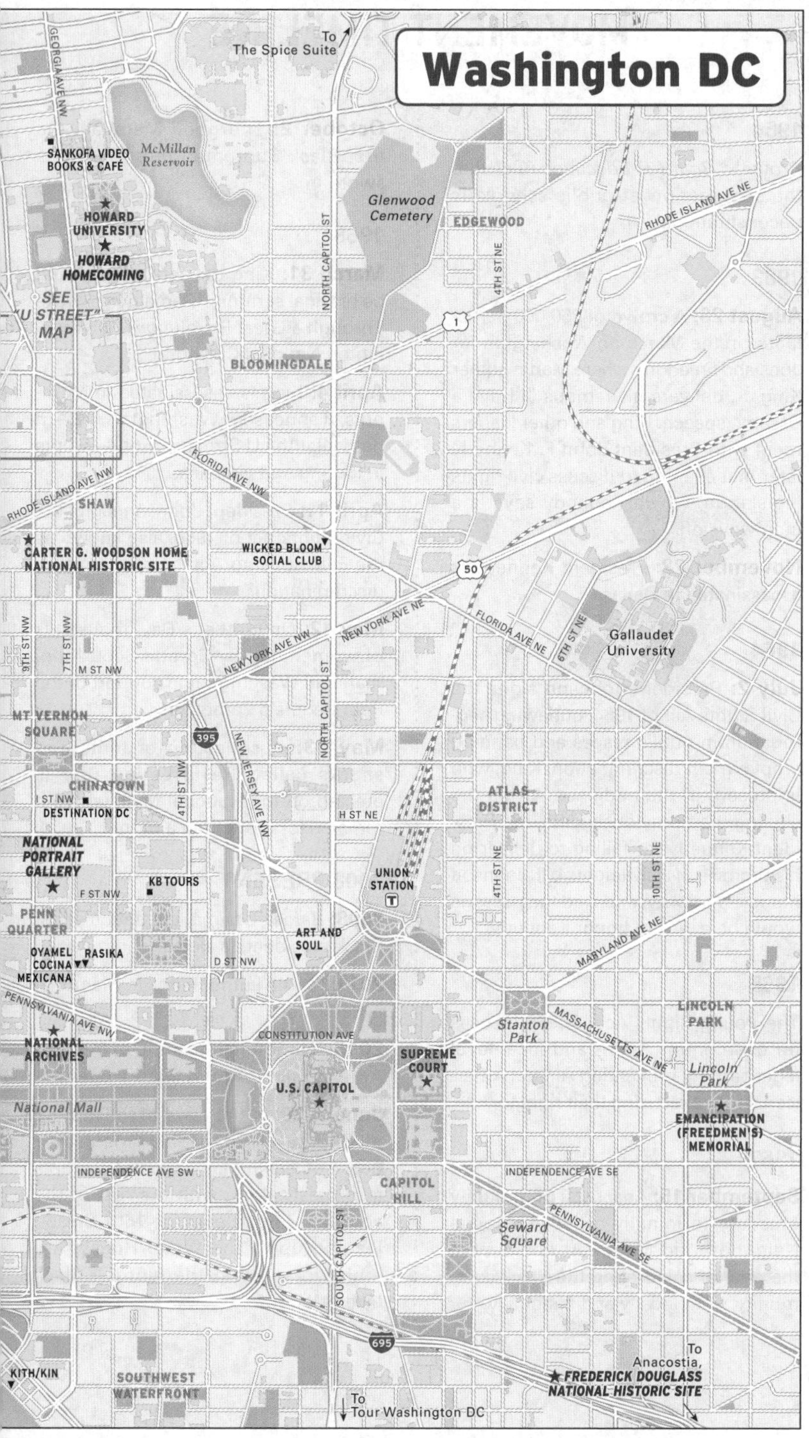
Washington DC
To The Spice Suite
McMillan Reservoir
SANKOFA VIDEO BOOKS & CAFÉ
HOWARD UNIVERSITY
HOWARD HOMECOMING
SEE "U STREET" MAP
Glenwood Cemetery
EDGEWOOD
RHODE ISLAND AVE NE
4TH ST NE
NORTH CAPITOL ST
GEORGIA AVE NW
BLOOMINGDALE
FLORIDA AVE NW
RHODE ISLAND AVE NW
SHAW
CARTER G. WOODSON HOME NATIONAL HISTORIC SITE
WICKED BLOOM SOCIAL CLUB
NEW YORK AVE NE
NEW YORK AVE NW
FLORIDA AVE NE
6TH ST NE
Gallaudet University
9TH ST NW
7TH ST NW
M ST NW
MT VERNON SQUARE
NEW JERSEY AVE NW
4TH ST NW
CHINATOWN
I ST NW
DESTINATION DC
ATLAS DISTRICT
H ST NE
NATIONAL PORTRAIT GALLERY
F ST NW
KB TOURS
UNION STATION
10TH ST NE
PENN QUARTER
ART AND SOUL
OYAMEL COCINA MEXICANA
RASIKA
D ST NW
MARYLAND AVE NE
PENNSYLVANIA AVE NW
Stanton Park
MASSACHUSETTS AVE NE
LINCOLN PARK
NATIONAL ARCHIVES
CONSTITUTION AVE
SUPREME COURT
U.S. CAPITOL
Lincoln Park
National Mall
EMANCIPATION (FREEDMEN'S) MEMORIAL
INDEPENDENCE AVE SW
INDEPENDENCE AVE SE
CAPITOL HILL
SOUTH CAPITOL ST
Seward Square
PENNSYLVANIA AVE SE
KITH/KIN
SOUTHWEST WATERFRONT
To Tour Washington DC
To Anacostia, FREDERICK DOUGLASS NATIONAL HISTORIC SITE
1
50
395
695

MOVEMENT TIMELINE

1954

Brown v. Board of Education rules that the segregation of public schools is unconstitutional.

1963

August 28: A crowd of 250,000 participates in the March on Washington for Jobs and Freedom, where Martin Luther King Jr. delivers his famous "I Have a Dream" speech. King and other leaders meet with President John F. Kennedy later that evening to discuss civil rights legislation, which Kennedy says is a long ways off.

November 22: President Kennedy is assassinated in Dallas.

1964

July 2: President Johnson signs the Civil Rights Act of 1964, outlawing segregation in public places and banning employment discrimination. King, who is present in the audience during the signing, had previously criticized President Kennedy for failing to deliver on his promise of a civil rights bill. Johnson made it a priority, and said the passage would be a way to honor Kennedy.

1965

The Voting Rights Act of 1965 focuses on overcoming state- and local-level legal barriers preventing African Americans from exercising their right to vote.

1967

September 15: Anacostia Community Museum (originally called Anacostia Neighborhood Museum) opens with the goal of celebrating the Black community, both locally and nationally.

October 2: Thurgood Marshall, the first Black Supreme Court justice, is sworn in.

1968

March 31: King delivers what would be his final sermon, "Remaining Awake Through a Great Revolution," at Washington National Cathedral.

April 4: King is assassinated in Memphis, Tennessee. Washington DC—in particular the U Street corridor—erupts in looting and violence.

April 11: President Johnson signs the Civil Rights Act of 1968, also known as the Fair Housing Act, barring housing discrimination.

May 12: On Mother's Day, thousands of women, led by Coretta Scott King, march in Washington in support of the Poor People's Campaign.

May 13: A collection of tents and shacks called Resurrection City is erected on the National Mall, where it remains for more than a month.

2008-PRESENT

2008: Barack Obama, the nation's first Black president, is elected.

2011: Martin Luther King, Jr. Memorial is dedicated.

2016: National Museum of African American History and Culture opens.

June 2020: In the wake of the murder of George Floyd, a Black man, by a police officer in Minneapolis, DC erupts in protest, along with the rest of the country. Two blocks of 16th Street, leading up to the White House, are emblazoned with the words "Black Lives Matter."

the Lincoln Memorial, containing a high concentration of attractions, including the National Museum of African American History and Culture. Directly north of the National Mall, **Downtown and Penn Quarter** is where the White House and National Portrait Gallery are located. **Dupont Circle** is northwest of downtown. Directly east of the Mall is **Capitol Hill and Atlas District,** home to the Capitol Building and the Supreme Court.

North of downtown is **U Street and Shaw,** the historically Black area that's home to Howard University, an HBCU, along with nightlife venues. Today, U Street is the site of the annual Funk Parade, held each May, which celebrates the local community.

Anacostia, in southwest Washington, began in 1854 as a suburb, and in 1877 Frederick Douglass became its first Black resident. You can visit Douglass's home, known as Frederick Douglass National Historic Site, today, along with the Anacostia Community Museum, which is dedicated to amplifying urban issues that affect local residents along with urban residents nationwide. This neighborhood also has the city's greatest concentration of Black-owned businesses.

PLANNING YOUR TIME

Take a good three days to enjoy the sights in Washington DC, but if you'd like to stay a week, there's plenty to do and see. It's easy to spend a day in the NMAAHC alone.

March through Labor Day is considered **high season.** If you're wondering what to pack, note that visitors do not have to dress like well-heeled lobbyists to visit the Capitol, the White House, or the Supreme Court; however, wearing business attire or your "Sunday best" is respectful (and may get you further in a meeting with your elected official).

Timed-entry passes for **NMAAHC** are made available the first Wednesday of every month. If you'll be visiting during high season, it's smart to secure passes two months in advance. Reservations are also encouraged for the **National Archives,** especially May through Labor Day. And if you want to meet with lawmakers at the **U.S. Capitol,** you'll have to contact your senator or representative in advance.

If you're planning a visit in summer 2021, note that the portraits of Barack and Michelle Obama won't be on view in the **National Portrait Gallery** at that time, when they are scheduled to tour the nation.

The official tourism office for Washington DC is **Destination DC** (901 7th St. NW; tel. 202/789-7000; www.washington.org).

CONNECT WITH

Richmond, Virginia, is your closest destination in this guide, so it's a good place to head next if you're starting your trip in DC.

PEOPLE WHO MADE THE MOVEMENT

GROUPS

"Big Six" of the Civil Rights Movement: This group was responsible for the March on Washington. It consisted of Martin Luther King Jr. (Southern Christian Leadership Conference); John Lewis (SNCC); labor organizer A. Phillip Randolph (founder of the Brotherhood of Sleeping Car Porters and Maids); Roy Wilkins (NAACP); Whitney M. Young Jr. (National Urban League); and Congress of Racial Equality (CORE) co-founder James Farmer. A seventh figure, Bayard Rustin, served as chief organizer.

National Council of Negro Women: Organization founded in 1935 to improve the lives of African American women, families, and communities. Originally headquartered in Washington DC, at the Mary Bethune Council House (known as the Council House), the organization is still active today.

1960s MOVEMENT LEADERS

Dr. Martin Luther King Jr.: The legendary leader led the momentous March on Washington for Jobs and Freedom on August 28, 1963, where he delivered his famous "I Have a Dream" speech to a crowd of 250,000. After the march, King and other leaders met with President John F. Kennedy to discuss civil rights legislation. King was awarded the Nobel Peace Prize in October 1964.

Stokely Carmichael: The Freedom Rider, one-time head of SNCC, and leader of the Black Power movement was in Washington DC the night of King's assassination and tried to stem the violence that erupted along the U Street corridor in response to it.

Frederick Douglass

Rev. Jesse L. Jackson: Civil rights activist and minister who ran for president in 1984 and 1988.

EARLIER AND LATER FIGURES

Frederick Douglass: Formerly enslaved, Douglass became a leading abolitionist who lived in Anacostia.

Mary McLeod Bethune: Bethune was an educator, activist, and special advisor to President Franklin D. Roosevelt.

Carter G. Woodson: Liberal arts dean of Howard University who sought to preserve Black history. In 1926, Woodson established Negro History Week, which eventually became Black History Month.

Thurgood Marshall: Confirmed in 1967, Marshall became the first Black Supreme Court justice and is known for prioritizing civil rights.

Barack and Michelle Obama: Barack Obama became the nation's first Black president when he was elected in 2008. His portrait, along with that of First Lady Michelle Obama, hangs in the National Portrait Gallery.

Three Days in Washington DC

Three days in Washington DC will show you several layers of the city's Black history. Visiting the National Mall, you can stand on the site where Martin Luther King Jr. delivered his historic "I Have a Dream" speech, then head over to the National Portrait Gallery to view stunning portraits of Barack Obama and Michelle Obama, the nation's first Black president and first lady. You'll also see the Black neighborhoods of U Street, which thrived as a center of Black commerce during Jim Crow, and Anacostia, where Frederick Douglass once lived.

Make reservations to visit the **National Museum of African American History and Culture** (Day 2) as far in advance as possible. (Two months is a good rule of thumb.) Reservations are also recommended to tour the **Frederick Douglass National Historic Site** (Day 3), especially if you'll be visiting on a weekend.

DAY 1: NATIONAL MALL AND U STREET

1 Start your visit to DC by standing where King stood at the **Lincoln Memorial** when he delivered his enduring "I Have a Dream" speech on August 28, 1963.

2 Next, take an early morning stroll over to the **Martin Luther King, Jr. Memorial.** Take some time to quietly contemplate the meaning of his timeless, always urgent words, which are inscribed as quotes on several walls that comprise this memorial.

3 Break for lunch at **Rasika** for award-winning Indian food. Alternatively, the steps of the National Portrait Gallery (your next stop and just steps away) are a great place for an alfresco picnic.

4 At the **National Portrait Gallery,** contemplate the legacy of Michelle Obama, a descendant of enslaved Black people who became our Forever First Lady when she moved into the White House. Michelle Obama's portrait hangs in the gallery as does a portrait of Barack Obama.

5 Take the Metro up to U Street and listen for the beat of go-go music, banged out on buckets by local residents, as you exit the station. Beloved local favorite **Ben's Chili Bowl** on U Street is a sure bet for dinner.

DAY 2: NATIONAL MUSEUM OF AFRICAN AMERICAN HISTORY AND CULTURE

Spend an entire day on a journey of the Black experience in America at this landmark museum.

1 Before you enter the building, notice the stunning **exterior**: it's inspired by the crown from the Yoruba culture of West Africa.

2 Begin your tour on the **concourse-level galleries,** which start with the story of Black enslavement. Emmett Till's casket—arguably the most moving artifact in the entire museum—is on display here.

3 Break for lunch at **Sweet Home Café,** which showcases African American foodways, in Concourse 0.

4 Spend the rest of your day exploring the **third- and fourth-floor galleries,** which cover topics from sports to music to dance and language.

DAY 3: ANACOSTIA

1 Begin with a 9am tour (reservations recommended, especially on weekends) of **Frederick Douglass National Historic Site** to see where the neighborhood's first Black resident lived and conducted business.

2 Grab a coffee and a bite to eat at the Anacostia branch of **Busboys and Poets** located near the Frederick Douglass Site.

3 Patronize some of the neighborhood's Black-owned businesses at the **Anacostia Arts Center,** steps away from Busboys and Poets. Try Nubian Hueman for clothing or Mahogany Books for a selection of reads on antiracism, among other topics.

4 Your last stop in Anacostia is the **Anacostia Community Museum,** which brings the power and passion of museums to the people where they live and thrive.

Sights

NATIONAL MALL

Lincoln Memorial

2 Lincoln Memorial Circle NW; tel. 202/426-6841; Metro: Arlington Cemetery (Blue line) or Smithsonian (Blue, Orange, and Silver lines)

No visit to Washington DC is complete without a visit to this memorial, an expansive hilltop retreat where the 16th president is depicted in a moment of solemn reflection, staring forward at a nation that was struggling to live up to its ideals and remain unified.

From this site, Dr. Martin Luther King Jr. gave the world his famous **"I Have A Dream"** speech on August 28, 1963. It was a hot, humid day when a multiracial crowd of 250,000 convened for the March on Washington for Jobs and Freedom. People carried signs with messages like "End Police Brutality Now!" "Integrate Schools Now!" and "First Class Citizenship Now!" Five thousand law enforcement officers were on standby to keep order and guard against dissident groups. Marchgoers flocked toward the memorial, singing "We Shall Overcome."

This was also the anniversary of the seminal precipitating event for the civil rights movement: the murder of 14-year-old Emmett Till.

The three-hour event was helmed by the Big Six of civil rights movement leadership and featured notable guests, including writers (James Baldwin), musicians (Sammy Davis Jr., Joan Baez, and Bob Dylan); actors (Ossie Davis, Marlon Brando, and Ruby Dee), athletes (Jackie Robinson), and many, many more. The march's aim was to put pressure on Washington to pass pending civil rights

ABOUT THE "DREAM"

King's famous "I Have a Dream" speech was originally titled "Normalcy, Never Again." While he had used "dream" imagery before, he didn't plan to do so when he took the podium at the March on Washington—until Black church-style call-and-response, a diasporic tradition, took over. King's advisor and speechwriter, Clarence Jones, described what happened to the *Wall Street Journal*: "[King's] favorite gospel singer, Mahalia Jackson, who was on the podium . . . shouted to him, 'Tell 'em about the dream, Martin, tell 'em about the dream!" Jones then described how King set his written speech aside and looked down on the thousands assembled below him. "And I turned to the person standing next to me, whoever that is I can't remember," says Jones. "I said, these people out there, they don't know it, but they're about ready to go to church."[1]

And so, when Mahalia Jackson coaxed him in love, support, and awe as a good church sister would, King obliged.

legislation and protest racial discrimination and economic inequality. In the aftermath, states ratified the 24th Amendment, which abolished the poll tax. The tax blocked low-income people of all races from being able to afford the privilege of voting, effectively disenfranchising entire swaths of the Black community.

That evening after the march, civil rights leaders met President John F. Kennedy and Vice President Lyndon B. Johnson in the Oval Office. Those leaders included: Floyd McKissick (CORE); Mathew Ahmann (National Catholic Conference for Interracial Justice); Whitney Young (National Urban League); Martin Luther King Jr. (SCLC); John Lewis (SNCC); Rabbi Joachim Prinz (American Jewish Congress); A. Philip Randolph; and Roy Wilkins (NAACP). The president warned of a long road ahead to get civil rights legislation passed, and all agreed civil rights legislation would need bipartisan support. After Kennedy's assassination later that year, Johnson saw to it that the most comprehensive civil rights law ever, the Civil Rights Act of 1964, became law. King was awarded the Nobel Peace Prize in October 1964.

The memorial, which is a stop on the official U.S. Civil Rights Trail, consists of a massive seated Abraham Lincoln surrounded by inscriptions of his Gettysburg Address and Second Inaugural Address, along with a pair of Jules Guerin murals. One, entitled "Emancipation," depicts the Angel of Truth freeing enslaved Black people from bondage. The second, "Unity," shows the Angel of Truth joining the hands of two figures, one representing the North and one representing the South. Lincoln looks out over a reflecting pool that extends more than 2,000 feet toward the Washington Monument.

There is a spot on the memorial, halfway up the daunting stone steps that lead to Lincoln, where an inscription, added in 2003 to commemorate the 40th anniversary of King's assassination, marks the site where King stood as he addressed the crowd. This is a good place to stand tall, gaze across the reflecting pool, and dream for yourself. Please remember the civil rights agenda was about so much more than softly focused dreams; it was about the hard work of equity and justice.

★ Martin Luther King, Jr. Memorial

1964 Independence Ave. SW; tel. 202/426-6841; Metro: Smithsonian (Blue, Orange, and Silver lines)

"With this faith, we will be able to hew out of the mountain of despair a stone of hope,"[2] King said in his famous 1963 "I Have A Dream" speech. Every year, millions of people come to behold the 30-foot-tall monument of the slain civil rights leader—the first National Mall memorial to honor a Black person—emerging from a mountain.

The monument was spearheaded by King's fraternity, Alpha Phi Alpha, authorized by Congress in 1996, and dedicated in 2011. Visitors enter through the massive pink granite Mountain of Despair, which has scrape marks denoting struggle. The Stone of Hope contains a carving of King looking out intensely with a furrowed brow and unwavering gaze. (Sculptor Lei Yixin based King's visage on a composite of photographs.) The great orator's arms are folded into the stone, and he is holding what the sculptor says is a rolled-up "Dream" speech. A 450-foot wall behind the monument is inscribed with quotations from King's speeches, writings, and sermons.

A great time to visit is springtime, when more than 3,000 cherry blossoms reach peak bloom along the Tidal Basin. Better yet, visit any day during golden hour at dawn or dusk, when the lighting lends itself to a contemplative mood. Take some time here to consider the movement, its martyrs, and what they wrought. It is all a wonder to behold.

This monument, a stop on the official U.S. Civil Rights Trail, resides in West Potomac Park at the Tidal Basin between the Jefferson and Lincoln memorials. From Smithsonian Metro, it's a 15-20-minute walk following Independence Avenue to the west. You'll find a bookstore, restrooms, and drinking fountains across West Basin Drive near the main entrance.

TOP EXPERIENCE

★ National Museum of African American History and Culture

1400 Constitution Ave. NW; tel. 844/750-3012; www.nmaahc.si.edu; daily 10am-5:30pm; free; Metro: Smithsonian (Blue, Orange, and Silver lines)

Museum? Yes. But the National Museum of African American History and Culture (NMAAHC) is so much more than that, according to Lonnie G. Bunch III, secretary of the Smithsonian and the museum's inaugural director: It is a pilgrimage.

The museum's six floors of exhibit space hold about 3,000 objects and feature 12 exhibitions with several award-winning interactive kiosks and videos. Exceptional finds include the open metal casket used to display teen lynching victim Emmett Till in Concourse 2. Featured art includes works by Charles Alston, John Biggers, Elizabeth Catlett, Jacob Lawrence, Lorna Simpson, Romare Bearden, and Henry O. Tanner.

The building itself, designed by David Adjaye and lead architect Phil Freelon, is stunning: an architectural tour de force whose facade is inspired by the three-tiered corona crown from the Yoruba culture of West Africa. Patterned exterior panels allow light through their openings, and the corona glows at night with the grandeur befitting its prominence on the National Mall. By calling forth the roots of Black culture—Africa herself—a visit here is a journey home, to where it all began.

The museum is a stop on the official U.S. Civil Rights Trail.

GET INTO THE RHYTHM

The **March on Washington for Jobs and Freedom**, held on a hot summer day in August 1963, was marked by positivity and hopefulness. As crowds moved toward the Lincoln Memorial, holding signs and placards, they engaged in singalongs and fellowship. The following songs filled the air with the spirit of determination:

- **Marian Anderson, "He's Got the Whole World in His Hands"**: The last time the world-famous contralto sang for the nation at the Lincoln Memorial (1939), she did so because the Daughters of the American Revolution had denied the world-famous singer the right to sing at Constitution Hall.
- **Eva Jessye Choir, "We Shall Overcome" and "Freedom Is the Thing We're Talking About"**: King selected this choir to perform the movement's anthem, "We Shall Overcome," at the March on Washington. Kansas-born Jessye, one of the first Black women to direct a professional choral group, was the choral director for George Gershwin's 1935 folk opera, *Porgy and Bess.*
- **Mahalia Jackson, "How I Got Over"**: Jackson performed this transcendent Clara Ward-composed gospel song that reflects on past trials while foreshadowing victory and thanking God. She also delivered a moving rendition of "I've Been 'Buked and I've Been Scorned," which addresses the disrespect and condemnation that's piled on for standing up for what is right—and continuing to stand nevertheless.
- **Freedom Singers (SNCC), "We Shall Not Be Moved"**: This group included veterans of the Albany Movement, who fought for desegregation and voters' rights in Georgia. The group led spectators in a rousing performance full of purposeful movement and hand clapping.
- **Bob Dylan, "Only a Pawn in Their Game"**: Dylan's lyrics held White authority figures accountable for their role in Black pain and complicity by poor Whites.
- **Joan Baez, "We Shall Overcome"**: The folk singer strummed her guitar, leading a hopeful crowd in the anthem of the civil rights movement.

KING'S RADICAL AGENDA

Resurrection City on May 28, 1961

Real talk: King had a radical economic agenda that gets tangled up in the gauzy goodness of dreams and such. And while the spotlight followed King, his goal was to shine a light on the common man, be they Black sanitation employees, Native Americans, or Latino farm workers.

By the time King traveled to Memphis to support striking Black sanitation workers, he was in the midst of mounting the **Poor People's Campaign** to make a serious shift into addressing the unequal structure of the American economy. The prescient King espoused a radical redistribution of wealth, workers' rights, a living wage, and universal basic income. Economic access was just as critical in dismantling inequality and poverty as the right to vote and desegregation.

King's assassination did not halt the campaign: Under the guidance of Rev. Ralph Abernathy, the group pressed on. Led by Coretta Scott King, thousands of women marched in Washington on Mother's Day, 1968. On May 13, 1968, **Resurrection City**, a grouping of tents and shacks, was constructed on the National Mall on 15 acres near the Reflecting Pool. More than 3,000 demonstrators weathered the elements here for more than a month. Folks came from all over, bused in from places like Mississippi. Celebrities came out to support, including Sidney Poitier, Marlon Brando, and Barbra Streisand. When Attorney General Robert Kennedy was assassinated on June 6, 1968, the motorcade drove through Resurrection City as a sign of respect. The Department of Interior shut it down in June.

Was the Poor People's Campaign successful? As a result, hundreds of counties would now receive surplus food, and job guarantees were made. Yet even today, a living wage is still not the norm. It takes months for a White woman earn to earn as much as a White man—and even longer for Black, brown, and Native American women to do so—and in that order. These issues still being debated today, and neo-civil rights movements, from Black Lives Matter to the movement for Black women's reproductive justice, continue to build on what began in the '60s.

TICKETS

Demand for NMAAHC is intense, and the sprawling 85,000-square-foot exhibition space fills to capacity on a daily basis. Timed-entry passes must be ordered online or by phone. The wait can take up to 30 minutes online and even longer on the phone. Timed passes are made available the first Wednesday of the month, so if you're planning a trip to DC, it helps to reserve yours well in advance. Two months prior is a good rule of thumb. Advance reservations are recommended, especially for groups larger than 10.

Another option is to reserve a same-day timed pass online, available at 6:30am daily. During peak season (March through Labor Day), walk-up entry without a timed pass is available Monday through Friday after 1pm. In off-peak season (Sept.-Feb.), walk-up entry without a timed pass is available 10am-5:30pm.

Veterans, active-duty soldiers, and first responders don't need a pass, just official ID. They also can bring one guest. If the museum is at capacity during a given visit, they may be asked to wait for the crowd to die down before entering.

PLANNING YOUR VISIT

The massive NMAAHC requires more than one visit, and it's easy to spend an entire day here. Visitors are urged to start their tours on the bottom-floor history galleries, which start with the story of Black enslavement, and work their way up to the (very fun) culture galleries on the fourth floor. A good strategy is to explore the concourse-level galleries, then break for lunch at **Sweet Home Café** (Concourse 0; entrees $8-18), and end the day with the third- and fourth-floor galleries. (The fifth floor holds offices.) The civil rights movement is covered mostly in Concourse 2 and some of Concourse 3, so visitors interested in that period of history may want to focus their time there (though aspects of the movement show up in exhibits throughout the museum).

Free lockers are available to store items. The museum is wheelchair accessible and has a limited number of them available for free use on a first-come, first-served basis. No food or drink is allowed in the museum, though patrons may bring bottled water.

INSIDE THE MUSEUM

Visitors enter the museum on the first floor, then descend three stories underground. The story begins here, in the History Galleries in Concourses 1-3. In **Concourse 3,** an oversize image depicts the West African Queen Nzinga, who made alliances with Europeans to save her people from enslavement. A disturbing quote by poet William Cowper is superimposed at the bottom of her likeness: "While I am sickened at the purchase of slaves . . . I must be mum, for how could we do without sugar and rum?"

Segregation and the civil rights movement are covered in **Concourses 2 and 3.** Artifacts here include a yellow and gray floral dress made by Rosa Parks, a seamstress, and shards of colored glass from the 16th Street Baptist Church in Birmingham, the 1963 bombing of which killed four little girls. Visitors can hear the voices of activists such as John Lewis, who marched from Selma to Montgomery to secure Black voting rights and served as the youngest speaker at 1963 March on Washington. It's also possible to step inside a restored Southern Railway train car, which was segregated when it was in use, and see for yourself that the accommodations meant for African Americans were inferior to those meant for Whites. A modern interpretation of a Woolworth's lunch counter, complete with an interactive media countertop, allows patrons to learn the strategy and tactics of nonviolent protest. But perhaps the most compelling artifact in the entire museum is Emmett Till's casket. It was Till's Mississippi murder and his mother's decision to

Photos (top to bottom): Lincoln Memorial; Martin Luther King, Jr. Memorial; National Museum of African American History and Culture

leave his casket open so mourners in Chicago could see his mutilated body—a heartbreaking and courageous act—that ignited the modern-day civil rights movement. Till's family gave the metal coffin to the museum after his remains were exhumed from Burr Oak Cemetery in suburban Chicago in 2005 so an autopsy could be performed—at last. The Justice Department decided to open a new investigation to explore additional leads.

The **second floor** holds a family history center where individuals and groups may learn how to access databases and explore their family history. The museum provides free access to databases such as Ancestry.com, and staff will take an appointment to work with you on how to search databases and use other genealogical research techniques once you leave the museum.

Black athleticism is featured on the **third floor** in a gallery called Sports: Leveling the Playing Field. Also on the third floor, The Power of Place contains a series of "place studies" that explore how location feeds the Black experience.

Now, let's talk about how much fun the **fourth-floor** "culture galleries" are. In the popular "Musical Crossroads" gallery, the rehearsal piano Thomas Dorsey played at Chicago's Pilgrim Baptist Church introduces the soul-stirring power of gospel music. (After all, it was sacred songs like "We Shall Overcome" that tightened the ties that bind.) Other artifacts include Chuck Berry's red Eldorado Cadillac and a Louis Armstrong 1946 Selmer trumpet, inscribed with his name. On the quirky end of things, you'll find a replica Parliament-Funkadelic mothership.

The Neighborhood Record Store in the Musical Crossroads gallery is a communal space to share the love of music and musical periods. Browse through record covers and play with a digital touch screen to cycle through songs, artists, themes, regions, and periods. You might wanna bust a move when you remember the songs you've always loved, some you forgot, and others newly discovered. The artistry of album covers says a lot too.

The circular space that denotes the Cultural Expressions gallery covers African American foodways, artistry, dance, and language, both spoken and written. It extends into the Africa diaspora. One of Mary Jackson's Gullah sweetgrass baskets is on display here.

National Archives

701 Constitution Ave.; tel. 202/357-5000; www.museum.archives.gov; daily 10am-5:30pm; free; Metro: Archives-Navy Memorial-Penn Quarter, (Green and Yellow lines)

When King gave his final speech at Mason Temple on April 3, 1968, he drew enthusiastic applause when he said, "All we say to America is to be true to what you said on paper."[3] Well, those papers are right here at the National Archives at the heart of the National Mall, in a grand temple-style Greek Revival building featuring 72 Corinthian columns. In the Rotunda for the Charters of Freedom, the Constitution is on display, a sacred space befitting its role of showcasing the country's most important document. So are the Declaration of Independence and Bill of Rights.

The original Emancipation Proclamation is here, too, though it is not allowed out more than 30 hours a year and can usually be seen on Martin Luther King Jr. Day. Otherwise, visitors may view a facsimile of the document that shows how President Lincoln freed enslaved Black people living in secessionist states. Archives from the civil rights movement include a letter to President Eisenhower from 12-year-old Marilyn Albertson seeking his help in the Little Rock school desegregation crisis.

The archives consist of permanent and temporary exhibits, and it is possible to register to do research and view some original documents and letters under careful watch. Walk-up access is possible, but reservations are encouraged, especially during high season from March through Labor Day. At 9:45am Monday-Friday, reserved guided tours are offered. Seven days a week, timed entries start at 10:30am, and the last entry is 90 minutes before close. If you have a tour reservation, head to the Special Events door on Constitution Avenue and 7th Street. People without time-entry reservations must enter at 9th Street and Constitution Avenue.

DOWNTOWN AND PENN QUARTER

The White House

1600 Pennsylvania Ave. NW; tel. 202/456-7041; www.whitehouse.gov; self-guided tours (you must apply in advance) Tues.-Thurs. 7:30am-11:30am, Fri.-Sat. 7:30am-1:30pm; free; Metro: McPherson Square Station (Blue, Orange, and Silver lines), Farragut North (Red line)

The history of the White House, official residence of the U.S. president, is not a proud one: Enslaved and free Black people provided most of the labor to construct it, and several presidents used enslaved labor in the building's day-to-day operations. This includes Thomas Jefferson, who relied on three enslaved teenage girls (Ursula Granger Hughes, Edith Fossett, and Frances Hern) for cooking. Other enslaved Black people worked alongside White laborers and freedmen in Jefferson's White House, cutting timber, quarrying stone, and making bricks. Historian Bob Arnebeck curated a list of 200 names of enslaved Black people who worked in the White House and Capitol from 1792-1800. His list is not exhaustive.

Jim Crow traditions extended to the White House too, and Black people were rarely welcome here. Frederick Douglass and Sojourner Truth were received here during President Abraham Lincoln's term in the 19th century. But when President Theodore Roosevelt invited Booker T. Washington to eat dinner in 1901, all hell broke loose. Southern politicians and news outlets were apoplectic—and mean. It took decades for another African American to be invited back.

There is, however, a history of Black civil rights leaders meeting with U.S. presidents. Notably, after the 1963 March on Washington for Jobs and Freedom, civil rights leaders, including King, John Lewis (SNCC), A. Philip Randolph, and Roy Wilkins met with President Kennedy and Vice President Johnson in the Oval Office to discuss what it would take to get a comprehensive civil rights bill passed. Other African Americans made their way into the White House—as entertainers—and Black children were invited to the annual White House Easter Egg Roll, an event that began in the Rutherford B. Hayes administration in 1878. The first Black White House executive was E. Frederic Morrow, an administrative officer for special projects from 1955-1961.

Given this backstory, the idea of a Black family living at 1600 Pennsylvania Avenue NW is a big deal—but that's exactly what came to pass after the 2008 election of Barack Obama, when Barack, Michelle, Malia, Sasha, and First Grandmother Marian Shields Robinson moved in. Michelle knew it too. In 2016 she poignantly and optimistically stated, "I wake up every morning in a house that was built by slaves. And I watch my daughters, two beautiful, intelligent, Black young women, playing with their dogs on the White House lawn . . . So, look, don't let anyone ever tell you that this country isn't great, that somehow, we need to make it great again. Because this right now is the greatest country on earth."[4]

The conversation continued in June 2020, in the wake of the murder of George Floyd, a Black man, by a police officer in Minneapolis. Two blocks of 16th street leading up to the presidential residence were emblazoned with giant yellow letters reading **"Black Lives Matter,"** a clear message from DC Mayor Muriel Bowser to the 45th president—and the world. It was a long time coming.

If you want to visit public areas of the White House, you'll need to make a request through your congressperson (online or call) up to three months, and no less than three weeks, before your requested date. Free self-guided tours are offered on a first-come, first-serve basis. They take about 35-45 minutes, but you can take as long as you'd like. Space is limited.

★ National Portrait Gallery

8th and F Streets NW; tel. 202/633-8300; www.npg.si.edu; daily 11:30am-7pm; free; Metro: Gallery Place/Chinatown Station (Red, Green, and Yellow lines)

The National Portrait Gallery is the nation's only museum dedicated to collecting and displaying paintings, drawings, photos, engravings, sculptures, and other art forms that show human expression and likenesses. It also houses the only complete collection of presidential portraits outside the White House, including Kehinde Wiley's vibrant, large-scale rendering of 44th President Barack Obama and Amy Sherald's oil-on-linen portrait of First Lady Michelle Obama.

Both portraits of the beloved first couple were heralded for breaking out of staid patterns previously used to depict the nation's most eminent citizens and have been wildly popular since being unveiled in February 2018. (Note that if you're planning a visit in summer of 2021, these portraits are scheduled to tour the nation at that time.)

Wiley's Barack Obama portrait is on display in the America's Presidents gallery.

Photos (top to bottom): National Archives; The White House; Michelle Obama's portrait by Amy Sherald

Wiley has reinvented portraiture by styling young Black men in the vein of European royalty. His oil-on-canvas painting of Obama shows the president seated with arms crossed in front of a decidedly unconventional backdrop of foliage and chrysanthemums, the official flower of Chicago. The portrait of Mrs. Obama, which is on display in the 20th Century Americans exhibition, caused a social media sensation at its debut, when an onlooker snapped a photo of two-year-old Parker Curry staring awestruck, mouth agape, at the portrait of the first lady. The image went viral, and the following year Parker published a children's book, *Parker Looks Up,* and developed a special friendship with the former first lady (forever first lady to some of us).

In addition to the Obama portraits, the vast collection contains more than 23,000 media forms and features activists, artists, politicians, scientists, and inventors, including a treasure trove of works that document the civil rights movement. A black-and-white photo by Charmian Reading shows Fannie Lou Hamer participating in the March Against Fear from Memphis to Jackson, Mississippi, in June 1966, while screen prints by artist Ben Shahn depict James Chaney, Andrew Goodman, and Michael Schwerner, the three Freedom Summer activists who were slain by Klansmen in Mississippi. Rev. Jesse L. Jackson is featured in opaque paint on paperboard in a creation commissioned in 1970 by the American master, Jacob Lawrence, noted for his rendering of the Black experience. Hosea Williams—who King called "my wild man, my Castro"[5] because of his prodigious skill as a SCLC organizer—is seen in a dual image photo wearing a work shirt, making expressive gestures and glistening with sweat. Also in the collection is a photograph of President Johnson signing the Civil Rights Act of 1964.

About 900 works are on display at any given time, and you can search the website to find out what's on view during your visit. There are 17 galleries that are arranged in chronological order, making it easy to find pieces from specific eras. Plan on spending at least an hour or two here—there's so much to see. The front stairs are a great place to eat lunch, while the courtyard is a sheltered rainy-day hideaway.

Black Lives Matter Plaza

The National Portrait Gallery is off the Gallery Place/Chinatown Metro stop, a block from the 7th and 9th Street Metro exits. The building shares space with the Smithsonian American Art Museum.

CAPITOL HILL AND ATLAS DISTRICT

U.S. Capitol

First St. SE; tel. 202/226-8000; www.visitthecapitol.gov; Mon.-Sat. 8:30am-4:30pm; free; Metro: Union Station (Red line), Capitol South Station (Blue, Orange, and Silver lines)

The U.S. Capitol is where presidents are inaugurated, State of the Union speeches are given, and the U.S. Congress makes laws (which either get us closer our written ideals or farther away from them, depending on the administration and state of cultural wars at the time). When the American people feel like our legislators are getting it wrong, the Capitol is also where activists organize rallies and protests to let 'em know.

CAPITOL VISITOR CENTER

Free, guided tours of the **Capitol Visitor Center** (Mon.-Sat. 8:30am-4pm) take 45 minutes and are available from 8:40am-3:20pm. Tours include a visit to the Crypt, the Rotunda, and National Statuary Hall. Advance reservations are encouraged and may be made online up to 90 days in advance. A very limited number of same-day passes are available at the lower level information desks and will require a wait.

The **Crypt** is on the first floor of the Capitol in a large circular area featuring 40 Doric columns and sandstone arches that support the floor of the Rotunda. Inside, you'll find 13 statues from the National Statuary Hall Collection, which represents the original colonies, plus a replica of the Magna Carta.

The Capitol **Rotunda** is a large domed, circular room on the second floor in the center of the Capitol. The room, filled with natural light, is used for important ceremonies. Rosa Parks lay in honor here on October 30-31, 2005. A bust of King is also on display. Sculpted by African American artist John Wilson, the bronze sculpture is

U.S. Capitol

CIVIL RIGHTS LEGISLATION

This thing called democracy, well, it sometimes works . . . eventually. Progress takes time, but as the following list of laws and polices shows, African Americans' need for and insistence on equity is tied directly to the best notion of what the United States represents.

ENACTED LEGISLATION

- **Thirteenth Amendment** (1865): Abolished slavery and involuntary servitude, except as punishment for a crime.
- **Civil Rights Act** (1866): Made citizens of all male persons born in the United States, "without distinction of race or color, or previous condition of slavery or involuntary servitude."
- **Fourteenth Amendment** (1868): Granted citizenship and equal civil and legal rights to African Americans and formerly enslaved freed men after the Civil War.
- **Fifteenth Amendment** (1870): Prohibited federal and state governments from denying the right to vote based on race, color, or "previous condition of servitude."
- **Civil Rights Act** (1871): Allowed the president to suspend the writ of habeas corpus to combat the Ku Klux Klan and other White supremacy groups.
- **Civil Rights Act** (1875): Enacted during Reconstruction, this act gave African Americans equal treatment in public accommodations and public transportation and prohibited our exclusion from juries.
- **Nineteenth Amendment** (1920): Guaranteed all women the right to vote. (The White-led suffrage movement had no room for Black women, so they made room for themselves and embraced the vote with zeal and courage.)
- **Civil Rights Act** (1957): Allowed federal prosecutors to get court injunctions against interference with the right to vote.
- **Civil Rights Act** (1960): Established federal inspection of voter registration polls and levied penalties for anyone who blocked someone's attempt to register to vote.
- **Twenty-Fourth Amendment** (1964): Forbid states and the federal government levying poll taxes in national elections.
- **Civil Rights Act** (1964): Ended segregation in public places and banned employment discrimination on the basis of race, color,

religion, sex, or national origin. Representative Howard Smith (D-VA) introduced the Smith Amendment to Title VII of the Civil Rights Act to exclude discrimination on the basis of sex. He wasn't doing women a favor: Smith opposed civil rights and hoped this addition would diminish and defeat the bill. Fortunately, it didn't.

- **Voting Rights Act** (1965): Focused on overcoming state- and local-level legal barriers preventing African Americans from exercising their right to vote.
- **Civil Rights Act, aka Fair Housing Act** (1968): Barred housing discrimination based on the "refusal to sell or rent a dwelling to any person because of his race, color, religion, or national origin."

ASKED BUT NOT YET ANSWERED

- **Emmett Till Antilynching Act**: At this writing, lynching is *not* a federal crime in the United States. In 2019, bills making lynching a hate crime passed both houses, but the Senate couldn't reconcile them. Republican Senator Rand Paul (R-KY) was the holdup as of August 2020. The first anti-lynching act was introduced in 1918 by Congressman Leonidas Dyer (R-MO) and failed to pass many times. The most recent bill was introduced by Congressman Bobby Rush (D-IL) in 2019.
- **H.R. 40, Study of Reparations**: Late Congressman John Conyers (D-MI) introduced this bill to simply *study* the issue of reparations for descendants of enslaved African Americans. For three decades, Congress has refused to pass it.
- **Restoration of 1965 Voting Rights Act**: *Shelby v. Holder* (2013) invalidated portions of the law that protected African Americans' right to vote. When Congressman John Lewis (D-GA) passed away in 2020, advocates immediately suggested Congress honor him restoring the law he for which he fought—valiantly.
- **CROWN (Create a Respectful and Open World for Natural Hair) Act**: The aim of this act, which was created in 2019, is to get legislatures to ban race-based discrimination based on hair texture. (Workplace and school-based policies jeorpardize Black people's ability to wear our hair the way it grows out of our head naturally: We have lost jobs and been kicked out of school for our hair styles.) The CROWN Act has passed in several states and failed in others, but the movement continues to push for full enactment everywhere.

36 inches high on a 66-inch Belgian black marble base.

The **National Statuary Hall,** a large, two-story, semicircular room south of the Rotunda, is a popular place. Here, Rosa Parks, diminutive in life, is memorialized in a nearly 9-foot-tall, 2,700-pound bronze sculpture. In a stunning display of symbolism, Parks is depicted sitting down with her legs and arms crossed, holding her purse. Her back is against a tall column, as if saying she will not be moved.

Depending on group size and general business at the Capitol, your tour may include a visit to the **old Supreme Court and Senate chambers.** If you consider that the court chamber is where original constitutional law cases were heard, the site is hauntingly breathtaking. This is where John Adams, a vocal opponent of slavery, argued in February 1841 that the Mende people who were captured from the African continent and held captive were taken illegally and should be allowed to go home. In *U.S. v. The Amistad*, the Supreme Court ruled 7-1 in their favor. Thirty-five surviving captives sailed home on the ship Gentleman in November 1841.

Though not a part of the guided Capitol tour, it is possible to visit galleries for the House of Representatives or the Senate when they are in session by securing a pass from your representative. International visitors should visit the House and Senate Appointment Desks in the upper level of the Capitol Visitor Center to secure a pass. Get to the House and Senate Galleries through the Capitol Visitor Center upper level. **House Gallery** visits are Monday-Friday 9am-4pm. Depending on demand, the last entry may be before 4pm, so be sure to get there in advance. **Senate Gallery** visits are open during scheduled recesses of a week or more and take place Monday-Friday 9am-4:15pm. The gallery closes at 4:30pm on recess days. Call 202/224-0057 to find out if the Senate Gallery is open.

VISITING YOUR REPRESENTATIVES

Watching politicians on television, Americans sometimes forget the bedrock principle of democracy: that those elected representatives work for the people, not the other way around. So, when a citizen visits Washington DC, a good first stop is a congressional office. Regular folks can make appointments to meet with lawmakers or legislative staff members to share concerns, get updates on important issues, or otherwise provide good old-fashioned citizen supervision. Call or email your lawmaker to get an appointment. Visit www.house.gov/representatives to find your representative or www.senate.gov to find and contact your senator. You may also book Capitol tours through your representatives and senators. Visiting those halls of power, with or without an appointment, means stumbling upon impromptu press conferences, exchanging ideas with visitors from across the country, and possibly lining up for lunch at the same cafeteria chow line as a former presidential candidate.

House members keep their offices in three buildings on the south side of the U.S. Capitol, while U.S. senators have offices on the north side of the Capitol. Those buildings hold the fabled "corridors of power" you may have heard about your whole life. This is where congressional hearings, which are open to the public, are held, and a quick pop-in visit can teach citizens more than any book about partisanship and the workings of government. Visit either www.house.gov or www.senate.gov to find out day-of committee and floor happenings. If you arrive early for a hearing, you might be surprised to see working-class folks in bicycle shorts and T-shirts lined up to get inside. Wealthy lawyers and lobbyists hire these bicycle messengers to hold their place in line so that they can stroll in at the last minute to seize the prime gallery seats in the front rows.

Supreme Court

1 First St. NE; tel. 202/479-3030; www.supremecourt.gov; Mon.-Fri. 9am-4:30pm; free; Metro: Union Station (Red line), Capitol South Station (Blue, Orange, and Silver lines)

The notion of "separate but equal" was created here. And it later died here.

History is made at the Supreme Court of the United States, and it's not always the glorious kind. Inside this hallowed chamber, some downright ugly rulings have held back the causes of human dignity, equal protection, and civil rights, while other decisions have cleared the path for slow, gradual progress. The court's vicissitude on matters of civil rights is well documented, from the dehumanizing 1857 *Dred Scott v. Sanford* decision, which ruled African Americans could not be considered U.S. citizens, to the 1954 landmark *Brown v. Board of Education* ruling, which declared that segregation must end in public schools. (Southern cities willfully resisted the *Brown* decision, and the civil rights movement turned up the heat to force the issue. The nation's definitions of freedom, justice, and equality have been in a process of continuous evolution since.)

The court meets between October and June. A limited number of gallery seats are set aside for regular folks, making it possible to see the nine justices in action. Otherwise, visitors are encouraged to take a self-guided tour of public areas and engage with programming, court lectures, exhibitions, and a visitor film. Visitors can also seek tickets through their congressional offices for educational tours of the nation's highest court. It's also possible to read about cases, past or present, through www.supremecourt.gov or independent sites like www.oyez.com.

The U.S. Supreme Court is a stop on the official U.S. Civil Rights Trail.

VISITING THE SUPREME COURT

The Supreme Court is open to the public on weekdays (9am-4:30pm). You can explore the first-floor Great Hall, which contains a statue of John Marshall, the fourth chief justice who helped establish the judicial branch's ability to review the constitutionality of actions by the federal and legislative branches, and the ground floor, which features exhibits showcasing

Supreme Court

CIVIL RIGHTS SUPREME COURT CASES

Over the years, various Supreme Court cases have either advanced or harmed civil rights causes. Below are some of the movement's biggest wins and losses:

- **LOSS**: *Dred Scott v. Sandford* (1857): Denied citizenship to enslaved Black people.
- **LOSS**: Civil Rights Cases (1883): Ruled the Civil Rights Act of 1875 unconstitutional, allowing private sector segregation.
- **LOSS**: *Plessy v. Ferguson* (1896): Endorsed segregation by "separate but equal" principle.
- **WIN**: *Powell v. Alabama* (1932): Overturned convictions of nine Black teens accused of rape in 1931, and guaranteed right to fair trial.
- **WIN**: *Murray v. Maryland* (1936): Desegregated University of Maryland's Law School.
- **WIN**: *Gaines v. Canada* (1938): Ordered the University of Missouri law school to accept Black students.
- **WIN**: *Smith v. Allwright* (1944): Thurgood Marshall successfully challenged "White primaries" that blocked Southern Black people from voting.
- **WIN**: *Morgan v. Virginia* (1946): Overturned law enforcing segregation on interstate buses and trains.
- **WIN**: *Shelley v Kraemer* (1948): Stopped enforcement of racially restrictive covenants, which blocked Black people from buying homes in so-called "White" neighborhoods.
- **WIN**: *Sweatt v. Painter* and *McLaurin v. Oklahoma* (1950): Required states to admit Black students to their graduate and professional schools.

the history of the court and a short film featuring interviews with several justices, starting every 15 minutes in the theater.

Thirty-minute lectures on the workings of the court occur when court is not in session. They begin daily at 9:30am and start every hour on the half hour until the last lecture at 3:30pm.

VIEWING A COURT SESSION

Since the Supreme Court's arguments are not televised, attending an oral argument offers citizens rare insight into court proceedings.

Court chambers are reminiscent of a church, with the chief justice and eight associate justices seated behind a raised mahogany bench, under the watchful eye of marble friezes of "lawgivers" like Moses, Confucius, and Solon. Attorneys presenting arguments sit at tables in front of the justices, with members of the public gallery

- **WIN**: *Brown v. Board of Education* (1954): Ruled separation of Black and White students in public schools unconstitutional.
- **WIN**: *Cooper v. Aaron* (1958): Ruled that the state of Arkansas could not undermine *Brown v. Board of Education.*
- **WIN**: *Boynton v. Virginia* (1960): Declared segregation of interstate transportation facilities unconstitutional. (The Freedom Rides that took place the following year tested this decision.)
- **WIN**: *Bailey v. Patterson* (1962): Prohibited racial segregation of interstate and intrastate transportation facilities.
- **WIN**: *Heart of Atlanta Motel, Inc. v. United States* (1964): Ruled that the motel had no right to select its guests, free from government oversight regulation.
- **WIN**: *Harper v. Virginia State Board of Elections* (1966): Overturned a precedent that allowed poll taxes in national elections.
- **WIN**: *Loving v. Virginia* (1967): Ruled bans on interracial marriage unconstitutional.
- **WIN**: *Roe v. Wade* (1973): Protected a woman's right to choose an abortion (or not). The decision was very significant for Black women, who have not traditionally enjoyed bodily autonomy.
- **LOSS**: *Shelby v. Holder* (2013): Ruled that jurisdictions with past patterns of bad behavior, including vast swaths of the South, are no longer required to seek preclearance to change voting policies.
- **WIN**: *Bostock v. Clayton County* (2020): Applied Title VII of the Civil Rights Act of 1964, which forbid discrimination "on the basis of sex," to outlaw anti-LGBTQ employment discrimination—one of several ways the landmark act has benefited other groups in addition to the African American community.

behind them. To the left, at tables partially obscured by columns, are journalists there to document the proceedings, while officers of the court and guests of the justices are seated on the opposite side.

First-time observers often are struck by how few words the opposing attorneys are allowed to utter before justices begin jumping in with pointed questions that often reveal their leanings. Some judges might ask rapid-fire questions, while pressing the advocates to defend their written arguments; others are more reserved. In decades past, Thurgood Marshall, the first Black Supreme Court justice, was known as "the great dissenter" for opposing majority Supreme Court decisions he deemed violations of civil and human rights. He supported affirmative action and aspired to preserve civil rights wins.

Since the court waits weeks or months before issuing its written rulings, a trip to the Supreme Court often inspires feverish debates among members of the gallery as they exit the courthouse and find themselves surrounded by competing groups of protesters demanding, "How'd it go? How'd it go?" Once that written ruling is finally issued, the law becomes "settled"—until the next shake-up, at least.

Because seating is limited and first-come, first-served, would-be observers begin forming lines early in the morning on the plaza outside the building. One line is for those who want to sit through an entire argument; the other is for those wanting to be let inside for a brief, three-minute glimpse. Seating for the first argument begins at 9:30am Monday-Friday. For the most controversial cases, including matters of civil rights or anything involving competing interest groups, seats are hot-ticket items, so don't be surprised if the lines are long. You're more likely to get a seat for one of the lower-profile cases.

To find out what cases are being heard, navigate to www.supremecourt.gov, where you'll find a calendar and list of current cases. (Tip: the privately run www.SCOTUSblog.com is much more user-friendly and provides links to cases, summaries, and analyses, plus a podcast.)

Emancipation (Freedmen's) Memorial

E Capitol St. NE, Lincoln Park; tel. 202/690-5155; www.nps.gov/cahi; Metro: Eastern Market Station (Blue, Orange, and Silver lines)

This bronze statue in Lincoln Park shows President Lincoln holding a copy of the Emancipation Proclamation in one hand while standing over a formerly enslaved Black man. The Black man, who kneels, freed from shackles, is modeled on Archer Alexander, the last person caught under the Fugitive Slave Act.

The statue was funded largely by formerly enslaved Black people, including a Virginia woman named Charlotte Scott, who donated the first $5 she earned as a free person in tribute to Lincoln, according to the National Park Service. It was unveiled in 1876, on the 11th anniversary of Lincoln's death, with remarks by noted Black abolitionist Frederick Douglass before a crowd that included President Ulysses S. Grant. According to Yale University historian David W. Bight, Black organizations and leaders celebrated the statue's dedication with a huge parade that was attended by Supreme Court justices and Howard University law dean and master of ceremonies John Mercer Langston, among others.[6] A young Black poet named Cordelia Ray recited a poem called "Lincoln."

The statue is controversial, and has long been criticized by some for its apparent depiction of Lincoln, who signed the Emancipation Proclamation executive order, singlehandedly freeing a Black man, as if that man had no agency or sense of self. Douglass himself noted at the unveiling ceremony that Lincoln was "ready and willing at any time during the first years of his administration to deny, postpone, and sacrifice the rights of humanity in the Colored people to promote the welfare of the White people of this country."[7] In 2020, in the wake of the police killings of several African Americans across the country and the subsequent removal of Confederate statues in several locations, critics of the Emancipation Memorial called for its removal as well.

One argument for removing the memorial and displaying (and contextualizing) it in a museum comes from Congresswoman Eleanor Holmes Norton, DC's nonvoting delegate. "Although formerly enslaved Americans paid for this statue to be built in 1876, the design and sculpting process was done without their input, and it shows," she stated.[8] In the summer of 2020, she announced her intention to work with the NPS to remove it or introduce legislation to do so.

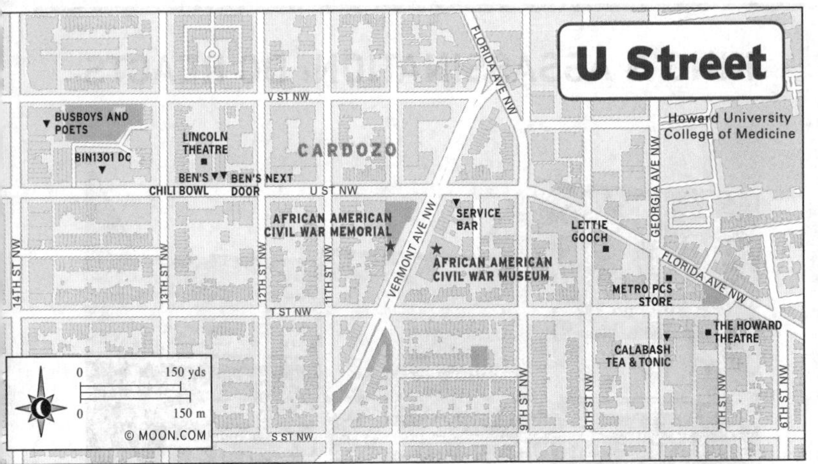

U STREET AND SHAW

Carter G. Woodson Home National Historic Site

1538 9th St. NW; tel. 202/426-5961; www.nps.gov/cawo; Thurs.-Sat. 9am-5pm; free; Metro: Shaw-Howard University (Green and Yellow lines)

The son of formerly enslaved parents, the self-taught Carter G. Woodson earned a doctorate degree at Harvard and eventually served as liberal arts dean at Howard University. Woodson sought to secure an accurate history of African Americans. In this home, he published *The Journal of Negro History* and *The Negro History Bulletin*, part of an effort to popularize the study of the African American experience. In 1926, he established Negro History Week, now celebrated as Black History Month. Until he came along, finding accurate information about the history and lived experience of African Americans was rare.

Woodson's Victorian row house has characteristics of Italianate style, with ornamented windows, a decorative cast iron stoop railing, and hard-burned brick masonry. In the basement, Woodson stored papers and artifacts linked to the history of African Americans and the African diaspora. Woodson worked tirelessly to get the story of Black America into the hands of everyday Black Americans, and one first-floor room was used for packing and shipping Black history periodicals and literature.

Woodson's work isn't quite as present in the home as visitors might hope, but as you walk through, try to imagine the work that took place here. Profound thinkers and scholars worked in this home office or consulted with Woodson, as did Harlem Renaissance poet Langston Hughes and author Zora Neale Hurston. Powerful women thought leaders supported his work, including educator and civil rights activist Mary McLeod Bethune, who served as the first female president of the association he founded.

A National Historic Landmark, Woodson's home is open to the public for tours, but space is limited to 20 people. Guided tours take about 45 minutes on a first-come first-served basis. Reservations ($1) are accepted. They occur at 9am, 10am, 11am, 1pm, 2pm, 3pm, and 4pm Thursday-Saturday. Reserve a spot at www.recreation.gov or call 877/444-6777. The staff at the Frederick Douglass National Historic Site operates this facility, so you may call there for reservations too: 202/426-5961.

KING'S ASSASSINATION: DC REACTS

Firefighters spray water on shops that were burned during the riots that followed Martin Luther King Jr.'s assassination.

As news about King's assassination on April 4, 1968, spread, segregated Black areas like the U Street corridor, which served as a cultural and nightlife hub from the 1920s through the '40s, suffered from the mighty howl of anger and hurt unleashed, and enraged residents filled the streets. It seemed that generations of racial oppression and pride swallowing was too much for Black residents living in both the shadow and the glow of the capitol.

Stokely Carmichael (who changed his name to Kwame Ture), former head of SNCC, was out there, trying to keep things calm. Stores where Black people felt they had been taken advantage of were looted. Buildings burned. Police used tear gas, and even though officers were told not to shoot, they did. Eventually, a thousand troops moved in and occupied the city. Hundreds of businesses along 14th Street suffered fire and looting damage. Many of the affected stores never reopened.

Other segregated Black neighborhoods in cities nationwide saw uprisings, including Detroit, Baltimore, Chicago, New York, and Wilmington, Delaware. In all, the destruction that unfurled over four days in DC was concentrated in Washington's segregated Black communities, and while the city recovered, it took years to do so. The blight reminding residents of the pain of that period has faded with new development in the hardest-hit areas—14th and Seventh Streets NW and H Street NE. The new enemy? Rising costs and cultural erasure powered by gentrification.

African American Civil War Museum

1925 Vermont Ave. NW; tel. 202/667-2667; www.afroamcivilwar.org; Mon. 10am-5pm, Tues.-Fri. 10am-6:30pm, Sat. 10am-4pm, Sun. noon-4pm; free; Metro: U St./African American Civil War Memorial/Cardozo (Green and Yellow lines)

The African American Civil War Museum opened in January 1999 to rectify the erasure and depresencing of Black soldiers and sailors in the narrative of the nation's armed forces. The museum does so much more than that: The stories told in this 14,000-square-foot institution reveal the unbreakable pride felt by African Americans in the country that they built.

Narrative displays, illustrations, and photographs reveal the untold story of the Black presence in the Civil War and beyond. A rendering of the first Black congressmen elected during Reconstruction (1865-1877) is shown, as well as a photo and narrative of P. B. S. Pinchback, a Union Army officer who became the first Black governor of Louisiana in 1872. Though biracial and light enough to pass for White, he never denied having a Black mother.

Other exhibits also touch on the economics of enslavement and the Tuskegee Airmen, the first Black military aviators in the U.S. Army Air Corps, the precursor of the U.S. Air Force. Historic interpreters dressed in period soldier garb, complete with unloaded rifles, provide context as they guide guests through the museum. The museum also offers genealogical research assistance (via the website or an onsite kiosk) so you can search for family members who served as soldiers and sailors in the Civil War.

The museum is located in the historic Grimke School, named for civil rights leader Archibald Grimke, who once led the DC NAACP chapter and was the second Black person to graduate from Harvard Law School. Guided tours are available with a reservation. Plan to take at least an hour to fully appreciate what the museum has to offer.

African American Civil War Memorial

corner of Vermont Ave., 10th St. and U St. NW; tel. 202/426-6841; www.nps.gov/afam; Metro: U St./African American Civil War Memorial/Cardozo (Green and Yellow lines)

This memorial statue by African American sculptor Ed Hamilton is dedicated to more than 200,000 Black soldiers and sailors who fought in the Civil War and helped free more than four million enslaved Black people. The nine-foot bronze statue, called *The Spirit of Freedom,* features servicemen from both the Army and Navy and a soldier and his family in back with the Spirit of Freedom watching over them.

Completed in 1997, the memorial is the first to honor Black people who fought for the Union after President Lincoln issued the Emancipation Proclamation and created Black regiments in the Army and Navy. A granite wall inscribed with names of those in the United States Colored Troops, along with their White officers, accompanies the statue.

The memorial is located across the street from the African American Civil War Museum.

Howard University

2400 6th St. NW; tel. 202/806-6100; www.home.howard.edu; Shaw-Howard University (Green and Yellow lines)

This historically Black university (located in the historically Black Shaw community) was founded in 1867 and named for General Oliver Otis Howard, then head of the Freedmen's Bureau. This location provided food, education, and shelter for formerly enslaved Black people during Reconstruction. Howard persuaded Congress to put up the money for the school.

Several Black fraternities and sororities were founded at Howard: Alpha Kappa Alpha (1908), Omega Psi Phi (1911), Delta

Sigma Theta (1913), Phi Beta Sigma (1914), and Zeta Phi Beta (1920). The Delta's founding members participated in the 1913 Women's Suffrage March. Notable Bisons include the first Black Supreme Court Justice Thurgood Marshall; civil rights leader Stokely Carmichael; sociologist E. Franklin Frazier; civil rights leader Andrew Young; Nobel Prize-winning author Toni Morrison; and 2020 Democratic vice presidential nominee Kamala Harris. Howard Law School Dean Charles Hamilton Houston taught a generation of great legal minds (including Marshall) and was known as the "Man Who Killed Jim Crow" for his role in almost every civil rights case before the Supreme Court from 1930 to *Brown v. Board of Education* (1954).

Today, the prevailing mood on the Howard campus (which is a stop on the official U.S. Civil Rights Trail) is one of determination and purpose. The institution explodes the myth of a monolithic Black experience because Black students represent the diaspora: Several presidents on the African continent have been educated here, and even those reared in the United States hail from different social classes, geographies, and lived experiences. This is an environment that embraces cultural diversity: While Howard was established to educate Black people, the student body, comprised of more than 6,000 students, is multiracial and global.

Howard's famous **Yard,** an open space on the northern end of the campus, is a center of Howard's celebrated homecoming and where the entertainment extravaganza that is Yardfest occurs. You'll see fraternity and sorority members here, posted up near tall trees designated for each group. The greenspace is surrounded by nine buildings and is listed as a National Historic Landmark along with three other campus buildings: **Andrew Rankin Memorial Chapel, Frederick Douglass Memorial Hall,** and **Founders Library** (a Georgian-style building where a lot of the work for *Brown v. Board of Education* took place). Andrew Rankin Memorial Chapel contains splendid stained-glass windows featuring the first three chapel deans, Dr. Howard W. Thurman (a Morehouse man, early proponent of Gandhian principles of nonviolence, and spiritual advisor to King), Dr. Daniel G. Hill, and Dr. Evans E. Crawford.

Two-hour campus tours for students, families, and groups interested in the Howard experience occur Monday-Friday at 10am, noon, and 2pm. Tours are led by savvy student ambassadors. Large groups are required to have one chaperone for every 25 students. To make a reservation, contact the Office of Admission or email campustour@howard.edu.

Meridian Hill Park (Malcolm X Park)

16th & W Streets NW; U Street/Columbia Heights (Green and Yellow lines)

Angela Davis gets credit for dubbing this park "Malcolm X Park" in the 1960s, when it became a gathering spot for Black activists. But Meridian Hill Park was a sacred space for Native Americans first. In the early 1800s, it was named for Commodore David Porter's house, Meridian Hill, at the prime meridian or what is now 16th Street. Before Greenwich time was used to map the continent, this was the starting point.

Today, the park features statuary such as Joan of Arc and Dante and acres of peaceful refuge and space to stretch and be creative through African dance, drum circles, yoga, or just relaxing on the grass. Accessible during daylight hours, the park features a multitiered cascading fountain that looks pretty awesome when it is actually working. Officially, the National Park Service calls this place Meridian Hill, but locals frequently call it Malcolm X. All power to the people—Malcolm X Park it is.

Meridian Hill Park (Malcolm X Park)

ANACOSTIA

★ Frederick Douglass National Historic Site

1411 W St. SE; tel. 202/426-5961; www.nps.gov/frdo; free; Metro: Anacostia Station (Green line)

Frederick Douglass's Victorian house on a hill is a likely metaphor for his rise to prominence. Born enslaved in 1818, Douglass escaped bondage and became a leading abolitionist, suffragist, orator, author, and diplomat who sowed the seeds of what would become the modern civil rights movement.

During Douglass's time, a butler greeted guests at his home at Cedar Hill, Anacostia. In the 14-room property, visitors can see rooms like the East Parlor (featuring several statues from Roman mythology), West Parlor, library (full of books—lots of books), and kitchen. The indoor kitchen, unusual for the time, burned coal instead of wood, which slowed the process of getting the home insured. Furnishings include the wooden rolltop desk where Douglass wrote speeches and his autobiography. His chair at the dining room table has wheels that allowed him to move around when telling stories in an animated fashion.

In the visitor center at the foot of the house, visitors can view a 19-minute film about Douglass. There's also a tactile statue of Frederick Douglass. A ramp leads up the incline to the house, and a wheelchair is available for use.

You must visit the house on a **tour;** it's not possible to walk through on your own. National Park Service rangers lead guided free 30-minute tours of the first and second floors at scheduled times. Reservations are recommended (especially on weekends, which are busy), but not required, for standard tours for groups up to 10 people. Standard tours occur at 9am, 12:15pm, 1:15pm, 3pm, 3:30pm, and 4pm daily, April-October. Tours for groups of 11-60 people are at 9:30am, 10:45am, and 2pm daily. Reservations are required for group tours and cost $1 for each reserved ticket or a $10 flat fee for school groups.

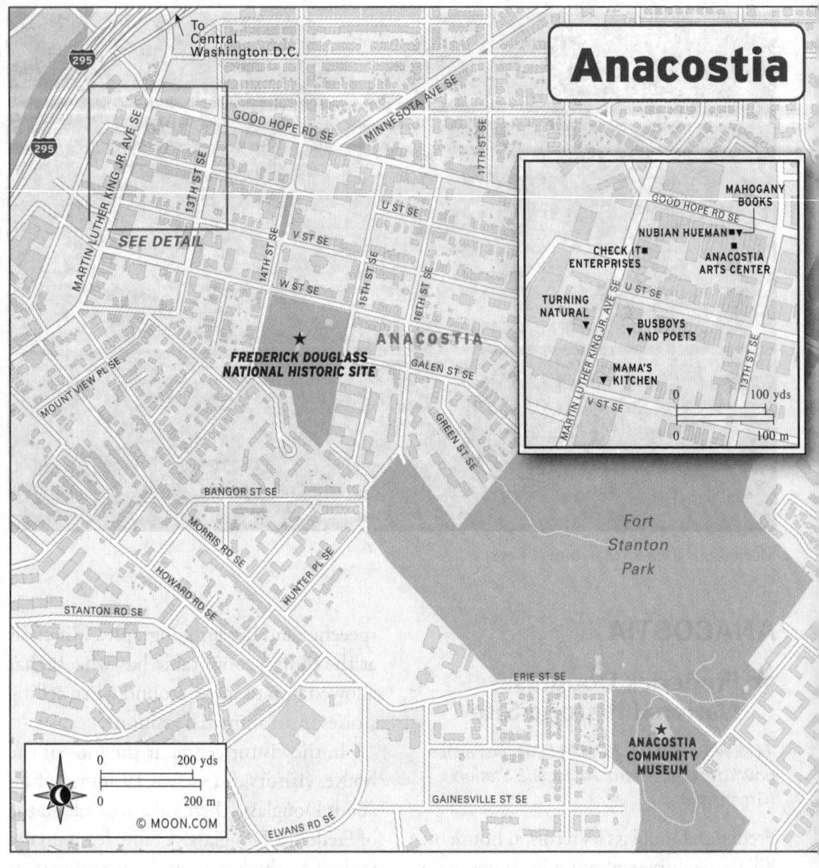

Anacostia Community Museum

1901 Fort Pl. SE; tel. 202/633-4820; www.anacostia.si.edu; Tues. 10am-8pm; Wed.-Mon. 10am-5pm; free; Metro: Anacostia Station (Green line)

Originally called The Anacostia Neighborhood Museum, this Smithsonian Institution community museum, which debuted in 1967, emerged from the realization that African Americans weren't going to museums on the mall, in part because African Americans have not always been made to feel comfortable in museums and couldn't always see themselves in narratives on display. Charged by the wins and losses of the '60s civil rights movement, and by a revolutionary embrace of Black power, the institution treated the history of the Black community as if it mattered—because it did.

The museum focuses on urban issues that impact DC residents and city dwellers everywhere. The facility features artifacts, photos, and news footage; an art and artifact collection; and an appointment-only library with about 8,000 books. See news footage of events like King marching in a parade in Shaw as he campaigned for home rule, so DC taxpayers could control their own affairs without undue federal oversight. A past exhibit called "A Right to City" explored economic investment and disinvestment across six DC neighborhoods. Another exhibit showcased works by Spiral, a Black artist collective that formed just before the March on Washington for Jobs and Freedom in 1963, lasting two years. Comprised of artists such as Emma Amos, Charles Alston, and Romare Bearden, Spiral held regular talks about art and activism in New York's Greenwich Village. Archival records include photographs, artwork, and ephemera linked to people like abolitionist Frederick Douglass and Tobias Henson, an 18th-century Washingtonian who purchased his freedom, then his wife's.

A special facet of this museum is that community members can see themselves reflected back in the exhibitions on display. Under the direction of founding director John Kinard, the museum began collecting oral histories and created a neighborhood archive. "Your Community, Your Story: Celebrating Five Decades of the Anacostia Community Museum, 1967-2017," which kicked off with a community block party, exhibited audio and video narratives from residents. During the coronavirus pandemic in 2020, the museum observed the city's stay-at-home order but encouraged residents tell their stories via video or phone in an initiative called #MomentsofResilience.

Docent-led tours are available for groups of five or more. Tours for school groups go 60-90 minutes long. Call 202/633-4868 to secure a tour reservation.

OTHER NEIGHBORHOODS

Mary McLeod Bethune Council House

1318 Vermont Ave. NW.; tel. 202/673-2402; www.nps.gov/mamc; Thurs.-Sat. 9am-4pm; free; Metro: Shaw-Howard U (Green line)

This northwest DC brick row house was the last home of the eminent educator and civil rights activist Mary McLeod Bethune. Born to formerly enslaved parents, Bethune was an accomplished educator and activist who served as a special advisor to President Franklin D. Roosevelt. In 1904, she founded Daytona Normal and Industrial Institute, which later became Bethune-Cookman College.

Bethune's home, known as the Council House, was also the first headquarters for the **National Council of Negro Women** (www.ncnw.org), an umbrella organization founded in 1935 to improve the lives of African American women, families, and communities. Council members met at this site in the 1940s through the 1960s. They even gathered here, in the front yard, before heading out to the 1963 March on Washington for Jobs and Freedom (though organization leader Dorothy Height was concerned about sexism in the movement, in particular, male leaders' resistance to having women speak at the rally).

Today, Bethune's 15-room Logan Circle home functions as a museum operated by the National Park Service. The home was damaged by fire, but replacement furnishings recreate its original feel. A pair of brass menorahs, gifted by a Jewish women's organization, rests on the parlor fireplace mantel. Vintage photography shows Black women sitting in the parlor with the menorahs nearby: a symbol of solidarity. An array of international flags sits on a grand piano, recognizing the council's efforts to improve the status of women around the globe. In another area of the home, a Bible sits open on a side table—not Bethune's actual Bible, but a symbol of her steadfast faith in God.

Rangers lead guided tours from 9am-4pm Thursday, Friday, and Saturday every hour on the hour, except for noon. Limit 25 guests per tour. This site is not wheelchair accessible and involves climbing stairs.

The council, meanwhile, is still active today. Some of its recent activities include literacy initiatives, public education, and the annual Black Family Reunion, held on the National Mall.

The Shaw-Howard U Metro stop is a few blocks north of Logan Circle, where this sight is located. Logan Circle is a

walkable community full of stylish shops and restaurants.

Washington National Cathedral

3101 Wisconsin Ave. NW; tel. 202/537-6200; www.cathedral.org; Mon.-Fri. 10am-5pm, Sat. 10am-4pm, Sun. services 8am, 12:45pm, 4pm; adults $12, seniors and students $8

In the age of Black Lives Matter, the admonition to "stay woke" might sound brand new—but it's a concept King eloquently spoke about in his final sermon, "Remaining Awake Through a Great Revolution," at this cathedral on March 31, 1968. Speaking from the cathedral's Canterbury Pulpit, King evoked the fictional Rip Van Winkle, who dozed off when George III was King of England, only to awake 20 years later to find out that George Washington was president of the United States. "He was completely lost," said King. "He did not know who he was."[9]

King's sermon took the crowd on journey of ideas and events: He summoned Jesus, Abraham Lincoln, and the English poet and scholar John Donne; his travels to India with his wife; Vietnam; and the Old Testament. He spoke of poverty and injustice at home and around the world. He left us with this enduring consideration: "We are tied together in the single garment of destiny, caught in an inescapable network of mutuality. And whatever affects one directly affects all indirectly."

The Gothic-style building still features the Canterbury Pulpit, from which King preached. The pulpit is built with stones from Canterbury Cathedral in England and depicts historical scenes of the translation of the Bible into English. A smaller niche statue depicts King in the Canterbury Pulpit with the words "I

Photos (top to bottom): Frederick Douglass National Historic Site; Washington National Cathedral; Washington National Cathedral's Canterbury Pulpit, where King spoke in 1968

Have A Dream." A carving of Rosa Parks is included in the cathedral's Human Rights Porch, near the front entrance.

Fun fact: A stone carving of Star Wars' Darth Vader, voiced by James Earl Jones, is featured on the north "dark" side of the cathedral.

Admission to the Cathedral includes a 30-minute docent-led **tour,** which is generally offered five times daily Monday-Saturday. Limited self-guided tours are available on Sunday afternoons with no admission charge. Advance reservations are needed for groups of 15 or more.

The closest Metro stops are Tenleytown and Woodley Park on the Red line, about 1.5 miles from the cathedral. You can also take a 30N, 30S, 31, or 33 bus going south on Wisconsin Avenue. The cathedral is on the left.

Tours and Local Guides

If you really want to dig into the civil rights story that lives in DC, consider a tour with a local guide. (Bonus: You'll get a ride to all the city's gems and can beeline back to any places you want to explore in greater depth.)

KB Tours, listed below, focuses exclusively on Black history in the city. There are also more general tour companies that offer African American-themed tours among their other offerings. These include **Tour Washington DC** (2312 Thornknoll Dr.; tel. 202/800-3119 or 888/796-8763; www.tourwashingtondc.com; $80 per person for a half-day tour), which also offers customizable multiday tours for groups; and **USA Guided Tours** (1155 F St. NW; tel. 844/390-3855; www.usaguidedtours.com/african-american-history-tour; $89 per person for a 3.5-hour tour). The bonus of KB Tours is a timed-entry NMAAHC ticket that allows visitors to explore the museum to their heart's content.

BUS TOUR

KB TOURS: AFRICAN AMERICAN HERITAGE TOURS

2312 Thornknoll Dr.; tel. 202/355-5579; www.kbtours.com; 9:30am daily; $80-100

DC native Kenny Burns started this company in 1996 after noticing a gap in DC-based heritage tours: "Nobody was talking about Black history," he says. As a tour guide, Burns delights in finding unknown details about heavy hitters in civil rights and Black history, explaining, "I like to give people facts they never heard about." One of Burns's favorite tour activities is helping visitors engage with the quotes inscribed on the King memorial, and connecting their discussion to contemporary issues.

Tours, which last four hours and are led by licensed tour guides and drivers, meet at Navy Memorial (701 Pennsylvania Ave. NW). Tours take place in a van or bus, and visitors are allowed to hop on and off to briefly engage with sites, which include places like the Frederick Douglass home, Dr. Martin Luther King, Jr. Memorial, and African American Civil War Museum. All tours include a timed-entry ticket to the National Museum of African American History and Culture, which is the last stop, so visitors have time to explore the museum.

Tours depart at 9:30am daily. There's also an evening version that departs 7pm Monday-Sunday. Reservations are required for all tours and must be made at least 24 hours in advance of the tour date.

Shopping

There's no dearth of places to spend money on souvenirs in Washington DC, but if the message of the movement means something to you, seriously consider spending your dollars in historic Black communities like Anacostia, which has the city's highest concentration of Black-owned businesses. The **Museum Store at the National Museum of African American History and Culture** is also worth a visit and often has a queue of people waiting to access its beautifully curated lineup of books, jewelry, apparel, and more.

U STREET AND SHAW

Clothing

LETTIE GOOCH

1921 8th St. NW #110; tel. 202/332-4242; www.lettiegooch.com; Mon.-Fri. noon-7pm, Sat. 11am-8pm, Sun. noon-6pm

Flirty, fun, hip dresses; chic loungewear; and face masks are just a few of the fun items on offer in this Shaw neighborhood boutique. Look for jewelry as well, from textured brass earrings to silver bar necklaces. The shop specializes in hand-picked items and is a great place to find gifts. The name may hearken to a time gone by, but the style found here is all about now.

Books and Media

SANKOFA VIDEO BOOKS & CAFE

2714 Georgia Ave. NW; tel. 202/234-4755; www.events.sankofa.com; Mon.-Fri. 11am-8pm, Sat.-Sun. 11am-6pm

The Black-owned bookstore and café doubles as a welcoming community space near Howard University. Sankofa takes its name from the mythic bird that looks back as it moves forward, a lesson for the Black community. The business started out in 1998 as a video distributor; today, they sell DVDs and videos featuring pan-African themes produced by the owners, Haile and Shirikiana Gerima, along with books (including a good selection of reads by Black authors), games, puzzles, stationery, and notebooks. The **café** (tel. 202/332-1084) serves everything from breakfast items to paninis and pizza.

DUPONT CIRCLE

Beauty Products

THE BROWN BEAUTY CO-OP

1365 Connecticut Ave. NW; tel. 202/506-2582; www.brownbeautyco-op.com; Tues.-Sat. 11am-7pm

This natural hair care products emporium in Dupont Circle sells "brown girl approved" clean skincare and cosmetics. The shop owners see themselves as filling a need: Despite all the buzz among Black women about natural haircare and styles, they realized that nowhere outside of salons saw to their needs. The beauty cooperative is a welcoming haven for those who are happy to be nappy and down to be brown.

Brown Beauty Co-Op in Dupont Circle

GO-GO DC

Go-Go music, a subgenre of funk that took off in the '70s and features guitars, keyboards, horns, cowbells, and congas, is the distinctive soundtrack of Black DC. You'll feel the beat as you exit Metro stops, where young men bang it out with buckets and sticks. Go-Go also lends itself to call-and-response to lead off chants for justice, so when Black America howls in pain and anger over racial injustice, The District is likely to respond with Go-Go.

Musician Chuck Brown gets credit for giving Go-Go liftoff. Spike Lee featured this music in the Black college cult classic *School Daze* (1988). (Remember "Da Butt"?) In DC, Go-Go was the center of a local controversy in 2019, when Donald Campbell, owner of a Shaw neighborhood **Metro PCS Store** (1915 7th St. NW; tel. 202/462-2584; Mon.-Sat. 10am-8pm, Sun. noon-6pm) that had been cranking out Go-Go music since 1995, was forced by a new corporate owner to move his speakers inside. Folks were so upset that a movement—**#DontMuteDC**—emerged. The clash over sound highlighted tensions between long-standing Black residents and newer, Whiter residents in what was, until recently, the nation's most gentrified city, according to the National Community Reinvestment Coalition. (As of 2020, San Francisco is now on top.) Long-term residents felt that turning down the volume of a Black art form effectively makes this area of the city less funky. Who wants that?

The music is back now, and Campbell is working with corporations and neighbors on sound issues. If you want to support Black-owned businesses and the idea that people who have long nurtured a space deserve a place in its future, don't just stand there and soak up the beat: Stop in to Campbell's store and buy a CD featuring Go-Go music (or purchase another item to support the community). Go-Go music makes great cookout music or a funky beat for kicking it old school with your friends.

ANACOSTIA

Anacostia has DC's highest concentration of Black-owned businesses, some of which are located in the **Anacostia Arts Center** (1231 Good Hope Rd. SE; http://anacostiaartscenter.com), a hub of small, creative businesses. The center has a fun atmosphere, complete with a theater and communal spaces.

Clothing

NUBIAN HUEMAN

1231 Good Hope Rd. SE; tel. 202/394-3386; www.nubianhueman.com; Tues.-Sat. noon-7pm, Sun. noon-4pm

This modern boutique inside the Anacostia Arts Center celebrates the African diaspora by featuring unique clothing, accessories, and beauty items from around the world. Owner and chief curator Anika Hobbs sources products from about 400 artists and 30 countries. Hobbs is the force behind the Black Love Experience, a celebration of Black culture that takes place in DC every February. This is where you get your butters—as in shea butter that makes your skin supple.

CHECK IT ENTERPRISES

1920 Martin Luther King Jr. Ave. SE; tel. 202/889-1532; www.checkitenterprises.com; Mon.-Fri. 10am-7pm, Sat. 11am-5pm

Get your official #DontMuteDC shirts (and other message clothing and hats) inside this store plus community resource center. Check It began when a group of LBGTQ former gang members decided to change their lives. Today, the venue, which also serves as an event space, is a safe haven for LBGTQ residents, young entrepreneurs, and citizens returning home from prison. Plans are in the works to turn the space into a Go-Go museum and café.

Books

MAHOGANY BOOKS

1231 Good Hope Rd. SE; tel. 202/844-2062; www.mahoganybooks.com; Tues.-Fri. noon-7pm, Sat. 11am-7pm, Sun. noon-4pm

This award-winning bookseller prides itself on promoting reading, writing, and cultural awareness. At Mahogany, they've always known Black Lives Matter, but if the realization of structural inequality is vexing you, this bookstore specializes in books that will help you and the children you love understand antiracism and so much more. This sanctum of knowledge is located inside the Anacostia Arts Center.

OTHER NEIGHBORHOODS

Food Products

THE SPICE SUITE

6902 4th St. NW; tel. 202/506-3436; www.thespicesuite.com; Fri.-Sun. 7am-2pm

A labor of love for founder Angel Anderson, this haven of flavor specializes in spice boxes that will help you expand your cooking repertoire. For example, one box contains brown sugar sub, lemon pepper spice, mixed pepper, spicy classic, and garlicky and classic signature blends. The Spice Suite also sells fashionable dinner plates, among other items. Find this gem on Instagram @TheSpiceSuite.

This shop is located about five miles north of the U Street/Shaw area. Take U.S. 29 heading north, then turn onto Piney Branch Road NW to get here. It's about a 20-minute drive. You can also get to the Takoma neighborhood on the Metro Red line.

Theater

As an international city, DC showcases performances by diverse artists from around the world. You can see Black artist groups from across the country, including Alvin Ailey's American Dance Theater, Dance Theater of Harlem, and Blacks in Wax, an annual performance of vignettes about influential people in Black history, performed at the **John F. Kennedy Center for the Performing Arts** (2700 F St. NW; 202/416-8000; www.kennedy-center.org), which showcases more than 2,000 performances and exhibits per year. Artists like Earth, Wind & Fire and opera star J'Nai Bridges have also taken the stage here.

The Howard Theatre

620 T St. NW; tel. 202/803-2899; www.thehowardtheatre.com; prices vary

When it first opened in 1910, the Howard Theatre, located on the corner of 7th Street and T Street NW in historic Black Broadway, was billed as the "largest colored theater in the world." Legendary producer Quincy Jones said no proper Chitlin' Circuit journey began without a stop here.

Native son Duke Ellington brought in the big band jazz era here, and the list of 20th century musical greats who appeared

BLACK BROADWAY

Both Howard Theatre and Lincoln Theatre are located on or near **U Street and 14th Street,** which was such a hub of Black cultural and social activity during the Jim Crow era that it came to be known as Black Broadway. (At the dawn of the 20th century, DC was segregated, but African Americans could own businesses in this bustling area that saw to the needs of the Black community.) The Black Broadway area was home to jazz clubs, civil rights organizations, and institutions such as Black-owned Industrial Savings Bank (which loaned many of those entrepreneurs the capital to start up), Murray Brothers Printing Company/Palace Casino, the Mary McLeod Bethune Council House, and the 12th Street YMCA, where Thurgood Marshall held meetings about civil rights legislation. Intellectual life flourished here too. When Alain Locke's *The New Negro* came out in 1925, half the book included works by Washingtonians, though Locke is considered Father of the Harlem Renaissance.

It is often said that desegregation, which allowed Black people to shop outside designated areas, failed communities such as Black Broadway. U Street's economy collapsed after desegregation, according to the National Trust for Historic Preservation.[10] When White-owned businesses moved in, the story of Black Broadway faded away, except in the memory and telling of those who were there. Fortunately, Washington native Shellée M. Haynesworth produced a multimedia public history project called ***Black Broadway on U: A Transmedia Project*** (www.blackbroadwayonu.com) to help us meet and/or remember this historic treasure.

at this theater is seemingly endless: Jones, Lionel Hampton, Dizzy Gillespie, Ella Fitzgerald, Billie Holliday, Miles Davis, The Supremes, Aretha Franklin, Marvin Gaye, and more. Since segregation kept Black artists from performing where they wanted, this was also where entertainers got their first significant exposure and were able to develop their various crafts. A lot of talented artists emerged from amateur nights at Howard Theatre, including Fitzgerald, Billy Eckstine, and Bill "Ink Spots" Kenny. The theater also hosted vaudeville acts, musicals, and lectures.

Initially, patrons came from the Black bourgeois. Later, White audience members came to enjoy too. The theater fell into disrepair after the riots that broke out following King's assassination in 1968. After a 32-year hiatus and a $29 million renovation, the beautifully restored venue reopened in 2012.

Today, a range of acts perform in this supper club scene, and a diverse audience fills the seats. Eat dinner in the main floor dining room before you see the show. Or enjoy some pricier seats in booths in the back.

The theater is located south of Howard University near LeDroit Park.

Lincoln Theatre

1215 U St. NW; tel. 202/888-0050; www.thelincolndc.com; Mon.-Fri. 1pm-7pm; $25-150

Built in 1922, the Lincoln Theatre served as a cultural center in DC before the Harlem Renaissance, a far-reaching cultural

Photos (top to bottom): John F. Kennedy Center for the Performing Arts; the Howard Theatre; the Linco Theatre

awakening that ushered in a golden age for Black artists, writers, and musicians. The likes of Pearl Bailey, Nat King Cole, and Louis Armstrong have performed at the Lincoln Theatre. An eclectic array of performances happen here, including appearances by Janelle Monáe, Andra Day, Ms. Lauryn Hill, and Nas. This venue invites all ages unless otherwise posted. Drinks and some light snacks are sold.

Festivals and Events

In DC, events that celebrate the Black experience and expression, institutions, and lifestyles are forms of freedom lived out loud.

JANUARY

MARTIN LUTHER KING JR. DAY

Various locations; www.mlkholidaydc.org; third Mon. in Jan.

King Day is a big deal in DC. On his federally recognized birthday the third Monday in January, the city comes alive with activities that include a prayer breakfast, a Peace Walk, and parade through historic downtown Anacostia, and a number of activities that honor a larger-than-life icon. The parade actually began six years before King Day became a holiday. Past parades have ended with a health and community fair at Gateway Pavilion (2730 Martin Luther King Jr. Ave. SE).

DC residents also take seriously the community service aspect of this day, engaging in everything from cultivating community gardens to writing letters to people in nursing homes. When the Obamas were living in the White House, they cherished the occasion by making it a day "on" not a day "off" by showing up at various venues to volunteer.

Visit www.mlkholidaydc.org to create your DC-based King Day repertoire.

FEBRUARY-MARCH

BLACK LOVE EXPERIENCE

The ARC, 1901 Mississippi Ave. SE; www.blackloveexperience.com; Feb. or March, Sat. 7pm-midnight; $55 and $250 for a VIP ticket

Relax and recharge at the annual Black Love Experience, a celebration of Black culture envisioned by DC's Anika Hobbs, chief curator at the Nubian Hueman retail store. Every year, DC residents collide at the Town Hall Education Arts Recreation Campus (The ARC) 16.5-acre site in Anacostia, to celebrate Black excellence through music, art, wellness, and commerce with Black-owned businesses. Black Love Experience features main-stage musicians, while other creative spaces include podcasts, medication, reiki and apothecary demonstrations, and exhibits. Interactive sessions may include meditation and self-care. Black Love Experience has previously featured writing workshops, wine tastings, and even a date whisperer. One year, artist Shani Crowe of the celebrated "BRAIDS" solo show demonstrated hairstyling techniques as depicted in her photography series on braids. Hobbs and her team make an effort to deliver what they believe the community craves. The event, which typically occurs in February or March, has also made space to discuss love and healthy relationships. Check the Black Love Experience website for details.

VOICES OF THE MOVEMENT:
REV. JESSE L. JACKSON

"We should be obsessed with voter registration. It is a measure of our political power. We begin to grow in conscience when we vote."

—**REV. JESSE L. JACKSON,** a member of King's inner circle, led the SCLC's Operation Breadbasket in Chicago, founded People United to Save Humanity (now RainbowPUSH Coalition), and ran for president in 1984 and 1988.

Jackson's progressive campaigns were influential, boosting voter registration and shifting notions of who could become president. His involvement in District politics included serving as a shadow U.S. senator for Washington DC from 1991-1997. His goal: to win statehood for DC, a quest that is ongoing.

By urging the New York Stock Exchange to close on Martin Luther King Jr. Day (along with his son, Jonathan), Jackson helped ensure the holiday is commemorated nationwide. "In those days, over 100 million people viewed the opening and closing bell," says Richard A. "Dick" Grasso, then NYSE chairman and chief executive. "When you make a decision not to open the market in reverence to Dr. King, people stand up and pay attention."

While King Day, for many, is a day of service, Jackson reminds us that "King was about empowerment and social change, not just social service." Jonathan explains: "My father's focus has been on economic justice: not only integrating the counter but being able to purchase at the counter."

Rev. Jesse L. Jackson marches for jobs in Washington DC, 1975.

MAY

FUNK PARADE

www.funkparade.com; second Sat. in May; parade free, festival wristbands $10-20

When King came to DC in 1965, hoping to put a stop to the disenfranchisement of the city's mostly Black residents, he walked down U Street, a historic place of joy and gathering. The area has seen its ups and downs, but the Funk Parade celebrates the spirit of U Street annually during a day-long fair, parade, and music festival. Thousands of Washingtonians of every stripe flood the streets for a day of pure joy and release on several stages and performance areas. The festival starts at 1pm; the parade kicks off at 5pm; and the Night Music Festival begins at 7pm. Proceeds benefit local causes. The parade starts at Howard Theatre at 620 T Street NW to the historic Lincoln Theatre at 1215 U Street NW, a half mile away. Funk Parade is held from 9th St NW to 14th St. NW. Follow the parade on Twitter (@FunkParade) or Instagram (dcfunkparade).

JUNE-JULY

JUNETEENTH AT THE NATIONAL MUSEUM OF AFRICAN AMERICAN HISTORY AND CULTURE

1400 Constitution Ave.; tel. 844/750-3012; www.nmaahc.si.edu; June 19; free

At NMAAHC, Juneteenth programming varies from year to year as the museum uses its collections, experts, and talent to explore Black freedom. Past programming has included a performance of the Black national anthem, "Lift Every Voice and Sing," by vocalist Rochelle Rice; the sharing of recipes and insights about African American culinary traditions; the teaching of genealogical research skills; and presentations and storytelling about the significance of Juneteenth. In 2020, during the coronavirus pandemic, Juneteenth at NMAAHC went virtual, and the museum produced a Google Arts and Culture story using photos from the museum's collection to illustrate what some call the United States' Second Independence Day. Visit the museum's events page to find out how to participate and celebrate what it means to be truly free.

DC JAZZ FESTIVAL

Various locations; www.dcjazzfest.org; June

As the birthplace of Duke Ellington, DC's jazz history runs deep. Over 10 days, acclaimed and emerging artists alike converge for a celebration of a uniquely American art form that is a product of the Black experience. This annual festival features more than 150 performances in over 40 music venues around town. In the past, finales have been held at the DC JazzFest at The Wharf (760 Main St. NW), a hot waterfront destination featuring shopping, dining, and entertainment in southwest DC. That event features three free outdoor stages and two ticketed indoor stages. Jazz in the 'Hoods allows audiences to watch performances in 25 neighborhoods. The festival takes place every summer, typically in June.

DC BLACK THEATRE & ARTS FESTIVAL

THEARC Theater, 1901 Mississippi Ave. SE, and Anacostia Playhouse, 2020 Shannon Pl. SE; tel. 202/889-5901; www.dcblacktheatrefestival.com; typically June or July, 3pm-10pm

This annual 10-day arts festival showcases more than 150 performances from writers, filmmakers, and musicians from across the globe in the east-of-the-Anacostia performance space known as THEARC. Works include plays, monologues, workshops, readings of new works, and the five-day One-Act Battle featuring plays that must not go over 20 minutes. Past shows include *Chocolate Lounge: A Performers of Color Burlesques/Variety Show* and learning

DC Jazz Festival

opportunities such as an ancient rhythm djembe drum class. Short films screened have included *Black Like Her, We Family,* and *Sounds of the Summer.* A New Works reading series allows new and established artists to incubate and discuss ideas for their dramatic works, and it's free to attend.

AUGUST-SEPTEMBER

DC VEGFEST

Nationals Stadium, 1500 S Capitol St. SE; tel. 301/891-2458; www.dcvegfest.com; Aug. or Sept.; free

This annual one-day event, held in August or September, is billed as the largest vegan gathering on the East Coast, drawing a diverse audience of 25,000 likeminded people who are interested in personal and community health, food justice and access, and the welfare of animals. Inside Nationals Stadium, a big, white tent houses a variety of vendors and an entertainment space featuring musicians and comedians. The festival also features cooking demonstrations, celebrity speakers, physician advice, talks about urban gardening, a kids' zone, and more. What can you eat here? How about vegan nacho mac and cheese, ginger miso noodle salad, or jerk barbecue chickpeas? The festival is great for anyone curious about the vegan lifestyle or who might consider themselves a "pre-vegan."

Get there on Metro: Board or transfer to the Green Line and take the Navy Yard stop and walk a block. If you drive, public parking is available in Nationals Park parking garage on a first-come, first-served basis. Plentiful bike racks are available.

OCTOBER

★ HOWARD HOMECOMING

Howard University Campus, 2400 6th St. NW; tel. 202-806-6100; www.homecoming.howard.edu; mid-October

Howard University is the "Most Searched HBCU" and the "Most Searched Homecoming," according to Google, so that should give you an indication of how people feel about homecoming every fall, usually in October. For students and alumni, homecoming means returning to the Mecca, as Bisons call it, which

CONGRESSIONAL BLACK CAUCUS WEEKEND

Held every fall, the annual **Congressional Black Caucus Foundation Legislative Conference** (1720 Massachusetts Ave. NW; tel. 202/263-2800; www.cbcfinc.org; standard package $670-840) is the leading policy conference on African American issues. In fact, the CBC is who led the charge to make King's January birthday a federal holiday in 1983. Their fall meeting draws more than 10,000 attendees, including local, state, and national legislators as well as concerned citizens in a robust series of programming that addresses civil rights, social justice, economic development, education, and public health.

More than 100 policy sessions generally include panel discussions and keynote speakers. Third-party organizations stage simultaneous events at the Walter E. Washington Convention Center (801 Mt. Vernon Pl. NW). One, the Black Millennial Convention, focused on civil engagement. Corporate sponsors, such as Wall Street banks, may host sessions on the state of Black wealth.

The big draw at this annual event is the opening press conference that formally introduces the congresspersons who serve as the year's conference co-chairs. Pay attention because whatever they're talking about at this conference this week sets the tone for the public conversation and news cycles the next several days. Themes explored here have elevated Black Lives Matter and the legacy of 400 years of Black people in America. The prayer breakfast and Phoenix Awards Dinner are also high points of this event, which draws people from all walks of life.

To be sure, keeping the world safe and sane for African Americans is hard work, but caucusgoers party hard during this event that is akin to a reunion of cool smart people. With scores of parties and receptions to attend nightly, many people approach this weekend as an HBCU-style party for grown folks. It's wild.

includes a week-long celebration of college memories and the Black experience. Among featured festivities, **International Yardfest** is a free concert on the green that includes big-name musical acts. The event takes places the Friday of homecoming week from noon to 5pm in the upper quadrangle of the main campus. Over the years, stars such as Biggie Smalls, Drake, and Rick Ross have headlined.

Homecoming events also include step shows, a gospel concert, and fashion and art shows. On the Saturday of the big game, a parade kicks off the day around 9am, featuring the Showtime Band, high school marching bands playing and entertaining in the Black tradition, community dance teams, and more. Later that afternoon, the Bison football team takes the field. Note that game-day **tickets** ($40 general admission), which go on sale in April, typically sell out quickly. Buy them through the school's athletics portal (www.bisontickets.com). Check the Howard Homecoming website for more details. You can also follow along on Instagram and Twitter: @BisonHomecoming.

NOVEMBER

DMV BLACK RESTAURANT WEEK

Various locations; www.dmvbrw.com

Erinn Tucker, PhD, faculty director of the Global Hospitality Leadership master's program at Georgetown University, and partners Andra Johnson and chef Furard Tate shared a concern about the African American dining experience in the wake of events in which African Americans were profiled for their dining habits. (Such events included a White woman calling police on Black people who were peacefully barbecuing in Oakland, California, and the arrest of two Black men in a Philadelphia Starbucks in 2018.) "I started reading articles that asked, 'Where are the Black chefs?' and 'Where are Black owners?' I've been in this space for 20 years. They're here. This area is so rich in talent and resources, but there's not a platform," Tucker said. In response, Tucker, Johnson, and Tate co-founded DMV Black Restaurant Week in 2018 in order to engage people inside and outside the hospitality industry. Forty restaurants in DC, Maryland, and Virginia (hence the name) participate in the event, which is held the second or third week of each November.

During DMV Black Restaurant Week, signature events feature industry experts in scheduled locations around the region. You can also enjoy a prix-fixe menu at select restaurants or receive discounts on catering or food purchases. (The beauty of this is that all kinds of Black entrepreneurs, including those who do not have a brick-and-mortar space, can participate.)

This enterprise extends far beyond a week of eating and enjoying the fruits of Black excellence. Organizers host events throughout the year to educate, support, and amplify Black food and hospitality-based businesses. Bookmark the DMV Black Restaurant Week website to see what's on the menu.

Food

DC offers something for every palate, from Southern to vegetarian. And if you've ever wondered what food around the world tastes like, this is a place to expand your dining horizons.

NATIONAL MALL

Eateries, including quirky food trucks, abound near the National Mall. In addition to the following, restaurants worth checking out include **Art and Soul** (415 New Jersey Ave. NW) run by Oprah Winfrey's chef pal, Art Smith, a fried chicken virtuoso. **Rasika** (633 D St. NW) serves award-winning Indian food, including vegetarian options. And if you believe a person's heart connects to food flavors, then you'll want to taste what the amazing Chef Jose Andres has got going on at **Oyamel Cocina Mexicana** (401 7th St. NW). (None of these are Black-owned.)

Southern and Soul Food

SWEET HOME CAFÉ

1400 Constitution Ave. NW; tel. 844/750-3012; www.nmaahc.si.edu; daily 10am-5:30pm; free

Located in Concourse 0 of the National Museum of African American History and Culture, Sweet Home Café showcases African American foodways: from the agricultural South, Gullah-style cooking and ingredients such as grits, pecans, and peaches; from the Creole coast, a blend of ingredients and techniques from West African, Native American, French, Portuguese, Spanish, and Acadian influences; from the Northern states where Caribbean and

West Indian foodways immigrated with its people; and from the Western range where Native American and Mexican traditions fed Black people headed westward to seek their fortunes.

What to eat? Maybe you'd like to start with Sweet Home Café's Buttermilk Fried Chicken, which is both crunchy and juicy. Barbecued pulled pork sandwiches taste great with slaw. Or try pan-fried Louisiana Catfish Po' Boy or Original Brunswick Stew, or make side dishes such as collard greens and macaroni and cheese the star of your plate. By serving food that's prepared authentically or presented as contemporary recipes, Sweet Home Café reminds you of where you are and where Black America has been with each bite. The experience is backed up by a wall-size black-and-white photograph of the Greensboro Four. Ezell Blair Jr., David Richmond, Franklin McCain, and Joseph McNeil, who sat in protest at a Woolworth's counter in 1960, helped set off the sit-in movement.

You must go through the museum's main entrance to access this space. The always-bustling café is huge, seating 400. Walk up and get in line at the regional food specialty station of your choice. Sometimes Sweet Home Café gets a little busy, so the line might start outside the café itself. Don't worry about the wait: The food will be worth it.

DOWNTOWN AND PENN QUARTER

Southern and Soul Food

GEORGIA BROWN'S

950 15th St. NW; tel. 202/393-4499; www.gbrowns.com; Mon.-Thurs. 11:30am-10pm, Fri.-Sat. 11:30am-11pm, Sun. 10am-4pm and 5:30pm-10pm; $10-28

If you're looking for shrimp, grits, and a show, Georgia Brown's might be the place for you. Here you'll find Southern coastal classics, such as Charleston she-crab soup, Carolina gumbo, and crab-stuffed "Devil" shrimp. Other dishes include crispy baby back ribs, short rib pot roast, and Beyond Meatloaf, a vegetarian option. Enjoy a jazz band and crafty cocktails during Sunday brunch and be sure to have some "proper desserts" that include peach cobbler and homemade ice cream. Sunday brunch features live jazz; Wednesday from 6pm-10pm also features live jazz.

U STREET AND SHAW

American

BEN'S CHILI BOWL

1213 U St. NW; tel. 202/667-0909; www.benschilibowl.com; Mon.-Thurs. 7am-2:30am, Fri.-Sat. 7am-4am, Sun. 11am-midnight; entrees $7-12

When the news of King's assassination on April 4, 1968, reached Washington DC, Ben's Chili Bowl owners Ben and Virginia Ali were in their restaurant—someone ran in and told them. However, as the area around them erupted with riots and looting, Ben's remained untouched, so beloved was the eatery founded by the Alis in 1958.

What makes Ben's so special? Start with the regional delicacy known as the "half-smoke," bigger than a hotdog, spicier and coarser, too, Yes, there's chili and burgers and fries, even vegetarian options such as veggie dogs and vegan chili. Drinks include handspun thick n' creamy milkshakes in a range of flavors, including cherry, maple, vanilla, and Oreo. Movement folk who ate here include King, Harry Belafonte, and Rev. Jesse L. Jackson. Jazz greats Duke Ellington, Ella Fitzgerald, and Miles Davis also enjoyed it here. Those who attended the 1963 March on Washington for Jobs and Freedom also gained sustenance and solidarity at Ben's.

To this day, people around DC care a great deal about what happens at Ben's Chili Bowl. During the 2020 coronavirus pandemic and the subsequent shutdown

Photos (top to bottom): Ben's Chili Bowl; tea blends at Calabash Tea & Tonic; Calabash Tea & Tonic

of restaurants and other businesses across the country, the eatery was in harm's way again, as were many Black-owned businesses across the country. On first try, the Alis did not receive funding from the federal program designed help people keep paying their bills. DC rallied and Ben's got funding in the next round.

BUSBOYS AND POETS

2021 14th St. NW; tel. 202/387-7638; www.busboysandpoets.com; Mon.-Fri. 8am-10pm, Sat.-Sun. 10am-11pm; $7-17

This full-service restaurant, bar, coffee shop, and bookstore is not Black-owned but was designed to foster racial and community connection. It is named in reference to poet Langston Hughes, who worked as a busboy before making his name. The menu offers small plates that include vegetarian selections, like sweet potato hash, vegan quesadilla, and shrimp tacos. There's also a nice selection of soups, salads, paninis, burgers, pizza, and more. But you don't come here for the food: What's most special about this place is the community feel. When there's a symposium on race, a spoken-word performance, or an appearance by intellectual Cornel West or poet Nikki Giovanni, it's your soul that will be fed.

Grab a justice-focused book and a bite or sit back and enjoy a performance on open-mic night at this U Street Corridor location, or venture out to other locations throughout the area, one of which is in Anacostia (2004 Martin Luther King Jr. Ave. SE; tel. 202/889-1374; Mon-Thurs. 9am-9pm, Fri. 9am-11pm, Sat. 10am-11pm, Sun. 10am-9pm) near the Frederick Douglass National Historic Site.

Southern and Soul Food

FLORIDA AVENUE GRILL

1100 Florida Ave. NW; tel. 202/265-1586; www.floridaavenuegrill.com; Tues.-Sat. 8am-9pm, Sun. 8am-4:30pm; $8-16

"The Grill" founder Lacey C. Wilson Sr. saved his tips as a shoeshine man on Capitol Hill to open up a restaurant in 1944 where Black people could eat good food and feel at home, free from racial tension. He and his wife Bertha did just that, and the soul food institution continues today. Breakfast is served all day. Fish & Grits come with either catfish, croaker, or salmon. There's hot buttered biscuits, and pork and beef half-smokes, a regional specialty sausage that's bigger and spicier than hot dogs. Soul food dinners feature Miss B's Southern Chicken Salad, steamed pigs feet, chitterlings, and an array of fresh cooked vegetables.

Originally a two-bar-stool business, Florida Avenue Grill has grown into a DC staple. The restaurant gets crowded, and the service can be a touch slow, but the upbeat atmosphere and homestyle cooking make up for it.

Tea

CALABASH TEA & TONIC

1847 7th St. NW; tel. 202/525-5386; www.calabashtea.com; Tues.-Sat. 9am-8pm, Sun. 9am-6pm; $3-7

Whether you need to calm your nerves or enjoy some immune-boosting health benefits, Calabash Tea & Tonic, an award-winning tea house, can brew you a luxurious cup of 100 types of teas for here or to go. Selections come in a range from chai, herbal, and green to black teas. Try blends like the Idris Chai—spicy, sweet, chocolatey, and strong—or the best-selling coconut-infused Mandingo Chai, which is rich, spicy, and sweet. Tonics feature herbal extracts designed to deliver a concentrated form of tea benefits. The menu includes Jamaican baked goods and veggie patties. The quiet, intimate environment makes this a great place to meet a friend for an afternoon catch-up session.

ANACOSTIA

In addition to the below eateries, you'll

find a branch of local chain **Busboys and Poets** (2004 Martin Luther King Jr. Ave. SE; tel. 202/889-1374; busboysandpoets.com; Mon.-Thurs. 9am-9pm, Fri. 9am-11pm, Sat. 10am-11pm, Sun. 10am-9pm) in Anacostia.

Pizza

MAMA'S KITCHEN

2028 Martin Luther King Jr. Ave. SE; tel. 202/678-6262; www.mamaskitchenmenu.com; Sun. noon-midnight, Mon. 11am-midnight, Tues.-Thurs. 11am-midnight, Fri. 11am-1am; $10-17

This east of the river pizza spot is owned by Turkish immigrant Fatma Nayir. Pizza combos run from the sausage-and-pepperoni supreme to the ham, bell pepper, and pineapple Hawaiian. Appetizers, salads, and other items are also available.

Juice Bar

TURNING NATURAL

2025 Martin Luther King Jr. Ave. SE; tel. 202/800-8828; www.turningnatural.com; Mon.-Fri. 9am-5pm, Sat.-Sun. 9am-3pm; $6-13

Jerri Evans's Turning Natural juice bar aims to create a movement around making healthy choices. The former aeronautical engineer serves up tasty juices made from the freshest ingredients. One concoction is a tribute to legendary DC DJ Petey Greene, a radio talk show host who used the airwaves at WOL-AM here in DC to calm a city in the throes of an uprising the night King died. Called Petey Green, the drink is made of apple, ginger, kale, celery, collard greens, cucumbers, cilantro, parsley, lemon, and pineapple.

OTHER NEIGHBORHOODS

Afro-Caribbean

KITH/KIN

801 Wharf St. SW; tel. 202/878-8566; www.kithandkindc.com; Mon.-Thurs. 6:30am-10:30am, noon-2:30pm, 5pm-10:30pm; Sat. 6:30am-11am, noon-2:30pm, 5pm-11pm; Sun. 6:30am-11am, noon-2:30pm, 5pm-10:30pm

On the waterfront at the Intercontinental Washington in the Wharf, this 120-seat Afro-Caribbean restaurant with a patio is a destination for DC diners. Featured dishes have included Trinidadian curry, jerk chicken, and braised cabbage. The beverage menu is eclectic and sophisticated, including Chef Kwame's Favorite, made with Filibuster Gin, elderflower, lime, honey, and tonic; One Love, with Plantation Pineapple Stiggins' Rum, hibiscus, passion fruit, lime, pineapple, and peach bitters. Floor-to-ceiling windows make for great people-watching while you sip and savor.

Chef Kwame Onwuachi's backstory is enough to draw you into this place—at one point, the Top Chef 13th season star started his own catering company with $20,000 earned by selling candy on the subway. Onwuachi chronicles the twists and turns of growing up and growing wise in *Notes from a Young Black Chef: A Memoir* (2019).

Nightlife

Here in DC, the convergence of politics, culture, and people from around the globe creates a winning atmosphere for the elevation of the art of the cocktail. For those who prefer intimate spaces to kick back, have a drink, and enjoy friends and live entertainment, DC has plenty of late-night options. Consider dedicating some quality time eating, drinking and chilling on U Street.

U STREET AND SHAW

Cocktail Bar

SERVICE BAR

926-928 U St. NW; tel. 202/462-7232; www.servicebardc.com; Wed.-Thurs. 5pm-10pm, Fri.-Sun. 4pm-11:30pm

A best-kept-secret kind of place, Service Bar is a cozy spot with DJs and a rotating list of seasonal cocktails, like Hipster in Heaven, made with mint leaves, vanilla syrup, lemon, Fernet, stout, and brandy, and The Purple Messiah, made with Concord grape, huckleberry, umeboshi, white rum, and citrus. The menu ranges from chilaquiles with pulled duck to fried chicken. The space is visually interesting, with blue accents and a variety of objets d'art. Think about reserving Service Bar's neon-lit Snug Room, an eight-seat private room that is exactly what it sounds like. While enjoying your privacy, guests have direct bartender access through a window. Snug Room requires a $150 minimum spend.

Bars

BIN1301 DC

1301 U St. NW; www.bin1301dc.com; Mon.-Thurs. 5pm-2am, Fri. 5pm-3am, Sat. noon-3am, Sun. noon-midnight

Come for the extensive wine and beer menu and stay for live music and DJ sets. That includes Wine Down Wednesdays, where you can take time for a midweek groove thang, and other themed nights. Stop in for Monday and Tuesday night Happy Hour from 5pm-8pm. Graze on whitefish salad, bruschetta, or Asian skirt steak skewers with shredded cabbage and julienned carrots.

BEN'S NEXT DOOR

1211 U St. NW; tel. 202/667-8880; www.bensnextdoor.com; Wed.-Sun. noon-10pm

From the folks who have faithfully served DC for decades at Ben's Chili Bowl, this is a relaxing spot with nine flat-screen TVs, a 53-foot bar, and a menu with considerable options, including shrimp and grits and brined chicken and waffles. Billed as a place to chill and vibe, the beverage menu won't disappoint. Ben's Next Door features a wide selection of wine, beer, cocktails, and even frozen cocktails. In addition to a full bar, the spot has plenty of table space, a friendly service vibe, and artwork that adorns the walls, topping off that feeling of being someplace special.

cocktail at Service Bar

chicken and waffles at Ben's Next Door

DUPONT CIRCLE

Club

THE CAGED BIRD

1723 Connecticut Ave. NW; tel. 202/733-3555; Tues.-Wed. 5pm-midnight, Thurs. 5pm-1am, Fri. 5pm-3am, Sat.-Sun. 11am-6pm

This Dupont Circle restaurant/lounge/meeting spot represents the labor and passion of co-owner and executive chef Meshach Cisero. The Caged Bird features full bars on two floors and a DJ booth on the bottom level where most of the action happens. Brunch leans toward Cajun shrimp and avocado toast, while dinner may include blackened salmon, Caged Bird chicken wings, or the Cajun black bean burger, among other options. The socially woke ethos of this place is summed up by a framed T-shirt on display that reads "Emmett, Amadou, Sean, Oscar, Trayvon and Jordan." In addition to spoken-word poetry, trivia, and spades card-playing nights, The Caged Bird is just as likely to run a drive for school supplies. The venue's name is in tribute to Maya Angelou's 1969 masterpiece, *I Know Why the Caged Bird Sings.*

OTHER NEIGHBORHOODS

Cocktail Bars

WICKED BLOOM SOCIAL CLUB

1540 N Capitol NW; tel. 202/750-6375; www.wickedbloomdc.com; Mon.-Thurs. 5pm-midnight, Fri.-Sat. 5pm-2am

Trendy and sophisticated, this cozy cocktail bar features a variety of rap-music inspired drinks, including Mama Said Knock You Out, made with Rhum agricole, grapefruit, lime, and habanero, stirred; and Teach Me How to Dougie, made with rye, bittersweet vermouth, and bitters, stirred. The intimate speakeasy feel is accentuated by wood accents and books, and beautiful black-and-white painted roses grace a long wall. The atmosphere is chill in a Black *Cheers* kind of way: They're glad you came.

Foodwise, consider loaded pork rinds, tacos, a variety of vegetarian Impossible Burgers, or DCity pit smoked chicken wings served with buttermilk ranch and your choice of sauce. Wicked Bloom is located about a mile northeast of downtown DC.

Accommodations

DOWNTOWN AND PENN QUARTER

Over $200

EATON DC

1201 K St. NW; 202/289-7600; www.eatonworkshop.com/hotel; $359-499 weekdays, $179-279 weekends (Fri.-Sat.)

Eaton DC bills itself as an experience in consciousness that welcomes changemakers and creative types. Eaton's 209 bespoke hotel rooms are designed to inspire, with mosaic tiled showers, Bluetooth record players to play vinyl records, and plush organic cotton pillowtop beds. Minibars carry sustainable snacks and the menu is "vegetable forward." The hotel offers wellness and community-building opportunities for creatives and travelers. **American Son** restaurant (Mon.-Fri. 3-9pm, Sat.-Sun. 9am-9pm) offers an Asian take on American dishes, serves brunch on weekends, and hosts a daily happy hour from 3pm-6pm.

Located in downtown DC, Eaton Hotel is a mile and a half from the National Mall and less than a mile from the White House.

WILLARD INTERCONTINENTAL HOTEL

1401 Pennsylvania Ave. NW; tel. 800/424-6835; www.washington.intercontinental.com; $300

This 200-year-old hotel is in downtown Washington DC, two blocks from the White House and a 10-minute walk from the National Museum of African American History and Culture. The hotel has 335 rooms and is four miles from Ronald Reagan National Airport.

DUPONT CIRCLE

$100-200

AWKAABA DC BED AND BREAKFAST

1708 16th St. NW; tel. 866/466-3855; www.dcakwaaba.com; $175-235

This 1890s townhouse features eight rooms influenced by Black literature and authors, with themed rooms named for literary greats Langston Hughes, Zora Neale Hurston, Walter Mosley, and Toni Morrison. Other suites evoke romance, inspiration, poetry, and modern classics. Hearty, healthful breakfasts include whole-wheat blueberry pancakes, eggs, and turkey bacon.

This B&B in Dupont Circle is a 20-minute walk from historic U Street and the African American Civil War Memorial and Museum, and a 10-minute drive northwest of the National Mall. Oh, yeah, Awkaaba is Twi for "welcome."

THE INN AT DUPONT SOUTH

1312 19th St. NW; tel. 202/359-8432; www.thedupontcollection.com; $100-235

This eight-room bed and breakfast in a Victorian home is a 15-minute drive to the National Mall and only five miles from Reagan National Airport.

Transportation

GETTING THERE

Air

Three airports serve the Washington DC area. **Reagan National Airport** is relatively close to the capitol and DC's tourist attractions. **Washington Dulles International Airport** is the go-to for international flights. Finally, going through **Baltimore/Washington International Thurgood Marshall Airport** in nearby Maryland, 32 miles northeast of Washington DC, can be a less expensive travel option.

REAGAN NATIONAL AIRPORT

2401 Smith Blvd., Arlington, VA; tel. 703/417-8000; www.dca-airport.com

Reagan National Airport is on the Metro system's Blue and Yellow lines. It takes about 20 minutes to get downtown from Reagan on Metro. A cab ride downtown takes around 10 minutes and costs about $16.

WASHINGTON DULLES INTERNATIONAL AIRPORT

1 Saarinen Circle, Dulles, VA; tel. 703/572-2700; www.flydulles.com

From Washington Dulles International Airport into the city, connect to Metrorail using **Metrobus** ($7.50 pp, $3.75 seniors and people with disabilities); the 5A takes you to Rosslyn Metrorail station on the Orange, Silver, and Blue lines with one stop in between. Check the 5A schedule (www.wmata.com/schedules) to see when the bus leaves the airport.

You may also take the **Silver Line Express** bus to the Wiehle-Reston East Metrorail station on the Silver line. Visit the Silver Line Express site for a schedule (www.flydulles.com/iad/silver-line-express-bus-metrorail-service-updates) and to ensure this service is being offered; the coronavirus pandemic may affect operations.

A cab ride to downtown takes about 30 minutes and will run you $55-65.

BALTIMORE/WASHINGTON INTERNATIONAL THURGOOD MARSHALL AIRPORT

7050 Friendship Rd., Baltimore, MD; tel. 410/859-7683; bwiairport.com

BMI offers a free Amtrak and MARC Rail Service shuttle that makes pickups every six minutes during the day, and every 25 minutes 1am-5am. Free shuttles pick up passengers on the lower level of the airport, just outside of baggage claim at four designated stops, and drop them at BWI Marshall Airport Rail Station. Amtrak and MARC Rail service is available from the rail station to Union Station in Washington DC. From there, an Amtrak train ticket into the District costs as low as $11 for a ride that takes about a half hour.

A taxi into downtown Washington DC from BWI costs about $90-100, though rates vary.

Train

Amtrak (www.amtrak.com) at DC's **Union Station** (50 Massachusetts Ave. NE; tel. 800/872-7245) is conveniently located less than half a mile north of the eastern edge of the National Mall, near attractions, restaurants, and hotels. You can access free Wi-Fi once you've boarded your train. The 125 Northeast Regional gets to **Richmond,** Virginia, in about four hours on a $22 ticket.

Bus

Greyhound (www.greyhound.com) also operates at **Union Station** (50 Massachusetts Ave. NE; tel. 202/289-5141). From **Richmond,** Virginia, it's a 2.5 hour

Union Station

trip ($25). You can also reach Washington DC from **Atlanta,** with a transfer in Richmond, for as little as $55—but the journey takes around 15 hours. Coming to DC from **New York?** Tickets start at $26 for the 4.5-6-hour journey.

Car

From **Richmond,** Virginia, take **I-95 North** for 110 miles (2 hours) to reach Washington DC.

GETTING AROUND

Here's the good news: With so many bucket-list attractions concentrated in and around the National Mall, Washington DC is one of the most walkable cities in the world. But it does take some serious stamina and good, comfortable walking shoes. Hoofing it—literally making your own march on Washington—can give you an intimate, awe-inspiring appreciation of the nation's capital. And it just might kick-start a new exercise regimen.

There is no debate that the Metro system is by far the best way to get around, though most visitors will use some combination of public transportation, taxicabs, Segways, scooters, bicycle-powered rickshaws, and good old-fashioned shoe leather. If you're driving into the District, consider picking a parking spot, then using the Metro, taxis, ride apps, or even scooters to get around. That would be easier and less frustrating than trying to scope out parking everywhere you go.

Parking

Parking garages are available near the National Mall and downtown. Rates across town vary by location, but most offer spaces for 24 hours at less than $40. On the National Mall, the **Reagan Building and International Trade Center** (1300 Pennsylvania Ave. NW; tel. 202/759-0074) almost always has parking, especially on weekends or early in the morning. The cost is $35 for 24 hours, and hourly rates or blocks are available. Go to www.rrbitc.com/parking for details. **Colonial Parking** (tel. 202/295.8100; www.ecolonial.com) has garages around town with rates that vary by location.

The National Park Service has 1,200 metered parking spaces along the National

Mall at a cost of $2.30 per hour for a maximum of three hours, daily 7am-8pm. These rates include weekends and holidays, except Christmas. Pay stations accept credit and debit cards, or you may pay through the **Parkmobile app** (us.parkmobile.com). No cash accepted. Metered parking spaces are available at: Constitution Avenue NW between 15th Street NW and 22nd Street NW; Independence Avenue SW between 15th Street and Maine Avenue; Jefferson Drive SW; Madison Drive NW; Ohio Drive SW between 23rd Street SW and Inlet Bridge; Parkway Drive NW; and West Basin Drive SW. There are 400 free parking spots at Hains Point in East Potomac Park. Accessible parking is available at the Tidal Basin, where you may go to see the King Memorial.

Public Transit

METRO

Washington DC's Metro, **Washington Metropolitan Area Transit Authority** (tel. 202/637-7000; www.wmata.com; Mon.-Thurs. 5am-11:30pm, Fri. 5am-1am, Sat. 7am-1am, Sun. 8am-11pm) is a great way to get around. The subway and elevated train lines are clean, convenient, and user-friendly. It's a welcome contrast to the gritty, labyrinthine, more intimidating subway system of New York City or Chicago's L.

The system is easy to navigate (even when train-to-train transfers are required) and faster—and often cheaper—than a cab ride. The cost of Metro fares vary depending upon the time of day and the distance between stations. Peak fares are in effect on weekdays 5am-9:30am and later between 3pm-7pm. A typical one-way trip costs just a few dollars.

Be warned: Eating and drinking are prohibited on trains, and every District resident has a story of seeing young people escorted off trains with a citation for eating from a bag of potato chips. Also, stations are busy places, so be sure to follow the unofficial District of Columbia motto: "Stand on the right. Walk on the left."

During the coronavirus pandemic conditions, face coverings were required in all Metro stations, trains, buses, and MetroAccess vehicles. For up-to-date coronavirus precautions, go to www.wmata.com/covid19.

The **National Mall** is served by the **Green, Orange, Red, Silver** and **Yellow** lines. Stops include Federal Center (at 3rd and D Streets SW); L'Enfant Plaza (at Maryland Avenue and 7th Street SW); Archives-Navy Memorial (at Pennsylvania Avenue and 7th Street NW); Smithsonian (at 12th Street on the Mall SW); and Federal Triangle (along 12th Street between Pennsylvania and Constitution Avenues NW); Farragut West (at 17th and I or 18th and I Streets NW); Foggy Bottom/George Washington University (23rd and I Streets NW); and Arlington Cemetery across Arlington Memorial Bridge over the Potomac River.

Downtown/Penn Quarter is served by the **Blue, Orange, Red,** and **Silver** lines.

In the **Capitol Hill and Atlas District,** the Capitol South Station is served by the **Orange, Silver,** and **Blue** lines.

In **U Street and Shaw,** the Shaw-Howard University station is served by the **Green** and **Yellow** lines.

Dupont Circle is served by the **Red** line.

In **Anacostia,** the Anacostia Station is served by the **Green** line.

Taxi and Ride-Hailing Apps

If you need a cab, call **Taxi Transportation Service** (tel. 202/398-0500; www.dctaxionline.com). **Uber** and **Lyft** are also definite go-to options in DC.

The Road Ahead

In 1965, singer Sam Cooke crooned "a change gon' come." And it did. The civil rights movement succeeded in strengthening constitutional protections through the passage of the Civil Rights Act of 1964, the Voting Rights Act of 1965, and the Fair Housing Act of 1968. But while much progress has been made, the structural underpinnings of racism endure today, and hard-won gains must be fought for again.

As a result of the 2013 Supreme Court case *Shelby v. Holder*, preclearance protections provided by the Civil Rights Act of 1965 more than 50 years ago have been removed, leaving voting rights at the mercy of those who don't believe Black people should have a say-so in this country. Voting has been tampered with in states such as Georgia, North Carolina, and Wisconsin, proof that vigilance must be maintained to protect—and restore—these rights.

And then there's police brutality and the overall policing of Black bodies. The 2012 killing of 17-year-old Trayvon Martin, and the subsequent acquittal of George Zimmerman, the wannabe cop who murdered him, ushered in a new era of awareness of the depth of racism. And in 2020, the modern-day lynching of Black people (Ahmaud Arbery, Breonna Taylor, George Floyd, and others) elicited widespread disgust.

The challenges don't end with policing and voting rights. Take the lack of wealth held by African Americans in general as another example of inequality. In 2020, The Urban Institute found that Black college graduates younger than 35 have a lower rate of homeownership than White high school dropouts. African Americans tend to suffer from lower credit scores because reporting agencies don't count the things Black people actually pay for—like rent and cell phones. There are problems in education as well, with research proving that Black female students are punished more severely than their White counterparts. And the 2020 coronavirus pandemic highlighted long-standing disparate health impacts as Black people succumbed to the virus faster, and in greater numbers.

Because of these ongoing issues, a new generation is making a deeper connection from the eras of Black enslavement and Jim Crow to the civil rights movement and beyond. We continue to unpack and attack social policies like mass incarceration, technological redlining, and the right to control our own bodies, whether through reproductive justice or the right to wear our Black hair—our crowns—naturally. The multigenerational force that is Black Lives Matter is one example of the movement's evolution.

This time around, the "respectability politics" embraced by the previous generation of African Americans, who showed up to the struggle in their "good" clothes, has been cast aside. In its place: a contemporary energy that is even more inclusive with regard to gender, sexuality, and class. In addition to Black Lives Matter, the civil rights movement has inspired countless modern movements, from the March For Our Lives to end gun violence and the Occupy movement, to the ongoing fight for women's rights. In some cases, such movements have benefited directly from the work done by civil rights activists. For example, in June 2020, the humanity of LGBTQ individuals got a boost from the Civil Rights Act of 1964. Because Title VII of that act bars discrimination "because of sex," the U.S. Supreme Court ruled discrimination against them illegal.

It's true that much work remains to be done. Statues of enslavers and other oppressors must come down. Leaders like President Woodrow Wilson cannot continue to be uncritically celebrated without accounting for their deep-seated racism. We know we need to dismantle structural inequity, and it's time to get serious and do the work from the White House, Congress, and the Supreme Court on down to the local level. The case for reparations has been well made, so we can start work on that too. But here's the good news: While the opposition stirs up age-old hate, the resistance—*our* resistance—has only gotten smarter, and further grounded in evidence-based strategies for equity and justice.

Previous: a Black Lives Matter protest in Hoboken, New Jersey, in 2020

MOVEMENTS AND ORGANIZATIONS

Has this journey inspired you to keep the "move" in movement and contribute to the Black freedom struggle that continues today? If so, the following resources are a few places to invest your time, money, and attention.

Black Lives Matter

www.blacklivesmatter.com

This is not a semantic argument, and if you can see that, maybe you'll also want to contribute to a global, intersectional liberation movement that works to dismantle systems and practices that harm Black people, including queer and trans people, undocumented and disabled people, women, and the formerly incarcerated. Visit the website to donate to the fight against state-sanctioned violence and end White supremacy.

National Association for the Advancement of Colored People (NAACP)

www.naacp.org

The NAACP is still in the business of fighting racism by advocating for the political, educational, social, and economic equality of all people. In addition to advocacy and legal work, the organization hosts the yearlong Afro-Academic, Cultural, Technological and Scientific Olympics (ACT-SO), a series of competitions in STEM, humanities, business, and performing, visual, and culinary arts to nurture Black youth excellence. The NAACP accepts donations to continue its work. Email development@naacpnet.org.

support for Black Lives Matter painted in Charlotte, North Carolina

THE ROAD AHEAD

Higher Heights

www.higherheightsforamericapac.org

Listen to Black women—and elect them too. Higher Heights is working to increase the number of Black women elected officials and support progressive policies. The organization prepares Black women to run for office by offering training, research, and messaging. The Higher Heights PAC is focused on getting more Black women elected in the 100 most populated cities. Visit the website for more information and volunteer opportunities, and follow #BlackWomenLead on Twitter.

National Bail Out

www.nationalbailout.org

Money bail disadvantages low-income people and people of color whose lives get turned topsy-turvy when they cannot afford to pay. National Bail Out organizes Mama's Day Bail Outs so Black women can spend time with their families on Mother's Day. This initiative highlights the injustice of a bail system that privileges the privileged who pay bail, go home, and keep working and supporting families while preparing for their cases. Too many Americans don't have this option and it is devastating.

Cite Black Women

www.citeblackwomencollective.org

Black thinkers often witness the theft of their work, but the time has come to give credit where it's due. Dr. Christen A. Smith at the University of Texas at Austin created this movement after hearing her research parroted at an academic conference without attribution one too many times. If you heard a good thing from a Black woman, it won't cost you anything to give her the credit for it.

The guiding principles of #CiteBlackWomen are: Read Black women's work; integrate Black women into the core of your syllabus; acknowledge Black women's intellectual production; make space for Black women to speak; and give Black women space and time to breathe. Visit the website and listen to the "Cite Black Women" podcast.

Cite Black Authors

www.citeblackauthors.com

The folks at Cite Black Authors maintain that scholarly citation is often passive and racially imbalanced. This site, a curated database of articles by Black scholars in various disciplines, invites you to reconsider your sources and citations.

We Need Diverse Books

https://diversebooks.org

We Need Diverse Books (WNDB) advocates for more diverse characters and experiences in children's books so that youth of all races, ethnicities, abilities, genders, and sexualites can see themselves reflected in what they read. WNDB brings diverse authors and stories to schools and develops educational materials with the School Library Journal and American Booksellers Association. Support their mission through smile.amazon.com and typing in "We Need Diverse Books" so a percentage of your purchases on Amazon benefit this initiative, or donate on their website.

Girl Trek

www.girltrek.org

Are you a Black woman? Do something good for yourself and join Girl Trek, an accountability movement that invites Black women to commit to walking regularly to improve their health. African Americans suffer disproportionately from poor health outcomes, but walking groups in cities around the country are a way to build momentum around healthy living. Girl Trek has led themed campaigns, such as the Black History Bootcamp, which involves

HASHTAGS AND HANDLES

Follow these leaders and organizations for information and inspiration.

- **#BlackLivesMatter**: The new movement for civil rights and social justice went back and got anybody left behind the first time, and includes a global perspective.
- **#CiteBlackWomen**: A movement to encourage people to give Black women thinkers credit for their intellectual output because, to paraphrase Zora Neale Hurston, we are not your mule.
- **@BeKing**: The Twitter handle of Rev. Bernice King, youngest daughter of Martin Luther King Jr. and Coretta Scott King.
- **@eji_org**: The Equal Justice Initiative keeps track of racial injustice and efforts to overcome racial inequality.
- **@NMAAHC**: The National Museum of African American History and Culture (NMAAHC) offers On The Day (OTD), which tracks events in Black history, from the establishment of the first African American baseball league to businesses that rebuilt after the 1921 Tulsa Race Massacre.
- **@dribram**: Twitter handle of antiracism scholar Ibram X. Kendi.
- **@colorofchange**: Racial justice movement that mounts campaigns to end anti-Blackness.
- **@keishablain**: Award-winning president of the African American Intellectual History Society on Twitter.

21 days of walking to remember where we come from. The organization offers tools such as 100 Radical Acts of Self-Care, activities that include movement (30 minutes of sweat), sanity (listen to a historic speech), soul (listen to the sounds of nature), and joy (have a porch picnic).

BUY BLACK

Actress and producer Issa Rae isn't the only one "rooting for everybody Black." Even if you don't have plans to hit the trail right away, you can still support some of the Black-owned businesses featured in this guide by buying online. Taking it a step further, you might also consider making deposits in banks committed to investing in underserved communities, including the Black-owned Boston-based **OneUnited Bank and Hope Credit Union Enterprise Corporation** (www.hopecu.org).

Food Items

- **Lillie's of Charleston** (Charleston; www.lilliesofcharleston.com) offers barbecue and hot sauces, spice mixes, and gift boxes.
- **Cocoa Belle Chocolates** (Little Rock; www.cocoabellechocolates.

com) features the creativity and whimsy of Little Rock's Carmen Portillo, the only certified chocolatier in the entire state of Arkansas.

- **Phillip Ashley Chocolates** (Memphis; www.phillipashleychocolates.com) is your go-to for high-end fair-trade chocolate creations.
- **Nick Wallace** (www.nickwallaceculinary.com), an award-winning Mississippi-born chef, sells T-shirts and his own spice blend through his website.

Clothing and Accessories

- **Mo's Bows** (Memphis; www.mosbowsmemphis.com) offers a range of bespoke neckties, bowties, face masks, and pocket squares so you can look your spiffiest.
- **Tags Boutique** (Atlanta; www.tagsatl.com), run by Kandi Burruss of *Real Housewives of Atlanta,* sells the latest seasonal fashions for women.
- **Pressed** (Atlanta; www.pressedatl.com), owned by hip-hop artist Rasheeda, offers fly fashion: clothing as well as sneakers and accessories.
- **Equal Justice Initiative** (Montgomery; www.shop.eji.org) is the place to get your T-shirt emblazoned with a quote from EJI founder Bryan Stevenson: "The opposite of poverty is not wealth. The opposite of poverty is justice."
- **Cheryl Pesce: The Lifestyle Store** (Memphis; https://cherylpesce.com) offers feminist T-shirts, artisan-made jewelry, home goods, dolls, and more.
- **KickSpins** (Memphis; www.kickspinsmemphis.com), run by musician and producer Tonya Dyson, sells Memphis soul apparel along with items like clocks and bookends made from upcycled vinyl records.
- **College Crib** (Nashville; www.collegecrib.com) sells all the gear you need to properly represent your Greek-letter organization.
- **Nubian Hueman** (Washington DC; www.nubianhueman.com) accepts online orders for its diverse array of products, from Stoop & Stank T-shirts to accessories and beauty products.
- **Takara** (Chicago; www.shoptakara.com) features handcrafted jewelry that makes a bold statement. Designer Takara Beathea-Gudell offers pins cut in Black woman silhouettes, CROWN Act bookmarks, and a range of museum-quality earrings, cuffs, and necklaces. (Beathea-Gudell's Chicago store is not covered in this guide, but her wares are well worth a look.)
- **Gift Wraps** (www.the-gift-wraps.myshopify.com): It's amazing that Louisiana's 1700s Tignon laws forced style-forward Black women to cover their hair, but we've managed to do it with such flair ever since. Gift Wraps, founded by Kenya Adjekum Bradshaw and Rochelle Griffin, specializes in head wraps, jewelry, and accessories, including backpacks for men women made with Kente patterns. In Memphis? Find Gift Wraps at Cheryl Pesce Lifestyle Store (1350 Concourse Ave., Suite 125) and Natural Affair Beauty Lounge (2869 Poplar Ave.).

Home Goods

- **SustainAble Home Goods** (Atlanta; www.yoursustainablehome.com) has a Black Makers Collection featuring jewelry, art, and other items from the African diaspora. The Atlanta-based home goods store offers free shipping for orders over $65.

- **Woodcuts Gallery & Framing** (Nashville; www.woodcutsfineartgallery.com) specializes in African American art—prints as well as original pieces.

Books

- **Mahogany Books** (Washington DC; www.mahoganybooks.com) is a go-to vendor for books on anti-racism. The folks here believe that a book is only the beginning.

Get Educated

Most of the books, films, and other resources listed below are by Black writers, academics, and thought leaders. In the same way that patronizing Black-owned businesses is an investment in Black economic power, innovation, and creativity, purchasing books by diverse authors is a way to show support for the principles people fought for—and are still fighting for.

FURTHER READING

Anti-Racism

Unless they're accompanied by direct action, our national compulsion to signal virtue through hashtags and statements are empty gestures. Undoing the racism and inequality takes more than symbolism. Thanks to thought-provoking intellects like historian Ibram X. Kendi, who has introduced us to the practice of anti-racism, we know what the real work entails.

In addition to the books below, check out **Momentum** (https://momentum.medium.com), a Medium blog that covers "the fight against anti-Black racism." One facet of the blog keeps track of problematic Civil War memorials erected well after the war as emblems of racial intimidation.

***How to Be an Antiracist,* by Ibram X. Kendi** (One World; 2019): Kendi provides actionable steps for going from merely believing that racism is bad to actively being antiracist.

***White Fragility: Why It's So Hard for White People to Talk About Racism,* by Robin DiAngelo** (Beacon Press; 2018): DiAngelo, a White academic, consultant, and facilitator, puts the responsibility for White supremacy in the hands of people who must solve it: White people, exposing White America's insultation from and discomfort with racism.

***So You Want to Talk About Race?* by Ijeoma Oluo** (Seal Press; 2018): Not every person has the same experience with and facility for discussing racism, so Oluo teaches us how to talk to one another.

Modern Issues

***Stamped From the Beginning: The Definitive History of Racist Ideas in America,* by Ibram X. Kendi** (Bold Type Books; 2016): This National Book Award winner chronicles the history of racist ideas in America.

***From #BlackLivesMatter to Black Liberation,* by Keeanga-Yamahtta Taylor** (Haymarket Books; 2016): The award-winning book explores the history of structural racism as a way to understand contemporary movements for Black liberation.

***Freedom Is a Constant Struggle: Ferguson, Palestine, and the Foundations of a Movement,* by Angela Y. Davis** (Haymarket Books; 2016): This collection of essays, speeches, and interviews makes the critical connection from domestic liberation struggles to global ones. Davis, the activist, scholar, author, and speaker, implores us to build a movement for human liberation.

***The New Jim Crow,* by Michelle Alexander** (The New Press; 2010): Before the "defund police" movement, there was this book, the bible of criminal justice reform. Attorney Michelle Alexander has given us a clear-eyed evidence-based argument for challenging America's addiction to mass incarceration.

***Race After Technology: Abolitionist Tools for the New Jim Code,* by Benjamin Ruha** (Polity; 2019): Don't believe the hype when it comes to the ability of lifestyle apps and other technology to transform our lives. This book shows how almighty algorithms that are touted as bias-free simply replicate the experiences of the people who program them, transferring discriminatory results over to the physical world.

***Algorithms of Oppression: How Search Engines Reinforce Racism,* by Safiya Umoja Noble** (NYP Press; 2018): Search engines are not the equal playing field they are portrayed to be. Noble's research shows how search engine results expose how racism and sexism flourish online.

***Caste: The Origins of Our Discontents,* by Isabel Wilkerson** (Random House, 2020): The Pulitzer Prize-winning journalist explains how racial hierarchies have perpetuated a caste system and explodes the myth of the "meritocracy" that places African Americans at the bottom.

Civil Rights History

***Eyes on the Prize: America's Civil Rights Years, 1954-1965,* by Juan Williams** (Penguin; 2013): This definitive account of the civil rights movement covers everything from the Montgomery bus boycott to the desegregation of Little Rock Central High School to the Selma-Montgomery march.

***The Color of Law: A Forgotten History of How Our Government Segregated America,* by Richard Rothstein** (Liveright; 2017): Rothstein explains how people and systems conspired to use federal housing policies to diminish Black wealth.

***Local People: The Struggle for Civil Rights in Mississippi,* by John Dittmer** (University of Illinois Press; 1995): Dittmer traces the battle against White supremacy in Mississippi, including efforts by Black World War II veterans (think: Medgar Evers) to register to vote, the Freedom Rides, the March Against Fear, and beyond.

***I've Got the Light of Freedom: The Organizing Tradition and the Mississippi Freedom Struggle,* by Charles M. Payne** (University of California Press; 2007): Tracing the early history of the civil rights movement, Payne excavates the workings of the Mississippi freedom struggle, allowing the people who powered the movement to speak for themselves.

***An Unseen Light: Black Struggles for Freedom in Memphis, Tennessee,* by Aram Goudsouzian and Charles W. McKinney** (University Press of Kentucky; 2018): There's so much more to Memphis's political and social history than King's assassination. Memphis, a largely poor, majority Black city, is where civil and labor rights converged, and is still dogged by the inequalities that brought King to the city to support the 1968 sanitation workers strike.

***But for Birmingham: The Local and National Movements in the Civil Rights Struggle,* by Glenn T. Eskew** (The University of North Carolina Press; 1997): This Georgia State University professor gives the blow-by-blow of the Birmingham Campaign, which produced events and imagery that shifted the public's view of civil rights. Eskew also explores the internal politics of Birmingham and leadership circles with both the White and Black communities, especially tensions between the Black elite and Black workaday folks.

Other History

***The Warmth of Other Suns,* by Isabel Wilkerson** (Random House; 2010): A chronicle of the Great Migration (1915-1970), when African Americans left the suffocating South for better opportunities in the North.

Memoir and Essay

***Walking with the Wind: A Memoir of the Movement,* by John Lewis** (Simon & Schuster; 1998): Lewis's memoir details his journey from his childhood as a sharecropper's son to his participation in the civil rights movement where he provides vivid details of being inside the struggle.

***Death of Innocence: The Story of the Hate Crime That Changed America,* by Mamie Till-Mobley with Christopher Benson** (One World; 2004): How did Mamie Till-Mobley, Emmett Till's mother, find the will to keep living after the lynching of her son? She tells her story in her own words.

***Coming of Age in Mississippi: The Classic Autobiography of Growing Up Poor and Black in the Rural South,* by Anne Moody** (Dell; 1968): This moving memoir of growing up in rural Mississippi also includes Moody's account of working for Congress of Racial Equality (CORE) at the Canton Freedom House.

***Notes on a Native Son,* by James Baldwin** (Beacon Press; 2012): This collection of essays describes the Black condition leading into the midcentury civil rights movement. Baldwin was in his 20s when these powerful pieces of social criticism were first published. They have proved elastic and prophetic.

Biography

***The Radical King,* by Cornel West** (Beacon Press; 2015): The celebration of King as a great speaker and likable guy belies the reality of his radical agenda. King was a democratic socialist who backed what many may consider revolutionary ideas, including guaranteed income and a living wage. His agenda included race and class so everyone with a stake in a better more economically just America could benefit.

***The Sword and the Shield: The Revolutionary Lives of Malcolm X and Martin Luther King Jr.,* by Peniel E. Joseph** (Basic Books; 2020): This biography of Martin Luther King Jr. and Malcolm X, two leaders who are considered ideological polar opposites, render their evolution in the fullness and complexity they deserve.

***Stokely: A Life,* by Peniel E. Joseph** (Basic Civitas Books; 2014): This biography of Trinidad-born, Howard-educated Stokely Carmichael traces his pathway to and through civil rights activism.

***Ella Baker & the Black Freedom Movement,* by Barbara Ransby** (University of North Carolina Press; 2005): A comprehensive history of the 50-year career of Ella Baker, whom many have called the most influential woman in the movement. Ransby covers the intersectional struggle of being Black and female in a movement dominated by male leaders. This book helps us understand the philosophy of Baker's bottoms-up style of leadership and the political and labor influences that informed her work.

Books by Martin Luther King Jr.

King, the powerful orator, possessed a firm spiritual and intellectual grounding in the philosophies he espoused for making the United States live up to its ideals. Read his books to get inside his head.

Stride Toward Freedom: The Montgomery Story (1958): King chronicles the people and tactics of the successful Montgomery Bus Boycott (1955-1956) and introduces the world to his principles of nonviolence.

Strength to Love (1963): This collection of sermons provides insight into King's Christian faith and use of nonviolence to reshape society. Classic sermons found here include "Loving Your Enemies," "Antidotes for Fear," and "Transformed Nonconformist."

Why We Can't Wait (1964): King started this book after the 1963 Birmingham Campaign. In it, he explains the circumstances that led African Americans to resist oppression and gives an honest assessment of what was gained and lost during the campaign's violent clashes.

Where Do We Go From Here: Chaos or Community? (1967): King's final manuscript, which narrates his vision for better jobs, higher wages, housing, and quality education, resonates through the ages.

Books by Other Black Leaders

***The Red Record: Tabulated Statistics and the Alleged Causes of Lynching in the United States,* by Ida B. Wells** (1895): Wells's copious documentation of 19th-century racial terrorism shows the real causes of lynching. Her reporting foreshadowed Carolyn Bryant, the White woman who got Emmett Till murdered in 1955, as well as the continued weaponizing of White privilege in contemporary America.

***The Souls of Black Folk,* by W.E.B. DuBois** (1903): DuBois posits that the problem of the 20th century is the problem of the color line and offers a lexicon to assess the lived experience of Black Americans.

Poetry

***The Talk,* by Jabari Asim:** Find this 2014 poem about explaining police brutality to children at the *Washington Post* (www.washingtonpost.com).

***I, Too,* by Langston Hughes:** Hughes's poem is an enduring reminder that this is our home too.

***I saw Emmett Till this week at the grocery store,* by Eve L. Ewing:** Imagine if Emmett lived. Ewing does.

Books for Young Adults

***STAMPED: Racism, Antiracism and You,* by Ibram X. Kendi and Jason Reynolds** (Little, Brown Books for Young Readers; 2020): A remix of the National Book Award-winning *Stamped from the Beginning* (2016), the authors explore the history of racists ideas in the United States and set the scene for an anti-racist future.

***Turning 15 on the Road to Freedom: My Story of the 1965 Selma Voting Rights March,* by Lynda Blackmon Lowery** (Dial Books; 2015): Lowery was the youngest marcher in the 1965 Selma to Montgomery march for voting rights. She brings her story to life in this book for young readers.

Books for Children

***Antiracist Baby,* by Ibram X. Kendi with illustrations by Ashley Lukashevsky** (Kokila; 2020): Children are not born racist, and it's up to us to make sure they don't learn to be that way.

***Preaching to the Chickens: The Story of Young John Lewis,* by Jabari Asim, illustrated by E.B. Lewis** (Nancy Paulson Books; 2016): Before he joined the Nashville Sit-in Movement and became a Freedom Rider—and well before he became a congressman—John Lewis was a little boy living in rural Alabama. This lovingly illustrated story of Lewis's childhood shows how the dreams of children can be righteous and realized.

***The Worst First Day: Bullied While Desegregating Central High: An Illustrated Autobiography,* by Elizabeth Eckford, Dr. Eurydice Stanley, and Grace Stanley** (Lamp Press; 2018): Little Rock Nine's Elizabeth Eckford describes her first day at Little Rock Central High School. Black-and-white photos of the time underscore the horrors she endured.

***The Youngest Marcher: The Story of Audrey Faye Hendricks, a Young Civil Rights Activist,* by Cynthia Levinson, illustrated by Vanessa Brantley-Newton** (Atheneum Books for Young Readers; 2017): Meet the youngest Birmingham foot soldier who, at age nine, was jailed for heeding a call to justice.

***A Ride to Remember: A Civil Rights Story,* by Sharon Langley and Amy Nathan** (Abrams Books for Young Readers; 2020): The same day the March on Washington for Jobs and Freedom took place, Sharon Langley became the first Black child to ride the merry-go-round at Gwynn Oak Amusement Park in Maryland thanks to a years-long interracial effort by CORE with help from the NAACP to desegregate the amusement park.

***Ruby Bridges Goes to School: My True Story,* by Ruby Bridges** (Cartwheel Books; 2009): Bridges was a six-year-old first-grader when she became a civil rights pioneer—the first child to desegregate a New Orleans school in 1960.

FILMS

Documentaries

I Am Not Your Negro (2016): Visionary author James Baldwin's unfinished manuscript *Remember This House* is rendered visually in this Raoul Peck documentary. Baldwin remembers civil rights leaders Medgar Evers, Malcolm X, and Martin Luther King Jr., and makes powerful observations about the American democratic experiment.

4 Little Girls (1997): Director Spike Lee's documentary is a tribute to the Addie Mae Collins, Denise McNair, Carole Robertson, and Cynthia Wesley, the four girls murdered in the September 15, 1963, 16th Street Baptist Church bombing.

Eyes on the Prize (1987): This 14-part documentary about the civil rights movement and the everyday people who stood up to racial oppression is visually stunning and every bit as definitive as the book upon which is it based.

The Road Ahead

Good Trouble (2020): Director Dawn Porter uses interviews and archival footage to explore Georgia Congressman John Lewis's 60-plus years of social activism and a legislative body of work that covered civil and voting rights, gun control, healthcare reform, and immigration.

Freedom Riders (2011): Based on the book *Freedom Riders: 1961 and the Struggle for Racial Justice* by Raymond Arsenault, this documentary focuses on six months in 1961, when an interracial group of more than 400 activists took to the roads on interstate buses to protest segregation.

The Murder of Emmett Till (2003): Stanley Nelson directs this TV documentary about a 14-year-old Chicago boy who went to visit his relatives in Mississippi in 1955 and was tortured and murdered by White men who were subsequently acquitted by an all-White, all-male jury.

Slavery By Another Name (2012): Black history scholars such as Khalil Muhammad, Mary Ellen Curtin, Adam Green, and Risa Goluboff are interviewed in a documentary that explores efforts to re-enslave African Americans since the Civil War.

The Black Power Mixtape 1967-1975 (2011): In the late 1960s, Swedish journalists came to the United States and recorded interviews with activists such as Stokely Carmichael, Bobby Seale, Angela Davis, and Eldridge Cleaver. Decades later, these recordings help us understand the Black Power Movement. This documentary features music by Questlove and Om'Mas Keith with commentary from Black entertainers and activists such as Erykah Badu, Harry Belafonte, and Melvin Van Peebles.

Soundtrack for a Revolution (2009): Artists such as John Legend, Joss Stone, Wyclef Jean, and The Roots are featured in this musical journey. The film explores the roots of freedom songs, from enslavement to the Black church to protests in jail cells, mass meetings, and marches.

Through a Lens Darkly: Black Photographers and the Emergence of a People (2014): Many museums in this guide touch on the demeaning imagery used to paint a false image of Black people, which, in turn, undergirded social norms, policies, and laws that threatened Black progress. This documentary explores the effects of this imagery.

More than a Month (2012): Black filmmaker Shukree Hassan Tilghman travels the country posing the question: "Should Black History Month cease to exist?" The cinema verité-style documentary calls forth a variety of answers that explore whether Black history is adequately taught in America's schools, whether it represents a false or demeaning sense of exceptionalism, or if Black history is just American history, period. Watch and decide for yourself.

The African Americans: Many Rivers to Cross (2013): Henry Louis Gates Jr. explores what it means to be African American in this expansive Emmy-award-winning series. This series includes interviews with top historians and key figures, plus visits to historical sites.

13th (2016): Director Ava DuVernay explores the connection between the Thirteenth Amendment and mass incarceration epidemic.

Other Films

When They See Us (2019): DuVernay's four-part Netflix drama about five Black and Latino teenage boys who were falsely convicted of the 1989 rape of a White woman in New York City's Central Park is a blistering and necessary look at how systemic racism works. If you didn't know before watching this, now you know.

Selma (2014): DuVernay directed this breathtaking Paul Webb drama that recounts the story of the 1965 Selma to Montgomery march. This film helps you get to know the names and faces of movement makers, who are played by Hollywood favorites including David Oyelowo (Martin Luther King Jr.), Carmen Ejogo (Coretta Scott King), Common (James Bevel), André Holland (Andrew Young), and Lorraine Toussaint (Amelia Boynton), among many others.

The Best of Enemies (2019): Based on the real-life story of activist Ann Atwater (Taraji P. Henson) and Ku Klux Klansman C. P. Ellis (Sam Rockwell) in Durham, North Carolina. The duo clash over school integration as they work to decide where Black students in East Durham will attend school following a fire.

Lee Daniels' The Butler (2013): This film based on a *Washington Post* article tells the story of White House butler Cecil Gaines (Forest Whitaker), who served eight presidents. The civil rights movement is depicted alongside a tale of family tensions.

The Vernon Johns Story: The Road to Freedom (1994): Rev. Vernon Johns (James Earl Jones) was an early adopter to civil rights causes and set the tone for King, who succeeded him as pastor of what was then Dexter Avenue Baptist Church.

Just Mercy (2019): Attorney and Legacy Museum founder Bryan Stevenson's quest to seek justice for Walter McMillian, a Black man sentenced to death for a murder he did not commit, is captured in this searing film, which lays bare the racism and politics embedded in America's justice system. The film is based on a case detailed in Stevenson's 2014 book of the same name.

10,000 Black Men Named George (2002): A fictionalized account of how A. Philip Randolph organized the Brotherhood of Sleeping Car Porters and Maids in the 1920s.

The Hate U Give (2018): Based on Mississippi writer Angie Thomas's best-selling young adult novel about race, activism and policing.

Podcasts

1619: Pulitzer Prize-winning journalist Nikole Hannah-Jones hosts this podcast series that builds on The 1619 Project, a *New York Times* initiative named for the year that the first enslaved Africans arrived in Virginia.

Code Switch (NPR): Explores how race and identity affects us all.

The Diversity Gap: Bethany Wilkinson excavates the space between good intentions and meaningful change.

Uncivil: Hosted by journalists Jack Hitt and Chenjerai Kumanyika, this show explores America's divisions and challenges what you think you know about U.S. history.

Nice White Parents: This five-part series by the *New York Times* Serial Productions delves into the problems with public schools, including the history of segregation.

Pod Save The People With DeRay: Organizer and activist DeRay McKesson, who rose to prominence during the Ferguson uprising, hosts conversations on news, politics, and social justice topics with Kaya Henderson, Debra Balenger, Sam Sinyangwe, and featured guests.

History

Before the Movement

ENSLAVEMENT

The history of Black resistance stretches way back to enslavement. The stories told by schools and history books don't usually include early efforts to resist enslavement, as if they never occurred. But they did. Captured Africans, including women, rebelled on transatlantic slave ships and continued to do so when they got here, setting the stage for later activism. Enslaved Black people rebelled against the system in other ways too, working and buying their freedom, and

then working some more to purchase freedom for family members. This sense of self-possession guided African Americans during Reconstruction and into the Jim Crow era when Black people pursued education and opportunity.

A WAR ABOUT FREEDOM (1861-1865)

As with resistance to enslavement, stories of the Civil War often leave out participation by Black soldiers. White supremacist ideology insisted Black soldiers could not be good soldiers, but the 1st Kansas Colored Volunteers dispelled that notion in October 1862, when they handily dispatched Confederates at the Battle of Island Mound, Missouri. By August 1863, 14 Black regiments were formed.

Multiple Black regiments entered Richmond, the capital of the Confederacy, on April 2, 1865, according to Marquett Milton, a history interpreter. Days earlier, they defeated the Confederates in Petersburg, Virginia. On April 9, 1865, the 25th Army Corps forced Robert E. Lee to surrender at Appomattox on April 9, 1865, effectively ending the Civil War. It took a while for news to spread, so the final fight, the Battle of Palmito Ranch near Brownsville, Texas, went forward on May 12-13, 1865. And as we well know, Black people in Texas didn't get word they were free until June, annually celebrated as Juneteenth.

When the war was over, African Americans were awarded with three amendments: Thirteenth (abolishes enslavement), Fourteenth (grants African Americans citizenship), and Fifteenth (gives Black men the right to vote). Women of every race didn't get the right to vote until the Nineteenth Amendment went into effect in 1920.

RECONSTRUCTION: REBUILDING AND CLIMBING (1865-1877)

Right after the Civil War ended, Southern Whites instituted Black codes that gave African Americans the right to legally marry and own property, but not to testify against a White person in court, or to serve as jurors or in militias. Those codes were repealed in 1866 after the rebuilding period known as Reconstruction, when the U.S. government maintained a presence in the South. The nation's laws were rewritten to guarantee the rights of formerly enslaved Black people who could now vote (men only) and assume public office. A handful of Black men were elected to the 41st and 42nd U.S. Congress. Hiram Revels of Mississippi became the first Black U.S. senator in 1870. Blanche K. Bruce became a senator five years later.

During this period, the Freedmen's Bureau was established to help newly freed Black people and poor Whites in the South obtain food, shelter, health care, and clothing. However, the bureau was soon undermined by President Andrew Johnson, who vetoed a bill extending the length of time the bureau could do its work by evoking the tired ol' states' rights argument that persists today. Johnson said the bureau cost too much and helped Black people to the exclusion of other groups. Congress also created the Freedmen's Bank to serve Black soldiers who had no bank to secure their pay. The bank was poorly run and eventually shuttered, taking small yet hard-earned deposits of its Black customers who believed the bank was federally backed. (This really did a number on Black depositors who stopped trusting banks.)

During this period, significant Constitutional amendments tied to citizenship were enacted. The Fourteenth Amendment established birthright citizenship, meaning if you are born in the United States, you are automatically a citizen. That same amendment provided for equal protection under

Previous: Activists march in support of the Poor People's Campaign, Washington DC, 1968

REDLINING

Between 1935-1940, maps created by the Home Owners' Loan Corporation were used by banks, insurers, and the government to determine the creditworthiness of communities. People living in areas shaded red were the least likely to secure mortgages. According to the Mapping Inequality online redlining resource, the "infiltration of negroes" informed the grades of neighborhoods in Birmingham, Oakland, Charlotte, Youngstown, Indianapolis, Cleveland, Los Angeles, and Chicago. Areas such as Little Rock's West 9th Street area show up prominently on maps.

Across the country, redlining systematically denied the wealth-building potential of homeownership to African Americans. The effects of this outlawed practice linger to this day. The net worth of a contemporary White family is 10 times that of Black families.

the law, which would prove pivotal in landmark desegregation cases decided during the midcentury civil rights movement. The Fifteenth Amendment secured the right to vote for Black men by barring racial discrimination in voting. (No women were allowed to vote until the Nineteenth amendment was passed in 1920.)

JIM CROW: SEPARATE BUT CERTAINLY NOT EQUAL

With the end of Reconstruction came an era called Jim Crow (a term used to diminish the humanity of Black people since at least the 1830s). Under Jim Crow, state and local laws that enforced segregation came into effect. These laws and policies upheld a racial caste system that permanently relegated African Americans to the bottom of society. Despite constitutional amendments and the Civil Rights Act of 1875, *Plessy v. Ferguson* codified racial separation by insisting separate could be equal in American institutions, including schools, public transportation, and the U.S. military. Separate *and inferior* is more like it. The perceived breach of these unfair laws, paired with demeaning and racially intimidating social customs, could—and did—get Black people killed.

The Civil Rights Movement

People who study and care about the civil rights movement will caution that events of the 1950s and '60s do not fully represent the totality of the fight for civil rights in the United States. They are right. But as a period that saw concrete results out of sustained activism across the South it certainly bears witnessing. The major goals of this era included desegregation, voting rights, and the general ceasing of violence and discrimination against Black people. There were wins and setbacks along the way, and the movement ultimately culminated with the passage of several important pieces of legislation.

Notably, this period saw the rise and assassination of Martin Luther King Jr. and the rise and assassination of another key leader in the Black freedom struggle: **Malcolm X** (El-Hajj Malik El-Shabazz), who was assassinated February 21, 1965, by members of the Nation of Islam. (Because Malcolm X lived his life outside the South, he is not covered in detail in this guide.) While these men didn't always see eye to eye on issues such as the use of nonviolent direct action, each man evolved in experience, instinct, and philosophy, and some would argue that they were more together than apart.

BROWN V. BOARD OF EDUCATION (1954)

Brown v. Board of Education, one of the most famous Supreme Court cases of all time, ruled the segregation of public schools illegal. Fewer people know about the events that preceded it, or the details of those that followed.

A 1951 decision foreshadowed *Brown* when a U.S. District Court of Appeals ordered the University of North Carolina at Chapel Hill to desegregate. Integration by a few Black students at the undergraduate and graduate levels over the next few years was uneventful. Also in 1951, 16-year-old Barbara Johns was fed up with the substandard condition of her Black high school, Robert Russa Moton High in Farmville, Virginia, especially in comparison to the neighboring White school. Johns persuaded her fellow high school students to strike for a better school. In addition to striking, the students reached out to NAACP attorneys, who convinced them to shift their demands away from better facilities and toward desegregation.

The NAACP filed a lawsuit, *Dorothy Davis et al. v. County School Board of Prince Edward County,* on the Farmville students' behalf. That lawsuit was one of five lawsuits that comprised *Brown v. Board of Education.* Of all five cases, the Farmville students' lawsuit was the only one spearheaded by students.

Although *Brown v. Board of Education* ruled segregation of public schools illegal, in practice, it was a long road to the desegregation of public schools in the South. After *Brown,* Virginia Governor Thomas B. Stanley stated, "I shall use every legal means at my command to continue segregated schools in Virginia." In some places, including Farmville and Little Rock, Arkansas, White politicians preferred to close all schools entirely rather than desegregate. (Little Rock's schools closed for a year; Farmville's for five years.) Farmville schools remained segregated until 1964.

MURDER OF EMMETT TILL (1955)

Meanwhile, the Mississippi Delta was one place where the lynching of Black people occurred for any number of reasons in the Jim Crow era. In 1955, Emmett Till, a 14-year-old Black boy from Chicago's South Side who was known affectionally as "Bobo," became the widest known victim of this crime.

Carolyn Bryant accused the teenager of flirting with her at Bryant's Grocery & Meat Market, a store owned by her husband near rural Money, Mississippi, in the summer of 1955. (Later in life, Bryant reportedly admitted that her accusation was false.) Three nights later, Bryant's husband, Roy, and his half-brother, J. W. Milam, dragged Till from his great uncle's house and murdered him, shooting the child in the head, tying a 75-pound cotton gin fan to his body, and throwing him in a nearby river.

Till's funeral took place at Roberts Temple Church of God in Christ in Chicago. His mom, Mamie Till-Mobley, made the courageous decision to funeralize her son with an open casket, deliberately revealing his brutalized body. "I think everybody needed to know what had happened to Emmett Till," she said.

Photos of Till's body in the open casket were published in *Jet* magazine. The gruesome images, particularly those of Till's head and face, became a catalyst for civil rights activism.

HISTORY

ORGANIZATIONS THAT MADE THE MOVEMENT

An alphabet soup of organizations turns up everywhere in the story of the civil rights movement. Their membership provided leadership, boots on the ground, and the moral and philosophical underpinning of the nonviolent direct action employed during the mid-20th-century movement. Here's a cheat sheet to know what they were all about.

NATIONAL ASSOCIATION FOR THE ADVANCEMENT OF COLORED PEOPLE (NAACP)

Founded by an interracial group of thought leaders in 1909, this civil rights organization works to remove all barriers of racial discrimination. The NAACP has an impressive record of legal wins that have helped dismantle racial segregation and ensure that African Americans and other marginalized citizens get equal protection under the law.

FELLOWSHIP OF RECONCILIATION (FOR)

An international peace and justice organization founded in 1914 in England and in the states in 1915. Members, including Quakers and other faith traditions, are pacifists. Bayard Rustin worked with FOR, as did Rev. James Lawson and other activists, and FOR is regarded as the parent organization of the Congress of Racial Equality (CORE). Though linked to the movement, FOR shifted its focus to speaking out against the Vietnam War.

CONGRESS OF RACIAL EQUALITY (CORE)

CORE was founded by James Farmer in 1942 in Chicago after he left the Fellowship of Reconciliation. CORE organized the 1947 Journey of Rec-

MONTGOMERY BUS BOYCOTT (1955-1956)

Four months after Till's murder, in Montgomery, Alabama, Rosa Parks, a department store seamstress and NAACP leader, refused to surrender her seat to a White male passenger. (At the time, many Southern cities, including Montgomery, required Black passengers to sit in the back seats of buses.) Parks's subsequent arrest sparked a wave of protest and activism, including the formation of the Montgomery Improvement Association (which, in turn, led to the formation of the Southern Christian Leadership Conference, or SCLC, in 1957). Under the leadership of a young Rev. Martin Luther King Jr., who, at the time, was pastor of Montgomery's Dexter Avenue Baptist Church—his first pastorate—the MIA coordinated a 13-month boycott of Montgomery's buses. The boycott ended in 1956, when the Supreme Court ruled segregation on municipal buses unconstitutional in *Browder v. Gayle.*

Before her death in 2005, Parks was awarded the Presidential Medal of Freedom, the highest honor given to a civilian. The national attention the boycott brought to Montgomery raised the profile on the civil rights struggle in the South. The movement would leverage these optics throughout the struggle.

onciliation, in which interracial activists rode buses to test the Supreme Court's *Morgan v. Virginia* ruling on interstate buses (1946), as well as the 1961 Freedom Rides. An early leader in nonviolent direct action, CORE later abandoned these beliefs and embraced a Black nationalist ideology.

ALABAMA CHRISTIAN MOVEMENT FOR HUMAN RIGHTS (ACMHR)

Formed in 1956 after Alabama officials outlawed the NAACP, the organization's goals included getting rid of second-class citizenship and pressing for freedom and democracy. Founded by Rev. Fred Shuttlesworth, ACMHR asked King to come to Birmingham to partner in the Birmingham Campaign.

SOUTHERN CHRISTIAN LEADERSHIP CONFERENCE (SCLC)

Co-founded in 1957 by King and others after the success of the 1955-1956 Montgomery Bus Boycott in order to coordinate local protests aimed at dismantling segregation. The stated goal of the SCLC, which is still headquartered in Atlanta, was to redeem "the soul of America."

STUDENT NONVIOLENT COORDINATING COMMITTEE (SNCC)

Pronounced "snick," this civil rights organization was founded in 1960 to give students a greater voice in leadership on civil rights issues. King hoped it would remain a part of the SCLC, but it operated independently.

COUNCIL OF FEDERATED ORGANIZATIONS (COFO)

COFO (pronounced "coe-FOH") is a coalition of national and regional groups fighting for civil rights in Mississippi. It was established in 1962 to optimize the results of SNCC, CORE, and the NAACP.

SCHOOL DESEGREGATION

Several events supplied a spark that ignited the civil rights movement of the 1950s and '60s. The Mississippi lynching of Emmett Till was one of them. *Brown v Board of Education* was another. But it did not suffice for the highest court in the nation to ban segregated schools: Now the law had to be enforced.

The *Brown v. Board of Education* decision ushered in a new era of resistance—from White people in the South who did everything they could to resist desegregating public schools, and from Black people, who persisted. African Americans would not let the issue go, because desegregation meant that Black children could have access to better facilities and learning materials. Separate but equal was never the case.

In a number of Southern cities, White officials chose to interpret the Brown decision in a manner that allowed them to put off dealing with the issue. In 1955, the Supreme Court followed up with *Brown II,* a court order mandating that school systems desegregate "with all deliberate speed." Still, it wasn't until 1957 that the nine Black students known as the Little Rock Nine were able to attend their first day of classes at the best high school in town, Little Rock Central High—and it took an army to get them through the school doors.

Also in 1957, under a plan for gradual integration, a group of six-year-olds

THE BROTHERHOOD OF SLEEPING CAR PORTERS AND MAIDS

The Pullman Porters were a cadre of Black male servants working tirelessly on sleeping car trains owned by White industrialist George Pullman. Though low-paid and maltreated, Pullman Porters successfully unionized as the Brotherhood of Sleeping Car Porters and Maids in 1925 and served as an early form of social media for the Great Migration. Working on train routes across the nation, the porters distributed Black periodicals like the *Chicago Defender* and shared news as part of an informal but effective information network.

The Pullman Porters play a role in the movement: Founder A. Phillip Randolph was one of the "Big Six" of the civil rights movement, and E. D. Nixon, head of the Montgomery branch of the Pullman Porters and president of the local NAACP, helped bail Rosa Parks out of jail.

desegregated eight Nashville schools. The Ku Klux Klan terrorized the children, driving by and cursing at them as they proceeded to school escorted by their parents, according to writer Jessica Bliss in the *Tennessean*. One of those children was Joy Kelly Smith, daughter of Rev. Kelly Miller Smith Sr., First Baptist Church pastor and National Christian Leadership Council founder. One night, a bomb went off at a local elementary school.

A 1960 NAACP Legal Defense Fund lawsuit called *Northcross v. Memphis Board of Education* led to the desegregation of Memphis schools. Under a grade-a-year plan, first-graders would go first, and students were assigned in such a manner that no more than four Black students could attend an all-White school at one time. In 1961, 13 Black children desegregated Memphis's schools with no exposure to violence. Among them were children of civil rights leaders, including Dwania Kyles, daughter of Rev. Samuel Kyles, who was just five years old at the time, and Michael Willis (now Menelik Fombi), son of attorney A. W. Willis. (Read Kyles's recollection of the events on page 304.)

On August 30, 1961, Atlanta public schools were integrated when nine Black students entered four all-White high schools. The ugliness that accompanied integration elsewhere in the South did not occur here. Instead, students were peacefully shadowed by parents, police, journalists, and other onlookers.

In Alabama, civil rights attorney Fred Gray filed *Lee v. Macon County Board of Education* in January 1963 to compel the integration of all-White Tuskegee High School in Macon County. Public schools at every level from primary to college were rolled into the lawsuit in which a three-judge panel that included Judge Frank M. Johnson issued an order to desegregate. The decision was upheld by the U.S. Supreme Court's *Wallace v. United States.* Gray filed the lawsuit a week before George Wallace assumed the governorship of Alabama and famously declared "segregation now . . . segregation tomorrow . . . segregation forever" in his inauguration speech.

The Civil Rights Act of 1964, enacted because of pressure by civil rights activists, included provisions to hold back on federal funding for schools that insisted on segregation. And in 1971, the Supreme Court authorized busing as a means of fully and meaningfully integrating schools across the country.

THE SIT-IN MOVEMENT (1960)

The sit-in movement was another massive effort at desegregation. It took courage for four Black college students (David Richmond, Franklin McCain, Ezell Blair Jr. (Jibreel Khazan), and Joe McNeil) to resist the forces and dangers of Jim Crow and refuse to leave the Woolworth's lunch counter on February 1, 1960. Theirs was the earliest widely known sit-in, and it gets a lot of credit for starting a movement that spread quickly across the South.

Nashville is one place where the movement caught on with gusto. In 1959, Rev. James Lawson, inspired by Gandhi and time spent in India, had started training local students in nonviolent protest. Just a couple of weeks after the Greensboro sit-in, students trained by Lawson occupied lunch counters at Woolworth, Kress, and McLellan stores and were denied service at all three. More sit-ins followed in Nashville, where students including Diane Nash, John Lewis, and Bernard Lafayette emerged as leaders. John Lewis, the future Georgia congressman, was arrested for the first of dozens of times in Nashville. Upon arrest and conviction, many activists, including Nash, opted for jail time rather than paying a fine they felt would support a corrupt system, a tactic that came to be known as **"Jail. No Bail."**

Following the Greensboro and Nashville sit-ins, in April 1960, Ella Baker, with participation from King and Lawson, convened a meeting of students at Shaw University in Raleigh, with student activists from Nashville and elsewhere in attendance. At this meeting, the **Student Nonviolent Coordinating Committee (SNCC)** was founded.

On July 25, 1960, Woolworth's management in New York City agreed to desegregate lunch counters. Woolworth's cook Geneva Tisdale, 28, was the first Black person to eat at the Greensboro lunch counter. Her meal was an egg salad sandwich she made herself.

In spite of the 1960 agreement to desegregate lunch counters, the Woolworth's counter in Jackson, Mississippi, remained segregated for several years. A sit-in at this lunch counter in 1963 is regarded as the most violent of the movement.

FREEDOM RIDES (OR DIE TRYING) (1961)

In yet another example of desegregation efforts, back in 1947, the Congress of Racial Equality (CORE) had initiated the "Freedom Rides" to test the veracity of the 1946 Supreme Court decision *Morgan v. Virginia,* which overturned laws enforcing segregation on interstate buses and trains. The test involved interracial teams who rode interstate buses in the Upper South to make sure the law was being followed. In 1960, *Morgan v. Virginia* was bolstered by *Boynton v. Virginia,* which officially desegregated interstate transportation facilities. In 1961, Freedom Riders again took to interstate buses to test this new ruling.

After receiving training in nonviolent tactics, two interracial groups of Freedom Riders (13 riders total) left Washington DC on May 4, 1961. The majority of the Freedom Riders came from 40 states and ranged in age from 18-30, according to Marian Smith Holmes in *Smithsonian Magazine.* Half were Black and a quarter were women. The Freedom Riders planned to end their campaign in New Orleans, where they would attend a May 17 seventh-anniversary celebration of the *Brown v. Board of Education* decision.

The Freedom Riders encountered extreme violence on their rides. One bus was bombed in Anniston, Alabama, on May 14,

HISTORY

1961 (Mother's Day). Another group was beaten by the Ku Klux Klan in Birmingham, where local police commissioner Eugene "Bull" Connor gave a White mob free reign to attack. At this point, CORE, reacting to the violence (and unable to find a driver), suspended the campaign, and the Freedom Riders flew to New Orleans to complete their journey. This was when Diane Nash, a student leader of the successful Nashville sit-in campaign, stepped in, organizing fellow students to go to Birmingham to pick up where the original Riders had left off. Among the students who joined Nash were Nashville sit-in veterans John Lewis and Bernard Lafayette.

When the Freedom Riders reached Jackson, a number of were arrested and sentenced to time at the notorious **Mississippi State Penitentiary, aka Parchman Farm.** In prison, the Freedom Riders sang freedom songs so loudly and persistently that they were punished by having their mattresses taken away, among other more severe indignities. They also used the time to talk about the purpose of the movement, turning the jail into a university, Rev. James Lawson says.

The Freedom Riders kept the campaign going through the fall, when the Interstate Commerce Commission's enhanced regulations to enforce existing federal law banning segregated facilities went into effect. New regulations included $500 fines for segregated facilities and removing White and Colored signs from transportation facilities.

BIRMINGHAM CAMPAIGN (1963)

A number of significant movements occurred in 1963, some productive and some tragic. In April, King and Rev. Fred L. Shuttlesworth initiated the Birmingham Campaign, also known as Project C, for confrontation, to dismantle segregation in what was known as "the most segregated city in America." Black residents wanted the same rights as Whites, such as the ability to try on clothes in a store or return what didn't fit. They wanted the right to work in those same stores and the right to vote. They wanted public accommodations, including the ability to sit at a lunch counter or sit anywhere on a bus.

The plan entailed mounting a massive and nonviolent direct-action campaign to put pressure on White merchants during Easter season, second only to Christmas for shopping. (Because so few Black people could vote, putting pressure on the local economy was deemed the best action.) The plans also consisted of meetings, sit-ins, and marches, including a controversial Children's Crusade, in which 1,000 Black children, some as young as age six, marched. During this campaign, King was jailed and penned his famous "Letter from a Birmingham Jail."

Birmingham's notorious Commissioner of Public Safety Eugene "Bull" Connor was a leader in the violent reaction to the Birmingham Campaign. Video footage captured law enforcement blasting high-pressure water cannons at protestors, beating them with nightsticks, and other atrocities. As with Till's lynching, media coverage of this cruelty raised national awareness of civil rights issues, and the city of Birmingham took some steps toward desegregation.

A few months later, in June 1963, civil rights leader Medgar Evers was assassinated in front of his home in Jackson, Mississippi, becoming one of the movement's early martyrs.

MARCH ON WASHINGTON FOR JOBS AND FREEDOM (1963)

More than 250,000 people of all races came out to support the March on Washington for Jobs and Freedom in August 1963. The march was organized by the Big Six of the civil rights movement: A. Philip Randolph

(Brotherhood of Sleeping Car Porters and Maids), Whitney M. Young Jr. (National Urban League), Martin Luther King Jr. (Southern Christian Leadership Conference), James Farmer (Congress of Racial Equality), Roy Wilkins (National Association for the Advancement of Colored People), and John Lewis (Student Nonviolent Coordinating Committee). Bayard Rustin was chief organizer of the march.

Marchers gathered to press for civil rights, voting rights, and racial equality. An important goal of the March on Washington was to push the federal government to raise the minimum wage from $1.17 an hour to $2 an hour. March organizers also pushed for a national job-training program for Black people and Whites, so unemployed workers could work at jobs that paid decent money. After the march, King and other leaders met with President John F. Kennedy and Vice President Lyndon B. Johnson in the Oval Office to discuss a civil rights bill, which Kennedy warned was way off.

According to the Economic Policy Institute, civil rights demands were met by the passage of the Civil Rights Act of 1964 and the Voting Rights Act of 1965. However, Black Americans and others are still waiting on answers to economic disparities exacerbated by structural racism that produces unequal access to housing, education, and jobs.

FREEDOM SUMMER (1964)

Desegregation was not the only goal of the civil rights movement: Voting rights were hugely important as well. One poignant example of the sanctity of voting for African Americans occurred in Fayette County, Tennessee, when Black sharecroppers risked homelessness and lived in tents starting in 1959 rather than bow to White intimidation and back off trying to vote.

In Mississippi, where only a small minority of Black people were able to register to vote in the early 1960s, SNCC activist Bob Moses proposed a summer-long campaign known as Freedom Summer, in which college-age volunteers from the North, most of them White, were invited to Mississippi to help with voter registration efforts.

Organizers were transparent about conditions in Mississippi, according to the King Institute at Stanford University. Volunteers had to commit to the doctrine of nonviolence, get state driver's licenses, and were informed that they might face arrest. Volunteers also taught locals civics education in newly formed Freedom Schools and promoted the recently established **Mississippi Freedom Democratic Party** (MFDP). Founded by organizations affiliated with the Council of Federated Organizations (COFO), the MFDP was an integrated parallel party to the regular state Democratic Party, which barred Black people from participating in its meetings.

Nothing about Freedom Summer was free: Civil rights workers Michael Schwerner, James Chaney, and Andrew Goodman paid with their lives after they were arrested for "speeding" near Philadelphia, Mississippi, and were murdered by the Ku Klux Klan. The initiative was also unsuccessful in registering large numbers of voters. However, it is credited in helping pass the Civil Rights Act of 1964 and the Voting Rights Act of 1965.

In the fall of 1965, the MFDP sent delegates to the Democratic National Convention in Atlantic City to beseech the credentials committee to recognize their party and seat their delegates. An eloquent MFDP delegate and spokesperson, Fannie Lou Hamer told the DNC, "If the Freedom Democratic Party is not seated now, I question America. Is this America, the land of the free and the home of the brave, where we have to sleep with our telephones off the hooks because our lives be threatened daily, because we want to live as decent human beings, in America?" The Democrats offered the MFDP two seats,

THE NONVIOLENT STRATEGY

In considering King's legacy, many people lean into the comforting narrative of nonviolent resistance in the quest for equality and justice. But the Nobel Peace Prize winner's actions and body of work were more radical than a commitment to not hitting back the people who hit him first. Nonviolent direct action facilitated the movement's moral high ground and provided a creative friction that revealed the true motivations of White supremacists: Think about images of water hoses trained on nonviolent protestors in Birmingham, or the vicious dogs and police wielding batons as they beat civil rights activists, many of them children. Who looks like the bad guy here?

but, as Hamer put it, "We didn't come all this way for no two seats when all of us is tired." The MFDP unanimously voted to decline the offer.

CIVIL RIGHTS ACT (1964)

Several events, including Freedom Summer, are credited with encouraging the passage of the Civil Rights Act of 1964. President Kennedy had proposed a civil rights act during a June 6, 1963, nationally televised appearance, and after his assassination in November 1963, President Johnson made it his mission to see it through. It wasn't easy: The House tried to tie it up in the rules committee, and the Senate tried to talk it to death through filibuster. Senator Hubert Humphrey (D-MN), with help from Johnson, overcame the filibuster, and Senate Minority Leader Everett Dirksen (D-IL) got Republicans to support the bill.

The Civil Rights Act of 1964 is an exquisite law. It prohibits discrimination in public accommodations and employment and makes way for integrated schools.

SELMA VOTING RIGHTS MARCHES (1965)

By 1965, voter registration was a main goal of civil rights activists. Despite the fact that the Fifteenth Amendment gave Black men the right to vote and the Nineteenth gave all women that right, few Black people had been able to actually do so due to racial terror and segregationist laws. African Americans who persisted in registering regardless of nonsensical tests and poll taxes risked violence. Some were even killed. On June 23, 1964, the Twenty-Fourth amendment made it illegal to make citizens pay for the privilege of voting. That was a start. Still, Black people were vastly under-registered. In Selma, for example, only 335 citizens (among 15,000 eligible voters) were registered to vote.

It was in this environment that voting rights activists in Selma, led by John Lewis and Hosea Williams, staged a march to the state capital in Montgomery to demand voting rights. Demonstrators got as far as the Edmund Pettus Bridge, where they were attacked by law enforcement using tear gas, batons, and whips. The date, March 7, 1965, would be remembered as **Bloody Sunday.**

A subsequent Selma to Montgomery march, led by King, was completed on March 25, 1965. Men, women, children, ministers, and White allies joined in, and the crowd swelled to 25,000 by the time they made it to the state capitol. This march provided visibility and voice, along with pressure to pass a law that would destroy all barriers to voting.

VOTING RIGHTS ACT (1965)

Following the Selma to Montgomery march, President Johnson signed the Voting Rights Act of 1965 on August 6, 1965. The new law put teeth in the Fifteenth Amendment by removing restrictions tied to race or language. It also provided for federal examiners to register voters in problem areas and outlawed literacy tests as a qualifier for voting. Places with past patterns of discrimination had to secure preclearance to change voting patterns and practices. By the next year, 11,000 Black people had successfully registered to vote in Selma, and five African Americans ran for public office in Dallas County.

MARCH AGAINST FEAR (1966)

Even after the passage of the Voting Rights Act, Black people faced violence when attempting to register to vote. To encourage Black voter registration efforts, activist James Meredith (who had previously desegregated the University of Mississippi, becoming the first Black student to attend) staged a small march from Memphis to Jackson, Mississippi. When he was shot on the second day of his march and had to be hospitalized, other civil rights leaders stepped in to complete the trek.

Among the leaders who stepped in was SNCC chairman Stokely Carmichael, who evoked the phrase **"Black Power"** during a speech in Greenwood, Mississippi—much to the chagrin of movement elders. Some leaders, including King, believed the phrasing would be misinterpreted. However, many felt (and continue to feel) that the call for Black political and economic independence and cultural pride was a natural next step in the movement.

KING'S ASSASSINATION (1968)

On February 12, 1968, more than 1,300 sanitation workers in Memphis went on strike following the death of Black employees Echol Cole and Robert Walker, who were crushed to death in a malfunctioning garbage truck on February 1, 1968. For workers, their tragic deaths were the last straw in a series of many indignities.

At this time, King was in the process of mounting his **Poor People's Campaign,** seeking to address financial inequality for Native Americans, Latino farm workers, and other groups, in addition to Black people. The sanitation workers' strike drew King to Memphis to support and amplify their cause.

It was in Memphis that King's tragic assassination took place on the balcony of the Lorraine Motel. King was shot by a sniper named James Earl Ray, who had lain in wait across the way. King was 39 years old.

Black America was devastated and demoralized by King's assassination. All notions of nonviolent resistance went right out the window, and uprisings, including looting and arson, occurred in more than 200 cities. The Kerner Commission's watershed report released earlier that year put the unrest in context: "Segregation and poverty have created in the racial ghetto a destructive environment totally unknown to most white Americans," the report reads. "What white Americans have never fully understood—but what the Negro can never forget—is that white society is deeply implicated in the ghetto. White institutions created it, white institutions maintain it, and white society condones it."

Just a week after King's tragic assassination, President Johnson signed the Civil Rights Act of 1968, also known as the **Fair Housing Act,** which barred housing discrimination—an action that is often listed as the final act of the civil rights movement.

SHELBY V. HOLDER

In 2013, the Supreme Court struck a blow to the Civil Rights Act of 1965 with *Shelby v. Holder,* which removed the requirement to get federal clearance to change election laws. Current efforts to fight voter suppression, such as the work by Obama administration Attorney General Eric Holder, represent the latest front to keep Black voters fully enfranchised. In his eulogy for John Lewis, the beloved civil rights icon, in 2020, President Barack Obama implored us to honor Lewis by reviving the law he risked his life for.

After the Movement: 1968-Today

Since 1968, efforts have been made to honor the people who made the movement, many of whom were children, who took a chance on change. In 1999, the Little Rock Nine were awarded the Congressional Medal of Freedom by President Bill Clinton. Several civil rights-themed and Black history museums now hold our most precious stories and artifacts to help contextualize the Black experience in America, including Memphis's National Civil Rights Museum at the Lorraine Motel (opened in 1991); the Birmingham Civil Rights Institute (opened in 1992); the National Museum of African American History and Culture (opened in 2016) in Washington DC; Jackson's Mississippi Civil Rights Museum (opened in 2017); and the Legacy Museum: From Enslavement to Mass Incarceration and the National Memorial for Peace and Justice in Montgomery (opened in 2018). Charleston's International African American Museum, slated to open in 2022, will be a jewel in the crown of these cultural repositories.

Meanwhile, African Americans have continued to resist oppression as social movements challenge racism; demand fair wages, health care, and adequate housing; and tackle structural inequality across the board. African Americans have also run for public office at every level of government.

SWANN V. CHARLOTTE-MECKLENBURG BOARD OF EDUCATION (1971) AND DESEGREGATION BUSING

It's important to understand the difference between desegregation, which refers to the end of legally enforced segregation, and integration, in which institutions actually become more racially mixed. Because of housing inequality, many school districts remained de-facto segregated long after the *Brown* decision. The 1971 Supreme Court decision *Swann v. Charlotte-Mecklenburg Board of Education* permitted the use of busing students to schools outside their district as a method of achieving racial balance. Many Whites opposed busing, and the policy resulted in a "White flight" from some cities.

SHIRLEY CHISHOLM'S PRESIDENTIAL RUN (1972)

The 1970s also ushered in a wave of elections of Black mayors in major cities, including Gary, Indiana; Chicago; and Atlanta, Georgia, as well as Washington DC, where civil rights activist Marion Barry was elected mayor in 1978. They brought with them significant policy changes and programs benefitting Black people.

On a national level, Shirley Chisolm became the first Black person to run for president, seeking the Democratic Party nomination in 1972. The daughter of immigrants from Barbados and Guyana, Chisholm was the first Black woman elected to the U.S. Congress. She co-founded the Congressional Black Caucus and the National Women's Political Caucus. Her campaign lacked full support because Chisolm was subject to racism from Whites, and sexism from both Black and White men. She served in Congress for several years after her unsuccessful run. She continues to inspire women, especially Black women with her wise assertions, including, "If they don't give you a seat at the table, bring a folding chair."

EQUAL RIGHTS AMENDMENT (1972)

First proposed by the National Woman's Party in 1923, the Equal Rights Amendment sought to ensure the legal equality of the sexes. It passed the House of Representatives in 1971 and the Senate in 1972. A minimum of 38 states needed to ratify it before it would become law, and by 1977, only 35 states had done so. Congress set an initial ratification deadline of March 22, 1979, and then extended it to June 30, 1982, for the state legislatures to consider the ERA.

Although the ERA (like the women's movement in general) has often been framed inaccurately as a White woman's amendment, the law would be particularly auspicious for Black women, many of whom work outside the home and are more likely to be breadwinners than White and Latina women. We earn 62 cents to every dollar a White man earns. Equal Pay Day tracking shows we must work well into the calendar to earn what White men do at the end of the year regardless of the type of work we're doing. Advocates acknowledge that the Equal Pay Act and Title IX has antidiscrimination provisions, but as we have seen with the Voting Rights Act, they are subject to rollback. A Constitutional amendment explicitly barring gender discrimination would safeguard these protections.

Because it lacked votes, the amendment was considered dead until recently when advocates suggested an imposed deadline should never have been required, since other constitutional amendments never had a deadline for ratification. Since then, Nevada, Illinois, and Virginia have voted to ratify the amendment. The #MeToo movement was part of what helped put the proposal back in the spotlight.

JESSE L. JACKSON'S PRESIDENTIAL RUNS (1984 AND 1988)

King's protégé and civil rights activist, Rev. Jesse L. Jackson became a contender for president in 1984 and 1988.

Jackson's presidential platform was considered radical at the time, calling for universal health care, a nuclear freeze, reparations, and recognition of the LGBT community. His campaigns came with a powerful voter registration push that boosted the numbers of Black voters and in 1984 provided him surprising voting margins necessary to stay in the race as a contender. In 1988, when he challenged Michael Dukakis for the Democratic nomination, he received three times as many White votes as he did in his first campaign.

While Jackson's progressive, multiracial campaigns were ultimately unsuccessful, symbolically, they shifted the public's perceptions around who could be president. His presence and ideas offered concrete benefits too. For example, he challenged the Democratic Party's winner-take-all rules on the assignment of delegates after the 1984 election. Jackson's leadership resulted in changing Democratic Party rules, which made it possible for both Hillary Clinton and Barack Obama to be viable candidates, a crucial step in Obama's win as first Black president.

As a shadow senator for Washington DC from 1991-1997, Jackson sought to win statehood for the District so that the majority Black taxpayers could be self-determining. The statehood quest continues to this day.

Jackson's accomplishments in civil rights and social justice extends to global movements for human rights: He enjoyed a close relationship with South African President Nelson Mandela and other global leaders and is regarded highly around the world.

ELECTION OF BARACK OBAMA (2008)

A popular saying in the Black community about being our ancestors' wildest dreams was realized on November 4, 2008, when Barack Hussein Obama became the United States' 44th president and its first Black chief executive.

Obama's civil rights record includes embracing marriage equality in 2012, ending the "don't ask, don't tell policy" of LGBT people in the military, and expanding the hate crime statute to cover anti-gay bias. He refused to support the Defense of Marriage Act previously signed by President Bill Clinton, denying federal benefits to same-sex couples who got married in states that recognized these unions. He set the tone for the Supreme Court to invalidate the law in 2013, making same-sex marriage legal everywhere. The Fair Sentencing Act of 2010 reduced racial disparities in sentencing for crack and cocaine convictions. After becoming the first U.S. president to visit a federal prison, Obama issued a guidance to reduce the use of solitary confinement, particularly for young people and mentally ill people. The Affordable Care Act that extended health insurance to millions of Americans is the crowning achievement of his two terms as president. He is not without critics on many other issues, such as immigration enforcement, but when Obama left office, unemployment was low, his ratings were high, and more people had access to good healthcare.

FORMATION OF BLACK LIVES MATTER (2013)

If you had looked at the Facebook timelines of Black Americans on July 2013 when George Zimmerman was acquitted in the killing of 17-year-old Trayvon Martin in Sanford, Florida, you would have seen a different America. We were angry, demoralized, and fearful for our children and those living in our communities at large. This verdict affirmed our vulnerability: Our own children couldn't even go to the store and buy candy and a drink, which is what the teenager had done the night he was headed home minding his own Black business. Collectively, we committed ourselves to a wait-and-see approach to see if the justice system would do what it's supposed to do. Times had changed, right? We got our first Black president, right? But, oh, that system gloriously failed us—again. It was like the civil rights movement never happened.

Alicia Garza named the collective mood when she first used the phrase "Black lives matter" in a Facebook post. Her friend Patrisse Cullors made it into a hashtag. In the second half of 2013, the hashtag appeared about 30 times a day, according to Pew Research, gaining traction in 2014 when Michael Brown, an 18-year-old Ferguson, Missouri, teen was shot and killed by White police officer Darren Wilson. When patterns of state-sanctioned violence against Black people emerged in cases such as Eric Garner's death by police chokehold and Freddie Gray's death in the custody of Baltimore police officers, #BlackLivesMatter captured a particular kind of zeitgeist.

The organization #BlackLivesMatter, founded in 2013 by Garza, Cullors, and Opal Tometi, draws on the egalitarian organizing style of Ella Baker in a global effort to defeat White supremacy. The inclusive movement affirms all Black lives, including queer and trans people, disabled people, undocumented people, the formerly incarcerated, and women. #BlackLivesMatter has chapters from Boston to Long Beach and in Canada. Former NFL quarterback Colin Kaepernick lent his voice to the youthful yet multigenerational movement and repeatedly took a knee during the national anthem to protest police brutality. He lost his job in the NFL because of it.

One doesn't have to belong to #BlackLivesMatter to believe it. Leading activists, grassroots social justice warriors, workaday Black folks, and our advocates fully embrace what it means.

2020 PROTESTS

As the year 2020 dawned, an all-too-familiar pattern of state-sanctioned violence against African Americans continued to play out across the nation: Ahmaud Arbery, 25, was on a jog when White neighbors chased and killed him on February 23. Breonna Taylor, 26, a first responder, was shot and killed by police entering her home on a no-knock warrant on May 13. There were others, too. And when George Floyd, a 46-year-old Black man, was suffocated to death by a White Minneapolis police officer on May 25, something broke open in America. On lockdown due to the coronavirus pandemic, Black people were already struggling to breathe, literally and metaphorically, due to the disproportionate impact of the virus, which was killing a disproportionate number of us because of preexisting conditions linked to structural racism. Despite directives to stay socially distanced, the moment was too dire to stay off the streets. Daily demonstrations spread across the country, even in places like Portland, Oregon, with a small (5.8 percent) Black population. Some analysts surmised that the mostly peaceful Black Lives Matter demonstrations were the largest movement in U.S. history. As of July 3, 2020, the *New York Times* reported that more than 4,700 demonstrations had taken place since they began in Minneapolis on May 26.

Corporate America seemed to get the message: Organizations such as NASCAR, the NFL, and JPMorgan Chase issued statements in support of Black Lives Matter, though many people expressed skepticism about their motives. More than 190 technology sector companies issued statements of support, according to Sherrell Dorsey, founder of The Plug, which reports on the Black innovation economy. As an accountability measure, her team created a graphic showing the percent of Black people employed by the companies that spoke up. The image resonated with African Americans working in the tech sector, and it was shared widely. With the exception of large companies such as Amazon or Nike, the numbers didn't hold up when considering the total population of African Americans.

Public opinion about the Black Lives Matter movement shifted during summer 2020. A *Washington Post*-ABC poll reported that 69 percent of Americans believe the criminal justice system treats African Americans and other minorities unequal to White people. More than half (55 percent) of those polled said the recent killings of unarmed Black people was "a sign of broader problems in the treatment of black people by police."

Meanwhile, the state-sanctioned violence against African Americans has not stopped.

ESSENTIALS

Transportation

There's no "best" entry point to the Civil Rights Trail: You'll probably choose your starting point based on your interests and proximity to your home base. Long-distance buses and trains do serve the South, but they can be slow, so most travelers will probably arrive by air or car.

GETTING THERE

Air

The large cities in this guide all have airports served by major airlines, including **Charleston** (Charleston International Airport; tel. 843/767-7000; www.iflychs.com), **Atlanta** (Hartsfield-Jackson Atlanta International Airport; tel. 800/897-1910; www.atl.com); **Birmingham** (Birmingham-Shuttlesworth International Airport; tel. 205/322-2100; www.flybirmingham.com), **Jackson, Mississippi** (Jackson-Medgar Wiley Evers International Airport; tel. 601/939-5631; www.jmaa.com); **Little Rock** (Bill and Hillary Clinton National Airport/Adams Field; tel. 501/372-3439; www.clintonairport.com); **Memphis** (Memphis International Airport; tel. 901/922-8000; www.flymemphis.com), **Nashville** (Nashville International Airport; tel. 615/275-1675; www.flynashville.com); **Raleigh** (Raleigh-Durham International Airport; tel. 919/840-2123; www.rdu.com), **Richmond** (Richmond International Airport; tel. 804/226-3000; www.flyrichmond.com), and **Washington DC** (Washington Dulles International Airport; tel. 703/572-2700; www.flydulles.com). Reagan National Airport (tel. 703/417-8000; www.dca-airport.com) also serves Washington DC.

Atlanta's Hartsfield-Jackson Airport typically rates as the busiest airport with more than 100 million passengers annually. There's a high likelihood you'll connect through here to get almost anywhere you'll need to go on the trail, depending on your originating airport.

Selma, Montgomery, and the **Mississippi Delta** are the only destinations that lack large airports. Montgomery Regional Airport (tel. 334/281.5040; www.flymgm.com) serves Montgomery and Selma, or you can fly into a larger airport in Birmingham. To reach the Delta, fly into Memphis or Jackson.

Follow the **Federal Aviation Administration** (@FAA) on Twitter to get updated traffic reports and a snapshot of airports with slow traffic.

Train

Amtrak (www.amtrak.com; tel. 800/872-7245) has several lines that link destinations on this route:

- The **City of New Orleans** route connects Chicago and New Orleans, with stops in Memphis as well as Greenwood and Jackson, Mississippi.
- The **Carolinian/Piedmont** route connects New York with Charlotte, Virginia, with stops in Washington DC; Richmond, Virginia; and Durham, Greensboro, and Raleigh, North Carolina.
- The **Crescent** route connects New York and New Orleans, with stops in Washington DC; Greensboro, North Carolina; Atlanta; and Birmingham.

- The **Silver Service/Palmetto Route** connects New York and Miami, with stops in Washington DC; Richmond, Virginia; Raleigh, North Carolina; and North Charleston, South Carolina.

The train is known for going slow in many corridors, so this is only an option for folks with time on their hands. There's Wi-Fi and outlets to plug in devices, plus free coffee in business class. Purchase tickets in advance online or over the phone. You can also purchase tickets at staffed Amtrak stations (not all stations are staffed) or onboard the train.

Bus

Nearly every city and town covered in this guide, including Selma, Alabama, and the rural town of Farmville, Virginia, has a **Greyhound** (www.greyhound.com) station. The Delta is the exception: While the Greyhound stops in Clarksdale, Cleveland, and Indianola, Mississippi, it does not stop in every single destination covered in the Delta chapter. Selma has no direct connections to other destinations in this guide other than Montgomery.

Greyhound moves at a snail's pace compared with other transportation options, but if it's your jam, by all means indulge. Buy tickets online or in person at the station.

GETTING AROUND

The trail is a car-centric activity, especially in the Delta, where public transit options are limited. Even within cities, a car is generally your best option for getting from site to site.

Driving Between Destinations

Driving is the best option if you want to hit multiple destinations on the trail. Make sure you have a phone number for roadside service and check your windshield-wiper fluids and freon: We can't have the air conditioning going out on you in this unholy heat. Keep safety in mind too: Before heading into rural areas, gas up, and make sure your car has a spare tire and is ready for the road. Have a phone charger on hand, or identify the USB port in your vehicle, and don't forget an auxiliary cord.

Washington DC, Georgia, Tennessee, and Virginia all ban cell phone use while driving. If using Google, Waze, or other phone-based apps for navigation, check to see if your device interface syncs with your vehicle so you're hands-free all the way. If you're in an older car, get an inexpensive holder for your phone so you can pay attention to the road.

On this trip, you may find yourself driving pretty long stretches. If you feel tired, don't push it: Rest areas are great places to take breaks, catch catnaps, or wait out torrential spring and summer rains. (When those buckets of water are falling from the sky, sometimes the best thing to do park in safe area and let it pass.)

In Mississippi, it is wise to honor posted traffic speeds, as local police are known for their vigilance. (Conventional wisdom has it that your fines and fees boost the civic bottom line. Don't let them.) Also, drivers should use caution in pulling to the side of interstate road shoulders to avoid oncoming traffic. Just don't if you can avoid it.

City Transit

Cities generally have bus systems, and some, including Memphis and Charleston, also have trolleys or trolley tours, but as a rule of thumb, car culture rules in this part of the country, especially in rural areas like the Delta. Washington DC, whose excellent Metro system is affordable and easy to navigate, is the exception to this rule. Some neighborhoods are walkable, and it's likely that you'll do a lot of walking on this trip.

Uber and **Lyft** operate nearly everywhere, though you may have to wait for a ride in the Delta, where there seems to be a shortage of drivers. Venues are spaced out here, so you'll do better with your own car anyways.

Many tours, including multi-campus HBCU tours, were suspended during the coronavirus pandemic. Check with the individual tour companies and campuses to confirm whether tours have resumed.

CIVIL RIGHTS TOURS

Individual chapters of this guide include destination-specific tours. There are also multiday bus tours focusing on civil rights history that include multiple destinations on the trail:

SOJOURN TO THE PAST

tel. 650/952.1510; www.sojournproject.org, info@sojournproject.com; $3,200 pp for an eight-day tour

Based in Millbrae, California, and founded by former high school teacher Jeff Steinberg, Sojourn to the Past offers immersive civil rights movement tours for students and teachers that include a curriculum, footage, photos, and books. Eight-day bus tours launch from various states across the South. Past tours have included meetings with movement heroes like the late Congressman John Lewis and Reena Evers-Everette, daughter of Medgar Evers, the NAACP field secretary who was slain in Jackson in 1963. (Evers-Everette is the chair of Sojourn's board.) Visitors partake in immersive experiences; for example, standing in the driveway where Medgar Evers was shot down, after reading *Watch Me Fly,* a memoir written by his wife, Myrlie Evers-Williams, that describes that horrible day.

Tours include high-end bus transportation, food, lodging, and any site-specific security. Sojourn to the Past works mostly with school groups, but individuals (including adults) can book tours too. Their season revolves around the school year.

FREEDOM LIFTED

tel. 269/870-0008; www.freedomlifted.com; $1,100-1,200 pp for a four-day tour

Freedom Lifted founder Mia Henry, an educator and movement builder, got bitten by the heritage tours bug in 2011, when she joined a civil rights tour to commemorate the 50th anniversary of the Freedom Rides with Dr. Bernard Lafayette. Henry envisioned a tour company that would cover several cities throughout the South, taking to heart lessons of the civil rights movement by inviting voices of that time to meet and talk with school-age children.

Freedom Lifted appears to be Henry's dream realized. Much more than a tour, it's an immersive educational experience centering on the civil rights movement. Henry seeks to connect the past with the present by creating the ultimate experiential education about Black resistance to White supremacy. In addition to visiting historic sites, travelers get a taste of regional flavors at local restaurants, including those that are Black-owned. Henry has cultivated rich relationships with civil rights workers and knowledgeable residents who tell uniquely local stories about the movement. Her mother, Rugenia Moore Henry, a foot solider during the Birmingham Campaign in 1963 and one of the first Black children at her junior high in Gadsden, Alabama, is a frequent speaker on tours, as is Catherine Burk-Brooks, a Birmingham-based Freedom Rider.

Tour stops include Birmingham, Memphis, the Mississippi Delta, Tuskegee, Atlanta, North Carolina, Selma, and Montgomery. Tour buses are stocked with books and other learning materials that facilitate discussions. Tours typically include 15-40 people.

BIKE TOUR

TRIANGLE BIKE WORKS

www.spokenrevolutions.org; tel. 919/408-7913; $800

Based in Carrboro, North Carolina, Triangle Bike Works trains junior high and high school students in the sport of cycling and bicycle maintenance so they can go the distance. Every summer, 20 high school students join founder Kevin Hicks on a two-week-long distance journey along back roads and state highways to historical sites where they learn hidden and not-so-hidden facts about Black history. Past journeys have included Atlanta's Martin Luther King National Historical Park, Greenville, South Carolina, and Natchez, Mississippi. Hicks provides the bikes, gear, food, and anything the kids needs for a successful trip that covers 50 to 70 miles a day for a cost of $800. "It's all about building faith and trust in the person ahead of you. The goal is to create critical thinkers so they can plot a course for a better future," says Hicks, who created this opportunity because he felt local school kids weren't getting the exposure to and context of their history. The majority of youth cyclists are Black, though Hicks wants to expand into Latino history because that has not been fully told either.

HBCU TOURS

Historically Black colleges and universities (HBCUs) are living monuments to Black excellence. They have existed since the founding of the Institute for Colored Youth (1837) and Lincoln University in Pennsylvania, and Wilberforce University (1856) in Ohio. These schools initially provided elementary and secondary education to Black students who had no previous training. Postsecondary classes took off in earnest in the early 1900s. Today, HBCUs, specifically Howard University and Meharry Medical College, stand out for educating a significant numbers of Black physicians and dentists, most Black doctoral degree holders, and a significant percentage of Black armed forces officers and Black judges.

There are more than 100 HBCUs in the U.S., many of them located near the civil rights trail. HBCUs are attended primarily, though not exclusively, by Black students: The campuses welcome a wide range of students from all races, ethnicities, and nationalities, as well as socioeconomic backgrounds.

Individual Campus Tours

Prospective students should check the website of each of the below institutions for information about campus tours. Many HBCUs have a direct connection to the civil rights movement, including those listed in boldface, which are covered in more detail in the destination chapters of this guide.

ATLANTA

Morehouse College
Spelman College
Clark Atlanta University
Morehouse School of Medicine
Interdenominational Theological Center

SELMA

Selma University

MONTGOMERY

Alabama State University
Trenholm State Community College

BIRMINGHAM

Lawson State Community College

JACKSON

Jackson State University

MISSISSIPPI DELTA

Coahoma Community College
(Clarksdale)

LITTLE ROCK

Arkansas Baptist College
Philander Smith College

MEMPHIS

Le Moyne-Owen College

NASHVILLE

American Baptist College
Fisk University
Meharry Medical College
Tennessee State University

GREENSBORO, NORTH CAROLINA

Bennett College
North Carolina A&T State University

RALEIGH, NORTH CAROLINA

Shaw University
Saint Augustine's University

DURHAM, NORTH CAROLINA

North Carolina Central University

RICHMOND, VIRGINIA

Virginia Union University

WASHINGTON DC

Howard University
University of the District of Columbia

OTHER HBCUS

Other HBCUs within proximity to cities or regions covered in this guide include Lane College (Jackson, Tennessee); Miles College (Fairfield, Alabama); Mississippi Valley State University (Itta Bena, Mississippi); Rust College (Holly Springs, Mississippi); **Tougaloo College** (Tougaloo, Mississippi); Hampton University (Hampton, Virginia); and Virginia State University (Petersburg, Virginia).

Multi-Campus Tours

It's possible for prospective students to join a tour that visits multiple HBCU campuses. Some organized tours also take side trips to civil rights sites.

PUSH Excel Black College Tours (tel. 773/256-2762; www.pushexcel.org; $1,500 per student), is part of the PUSH of Excellence program founded by Rev. Jesse L. Jackson to support Black students' ability to achieve higher education regardless of economic situation. The cost includes travel, lodging, and two meals a day for seven days. Every journey includes an exploration of civil rights history, including visits to museums and sites. PUSH Excel also hosts oratorical training and contests from kindergarten through college. Support this work by visiting www.pushexcel.org.

Another option for California students is the nonprofit **EST Black College Tours** (www.blackcollegetours.org; $1,750 per student), which offers tours for California-based high school students and community college students. This is a bonus for students in California's community college system, who have automatic transfer access to 40 HBCU partner schools across the country. Tours include trips to Black history and civil rights sites, such as Ebenezer Baptist Church in Birmingham.

Travel Tips

See page 18 for a list of recommended items to pack.

Children, military personnel, seniors, and students with valid ID receive discounted entry at a number of museums and sites on the trail.

SENIORS AND TRAVELERS WITH DISABILITIES

Seniors and travelers with limited mobility should note that this journey typically involves a great deal of walking. Some museums, such as the National Museum of African American History and Culture in Washington DC, do have loaner wheelchairs, though supplies are limited. When making hotel reservations, inquire to ensure the facility is prepared to accommodate your specific needs.

TRAVELING WITH CHILDREN

From the bars of the Birmingham jail that held Martin Luther King Jr. (visible in the Birmingham Civil Rights Institute) to water cannons once aimed at Black children in Birmingham's Kelly Ingram Park, sites and museum exhibits relating to civil rights and Black history can be deeply upsetting or confusing, and children may need some extra context to understand and process what they're seeing. A few tips for parents and guardians:

- Prepare children for the journey by giving them age-appropriate books and reading materials.
- Discuss potentially upsetting sites with children before visiting. For example, when preparing children to see the bars from King's jail cell, help them understand what being in jail helped King accomplish. Explain what it means to be a part of a movement, and how King and others had people on the outside looking out for them. Leave time for discussion during and after your visit too.
- In smaller museums, consider asking museum staff for spoiler alerts if you prefer to avoid disturbing imagery.
- Address children's questions, concerns, and fears about their own personal safety—as part of a movement or in everyday life.

Sites that deal with the most gruesome aspects of the civil rights story include Bryant's Grocery & Meat Market and the Emmett Till Intrepid Center in the Mississippi Delta, Charleston's Old Slave Mart Museum, and Montgomery's Legacy Museum and National Memorial for Peace and Justice.

This journey also offers many chances for Black children to feel proud of their heritage, and for all children to imagine how they, too, can make a difference. Virginia's Robert Russa Moton Museum, the former school where 16-year-old Barbara Johns staged a walkout in 1951, and still-functioning Little Rock Central High School are two places that invite children to locate themselves in this powerful narrative. The annual Children's Crusade march at the Birmingham Civil Rights Institute brings history to life by allowing kids to walk in the footsteps of child foot soldiers. The history of Black music, meanwhile, is an awesome point of entry into our story and is celebrated at a number of places on the trail, including Stax Museum of American Soul Music in Memphis and the popular Musical Crossroads gallery at the National Museum of African American History and Culture in Washington DC.

CORONAVIRUS AND THE U.S. CIVIL RIGHTS TRAIL

At the time of writing in early August of 2020, the coronavirus pandemic had significantly impacted the U.S., including the cities and states covered in this guide. Most, if not all, destinations required that face masks be worn in enclosed spaces, but the situation was constantly evolving.

BEFORE YOU GO

- Check the state and city websites listed below for updated local restrictions and the overall health status of the destination.
- If you plan to fly, check with your airline as well as the **Centers for Disease Control and Prevention** (www.cdc.gov) for updated recommendations and requirements.
- Check the website of any museums and other venues you wish to patronize to confirm that they're open and to learn about any specific visitation requirements, such as mandatory reservations.
- Pack **hand sanitizer,** a **thermometer,** and plenty of **face masks.** Road trippers may want to bring a **cooler** to limit the number of stops along their route.
- **Assess the risk** of entering crowded spaces or joining tours.
- Expect **disruptions** in general. Events may be postponed or cancelled, and some tours and venues may require reservations or enforce limits on the number of guests permitted at one time—or they may be closed entirely.

RESOURCES

The *New York Times* regularly updates a series of online maps that track the number of cases and deaths from coronavirus by state and county, which can be a good resource for travelers.

WOMEN TRAVELING ALONE

Culturally speaking, some people in the South may not understand why a woman is traveling alone or with other women. It's not for them to understand, but just smile and keep it moving.

LGBTQ TRAVELERS

The LGBTQ community has never been more vocal and visible in many of these cities, as evidenced by businesses like Montgomery's 1977 Books, which emphasizes authors who are queer, transgender, indigenous, or people of color. Still, this is the South, so when going off the beaten path, deep into rural areas, or patronizing mom-and-pop businesses, you may encounter less-than-welcoming attitudes. Atlanta is the most LGBTQ-friendly destination on the trail.

- **Charleston:** South Carolina Department of Health and Environmental Control (www.scdhec.gov) and City of Charleston (www.charleston-sc.gov)
- **Atlanta:** Georgia Department of Public Health (www.dpg.georgia.gov) and City of Atlanta (www.atlantaga.gov)
- **Selma, Montgomery, and Birmingham:** Alabama Public Health (www.alabamapublichealth.gov), City of Selma (www.selma-al.gov), City of Montgomery (www.mongtomery.al.gov), City of Birmingham (www.birmingham.al.gov)
- **Jackson and the Mississippi Delta:** Mississippi State Department of Health (www.msdh.ms.gov), City of Jackson (www.jacksonms.gov). Also see city websites for the specific Delta destinations you plan to visit.
- **Little Rock:** Arkansas Department of Health (www.healthyarkansas.gov), City of Little Rock (www.littlerock.gov)
- **Memphis and Nashville:** Tennessee Department of Health (www.tn.gov), A Safe Nashville (www.asafenashville.org), City of Memphis (www.memphistn.gov)
- **Greensboro, Raleigh, and Durham:** North Carolina Department of Health and Human Services (www.covid19.ncdhhs.gov), City of Greensboro (www.greensboro-nc.gov), City of Raleigh (www.raleighnc.gov), City of Durham (www.durhamnc.gov)
- **Richmond and Farmville:** Virginia Department of Health (www.vdh.virginia.gov), City of Richmond (www.ci.richmondva.us), (City of Farmville (www.farmvilleva.com)
- **Washington DC:** DC Government (www.dc.gov)

The **International LGBTQ+ Travel Association** (www.iglta.org) allows online searches by state so you can find resources that will facilitate travel planning. You'll also find a calendar of LGBTQ festivals and events, and an international gay pride calendar.

PEOPLE OF COLOR

Some may wonder whether traveling in the South as a person of color, or as a Black person specifically, requires extra safety precautions. However, to the extent it is dangerous to be Black in any certain place, that holds true all over the country. Think: Tamir Rice in Cleveland. Eric Garner in Staten Island. Rekia Boyd in Chicago. George Floyd in Minneapolis. There are no special prohibitions to offer other than the suggestion to be mindful of traffic laws and safety. Any other safety precautions are

TRAVEL TIPS

a natural part of being Black in America.

There are some online resources that cater to Black travelers. From the folks who brought us Blavity.com, **Travel Noire** (www.travelnoire.com) offers news, information, and a community that feeds our passion for travel while surfacing new places to explore around the world, with planning advice to get there. A members-only community (membership starting at $9/month) connects travelers to additional resources such as Black-owned hotels.

Nomadness (www.nomadnesstv.com) is a travel lifestyle brand and international community that founder Evita Robinson says pays homage to *The Negro Motorist Green Book*. (Look for Robinson's TED Talk, "Reclaiming the Globe," at www.ted.com.) Membership is by invitation only, and members are primarily Black women in a community that creates a safe space for millennials to revel in all things travel. Get acquainted with the community membership-free by liking the @nomadnesstraveltribe page on Facebook or following on Instagram @nomadnesstribe.

Other Black travel communities or personalities worth following on Instagram include **Black Adventuristas** (@blackadventuristas), **Soul Society** (@soulsociety), and **Jettasetting** (@jettasetting). The **Black Travel Movement** Facebook group is a community of Black people from across the globe who share the joy and freedom of traveling via photos, commentary, and advice.

Customs and Etiquette

Southerners, in general, are friendly and will say "hello" upon passing: Be nice, and just say "hi" back or nod with a smile. Also say "please" and "thank you." Southern culture thrives on small talk, so transactions, especially in more rural areas, may move a little slower. Be patient and go with the slower flow. Some people might ask where you are from, which might feel impertinent, but give the asker the benefit of the doubt: They likely want to know if you have folks in common and want to make a deeper connection.

VISITING CHURCHES

Several still-functioning Black churches are included on the trail and will be welcoming, but visitors are reminded to be mindful of sacred spaces as well as conservatism embedded in Black church tradition. Opt for modesty and neatness in dress: tank tops and shorts are a no-go. (It's not respectability politics, it's just good manners.)

FIREARMS

Some states allow the concealed carrying of guns, but not all businesses, like malls and museums, and other institutions allow firearms inside. Be mindful of signage if you're a gun owner. If the presence of guns bothers you, be aware of the cultural comfort with firearms so you can make the mental adjustment and feel secure.

Health and Safety

Make sure your health insurance is up-to-date before you hit the road—and by all means, make sure you understand the rules for seeing an out-of-network doctor or going to an emergency room so you don't face unexpected charges should you need medical help on the road.

If you have an emergency anywhere on this route, dial **911.**

HOSPITALS AND PHARMACIES

There are hospitals in all the major cities in this guide, as well as in Selma, Alabama, which is served by **Vaughn Regional Medical Center** (1015 Medical Center Pkwy., Selma; tel. 334/418-4100). In the Mississippi Delta, Greenwood is served by **Greenwood Leflore Hospital** (1401 River Rd., Greenwood; tel. 662/459-7000), while **Bolivar Medical Center** (901 E Sunflower Rd., Cleveland; tel. 662/846-0061) serves Cleveland.

National pharmacy chains can be found in every city along the trail, as well as in the smallest towns.

SUMMER WEATHER

Summer in the South is hot and humid. Stay hydrated and wear sunscreen to avoid overexposure.

SAFETY

Many sites covered in this guide are in the downtowns of their respective cities, or in closely monitored tourist areas where a modicum of safety is to be expected. Common sense, self-awareness, and listening to your gut are still great qualities to embrace.

Regardless of whether you're traversing well-traveled spots, residential areas, or rural roads, you are invited to be a traveler—not an explorer. Make a plan to get from Point A to Point B *before* you head into unfamiliar territory, and when driving into rural areas, gas up and make sure your car is basically ready for the road. Always share your itinerary with someone who is not traveling with you. (Text them or check in on a social media app, for example.) These heartfelt suggestions are not meant to deter you from experiencing your God-given right to move about freely, but the term Driving While Black doesn't exist for nothing, and most of us are aware of disturbing videos of Black and brown people being mistreated. This advice also goes for everyone, because safety matters for us all.

NOTES

CHAPTER 1: CHARLESTON

1. "Freedom Singer: 'Without Music, There Would Be No Movement,'" NPR's *Tell Me More,* August 28, 2013, https://www.wbur.org/npr/216422973/freedom-singer-without-music-there-would-be-no-movement.

CHAPTER 2: ATLANTA

1. Martin Luther King, Jr., "An Autobiography of Religious Development," (essay, Crozer Theological Seminary, 1950), Howard Gotlieb Archival Research Center, Boston University, Boston.
2. John Lewis, Office of the Fifth Congressional District of Georgia, https://johnlewis.house.gov/issues/civil-rights-and-civil-liberties.
3. John Lewis, Office of the Fifth Congressional District of Georgia, "Rep. John Lewis Responds to Supreme Court Decision on Gay and Transgender Civil Rights," Press Release, June 15, 2020, https://johnlewis.house.gov/media-center/press-releases/rep-john-lewis-responds-supreme-court-decision-gay-and-transgender-civil.

CHAPTER 3: SELMA

1. "The Civil Rights Movement in Selma, Alabama, 1865-1972," United States Department of the Interior National Park Service.

CHAPTER 4: MONTGOMERY

1. Martin Luther King, Jr., "I've Been to the Mountaintop," speech, Memphis, April 3, 1968, The Martin Luther King, Jr. Research and Education Institute, Stanford University, https://kinginstitute.stanford.edu/king-papers/documents/ive-been-mountaintop-address-delivered-bishop-charles-mason-temple.
2. *Williams v. Wallace,* 240 F. Supp. 100 (M.D. Ala. 1965).
3. "Judicial Courage and Commitment to the Rule of Law," United States Courts, https://www.uscourts.gov/about-federal-courts/educational-resources/annual-observances/african-american-history-month.
4. Martin Luther King, Jr., "Our God is Marching On!," speech, Montgomery, Alabama, March 25, 1965, The Martin Luther King, Jr. Research and Education Institute, Stanford University, https://kinginstitute.stanford.edu/our-god-marching.
5. Hugh A. Mulligan, "James Farmer Brings Days of Fear, Hate to Students," *Los Angeles Times,* June 3, 1990, https://www.latimes.com/archives/la-xpm-1990-06-03-mn-789-story.html.
6. John Lewis, Office of the Fifth Congressional District of Georgia, Press Release, September 12, 2019, https://johnlewis.house.gov/media-center/press-releases/rep-john-lewis-death-mrs-vera-harris.

CHAPTER 5: BIRMINGHAM

1. Charles E. Connerly, *The Most Segregated City in America: City Planning and Civil Rights in Birmingham,* 1920-1980 (Charlottesville: University of Virginia Press, 2013).

2. John F. Kennedy, Televised Address to the Nation on Civil Rights, televised address, June 11, 1963, John F. Kennedy Presidential Library and Museum, https://www.jfklibrary.org/learn/about-jfk/historic-speeches/televised-address-to-the-nation-on-civil-rights.
3. "The Iconic Wales Window Inside 16th Street Baptist Church," *Birmingham Times,* October 18, 2018, https://www.birminghamtimes.com/2018/10/the-iconic-wales-window-inside-16th-street-baptist-church/.
4. Greg Garrison, "Photographer was a man of a thousand images, best known for one (Life Stories: Tommy Langston)," *AL.com,* November 10, 2013, https://www.al.com/living/2013/11/photographer_was_man_of_a_thou.html.
5. Glenn T. Eskew, *But for Birmingham* (Chapel Hill, NC: The University of North Carolina Press, 1997), 144.
6. Angela Davis, "Terrorism is Part of Our History," speech, Oakland, California, September 16, 2013, Democracy Now!, https://www.democracynow.org/2013/9/16/terrorism_is_part_of_our_history.

CHAPTER 6: JACKSON

1. U.S. Department of Justice, Statement by the Honorable Robert F. Kennedy, Attorney General of the United States, May 24, 1961.

CHAPTER 7: MISSISSIPPI DELTA

1. Tina L. Lingon, "'Turn This Town Out': Stokely Carmichael, Black Power, and the March Against Fear," June 2016, National Archives: Rediscovering Black History, https://rediscovering-black-history.blogs.archives.gov/2016/06/07/turn-this-town-out-stokely-carmichael-black-power-and-the-march-against-fear.
2. Nikole Hannah-Jones, "Ghosts of Greenwood," *ProPublica,* July 8, 2014, https://www.propublica.org/article/ghosts-of-greenwood.
3. "Freedom Summer," Martin Luther King, Jr. Research and Education Institute, Stanford University, https://kinginstitute.stanford.edu/encyclopedia/freedom-summer.
4. Nikole Hannah-Jones, "Ghosts of Greenwood," ProPublica, July 8, 2014, https://www.propublica.org/article/ghosts-of-greenwood.
5. "Freedom Summer," Martin Luther King, Jr. Research and Education Institute, Stanford University, https://kinginstitute.stanford.edu/encyclopedia/freedom-summer.

CHAPTER 7: LITTLE ROCK

1. "September 12, 1958: Little Rock Public Schools Closed," 2020, Zinn Education Project, https://www.zinnedproject.org/news/tdih/little-rock-schools-closed/#:~:text=The%20Lost%20Year%20ended%20with,Read%20in%20full.
2. Daisy Bates, March on Washington, speech, Washington DC, August 28, 1963, Anna Julia Cooper Center, http://cooperproject.org/daisy-bates-speaks-at-the-1963-march-on-washington/.

CHAPTER 8: MEMPHIS

1. *Chesapeake, Ohio & Southwestern Railroad Company v Ida B. Wells,* 1885, testimony of Ida B. Wells, Digital Public Library of America, https://dp.la/primary-source-sets/ida-b-wells-and-anti-lynching-activism/sources/1113.

CHAPTER 9: NASHVILLE

1. "We Shall Overcome: Civil Rights and the Nashville Press, 1957-1968," Frist Art Museum, https://fristartmuseum.org/calendar/detail/we-shall-overcome-civil-rights-and-the-nashville-press.
2. "May 1961: Nashville Students and SNCC Pick Up Freedom Rides," SNCC Digital Gateway, https://snccdigital.org/events/freedom-rides.

CHAPTER 10: GREENSBORO, RALEIGH & DURHAM

1. Claude Sitton, "Negro Criticizes N.A.A.C.P. Tactics," *New York Times,* April 17, 1960.

CHAPTER 11: RICHMOND AND FARMVILLE

1. "Stanley Backs Segregation," *New York Times,* June 26, 1954.
2. Brendan King, "Historical marker unveiled honoring 'Richmond 34' arrested after 1960 Thalhimers sit-in," *WTVR News Richmond,* June 28, 2016, https://wtvr.com/2016/06/28/historical-marker-unveiled-honoring-richmond-34-arrested-after-1960-thalhimer-sit-in/.

CHAPTER 13: WASHINGTON DC

1. "How Martin Luther King Went Off Script in 'I Have a Dream,'" video file, 1:13, WSJ | Video, August 24, 2013, https://www.wsj.com/video/how-martin-luther-king-went-off-script-in-i-have-a-dream/BA42F5FB-83B7-4819-9752-062A91027D12.html.
2. Martin Luther King, Jr., "I Have a Dream," speech, Washington DC, August 28, 1963, The Martin Luther King, Jr. Institute for Research and Education, Stanford University, https://kinginstitute.stanford.edu/king-papers/documents/i-have-dream-address-delivered-march-washington-jobs-and-freedom.
3. Martin Luther King, Jr., "I've Been to the Mountaintop," speech, Memphis, April 3, 1968, The Martin Luther King, Jr. Institute for Research and Education, Stanford University, https://kinginstitute.stanford.edu/king-papers/documents/ive-been-mountaintop-address-delivered-bishop-charles-mason-temple.
4. Michelle Obama, Speech at the Democratic National Convention, Philadelphia, July 25, 2016.
5. Taylor Branch, *Pillar of Fire: America in the King Years: 1963-65* (New York: Simon & Schuster, 1998), 124.
6. David W. Blight, "Yes, the Freedman's Memorial uses racist imagery. But don't tear it down," *Washington Post,* June 25, 2020, https://www.washingtonpost.com/opinions/2020/06/25/yes-freedmens-memorial-uses-racist-imagery-dont-tear-it-down.
7. DeNeel Brown, "Frederick Douglass delivered a Lincoln reality check at Emancipation Memorial unveiling," *Washington Post,* June 27, 2020, https://www.washingtonpost.com/history/2020/06/27/emancipation-monument-in-washington-dc-targeted-by-protests.
8. Congresswoman Eleanor Holmes Norton, "Norton to Introduce Legislation Removing Emancipation Statue from Lincoln Park," Press Release, June 23, 2020.
9. Martin Luther King, Jr., "Remaining Awake Through a Great Revolution," speech, Washington DC, March 31, 1968, The Martin Luther King, Jr. Institute for Research and Education, Stanford University, https://kinginstitute.stanford.edu/king-papers/publications/knock-midnight-inspiration-great-sermons-reverend-martin-luther-king-jr-10.
10. "Explore Washington DC's Historic Black Broadway on U Street," National Trust for Historic Preservation, https://savingplaces.org/guides/explore-washington-dc-black-broadway#.X0RLoy2z2i5.

INDEX

A

B

C

D

E

F

I

J

K

L

M

N

OP

R

S

T

UV

W-Z

LIST OF MAPS

PHOTO CREDITS

All photos © Deborah D. Douglas except page v (top) © Phagenaars | Dreamstime.com; page v (middle) © lainhamer | Dreamstime.com; page v (bottom) © Demerzel21 | Dreamstime.com; page 1 © Carol M. Highsmith; page 2 © Appalachianviews | Dreamstime.com; page 4 (top) © F11photo | Dreamstime.com; page 4 (bottom) © Cliff Garten Studio, Visual Artists' Right Act, photography Jeremy Green; page 5 (bottom) © Glenn Nagel | Dreamstime.com; page 8 © Ritu Jethani | Dreamstime.com; page 9 © Carol M. Highsmith; page 11 © Birmingham Civil Rights Institute; page 15 © Warren K. Leffler; page 20 © SustainAble Home Goods; page 29 © Carol M. Highsmith; page 31 © Eyre Crowe; page 32 © Brady-Handy photograph collection, Library of Congress, Prints and Photographs Division; page 37 (middle) © James Kirkikis | Dreamstime.com; page 37 (bottom) © Brennan Wesley; image courtesy of the Gibbes Museum of Art; page 60 (top) © James Kirkikis | Dreamstime.com; page 64 © Carol M. Highsmith; page 65 © Marion S. Trikosko; page 68 © Historic American Buildings Survey; page 85 © SustainAble Home Goods; page 86 © Collection of the Smithsonian National Museum of African American History and Culture; page 97 © Peter Pettus; page 101 © Peter Pettus; page 106 © Stanley Wolfson; page 108 (bottom) © James Kirkikis | Dreamstime.com; page 117 © Carol M. Highsmith; page 120 © Carol M. Highsmith; page 123 (top) © Carol M. Highsmith; page 123 (bottom) © Carol M. Highsmith; page 135 (bottom) © Jacqueline Nix | Dreamstime.com; page 144 (top) © Jacqueline Nix | Dreamstime.com; page 144 (middle) © Katharina Notarianni | Dreamstime.com; page 147 (middle) © Carol M. Highsmith; page 160 (top) © Birmingham Civil Rights Institute; page 160 (middle) © Carol M. Highsmith; page 164 © Marion S. Trikosko; page 165 © Warren K. Leffler; page 170 (middle) © Birmingham Civil Rights Institute; page 176 (bottom) © Marion S. Trikosko; page 180 © Carol M. Highsmith; page 189 © Photo by Tom Beck. Courtesy of MDAH; page 190 (top) © Phagenaars| Dreamstiime.com; page 194 © Marion S. Trikosko; page 204 © Photo by Tom Beck. Courtesy of MDAH; page 209 © Roberto Galan | Dreamstime.com; page 215 © Photo by Tom Beck. Courtesy of MDAH; page 220 (bottom) © B.B. King Museum & Delta Interpretive Center; page 223 © Dave Mann; page 224 © Warren K. Leffler; page 233 © Warren K. Leffler; page 252 © Walter Albertin; page 261 © Thomas J. O'Halloran; page 264 (bottom) © Amadeustx | Dreamstime.com; page 276 © Arshia Khan; page 279 © F11photo | Dreamstime.com; page 280 (top) © Peek Creative Collective | Dreamstime.com; page 280 (middle) © Jeremy Green; page 280 (bottom) © Paul Mckinnon | Dreamstime.com; page 283 © Marion S. Trikosko; page 284 © The Afro-American press and its editors; page 287 (bottom) © R. Gino Santa Maria / Shutterfree, Llc | Dreamstime.com; page 291 © Cliff Garten Studio, Visual Artist's Right Act, photography Jeremy Green; page 293 (middle) © Marion Post Wolcott; page 293 (bottom right) © Calvin L. Leake | Dreamstime.com; page 297 (top) © Jack E. Boucher; page 297 (middle) © Carol M. Highsmith; page 299 © National Portrait Gallery, Smithsonian Institution; page 323 © Thomas J. O'Halloran; page 326 (middle) © TN Dept. of Tourist Development & Witness Walls; page 347 © photo courtesy Discover Durham; page 348 (top) © International Civil Rights Center & Museum; page 348 (bottom) © Aya Shabu; page 354 © Collection of the Smithsonian National Museum of African American History and Culture; page 358 (top) © International Civil Rights Center & Museum; page 358 (middle © Lynn Donovan; page 358 (bottom) © Greensboro History Museum; page 361 © Jayway photography; page 367 (top) © Art by Durham Civil Rights history project, photo courtesy Discover Durham; page 367 (middle) © Zimmytws | Dreamstime.com; page 367 (bottom) © Kelley Albert | Dreamstime.com; page 368 © Chuck Ruffin; page 373 (top) © Dame's Chicken and Waffles; page 373 (middle) © Harry Monds; page 373 (bottom) © Discover Durham; page 375 © From The New York Public Library; page 376 (top) © Zimmytws |

Dreamstime.com; page 376 (middle) © Keenan Hairston/VisitRaleigh.com; page 376 (bottom) © VisitRaleigh.com; page 378 © Collection of the Smithsonian National Museum of African American History and Culture; page 381 © Lucy Clark | Dreamstime.com; page 382 (top) © Robert R. Moton Museum; page 382 (middle) © Black History Museum & Cultural Center; page 382 (bottom) © Bill Crabtree Jr.; page 385 © Thomas J. O'Halloran; page 386 © Thomas J. O'Halloran; page 390 (top, middle, and bottom) © Robert R. Moton Museum; page 397 (top) © Visit Richmond; page 397 (middle) © Black History Museum & Cultural Center; page 397 (bottom) © Visit Richmond; page 399 (top) © Sarah Hauser; page 399 (middle) © Visit Richmond; page 399 (bottom) © Richard T Nowitz; page 401 © Nick Davis; page 403 (top) © Vagabond Restaurant & Speakeasy; page 403 (middle and bottom) © Kip Dawkins; page 405 © Marion S. Trikosko; page 406 (top) © Courtesy of Washington.org; page 406 (middle) © 3000ad | Dreamstime.com; page 406 (bottom left) © Joe Sohm | Dreamstime.com; page 406 (bottom right) © Ritu Jethani | Dreamstime.com; page 407 © Marion S. Trikosko; page 412 © J. W. Hurn; page 418 © Marion S. Trikosko; page 420 (top) © Brizardh | Dreamstime.com; page 420 (middle) © Sergii Figurnyi | Dreamstime.com; page 420 (bottom) © Courtesy of Washington.org; page 423 (top) © Courtesy of Washington.org; page 423 (middle) © Mkopka | Dreamstime.com; page 423 (bottom) © Michelle LaVaughn Robinson Obama By Amy Sherald, Oil on linen; page 424 © Courtesy of Washington.org; page 425 © Christian Offenberg | Dreamstime.com; page 429 © Rolf52 | Dreamstime.com; page 434 © Warren K. Leffler; page 437 © Courtesy of Washington.org; page 440 (top) © Joe Sohm | Dreamstime.com; page 440 (middle) © Courtesy of Washington.org; page 440 (bottom) © Washington National Cathedral; page 442 © Erin Martin; page 446 (top) © Justin Fegan | Dreamstime.com; page 446 (middle) © Richard Gunion | Dreamstime.com; page 446 (bottom) © Courtesy of Washington.org; page 448 © Thomas J. O'Halloran; page 450 © Courtesy of Washington.org; page 454 (top) © Courtesy of Washington.org; page 454 (middle and bottom) © Calabash Tea & Tonic; page 457 © "Rey Lopez"IG rlopez809; page 458 © Christie Jeon; page 461 © Courtesy of Washington.org; page 463 © Tisaeff | Dreamstime.com; page 465 © Walter Arce | Dreamstime.com; page 476 © Warren K. Leffler

Foldout Map Photo Credits

Top row, left to right: © Deborah D. Douglas; © Deborah D. Douglas; © Peter Pettus; © Carol M. Highsmith; photo by Tom Beck, courtesy of MDAH; © Deborah D. Douglas; © Deborah D. Douglas; © Cliff Garten Studio, Visual Artist's Right Act, photography Jeremy Green; © TN Dept. of Tourist Development & Witness Walls; photo courtesy Discover Durham; © Visit Richmond; © Rolf52 | Dreamstime.com

Black Lives Matter image: © Joe Sohm | Dreamstime.com

Demonstrators image: © National Archives / Handout

Timeline Photo Credits

Top row, left to right: © Deborah D. Douglas; © Dave Mann; © Warren K. Leffler; © Walter Albertin; © International Civil Rights Center & Museum; © photo by Tom Beck, courtesy of MDAH; © Deborah D. Douglas; © Warren K. Leffler; © Deborah D. Douglas; © Warren K. Leffler; © Warren K. Leffler; © Peter Pettus

Bottom row, left to right: © Marion S. Trikosko; © Thomas J. O'Halloran; Collection of the Smithsonian National Museum of African American History and Culture, gifted with pride from Ellen Brooks; Collection of the Smithsonian National Museum of African American History and Culture; © Peek Creative Collective | Dreamstime.com; © Pete Souza; © Joe Sohm | Dreamstime.com; © Deborah D. Douglas; © 3000ad | Dreamstime.com; photo by Tom Beck, courtesy of MDAH; © Deborah D. Douglas

ACKNOWLEDGMENTS

Love to my family and friends for your support, cheering me on, and connecting me to vital resources: Ernestine P. Stewart (my mama); Margaret Littman; Emily Wagster Pettus; Sarah Campbell; Jimmie Gates; Reagan Walker; Terri Sharpp; Mia Henry; Timla Washington; Constance Dyson; David Ewing; Cory Anderson; Sybil Hampton; Terri Sharpp; Tracey and Jamel Richardson; Sara Catania; Cynthia Greenlee; Janice Miller; Kimberly and David Rudd; Katelyn Hunger; Samuel Autman; the Davis Family, especially Lynn; Dornetha Taylor and Mr. Barash (in memoriam); Kabula Djenaba Abubakari; Jetta Bates; and Michele Weldon, Teresa Puente, Katie Orenstein, and The OpEd Project.

Thanks to my Moon Travel team. Nikki Ioakimedes, you are my DREAM editor.

Much appreciation to these individuals at institutions featured in this guide, especially in a pandemic: Cynthia Goodloe (Mississippi Veterans of the Civil Rights Movement); Pamela Junior (Mississippi Civil Rights Museum); Ruth Miller; Verdell Dawson (Tabernacle Baptist Church, Selma); Vickie Ashford Thompson (Greater Birmingham Convention & Visitors Bureau); Milton Howery; Cameron Patterson (Robert Russa Moton Museum); Jermaine House (National Museum of African American History and Culture); Morgan Powell and Heather Middleton (Music City); Julie Marshall; Miriam Kleinman (National Archives); Bryan McDade (Mosaic Templars Museum); Lucera Parker (Shaw University); Barbara Lau (Pauli Murray Center); Glenn Perkins (Greensboro History Museum); Ian Janetta (Metro); John Swaine and Will Harris (International Civil Rights Center and Museum); and Floyd Myers.

TRAVEL NOTES

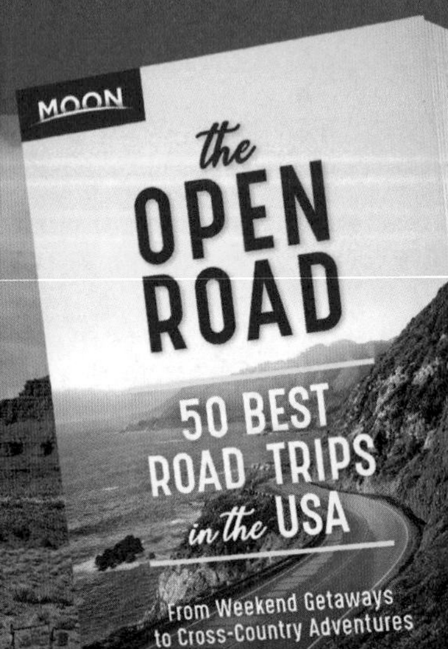
MOON
the OPEN ROAD
50 BEST ROAD TRIPS in the USA
From Weekend Getaways to Cross-Country Adventures
JESSICA DUNHAM

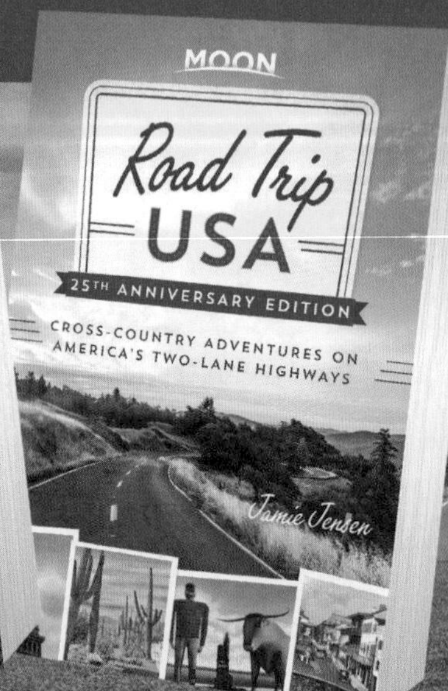
MOON
Road Trip USA
25TH ANNIVERSARY EDITION
CROSS-COUNTRY ADVENTURES ON AMERICA'S TWO-LANE HIGHWAYS
Jamie Jensen

MOON
Drive & Hike
APPALACHIAN TRAIL

MOON
CALIFORNIA
Road Trip
SAN FRANCISCO, YOSEMITE, LAS VEGAS, GRAND CANYON, LOS ANGELES, & THE PACIFIC COAST HIGHWAY
STUART THORNTON

MOON
NASHVILLE TO NEW ORLEANS
Road Trip
61
49

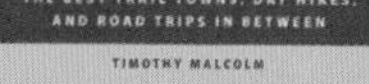
THE BEST TRAIL TOWNS, DAY HIKES, AND ROAD TRIPS IN BETWEEN
TIMOTHY MALCOLM

INCLUDING SHENANDOAH & GREAT SMOKY MOUNTAINS NATIONAL PARKS
JASON FRYE

MOON
NEW ENGLAND
Road Trip
BOSTON, ACADIA NATIONAL PARK, WHITE MOUNTAINS, BERKSHIRES, NEWPORT, AND CAPE COD
JEN ROSE SMITH

MOON
OREGON TRAIL
Road Trip
HISTORIC SITES, SMALL TOWNS, AND SCENIC LANDSCAPES ALONG THE LEGENDARY WESTWARD ROUTE
KATRINA EMERY

MOON
PACIFIC COAST HIGHWAY
Road Trip
CALIFORNIA, OREGON & WASHINGTON
IAN ANDERSON

ROAD TRIP GUIDES FROM MOON

MOON
Drive & Hike
PACIFIC CREST TRAIL
THE BEST TRAIL TOWNS, DAY HIKES, AND ROAD TRIPS IN BETWEEN
CAROLINE HINCHLIFF

MOON
PACIFIC NORTHWEST
Road Trip
SEATTLE, VANCOUVER, VICTORIA, THE OLYMPIC PENINSULA, PORTLAND, THE OREGON COAST & MOUNT RAINIER
ALLISON WILLIAMS

MOON
ROUTE 66
Road Trip
JESSICA DUNHAM

MOON
SOUTH FLORIDA & THE KEYS
Road Trip
WITH MIAMI, WALT DISNEY WORLD, TAMPA & THE EVERGLADES
JASON FERGUSON

MOON
SOUTHWEST
Road Trip
LAS VEGAS, ZION & BRYCE, MONUMENT VALLEY, SANTA FE & TAOS, AND THE GRAND CANYON
TIM HULL

MOON
U.S. CIVIL RIGHTS TRAIL
A TRAVELER'S GUIDE TO THE PEOPLE, PLACES, AND EVENTS THAT MADE THE MOVEMENT
Deborah Douglas • With Foreword by Bree Newsome Bass

MOON
VANCOUVER & CANADIAN ROCKIES
Road Trip
VICTORIA, BANFF, JASPER, CALGARY, THE OKANAGAN, WHISTLER & THE SEA-TO-SKY HIGHWAY
CAROLYN B. HELLER

MOON
YELLOWSTONE TO GLACIER NATIONAL PARK
Road Trip
JACKSON HOLE, CODY, THE GRAND TETONS & THE ROCKY MOUNTAIN FRONT
CARTER G. WALKER

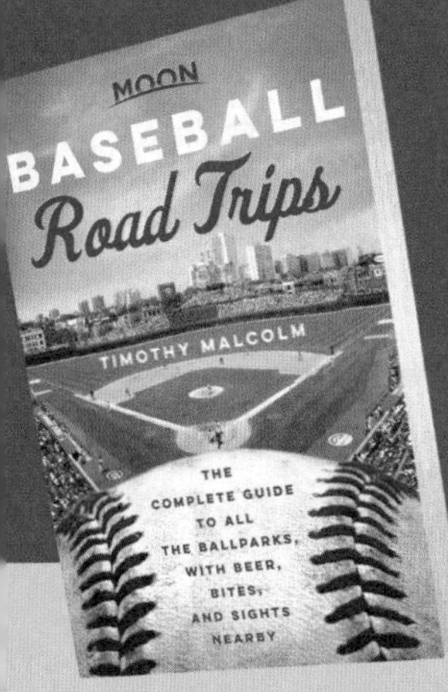

Moon Baseball Road Trips

The Complete Guide to All the Ballparks, with Beer, Bites, and Sights Nearby

Sunshine, hot dogs, friends, and the excitement of the game: Baseball is called America's pastime for a reason. Experience the best of the MLB cities and stadiums with strategic advice from road tripper and former baseball writer Timothy Malcolm.

MAP SYMBOLS

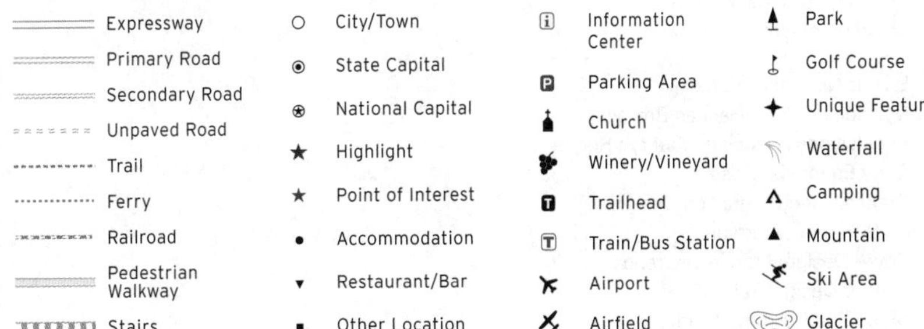

CONVERSION TABLES

°C = (°F - 32) / 1.8
°F = (°C x 1.8) + 32
1 inch = 2.54 centimeters (cm)
1 foot = 0.304 meters (m)
1 yard = 0.914 meters
1 mile = 1.6093 kilometers (km)
1 km = 0.6214 miles
1 fathom = 1.8288 m
1 chain = 20.1168 m
1 furlong = 201.168 m
1 acre = 0.4047 hectares
1 sq km = 100 hectares
1 sq mile = 2.59 square km
1 ounce = 28.35 grams
1 pound = 0.4536 kilograms
1 short ton = 0.90718 metric ton
1 short ton = 2,000 pounds
1 long ton = 1.016 metric tons
1 long ton = 2,240 pounds
1 metric ton = 1,000 kilograms
1 quart = 0.94635 liters
1 US gallon = 3.7854 liters
1 Imperial gallon = 4.5459 liters
1 nautical mile = 1.852 km

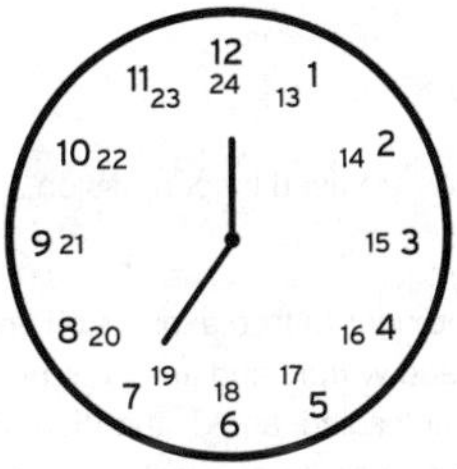

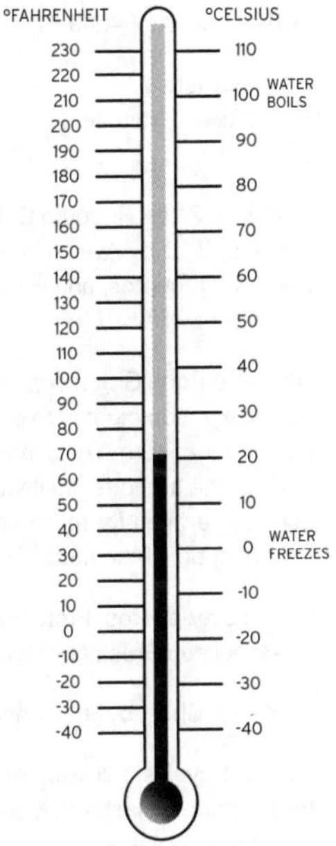

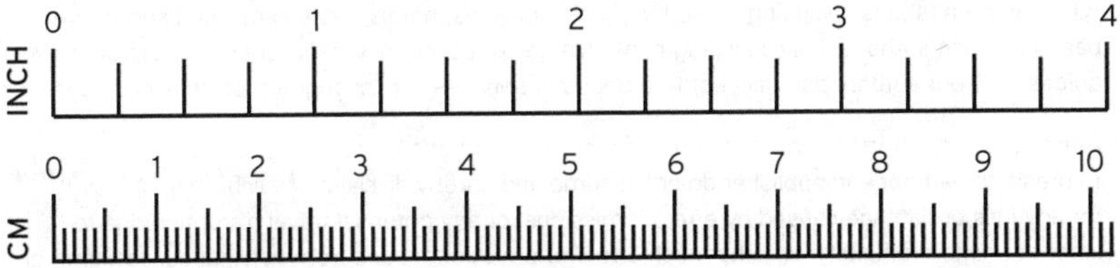

MOON U.S. CIVIL RIGHTS TRAIL
Avalon Travel
Hachette Book Group
1700 Fourth Street
Berkeley, CA 94710, USA
www.moon.com

Editor: Nikki Ioakimedes
Managing Editor: Hannah Brezack
Acquisitions Associate: Kathryn Roque
Copy Editor: Tia Ross
Graphics and Production Designer:
Suzanne Albertson
Cover Design: Marcie Lawrence
Interior Design: Tabitha Lahr
Moon Logo: Tim McGrath
Map Editor: Albert Angulo
Cartographer: John Culp
Foldout Map Design: Karin Dahl
Proofreader: Megan Anderluh

ISBN-13: 978-1-64049-915-7

Printing History
1st Edition © January 2021
5 4 3 2 1

Front cover photos: Protestors © National Archives / Handout, Getty Images; Montgomery Bus © Associated Press / Horace Cort, Photographer

Printed in China by RR Donnelley